THE GREENWOOD ENCYCLOPEDIA OF FOLKTALES AND FAIRY TALES

ADVISORY BOARD MEMBERS

THE GREENWOOD ENCYCLOPEDIA OF FOLKTALES AND FAIRY TALES

Volume 2: G–P

Edited by
Donald Haase

GREENWOOD PRESS
Westport, Connecticut · London

Library of Congress Cataloging-in-Publication Data

The Greenwood encyclopedia of folktales and fairy tales / edited by Donald Haase.
   p. cm.
  Includes bibliographical references and index.
  ISBN-13: 978-0-313-33441-2 ((set) : alk. paper)
  ISBN-13: 978-0-313-33442-9 ((vol. 1) : alk. paper)
  ISBN-13: 978-0-313-33443-6 ((vol. 2) : alk. paper)
  ISBN-13: 978-0-313-33444-3 ((vol. 3) : alk. paper)
  1. Folklore—Encyclopedias. 2. Tales—Encyclopedias. 3. Fairy
tales—Encyclopedias. I. Haase, Donald.
  GR74.G73 2008
  398.203—dc22   2007031698

British Library Cataloguing in Publication Data is available.

Library of Congress Catalog Card Number: 2007031698

ISBN-13: 978-0-313-33441-2 (set)
        978-0-313-33442-9 (vol. 1)
        978-0-313-33443-6 (vol. 2)
        978-0-313-33444-3 (vol. 3)

First published in 2008

Greenwood Press, 88 Post Road West, Westport, CT 06881
An imprint of Greenwood Publishing Group, Inc.
www.greenwood.com

Printed in the United States of America
∞™

The paper used in this book complies with the
Permanent Paper Standard issued by the National
Information Standards Organization (Z39.48–1984).

10 9 8 7 6 5 4 3 2 1

CONTENTS

LIST OF ENTRIES

Volume 2: G–P

G

Gaarder, Jostein (1952–)

The Norwegian Jostein Gaarder is best known as the author of *Sofies verden* (*Sophie's World*, 1991), a novel about the history of philosophy for young readers that was the world's bestselling work of fiction in 1995, and which has been translated into fifty-four languages.

Although primarily concerned with encouraging young readers to explore philosophical and existential questions, Gaarder utilizes elements from the fairy-tale tradition, with a postmodern twist, in much of his writing. Layering stories within stories, Gaarder often involves his young protagonists in a quest or search of some kind, which may take them through both space and time, as in *Julemysteriet* (*The Christmas Mystery*, 1992), and involves them with a cast of strange and mysterious creatures who often function as **magic helper**s, as in *Kabalmysteriet* (*The Solitaire Mystery*, 1990). *Froskeslottet* (*The Frog Castle*, 1988) relates how a young boy comes to grips with the death of his grandfather through adventures in a magic castle dream world and in nonsense sequences reminiscent of Lewis **Carroll**.

A high school philosophy teacher until 1991, Gaarder now writes full time and produces a new novel every two to three years. Most of his books have been translated into English, including *Sirkusdirektørens datter* (*The Ringmaster's Daughter*, 2001) and *Appelsinpiken* (*The Orange Girl*, 2003), which has been called a fairy tale for adults. Gaarder has won many literary prizes and, along with his wife, Siri Dannevig, established an international environment and sustainable development award, the Sophie Prize, in 1997. ***See also*** Postmodernism.

Further Reading: van Suntum, Lisa Rainwater. "Jostein Gaarder." *Twentieth Century Norwegian Writers.* Edited by Tanya Tresher. Detroit: Gale, 2004. 102–110.

Marte Hult

Gág, Wanda (1893–1946)

Wanda Gág translated and illustrated Wilhelm and Jacob **Grimm**s' fairy tales for the American audience in the middle of the twentieth century at a time when Walt **Disney** was presenting his animated versions. She grew up in a Bohemian family of nine in New Ulm,

Minnesota, and her German-speaking community and artistic parents had a strong influence on her work. After the death of her parents, Gág as the eldest took responsibility for the support of her siblings and studied art in Minneapolis and New York. She worked in commercial art, including drawing spot illustrations for journals such as *The Nation* and *Horn Book*, and also produced fine arts lithographs. Her illustrated autobiography *Growing Pains* (1940) describes her early years.

Her first book for children, the picturebook *Millions of Cats* (1928), a Newbery Honor Award book for 1929, has a fairy-tale structure and an old-fashioned look that characterizes her work. For instance, the horizontal hand-lettered text bears black-and-white pen-and-ink illustrations reminiscent of wood-block illustrations. In all, she loosely translated fifty-one of the Grimms' fairy tales in American idiom, in *Tales from Grimm* (1936), *Three Gay Tales from Grimm* (1943), and *More Tales from Grimm* (1947), the latter published posthumously. Her single-story volume *Snow White and the Seven Dwarfs* (1938) was published in response to the Disney film (1937) and preserved some of the details altered by the movie. *See also* Illustration.

Further Readings: Gág, Wanda. *Growing Pains: Diaries and Drawings for the Years 1908–1917.* New York: Coward-McCann, 1940; Hoyle, Karen Nelson. *Wanda Gág.* New York: Twayne, 1994.

George Bodmer

Gaiman, Neil (1960–)

Initially known for his Sandman series of comics and, later, **graphic novel**s, British/American writer Neil Gaiman has established himself firmly as an award-winning novelist and scriptwriter who has a cult following within the **fantasy** genre. A darkly intelligent, postmodern, and imaginative writer, he brings to his work an ongoing fascination with **intertextuality**, both in his strong invocations of literary texts and in his reliance on the patterns and **motif**s of **myth**, **legend**, and **folklore**.

Drawn by various high-profile comic-book artists but written throughout by Gaiman, the Sandman series (1988–96) is his strongest statement on the power both of narrative and of the narrator. Gaiman constructs a mythic realm called the "Dreaming," a realm of the unconscious, repository of the dreams, imaginings, and stories of humanity across time, rife with characters and events from **Bible tales**, Greek myth, folklore from many cultures, fairy tale, and literature from William **Shakespeare** to H. P. Lovecraft. The dense literary texture of the series allows self-conscious play with patterns of inevitability and predestination; the Sandman himself, the Dreamlord Morpheus, is very much bound, often tragically, by the rules of the patterns he controls. The Sandman series is itself a profoundly postmodern mythology, relying on recognition and resonance for its effect.

Gaiman's novelistic career started with *Good Omens* (1990), the comic biblical apocalypse written in collaboration with Terry **Pratchett**. However, Gaiman's interest in mythic narrative is more evident in *Neverwhere*, a **television** series (1996) and **novel** (1997) that peoples a grimy and dangerous underground London with myths, legends, and fairy-tale **archetype**s to be negotiated and overcome by a classic underdog hero. Even more like the fairy-tale is his novel *Stardust* (1999), in which a half-fairy hero must enter **faerie** on a quest for a fallen star, negotiating his way through the perils of witchcraft and power-hungry lords. A similar fairy-tale awareness underpins several of the tales in his 1998 short-story collection, *Smoke and Mirrors*, which includes "Glass, Snow, Apples," a retelling of the **Snow White** story with Snow White as a vampire. His more recent novels *American Gods* (2001) and *Anansi Boys* (2005) borrow wholesale from the mythic pantheons of multiple cultures to present gods and heroes updated to a gritty, contemporary American or British landscape. *Anansi Boys* is particularly interesting in its focus on the **trickster** figure of **Anansi** the spider, and its subtle and intelligent investigation into the nature of **storytelling**. The self-consciousness with which Gaiman refigures literary and folkloric themes lends itself to a certain comic irony, but nonetheless these are also dark and edgy narratives. This tendency is hardly muted in his children's books such as *Coraline* (2002) and *The Wolves in the Walls* (2003). While continuing Gaiman's collaboration with the visual, these books tend to stress the importance of childhood self-reliance in the face of strangely distorted fantasy worlds. Both of these works explore dreamscapes peopled with archetypes and symbols, a tendency seen again in the Gaiman-scripted film *Mirrormask* (2005). **See also** Amano Yoshitaka; Cartoons and Comics; Postmodernism.

Further Reading: Sanders, Joe. "Of Storytellers and Stories in Gaiman and Vess's 'A Midsummer Night's Dream.'" *Extrapolation: A Journal of Science Fiction and Fantasy* 45 (2004): 237–48.

Jessica Tiffin

Galland, Antoine (1646–1715)

From humble beginnings, Antoine Galland became a renowned French Orientalist and was the first to introduce the ***Arabian Nights*** and its narrator **Sheherazade** to western European audiences with his seminal translation, *Les mille et une nuits* (*Thousand and One Nights*, 1704–17), which was translated into English, German, Italian, Dutch, and Russian before the end of the century. A gifted student from Picardy, Galland made his way to Paris by 1661 and enrolled in the Collège du Plessis, where he began studying Arabic. His future as an Orientalist was sealed when in 1670 he became the secretary to the marquis de Nointel, ambassador of Louis XIV to the Ottomans in Constantinople. His position with Nointel led to further travels in Greece, Syria, and Palestine, where he collected ancient manuscripts, medals, and other objects. In 1675, he returned to France, and some two years later he traveled to Smyrna to bring back objects for the king's exhibition room. After a third extended trip to the Orient (1679–88), Galland definitively returned to France and served as an assistant to the Orientalist Barthélemy d'Herbelot, eventually publishing his monumental *Bibliothèque orientale* (*Oriental Library*, 1697) after Herbelot's death.

Before embarking on the *Nights*, Galland first translated *Voyages de **Sindbad*** in 1701, which was a separate manuscript from the *Nights*, but which he later included. Galland began publishing his collection of the *Nights* in 1704, working from one of the oldest extant manuscripts, which dated from fourteenth-century Syria. By 1706, the first seven volumes of the *Nights* appeared and became vastly popular. This popularity can be attributed to the fact that Galland's tales were published on the cusp of the fairy-tale vogue in the 1690s. Galland's publication gave the genre of the tale a new impetus and generated in its wake a whole era of Orientalist fairy tales by such authors as Jacques **Cazotte**, Thomas Simon Gueullette, Pétis de la Croix, and, later, Voltaire and Denis Diderot. Stylistically, Galland was inspired by authors such as Marie-Catherine d'**Aulnoy**, which gave his Oriental tales a *Louis-quatorzième* flavor. Galland eliminated what he viewed as repetitive details from stories, such as the description of the seven dresses of the vizier's daughter in the "Histoire de Nourredin Ali," as well as repetitive stories and the poems that punctuated many of the narratives, for which he was later criticized by Joseph Charles **Mardrus**. Many stories from the last volumes, such as the tales of **Aladdin** and **Ali Baba**, were in fact adaptations from oral and perhaps written stories by Hanna Diab, a Christian Maronite from Aleppo, whom Galland met in 1709. Thanks to Galland, the *Arabian Nights* became one of the most important foundational texts in western European literature. *See also* Burton, Richard Francis; Lane, Edward W.

Further Readings: Chraïbi, Aboubakr. "Galland's 'Ali Baba' and Other Arabic Versions." *The* Arabian Nights: *Past and Present.* Edited by Ulrich Marzolph. Spec. issue of *Marvels & Tales* 18 (2004): 159–69; Larzul, Sylvette. *Les traductions françaises des Mille et une Nuits: Étude des versions Galland, Trébutien et Mardrus.* Paris: L'Harmattan, 1996.

Anne E. Duggan

García Márquez, Gabriel (1928–)

Gabriel García Márquez is a Colombian novelist, short-story writer, and journalist whose works constitute the best-known example of Latin American **magical realism**. Born in Aracataca, a small coastal town in the north of Colombia, he was raised by paternal grandparents and aunts who told him, from a very early age, stories that seamlessly blended fantastic, supernatural events with realistic, everyday settings, narrated in a matter-of-fact way. The writer was later to acknowledge those early narrations as the main models for his own idiosyncratic style.

Gabriel García Márquez in his office at home, 1983. [Time & Life Pictures/Getty Images]

Although García Márquez started publishing in the late 1940s, it was the appearance of *Cien años de soledad* (*One Hundred Years of Solitude*) in 1967 that brought him international acclaim. The book was followed by numerous novels, short stories, journalistic writings, screenplays, and a volume of memoirs. He was awarded the Nobel Prize for Literature in 1982.

García Márquez's main subject matter in most of his novels and stories is Latin America: its history, its political upheavals, its ultimate destiny. However, although concerned with political questions and frequently dire social conditions, his best-known works are characterized by a mixture of **fantasy**, hyperbolic humor, and realism that find expression in a controlled, often austere style. Many of his works take place in the imaginary town of Macondo, which may be considered as microcosmic embodiment of Latin America as a whole.

Although García Márquez highlights the importance of the oral tales he heard as a child, his work shows the influence of diverse sources such as **myth**s, **folklore**, and fairy tales. The foundation of

Macondo, for example, is modeled on creation myths—the town's original inhabitants have to name their surrounding realities, like Adam and Eve in Eden. The notion of circular or cyclic time also plays an important role in his fictional universe. In *One Hundred Years of Solitude*, the literal consequence of breaking the taboo against **incest** is the **birth** of a child with a **pig**'s tail.

Occasionally, García Márquez will openly reveal his sources, as in the story "El avión de la bella durmiente" ("The Sleeping Beauty's Plane," 1992), evidently inspired by "**Sleeping Beauty**." More often, the references are not so obvious, and the reader is immersed in the writer's transformation (and often reversal) of an otherwise familiar plot. Such is the case in "La cándida Eréndira" ("Innocent Eréndira," 1972), an inversion of the traditional story of the captive **princess** in which the princess claims her freedom at the end by abandoning her rescuer.

Further Readings: Bell-Villada, Gene H., ed. *Conversations with García Márquez.* Jackson: University Press of Mississippi, 2005; Bloom, Harold, ed. *Gabriel García Márquez.* Philadelphia: Chelsea House, 1992; Grullon, Carmen Amantina. "Once There Was a Writer: The Narrative of Gabriel García Márquez and the Fairy Tale: A Comparative Study." Dissertation. University of Connecticut, 1994; Jain, Jasbir. "Innocent Eréndira: The Reversal of a Fairy Tale." *García Márquez and Latin America.* Edited by Alok Bhalla. New York: Envoy Press, 1987. 101–8.

Víctor Figueroa

Garner, Alan (1934–)

Alan Garner is a British novelist whose fiction engages extensively with the form and content of mythology, **folklore**, and, more broadly, the forces of history and tradition. Garner has lived in and around Alderley Edge in Cheshire for his entire life. It is an area rich with history that the author has himself explored in archaeological and archival terms, and it is his patient and detailed attention to place and land—and to the relationship of person and place—that forms the bedrock of his work. His first **novel**, *The Weirdstone of Brisingamen* (1960), employs the **legend** of the wizard of Alderley Edge, a precise situating of the writing, including at the level of diction, which continued through *The Moon of Gomrath* (1963) and *Elidor* (1965). Indeed, *The Owl Service* (1967), a novel that draws on the medieval Welsh tales of the *Mabinogion*, is to date the only extended fictional work of Garner's set beyond the Cheshire landscape.

Along with geography, the other dominant feature of Garner's work is its concern for the dialogue of historical and mythical time. This is particularly evident in *Red Shift* (1973), *Strandloper* (1996), and *Thursbitch* (2003), each of which attempts a complex interweaving of times past and present. In the introduction to *Alan Garner's Book of British Fairy Tales* (1984), Garner as editor laments the shift in the life of the fairy tale toward the educator, the scholar, and the nursery. Fairy tales are the property of all, a rooted body of narratives intended for **performance**. Their meaning is universal but lies beyond the reach of reason, in the ebb and flow of the language itself. Garner carefully adapts his sources according to these beliefs, with a view to passing on their singularity and continued importance. As with all of his work, respect for the particularities of tradition is coupled with a desire actively to engage with their continuance. Not surprisingly, it has been argued that much of Garner's own writing is in fact the product of a subtle process of creative **adaptation**, drawing in materials both local and international. His reach stretches from Celtic folklore (*The*

Weirdstone of Brisingamen; *Elidor*) to Australian aboriginal mythology (*Strandloper*), but he admits to being left cold by Greek and Roman **myth**s.

Garner has long resisted the designation of children's author, despite having adapted a large number of fairy tales, including *Alan Garner's Fairy Tales of Gold* (1980), with illustrations by Michael Foreman. Nevertheless, the figure of the child is accorded a privileged position in Garner's fiction, as having a nature open and available to the presence of the traditions of the past, an openness lost to, and threatened by, the modern adult world.

Further Readings: Garner, Alan. *The Voice That Thunders*. London: The Harvill Press, 1997; Philip, Neil. *A Fine Anger: A Critical Introduction to the Work of Alan Garner*. London: Collins, 1981; Rose, Jacqueline. *The Case of Peter Pan or, The Impossibility of Children's Fiction*. Revised edition. London: Macmillan, 1994.

Stephen Benson

Gautier, Théophile (1811–1872)

A French poet, critic, playwright, and established journalist, Théophile Gautier contributed to the development of the fantastic tale. His family moved to Paris from Tarbes in 1814, and in 1822, Gautier made the acquaintance of Gérard de Nerval, who would become a lifelong friend. Initially an avid defender of Romanticism, Gautier later became a spokesman of "art for art's sake." Gautier's interest in the fantastic was sparked by the French publication of E. T. A. **Hoffmann**'s tales, and the first of his several articles on Hoffmann appeared in 1830. His tales clearly bear Hoffmann's influence: in "La cafetière" ("The Coffeepot," 1831), figures slip out of their paintings to dance; his 1832 "Onuphrius" is subtitled "ou les vexations fantastiques d'un admirateur d'Hoffmann" ("or the Fantastic Vexations of an Admirer of Hoffmann"); and "Le pied de momie" ("The Mummy's Foot," 1840) might be considered Gautier's "Sandman."

Gautier also came under the spell of the ***Arabian Nights*** and the Orient. In "La mille et deuxième nuit" ("The Thousand and Second Night," 1842), the sultana **Sheherazade** approaches the narrator because she has run out of stories. Gautier also conceived several fantastic ballets, including *Giselle, ou Les Wilis* (1841), based on Slavic lore filtered through a poem by Heinrich Heine, and *La Péri* (1843). *See also* French Tales.

Further Readings: Fortin, Jutta. "Brides of the Fantastic: Gautier's 'Le Pied de momie' and Hoffmann's 'Der Sandmann.'" *Comparative Literature Studies* 41 (2004): 257–75; Smith, Albert Brewster. *Théophile Gautier and the Fantastic*. University, MS: Romance Monographs, 1977.

Anne E. Duggan

Gay and Lesbian Tales

It is a truism that a love story is the central focus of many (and perhaps most of the best-known) folktales and fairy tales. However, the fact that the love described is almost invariably heterosexual is rarely acknowledged or analyzed. While there are isolated examples of folkloric narratives with homoerotic themes, and while a "**folklore**" (stories, jokes, epithets, etc.) has emerged within contemporary gay and lesbian groups, the representation of same-sex desire is largely absent from most folktale and fairy-tale traditions. This is hardly surprising given the taboos surrounding homosexuality in most cultures. Still, as the effects of heterosexist portrayals of love on generations of gays and lesbians come into sharper focus, so too has the adverse role folktale and fairy-tale plots have played. Intentionally or not, they have been used to enforce what has been termed "compulsory heterosexuality," the cultural expectation that all individuals are innately and immutably heterosexual, and that same-sex object choice is "unnatural." In response, several contemporary writers have rewritten folktale and fairy-tale plots so as to reflect same-sex desires and relationships. Their small but growing corpus can rightfully be called "gay and lesbian tales."

But even before the advent of this corpus, folktales and fairy tales portrayed anything but a monolithic image of **sexuality**. If viewed from the perspective of homosociality, the same-**gender** affective bonds that are not primarily (although potentially) erotic, many tales offer depictions of same-sex emotional attachments that complicate the stereotypical notion that their sole focus is heterosexual desire. Beyond the love and the rivalry among siblings, parents and children, stepparents and stepchildren, there are the innumerable tales in which same-gender friends and rivals are the salient feature of the plot. The ways in which these same-gender (or homosocial) relationships are portrayed are inevitably linked to cultural expectations, which, at their root, concern homosexuality, whether this is articulated as such or not. This becomes exceedingly clear in folktales and fairy tales that feature **cross-dressing** characters, such as Giovan Francesco **Straparola**'s "Costanzo-Costanza," Giambattista **Basile**'s "Le tre corone" ("The Three Crowns"), Marie-Jeanne **Lhéritier de Villandon**'s "Marmoisan," Marie-Catherine d'**Aulnoy**'s "Belle-Belle, ou le chevalier Fortuné" ("Belle-Belle or the Fortunate Knight"). In such narratives, the cross-dressing **motif** is used to create homoerotic suspense wherein a character is attracted to the cross-dressed hero(ine) even though s/he seems to be of the same gender. In the end, the disguise is exposed, and a heterosexual **marriage** dissipates the possibility of homoerotic "disorder." Homoerotic elements have also been noted in tales by Hans Christian **Andersen** and Oscar **Wilde**, motivated in part by an attempt to find links between the sexuality of these authors and their writings. If approached metaphorically and contextually, Andersen's and Wilde's stories do indeed contain ambiguous characters, situations, and descriptions that evince homoerotic overtones. Within their cultural context, Wilde's fairy tales—even more clearly than Andersen's—can be interpreted in this way, with their valorization of intense male friendship, nonreproductivity, and aestheticism (see, for instance, "The Happy Prince" and "The Devoted Friend").

Contemporary gay and lesbian fairy tales, which deal explicitly with same-sex desire and relationships, are the product of the post-Stonewall era. In the wake of the famous 1969 riots in New York City (precipitated by a police raid on the Stonewall Inn), gays and lesbians demanded the right to visibility and equality, and, at the same time, began on the one hand to scrutinize the heterosexist culture in which they lived and on the other to use various art forms to express their own experiences. It is this context that explains the fairly recent appearance of gay and lesbian fairy tales. The fairy-tale form also offers the appeal of lending itself readily to the camp aesthetic that is exploited in many gay and lesbian circles. The fantastical characters and situations typical of the genre are so many ready-made elements of the self-conscious exaggeration and theatricality that are prized in camp. At the same time, by transforming well-known constructs of gender and sexuality, writers of gay and lesbian fairy tales have engaged in the practice of what is called "queerness," the deliberate alteration and making "strange" of the seemingly "natural" constructs of patriarchal and heterosexual culture so as to expose their arbitrariness. As well-known cultural **archetype**s whose representations of gender and sexuality are usually taken for granted, folktales and fairy tales can be readily "queered."

The first to explore the "queer" potential of fairy tales was Olga **Broumas**, whose 1977 collection of poems, *Beginning with O*, recalls in many ways Anne **Sexton**'s earlier collection *Transformations* (1971). However, unlike Sexton's **adaptation**s, Broumas's rewritings of selected tales by the **Grimm**s stage a variety of relationships between **women**, including scenes of lesbian love. Peter Cashorali's two volumes of prose tales, *Fairy Tales: Traditional Stories Retold for Gay Men* (1995) and *Gay Fairy and Folk Tales: More Traditional Stories Retold for Gay Men* (1997), are retellings of a wide variety of stories from many national traditions. While he carefully notes the sources for each tale, Cashorali sets most of them in various setting of contemporary gay subculture and addresses numerous issues confronting gay **men**: coming out, dealing with troubled **family** relationships, surviving the AIDS epidemic, to name a few. Emma **Donoghue**'s *Kissing the Witch: Old Tales in New Skins* (1997) is overall less pragmatic and more lyrical than Cashorali's collections, with twelve linked stories each told by a character in the previous tale, usually a woman. Not only does Donoghue disrupt the predictable plots of heterosexual desire, she also questions the moral binary so frequent in traditional folktales and fairy tales, with old and "evil" women becoming objects of love for younger women. In the growing body of gay and lesbian **children's literature**, intended to sensitize children to sexual diversity, at least two recent picture books qualify as fairy tales: Linda de Haan and Stern Nijland's *King and King* (2002) and Harvey Fierstein and Henry Cole's *The Sissy Duckling* (2002). Both of these rewrite fairy-tale-like motifs to promote acceptance of gays and lesbians. Beyond the corpus of gay and lesbian fairy tales, "queer" interpretations have only begun to be pursued. Such an approach would seek to reconsider heterosexist assumptions in both "classic" folktales and fairy tales and in the field of folktale and fairy-tale scholarship. *See also* Erotic Tales.

F*urther Readings:* Duffy, John-Charles. "Gay-Related Themes in the Fairy Tales of Oscar Wilde." *Victorian Literature and Culture* 29.2 (2001): 327–49; Newall, Venetia. "Folklore and Male Homosexuality." *Folklore* 97.2 (1986): 123–47; Wood, Naomi. "Creating the Sensual Child: Paterian Aesthetics, Pederasty, and Oscar Wilde's Fairy Tales." *Marvels & Tales* 16 (2002): 156–70.

Lewis C. Seifert

Gender

Gender, or the cultural constructions accompanying biological **sex**, is a fundamental organizing category in folktales and fairy tales in addition to all of social life. Gender can be defined as the behavioral, psychological, and expressive traits associated with a sex. Masculine traits map to the male sex whereas feminine traits map to the female sex. Yet the widely accepted heuristic aligning gender with culture and sex with biology is complicated by the further introduction of **sexuality** as a factor, in addition to recent feminist work problematizing the assumed naturalness of gender, sex, and sexuality. None of these categories or identities is fixed in time or space, individually or culturally. Many Western cultures tend to have only masculine and feminine genders available, while some non-Western cultures allow for the existence of a third gender. Since gender is malleable and culturally relative, it is an especially important component of narratives and narrative analysis. Some key interactions of folktales and fairy tales with gender occur within tale texts (such as gendered plots and characters), tale contexts (the gender of storytellers and implied gender of genres), and tale scholarship (feminist criticism of gender roles and revisions thereof).

The plots of many folktales and fairy tales can be classified along gender lines as masculine or feminine stories. The ordering of the index of **tale type**s supports this construction but risks gender bias in its inconsistent labeling of female characters, sometimes omitting entire actions that **women** perform. Bengt **Holbek**, in his *Interpretation of Fairy Tales* (1987), distinguishes between masculine and feminine fairy tales depending on the gender of the protagonist. In addition, using data from the nineteenth-century Danish folktale collector Evald **Tang Kristensen**, Holbek discusses the correlations between the gender of storytellers and the gender of the characters within the tales.

Characters in fairy tales often exhibit strongly gendered behavior. Male protagonists are frequently sent on quests, whereas female protagonists encounter tasks in the domestic sphere. These boundaries are mutable, however, as some tales (notably ATU types in the 880s) feature **cross-dressing**. Many female characters occupying a role of power are demonized as antagonists; this is especially the case with the stepmother and the **witch**. There can be a correspondence between the genders of the major tale characters. For instance, in ATU 510, **Cinderella**, the heroine, must outwit her wicked stepmother, aided by the benevolent female donor figure who is either her dead **mother** or a fairy godmother, to attend a social function that leads to **marriage**.

On a contextual level, folktales and fairy tales are frequently aligned with storytellers of different genders in different cultures, regions, and time periods. One problem with trying to study the correlation between gender and **storytelling**, though, is the lack of details about **informant**s' lives in many collections. Two positive examples are Hasan El-Shamy's *Folktales of Egypt* (1980) and Ibrahim Muhawi and Sharif Kanaana's *Speak, Bird, Speak Again: Palestinian Arab Folktales* (1989). These not only provide comprehensive information about the storytellers but also hypothesize about why so many of the storytellers are women. Both studies, which link women's roles in child-rearing and the domestic sphere to their interactions with folktales, would not be possible without attention to gender in the larger cultural context. Similarly, Linda **Dégh**'s *Folktales and Society: Story-Telling in a Hungarian Peasant Community* (1969) examines larger social trends, including the gendered domains of occupations and performances that lead to a preponderance of male storytellers. Both Dégh and Holbek discuss the stylistic and thematic differences between male and female storytellers, though both acknowledge that this area remains largely unexplored. Gender bias in collections—conscious or unconscious, on the part of the collector or the informant—is also a factor, especially in communities where a collector may have more- or less-restricted access to certain spheres of social life.

Various subgenres have themselves assumed gendered identities at times. Fairy tales have become a feminized genre in contemporary English-speaking countries, along with being assimilated into **children's literature**. In her study *From the Beast to the Blonde: On Fairy Tales and Their Tellers* (1994), Marina **Warner** traces the roots of the old wives' tales and other gendered associations with fairy-tale narrators. Warner also discusses the seventeenth- and eighteenth-century **French tales** representing the *conte de fées*, over half of which were authored by women who used the genre as a medium to critique gender roles.

On a metatextual level, feminist criticism of the gender roles expressed in fairy tales has passed through a variety of stages. Feminist scholars initially protested the passive portrayal of heroines and the allocation of **punishment and reward** according to gender roles. For instance, the protagonist in ATU 480, **The Kind and the Unkind Girls**, is rewarded with wealth and sometimes marriage for demonstrating domestic competence. Moreover, feminists have critiqued the role that folktales and fairy tales play in socialization with their static depictions of gender roles. Jack **Zipes**'s *Don't Bet on the Prince: Contemporary Feminist Fairy Tales in North American and England* (1986) provides a dual approach to this problem: the scholarly essays evaluate some of the ways gender roles are integrated into fairy tales, while the collected tales provide alternative models of gendered behavior.

Retellings of folktales and fairy tales often focus on gender as a key point for revision. Some of these **adaptation**s reverse gender roles by placing females in traditionally male roles, having them slay **dragon**s and rescue captives. Other retellings seek to valorize neglected feminine roles by emphasizing the strength needed to perform stereotypically feminine or nurturing occupations. Overall, critical attention to gender in folktales and fairy tales has generated a host of scholarship as well as new texts that seek to rectify sexism. **See also** Collecting, Collectors; Erotic Tales; Feminism; Feminist Tales; Gay and Lesbian Tales; Men.

Further Readings: Apo, Satu, Aili Nenola, and Laura Stark-Arola, eds. *Gender and Folklore: Perspectives on Finnish and Karelian Culture.* Helsinki: Finnish Literature Society, 1998; Bacchilega, Cristina. *Postmodern Fairy Tales: Gender and Narrative Strategies.* Philadelphia: University of Pennsylvania Press, 1997; Haase, Donald. "Feminist Fairy-Tale Scholarship." *Fairy Tales and Feminism: New Approaches.* Edited by Donald Haase. Detroit: Wayne State University Press, 2004. 1–36; Järv, Risto. "The Gender of the Heroes, Storytellers, and Collectors of Estonian Fairy Tales." *Folklore: Electronic Journal of Folklore* 29 (August 2005): 45–60. http://www.folklore.ee/folklore/vol29/gender.pdf; Stone, Kay. "The Misuses of Enchantment: Controversies on the Significance of Fairy Tales." *Women's Folklore, Women's Culture.* Edited by Rosan A. Jordan and Susan J. Kalcik. Philadelphia: University of Pennsylvania Press, 1985. 125–45.

Jeana Jorgensen

German Tales

Germany has been at the center of folktale and fairy-tale research and production since Jacob and Wilhelm **Grimm**'s pivotal work, the ***Kinder- und Hausmärchen*** (*Children's and Household Tales*, 1812–15). That collection, which has since gained canonical status, developed at a specific historical confluence of sociopolitical, pedagogical, mercantile, publishing, and theoretical concerns. Since the Grimm's landmark work, folktales and fairy tales have become a fundamental part of German culture.

Fairy and Folktales in Print

Before the Grimms, generic boundaries between **folktale**, **fairy tale**, **saga**, **legend**, and **epic** were fluid. With the 1447 invention of the printing press, reading materials became more widely available, and while there were not fully developed tales as they came to be known later, several fairy-tale **motif**s appeared in these genres as early as the fifteenth century. Literate clergy with access to texts had already been exploiting the tales' didactic potential for religious instruction. The ***Gesta Romanorum*** (*The Deeds of the Romans*), a collection of **anecdote**s with appended religious **moral**s, was an important source for homiletic texts and introduced German-speaking congregants to stories such as "Tales about Toads." "Aschenprödlin" ("**Cinderella**") appeared in a 1521 biblical exegesis by Martin Luther, and others of his sermons contained motifs from "The Brave Little Tailor." Writers of courtly and heroic epics often embedded fairy-tale motifs into those longer, novelistic works.

The most common print vehicle in the sixteenth and seventeenth centuries was the *Volksbücher*, the inexpensive **chapbook**s of short tales expanded into multipage stories; especially popular were tales of wrongly-accused **women** suffering trials of patience (Griseldis, Genovefa). By the middle of the sixteenth century, writers, dramatists, and satirists such as Martin Montanus, Hans Sachs, and Johann Fischart were incorporating fairy-tale motifs into their works. In his 1557 "Wegkürtzer" ("The Journey Quickened"), Montanus included the tale "Das Erdtkülin," an early version of ATU 510A, Cinderella, and thereby predating the Giambattista **Basile**'s "Cennerentola" by almost eighty years. Motifs in Sachs's dramatized **fable**s and **jest**s included "The Knapsack, the Hat, and the Horn," "Eve's Unequal Children," "The Seven Swans," and "The Raven," among others. Fischart wrote a version of "Rumpelstiltskin" in 1572. This trend continued into the seventeenth century as baroque writers such as Johannes Praetorius, Jakob Grimmelshausen, Gabriel Rollenhagen, and Johann Michael Moscherosch included fairy-tale motifs in longer works; scholars have identified a version of "The **Frog King**, or Iron Heinrich" already in 1595 in Rollenhagen; "The Mouse, the Bird, and the Sausage" and "Godfather Death" in Moscherosch in 1650; numerous Rübezahl stories in Praetorius's 1662 works; and "Bearskin" in Grimmelshausen in 1670.

By the middle of the eighteenth century, Europe was in the throes of the Enlightenment, with its insistence on rationality and reason. Nonetheless, or perhaps in response, interest in fairy tales, especially in the French *conte de fées* and Oriental tales, boomed in Germany among the literate upper classes. Marie-Catherine d'**Aulnoy**'s *Les contes des fées* (1697) were circulating in the original, as was Antoine **Galland**'s translation of the *Arabian Nights*, *Les mille et une nuits* (1704–17; German translation, 1711), along with other "pseudo-Oriental" magic tales by Jacques **Cazotte** and Thomas-Simon Gueulette. The bourgeoisie, generally unable to read French, created a demand for translations; by the end of the century, Friedrich Bertuch's twelve-volume *Blaue Bibliothek aller Nationen* (*Blue Library of All Nations*, 1790–96) brought *la bibliothèque bleue* to Germany. Bertuch also planned a less costly edition for broader distribution.

German writers—encouraged by the financial successes of the tales of fairies from France—began to write their own **literary fairy tale**s or adapt foreign tales for a specifically German readership, although the generic boundaries remained inchoate. Manfred Grätz has called Gottlieb Wilhelm Rabener's 1755 "Märgen vom Ersten Aprile" ("Fairy Tale from April First") the first true German fairy tale; he considers Georg Christof Weitzler's "Mährchen vom Ritter mit dem Blasebalg" ("Tale of the Knight with the Bagpipe," 1763) the earliest complete German **wonder tale** for which no foreign source can be established and which foreshadows the Grimms' *Volksmärchen* (folktale) model. Grätz claims Wilhelm Christhelf Mylius's rendition in 1777 of Anthony **Hamilton**'s mostly Oriental tales to be the first clear attempt at adapting tales to German popular culture, as well as to address the lower classes rather than the nobility and privileged bourgeoisie.

German writers were only slowly beginning to distance themselves from the French tradition. Christoph Martin **Wieland,** for example, in his *Die Abentheuer des Don Sylvio von Rosalva* (*The Adventures of Don Sylvio of Rosalva*, 1764) made fun of the ludicrous fantastic elements in the *contes*, but also included his own literary fairy tale, "Geschichte des Prinzen Biribinker" ("Story of Prince Biribinker"). Johann Karl August **Musäus** overtly established his work as drawn from an indigenous German **oral tradition** when he stressed his tales were originals from the fatherland (*vaterländische Originale*) and titled them

Volksmärchen der Deutschen (*Folktales of the Germans*, 1782–86). His five-volume collection of Thuringian, Silesian, and Bohemian folk material was hugely successful before the Grimms. In 1789, Benedikte **Naubert** began publishing her four-volume *Neue Volksmärchen der Deutschen* (*New German Folktales*), using English, French, and pseudo-Oriental sources. She anticipated many of the themes and narrative strategies of later women's works. While women had clearly been established as storytellers, Naubert was the first to put women in the role of writer.

With Johann Joachim Schwabe's 1756–57 German translation of Jeanne-Marie **Leprince de Beaumont's** *Le magasin des enfants* (*The Young Misses' Magazine*), fairy tales clearly entered the realm of **children's literature**. Book production was happening in synergy with debates of philosophers and educators about fairy tales' uses and usefulness for children. Schoolbooks written during the Enlightenment contained predominantly moralizing **religious tale**s and fables, but also sundry stories of world history and a few assorted French fairy tales. Two camps had emerged regarding fairy tales as suitable children's reading: one that feared superstitions and fantastic elements frightened and distracted children from their duties and the teachings of the church, and the other that saw the tales socializing children to be upright citizens and promoting their creative imagination. When translated child-appropriate selections of the *Le cabinet des fées* (*The Fairies' Cabinet*) appeared between 1763–66, they bore an appended moral caveat to stress their pedagogical value. Other collections, such as Johann Gottlieb Schummel's *Kinderspiele und Gespräche* (*Children's Games and Conversations*, 1776, containing tales from Carlo **Gozzi**), used the fantastic elements to present religious morals. The author of *Einige Feenmährchen für Kinder* (*Some Fairy Tales for Children*, 1780, mostly translations of child-appropriate *contes*) explicitly stated the tales' didactic and creative potential.

In the years shortly before the turn of the nineteenth century, writers continued to mediate the French tales for children but began turning to indigenous German models. An important hybrid work between translation, adaptation, and revival of German folk materials were Ludwig **Tieck**'s *Volksmährchen* (*Folktales*, 3 vols., 1797) and *Romantische Dichtungen* (*Romantic Literature*, 1799). In those collections, he presented tales from Charles **Perrault**, including "**Bluebeard**," "**Little Red Riding Hood**," and "The Master Cat, or **Puss in Boots**." Perrault had already been received positively in Germany for his children's tales; Bertuch, for example, in his introduction to the *Blue Library*, had praised the Frenchman for bringing fairy tales to children, especially young girls, and extolled the tales for their purity and decency, a "catechism for habits of good breeding." In addition to Perrault's tales, Tieck also included stories from German chapbooks and **jest**s, such as "Leben und Tod der heiligen Genoveva" ("Life and Death of Saint Genovefa") and "Sehr wundersame Historie von der schönen Melusina" ("The Very Wonderous History of the Beautiful Melusine").

The fairy tale became tremendously successful as children's literature in the nineteenth century for sociopolitical, publishing, and pedagogical reasons. The middle class was burgeoning; the development of the bourgeois nuclear family and the genesis of the children's room around the turn of the century precipitated major social changes within the family structure. Mandatory schooling led to a need for reading materials and to greater literacy: in 1830, the literacy rate in Germany was only 30 percent; by 1850, it was 50 percent, and 90 percent by 1890—a growth rate of approximately a half-million new readers per year. Some educators, folklorists, and writers were already penning collections specifically for children, such as Albert Ludwig Grimm's *Kindermärchen* (*Children's Fairy Tales*, 1808) and Johann Gustaf Büsching's *Volks-Sagen, Märchen und Legenden* (*Folk Sagas, Fairy Tales, and Legends*) in 1812—nine months ahead of Jacob and Wilhelm Grimms' collection. It was at this juncture that the Grimm brothers would compile the *Children's and Household Tales*, their self-proclaimed *Erziehungsbuch* (educational primer). It would become the best-known German book internationally and the most published book in German after the Bible; it would go through seventeen editions in almost forty years, in a three-year cycle alternating between ten abridged and seven complete editions. By the 1830s and the publication of their third edition, many of the Grimms' tales were part of the school reading curriculum. The *Children's and Household Tales* set into motion a flurry of collecting, writing, tale-swapping, and pirated editions of various market-successful collections.

Female writers and **collectors** also played an important part in the German folktale and fairy-tale tradition. Over the course of the eighteenth and nineteenth centuries, women published at least 800 fairy tales and collections, far outnumbering male authors and compilers of fairy-tale books. By 1800, the family and romance novel had become the domain of female writers; by 1810, writers such as Sophie Albrecht, Julie Berger, Caroline Auguste Fischer, Therese Huber, Caroline de la Motte Fouqué, Caroline Pichler, Dorothea Schlegel, Sophie Tieck-Bernhardi, and Johanna Isabella von Wallenrodt had published individual fairy-tale and legend reworkings that struck a compromise between the generic demands of the fairy tale and the narrative structure of the romance novel. Starting with Naubert's *New German Folktales*, women also participated in the documentation of tales from the Germanic past and became avid collectors of local tales and legends, often adapted for children. Other writers mediated the tales written by French women in the late seventeenth century or produced translations and compilations from the *Arabian Nights*.

The fairy tale as children's literature and the popular reception of the Grimms continued unabated into the twentieth century. In the first third of the century, the fairy tale had been established indisputably as appropriate children's reading and was the best represented genre. Most collections were of nineteenth-century provenience (Grimms, Ludwig **Bechstein**, and Hans Christian **Andersen**), along with the *Arabian Nights* and the Romantics' *Kunstmärchen* (literary fairy tales). At the turn of the century, floods of tales and newly arranged anthologies came to bookshelves; the *Gesamtverzeichnis des deutschsprachigen Schrifttums* (*The Registry of German-Language Literature*) shows that between 1911 and 1965, approximately twelve new fairy-tale books appeared each year, including translations from other linguistic and cultural traditions. New media such as radio, **television**, **film, and video** broadened the audience, often bowdlerizing the originals. Those media made fairy tales the stuff of advertisements, commercials, and children's films. Fairy tales were now firmly established in the school curriculum.

Folklore and Fairy Tales in the Service of Nation-Building and Sociopolitical Ideologies

The history of the fairy tale and folktale in Germany has been intertwined with sociopolitical, pedagogical, folkloristic, and ideological agendas since the Enlightenment. In 1778, the literary critic and philosopher Johann Gottfried Herder espoused the ideas of the *Volk*—the **folk** united by common culture and language—and *Naturpoesie*, the natural poetic creations that bubbled up from the folk, in contrast to *Kunstpoesie*, the artificial poetry of individual writers. Herder called upon his countrymen to recapture the folk's poetic artistry from the

Nordic-Germanic past in all its forms, including mythology, legends, sagas, and folktales. When Herder was named school superintendent in Weimar in 1790, his folkloristic interests became pedagogical and he began making plans to integrate fairy-tale and fable collections into the school curriculum. His notions about **folklore** had a lasting impact on collecting and publishing activities long after.

Herder's ideas exercised a great influence on the Romantics at the turn of the century, when Germany was in the grips of the Napoleonic occupation and intellectuals sought means to assert the superiority of the Germans over their occupiers. The Romantics looked back to the **Middle Ages** and even farther, to the Nordic-Germanic, pre-Christian times when, they believed, a unified German identity existed. Lionizing the poetic soul of the folk, they began recovering the cultural remnants the Enlightenment had scorned: folk songs and folktales, chapbooks, Nordic-Germanic mythology, sagas, legends, and fairy tales. The Romantic movement, at its core nationalistic, heralded the fairy tale's emancipation from the French influence that had dominated German literature: the Romantic literary fairy tale was born. Important Romantic writers include Achim von Arnim, Clemens **Brentano**, Joseph Freiherr von **Eichendorff**, E. T. A. **Hoffmann**, Friedrich von Hardenberg (**Novalis**), Ludwig Tieck, Friedrich de la Motte **Fouqué,** Adalbert von **Chamisso,** Amalie von **Helvig,** Bettina von **Arnim**—and the Brothers Grimm.

The *Children's and Household Tales* did not develop in a vacuum but at a confluence of nationalistic, philological, and political agendas. The Grimms believed that the cultural concept of a nation hinges on a common language, a common set of beliefs, and a common cultural heritage shared by a people. That ideology prompted their work on reconstructing that identity and a national consciousness through the recovery of the pre-Christian, Nordic-Germanic pagan mythic world, as evidenced in the tales they believed were remnants of that world. Their theorizing precipitated a flurry of collecting, as other collectors set off to document tales, sagas, and legends claiming provenience in the oral tradition and to recapture the common bonds of language and culture in far-flung German lands—German-speaking Switzerland, Austria, Silesia, Bavaria, Lower Saxony, Transylvania, and many others.

In the conservative restoration period after the failed 1848 revolution, educators, folklorists, and writers took up the cause of the Grimm heritage, and fairy tales were called upon increasingly to play a role in defining the national identity. In an essay in the patriotic journal *Germania*, Ludwig Bechstein (whose own two fairy-tale collections actually outpaced the Grimms' in sales until the 1890s) praised Jacob Grimm for making the connection between tales and Germanic mythology and suggested that the youth of the nation needed fairy tales to distract them from contemporary political realities. In 1851, Friederich August Wilhelm Diesterweg, one of the century's most influential educators promoting universal public education, argued for uncovering the treasures of the German national language in folk songs, fairy tales, folk epics, and proverbs, and declared them important tools in the German national upbringing. Heinrich Pröhle, the most important folklore researcher in northern Germany, opined: "Oh, how lovely when you can so easily teach children to love their fatherland, to hold its borders holy, to respect their folk, and never to forget the heroic deeds of their fathers."

The fairy tale's fate in the twentieth century was most dramatically impacted by the two world wars and the subsequent division of Germany into two independent nations. Early in the century, the Grimms' collection and other folktales continued to be considered essential for the development of the German national identity. As in previous centuries, some educational reformers opposed fairy tales; while they praised the folktale, they argued new tales had to be told that would address contemporary events from the child's view. After the horrors of World War I, writers such as Hermynia **Zur Mühlen** began penning socialist and proletarian fairy tales for children.

The ground was already being tilled during the Weimar Republic for the *Blut und Boden* (blood and soil) folk literature to come in the National Socialist regime. Already in the 1920s, "folklorists" Werner von Bülow, Karl von Spieß, and Georg Schott were harking back to Herder and the Romantic ideas of the pre-Christian Nordic-Germanic religion to validate their racist and xenophobic attitudes. Two titles from 1925 made clear the direction their folklore research would take: von Bülow stressed the connection between fairy tales and Germanic religion in *Märchendeutungen durch Runen: Die Geheimsprache der deutschen Märchen*; *Ein Beitrag zur Entwicklungsgeschichte der deutschen Religion* (*Fairy Tale Interpretations with Runes: The Secret Language of the German Fairy Tales; A Contribution to the Evolution of German Religion*). Schott found prophetic messages for Germany's destiny in the tales in his *Weissagung und Erfüllung in deutschen Volksmärchen* (*Prophesy and Fulfillment in German Folktales*); among other outlandish interpretations, he compared "Cinderella" to the dire situation of the Germans during the Depression and claimed the unhappy ending of "The Companionship of the Cat and the Mouse" was due to nature's abhorrence of unions between different races.

Citing Herder's notion of the folk and the revival of the folk spirit during the Romantic movement, the Nazis promoted German folk education and saw the folktale as a means to their racial and political ends. Hitler regarded the "folkish" state as the central point of his political thought. In 1934, the Minister of Science, Education, and Folk Culture decreed school teachers focus on Nordic-Germanic folklore and organize the school curriculum around "a unified worldview" that reflected the old Germanic peasant culture and Nordic-Germanic roots. During the 1930s, as a means to support the idea of a super race united by language, culture, and tradition, a mass of folklore and fairy-tale literature was published in Germany, with titles such as *German Heroic Tales* and *Germanic-Nordic Fairy Tales*. The Grimms' collection figured prominently in this effort. Nazi folklorists' works also proliferated: von Spieß called for "purifying" the German folktale of "foreign influences" to reveal the "true mirror of the German folk soul," while Friedrich Panzer suggested all previous folklore theories should be abandoned in favor of the singularity of the German folktale. Matthes Ziegler, director of the Working Group for German Folklore, described in his book *Die Frau im Märchen* (*The Woman in Fairy Tales*, 1937) the German folktale heroine as the ideal Germanic woman, ready to serve and obey, with a "healthy peasant spirit," while Josef Prestel declared the *Children's and Household Tales* "the most important of our holy scriptures."

The Anglo-American occupational forces after World War II believed that the German love of Grimms' fairy tales had contributed to Nazi atrocities. The British limited the exposure to the tales in schools and imposed a prohibition on publishing new fairy-tale editions; whole library collections of fairy tales were shipped off to England and America. In the first years of the Federal Republic and the German Democratic Republic (GDR), the dominant discourse among Germans affirmed what the allied forces had contended: the classic German fairy tales were profoundly repressive, fueled prejudices and xenophobia, and glorified cruelty and militarism. After 1945, critics in both countries debated how fairy tales could play a role in a new children's literature.

The GDR—with its goal of educating the new socialist citizen—had special concerns, and folktales were once again pressed into service to meet political and ideological needs. Initial discussions took a critical stance toward tales. One argument echoed those of centuries past: that the tales were full of archaic superstitions and prejudices. The second tack maintained that tales' use of fantastic elements overstimulated children's imaginations and encouraged utopian longings—things not conducive to the new socialist consciousness. The third argument was that Grimms' tales had fostered German chauvinism and militarism and should be abandoned. The fourth consideration was that their antiquated language and unconventional grammar made tales inappropriate in the classroom.

In the 1950s, partially because of the reception of folklore research in the Soviet Union (which saw folklore as weapons of class conflict), GDR folklorists were working to uncover the "emancipatory democratic character" of the social criticism in folk literature and the national cultural heritage in the artistic creations of the proletariat. When Arnold Zweig assumed the presidency of the German Academy of the Arts in East Berlin, his critique of "The Knapsack, the Hat, and the Horn" paved the way for the Grimms' rehabilitation in East Germany. He argued that fairy tales were not necessarily reactionary, but needed simply to be suffused with the correct ideology. He envisioned ways in which the tales could contribute to the "progressive socialist vision of the future," and made connections to the socialist children's fairy tales of Hermynia Zur Mühlen, Berta Lask, and Lisa Tetzner in the 1930s. Their tales became the standard for children's fairy tales in the GDR in the 1950s.

Between 1945 and 1951, no complete collection of the *Children's and Household Tales* appeared in East Germany, but a new, "improved" edition came out in 1952 with less violence, more happy endings, and no nighttime prayers. The first unexpurgated version was released in 1955; it was to serve as the main source for the motifs and constellations of figures for new, antiauthoritarian fairy tales that socialist writers were expected to produce. The fantastic elements of the fairy tales were to be superimposed on realistic representation of social realities.

By 1984, the mature socialist was ready to have the entire Grimms' collection (although some schoolteachers worried about how to handle certain non-socialist characters, such as **king**s, **princess**es, and other royalty). Besides the classic tales, East German publishing houses also released tales from other countries, predominantly Russia and the peoples of the Soviet Union; they thereby promoted the international heritage of folk literature with the tales of the "socialist brother nations" (*sozialistische Brudervölker*) and dispelled the Nazi hegemonic notion that there was only one true tradition, that of the Nordic-Germanic ancestors and the Grimms.

In contrast to the GDR, where the new political ideology drove folktale and fairy-tale scholarship, West Germany was much slower to question the theoretical premises and scholarly practices of traditional studies. In the East, folklore was conceived of as an independent historical discipline; in the West, folklorists came mainly from German philology, which was deeply indebted to the Grimms and had little contact with the social sciences. Whereas East German scholars had been attempting since the founding of the GDR to elevate the proletariat's experiences and artistic outpourings as represented in folklore, West German scholars often were still in the thrall of Wilhelm Heinrich Riehl's conservative approach, which deliberately excluded the proletariat and focused instead on the landed peasantry. Radical change did not come in the West until the student revolts at the end of the 1960s, which ended in a reorientation of the discipline; West German scholars began to move away from collecting and cataloguing material and focus instead on the meaning of the material for the producers and the recipients. The "folk" was replaced by "culture" in all its varied manifestations.

Evolution of Theories and Methods of Folktale and Fairy-Tale Scholarship

The science of folklore really began with the Grimms, and since their time, German-speaking scholars have fundamentally shaped the discipline. Some scholars have focused specifically on the Grimms' work, while others have expanded the theories and methods the Grimms developed. The brothers have been credited with making folktales worthy of scholarly and literary attention; the tales they assembled and refined in the *Children's and Household Tales* have come to define the generic parameters of the folktale and wonder tale. Their editorial practices and socializing agenda have undergone years of critical scrutiny. Their work with that collection and Germanic **myths**, sagas, and legends established the methodology for mining literary and oral sources; their critical apparatus created the framework for the **comparative method** of literary and folklore research. The Grimms also laid the groundwork for **mythological approaches** by suggesting that folktales were remnants of pre-Christian religion and myths from Indo-European peoples. Wilhelm Grimm argued for an oral source but did not completely discount the possibility of literary influences on tales.

In 1859, Theodor **Benfey** postulated a written rather than oral tradition for folklore/fairy tale origins, the Indian theory. After studying the *Panchatantra* (c. 200 CE), he argued the tales had been disseminated through texts at the time of the Crusades, migrating from India westward over the next centuries. Benfey's theory was overshadowed when older collections from earlier and geographically distant cultures surfaced, although the idea of a literary tradition is still of current scholarly consideration.

At the same time, scholars from multiple disciplines attempted to explain the similarities between tales from geographically divergent cultures and languages. These attempts led to the theory of **polygenesis**—that tales had sprung up independently around the world, due to commonalities in the human experience and psyche. Wilhelm Grimm had already anticipated this theory, which was supported by numerous disciplines in the social sciences. Adolf Bastian, for example, worked from an ethnological position and posited the idea of the *Elementargedanke* (primal thought), while proponents of **anthropological approaches** and **psychological approaches** argued that all primitive people viewed the world in the same way and hence created the same basic stories.

The twentieth century saw a refinement and expansion of approaches and theories. The early twentieth-century cataloguing of the vast amounts of oral and print material collected in the previous century facilitated some of this scholarship. The comparative method produced a large number of reference works. The seminal work for the European narrative tradition is *The Types of International Folktales: A Classification and Bibliography* (started in 1910 by Antti **Aarne**, twice revised by Stith **Thompson,** and again in 2004 by Hans-Jörg Uther). Johannes **Bolte** and Jiří **Polívka**'s five-volume *Anmerkungen zu den Kinder- und Hausmärchen der Brüder Grimm* (*Annotations to Grimms' Children's and Household Tales*, 1913–32) includes all of the known international variants of the Grimms' tales to 1918.

The Gordian knot of much scholarly debate has to do with the tales' age, their transmission through oral or print sources, and their dissemination routes. The **historic-geographic method** proposed a wavelike oral tradition rippling from a central point of origin over an ever-larger geographical area; the greater the area in which a tale was found, the more likely that it appeared independently. Since this method assumed an oral tradition transmitted from the folk to the upper classes, printed tales were considered contaminated oral versions. Other folklorists and scholars have argued instead for the primacy of print versions in the dissemination of tales. In 1922, Hans Naumann posited dissemination not from the folk to the upper classes, but rather in the opposite direction (*gesunkenes Kulturgut*). Albert Wesselski expanded this view in the 1920s and 1930s, arguing in favor of a book history for the dissemination of fairy tales, believing that the literary sources played a more significant role than oral versions in the transmission of tales.

Other branches of folklore and fairy-tale scholarship, using various historical approaches, have focused on what tales reveal about the times and societies in which they evolved. In 1956, for example, Lutz Röhrich explored to what extent tales give evidence of the magical beliefs, relationships between humans and animals, customs, space and time, and the social milieu in early Europe. **Sociohistorical approaches** situate individual tales in a specific time and place that tell about social conditions and the people who wrote and told them.

Folk-narrative theory has shifted the focus from the told to the teller and addressed issues of working with **informant**s. Friedrich Ranke did pioneering work in 1933: he was interested in how the tales functioned for their contemporary tellers. Ranke argued for an exact recording rather than editorial interventions. Later developments in narrative theory have introduced the ideas of **performance** and **context** to include information about the names, ages, professions of the informants, and their attitudes about what they are narrating.

Psychological approaches tend to be hermetic because they typically focus only on tales in the Grimms' collection. Freudian interpretations explore sexual and maturation symbolism and employ tales in the analysis of various neuroses, while Jungian analysts work from Carl Gustav **Jung**'s idea of the collective unconscious, a theory built on Bastian's postulates.

There has also been extensive scholarship conducted under the broad umbrella of recovery work. Heinz Rölleke and others have created a huge amount of scholarship on the editorial and collecting histories of the Grimms. Based on his exhaustive research on the Grimms' informants and sources, Rölleke has dispelled myths that the tales were collected in the field and that they were from an illiterate peasant oral tradition. Feminist recovery work has focused on documenting women's contribution to the German fairy-tale tradition.

There is often a symbiotic relationship between theories and methods, and theories and ideological positions. The debates over the age of the tales (ancient or relatively modern); about **monogenesis** versus polygenesis; oral versus print **diffusion**; and the direction of transmission from the upper classes to the lower classes, or vice versa, continue to occupy scholars and researchers. *See also* DEFA Fairy-Tale Films.

Further Readings: Bottigheimer, Ruth B., ed. *Fairy Tales and Society: Illusion, Allusion, and Paradigm.* Philadelphia: University of Pennsylvania Press, 1986; Dow, James R., and Hannjost Lixfeld, trans. and eds. *German Volkskunde: A Decade of Theoretical Confrontation, Debate, and Reorientation (1967–1977).* Bloomington: Indiana University Press, 1986; Grätz, Manfred. *Das Märchen in der deutschen Aufklärung: Vom Feenmärchen zum Volksmärchen.* Suttgart: Metzler, 1988; Haase, Donald, ed. *The Reception of Grimms' Fairy Tales: Responses, Reactions, Revisions.* Detroit: Wayne State University Press, 1993; Jarvis, Shawn C., and Jeannine Blackwell, eds. and trans. *The Queen's Mirror: Fairy Tales by German Women, 1780–1900.* Lincoln: University of Nebraska Press, 2001; Kamenetsky, Christa.

"Folktale and Ideology in the Third Reich." *Journal of American Folklore* 90 (1977): 168–78; Röth, Diether, and Walter Kahn, eds. *Märchen und Märchenforschung in Europa: Ein Handbuch.* Frankfurt a.M.: Haag und Herchen, 1993.

Shawn C. Jarvis

Gesta Romanorum

The title of the *Gesta Romanorum—Deeds of the Romans*—might suggest events tied to Roman history, but many of the deeds included in this medieval collection come from later chronicles both in Latin and in German. Although the earliest manuscript dates from 1342, the tales were very likely already being collected and recorded in the late thirteenth century. Taken together, the diverse printings and manuscripts of the *Gesta Romanorum* comprise a collection of 283 stories. Variously called a collection of **exempla**, **anecdote**s, allegories, or **fable**s, the *Gesta Romanorum* was created mainly to supply medieval European preachers with a group of tales that elucidated particular moral lessons. In time, the moralizations of the tales became of secondary importance while the tales themselves grew in literary significance. Accordingly, the *Gesta Romanorum* is recognized both as a collection of early European tales in its own right and as an important and popular sources for such authors as Giovanni **Boccaccio** (in *Decameron*), Geoffrey **Chaucer** (in "The Man of Law's Tale"), John Gower (in his version of *Apollonius of Tyre* within his *Confessio amantis*), and William **Shakespeare** (in *King Lear*).

The collection has no clear originary context, and scholars continue to debate the manuscript's history as well as the existence of subgroupings of tales within the whole. It seems most likely that early collections of the tales became so popular that they were circulated from region to region, where local additions were probably made. The first printed edition may therefore include selections from a number of manuscripts. The popularity of the work is evidenced by the knowledge of more than 200 Latin manuscripts plus numerous reworkings of the tales in English and German. The first English edition was issued by Wynkyn de Worde around 1510, and the 1824 edition by Charles Swan (updated with revisions and commentary by Wynnard Hooper in 1876) is still widely used. The 1872 critical edition in German by Hermann Österley remains a major study of the work.

The *Gesta Romanorum* develops folkloric **motif**s common in both oral and written traditions. There are tales centering on tests, tasks, or the answering of seemingly impossible questions; characters prompted by sudden, inexplicable, and urgent desires; plotlines that follow the fortunes or behaviors of parallel characters (two knights, three daughters, three lazy men, or four princes); moral lapses such as mistreating stepchildren or committing adultery or **incest**; and challenges that arise in such unexpected ways as meeting a solitary figure on the road or falling into a **dragon**'s pit. But standard folktale and fairy-tale motifs of the *Gesta Romanorum* are nearly always explicitly allegorized in the Christian applications that follow. The stranger on the road is likely to be an angel sent from God; the dragon in the pit, the **devil**. The tales are also keyed to the Christian doctrine of the forgiveness of sins—along with its ritualized movement through penitence, confession, and penance—thus presenting material ready-made for the instructional purposes of the **clergy** for whom the tales were collected. ***See also*** Middle Ages.

Further Reading: Marchalonis, Shirley. "Medieval Symbols and the *Gesta Romanorum.*" *Chaucer Review* 8 (1974): 311–19.

Lori Schroeder Haslem

Ghost Story

The ghost story is a narrative genre characterized by the presence of a dead person, either as an apparent or disguised element—the ghost. As a **folktale**, the ghost story is widespread and performs a variety of functions ranging from entertainment to corrective education. As a genre, the ghost story can be related to numerous other narrative types—such as the **cautionary tale**, **didactic tale**, **legend**, and **memorate**—in which ghosts may also appear.

Ghost stories appear to have existed since ancient civilizations and are often related to folk beliefs concerning places, buildings, cremation grounds, graveyards, wells, and mountains or other geographical phenomena in nature. They are also informed by beliefs about the nature of ghosts. An almost universally prevalent idea is that ghosts are the spirits of people who died with strong unfulfilled wishes that they still seek to realize. Ghosts can be male or female, appear in human and nonhuman forms, and are capable of both good and bad acts. More powerful than the natural beings they were in life, ghosts often cannot be overcome by rational means but must be appeased in other ways.

Typically, ghost stories are woven around the figure of a single ghost, who may therefore develop a personality of its own through the narrative. Ghosts, their personalities, and their interaction with others reflect the fears and anxieties of the narrators and their audiences. As a tale of the supernatural, the ghost story may inspire fear, but—based on cultural and religious ideas about right and wrong, life and death, this world and the otherworld—it may also be deeply moving.

Further Reading: Stiffler, Muriel W. *The German Ghost Story as Genre.* New York: Peter Lang, 1993.

Sadhana Naithani

Gilgamesh

Gilgamesh is the name of the main character of a literary **epic** that is one of the world's oldest recorded stories. Fragments of myths and tales about Gilgamesh were inscribed in cuneiform in the Sumerian language around 2000 BCE on clay tablets found in the ancient cities of Mesopotamia, Levant, and Anatolia, However, the epic is best known via the standardized Akkadian version recorded on tablets during the seventh century BCE and discovered in the library of Assurbanipal, king of Assyria, in Nineveh. Archaeological findings tell us that Gilgamesh, named on the Sumerian king list, was the fifth king of the first dynasty of Uruk in Babylonia around 2700 BCE.

Many **motif**s and **tale type**s in the epic of Gilgamesh suggest that it has been a bridge to Western folktales and fairy tales. Orientalists have emphasized biblical parallels, pointing out for example that the story of the Deluge in the Gilgamesh epic shows parallels with the story of the Great Flood in the Old Testament. Others have seen a link between the Gilgamesh epic and Homer's *Iliad*. The epic has also been identified as a solar **myth** that originated in Palestine, became part of the biblical tradition, and, via Asia Minor, impacted the

Greek **legend**s. Parallels to ATU 300, The **Dragon**-Slayer, have supported the idea that this important tale type originated in Mesopotamia or Anatolia.

A brief plot summary reveals distinct parallels with recognized folktale types and motifs. Set in ancient Uruk, the epic tells of the tyrant Gilgamesh, a demigod who makes his people suffer (Motif A500, Demigods and culture heroes). The Goddess Ea sends Enkidu, a half human-half beast, to the world (Motif A1241, Man made from clay; Motif F521.1, Man covered with hair like an animal). At first, Enkidu and Gilgamesh fight, but later they become close friends (ATU 303, The Twins or Blood Brothers; Motif P311.1, Combatants become sworn brethren). Together they fight and slay Humbaba, the guardian monster of the Forest of Cedar, who exhales fire (Motif B14.1, Chimera) and is protected by the aura of seven magical layers (Motif D1050, Magic clothes; Motif D2071.0.1, Evil eye covered with seven veils). When the heroic Gilgamesh spurns the goddess Ishtar (Motif K2111, Potiphar's wife), she sends the Bull of Heaven to destroy Uruk (Motif G372, "Rain" as ogre in bull form). Again, Enkidu and Gilgamesh slay the beast. When Enkidu is later punished by the gods and dies, the epic turns to Gilgamesh's quest to find the secrets of life and **death** (Motif E481, Land of the dead; Motif F80, Journey to the lower world). One of this epic's principle themes, the quest for immortality, is very common in ancient mythologies and later folktales. ***See also*** Bible, Bible Tale; Oral Theory.

Further Readings: George, Andrew, trans. *The Epic of Gilgamesh: The Babylonian Epic Poem and Other Texts in Akkadian and Sumerian.* Middlesex: Penguin, 1999; Heidel, Alexander. *The Gilgamesh Epic and Old Testament Parallels*: *A Translation and Interpretation of the Gilgamesh Epic and Related Babylonian and Assyrian Documents.* 2nd edition. Chicago: University of Chicago Press, 1949.

Hande Birkalan-Gedik

Glinka, Mikhail (1804–1857)

Mikhail Glinka is often referred to as the father of Russian classical **music**. He was the first Russian composer to create romances, **opera**s, and other pieces using Russian folk **motif**s and themes. Born into a wealthy family, Glinka's musical interest arose already in his early years. The sounds of the village church bells and the songs of passing peasant choirs influenced him, as did listening to his uncle's orchestra of serf musicians. His studies in schools for children of nobility included piano and violin lessons. From 1830 to 1834, Glinka visited Italy, Germany, and Austria and met with famous composers like Gaetano Donizetti, Felix Mendelssohn, and Hector Berlioz. It was in Italy that he first thought of composing a Russian opera, which led in 1836 to *Ivan Susanin: Zhizn' dlya tsarya (Ivan Susanin: A Life for the Tsar)*, the first of Glinka's two operas.

The story of the brave peasant Ivan Susanin, who saves the life of the tsar by sacrificing his own, has been considered a celebration of Russian patriotism. Musically, it represents a mixture of Russian and Polish folk music with reminiscences of Italian opera. Glinka's second opera, *Ruslan i Lyudmila (Ruslan and Lyudmila,* 1842), is based on the popular and provocative fairy-tale poem by Aleksandr **Pushkin**. Although it did not enjoy the immediate success of *Ivan Susanin*, it has been considered musically superior, especially when it comes to the portrayal of characters. ***See also*** Russian Tales.

Further Readings: Abraham, Gerald. *Studies in Russian Music.* Freeport, NY: Books for Libraries Press, 1968; Stites, Richard. "The Domestic Muse: Music at Home in the Twilight of Serfdom." *Intersections and Transportations: Russian Music, Literature, and Society.* Edited by Andrew Baruch Wachtel.

Evanston, IL: Northwestern University Press, 1998. 187–205; Taruskin, Richard. "Glinka's Ambiguous Legacy and the Birth Pangs of Russian Opera." *19th Century Music* 1.2 (1977): 142–62.

Janina Orlov

Goethe, Johann Wolfgang von (1749–1832)

Fairy tales play only a minor part in the context of Johann Wolfgang von Goethe's extensive and manifold literary works, but the three pieces Germany's most eminent poet and dramatist did write were of seminal importance for the development of the **literary fairy tale**. "Der neue Paris" ("The New Paris") was published in 1821 as part of Goethe's autobiography, *Dichtung und Wahrheit* (*Poetry and Truth*); "Die neue Melusine" ("The New Melusine") is featured in *Wilhelm Meisters Wanderjahre* (*Wilhelm Meister's Journeyman Years*, 1821); and "Das Märchen" ("The Fairy Tale") is included in *Unterhaltungen deutscher Ausgewanderten* (*Conversations of German Refugees*, 1795).

Both "The New Paris" and "The New Melusine" are first-person narratives in which Goethe skillfully blurs the boundaries between magic and reality. The tales' protagonists are imperfect characters: a young boy not yet capable of controlling his emotions (Paris) and a light-minded and unreliable adventurer (Melusine). Goethe frequently makes the trivial and the fabulous collide with great comic effect. Neither tale, however, features a happy ending, leaving the heroes in exactly the same circumstances as before. "The New Paris" is the dream tale of a boy who, opening a secret door in the Frankfurt fortifications, finds himself in a pleasant garden where he is entertained by beautiful nymphs. The story's open-endedness suggests continuation, which is, in Goethe's view, a distinguishing characteristic of fairy tales. In "The New Melusine," the human narrator is chosen to marry a pretty **dwarf** princess to stop the ongoing miniaturization of the whole race of little people. After temporarily becoming a dwarf himself, he eventually regains his human height. The story's style and characters are strongly reminiscent of the *Arabian Nights*.

"The Fairy Tale," first translated into English as "The Tale" by Thomas Carlyle in 1832, has been described as one of the most enigmatic and ambiguous prose texts in world literature. According to Goethe, it was intended to be significant and insignificant at the same time, simultaneously reminding the listener of everything and nothing. Goethe was fond of collecting his contemporaries' interpretations of the text without ever himself giving any hint as to its meaning.

Goethe defined "**fairy tale**s" as stories narrating impossible events happening in reality, whereas novels present events that may be possible. In both genres, however, the underlying conditions may be impossible or nearly impossible. Goethe, therefore, considered all fiction to be **märchen** in the sense that it is regularly based on the marvelous and the impossible. He took into account not only classical fairy tales such as the *Arabian Nights*, which he valued most, but also admired **legend**s, **myth**s from **classical antiquity** and the Northern tradition, as well as wondrous tales from the **Bible** and other cultural contexts, and he frequently made use of their symbolism in his own writings. To be sure, Goethe kept this literary approach strictly confined to fiction. As a natural philosopher, he did not tolerate any superstition. *See also* Kreutzwald, Friedrich Reinhold; Reynard the Fox.

Further Readings: Mommsen, Katharina. *Goethe und 1001 Nacht*. Berlin: Akademie-Verlag, 1960; Morgan, Peter. "The Fairy-Tale as Radical Perspective: Enlightenment as Barrier and Bridge to Civic Values in Goethe's *Märchen*." *Orbis Litterarum* 40 (1985): 222–43.

Willi Höfig

Gonzenbach, Laura (1842–1878)

A Swiss-German woman born in Sicily, Laura Gonzenbach was an amateur collector best known for her two-volume collection of Sicilian folktales published in German in 1870 as *Sicilianische Märchen* (*Sicilian Fairy Tales*). Predating Sicilian folklorist Giuseppe **Pitrè**'s four-volume *Fiabe, novelle, e racconti popolari Siciliani* (*Fairy Tales, Novellas, and Popular Tales of Sicily*, 1875) by several years, *Sicilian Fairy Tales* is one of the few nineteenth-century folktale collections made by a woman. It contains predominantly fairy tales and romantic **novella**s, and although both male and female protagonists are represented, the majority of these narratives are feminine tales with female protagonists. These stories present a decidedly lower-class, feminine perspective, and **women**'s struggle against oppression in various forms is a major theme.

Gonzenbach was born to Swiss-German parents in Messina, Sicily, in 1842; her family was part of a German-speaking community in Sicily. She was well educated and spoke many languages, including German, French, Italian, and Sicilian. Her father was both a merchant and the Swiss consul in Messina, and her sister, Magdelena Gonzenbach, founded a school for girls in Messina. Laura Gonzenbach was motivated to collect these stories when historian and theologian Otto Hartwig requested that she send him a few tales for inclusion in his history of Sicily. In 1868, she collected and sent to Hartwig ninety-two stories told by Sicilian peasant women and translated from Sicilian into literary German. Hartwig edited and published this collection, along with comparative notes by folklorist Reinhold **Köhler**. The vast majority of Gonzenbach's **informant**s were women from eastern Sicily, including Messina, its surrounding region, the countryside to the southeast of Mount Etna, and Catania. Two tales were narrated by a man, Alessandro Grasso, who learned his repertoire of feminine tales from his mother. Otherwise, very little is known about the narrators, the circumstances, the methods of collection, or the natural **storytelling** context; any original manuscripts or notes Gonzenbach might have taken were destroyed in Messina's 1908 earthquake.

Although Gonzenbach was regarded as a talented storyteller, she was not trained as a folklorist, which is one reason scholars have long ignored her work. No transcripts exist, so it is impossible to know what alterations she made during **translation**. In a letter from Gonzenbach to Hartwig published in the collection's introduction, she assures him that her transcriptions of the oral tales were faithful. After more than a century of relative obscurity, Luisa Rubini translated the complete collection into Italian as *Fiabe Siciliane* (*Sicilian Folktales*, 1999), and Jack **Zipes** translated the collection into English in two volumes under the titles *Beautiful Angiola: The Great Treasury of Sicilian Folk and Fairy Tales Collected by Laura Gonzenbach* (2004) and *The Robber with a Witch's Head: More Stories from the Great Treasury of Sicilian Folk and Fairy Tales Collected by Laura Gonzenbach* (2004). In 2006, Zipes's two-volume English translation appeared in one volume, with two additional Sicilian tales, under the title *Beautiful Angiola: The Lost Sicilian Folk and Fairy Tales of Laura Gonzenbach*. *See also* Collecting, Collectors; Editing, Editors; Italian Tales.

Further Readings: Rubini, Luisa. *Fiabe e mercanti in Sicilia: La raccolta di Laura Gonzenbach, la comunità di lingua tedesca a Messina nell'Ottocento*. Florence: Olschki, 1998; Zipes, Jack. "Laura Gonzenbach's Buried Treasure." *Beautiful Angiola: The Lost Sicilian Folk and Fairy Tales of Laura Gonzenbach*. Translated and edited by Jack Zipes. New York: Routledge, 2006. xi–xxvii.

Linda J. Lee

Gozzi, Carlo (1720–1806)

The Venetian playwright and memorialist Carlo Gozzi was a lively participant in literary debates of his time, taking the position of a political conservative and literary traditionalist and in particular criticizing the theatrical reforms—in the direction of bourgeois realism—of his fellow Venetian, Carlo Goldoni. Today, he is best known for his ten *Fiabe teatrali* (*Fairy Tales for the Theater*). Published between 1761 and 1770, the *Fiabe* inaugurated the genre of the fairy-tale play and hold continuing interest for both their ideological content and the eclectic theatrical style expressed therein.

The first of the *Fiabe* was *L'amore delle tre arance* (*The Love of the Three Oranges*), based on the last tale (5.9) of Giambattista **Basile**'s *Lo cunto de li cunti* (*The Tale of Tales*, 1634–36). It was soon followed by *Turandot*; *Il corvo* (*The Crow*, based on Basile's 4.9); *Il re cervo* (*The King Stag*); *Il mostro turchino* (*The Blue Monster*); *La donna serpente* (*The Serpent Woman*); *L'augellin belverde* (*The Green Bird*); *I pitocchi fortunati* (*The Fortunate Beggars*); *La Zobeide*; and *Zeim re dei geni* (*Zeim, King of the Genies*). Besides Basile, sources for Gozzi's material included the *commedia dell'arte*, improvised comedy that had its origins in the late Renaissance; eastern collections such as the **Arabian Nights**, together with their French-Orientalist derivatives; and **oral traditions**.

The particular flavor of Gozzi's plays results from a hybrid style in which fairy-tale characters and plots merge with the conventions, masks, and improvisational techniques of the *commedia*. On the whole, the somewhat melodramatic plots of the plays are moved forward by serious fairy-tale characters who speak in Italian and sometimes in verse, and offer heavy-handed ideological pronouncements. The stock characters of the *commedia* (Harlequin and others), on the other hand, tend to jest lightheartedly, interact occasionally with the audience, and speak in a mix of Italian and dialect.

Gozzi's attempt to recover the marvelous that had so dominated the poetics of the seventeenth century and to revitalize older comic forms often yields curiously cerebral results, far from the effervescence of either Basile's tales or early *commedia* scenarios. Likewise, the common fairy-tale progression toward social betterment is often substituted by the reinforcement of rigidly hierarchical social structures and values, such as conjugal faithfulness, resignation to the work of Providence, and submission to the powerful. At the same time, however, the ever-present dialectic in these plays between order and disorder creates a dramatic tension that in many cases undermines overt ideological certainties.

Gozzi received less critical acclaim at home than he did outside of Italy. The consummate theatricality of his work, with its spectacularly eclectic combination of styles, traditions, and messages have influenced many other artists, in particular in the field of **opera**. It may suffice to mention the magic plays and singspiels that climaxed with Wolfgang Mozart's *Die Zauberflöte* (*The Magic Flute*, 1791); Sergey Prokofiev's *Liubov' k trem apel'sinam* (*The Love for Three Oranges*, 1919); and both Ferruccio Busoni's and Giacomo Puccini's versions of *Turandot* (1921 and 1926, respectively). *See also* Italian Tales; Theater.

Further Readings: Bermel, Albert, and Ted Emery, trans. and ed. *Five Tales for the Theatre*. Chicago: University of Chicago Press, 1989; Bosisio, Paolo. *Fiabe teatrali*. Rome: Bulzoni, 1984.

Nancy Canepa

Grace, Patricia (1937–)

A leading New Zealand writer, Patricia Grace draws on the Maori **oral tradition** of **storytelling** in fiction that focuses on Maori life and culture. Of Te Ati Awa, Ngati Raukawa, and Ngati Toa descent, Grace was born in Wellington, trained as a teacher, and taught in several areas of New Zealand while raising her seven children. Her short stories, novels, and **children's literature** reveal varieties of Maori experience and narrative voices, and recognize the importance of maintaining communal **memory** through **myth**. Her second **novel**, *Potiki* (1986), like much of her work—and like the work of fellow Maori writer Witi **Ihimaera**—weaves Maori mythology and storytelling into a contemporary plot that contrasts old Maori ways with the new. Grace also uses Maori myth more directly by, for example, retelling the Maori myth of creation in "Sun's Marbles," from her fourth collection of short stories, *The Sky People* (1994).

Her award-winning children's picture book, *The Kuia and the Spider/Te Kuia me te Pungawerewere* (1981), illustrated by Robyn Kahukiwa and published in English and Maori, is a **folktale** recounting a **spinning** contest between a spider and an old woman. Grace's text also accompanies Kahukiwa's illustrations of mythological Maori women in *Wahine Toa* (1984). *See also* Australian and Aotearoan/New Zealand Tales; Pacific Island Tales.

Further Readings: "Grace, Patricia." New Zealand Book Council Web site. 2005. http://www.bookcouncil. org.nz/writers/gracep.html; Robinson, Roger. "Grace, Patricia." *The Oxford Companion to New Zealand Literature*. Edited by Roger Robinson and Nelson Wattie. Melbourne: Oxford University Press, 1998.

Adrienne E. Gavin

Graphic Novel

Graphic novels and comic books are a form of printed narrative based on sequential art. Over the years, people have used this form in different ways related to folktales and fairy tales. While each work treats folktale material differently, it is possible to put them into three different categories: direct retellings, **adaptation**s, and pastiches.

The simplest of these forms is the direct retelling. In the direct retelling, the setting and characters are the same as in the original source material. Over the years, a number of different publications have presented direct retellings of fairy tales from well-known sources, such as the tales Jacob and Wilhelm **Grimm**. These direct retellings sometimes exist as individually published comics and sometimes as parts of larger collections. An example of the former is David Wenzel and Douglas Wheeler's *Fairy Tales of the Brothers Grimm* (1995); examples of the latter include Walt Kelly's comic version of the story of the Gingerbread Man and David Mazzucchelli's comic version of the Japanese folktale of Urashima Taro, both from Art **Spiegelman** and Françoise Mouly's collection *Folklore & Fairy Tale Funnies* (2000) in the *Little Lit* series. One clear example of this sort of work comes from Charles **Vess'** *Book of Ballads and Sagas* (1995), which contains comic adaptations of traditional **ballad**s from the Child collection, presented alongside the original text. Direct retellings do not alter the story content, but attempt to faithfully retell folktales in the comic medium.

Adaptations take folktales or fairy beliefs as inspiration but adapt the setting or the characters in some way. These comics often blend genre conventions of folktales and fairy tales with the conventions of other genres either in form or in style. An example of the former comes in Neil **Gaiman** and Charles Vess' work *Stardust* (1997). *Stardust* presents a fairy-tale style plot regarding the journey of a young mortal into the lands of **faerie** in the form of an illustrated **novel**, with chapter breaks and changes in setting from chapter to chapter. While the material is clearly inspired by the fairy tale and ballad, it does not conform to fairy-tale conventions of style, thus reflecting the nature of the adaptation. An example of the adaptation of style comes from the comic *Scary Godmother* (1997–2006) by Jill Thompson. This series adapts concepts from the story of "**Cinderella**" for a modern humor comic. In this comic, the eponymous character acts as a helper figure for a young girl who calls on her for assistance with modern children's problems, such as getting shots at the doctor. While remaining faithful in the relationship between heroine and helper figure, the story recasts the relationship for the demands of humor, focusing on the absurdity of these requests in the modern world.

Another style of adaptation comes in the expansion of established material. In works of this style, familiar characters are used, but the stories told differ from published material. One of the best examples of this style of adaptation is the series Books of Faerie (1998–99). First published as individual comics, and then collected in two graphic novels, the Books of Faerie series deals with the characters of Titania and Oberon, famous from William **Shakespeare**'s *A Midsummer Night's Dream*. In both cases, the comic details the lives of the characters before their establishment as **king** and **queen** of faerie. While Books of Faerie does not contradict material published elsewhere, neither does it adapt this material; instead, it deals with periods in the lives of the characters that have not been detailed. In works of this style, the action is confined to characters from a single tale, though the action of the story lies outside the bounds of the original.

The final category of graphic novel adaptation encompasses pastiche. In a pastiche work, characters from different folktales and fairy tales interact with each other, and in some cases with characters from other genres of **folklore**. One of the best-known examples of this style is the comic series The Sandman (1988–96) by Neil Gaiman. In this series, characters from fairy tale and stories inspired by fairy beliefs, such as Robin Goodfellow from *A Midsummer Night's Dream* and **Harun al-Rashid** from the *Arabian Nights*, interact with characters from world mythology, such as the Norse god Loki and the Greek hero Orpheus, and even characters from the **Bible**, including Cain and Abel. This is characteristic of the pastiche, in which different tales are presumed to exist in the same world. Such is the case in the series Books of Magic (1994–2000), where the character Tam Lin from the popular ballad interacts with Oberon and Titania from *A Midsummer Night's Dream* in the modern world.

The pastiche comic series Fables (2002–) by Bill Willingham shows the most extensive use of folktale and fairy-tale material, with a number of references made in the text to the techniques of pastiche. In this series, several "fables"—that is, immortal characters from folktales—live in modern New York. What is interesting in terms of the pastiche quality of this work is the way in which different folktales with similar characters are grouped together. For instance, the character **Snow White** is implied to be from both "Snow White and the Seven Dwarves" and "Snow White and Rose Red," a contiguity not implied in the original tales. Similarly, the character of Prince Charming from "Snow White and the Seven Dwarves," "**Cinderella**," and "**Sleeping Beauty**" is shown to be the same person, his multiple **marriage**s explained by multiple divorces. In this comic, the folktales of diverse cultures are part of the same world, with characters from the *Arabian Nights* interacting with other fairy-tale characters throughout a number of issues. Several adaptations exist within this pastiche, including "The **Soldier** and **Death**" set in the Civil War and featuring a character from the comic. Such extensive use of pastiche is common in graphic novel treatments and shows well the ways in which fairy-tale material has been adapted for this new form of storytelling. *See also* Cartoons and Comics; Illustration; Japanese Popular Culture; Mizuno Junko; *Taketori monogatari*.

Further Readings: Castaldo, Annalisa. "'No More Yielding Than a Dream': The Construction of Shakespeare in *The Sandman*." *College Literature* 31.4 (2004): 94–110; Sanders, Joe. "Of Storytellers and Stories in Gaiman and Vess's 'A Midsummer Night's Dream.' "*Extrapolation: A Journal of Science Fiction and Fantasy* 45 (2004): 237–48; Spiegelman, Art, and Françoise Mouly, eds. *Folklore & Fairy Tale Funnies*. Little Lit. New York: HarperCollins, 2000.

B. Grantham Aldred

Grass, Günter (1927–)

Günter Grass, probably the most important contemporary German author, was born in the city of Danzig (now Gdańsk, Poland), which serves as a background for many of his **novel**s. He was drafted into the German army at the age of sixteen, studied sculpture and graphics in Düsseldorf and West Berlin (1948–56), and established himself as a writer in the late 1950s. An exponent of engaged literature, Grass is also active within and outside party politics. Between 1961 and 1972, he regularly campaigned for the Social Democrats, of which he was a member from 1982 to 1992; he also is a staunch advocate of minorities. Earning fame as a novelist, Grass has also published **poetry**, plays, short stories, and essays and has continued to be productive as a sculptor and graphic artist. His work has aroused much controversy, on political grounds as well as for reasons of decency. He has received many prestigious national and international awards, including the Nobel Prize for Literature in 1999.

Grass's novels reflect German historical realities, especially those of the recent past, which he gives fantastic and grotesque dimensions. His use of **myth** has been compared to the concept of mythical narratives developed by Claude Lévi-Strauss. Oskar Matzerath, the mischievous child protagonist of Grass's first novel, *Die Blechtrommel* (*The Tin Drum*, 1959), recalls in many ways the **tricksters**, **thumbling**s (ATU 700, Thumbling; ATU 327B, The Brothers and the Ogre), and unpromising heroes of folk narrative. Oskar is gifted with an adult mind at **birth** (see Motifs T585.2.1–2, T615.1, and T615.3), voluntarily stops to grow at the age of three, and possesses extravagant destructive powers; he is haunted by the black cook, a mysterious female figure from a widespread children's game rhyme which serves as a symbol of terror and guilt. **Folklore** elements in Grass's second novel, *Hundejahre* (*Dog Years*, 1963), include a prophetic miller as well as myth and local **legend**s. In two later works, Grass draws directly on Jacob and Wilhelm **Grimm**s' *Kinder- und Hausmärchen* (*Children's and Household Tales*, 1812–15) and shows that he is well acquainted with Grimm scholarship. The novel *Der Butt* (*The Flounder*, 1977), a panorama of world history from the Neolithic period up to the present, is an antipatriarchal revision of Grimms' tale "The **Fisherman and His Wife**" (ATU 555). In the sixth chapter of *The Flounder*, Grass stages a fictitious meeting of those involved in the tale's editing process, illustrating divergent Romantic conceptions of folk narrative. Grass's feminist counterversion to the Grimms' tale has been criticized from a rather narrow scholarly point of view, which not only comes close to denying the artist's creative liberty but also fails to recognize how popular tradition functions. In one of several narrative strands of the apocalyptic prose text *Die Rättin* (*The*

Rat, 1986), the Grimm brothers and their fairy-tale figures are linked with the dying forest; the legend of the Pied Piper of Hamelin and the myth of the sunken city of Vineta stand emblematically for doom and destruction. Through Ralph Manheim's translations, which have been both praised and criticized, Grass has inspired English-language novelists such as Salman **Rushdie**, John Irving, and Graham Swift. *See also* Feminism.

Further Readings: Brady, Philip, Timothy McFarland, and John J. White, eds. *Günter Grass's "Der Butt": Sexual Politics and the Male Myth of History.* Oxford: Clarendon Press, 1990; Mews, Siegfried, ed. *"The Fisherman and His Wife": Günter Grass's "The Flounder" in Critical Perspective.* New York: AMS Press, 1983; O'Neill, Patrick, ed. *Critical Essays on Günter Grass.* Boston: G. K. Hall & Co., 1987; Preece, Julian. *The Life and Work of Günter Grass: Literature, History, Politics.* New York: Palgrave Macmillan, 2004; Reddick, John. *"The Danzig Trilogy" of Günter Grass: A Study of The Tin Drum, Cat and Mouse, and Dog Years.* London: Secker & Warburg, 1975; Rölleke, Heinz. *Der wahre Butt: Die wundersamen Wandlungen des Märchens vom Fischer und seiner Frau.* Düsseldorf: Diederichs, 1978.

Christine Shojaei Kawan

Greek Tales

The term *paramythion/paramythi* (plural *paramythia*), which in ancient Greek means "exhortation" or "consolation," has come to mean in modern Greek "tale," "**folktale**" or "**fairy tale**." The term *mythos* (plural *mythoi*), whose meaning in ancient Greek is "verb" or "plot," is used by modern Greek folklorists to refer to **animal tale**s, **fable**s, and **fabliaux**.

The considerable corpus of Greek tales includes **variant**s told in any dialect or idiom, a variety that is paralleled by the literature of ancient, Byzantine, and modern Greece. Greek tales in general follow the narrative and aesthetic rules that inform the European folktale as defined by Max **Lüthi**. Local adaptations, however, offer a vivid narrative style, enriched with many formulaic elements that incorporate rhymes, charms, **proverbs**, and **riddle**s in the narrative, thereby creating an amusing dialogue with the audience. Such tales often display a particular taste for, and precise understanding of, matters of social morality, while some type of philosophy of life is usually stressed. The plot is always adapted to the surrounding context of landscape, customs, manners, and preexisting mythology. A traditional storyteller's major skill lies in drawing out his narration over many hours and even over succeeding evenings so as to keep the audience entertained, a feat he achieves by combining episodes, themes, and individual **motif**s drawn from various tale types. **Storytelling** competitions have always been very popular in traditional Greek communities. The considerable number of 509 Greek **oicotype**s, devised by Georgios A. **Megas**, and several oicomotifs indicate the size and importance of the procedure involved in the adapting of international **tale type**s to local cultural contexts. These **adaptation**s display a rational taste in matters of everyday life and produce highly canonical plots. Such adaptation procedures are most frequent in jocular narratives and formula tales, which deviate considerably from the international classification system.

Modern Greek tales derive from two influences: first, the evolution of Greek culture and language, which includes a long storytelling and literary tradition; and second, a long-lasting exchange with neighboring and conquering cultures, an inevitable feature given Greece's nodal position in relation to three continents.

Traces of storytelling in classical Greece are to be discerned in the literary record and in particular in the folktale motifs that occur within the texts themselves. Plato, among others, refers to the act of storytelling and especially to tales transmitted to infants and children by their mothers and nurses (*Laws* 10.887d; *Republic* 1.350e and 2.377b).

Although motifs and occasionally entire plots in major ancient literary works are of great relevance to any discussion of storytelling in ancient Greece, our evidence comes mainly from the mythic tradition upon which ancient Greek literature so firmly rests, where **myth** deals with gods, deities, and heroes. There must have been, however, a certain exchange between folk narratives and mythic traditions.

There are three representative paradigms of entire tale plots, which must have been fairly popular in Greek antiquity. The first paradigm consists of the tale of Meleager (ATU 1187), at whose **birth** his untimely **death** is foretold, which is to occur when the torch associated with his life is burnt. A recorded variant of the tale is told by Phoenix to Achilles (*Iliad* 10.529–99). In the second paradigm, Lucius **Apuleius**, the second-century CE Roman-African author, records the story of "**Cupid and Psyche**" (ATU 425, The Search for the Lost Husband), which follows the plot of the supernatural husband who is lost and then

Perseus slays Medusa. Illustration by Dugald Stewart Walker in *The Golden Porch: A Book of Greek Fairy Tales* by W. M. L. Hutchinson (New York: Longmans, Green and Co., 1925), frontispiece. [Courtesy of the Eloise Ramsey Collection of Literature for Young People, University Libraries, Wayne State University]

found. The story must have been very popular in **oral tradition**, as both iconography and texts dating to the text of Apuleius testify. In the third paradigm, the tale of Polyidus (ATU 612, The Three Snake Leaves), who resuscitates Glaukos by means of an herb, in the manner of a snake resuscitating its companion, was recorded by Apollodorus (*Library* 3.3). This, too, must have been a popular motif in oral tradition, while it also appears in the works of Aeschylus, Sophocles, and Euripides.

Aesop's fables, which were used in schools of rhetoric, are representative of many popular tales of animals and offer evidence of a continuous exchange between oral and literary tradition. A number of animal tales provide parallels to Aesop's fables, including such tale types as Torn-Off Tails (ATU 64), The Snake Trying to Surround the Crab Refuses to Straighten Himself Out (ATU 279*), and The Sheep Persuades the Wolf to Sing (ATU 122C).

Much folktale material, especially in the form of isolated motifs or episodes, can be seen in most mythological cycles found in classical Greek literature. Odysseus is a typical tale character and his adventures among the sirens (Motif B53), in the land of lotus-eaters (Motif

*F111.3), or in the land of Cyclops blinding Polyphemus (Motif F512.1.1, ATU 1137), are identifiable in many oral traditions, Greek and otherwise. The Homeric epics, Aesop's fables, dramatic poetry, Herodotus' *History*, Hesiod's *Theogony*, and later works, such as Apuleius' *Metamorphoses* and Apollodorus' *Library*, provide folktale motifs in abundance. These include, for instance, the journey to the world of the dead (the Homeric *nekyia*, Motif F81); the transformations of Proteus (Motif G311) and any aquatic deity; the talking horse of Achilles (Motif B211.3); the suitors' race (Motif H331.5.2.) to win Hippodamia, daughter of king Oinomaos, as a wife; many motifs in the story of Perseus, who was born of Danae through supernatural agency and abandoned in the sea with his mother; or in the Argonautic cycle.

Little is known of tales and storytelling during the Byzantine period. Some scholars believe that storytelling was addressed either to young children by their nurses or to an adult public by specialist storytellers. Whereas during the early Byzantine period, Homeric epics and Aesop's fables were used to entertain and instruct young listeners, the long process of Christianization gradually drew Byzantine storytelling away from tales of purely mythological content toward stories derived from biblical tradition. From early Byzantine times, an important source for the developing Christian oral tradition was the *Synaxaria* (*Lives of the Saints*), which are part of the liturgical texts of the Orthodox church and function as a counterpart to the western **exempla**. Another considerable step in the evolution of the Greek oral storytelling tradition was the development of Byzantine popular literature, which betrays evidence of a certain exchange between literary and oral tradition. Examples of this interplay are the epic of Digenis Akritas, of the twelfth century, which employs the long tradition of acritic songs and many motifs drawn from oral tradition. Another example of this interplay are the Byzantine versions of the extremely popular *Alexander Romance*, which combines pseudohistory with folktale motifs and themes. The question of how much late Byzantine romances contributed to the dissemination of plots, themes, and motifs derived from both western and eastern traditions is still a fruitful field for research.

Several texts from classical antiquity betray a secular exchange between Greek and Oriental cultures well before the development of Arabic cultures and the rise of Islam. Herodotus reports several stories from Egypt in his *History,* whereas Bellerophon's adventure with Proetos' wife (*Iliad* 6.155–205) is paralleled both by Joseph's adventure with Potaphar's wife (Gen. 39) and by the tale of The Two Brothers, transcribed in an Egyptian papyrus of 1250 BCE (see **Egyptian Tales**).

Oriental influences, via the Arab invasions, began to affect Greek folktales during the Byzantine period, although Greek storytelling was not influenced as much as storytelling in other southern European areas. Several plots, themes, and motifs are common to either Greek and Arab oral tradition, such as the swan maiden motif (Motif D361.1) and the various tale types that employ it. The introduction of specific plots into Greek oral tradition was probably due to oral modes of exchange rather than to any literary tradition. In modern times, especially during the four centuries of the Ottoman domination of Greece, Oriental influences on Greek tales sprang mainly from Turkish narrative traditions. Indeed, Turkish influence was decisive in the evolution of modern Greek tales. Thanks to the Turkish people's particular interest in folktales, this influence stimulated and enlivened oral narrative and enriched folktale material with new motifs and characters. Invasion and commercial exchanges, in addition to facilitating the circulation of distinct oral traditions, also brought about linguistic loans, whose forms echo the language of modern Greek folktales. The adoption of specific folktale characters, such as the *bey*, the *kadi*, the terrifying Arab, and even the *Hodjas* (an abbreviation for **Nasreddin** Hoça), is a particular example of this phenomenon. Such exchanges were also responsible for the appearance of purely new folktale figures, such as the evil and intelligent man lacking in facial hair (*spanos*), a purely Greek folktale figure, as the Austrian linguist Paul Kretschmer first perceived. New characters created from elements drawn from outside of the traditional confines of the folktale appeared, such as the figure of Karagiozis (the modern Greek version of Karagöz), an antihero of the shadow theatre, which contains elements from both Greek and Turkish traditions. The figure was initially addressed to an adult audience, but since World War II has been restricted to a children's audience.

Western influences on Greek tales are detectable above all in specific tale-type plots, such as the Greek variants of **Sleeping Beauty** (ATU 410), but are less obvious in oral Greek folktales. Such influences were introduced during the Crusades and the Frankish and Venetian invasions. **Italian tales** provide the closest parallel to the forms of Greek tales, particularly in regard to **novella** tales and dispersed common motifs in both traditions.

On the other hand, **children's literature** versions of folktales are directly related to the better-known public Greek collections of the Brothers **Grimm**, Charles **Perrault**, and Hans Christian **Andersen**. The children's versions underwent popular **translation**s and adaptation, and such versions were published either separately in the form of popular booklets and magazines for children or gathered in volumes of tale collections aimed at the educated and well-off urban elite. This process took place during the late nineteenth and early twentieth centuries, with the result that such elements entered Greek oral narrative only recently.

Scholarly research on modern Greek folktales started in the eighteenth century, with European travelers offering their own version of modern Greek traditions, including oral folktales. One of the first fieldworkers of this kind was the French trader and scholar Pierre Augustin de Guys, who described storytelling in his correspondence and preserved some variants of oral and literary folktales in his work *Voyage littéraire de la Grèce, ou Lettres sur les Grecs, anciens et modernes, avec un parallèle de leurs mœurs* (*Literary Journey of Greece, or Letters on the Greeks, Ancient and Modern, with a Comparison of Their Customs*, 3rd ed., 1783).

The first collection of transcribed oral Greek folktales, *Griechische und albanesische Märchen* (*Greek and Albanian Tales*), was published in 1864 by the Austrian consul based in Ioannina, Johann Georg von Hahn. In his transcription of these stories, von Hahn focused on content and attempted to associate the tales with various branches of primary Aryan mythology. Von Hahn's volume is also historically important since it represents a first attempt at classification based on patterns derived from Greek mythology. The annotated collection entitled *Contes populaires grecs* (*Greek Popular Tales*), published in 1879 by the French scholar Jean Pio, was based on von Hahn's personal collection and contained forty-seven tales originating in four different regions of Greece. The second collection was published in 1877 by Bernhard Schmidt. *Griechische Märchen* (*Greek Tales*) contains twenty-five stories, collected by Schmidt himself, mostly in the Ionian island of Zakynthos. This first period of scholarly investigation of Greek tales, motivated either by linguistic or historic interest, produced a considerable number of collections.

In nineteenth-century Greece, literary societies were deeply interested in folkloristic studies and **collecting** folktales, holding competitions, and publishing periodicals. Such periodicals are responsible for important corpora of tales from Thrace, Zakynthos, and Pontos. The Byzantinist Adamandios Adamandiou was a notable collector of the period, responsible for important transcriptions of tales and for gathering information on storytelling, especially from the Cycladic island of Tinos.

Greek scholarly research on Greek tales was shaped profoundly by Nikolaos Politis, the founder of **folklore** studies in Greece. In addition to deriving material from his own **field-work**, Politis established a network of local collectors, normally primary and high-school teachers, who provided him with transcribed oral material. Circulars promulgated by the Ministry of Education also supported the business of collecting oral literature. The establishment of the Hellenic Folklore Society in 1908 and the publication of its periodical, *Laographia*, from 1909, contributed greatly to the collection and publication of oral Greek tales. The establishment of the Folklore Archive (since renamed the Hellenic Folklore Research Centre) in 1918 stimulated the habit of depositing manuscript collections and carefully preserved the network of local collectors. Politis applied the **comparative method** and left behind an enormous number of studies about, and annotations of, modern Greek tales and mythology. He also initiated the project of creating a catalogue of Greek folktales compiled according to the international classification system developed by Antti **Aarne** and Stith **Thompson**. His work in this area was continued during his lifetime and after his death by Georgios A. Megas, who was his student.

In the first half of the twentieth century, the British archaeologist Richard M. Dawkins made a fundamental contribution to the recording and studying of Greek tales and dialects deriving in particular from Greek communities which then still populated large regions beyond Greek national borders, such as Asia Minor, Cappadocia, Pontos, and the Dodecanese islands (which were under Italian authority until 1948). In his eyes, the Greek tale tradition displayed a considerable autonomy, in spite of the merging surrounding influences.

The number of transcribed Greek folktale variants greatly increased with all the recording and gathering of tales during the twentieth century. In parallel with scholarly research, this collection of material continues today, thanks to the efforts of interested amateurs and local periodicals.

Along with the gathering of material and scholarly research into Greek folktale tradition, the late nineteenth and early twentieth centuries saw the development of the production of **literary fairy tale**s for children. This started with the appearance of translations of the tales of the Brothers Grimm, which were published either as independent volumes or as items in magazines, in particular in *Diaplasis ton Paidon* (*Children's Education*), which appeared regularly between 1879 and 1948. Original children's literature at this time was produced by writers such as Pinelopi Delta and Galateia Kazantzaki and was inspired either by northern European collections, such as those by the Brothers Grimm and Andersen, or by traditional Greek tales.

A "tradition" in large urban centres of the retelling of folktales developed in the 1950s upon the publication of cheap booklets of tales for children, enhanced by the popular radio program of Antigone **Metaxa-Krontera**, which presented adaptations of tales for children. This trend continues today by means of theatrical entertainments for children that blend tales and myth, and its most recent manifestation is the appearance of the "new storyteller" (*neoconteur*). The new storyteller draws from traditional material, but enriches it with a multicultural and universalizing approach, thereby attracting both children and adults. *See also* Albanian Tales; Classical Antiquity.

Further Readings: Angelopoulou, Anna, and Aigli Brouskou. *Catalogue raisonné des contes grecs: Types AT 700–749*. Paris: Maisonneuve et Larose, 1995; Dawkins, Richard M., ed. and trans. *Forty-Five*

Stories from the Dodekanese. Cambridge: Cambridge University Press, 1950; ———, trans. *Modern Greek Folktales*. 1953. Westport, CT: Greenwood Press, 1974; Kaliambou, Maria. *Heimat—Glaube—Familie: Wertevermittlung in griechischen Popularmärchen (1870–1970)*. Neuried: Ars Una, 2006; Lüthi, Max. *The European Folktale: Form and Nature*. Translated by J. D. Niles. Philadelphia: Institute for the Study of Human Issues, 1982; Megas, Georgios A. "Some Oral Greek Parallels to Aesop's Fables." *Humaniora: Essays in Literature—Foklore—Bibliography Honoring Archer Taylor on His Seventieth Birthday*. Edited by Wayland D. Hand and Gustave O. Arlt. Locust Valley, NY: J. J. Augustin, 1960. 195–207; Meraklis, Michael G. *Studien zum griechischen Märchen*. Translated and edited by Walter Puchner. Vienna: Selbstverlag des Osterreichischen Museums für Volkskunde, 1992; Papachristophorou, Marilena. "The *Arabian Nights* in Greece: A Comparative Survey of Greek Oral Tradition." *Fabula* 45 (2004): 311–29; Rohde, Erwin. *Der griechische Roman und seine Vorläufer*. New York: Georg Olms Verlag, 1974.

Marilena Papachristophorou

Gregory, Lady Isabella Augusta Persse (1852–1932)

Born in 1852 in County Galway, Isabella Augusta Persse came from a family closely connected to the English rule of Ireland. She was married in 1880 to then sixty-three-year-old Sir William Henry Gregory and was widowed in 1892. Prior to her husband's death, her writings, though favorable toward home rule for British imperial holdings, did not explicitly address the Irish case. Afterward, however, she emerged at the forefront of Irish cultural **nationalism**.

The change came in 1893 when she traveled to Insheer in the Aran Islands. The experience awoke in her an interest in Irish language and **folklore**, especially of the west of Ireland, where she lived. She met William Butler **Yeats** in 1896, and the two began **collecting** folklore together. In 1897, she met playwright Edward Martyn, with whom she and Yeats cofounded the Irish Literary Theatre (later the Abbey Theatre Company).

Between 1893 and the end of her life, Lady Gregory published no less than five books on the topic of Irish folklore. Foremost among them was her two-volume work, *Visions and Beliefs in the West of Ireland* (1920). Here, she combined her personal experiences with **folktale**s, **legend**s, and customs collected in the course of her **fieldwork** to produce an in-depth account of supernatural belief. Along with John Millington Synge's *The Aran Islands* (1907) and Yeats's *Celtic Twilight* (1893), *Visions and Beliefs in the West of Ireland* stands as one of the earliest examples of a folkloristic ethnography. *See also* Celtic Tales.

Further Readings: Gregory, Lady. *Visions and Beliefs in the West of Ireland*. New York: Oxford University Press, 1970; Tolbin, Colm. *Lady Gregory's Toothbrush*. Milwaukee: University of Wisconsin Press, 2002.

Adam Zolkover

Grimm, Jacob (1785–1863)

As the cofounder of German philology, Jacob Grimm gained a worldwide reputation as a distinguished linguist, jurist, and narrative scholar. Jacob's interest in the German language and its literature was initially inspired by the historical lectures given by Ludwig Wachler. This was reinforced by the work of his mentor and teacher (who was only a few years older than Jacob), Carl von Savigny, who specialized in historical and antiquarian studies of literature and law. With an encyclopedic fervor, Jacob subsequently devoted himself to tracing and documenting ancient German literary and linguistic milestones. Pivotal stimuli for his research also came from the circle of Heidelberg Romantics revolving around Clemens **Brentano** and Achim von Arnim, who were able to secure the assistance of the Jacob and Wilhelm **Grimm** for their edited collection of folksongs, *Des Knaben Wunderhorn* (*The Boy's Magic Horn*, 1805–8), beginning with the second volume. Like Johann Gottfried Herder, Jacob Grimm was of the opinion that at one time the people—the **folk**—had had a thriving oral narrative tradition, which now existed only in the form of tales in literary and historical sources from the "old days." Because these texts were often fragmentary, it would be possible to reconstruct them accurately only by comparing them to other documents to gain a more comprehensive picture. In contrast to Wilhelm Grimm, Jacob was particularly interested in the mythological-poetical dimension of these historical narratives. For this reason, he did not reiterate the misgivings of other chroniclers, poets, compilers, and **collectors** as to the **authenticity** of what was reported in these documents. Instead, he remained true to the nature and form of the narratives by reproducing them faithfully from the originals. He was opposed to a free poetic **adaptation** of older literary texts.

From 1811 onward, Jacob was continually involved in the publication of editions relating to historical Germanic linguistics, law, and **folklore**, including mythology, **folktale**s, and **legend**s: *Deutsche Grammatik* (*German Grammar*, 1819–37; an index volume was published in 1865); *Deutsche Rechtsalterthümer* (*German Legal Antiquities*, 1828); *Reinhart Fuchs* (**Reynard the Fox**, 1834), the first documentation of beast epics in the vernacular versions; *Deutsche Mythologie* (*German Mythology*, 1835); *Deutsche Weisthümer* (*German Works of Wisdom*, 1840–78); and *Geschichte der Deutschen Sprache* (*History of the German Language*, 1848). Primarily, however, Jacob's early works were coauthored with his brother Wilhelm **Grimm**. These included the following:

- *Die beiden ältesten deutschen Gedichte aus dem achten Jahrhundert: Das Lied von Hildebrand und Hadubrand und das Weißenbrunner Gebet* (*The Two Oldest German Poems from the Eighth Century: The Song of Hildebrand and Hadubrand and the Wessobrunner Prayer*, 1812).
- *Kinder- und Hausmärchen* (*Children's and Household Tales*, 1812–15).
- *Altdeutsche Wälder* (*Old German Forests*, 1813–16).
- *Der Arme Heinrich* (*Poor Henry*, 1815).
- *Lieder der alten Edda* (*Songs of the Elder Edda*, 1815).
- *Silva de romances viejos* (*Old Spanish Romances*, 1815).
- *Deutsche Sagen* (*German Legends*, 1816–18).
- *Irische Elfenmärchen* (*Irish Fairy Legends*, 1826).

They also undertook together the monumental work, *Deutsches Wörterbuch* (*German Dictionary*), whose first volume appeared in 1854. It was finally completed in 1961 through the collaboration of several generations of linguists.

Although Wilhelm was largely responsible for **editing** the *Children's and Household Tales* after the publication of the first edition in 1812 and 1815, Jacob took on the lion's share of editorial work for their joint publication of *German Legends*. The Grimm's differentiation between local legend (*Ortssage*) and historical legend (*historische Sage*) was a first attempt to combine very disparate material from different sources. Nevertheless, the characterization "historical" was open to misinterpretation because its use implied that anecdotal descriptions of historical events and people in legends held the same status as more authentic sources. On the whole, the subject matter and **motif**s of legends reflect the variety of medieval and modern folklore, even when some of the texts have been gleaned from secondary sources instead from the originals. Editing of the linguistic and narrative content of the originals was justified to avoid categorization of the texts as fiction. It is obvious that such a procedure contradicts the Grimms' self-proclaimed devotion to "Loyalty and Truth" in the preface to *German Legends,* and that it allows for subjective interpretations of literary sources. Instead of being reproduced literally, the subject matter was interpreted in a new way. During their lifetimes, the fame of the Brothers Grimm, in particular Jacob, is evident from the prefaces to regionally published volumes of folktales and legends from the nineteenth century: the brothers' work is addressed here in an exemplary way. It was not a rare occurrence for such collections to reprint some of the Grimms' legends in unmodified form. Even then they were regarded as trademarks, as they are to this day.

With the publication of his *German Mythology* in 1835, Jacob Grimm founded the study of German language and literature from a historical-religious perspective (*religionskundliche Germanistik*). Drawing on scant direct sources, medieval Latin literature, and explanations of the names of places and people and linguistic idiosyncrasies, Jacob attempted to reconstruct the Germanic religion. He also incorporated more recent (oral) narratives as well as legends and folktales due to his conviction that these accounts revealed a common collective **memory**: the older culture consisted only of fragments that had to be newly reassembled. His aim was to create a cultural history of times gone by as a history of religion. In thirty-eight chapters, he examined the religious world of the Germanic peoples, thereby creating a counterbalance to classical mythology through his defense of the basic principles of heathen antiquity. Nevertheless, the somewhat speculative nature of some of the etymological derivations led to numerous hasty conclusions, which peaked in the so-called mythological school of thought, a field of research concerned with the reconstruction of Indo-European **myth**s. *Deutsche Mythologie* was often translated and wholly or partially reprinted. In this way, Jacob Grimm contributed to a European renaissance in the examination of literary and oral narrative transmissions from bygone times. Not only has the *Children's and Household Tales* been of particular interest to researchers in the field of **children's literature** and youth literature for some time, it has also dominated the international literary scene for many years. In contrast, an intensive analysis of the content of *German Legends* began only a few decades ago. An assessment of the national and international impact of individual works such as *German Mythology* has only just begun. In the future, we can expect above all to see interesting results with regard to the development of a "patriotic education." *See also* Brothers Grimm in Biopics; German Tales; Mythological Approaches.

Further Readings: Bluhm, Lothar. *Die Brüder Grimm und der Beginn der Deutschen Philologie: Eine Studie zu Kommunikation und Wissenschaftsbildung.* Hildesheim: Weidmann, 1997; Denecke, Ludwig. *Jacob Grimm und sein Bruder Wilhelm.* Stuttgart: Metzler, 1971; Ginschel, Gudrun. *Der junge Jacob Grimm, 1805–1819.* 2nd expanded edition. Berlin: Akademie-Verlag, 1989; Hennig, Dieter, and Bernhard Lauer, eds. *200 Jahre Brüder Grimm: Dokumente ihres Lebens und Wirkens.* 3 volumes. Kassel: Weber & Weidemeyer, 1985; Kamenetsky, Christa. *The Brothers Grimm and Their Critics: Folktales and the Quest for Meaning.* Athens: Ohio University Press, 1992; Kellner, Beate. *Grimms Mythen: Studien zum Mythosbegriff und seiner Anwendung in Jacob Grimms Deutscher Mythologie.* Frankfurt a.M.:

Lang, 1994; Uther, Hans-Jörg. "Die Brüder Grimm als Sammler von Märchen und Sagen." *Kultur und Politik: Die Grimms*. Edited by Bernd Heidenreich and Ewald Grothe. Frankfurt a.M.: Societätsverlag, 2003. 67–107; Zipes, Jack. *The Brothers Grimm: From Enchanted Forests to the Modern World*. 2nd edition. New York: Palgrave MacMillan, 2002.

Hans-Jörg Uther

Grimm, Ludwig Emil (1790–1863)

The sixth of nine children, and the fifth to survive infancy, Ludwig Emil Grimm was the youngest brother of Wilhelm and Jacob **Grimm**, the compilers of the **Kinder- und Hausmärchen** (*Children's and Household Tales*, 1812–15). Beyond the connection to his two famous brothers, Ludwig was in his own right a well-known painter and engraver, having studied in Munich as a young man with the artist Karl Hess. He attended the Munich Academy, and beginning in 1832, taught art in Kassel.

Ludwig contributed seven **illustration**s to the Small Edition of the *Kinder- und Hausmärchen*, a selection of fifty fairy tales especially for children that first appeared in 1825 and was modeled on Edgar **Taylor**'s English translation of Grimms' stories, *German Popular Stories* (1823–26), which included illustrations by George **Cruikshank**. Ludwig was also responsible for the etching of Dorothea Viehmann, the Grimms' most famous **informant**, which appeared as the frontispiece to the second volume of the *Kinder- und Hausmärchen* beginning with its second edition in 1819. His portrait of Viehmann, a prolific contributor of tales to Grimms' collection, does not portray her as the urban, middle-class tailor's widow that she was, but rather as a kind-faced, elderly peasant woman. It thus serves as a reflection of the Grimm brothers' vision of the ideal German fairy-tale teller and of their commitment to the idea of the pastoral as the location of national identity.

Further Reading: Koszinowski, Ingrid, and Vera Leuschner, eds. *Ludwig Emil Grimm 1790–1863: Maler, Zeichner, Radierer*. Volume 2 of *200 Jahre Brüder Grimm*. Kassel: Weber und Weidemeyer, 1985.

Adam Zolkover

Grimm, Wilhelm (1786–1859)

Classical scholar, philologist, and cofounder of German philology and comparative narrative research, Wilhelm Grimm worked and lived together with his older brother Jacob **Grimm** in a lifelong cooperation. After attending secondary school in Kassel, Wilhelm studied law at the University of Marburg from 1802 to 1806. There the legal historian Carl von Savigny proved to be an attentive patron. In 1805, Jacob and Wilhelm Grimm had their first encounter with the poet Clemens **Brentano**, who was to play a significant role in influencing their subsequent way of life. Brentano aroused their interest in the importance of historical literary sources and arranged for their collaboration on *Des Knaben Wunderhorn* (*The Boy's Magic Horn*, 1805–8), a collection of folk songs gathered by Achim von Arnim, to whom Brentano recommended them highly as collaborators in 1807 (beginning with the second volume). The ideas of the philosopher Johann Gottfried Herder about folk poetry were another important influence on the Grimm brothers, as were oral sources.

At first, Wilhelm was unable to take up a regular profession due to asthma and a heart condition. Nevertheless, in 1814, he was granted the post of secretary in the royal library

(Kurfürstliche Bibliothek) in Kassel. He married Dorothea Wild in May of 1825 and had three children with her. When neither of the Brothers Grimm was appointed to be the new head librarian in 1829, they both requested to be dismissed from the Hessian civil service. Their wish was granted the following day. In early 1830, Wilhelm and his family moved to Göttingen, where his brother Jacob was already living. There he was appointed librarian and, in 1835, was made an associate professor of the faculty of philosophy. Together with Jacob and five other Göttinger professors (the "Göttinger Sieben"), Wilhelm signed a note of protest in 1837 against the revocation of the constitution of 1833. Their new employer, Ernst August II, Duke of Cumberland and King of Hannover, duly took the opportunity to immediately remove the professors from their posts. Furthermore, he banished three of the professors, including Jacob, from the state. Wilhelm stayed in Göttingen until October 1838, when he once more moved to be with his brother, this time in Kassel. In 1841, Wilhelm followed his brother Jacob to Berlin and was also made a professor there. He was to remain in the city until his death.

Wilhelm's main interest was in medieval poetry. In particular, his historical research on literature and linguistic studies are of lasting importance. *Die deutsche Heldensage* (*The German Heroic Legend*, 1829) is one of his major works. It was the first of its kind to comprise a collection of the oldest written records from the sixth to the sixteenth centuries as well as a treatise on the origin of heroic **legend**s and their reception. With its publication, Wilhelm and his brother explored new literary territory. Despite differing reactions to their editions, including sometimes heavy criticism, their version achieved wider acceptance than comparable works and secured the brothers' fame. Since the second edition of 1819, Wilhelm alone was responsible for the success of the **Kinder- und Hausmärchen** (*Children's and Household Tales*). His talent for narrative shaped the Grimm's signature style to such an extent that some of his interpretations of fairy tales were later published as model examples of books in the genre (for example, *Die Sterntaler* [*The Star Coins*] and *Schneeweiß chen und Rosenrot* [*Snow White and Rose Red*]). Wilhelm wrote a survey of the history of the folktale, which even today is still insufficiently appreciated by the literary world. This was published in a volume with annotations to the *Kinder- und Hausmärchen* (in 1822 and 1856). The publication of the two-volume *Deutsche Sagen* (*German Legends*) in 1816–18 provided the foundation for a scholarly examination of legends. Although the circulation of this edition was not particularly impressive (some copies of the book were still available in 1837) and it was heavily criticized by others working in the field, Grimm's work influenced subsequent collections published throughout Europe and later even further afield in conceptual terms. Some of the legends from this collection were also published in literary journals; the first legends to be reprinted appeared a couple of years later in school textbooks and calendars. A translation of the first, anonymous volume of Thomas Crofton **Croker**'s *Fairy Legends and Traditions of the South of Ireland* (1825), which included an extensive introduction to **fairy lore**, was released almost simultaneously in Germany (*Irische Elfenmärchen*). Reputedly, the Grimms' last joint editorial project was the *Deutsches Wörterbuch* (*German Dictionary*), which they began publishing in installments in 1852. This work, however, was only completed in 1961, nearly a century after Jacob's death.

The *Gattung Grimm* ("Grimm Genre")—as their form of the fairy tale is often called—holds an outstanding place in the literature written for children and adolescents, and *Kinder- und Hausmärchen* constitutes an indispensable contribution to world literature. Several of the Grimm's folktales continue to appear in all forms of popular media, and interest in their stories appears to be as strong as ever. In contrast, the *Irische Elfenmärchen* and the *Deutsche Sagen* remain in the background in terms of importance, despite the fact that individual stories from these anthologies, or even the anthologies as a whole, are published time and again. *See also* Brothers Grimm in Biopics; Collecting, Collectors; Editing, Editors; German Tales.

Further Readings: Bluhm, Lothar: *Grimm-Philologie: Beiträge zur Märchenforschung und Wissenschaftsgeschichte.* Hildesheim: Olms-Weidmann, 1995; Denecke, Ludwig: *Jacob Grimm und sein Bruder Wilhelm.* Stuttgart: Metzler, 1971; Grimm, Wilhelm. *Kleinere Schriften.* 4 volumes. Edited by Gustav Hinrichs. Volumes. 1–3. Berlin: Dümmler, 1881–83; volume 4: Gütersloh: Bertelsmann, 1887; Hennig, Dieter, and Bernhard Lauer, eds. *200 Jahre Brüder Grimm: Dokumente ihres Lebens und Wirkens.* 3 volumes. Kassel: Weber & Weidemeyer, 1985; Tatar, Maria. *The Hard Facts of the Grimms' Fairy Tales.* 2nd edition. Princeton, NJ: Princeton University Press, 2003; Uther, Hans-Jörg. "Fairy Tales as a Forerunner of European Children's Literature: Cross-Border Fairy Tale Materials and Fairy Tale Motifs." *Narodna umjetnost* 38.1 (2001): 121–33; Ward, Donald, ed. and trans. *The German Legends of the Brothers Grimm.* 2 vols. Philadelphia: Institute for the Study of Human Issues, 1981. 2: 341–84; Zipes, Jack. *The Brothers Grimm: From Enchanted Forests to the Modern World.* 2nd edition. New York: Palgrave MacMillan, 2002.

Hans-Jörg Uther

Grimm Brothers. *See* Brothers Grimm in Biopics; Grimm, Jacob; Grimm, Ludwig Emil; Grimm, Wilhelm; *Kinder- und Hausmärchen*

Grimms' Fairy Tales. *See Kinder- und Hausmärchen*

Gripari, Pierre (1925–1990)

One of the most successful writers for children in twentieth-century France, Pierre Gripari is especially known for his collections of humorously irreverent fairy tales. The son of a Greek father and a French mother, Gripari was an avid reader, notably of tales in the Russian tradition by Aleksandr **Afanas'ev** and Nikolai Gogol and, in the German tradition, by the Brothers **Grimm** and E. T. A. **Hoffmann**. A prolific and versatile writer, Gripari published his first and probably most-famous collection of fairy tales, *Les contes de la rue Broca* (*Tales of Broca Street*), early in his career, in 1967. While continuing to write in other genres for both children and adults, he published similar collections until the very end of his life: *Histoire du Prince Pipo, de Pipo le cheval et de la Princesse Popi* (*The Story of Prince Pipo, Pipo the Horse, and Princess Pipo*, 1976); *Contes de la Folie-Méricourt* (*Tales of Folie-Méricourt*, 1983); *Marelles* (1988); and *Contes d'ailleurs et d'autre part* (*Tales of Elsewhere and Otherwise*, 1990). Rather different both in style and intended readership is his novel, *Patrouille du conte* (*Tale Patrol*, 1983), which constitutes a sort of a manifesto on the (re)writing of fairy tales.

Gripari's fairy tales have received institutional consecration in France, where they are regularly included on school reading lists. While this recognition is a testament to the clever use of language and humor in his reworkings of common folktale and fairy-tale **motif**s, it is also somewhat paradoxical. In his recastings of well-known stories by Hans Christian **Andersen**, Charles **Dickens**, the Grimms, and Charles **Perrault** (as well as stories of his own invention), Gripari revels in standing conventional wisdom on its head. Many of his tales defy readerly expectations by introducing ambiguity into the Manichean ethical framework so typical of the best-loved tales: thus, God can be malicious, and the **devil** good. Moreover, the **fairies**, **witch**es, and **sorcerer**s who inhabit these tales are frequently injudicious in their use of magic, which is anything but a reliable force, either for "good" or for "evil." In settings that meld the vaguely archaic with the specificity of contemporary Paris, Gripari's protagonists by and large find happiness at the end of their adventures, but often in ways that contest settled folktale and fairy-tale precedents.

Gripari's *Tale Patrol* offers a metacommentary on the craft of writing fairy tales. This novel recounts the misadventures of a group of children who are sent out to reform the Kingdom of Fairy Tales. When the patrol's attempts to impose democracy and dispel superstition, racism, and sexism encounter unexpected and undesired results, its mission is declared a failure and the unit is disbanded. In this allegory of the process of rewriting fairy tales, Gripari strongly denounces attempts to reduce the genre to a utilitarian political or cultural agenda. They may be disturbing by contemporary standards, he contends, but therein lies their value.

Further Reading: Peyroutet, Jean-Luc. *Pierre Gripari et ses contes pour enfants*. Paris: Girandoles, 1994.

Lewis C. Seifert

Gripe, Maria (1923–)

One of Sweden's most prolific writers of fiction with children as protagonists, Maria Gripe is the author of nearly forty books from *I vår lilla stad* (*In Our Little Town*, 1954) to *Annas blomma* (*Anna's Flower*, 1997). Many of her main characters are presented in short series of three or four books, such as the Josephine and Hugo books, the Elvis Karlsson series, the Shadow series, and the series about Lotten. Her literary breakthrough came with *Josefin* in 1961, an exquisite child's eye view of reality. Her husband, Harald Gripe, illustrates many of her books.

The question of identity and how it is formed is central to Gripe's oeuvre. Recurring **motif**s in the young protagonists' search for identity are the **mirror** and especially the shadow, evidence of Hans Christian **Andersen**'s influence. Fairy-tale motifs intertwined with psychological realism are presented in a poetic style that often includes elements of **myth** and **fantasy**. In *Landet utanför* (*The Land Beyond*, 1967), Gripe examines the nature of reality itself, evidence of her studies in philosophy and the history of religion. The four books in the shadow series, published between 1982 and 1988, have received the most scholarly attention. Maria Gripe has received much critical acclaim for her work, including the Hans Christian Andersen Medal in 1974. In 2005, her publisher instituted the Maria Gripe Prize. *See also* Scandinavian Tales.

Further Readings: Lindström, Carina. *Sökande, spegling, metamorfos: Tre vägar genom Maria Gripes skuggserie*. Stockholm/Stehag: Symposion Graduale, 1994; Toijer-Nilsson, Ying. *Skuggornas förtrogna: Om Maria Gripe*. Stockholm: Albert Bonniers Förlag, 2000.

Marte Hult

Grundtvig, Svend (1824–1883)

Danish folklorist and philologist Svend Grundtvig translated Johann Gottfried Herder's ideas of the national soul and Jacob and Wilhelm **Grimm**'s archival interest in folk traditions into a Danish context. As a nineteen-year-old, Grundtvig published translations of English and Scottish traditional **ballad**s, and Danish folktales and ballads became the focus of his lifelong commitment to collection and study. In a manifesto to "Danish men and women" in 1843–44, Grundtvig strongly encouraged people to record the traditional ballads that were still in popular usage. In 1847, a plan to include all ballad **variant**s in the collections was propounded, and in 1854, Grundtvig urged people to collect all types of **folklore**, with the intention of creating a national "museum" of popular traditions.

Grundtvig was the founder of the study of **folklore** in Denmark, and the collections of retellings (restitutions) of folktales, **legend**s, and ballads inspired numerous contemporary poets and artists. In 1876, *Danske folkeæventyr* (*Danish Fairy Tales*), the first of three volumes of folktales, was published. Taking an interest in parallels between folktales and ballads, Grundtvig considered interactions between variants and tradition a feature of all popular traditions. This assumption led to a dynamic view of folktales as living organisms based on basic plots and deep structures, which make up traditions by being adapted to new contexts. In 1861, Grundtvig worked out an unpublished catalogue of folktales, supposedly the first in the world. *See also* Scandinavian Tales.

Further Reading: Rossel, Sven H., ed. *A History of Danish Literature*. Lincoln: University of Nebraska Press, 1992.

Helene Høyrup

H

Hair

While best known for its role in "Rapunzel"—the **Grimm** brothers' version of ATU 310, The Maiden in the Tower—hair, on both the head and the body, plays a significant part in many folktales. The role of hair can be divided into three categories: (1) the alteration of hair as story element, (2) the identification of a character by hair, and (3) hair as an important plot element.

The first category, alteration, includes stories in which hair turns golden as a result of disobedience (ATU 314, Goldener, and ATU 710, Our Lady's Child); stories where **women** grow beards to avoid **marriage** (ATU 706D, St. Wilgefortis and Her Beard); and stories in which people lose their hair after placing a hot cake under their hat (ATU 774J, Why St. Peter Became Bald). In addition, the cutting of hair is featured in several **motif**s identified in Stith **Thompson**'s *Motif-Index of Folk-Literature:* for disguise (Motif K1821.10), to escape a captor (Motif K538), as an insult (Motif P672.2), as a **punishment** (Motif Q488), and as preparation for war (Motif P552.5). In these **tale type**s and in other tales using these motifs, the alteration of hair is an essential part of the story.

"Rapunzel" illustrated by Walter Crane in *Household Stories, from the Collection of the Brothers Grimm*, trans. Lucy Crane (London: Macmillan & Co., 1882), p. 72. [Courtesy of the Eloise Ramsey Collection of Literature for Young People, University Libraries, Wayne State University]

Hair also serves as a means of identifying characters. Some characters bear names based on their hair, such as **Bluebeard** (ATU 312, Maiden-Killer) and King Thrushbeard (ATU 900), who are characterized by their facial hair. The children in ATU 707, The Three Golden Children, are known by their golden locks. Hair—even a single strand—as an identifier in folktales is distinct enough to justify its own motif: H75, Identification by a hair (with its subdivisions H75.1–7). Also featured in Thompson's motifs are H151.13, Disguised hero's golden hair discovered by spying **princess**; and H312.8, Bridegroom-to-be has to have three pecks, three quarts of gold, and an animal with a horn on his head pointing to the sky, and a large red hair.

Finally, there are tales in which hair plays an important role in the plot. While Rapunzel might be the best known, featuring as it does the memorable image of a girl's long locks being used as a ladder into a tower where she is held captive (Motif F848.1), there are other tales where hair plays a central—even titular—role. In the tale about Three Hairs from the **Devil**'s Beard (ATU 461), hair is featured as the goal of a test. In ATU 910C, Think Carefully Before You Begin a Task, an officer threatens to kill a barber if cut while shaving. The barber's apprentice takes the job, reasoning that if he makes a mistake, he could simply cut the throat of the officer immediately. In the tale type known as The Speaking Hair (ATU 780B), hair functions as an important character, announcing the unjust **death** and burial of the young girl to whom it is attached. Hair frequently has magical uses in folktales. For example, in some instances it is burned to summon victims (D2074.2.2) or to summon **fairies** (F398), and it other cases hair is set afire to kill victims outright (D2061.2.2.4.1).

Hair also plays a role in humorous and **bawdy tale**s. Tale type ATU 921C, for example, asks why the hair on the head is gray before the beard and offers the answer: because it's twenty years older. Tales of a bawdier nature joke about mistaking human pubic hair for that of an animal. For example, in some tales a culture hero's pubic hair is thought to be a bear's hair (Motif J1772.4), while in others a **peasant** in a tree mistakes the pubic hair of an ardent husband's wife for a calf's tail (Motif J1772.4.1).

Further Readings: Claudel, C. "Golden Hair." *Southern Folklore Quarterly* 5 (1941): 257–63; Ofek, Galia. "'Tie Her Up by the Hair': Dickens's Retelling of the Medusa and Rapunzel Myths." *Dickens Quarterly* 20 (2003): 184–99.

B. Grantham Aldred

Hamilton, Anthony (1646–1720)

Born in Ireland and educated in France, Anthony Hamilton settled permanently in France with the deposition and exile of James II. Perhaps best known for his fictionalized *Mémoires de la vie du comte de Grammont* (*Memoirs of the Life of the Count of Grammont*, 1713), inspired by the life of his brother-in-law, Hamilton produced among the first licentious fairy tales in France. He combined the burlesque with parodies of tales by Marie-Catherine d'**Aulnoy** and of the Oriental tale, which recently had come into fashion with the publication of Antoine **Galland**'s **translation** of the *Arabian Nights*. Hamilton's three fairy-tale **novel**s, *Le bélier* (*The Ram*), *L'histoire de Fleur d'Epine* (*The Story of Mayflower*), and *Les quatre facardins* (*The Four Facardins*), were written sometime between 1705 and 1715 and were published posthumously in 1730. However, the manuscripts of the tales circulated in Parisian high society well before they appeared in print.

With respect to both structure and motif, Hamilton borrows from earlier Italian and French fairy-tale collections as well as from the *Arabian Nights*. All three of his novels open with **frame narrative**s within which unfold embedded tales, and they play on the types of convoluted plots typical of d'Aulnoy. In fact, the very title *The Ram* is an explicit reference to d'Aulnoy's tale, "Le mouton" ("The Sheep," 1694). For this tale Hamilton creates a **legend** that explains how the estate of Les Moulineaux came to be known as Pontalie, blending chivalric, pastoral, Oriental, and precious references and themes. He satirizes the precious language typical of the style of the first vogue of the *conte de fées*, characterized by the use of hyperbole. **Parody** is accomplished through the accumulation of **motif**s, such as the persecuted stepdaughter, metamorphosis, and the discarded animal skin, as well as the ironic use of superlatives distinctive of precious language.

While *The Ram* makes references to the *Arabian Nights*, *The Story of Mayflower* and *The Four Facardins* draw more directly from the Orientalist tale tradition. *The Story of Mayflower* opens on the 999th night, when Dinarzade has finally tired of her sister **Sheherazade**'s stories and her problematic **marriage**, and she decides to relate her own tale to the sultan. *The Four Facardins* continues where *The Story of Mayflower* leaves off: the **prince** de Trébizonde will continue to tell the sultan tales. Hamilton begins his third fairy-tale novel with the narrator begging Sylvie to relieve him of his duty to her to write more absurd tales, for which he excuses himself, only to begin recounting, against his better judgment, how the prince scolds the sultan for his past behavior and then goes on to narrate his strange adventures. Just as Miguel de Cervantes Saavedra parodies the chivalric novel, Hamilton takes aim at the tale tradition, mocking Sheherazade's heroism, the sultan's cruelty, and Radiant's literally blinding eyes. Hamilton skillfully pits trope against trope in a self-reflexive style satirizing a literary genre that nevertheless has an irresistible charm. *See also* Erotic Tales; Salon.

Further Reading: Ennis, Mary Louise. "Fractured Fairy Tales: Parodies for the Salon and Foire." *Out of the Woods: The Origins of the Literary Fairy Tale in Italy and France*. Edited by Nancy L. Canepa. Detroit: Wayne State University Press, 1997. 221–46.

Anne E. Duggan

Hamilton, Virginia (1936–2002)

Virginia Hamilton, named to honor a slave grandfather who escaped from Virginia, grew up outside Yellow Springs, Ohio, on a small farm surrounded by the farms of other family members. After college, first at Antioch and then at Ohio State, and after ten years of the literary life in New York, she returned with her husband to live on the family land. There, where as a child she had listened to her mother and aunts tell stories, she settled down to write stories for the next generation of children. Hamilton had already won acclaim for her children's books, including a National Book Award, a Newbery Award, and an Edgar Allan Poe Award, and had already adapted folk **motif**s in books and short stories, when she wrote *The People Could Fly: American Black Folktales* (1985), with **illustration**s by Leo and Diane Dillon. This, her first collection of folktales, retold **animal tale**s, **legend**s from slave days, **tall tale**s, and **märchen**. This book won the Coretta Scott King Award and numerous other accolades.

Seven more books of African American, Caribbean, and African folktales followed. Hamilton continued to win awards, including the Laura Ingalls Wilder Medal, the Regina Medal, the NAACP Image Award, the Hans Christian Andersen Medal, and a MacArthur Fellowship. In retelling folktales, she used distinctive diction, grammatical structures, sentence rhythm, and vocabulary, but usually avoided nonstandard spelling, to suggest a variety of African American vernaculars, including Gullah and West Indies English. She also included informative notes about provenance, language, and other folkloric matters. *See also* African American Tales; African Tales.

Further Reading: Mikkelsen, Nina. *Virginia Hamilton.* New York: Twayne, 1994.

William Bernard McCarthy

Hansel and Gretel

"Hansel and Gretel" is a tale in the ***Kinder- und Hausmärchen*** (*Children's and Household Tales*, 1812–15) of Jacob and Wilhelm **Grimm**. The basic story of the Grimm version can be described as follows:

I. The family of a poor woodcutter is starving. The wife insists that her husband take the two children, Hansel and Gretel, into the forest and abandon them there. So the children can later find their way home, Hansel marks the path that they take, first with pebbles and then with breadcrumbs, which are eaten by birds.

II. Lost, the children wander until they find a house made of bread and cake. After the hungry children break off bits and eat, the **witch** who lives there invites them into her house for a meal and puts them to bed. The witch imprisons Hansel in a cage, intending to fatten him up for slaughter. Gretel is forced to do household chores, especially the cooking. When the witch, who is blind, feels Hansel's finger to see how fat he is getting, he holds out a bone to deceive her.

III. The witch decides to cook him anyway. After Gretel prepares the oven, the witch asks her to climb inside to see if it is ready. Gretel pretends she does not understand, so the witch crawls in to demonstrate. Gretel quickly shuts the oven, thus killing the witch.

IV. The children take the witch's treasure and return home, crossing a river on the back of a duck. When they reach home, their **father** welcomes them.

The Grimms credited "various tales from Hesse" (the region of Germany where they lived) as their source, but Grimm scholar Heinz Rölleke believes they got this tale from Dortchen Wild (both may be true). The Grimms (Wilhelm in particular) effected several different versions, from the prepublication manuscript of 1810 to the sixth edition of the *Kinder- und Hausmärchen* in 1850. The basic events remained unchanged, but the tale increased in length with the addition of psychological motivation and visual imagery. Some of the most interesting alterations are as follows: the characters of the parents were given more attention; in the fourth edition, the woodcutter's wife (who had been the children's own **mother**) was first called a stepmother. The birds are additions, as is Gretel's kindness to the duck as she asks it to help her and her brother cross the river.

In the Grimms' 1810 version, the children were called Little Brother and Little Sister, but since the first edition (1812), the tale and the children have been named Hansel (Hänsel) and Gretel (diminutives of Johannes and Margarete). Along with other forms of the same names (such as Hans and Gretchen) that appear in other German tales, these were deliberately chosen for their generic quality.

"Hansel and Gretel" remains one of the best-known Grimm tales both in Germany and elsewhere. Other important published versions include those in Ludwig **Bechstein**'s

Deutsches Märchenbuch (*German Fairy-Tale Book*, 1845), which offers a version quite similar to the Grimms' tale, and in August Stöber's *Elsässisches Volksbüchlein* (*Little Alsatian Chapbook*, 1842). The **opera** by Engelbert **Humperdinck** was first performed in 1893. The first English **translation** of Grimms' tales, published by Edgar **Taylor** in 1823 and 1826, confused "Hansel and Gretel" with two other similarly structured Grimm tales, "Der Liebste Roland" ("Sweetheart Roland"; ATU 1119 and 313) and "Brüderchen und Schwesterchen" ("Little Brother and Little Sister"; ATU 450). A proper English translation of the tale of "Hansel and Gretel" was published in 1853.

In every part of the tale there are references to **food** or to its absence, causing hunger and starvation. The main tension comes from the threat of **cannibalism**. Sociohistorical interpreters point to historical famines, while psychological interpreters see themes of deprivation and oral gratification. The central image of the tale is the attractive, edible house. Especially around Christmastime, the cookie-and-candy houses displayed in shops and magazines are reminders of this folktale.

In addition to the subject of food, the tale is notable for its exaggerated **family** dynamics. The brother and sister are repeatedly shown to be selflessly devoted to one another. However, the children's roles shift during the course of the tale. At the beginning, Hansel takes charge, plans how to mark the path, and comforts and protects his little sister. Later, Gretel dominates: it is she who kills the witch and arranges for the duck to help them get home. The relationship between the parents and the attitude of each parent toward the children depend on which edition is being read. In general, the father is led by his nagging wife to act against his will, and is happy at the end when the children return home. Interpreters reading from a psychoanalytic perspective have noted that after Gretel kills the witch, the stepmother is also dead, as if the two malicious **women** were manifestations of a single person.

Traditional Elements

The entire tale is a **folktale** with printed and oral analogs. Although "Hansel and Gretel" is the prototype for the **tale type** ATU 327A, an earlier version exists in Marie-Catherine d'**Aulnoy**'s tale "Finette Cendron" (1697). In this story, an impoverished **king** and **queen** deliberately lose their three daughters three times in the wilderness. The kindest and cleverest of the **sisters**, Finette, plants an acorn that grows quickly into a tall tree, which she climbs to see where they are. She discovers a mansion that turns out to belong to a hag and her husband, a giant **ogre**, who permit the girls to be their servants. Finette heats the oven and asks the ogre to test it with his tongue, so that he falls in and is incinerated. Then, as the girls arrange the ogress's hair, Finette cuts off her head (this is Motif K1013, False beauty-doctor, which is known worldwide). The sisters remain in the ogre's house, and the rest of the tale relates the story of "**Cinderella**."

The individual episodes and motifs are also traditional:

I. The children lost in the forest: Several versions of the episode of the children deliberately lost by their parents predate the Grimms' usage. In addition to "Finette Cendron," it appears in Martin Montanus's "The Little Earth-Cow" (1557), wherein one of two sisters is named Gretel; in Giambattista **Basile**'s "Ninnillo e Nennella" (1636); and in Charles **Perrault**'s "Le petit poucet" ("Little **Thumbling**," 1697). The episode of the paths marked with stones and crumbs represents an elaboration of the motif of the thread that Ariadne gives Theseus to use to get out of the Minoan labyrinth. This particular introduction is absent from Humperdinck's opera. In some **variants** taken from **oral tradition**, there is no parental involvement: the children become lost entirely by accident, or they have set out to seek their fortunes. Sometimes, the children seek a light that turns out to come from the house or camp of the villain.

II. Meeting the witch: ATU 327A is part of an international folktale cycle (ATU 327, The Children and the Ogre) in which a child or children fall under the power of an ogre and then escape by means of any of several clever tricks. Here, as in other tales—including ATU 327B, The **Brothers** and the Ogre, in Arab tradition; and ATU 327C, The Devil (Witch) Carries the Hero Home in a Sack—an exchange of food precipitates the crisis. The child who falls into the power of the cannibal figure (ogre, witch, **Baba Yaga**, etc.) either eats food that belongs to the cannibal or gives food to the cannibal. Precisely this danger is reflected in the common warning to children not to take candy from strangers. The witch's saving the children alive, intending to eat them later, is a narrative device that increases the suspense in various ogre tales.

III. "Show me how": Gretel's pretense of not understanding how to test the oven is characteristic of ATU 327A and also appears traditionally in other subtypes of ATU 327. With characters other than a child and an ogre (see **Trickster**), this episode constitutes ATU 1121, The Ogre's Wife Burned in Her Own Oven. In a tale from India (c. 1600), a villain kills people by having them dance on the edge of his boiling cauldron and then pushing them in. One potential victim pretends not to understand, so the villain demonstrates and is killed. An oven instead of a cauldron is apparently an alteration made to reflect local culinary practices (see **Oicotype**). Strictly speaking, "Finette Cendron" lacks the "show me how" element. However, when Finette asks the ogre to test the heat of the oven with his tongue, she throws in a great quantity of butter. This would make more sense if she were using a frying pan rather than an oven.

More generally, in the strategy of feigned ignorance, one character induces his or her adversary to "show me how I should do that" and uses the opportunity to kill the adversary. Other means of execution such as beheading (in Indian literature), slicing the throat while shaving, crushing to **death**, and hanging (in, for example, Punch-and-Judy puppet shows and ATU 327D, The Kiddelkaddelkar) are also employed. Sometimes, a third character warns the hero in advance about what his adversary intends to do, which makes the incident longer and reinforces it by repetition. Gretel, in contrast, figures out what to do by herself, and she does it so humbly that many summaries of the story do not convey how clever (rather than just lucky) she is.

IV. The children return home: The end of the tale can be brief (as in the Grimms' manuscript and first edition versions) or even nonexistent (as in "Finette Cendron," where the sisters stay at the ogre's house). The children often keep the witch's or ogre's treasure, thus rescuing their family from poverty.

Alternatively, this part of the tale can prolong the excitement. In that case, the chief ogre absents himself and the intruder kills his daughter or wife. Sometimes when the chief ogre returns, he finds cooked meat that he believes to be the flesh of the intruder. After he eats it, he discovers that he has eaten his own daughter. Meanwhile, the human child or children have run away. The chief ogre, furious, chases after them. The children may escape by means of a Magic Flight (ATU 313): they throw objects behind them that produce obstacles (such as a mountain or a body of water) to delay the pursuer (Motif D672, Obstacle flight), or they turn themselves into other shapes to fool the pursuer (Motif D671, Transformation flight). Especially in African ogre tales, the fugitives throw objects such as needles behind them to delay the pursuer (this is a natural rather than a magical flight). The river that Hansel and Gretel have to cross is a remnant of the Magic Flight motif.

Closely Related Tale Types

The folktale cycle ATU 327, The Children and the Ogre, includes ATU 327A, as described above, and the following tale types:

ATU 327B, The Brothers and the Ogre: A group of siblings (boys, girls, or mixed) come to an ogre's house and ask for hospitality. The ogre intends to kill them in their beds. The youngest of the visitors exchanges the bedplaces, nightcaps, etc., of the visitors with those of the ogre's own children. The ogre kills his children by mistake (compare with ATU 1119, The Ogre Kills His Mother [Wife]). The visitors run away and, although the ogre chases them, they manage to get home safely. This is often an introduction to ATU 328, The Boy Steals the Ogre's Treasure.

ATU 327C, The Devil (Witch) Carries the Hero Home in a Sack: A witch or an ogre catches a boy in a sack and carries him off. Initially the victim escapes, leaving an object so that the sack feels heavy. He is caught again and taken to the witch's house. As the witch's daughter prepares to kill him, the boy asks her to show him how he should arrange himself. When she does so, he kills her. He may cook her and serve the meat to her family. He taunts the witch, kills her, and returns home with her treasure.

ATU 327D, The Kiddlekaddlekar: Two children come to an ogre's house, where the ogre's wife tries to hide them. The ogre discovers them and intends to hang them. The girl pretends not to understand how to put her head in the noose, so the ogre demonstrates and hangs himself. He promises the children his kiddlekaddlekar (a magic cart) and his treasure if they will set him free. They do so. The ogre follows them home and unwittingly traps them in a cave. They kill the ogre and escape after a giant bird eats his corpse.

ATU 327F, The Witch and the Fisher Boy: Disguising her voice so she sounds like the boy's mother, a witch lures a boy and catches him. The witch's daughter tries to bake the boy, but he pushes her into the oven instead. The witch returns home and eats her own daughter. The boy, hiding in a tree, taunts her. The witch fells the tree, but birds rescue the boy and fly away with him.

In addition, there are miscellaneous variants that conform to the general pattern of ATU 327 but have few of its typical detail motifs. The tale types that comprise ATU 327 have a structure like that of ATU 313, which includes tales such as the Grimms' "Sweetheart Roland," "The Foundling," and "Okerlo" (a retelling of d'Aulnoy's "The Bee and the Orange Tree"), in that one or more protagonists come into the domain of, and then escape from, a malevolent supernatural figure. The chief distinction is that in ATU 327, the protagonists are children, while in ATU 313, where the protagonists are young adults, the tale typically ends with a celebration of marriage. *See also* Childhood and Children; Psychological Approaches; Sociohistorical Approaches.

Further Readings: Ashliman, D. L. *A Guide to Folktales in the English Language.* Westport, CT: Greenwood Press, 1987. 69–71; Böhm-Korff, Regina. *Deutung und Bedeutung von "Hänsel und Gretel."* Frankfurt a.M.: Peter Lang, 1991; Cosquin, Emmanuel. "Le conte de la chaudière bouillante et la feinte maladresse dans l'Inde et hors de l'Inde." *Études folkloriques: Recherches sur la migrations des contes populaires et leur point de départ.* Paris: E. Champion, 1922. 349–99; Ellis, John. *One Fairy Story Too Many: The Brothers Grimm and Their Tales.* Chicago: University of Chicago Press, 1983; Freudenberg, Rachel. "Illustrating Childhood—'Hansel and Gretel.'" *Marvels & Tales* 12 (1998): 263–318; Goldberg, Christine. "Gretel's Duck: The Escape from the Ogre in AaTh 327." *Fabula* 41 (2000): 42–51; Scherf, Walter. *Die Herausforderung des Dämons: Form und Funktion grausiger Kindermärchen; eine volkskundliche und tiefenpsychologische Darstellung der Struktur, Motivik und Rezeption von 27 untereinander verwandten Erzähltypen.* München: K. G. Saur, 1987; Uther, Hans-Jörg. *The Types of International Folktales: A Classification and Bibliography.* 3 volumes. Helsinki: Academia Scientiarum Fennica, 2004.

Christine Goldberg

Hardenberg, Friedrich von. *See* Novalis

Harris, Joel Chandler (1848–1908)

A white journalist from Georgia, Joel Chandler Harris sought out and recorded African American folk narratives, publishing a sampling first in 1879 in the *Atlanta Constitution*, then subsequently in a series of collections including *Uncle Remus*: *His Songs and Sayings; The Folklore of the Old Plantation* (1880), *Nights with Uncle Remus: Myths and Legends of the Old Plantation* (1883), and *Uncle Remus and His Friends: Old Plantation Stories, Songs, and Ballads, with Sketches of Negro Character* (1892). Harris spent part of his youth as a hired hand on a plantation where he encountered African American culture. As a virtual outcast from white society (a product of poverty and illegitimate birth), he found common cause with his coworkers, spending time listening to their stories, sayings, and songs, and developing the rudiments of the interest and skill that facilitated his later **collecting** activities.

Harris's collections were tailored primarily for a popular audience, slotted into the humor section of his publisher's catalogue. They were organized as **frame narrative**s, presenting an idealized view of race relations and hierarchy in the antebellum South. Nonetheless, Harris's scholarly interest in the material is clear. He is careful throughout his works to mention the accuracy with which he reproduces content and dialect, and criticizes other representations of African Americans—notably minstrel shows—for doing less. His collections are often retrospectively associated with the racist entertainment of the later nineteenth century, but in Harris' own estimation, they held a far greater value. *See also* African American Tales; Race and Ethnicity.

Further Reading: Harris, Joel Chandler, and Richard Chase, comp. *The Complete Tales of Uncle Remus.* Boston: Houghton Mifflin, 1955.

Adam Zolkover

Harry Potter Films

The **adaptation** to the silver screen of J. K. **Rowling**'s Harry Potter series was inevitable given the books' status as a popular phenomenon. However, the films also represent the recent resurgence of interest in cinematic **fantasy**, which has seen the film adaptations of J. R. R. **Tolkien**'s *The Lord of the Rings* and C. S. **Lewis**'s Chronicles of Narnia series. Rowling's mixture of magical adventure, quest, and school story tension is peculiarly suited to the cinema in its provision of recognizable visual cues, as is the clear-cut morality and symbol inherent in the adventures of the boy wizard and his nemesis Lord Voldemort. The films are also notable for their fidelity to the originals, which is to be expected considering Rowling's tight creative control during the process of adaptation. Necessarily, the films omit much of the day-to-day detail that conveys Rowling's magical world and that is the prime focus of her inventive wit. Lacking that slightly cluttered texture, the films feel more like straightforward adventure tales and less like alternative school stories. The necessary simplification of the plotline works with the generic expectations of action-adventure cinema to align the films more firmly than the books with the essentialist structures of the folkloric quest: challenge, struggle, and resolution.

The first two films were directed by Chris Columbus, whose experience with child actors was clearly relevant to the young cast. *Harry Potter and the Sorcerer's Stone* (2001) and *Harry Potter and the Chamber of Secrets* (2002) are the most pedestrian of the adaptations, with problems of pacing and fluency that partially detract from their undoubtedly sumptuous visual realization of the magical world of Hogwarts. More than any other Harry Potter directors, Columbus's films tend to exaggerate the visual appeal of the magical at the cost of plot complexity. At the same time, however, their slightly stilted storytelling allows for fairy-tale elements in Rowling's books to be retained in **motif**s such as repeated patterns of three and ritualized challenges such as the chess game.

A slightly different effect is seen in *Harry Potter and the Prisoner of Azkaban* (2004), directed by Alfonso Cuarón. This is a more coherent script, but it gains additional unity from the director's rather darker vision, which pulls the movie away from the innocent magic of **childhood** adventure into something closer to the gothic. Again, however, the film makes full use of the visual medium to bring magical creatures to life, and mythical monsters such as the hippogriff are considerably better-realized than the earlier films' attempts at centaurs and house-elves. *Harry Potter and the Goblet of Fire* (2005), directed by Mike Newell, presents the most pared-down script yet, losing several important subplots, but this is inevitable given the length of the novel, and the resulting film narrative is tightly paced. Cuarón's slightly grittier feel is abandoned in favor of the necessary ritualized repetition that characterizes the challenges faced in the Tri-Wizard Tournament and the ceremonial formality of Harry's confrontation with Voldemort at the end of his championship quest. *See also* Children's Literature; Film and Video.

Further Readings: Gupta, Suman. *Re-Reading Harry Potter*. New York: Houndmills: Palgrave Macmillan, 2003; Heilman, Elizabeth E., ed. *Harry Potter's World: Multidisciplinary Critical Perspectives*. New York: Routledge, 2003.

Jessica Tiffin

Hartzenbusch, Juan Eugenio (1806–1880)

Spanish playwright, critic, scholar, and prosodist Juan Eugenio Hartzenbusch owes the lion's share of his literary fame to *Los amantes de Teruel* (*The Lovers of Teruel*, 1837), a Romantic drama in verse and prose, but he also published two collections of **fable**s and stories that attest to his interest in folktales and fairy tales: *Fábulas puestas en verso castellano* (*Fables Set in Castilian Verse*, 1848) and *Cuentos y fábulas* (*Stories and Fables*, 1861).

Hartzenbusch intended his fables and stories not only to instruct but also to entertain. Among the most amusing and ironic tales from *Stories and Fables* are "El ratoncillo y el gato" ("The Mouse and the Cat"), "El maestro y las velas" ("The Teacher and the Candles"), "El sastre y el avaro" ("The Tailor and the Miser"), and "El reloj de sol" ("The Sundial"). Two particularly outstanding stories are "Palos de Moguer" and "La hermosura por castigo" ("Beauty as Punishment"). "Palos de Moguer" is an entertaining tale about an ongoing dispute between married couples in the Andalusian town of Palos de Moguer and how the *palos*—that is, "sticks," and by extension "beatings"—resolve the conflict and restore community. The **didactic tale** "Beauty as Punishment" is rich in irony and extrahuman events as it relates the pitfall of vanity in a beautiful woman. *See also* Spanish Tales.

Further Readings: Fedorcheck, Robert M., trans. *Stories of Enchantment from Nineteenth-Century Spain*. Lewisburg, PA: Bucknell University Press, 2002; Iranzo, Carmen. *Juan Eugenio Hartzenbusch*. Boston: Twayne, 1978.

Robert M. Fedorchek

Harun al-Rashid (766–809)

As the fifth caliph of the Abbasid dynasty (ruled 786–809), Harun al-Rashid has become the prototype of the just and considerate ruler in narratives originating from the Arab Muslim world, particularly in the tales of the ***Arabian Nights***.

In political terms, Harun al-Rashid's time was one of turmoil; it is considered a golden age in terms of commerce and culture. The capital of the dynasty, Baghdad, founded in

762, profited from the tremendous wealth acquired from the provinces and developed into a center of fine arts, particularly music and poetry. Harun's rule is closely linked to the family of the Barmakids, of whom several members held important administrative positions up to the date of their sudden and cruel dismissal in 803; Harun's vizier Ja'far has become the stereotypical representative of the Oriental adviser, particularly in Western Orientalist films.

Two centuries after his death, Harun and his era evolved to represent the focus of an uncritical tradition in Arabic sources attributing narratives from the most diverse origins to the time of his reign. While Harun does not figure prominently in those narratives, the allusion to his reign serves to create a fictional atmosphere of peace and prosperity. These characteristics also dominate Harun's image in the narratives of the *Arabian Nights*. In the tales, about sixty of which mention Harun in a central role, he is embellished with all of those traits that the audience would have appreciated in a ruler. At his court, Harun is driven by a constant urge to amuse himself and be entertained. Numerous tales begin with Harun leaving the palace in disguise to examine the daily problems of his subjects, and they end by having him restore justice, help the needy, unite lovers, and in general serve to make everybody in his realm happy. Meanwhile, his role in those narratives is static: he does not become, but he always is caliph. Similarly, the narratives do not deal with the actual role and function of his position but rather dwell on traits of character that Arabic culture had deemed important for a man of his position, such as an impressive stature in public life, a considerate and responsible attitude toward his subordinates, and a magnanimous behavior toward his subjects.

Harun opposed the claim to power voiced by the descendants of 'Ali, the Prophet Mohammed's cousin and son-in-law and father of his only surviving male descendants. In consequence, in Iranian tradition, wherein 'Ali and his descendants are venerated as the only rightful claimants to Mohammed's succession as the leader of the Islamic community, Harun has largely been replaced by the Safavid Shah 'Abbas (ruled 1588–1629) as the exemplary folktale ruler. *See also* *Arabian Nights* Films; Thief of Bagdad Films.

Further Readings: Gerhardt, Mia I. *The Art of Story-Telling: A Literary Study of the Thousand and One Nights*. Leiden: Brill, 1963. 419–70; Marzolph, Ulrich, and Richard van Leeuwen, eds. *The Arabian Nights Encyclopedia*. Volume 2. Santa Barbara: ABC-CLIO, 2004. 585–87.

Ulrich Marzolph

Hauff, Wilhelm (1802–1827)

The German-Swabian writer Wilhelm Hauff was unusually prolific considering his short life, for in addition to producing three collections of fairy tales, he also wrote three novels, several **novella**s, and a number of satires. Hauff is best known for his fairy tales, which exhibit not only the influence of the German Romantics E. T. A. **Hoffmann** and Ludwig **Tieck** but also that of Storm and Stress writers who penned tales about robber barons and knights. Hauff's tales fuse Romantic and realistic elements and move away from the artistic idealism of Romanticism toward a more realistic portrayal of life, from the magical-metaphysical sphere into the psychological one. In fact, the tales' rational and sometimes ironic tone already point toward the nineteenth-century bourgeois tradition that would later come to be known as the Biedermeier period.

Hauff's gift for storytelling was rooted in his childhood. As a child, he was a voracious reader who was particularly drawn to adventure fiction, which he retold orally to his siblings and friends, and later to the children of the Baron von Hügel family, for whom he worked as a house tutor. It was the von Hügel family that encouraged him to put his stories on paper. His tales, addressed to youth between the ages of twelve and fifteen years and written for their moral education, were collected in almanac form in three volumes between 1825 and 1827: *Die Karawane* (*The Caravan*, 1825), *Der Sheik von Alessandria und seine Sklaven* (*The Sheik of Alessandria and His Slaves*, 1826), and *Das Wirtshaus im Spessart* (*The Inn at Spessart*, 1827).

The tales in the collections move from interest in distant lands to the local setting. And within the tales themselves, Oriental and Teutonic **motif**s overlap. Given the longing of the Romantics for distant lands and the interest in the early nineteenth century in the exotic, it is not surprising that the setting of many of Hauff's tales is the Orient. Indeed, the model for the almanacs was the **Arabian Nights,** which had been available in Europe since Antoine **Galland**'s eighteenth-century French translation and, beginning in 1825, was starting to appear in a German translation by Maximilian Habicht. Each of Hauff's almanacs is organized around a **frame narrative** that gives the work its cohesion. The first collection focuses on a caravan of travelers moving through the desert and threatened by dangerous robbers. The tales in the second volume center on the celebration of the freeing of slaves in the palace of an Oriental **prince**, which fulfills an old prophecy. In the final volume, a group of travelers who meet by chance at an inn find themselves among a group of robbers; it focuses on their attempts to free themselves from their situation with acts of courage and ingenuity.

The popularity of Hauff's tales can be attributed to the fact that they are entertaining and full of adventure, with puzzling entanglements and unexpected twists and turns, and demystify the miraculous. Yet, the world that Hauff presents in the tales is not supernatural but fully natural, one filled with vivid and descriptive details of living spaces, costumes, meals, and customs.

Among Hauff's most popular fairy tales are stories such as "Kalif Storch" ("Caliph Stork"), "Der Zwerg Nase" ("Dwarf Long-Nose"), "Der kleine Muck" ("Little Muck"), and "Das kalte Herz" ("The Cold Heart"). These tales have also appeared from time to time in general collections of fairy tales or as separate illustrated editions. The protagonists in the tales "Dwarf Long Nose" (Long Nose), "Little Muck" (Muck), and "The Cold Heart" (Charcoal Peter) are all social outcasts: Long Nose because of his unusually long nose and grotesque and misshapen figure, Muck because of his bizarre figure and his eccentric dress, and the charcoal burner's son Peter because of his social standing. With the help of magic or supernatural forces, all three protagonists are able to raise their standings in society. Long Nose, after having learned the art of cooking with a secret herb he discovered under the spell of the old **witch**, becomes the head chef of the duke's court. Muck acquires a pair of slippers with which he can fly through the air and a magic wand with which he can find buried treasures, making it possible for him to be named the special runner for the **king**. After having suffered a series of losses over which he cannot express his emotions, Charcoal Peter elicits the help of a benevolent forest spirit to regain his human heart. In the end, however, all of these protagonists renounce the gifts acquired through magic and settle into a simple bourgeois existence in which they find happiness and contentment.

Such endings as these are consistent with Hauff's conservative Protestant values and reflect his worldview that, in a morally ordered universe, any desire to change the order of things in one's life is considered wrong and sinful. At the same time, it signals a literary response to the more conservative political climate in Germany during the period of Restoration that took place between the end of the Wars of Liberation and the Revolution of 1830. *See also* DEFA Fairy-Tale Films; German Tales.

Further Readings: Blamires, David. "The Meaning of Disfigurement in Wilhelm Hauff's 'Dwarf Nose.'" *Children's Literature in Education* 33 (2002): 297–307; Hauff, Wilhelm. *Fairy Tales.* Translated by Jean Rosemary Edwards. London: P. Hamlyn, 1961; ———. *Tales.* Translated by S. Mendel. 1890. Freeport, NY: Books for Libraries Press, 1970; Thum, Maureen. "Misreading the Cross-Writer: The Case of Wilhelm Hauff's 'Dwarf Long Nose.' "*Children's Literature* 25 (1997): 1–23.

Alfred L. Cobbs

Hau'ofa, Epeli (1939–)

Tongan writer Epeli Hau'ofa was born in Papua New Guinea to missionary parents. In a "story" on "**Oral Tradition**s and Writing," presented as an academic paper, Hau'ofa recalls his upbringing in Papua New Guinea and Tonga in an atmosphere "quickened" by **storytelling**, in which "the physical universe of island peoples was related and explained" through stories, and "serious discussions were always punctuated with funny **anecdote**s." Oceanian methods of storytelling are an integral part of Hau'ofa's generically varied writings, which place the lives of the Islands' common people center stage and emphasize the senses in which answers to the challenges Oceanians face might be found within their own traditional stories and storytelling forms.

Hau'ofa's expansive yet intimate relationship with Oceania is informed by his immersion in Pacific cultures, languages, and storytelling traditions; by his academic training in Tonga, Fiji, Canada, and Australia, where he received his PhD in social anthropology; and by a series of academic appointments and directorships. His early anthropological writing and his reflections on anthropology focus on issues of inequality in village life and on the limitations of social science writings about Oceanians. In monographs on overpopulation (*Our Crowded Islands*, 1977) and food distribution in Oceania (*Corned Beer and Tapioca*, 1979), Hau'ofa wrestles with the problem of Pacific Island dependency on foreign aid and encourages ecological approaches to physical and cultural resources.

Hau'ofa's fiction from this period draws upon Oceanian storytelling and **folk**dramatic forms that join humor (often ribald and absurdist) to social critique to satirize the narrowing of horizons that comes with participation in remittance economies. The story cycle *Tales of the Tikong* (1982) ridicules everyone from island elites who opportunistically invoke the neotraditionalist "Pacific Way," to liberal outsider preservationists in search of the "Essential Indigenous Personality" and static versions of culture, to idealistic Islanders transformed into "expert" beggars. In the scatological satire, *Kisses in the Nederends* (1987), regional pains are reconfigured as a boil on the anus of the author, who subjects himself to the ministrations of a series of charlatans offering "cures" that become increasingly painful and humiliating.

Hau'ofa's essay "Our Sea of Islands" (1993) offers a more hopeful vision of the Pacific Islands, not as tiny, isolated, resource-poor nation-states but as a vitally articulated and "world-enlarging" constellation of Island peoples, linked by shared values and a history of regional exchange. In "The Ocean in Us" (1997), Hau'ofa develops this sense of Oceania as "a world of social networks" whose creative vitality is "independent of the Pacific Islands world of official diplomacy and neocolonial dependency." "Pasts to Remember" (2000) extends this "aesthetic" to the reworking of Island stories or histories as distinctively Oceanian creations, drawing on the full range of oral resources.

Hauʻofa's ideas about the need for Islanders to avoid the conceptual "reservations" that have been set up for them and instead to build a welcoming space within which to develop their own stories have been materialized in the Oceania Centre for Arts and Culture at the University of the South Pacific in Suva, Fiji. Since 1997, Hauʻofa has directed this "home" for the arts, inviting visual, performing, and verbal artists to collaborate in producing new works, forms, sounds, and movements that are unmistakably Oceanian and ceaselessly inventive. *See also* Australian and Aotearoan/New Zealand Tales; Pacific Island Tales.

Further Readings: Keown, Michele. "Purifying the Abject Body: Satire and Scatology in Epeli Hauʻofa's *Kisses in the Nederends*." *Postcolonial Pacific Writing*. London: Routledge, 2005. 61–83; Subramani. "An Interview with Epeli Hauʻofa." *Inside Out: Literature, Cultural Politics, and Identity in the New Pacific*. Edited by Vilsoni Hereniko and Rob Wilson. Lanham, MD: Rowman and Littlefield, 1999. 39–53; ———. *South Pacific Literature: From Myth to Fabulation*. Suva, Fiji: Institute of Pacific Studies, University of the South Pacific, 1985; Teaiwa, Teresia. "Reading Gauguin's *Noa Noa* with Hauʻofa's *Kisses in the Nederends*: Militourism, Feminism and the Polynesian Body." *Inside Out: Literature, Cultural Politics, and Identity in the New Pacific*. Edited by Vilsoni Hereniko and Rob Wilson. Lanham, MD: Rowman and Littlefield, 1999. 249–63.

Paul Lyons

Hawthorne, Nathaniel (1804–1864)

The vacuum left by the Puritan proscription of fairy tales and folktales was cleverly filled by the American novelist Nathaniel Hawthorne. He did this in part by writing satirical adult stories such as "Feathertop" (1846), in which a Salem **witch** plays fairy godmother to the cinder-smoking scarecrow she foists on pretentious colonial pseudoaristocrats. However, it was in *A Wonder-Book for Girls and Boys* (1851), written a year after *The Scarlet Letter*, that Hawthorne tried to free old **myth**s of their "classical aspect" and give them "a Gothic or Romantic guise" that would truly make them "marvelously independent of all temporary models and circumstances."

To carry out this agenda, Hawthorne created an iconoclastic college student, Eustace Bright, as his prime storyteller. After entertaining child audiences with flower-names that "might better suit a group of fairies," Eustace protests that he has depleted his store of European imports: "I have already told you so many fairy tales that I doubt whether there is a single one which you have not heard at least twice over." Nor will he retell Washington Irving's pseudofolktale about an "idle fellow" called Rip Van Winkle. Instead, to the horror of a scholarly classicist, Eustace proceeds to "Gothicize" Greek myths. Thus, for instance, the giant Atlas, whom Hercules dupes, becomes a hood-winked giant out of **Grimm**s' fairy tales. Hawthorne dispensed with Eustace's playfully "Gothicizing" interventions in a sequel, *Tanglewood Tales for Girls and Boys* (1853).

Further Reading: Hundley, Clarence Carroll, Jr. "Fairy Tale Elements in the Short Fiction of Nathaniel Hawthorne." Dissertation. University of North Carolina at Greensboro, 1994.

U. C. Knoepflmacher

Hay, Sara Henderson (1906–1987)

Sara Henderson Hay was an award-winning American poet who, after graduating from Columbia University, worked for the publisher Charles Scribner's and Sons while writing

poetry. Her volumes of poetry include *Field of Honor* (1933), *This, My Letter* (1939), *The Delicate Balance* (1951), *The Stone and the Shell* (1959), and *A Footing on the Earth: New and Selected Poems* (1966). Of special importance is her *Story Hour* (1963), a volume that includes numerous poems based on classical **Grimm** fairy tales, as indicated by titles such as "Rapunzel" and "The Goosegirl." However, some of Hay's titles are mere allusions to the traditional fairy tales, as in "One of the Seven Has Something To Say" ("**Snow White**"); or they don't reveal their fairy-tale backgrounds at all, as in the case of "Juvenile Court" ("**Hansel and Gretel**") and "Interview" ("**Cinderella**"). Most of Hay's short poems reinterpret the Grimm tales by concentrating on individual **motif**s and relating them to concerns of modern society, including criminality, misogyny, **gender**, and **feminism**. The results are poetic **anti-fairy tale**s that lack the positive and hopeful endings of their prose originals. And yet, these critical approaches to the Grimm tales call the source texts to mind, thereby indicating how a better world might look after all.

Further Readings: Beaumont, Jeanne Marie, and Claudia Carlson, eds. *The Poets' Grimm: 20th Century Poems from Grimm Fairy Tales*. Ashland, OR: Story Line Press, 2003; Mieder, Wolfgang, ed. *Disenchantments: An Anthology of Modern Fairy Tale Poetry*. Hanover, NH: University Press of New England, 1985.

Wolfgang Mieder

Helakisa, Kaarina (1946–1998)

In the 1960s, Kaarina Helakisa brought an inventive and original voice to Finnish **children's literature** and the fairy-tale genre. Her stories are often fairy tales with connections to contemporary society. Helakisa published her debut book *Kaarina Helakisan satukirja* (*Kaarina Helakisa's Fairy-Tale Book*, 1964) at the age of eighteen. She illustrated this collection of fairy tales herself and based parts of it on William **Shakespeare**'s play *The Tempest*. Depictions of **women** of different ages as well as feminist themes become prominent especially in her production during the 1980s.

In *Kuninkaantyttären siivet* (*The Wings of the King's Daughter*, 1982), she uses fairy-tale themes to contemplate feminist topics. *Annan seitsämän elämää: Kertomuksia* (*Anna's Seven Lives: Stories*, 1987) also reflects the life and roles of present-day women. Here, Helakisa uses references to **folktale**s from the *Arabian Nights* to the Brothers **Grimm**. Her modern fairy tales are characterized by nonsense humor and innovative language, and she is considered as part of the modernization of the nursery-rhyme tradition in Finland. One of her later books is the humorous and colorful picturebook *Into, parrakas vauva* (*Into, the Bearded Baby,* 1985), illustrated by Pekka Vuori, in which a baby with a beard examines the wonders of the world during an adventurous journey. Helakisa also translated children's literature and wrote **television** plays and radio dramas, several of them **adaptation**s from her own stories and fairy tales. *See also* Feminism; Feminist Tales.

Further Readings: Loivamaa, Ismo, ed. *Kotimaisia lasten- ja nuortenkirjailijoita*. 2nd edition. Helsinki: BTJ Kirjastopalvelu, 1996; Nevala, Maria-Liisa, ed. *"Sain roolin johon en mahdu": Suomalaisen naiskirjallisuuden linjoja*. Helsinki: Otava, 1989.

Elina Druker

Helvig, Amalie von (1776–1831)

A writer and collector of **legend**s, **saga**s, and **literary fairy tale**s, Amalie von Helvig portrayed strong mythical and historical **women** in her works and created a kind of feminist

utopia in them. She enjoyed the patronage of Johann Wolfgang von **Goethe** and Friedrich Schiller and was a frequent contributor to numerous illustrious journals and almanacs.

Her writings fall into two periods: classical and Germanic/Romantic. Her greatest literary success was her debut, an **epic** poem in hexameter, "Die Schwestern von Lesbos" ("The Sisters of Lesbos"), published in 1800 in Schiller's *Musenalmanach* (*The Muses' Almanac*). In her second literary phase, she published *Taschenbuch der Sagen und Legenden* (*Pocket Book of Sagas and Legends*, 1812) in collaboration with Friedrich de la Motte **Fouqué** and with illustrations by Peter Cornelius. This was followed in 1817 by another *Pocket Book* with Nordic themes. Her 1814 *Sage von Wolfsbrunnen: Ein Märchen* (*The Saga of the Wolf's Well: A Fairy Tale*) is an interesting composite of both literary phases: it reflects the Romantic writers' interest in classical mythology and their fascination with the nature of the elements, while telling the tale of the soothsayer and arbitrator Velleda, a Germanic historical figure mentioned in Tacitus.

Von Helvig was an important liaison for introducing the Swedish Romantics' works in Germany. Her 1826 translation of Esaias Tegnér's *Frithiofs Saga* is still considered definitive. *See Also* Feminism; Feminist Tales; German Tales.

Further Reading: Helwig, Amalie von. "The Symbols." *The Queen's Mirror: Fairy Tales by German Women 1780–1900*. Edited and translated Shawn C. Jarvis and Jeannine Blackwell. Lincoln: University of Nebraska Press, 2001. 117–25.

Shawn C. Jarvis

Henson, Jim (1936–1990)

Jim Henson, an American puppeteer, writer, producer, and director of children's **television** and **film**, produced several works that drew extensively on fairy-tale and folktale sources. Born in Greenville, Mississippi, Jim Henson is best known for his creations the Muppets, a combination of puppets and marionettes that have appeared in three different television shows, *Sesame Street* (1968–), *The Muppet Show* (1976–81), and *Muppets Tonight* (1996–98), as well as in a number of feature films. Henson's puppet creations have varied in size from small hand puppets to large creatures operated by multiple people, and they have been frequently used alongside human actors. Before his death by pneumonia in 1990, Henson created several works with folktale sources.

In 1969, Henson directed *Hey, Cinderella!*—an **adaptation** of ATU 510A, Cinderella. Henson's version focuses the story on the fairy godmother character and the help she receives from a number of different sources, including Muppet characters such as Kermit the Frog. *Hey, Cinderella!* outlined the pattern that would recur in all of his Muppet folktale adaptations, with reflexive humor and original musical numbers, and Muppets playing characters alongside human actors.

The Muppet Musicians of Bremen (1972), a Muppet version of ATU 130, The Animals in Night Quarters, was Henson's second foray into folktales. Similar to *Hey, Cinderella!*, this adaptation featured music and humor and incorporated a frame narration by Kermit the Frog.

Henson's next fairy-tale project was *Tales from Muppetland: The Frog Prince* (1972), a version of ATU 440, The **Frog King** or Iron Henry. In this production, various roles were filled by Muppets, most evidently the title role, which was played by a new Muppet named Robin, who was said to be Kermit the Frog's nephew. Similar in form to his other Muppet productions, *Tales from Muppetland: The Frog Prince* was aired regularly on public television through the 1970s and 1980s.

During this period, Henson produced a recurring sketch called "Sesame Street News Flash" for his regular children's show on the Public Broadcasting Service's *Sesame Street*. In these sketches, Kermit the Frog, a Muppet portrayed by Henson himself, conducted a series of humorous interviews with Muppet versions of characters in **fable**s, nursery rhymes, and fairy tales. These sketches have continued to be a regular feature of *Sesame Street*, although no new ones have been produced since Henson's death.

In 1986, Henson coproduced the film *Labyrinth* with George Lucas, creating puppets based on the conceptual art of Brian **Froud**. This film drew on fairy beliefs about the abduction of small children and featured puppet versions of goblins and other fairy creatures. While not based on a traditional **tale type**, *Labyrinth* draws on fairy tales for its plot structure, beginning with absent parents, progressing through interdiction, lack, and helper-figure sequences.

Henson's most faithful work in folktales and fairy tales was produced in 1988 in the series called *The Storyteller*. In this series, Henson, using live actors and puppets, produced versions of European folktales that had been scripted by Anthony Minghella. Each episode was set in a **frame narrative** with actor John Hurt telling a story to both the audience and a talking puppet dog, which was voiced by Henson's son Brian. Minghella's retellings draw primarily, but not exclusively, on the **Grimm** brothers' *Kinder- und Hausmärchen* (*Children's and Household Tales*, 1812–15), although the exact sources are never clearly indicated. Drawing on the Grimms' stories and related tale types, Henson and Minghella's versions treat serious themes (for example, incest and power) and include no musical numbers. Moreover, the characters are not adapted to fit Henson's Muppets, despite the fact that the technique of combining live actors with puppetry continues. Henson retains the reflexive humor, however, with one of Sapsorrow's evil **sisters** in episode seven introducing herself as "Badsister."

The first episode in *The Storyteller*, "The Soldier and Death," is a version of ATU 330, The Smith and the Devil, set in Russia and featuring a magical sack. The second episode, "Fearnot," is an adaptation of ATU 326, The Youth Who Wanted to Learn What Fear Is. The third episode, "The Luck Child," is a version of ATU 930, The Prophecy, which uses the folk belief of the seventh son of a seventh son being lucky to justify the fortunes of the young hero. The fourth episode, "A Story Short," adapts ATU 1548, The Soup Stone, and features the storyteller character from the narrative frame of the series as the main character. Episode five, "Hans My Hedgehog," is an adaptation of the Grimm tale of the same name (ATU 441, Hans My Hedgehog). The sixth episode of the series, "The Three Ravens," is a version of ATU 451, The Maiden Who Seeks Her Brothers, with an interdiction of silence placed on the **princess** character. For a more comfortable fit with a television program's time constraints, the adaptation involves three **brothers** rather than twelve or seven. Episode seven, a version of ATU 510B, Peau d'Asne, is entitled "Sapsorrow" and features the dresses of gold, silver, and stars that are often associated with this tale. The eighth episode, "The Heartless Giant," is a **variant** of ATU 302, The Ogre's (Devil's) Heart in the Egg. The final episode of the series is entitled "The True Bride." An adaptation of ATU 425A, The Animal as Bridegroom, Henson's version features a lion as the **animal groom**.

The Storyteller is interesting as a series of folktale adaptations especially because of Henson's use of techniques of oral **storytelling** in the series. For instance, in "A Story Short," the storyteller character from the series framework serves as the main character, a technique common in oral **performance** but rare in theatrical adaptation. Another example comes from "The Heartless Giant." In this tale, the location of the heart of the giant, an egg, in a duck, in a well, in a church, on an island, in a lake, and on a mountain, is repeated as a formula by the narrator, as in oral variants of the tale.

Henson's association with folktales extended beyond his death, as illustrated in *Muppet Classic Theater*, which was released in 1994. Continuing the tradition of Muppet adaptations of folktale material, the project includes versions of "Three Little Pigs" (ATU 124, Blowing the House In) and "Rumpelstiltskin" (ATU 500, The Name of the Supernatural Helper). While these include the humor and musical numbers that are typical of Henson's earlier folktale adaptations, they differ by using casts consisting exclusively of Muppets. *See also* Jones, Terry; Puppet Theater.

Further Readings: Minghella, Anthony. *Jim Henson's "The Storyteller."* New York: Knopf, 1991; Zipes, Jack. "Once upon a Time beyond Disney: Contemporary Fairy-Tale Films for Children." *Happily Ever After: Fairy Tales Children, and the Culture Industry.* New York: Routledge, 1997. 89–110.

B. Grantham Aldred

Hesse, Hermann (1877–1962)

German poet and novelist Hermann Hesse was awarded the Nobel Prize for Literature in 1946. Hesse is known for his portrayal of the duality between spirit and nature, body, and mind, and the inner truths and external realities of the individual. His two novels *Siddhartha* (1922) and *Steppenwolf* (1927) reflect the integration of the semiotics of folktale and fairy tale into literary writing. However, the short works considered to be **märchen** reflect the induction of Hesse's philosophical beliefs into the genre of the fairy tale.

The story of *Siddhartha* is set on the Indian subcontinent in the time of Buddha. The fairy-tale nature of the **novel** draws mainly from the portrayal of a "spiritual India" and the search for happiness. It also reflects the status of India itself as it was considered a "fairy tale" in the European imagination. A cult book of the hippie generation, *Siddharta* was made into a film by Conrad Rooks in 1972 with Indian actors and shot entirely in northern India. The novel's continued international success can best be gauged from its publication in Nepali translation in Nepal in 2004.

Steppenwolf deals with the human and animal nature of the individual and portrays the artist and intellectual as an outcast. Hesse's literary technique and Romantic anticapitalist philosophy creates a fairy-tale atmosphere in which the boundaries between reality and **fantasy** are fluid. The novel does not have speaking animals as is common in the folktale, but they "speak" from the human body itself.

Hesse's "märchen," or "fairy tales," would not be described as such by everyone and are not written in the vein of the classical fairy-tale genre. Composed at different points of time, these stories reflect Hesse's ideas about art, artists, and society. Their philosophical bent remains similar to his novels, and the theme of the artist and his loneliness in society recurs. What remains of the fairy-tale genre in his writing is the aura of mystery embedded in the narratives. Characters seem to be disconnected from **time and place**, although they are symbolic of contemporary realities and Hesse's own distanced view of it. Influenced by the psychoanalytic theories of Carl Gustav **Jung**, Hesse's literary style can also be seen as a high point in the German tradition of the **literary fairy tale** since the time of E. T. A. **Hoffmann**.

Hesse's novels are recognized for their beautiful writing and the thoughts they contain. They are lyrical in nature and philosophically oriented in their content. The characters respond to social restrictions by the discovery and expression of the inner self. Their search for happiness is mystical and takes place between the poles of conflicting notions. Hesse's writings reveal influence of Friedrich Nietzsche and Buddhist mysticism. Western civilization seems doomed in Hesse's novels, so the search for higher truths leads to Eastern philosophy.

Hesse's relationship with India and Buddhism has its roots in his biography. His grandparents and parents had been missionaries in India, and he had heard of the land since his childhood. His later fascination with Buddhism expressed itself in writing, but his journey to India in 1911 ended in Sri Lanka, and he was quite disappointed by what he saw of colonial India. He regained his fascination intellectually, and it found expression in *Siddhartha*, where the image of India appears to be rooted in Buddhist folklore. Hesse defies ideological categorization, although his novels are often seen as a critique of bourgeois social behavior. His writings reflect much of his own personality and life. His style of writing presents social critique in a mystical and fairy-tale manner. *See also* Magical Realism.

Further Readings: Ashliman, D. L. "Hermann Hesse's Fairy Tales and Their Analogs in Folklore." *Wegbereiter der Moderne*. Edited by Helmut Koopmann and Clark Muenzer. Tübingen: Niemeyer, 1990. 88–113; The Hesse Society—Nepal. http://www.geocities.com/hesse_nepal; Hermann Hesse Portal. http://www.hermann-hesse.de/eng/; Zipes, Jack, trans. *The Fairy Tales of Hermann Hesse*. New York: Bantam, 1995.

Sadhana Naithani

Historic-Geographic Method

The historic-geographic method—also called "the Finnish method"—was the first scientifically ambitious method of **folktale** research. By comparative textual analysis, researchers sought to establish the geographic distribution, variation, history, place of origin, and original form of a single folktale or group of folktales.

Julius Krohn, a scholar of Finnish language and literature, laid down the foundations for the historic-geographic method in his studies of **epic** folk poems in the 1870s and 1880s. His son Kaarle Krohn expanded the method and applied it to the study of **animal tale**s in his work "Bär (Wolf) und Fuchs: Eine nordische Tiermärchenkette" ("The Bear [Wolf] and the Fox: A Nordic Animal-Tale Cycle," 1889). In 1913, Krohn's disciple Antti **Aarne** published *Leitfaden der vergleichenden Märchenforschung* (*Guide for the Comparative Investigation of Folktales*), a handbook written especially for folktale scholars. Krohn's own outline of the method, *Die folkloristiche Arbeitsmethode*, appeared in 1926 (and was published in English as *Folklore Methodology* in 1971).

Rooted in positivism, the systematic analysis of texts offered by the method usurped earlier speculations about the origins and dissemination of folktales. Scholars no longer considered folktales to be the receptacles of fragments of **myth** or products of primitive thinking. The notion that the genre had originated during a certain historical era or only in a certain region, such as India, was also discarded. Thus each narrative came to be viewed as having its own history. Over the centuries an individual folktale wandered from nation to nation assuming varying forms along the way. Only after having investigated the histories of many folktales could scholars begin to present plausible hypotheses about the whole genre's history in Europe.

The historic-geographic method required data gathered from a range of countries and language areas. The records considered most valuable were those acquired from oral narration. The idea of the antiquity of all **folklore** was a legacy of the Romantic era. The texts were then grouped geographically, and their variation was described meticulously by comparison. The aim of this was to determine the earlier and later forms of each trait. The criteria for establishing the precedence of a given form, however, were open to interpretation. Text **variant**s closely resembling each other could then be grouped together. A cluster of variants was referred to as a "redaction." In the best of cases, the researcher was able to construct a family tree depicting the folktale's temporal layers and regional **diffusion**. Thus he finally was able to present some suppositions about a folktale's origins: the time and place, as well as the **urform** (basic or original form).

The basis of the method could be found in nineteenth-century linguistics and philological text criticism. By systematic comparison, linguists had discovered the familial relations among different languages and how they had developed over time. In addition to this, Charles Darwin's theory of the laws of evolution was eagerly applied to cultural phenomena in the latter half of the nineteenth century. The transformations of folk poems and tales were assumed to obey psychological laws that influenced their singers and narrators—regardless of their own will or consciousness. These semimechanical "laws of thought" were, among others, forgetfulness, expansion, and the incorporation of elements from other narratives or poems.

The historic-geographic method and its modifications were most widely used in Nordic and Estonian folklore research. The best-known studies are Walter **Anderson**'s *Kaiser und Abt* (*The Emperor and the Abbot*, 1923), a study of ATU 922; Anna-Birgitta Rooth's *The Cinderella Cycle* (1951), a study of ATU 510; and Jan Öjvind Swahn's *The Tale of Cupid and Psyche* (1955), a study of ATU 425.

The 1930s saw the beginning of the end for the heyday of the Finnish method. Detractors (for example, Albert Wesselski) had found that the method failed to provide any certainty about a folktale's earliest stages of development. Although researchers were able to locate literary folktales accurately in history, they found it difficult to date items from **oral tradition** with any degree of certainty. In this way, the folktale's urform and place of origin could be only hypothetical, however rigorous the textual analysis. Moreover, there were not enough texts of a given folktale available from all of the areas where they had appeared, particularly outside of Europe. The paradigm's decline was hastened above all by the perception that the basic questions underlying the method were out of date. As scholarly interest in the historical development of a folktale waned, researchers began to turn their attention to how folktales were used by their narrators and narrative communities. Moreover, the old historicism bore little fruit for researchers whose analytical foci were the structures and meanings of folktales. In the 1960s and 1970s, research on the techniques of oral **performance** called into question the possibility of ever reconstructing an ancient urform from items recorded in the nineteenth and twentieth centuries.

Yet the historic-geographic method cannot be so easily be dismissed. Thanks to this method, folklorists working with vast quantities of texts have been able to describe more precisely the geographic distribution and variation of oral traditions. The most enduring achievements have been the method's by-products—the extensive narrative indices. The fourth edition of Aarne's index of **tale type**s was recently published by Hans-Jörg Uther (*The Types of International Folktales: A Classification and Bibliography*, 2004). In the years 1932 to 1936, Stith **Thompson** published an index of the constituents—that is, the motifs—of popular narrative (*Motif-Index of Folk-Literature*). The expanded edition appeared in 1955–1958. In addition to these international books of reference, hundreds of regional indices of numerous folklore genres have been compiled. **See also** Linguistic Approaches.

Further Readings: Goldberg, Christine. *The Tale of the Three Oranges.* Helsinki: Academia Scientiarum Fennica, 1997; Jason, Heda. *Motif, Type and Genre: A Manual for Compilation of Indices and a Bibliography of Indices and Indexing.* Helsinki: Academia Scientiarum Fennica, 2000; Krohn, Kaarle. *Folklore Methodology.* Translated by Roger L. Welsch. Austin: University of Texas Press, 1971; Röhrich, Lutz. "Geographisch-historische Methode." *Enzyklopädie des Märchens.* Edited by Kurt Ranke et al. Volume 5. Berlin: Walter de Gruyter, 1987. 1011–30.

Satu Apo

Hoban, Russell (1925–)

Russell Hoban is the author of many adult **novel**s such as the acclaimed *Riddley Walker* (1980), *Turtle Diary* (1975), *Pilgerman* (1983), and *The Medusa Frequency* (1987), as well as more than fifty books for children, including the enduringly popular Frances series (1960–70), *The Mouse and His Child* (1967), *La Corona and the Tin Frog* (1979), the Captain Najork (1974–75) books, and the young adult novel *The Trokeville Way* (1996). Hoban is a strikingly original writer whose innovations in language, genre, and theme have defied classification while garnering a diverse audience. Despite the immense variety and scope of Hoban's work (which extends from the engagingly warm and furry animals in many of his picture books to the grim, postapocalyptic landscape of *Riddley Walker*), the Hoban canon is unified by his concern with the interior lives of characters within the larger external world. Hoban's professed interest in classical mythology as a means of grounding and shaping the darker forces of society, culture, and technology is evident in many of his books, which often feature questing characters participating in their own modern (and postmodern) **myth**s. In his books for children, Hoban draws upon other classical literary forms such as **folktale**, **fairy tale,** and **fable** while consistently limning their boundaries with a subversive humor and deeply philosophical themes.

Hoban's first full-length novel, *The Mouse and His Child,* ostensibly for children, is a sophisticated, extended fable about a father and son pair of wind-up mice whose journey from a London toy shop through the brutal yet empowering outside world leads them on a quest to become "self-winding." While the circular shape of the quest, which begins and ends in a dollhouse, the cast of villains and helpers along the way, and even the "message" of the novel recall traditional elements of the fairy-tale journey from home and back, as well as the **Aesop**ian animal fable, the novel's emphasis on technology (the "animals" are wind-up toys), its starkly realistic and nuanced depiction of society (focused by the brutally commercial Manny Rat), and the complexity of its "**moral**" continually work to subvert the novel's use of such traditions.

Similarly, another much gentler animal fable, Hoban's *The Sea Thing Child,* written in 1972 as a chapter book and reissued as a picture book in 2000, engages its readers in a meditation on being and becoming that departs dramatically from the simplicity of traditional fables. This melancholy tale emphasizes the interiority of its individual characters rather than their relationships. While the sea-thing child finds a companion in the fiddler crab, each pursues a solitary struggle between fear and the desire for fulfillment. The story's ambiguous ending suggests that at least one of them is still struggling.

Hoban's interest in limning the boundaries between literary forms as well as between **fantasy** and reality is often postmodern in execution. In the surreal fairy tale *La Corona and the Tin Frog*, a tin frog falls in love with the picture of a beautiful "princess" on the inside of a cigar box and must jump into her picture to enter her world. The ending, in which the characters conspire to jump out of the story itself, evidences also its author's sly commentary on the equally fragile boundaries between literary text and the reader. *See also* Children's Literature; Postmodernism.

Further Reading: Allison, Alida, ed. *Russell Hoban/Forty Years: Essays on His Writings for Children.* New York: Garland, 2000.

Barbara Tannert-Smith

Hoffmann, E. T. A. (1776–1822)

Ernst Theodor Wilhelm Hoffmann, who took the middle name Amadeus in honor of the great composer, was a seminal figure of the late Romantic period in Germany. While Hoffmann is perhaps best known for his story *Nußknacker und Mausekönig* (*The Nutcracker and the Mouse King*, 1816), which served as the basis for Pyotr Il'ich **Tchaikovsky**'s celebrated ballet *The Nutcracker* (1892), his contributions to the genre of German *Schauerliteratur* (gothic literature) and the *Kunstmärchen* (**literary fairy tale**) made an indelible mark on the literary history of nineteenth-century Europe and continue to influence writers and thinkers today.

Hoffmann was born in Königsberg in East Prussia and practiced a wide variety of trades before settling into a relatively successful writing career, which ultimately spanned only thirteen years before the author died prematurely of a paralytic illness. Upon the completion of his law degree, Hoffmann began a seemingly promising career as a civil servant by serving in a variety of judiciary positions. This professional path was cut short, however, after he created unflattering caricatures of important figures in Posen, where he was employed as an assessor. As a result of this indiscretion, Hoffmann was transferred to Poland in 1804 and appointed a legal councilor in Warsaw. In 1805, he made his first public appearance as a conductor in Warsaw, where a number of his musical compositions were performed. By 1808, Hoffmann wished to devote himself entirely to a career in music and happily took the position of music director at the Bamberg Theater, which was unfortunately only short-lived. However, soon after his arrival in Bamberg, he published his first tale, "Ritter Gluck" ("Chevalier Gluck," 1809), and met the wine merchant, F. C. Kunz, who would later publish a number of his works.

While Hoffmann enjoyed some success with his stories, he was unable to sustain a comfortable lifestyle from his writing alone and therefore relied on teaching private music lessons as his means for earning a living. In 1808, he began giving voice lessons to Julia Marc, a girl of twelve, with whom he later fell in love. When "Julchen" left Bamberg at the age of sixteen to marry a banker from Hamburg, Hoffmann channeled his unrequited feelings of love into the feverish creation of a number of works over a span of few years. His satirical and fanciful work "Neueste Schicksale des Hundes Berganza" ("The Latest from the Life of the Dog Berganza," 1813) deals directly with his feelings of rejection, and the topic arises again, though more subtly, in his four-volume, self-ironic *Fantasiestücke in Callots Manier* (*Fantasy Pieces in the Manner of Jacques Callot*, 1814–15), which feature a number of Hoffmann's greatest fantastic works, including "Die Abenteur der Silvester-Nacht" ("Adventures of a New Year's Eve," 1814) and his renowned literary fairy tale *Der goldne Topf* (*The Golden Pot*, 1814).

The *Fantasy Pieces* are prime examples of Hoffmann's fantastic tales, in which supernatural beings appear alongside figures in the real world and often go unnoticed or are regarded with mere curiosity by members of the middle class. By contrast, these fantastic figures inspire fear in the artistic protagonist because he understands their import as the embodiment of the irrational aesthetic realm. As a result, the protagonist feels torn between the feverish intoxication of art and the mundane existence of the bourgeoisie, as in the case of Erasmus Spikher in "Die Geschichte vom verlorenen Spiegelbild" ("The Story of the Lost Reflection," 1815), who surrenders his **mirror** reflection to the **devil** in exchange for a life of artistic passion. Ultimately, Spikher's connection to the everyday world saves him from the enticements of the fantastic realm; he avoids a final pact with the devil and instead lives between the realms of art and the everyday.

In the case of the literary fairy tale *The Golden Pot*, the entire story takes place within the realm of the fantastic. This tale, which was greatly influenced by Friedrich de la Motte **Fouqué**'s "**Undine**" (1811), also served as the basis for an **opera** that he and Hoffmann created together. The fantastic world of elements and spirits serves as the backdrop for the adventures of the university student Anselmus. The young protagonist meets and falls in love with Serpentina, the daughter of a salamander, when she appears to him in the form of a snake. Based on his fear of the irrational elemental powers that Serpentina represents, however, Anselmus begins to doubt his beloved. He is consequently punished by Serpentina's **father**, who must live in Dresden as the archivist Lindhorst until all of his daughters have married, by being placed in a glass bottle on a shelf in the archivist's library. After Anselmus reiterates his feelings of love for Serpentina, he is released from the bottle and transported to her homeland of Atlantis, where the story ends in a happy union.

By contrast, the story "Das Fräulein von Scuderi" ("Mademoiselle de Scudèry," 1819) presents a more dismal fate when the artist protagonist succumbs to the draw of the irrational realm. In this gothic tale, the protagonist, Cardillac, is a jewelry maker who murders his customers to repossesses the precious works of art he has sold to them. Here the allure of art overcomes the protagonist and leads him to transgress against the ethical codes of the society in which he lives for the sake of art, a decision that ultimately results in his own **death**. Aspects of the uncanny also figure prominently in Hoffmann's best-known **novella**, "Der Sandmann" ("The Sandman," 1816), which Sigmund **Freud** later used to illustrate his theory of the uncanny. The story revolves around the young protagonist, Nathanael, who encounters an evil alchemist, Coppelius, as a child and is visited by him again as an adult in the figure of Coppola. Having just become engaged to Clara, who is the symbol of enlightened thought, Nathanael finds himself faltering between the **fantasy** world that Coppola represents and the rational thought that Clara embodies. When Coppola creates an automaton, Olimpia, to mesmerize Nathanael, he slowly loses all connections with the rational world and descends into a state of paranoia and fear. Ultimately, Nathanael rejects Clara's rationalism and instead succumbs to the overzealous artistic imagination that destroys him in the end. On top of a tower, Nathanael mistakes Clara for an automaton and attempts to throw her over the edge; he is stopped by her brother Lothar and springs to his own death instead, thus illustrating the danger of the fantastic realm of art.

While Hoffmann is often depicted as the tortured artist, many of his works focus on the necessary balance between artistic drive and the everyday as a prerequisite for artistic production. The search for this aesthetic balance, also known as his *Serapiontisches Prinzip* (the Serapiontic Principle), is the premise for Hoffmann's collection of tales *Die Serapions-Brüder* (*The Serapion Brethren*, 1819–21), in which he highlights the distinction between and integration of the artistic and bourgeois spheres in artistic production. For Hoffmann, typical bourgeois life, not to be mistaken with philistinism, tempers artistic fervor that verges on sentimentalism. Everyday bourgeois life provides important aesthetic material around which Hoffmann weaves elements of wonder that reach into the realm of the fantastic, enabling both spheres to exist simultaneously. This interplay between worlds serves as a common theme throughout Hoffmann's nearly four dozen stories, seven fairy tales, two novels, and numerous musical compositions. *See also* German Tales.

Further Readings: Brown, Hilda Meldrum. *E. T. A. Hoffmann and the Serapiontic Principle.* Rochester, NY: Camden House, 2006; Freud, Sigmund. "The Uncanny." *The Standard Edition of the Complete Psychological Works of Sigmund Freud.* Edited and translated by James Strachey. Volume 17. London: Hogarth, 1953. 219–52; McGlathery, James M. *E. T. A. Hoffmann.* New York: Twayne, 1997; Röder, Birgit. *A Study of the Major Novellas of E. T. A. Hoffmann.* Rochester, NY: Camden House, 2003.

Cynthia Chalupa

Hofmannsthal, Hugo von (1874–1929)

Austrian writer Hugo von Hofmannsthal wrote primarily poetry early in his career (under the pen name "Loris"), and later plays and libretti, but utilized prose narrative, particularly the fairy tale, throughout his life. His first published tale, "Das Märchen der 672. Nacht" ("The Fairy Tale of the 672nd Night," 1895), influenced by the **Arabian Nights**, follows the downward spiral of a wealthy merchant's son, who finally meets his death in a menacing corner of a mysterious town.

From about 1912 to 1919, Hofmannsthal worked on two versions of the same tale, *Die Frau ohne Schatten* (*The Woman without a Shadow*), one the libretto for an **opera** with Richard Strauss, the other a prose **novella**. Both are symbolic renderings of the interactions of two couples: a mortal emperor and his immortal wife, who casts no shadow, and the lower-class dyer Barak and his wife. The search for a shadow becomes a search for children and for true humanity.

Several fragmentary tales—among them "Der Goldene Apfel" ("The Golden Apple") and "Das Märchen der verschleierten Frau" ("The Tale of the Veiled Woman")—were published posthumously. Like his other tales, they are, in Hermann Broch's words, "Letztformen einer Spätform" ("last examples of a late genre"), influenced by the **literary fairy tale**s of German Romantics such as Johann Wolfgang von **Goethe**, **Novalis**, and Ludwig **Tieck**.

Further Readings: Broch, Hermann. "Die Prosaschriften." 1951. *Hugo von Hofmannsthal.* Edited by Sibylle Bauer. Darmstadt: Wissenschaftliche Buchgesellschaft, 1968. 87–120; Ritter, Ellen. "Hofmannsthal's Narrative Prose: The Problem of Individuation." *A Companion to the Works of Hofmannsthal.* Edited by Thomas A. Kovach. Rochester, NY: Camden House, 2002. 65–84.

Elizabeth Wanning Harries

Holbek, Bengt (1933–1992)

Bengt Holbek was a Danish folklorist whose interest in analyzing fairy tales informed his monumental dissertation at the University of Copenhagen. This was published as

Interpretation of Fairy Tales: Danish Folklore in a European Perspective (1987). Exceeding 600 pages, the book summarizes practically all prior fairy-tale scholarship and synthesizes previous theoretical contributions with the goal of articulating what fairy tales mean in specific social contexts.

One of Holbek's main goals was to understand the fantastic elements in fairy tales. He relied on **psychological approaches** to decode the marvelous as symbolic elements expressing human experiences. Holbek also synthesized structuralist scholarship (see **Structuralism**), creating multiple frames through which to view the actions in fairy tales. For instance, he condensed Vladimir **Propp**'s thirty-one functions into five moves, each consisting of closely related actions and each negotiating one of three oppositions: male/female, young/mature, and low/high status.

Holbek analyzed **Scandinavian tales**, particularly those collected in Jutland by Evald **Tang Kristensen** in the nineteenth century. "King Wivern," an **animal groom** tale, formed the centerpiece of Holbek's interpretation. Utilizing Alan **Dundes**'s motifemic analysis, Holbek demonstrated how equivalent symbols reveal ordinary people's concerns about family life and social hierarchies (see **Motifeme**). Holbek also utilized projection in a double sense: fairy tales projected as collective daydreaming and fairy-tale characters projecting as independent entities. Holbek's stimulating readings have provoked much thought and debate; the discussion among Francisco Vaz da Silva, Galit Hasan-Rokem, and John Lindow in the online journal *Cultural Analysis* in 2000 is but one conversation regarding Holbek's important contributions to fairy tales.

Further Readings: Hasan-Rokem, Galit. "Reflections on da Silva's Study of Holbek's Interpretation of Fairy-Tales." *Cultural Analysis* 1 (2000): 13–14. http://ist-socrates.berkeley.edu/~caforum/volume1/vol1_article1.html#response2; Lindow, John. "Response to Francisco Vaz da Silva, 'Bengt Holbek and the Study of Meanings in Fairy Tales.' "*Cultural Analysis* 1 (2000): 11–12. http://ist-socrates.berkeley.edu/~caforum/volume1/vol1_article1.html#response1; Vaz da Silva, Francisco. "Bengt Holbek and the Study of Meanings in Fairy Tales." *Cultural Analysis* 1 (2000): 3–14. http://ist-socrates.berkeley.edu/~caforum/volume1/pdf/silva.pdf.

Jeana Jorgensen

Honko, Lauri (1932–2002)

Lauri Honko was a prominent scholar of international repute in the field of oral narrative studies. In addition to folkloristics, the main interests of this interdisciplinary scholar included comparative religion, folk medicine, and cultural anthropology.

Lauri Honko was appointed professor of folkloristics and comparative religion at the University of Turku, Finland, in 1963. His famous monograph entitled *Geisterglaube in Ingermanland* (*Belief in the Supernatural in Ingria*) appeared in 1962. This was a methodologically ambitious study of the folk-belief traditions of the Finnish groups of Ingria, an area along the southern and eastern shores of the Gulf of Finland near St. Petersburg. The high quality of this research ensured the young scholar a firm position in the field of folk-narrative studies and comparative religion.

During his academic career, Honko worked as the director of the Nordic Institute of Folklore (1972–90), and he was nominated twice as the academy professor at the Academy of Finland (1975–78 and 1991–96). He also served as the chief editor of the Folklore Fellows' Communications and Folklore Fellows' Network. Honko was the president of the International Society for Folk Narrative Research for sixteen years between 1974 and 1989.

In the field of folk-narrative research, Honko elaborated methods of the tradition-ecological perspective, created an application of sociological role theory in the study of folklore, guided the debate on folkloristic theories of genre, fostered research on cultural identity, and developed the methods of folkloristic **fieldwork**. Honko focused on such traditional genres as belief **legend**s and **memorate**s, laments, and, toward the end of his life, **epic**s. He made long expeditions to the Saami people of northern Finland and to Russian Karelia, as well as to Tanzania, China, and India.

Honko devoted the last fifteen years of his life to researching epics, concentrating mainly on the Siri epic of the Tulu people of southern Karnataka, India. In December 1990, he and his Finnish-Indian team recorded on video and audiotape 15,683 lines of an epic performed by the singer and possession priest Gopala Naika. In 1998, this epic was published in Tulu and English in *The Siri Epic as Performed by Gopala Naika*. A third volume entitled *Textualizing the Siri Epic* (1998) is a comprehensive handbook on the methodology of the textualization process of oral epics.

Further Readings: Honko, Lauri, ed. *The Kalevala and the World's Traditional Epics*. Helsinki: Finnish Literature Society, 2002; ———, ed. *Religion, Myth, and Folklore in the World's Epics: The Kalevala and Its Predecessors*. Berlin: Mouton de Gruyter, 1990; ———, ed. *Textualization of Oral Epics*. Berlin: Mouton de Gruyter, 2000; ———, ed. *Thick Corpus, Organic Variation and Textuality in Oral Tradition*. Helsinki: Finnish Literature Society, 2000.

Lauri Harvilahti

Hopkinson, Nalo (1961–)

Caribbean-Canadian author Nalo Hopkinson draws imaginatively on **folklore** to explore and transform contemporary belief systems. In essays and interviews, Hopkinson describes her writing as blurring the boundaries of **fantasy**, science fiction, **magical realism**, and horror. For her, in the twentieth and twenty-first centuries, such speculative fiction seeks, as tales of magic did in the past, to shake things as they are. Like tales of magic, speculative fiction refuses straightforward mimesis and frees the imagination to work differently: as readers or listeners suspend disbelief, the supernatural crosses into the everyday and is accepted within it, loosening the hold of the prescribed and potentially admitting new possibilities. At the same time, like folktales and fairy tales, speculative fiction has culturally specific roots. Caribbean religious practices, children's games as well as folkloric characters, rituals, and plots function in Hopkinson's work as the otherworldly elements that disrupt norms and alert characters and readers to forgotten histories, social violence, and hope for **transformation**. While science fiction and fantasy are still predominantly Euro-American in their orientation, Hopkinson writes in "dark ink" and from a diasporic and intercultural framework.

Born in Jamaica, Nalo Hopkinson lived in Guyana, Jamaica, and Trinidad until the age of sixteen, when she moved to Connecticut and then to Toronto, where she still lives. She has published three **novel**s: *Brown Girl in the Ring* (1998), *Midnight Robber* (2000), and *The Salt Roads* (2003); one short-story collection, *Skin Folk* (2001); and several anthologies, *Whispers from the Cotton Tree Root: Caribbean Fabulist Fiction* (2000), *Mojo: Conjure Stories* (2003), and *So Long Been Dreaming: Postcolonial Science Fiction & Fantasy*, coedited with Uppinder Mehan (2004). As of 2006, she had completed another novel, *The Old Moon's Arms*, and was working with photographer David Findlay on a **graphic novel**, *Mr. Fox*.

The most visible connections between folktales and Hopkinson's fiction are in *Skin Folk*, the 2001 winner of the World Fantasy Convention's World Fantasy Award for Best Collection. In 2006, *Skin Folk* became available as an audio book, one of the first featuring a Caribbean-Canadian author. Informed by a poetics of transformation that works against prejudice and embraces eroticism, this volume offers revisions of specific tale types—**Little Red Riding Hood** (ATU 333) in "Riding the Red," **The Kind and the Unkind Girls** (ATU 480) in "Precious," Maiden-Killer or **Bluebeard** (ATU 312) in "The Glass Bottle Trick," Hans Christian **Andersen**'s "The Snow Queen" in "Under Glass"—and of Caribbean folktales, for instance "**Anansi** and Dry Bone." Hopkinson's Caribbean supernatural characters (duppy, soucouyant, and river goddess), her Creole-inflected language, and her attention to racial dynamics in all of these stories serves to creolize the fairy tale. *See also* Erotic Tales; Négritude, Créolité, and Folktale.

Further Readings: Bacchilega, Cristina. "Reflections on Recent English-Language Fairy-Tale Fiction by Women." *Fabula* 47 (2006): 201–10; Hopkinson, Nalo. "Essay: Dark Ink; Science Fiction Writers of Colour." 1998. *Nalo Hopkinson.* 2006. http://nalohopkinson.com/author_nalo_hopkinson/writing/on_writing/dark_ink/essay_dark_ink.html; Nalo Hopkinson's Web site. http://nalohopkinson.com/; Nelson, Alondra. "'Making the Impossible Possible.' Interview with Nalo Hopkinson." *Social Text* 20.2 (2002): 97–113.

Cristina Bacchilega

Housman, Laurence (1865–1959)

Laurence Housman was a British artist, novelist, playwright, and writer of literary fairy tales for adults. A younger brother of the poet A. E. Housman and the son of a solicitor, he was born in Worcestershire, England, and left with his older sister Clemence to study **art** at the Lambeth School of Art and the Royal College of Art in London. His first jobs were as an illustrator, notably for Christina Georgina **Rossetti**'s *Goblin Market* (1893), Jane Barlow's *The End of Elfinton* (1894), and Edith **Nesbit**'s *A Pomander of Verse* (1895). As an art critic for the *Manchester Guardian*, he championed illustrators and book design, especially the Pre-Raphaelite 1860s wood engravings of Arthur Boyd Houghton and Arthur Hughes, whose works influenced Housman's own style. He also contributed to the art nouveau movement and was associated with Aubrey Beardsley and the illustrated quarterly *The Yellow Book* (1894). With book designer and typographer Charles Ricketts, whom he met at Lambeth, Housman influenced late-Victorian book design and decorative bindings.

About this time, he began writing his own works, including a series of adult fairy tales, which include *A Farm in Fairyland* (1894), *The House of Joy* (1895), *The Field of Clover* (1898), and *The Blue Moon* (1904). The first two of these were self-illustrated (his images were engraved by his sister) and suggest a turning point, as Housman's elaborately detailed black-and-white style became more difficult as his eyesight failed. The final two were illustrated by his sister, who also later wrote three books herself. The writing style of these tales is likewise elaborate and informed by his liberal politics. Housman was one of the founders of the Fabian Society, was a socialist and pacifist, and worked for women's suffrage and the rights of gay people. After his poetry career faltered in the shadow of his older brother's fame, his first commercial success came in the anonymously published novel *An Englishwoman's Love-letters* (1900). In the first half of the twentieth century, he was probably best known as a playwright in Britain and the United States, although in the former his work was often censored for its frank discussion of **sexuality**, religion, and the royal family. His plays include *Bethlehem* (1902), *Prunella* (1906), which was successfully produced in New York, and *Victoria Regina* (1934).

Housman continued to write fiction and nonfiction throughout his life, returning frequently to the fairy tale. His retelling of the ***Arabian Nights*** tales, *Stories from the Arabian Nights* (1907), illustrated by Edmund Dulac, was especially popular. He edited the posthumous works of his brother, wrote an autobiography, *The Unexpected Years* (1936), and lived the final third of his life with his sister. *See also* Illustration.

Further Reading: Egan, Rodney K. *Laurence Housman*. Stroud: Catalpa, 1983.

George Bodmer

Humperdinck, Engelbert (1854–1921)

Engelbert Humperdinck, a teacher, **opera** critic, and award-winning composer, is most famous for his opera *Hänsel und Gretel* (***Hansel and Gretel***, 1893), his musical **adaptation** of the **Grimm** brothers' well-known fairy tale. The work began as four children's songs written for his sister Adelheid Wette's slightly altered and more optimistic version of the Grimms' story, in which she replaced the wicked stepmother with the children's real **mother** and added the characters of the **father**, the Sandman, the Dew Fairy, and angels. Humperdinck soon lengthened the piece to a singspiel, or operetta, consisting of sixteen songs with piano accompaniment. Realizing the work's potential, he then turned it into a full-scale opera, whose Weimar premiere was conducted by Richard Strauss. Its combination of Wagnerian techniques and traditional German folk melodies made the work an immediate success, not only in Germany but throughout Europe.

Humperdinck continued composing in this genre, writing the music for two more works based on Grimms' fairy tales: *Die sieben Geislein* (*The Seven Kids*, 1898), another adaptation by his sister; and *Dornröschen* (***Sleeping Beauty***, 1902). In 1910, he wrote the musical score for *Königskinder* (*The Royal Children*), a fairy-tale play by the librettist Elsa Bernstein-Porges, a work which Humperdinck considered his best. However, these three operas never attained the success of *Hansel and Gretel*, which remains a perennial holiday favorite. *See also* Music.

Further Reading: Denley, Ian. "Engelbert Humperdinck." *The New Grove Dictionary of Music and Musicians*. Edited by Stanley Sadie. 2nd edition. Volume 11. New York: Grove, 2001. 836–44.

Candace Beutell Gardner

Hurston, Zora Neale (1891–1960)

Zora Neale Hurston was a folklorist, anthropologist, playwright, and novelist who documented African American **folklore** and folklife. She was born in Notasulga, Alabama, in 1891, and spent her childhood in Eatonville, Florida. The Eatonville community influenced Hurston's intellectual endeavors and provided inspiration for many of her fictional stories.

In 1920, Hurston entered Howard University in Washington, D.C., but she struggled to support herself and ultimately dropped out. Through the encouragement of her peers, she moved to New York and became a figurehead of the Harlem Renaissance literary movement, cofounding the magazine *Fire!!* with Langston Hughes and Wallace Thurman, among

Zora Neale Hurston at the *New York Times* Book Fair, 1937. [Library of Congress]

other prominent African American writers. In New York, she attended Barnard College and studied under the renowned anthropologist Franz Boas, where she learned how to conduct ethnographic **fieldwork**. This experience stimulated Hurston's intellectual interest in the folktales she heard growing up in Eatonville.

Perhaps one of the most impressive aspects of Zora Neale Hurston's career was the context in which it took place. As both an African American and a woman in a white-dominated, patriarchal society, she faced many obstacles on the road to becoming a successful writer and folklorist in the early twentieth century. Her career spanned both world wars, the Great Depression, and segregation. Despite the hardships and uncertainties that faced Americans in those times, especially minorities, Hurston infiltrated both black and white society, collecting the **tall tales**, folk songs, dramas, rituals, and **motifs** of her **informant**s, which ranged from Floridian common folk and Haitian hoodoo doctors to aristocratic white southerners and businessmen. She obtained exclusive information that had not been previously disclosed to others.

During the Great Depression, Franklin Delano Roosevelt's New Deal program created the Works Progress Administration(WPA), which provided employment for writers and artists most affected by the dire economic circumstances. As a black woman, Hurston knew that she would seem less threatening within black communities than her white male counterparts working for the WPA. In this regard, Hurston did not let societal conventions obstruct her ability to overstep social boundaries in **collecting** material, and she utilized her race and gender to her advantage. Hurston's writing ability and resourcefulness led to work on the Federal Writers' Project, the literary division of the WPA, where she was assigned to cover southern folk traditions. The majority of her work was in Florida, where she collected folk songs, traditional tales, dances, and folk art of predominantly African American informants. Hurston also spent a great deal of time with hoodoo doctors in New Orleans, fascinated by the rituals and performances of conjure. She received a Guggenheim Fellowship to fund studies of these practices in New Orleans, and she eventually determined that traveling to Haiti and Jamaica would provide the greatest insight into hoodoo and conjure-ritualistic traditions. Her experiences in Florida as a child and as a writer, in addition to her fieldwork in New Orleans and the Caribbean, yielded two important folkloristic works: *Mules and Men* (1935) and *Tell My Horse* (1937).

In addition to hoodoo and conjure, tall tales and **legend**s were among the most frequently tapped folkloric source in Hurston's writings. *Mules and Men*, perhaps her most acclaimed folkloristic endeavor, was simply split into two parts: "Folk Tales" and "Hoodoo." American folk legends such as Br'er Fox, Br'er Deer, Br'er 'Gator, Br'er Dawg, Br'er Rabbit, and folk hero John Henry reappear in colorful detail. **Trickster** tales and **animal tale**s abound. Stories from European tradition, such as "Rawhead and Bloody Bones" and "Jack and the Beanstalk," are also infused with Hurston's witty analysis of black cultural heritage.

Hurston's documentation of hoodoo, a secretive, mystical practice, also vividly captured the rituals and practices of an obscure phenomenon.

Tell My Horse expanded upon the hoodoo lore first touched upon in *Mules and Men*. This book documented the rituals, magic, and secretive practices of conjure that were previously unknown to outsiders as well, but it was a more developed, thorough overview of hoodoo and conjure than previously provided in Hurston's earlier writings. *Every Tongue Got to Confess: Negro Folk-tales from the Gulf States* (1991) was published posthumously and also includes tales of hoodoo and conjure stemming from Hurston's treks through New Orleans and the Gulf states.

Hurston's fictional works, *Jonah's Gourd Vine* (1934), *Moses, Man of the Mountain* (1939), and, most notably, *Their Eyes Were Watching God* (1937), utilized African American folk traditions and tales to create unique, realistic accounts of the black experience in the Deep South. *Their Eyes Were Watching God*, set in Hurston's native Eatonville, Florida, relied on her reproduction of folkloric traditions. Hurston chose to phonetically voice her black characters in the hopes of achieving a greater sense of **authenticity**, a choice that garnered criticism from some African Americans, who believed that the dialectical voicing seemed derogatory.

One of Hurston's greatest talents was her ability to adapt the folklore of the people whom she studied into believable characters. Hurston filtered her fieldwork into fictional prose rich in the folkloric traditions that they were adapted from. In her autobiography, *Dust Tracks on a Road* (1942), Hurston divulges that as a child she greatly enjoyed reading **Bible** stories, Norse tales, and fairy tales (particularly the **Grimms**'), as well as Greek and Roman mythology. Her early affinity for folklore developed into ethnographic skill, and Hurston incorporated the themes of the traditional tales into her fiction and emphatically retold her collected folklore in her nonfiction works. ***See also*** African American Tales; Race and Ethnicity; Walker, Alice.

Further Readings: Carter-Sigglow, Janet. *Making Her Way with Thunder: A Reappraisal of Zora Neale Hurston's Narrative Art*. New York: P. Lang, 1994; Hill, Lynda Marion Hill. *Social Rituals and the Verbal Art of Zora Neale*. Washington, D.C.: Howard University Press, 1996; Hurston, Zora Neale. *Go Gator and Muddy the Water: Writings by Zora Neale Hurston from the Federal Writers' Project*. Edited by Pamela Bordelon. New York: Norton, 1999; Jacobs, Karen. "From 'Spy-Glass' to 'Horizon': Tracking the Anthropological Gaze in Zora Neal Hurston." *NOVEL: A Forum on Fiction* 30 (1997): 329–60.

Trevor J. Blank

Hybridity, Hybridization

Folktales and fairy tales that derive from heterogeneous sources, or are composed of different, incongruous elements, are sometimes called "hybrid," meaning that they mingle elements usually thought to be incompatible. In folktale or fairy-tale studies, the notion of hybridization has a quite different meaning from what it has in genetics, molecular biology, or chemistry. Hybrid tales often develop through the convergence of several diverse **storytelling** traditions. Sometimes they arise unexpectedly and are historically discontinuous and autonomous; sometimes they appear as something novel in a process of evolution. Hybrid folktales are new creations in both structural and functional terms, built up from previously existing narrative traditions, from which they recognizably draw.

Any folktale or fairy tale could be called hybrid with regard to its referential content because it mixes things recognizable in the world—houses, daughters, nightfall—with objects, characters, or incidents obviously fantastic—flying carpets, **women** with magic powers, or waking the dead. Disentangling and interpreting this mixture is the classic double problem of folktale studies: how are we to account for the surprising and shocking behavior of folktale characters, and how do we interpret the fantastic elements? Hybrid folktales generally, however, are narratives that transgress linguistic and symbol-system boundaries. Hybridization can be recognized at the lexical, grammatical, generic, and channel levels.

Lexical hybridization regularly occurs among border people, for example Mexican Americans, who play with the similarity of the sounds of words. José sends his brother Juan to buy gloves. When the English-speaking store clerk asks, "What do you want?" he answers, "*Si, guante*" (Yes, a glove).

"What do you say?"

"*Si, pa José*" (Yes, for José).

"Oh, you fool!"

"*Si, de esos de la correita azul*" (Yes, those with the blue thongs).

"Oh, you go to hell!"

"*Si, de esos me mando él*" (Yes, he sent me after those).

It is the lexical mix that does the work of this joke. Two languages, belonging to two social groups, are mixed within the limits of a distinct story. The Russian philosopher-critic M. M. Bakhtin called this phenomenon in literature an "intentional hybrid." Two distinct utterances, he said, are fused into one, but internally they are still in dialogue with each other. Although only the individual will of the storyteller is at work, there are "two consciousnesses, two language-intentions, two *voices,* and consequently two accents participating in an intentional and conscious artistic hybrid." In the joke, Spanish and English encounter each other as possessions of ethnic groups confronting one another. The lexical hybridization enables the joke to fulfill a new social and linguistic function appropriate to a border community, illustrating and commenting on its dual consciousness.

Grammatical hybridization postulates that people's rules for the creation of narratives are like the grammar of a language. In grammatical hybridization, though no rule is broken, some unexpected element, perhaps an episode from elsewhere, crosses a boundary. A narrator may follow his first story with a second part, which is actually another story sometimes told by itself. For example, a young woman, obliged to fulfill her mother's false boasts, is betrothed to a **prince** on the condition that she spins ninety rolls of flax in a month. When the **devil** helps her perform this and other tasks on the condition that she guess his name, the reader recognizes **tale type** ATU 500, The Name of the Supernatural Helper, better known as Rumpelstiltskin or Tom Tit Tot. But when the young woman begins to pine away from brooding over this impossible secret, and the **king** offers a reward to whoever can make her laugh, the narrator has brought in a suitor test (Motif H341, Making the princess laugh), which is part of several other international types but seldom found in this one. In a West African version of that same type (ATU 500), Spider finds out the names of the king's three daughters and confides the secret to Lizard, who, being the court herald, proclaims it and takes the girls. In a second part, Spider gets revenge on Lizard by dipping him in boiling water and reclaims the girls, saying they were stolen from him. Lizard is in no position to protest. This juxtaposition changes the meaning of the second trick by attaching it to the first one. Isn't such combining, in fact, the essence of individual creativity? If it is to be called hybridizing, then many narrators are hybridizers. In stories about the telling of tales, such as the ***Arabian Nights***, a narrator may follow or interrupt one tale with another, but such stories are **frame narrative**s, not hybrids.

The most familiar kind of narrative hybridization is generic, and the most familiar samples are **riddle** tales. Oedipus must answer the riddle propounded by the Sphinx; the riddle is incorporated in the story (Motif H541.1.1, Sphinx propounds riddle on pain of death). Medieval narratives, such as the *Prose Tristan*, also include riddles, subordinating the smaller genre to the larger. Medieval **ballad**s incorporate riddles as a sign of women's power. In "The Elfin Knight" ("Scarborough Fair," Child 2), a woman's suitor can win a lady's hand only by guessing riddles. In a modern tale from Mauritius, when a husband and wife are quarreling over whether to visit her parents, she proposes a riddle, "Eyes on a newborn." If her husband gives a successful answer, he will have the privilege of deciding whether they go and visit his in-laws. He fails the test and is obliged to follow his wife. Both the riddle and the story reverse the conventional dominance of a husband over his wife. All riddles play with accepted categories of thought; this story encloses that play in the less-threatening genre of narrative, combining two modes of thinking and speaking. Both The King and the Farmer's Son (ATU 921) and The Clever Farmgirl (ATU 875) make the performance of riddles a dramatic means of empowering a young hero or heroine, who can give clever answers to a king. The two genres enter into a dialogue, as the farmgirl and the king do in their respective stories.

The dialogue of genres is also revealed in stories about the composition of a song, such as The Singing Bone (ATU 780). Jacob and Wilehelm **Grimm**'s version of this tale contrasts a cunning and smart older brother with an innocent and naïve younger one, who successfully kills a wild boar as the king has demanded. The older brother kills his sibling and is awarded the king's daughter. Years later, a shepherd discovers one of the boy's bones, carves it into a mouthpiece for his horn, and hears the bone retell the whole story in song. Thus the song, not subordinated to the rest of the tale, is the very means of its climax. It is also a miniature of the narrative that encloses it.

Dialogue of genres is revealed again in the "neck riddle," which, despite its name, is actually a hybrid narrative. It parodies the riddle genre by making the answer to the riddle something that only the riddler can know. A well-known example is Samson's riddle (Judges 14.14), "Out of the eater came something to eat; out of the strong came something sweet." In the story, Samson's successful posing of the riddle, which ought to empower him, is actually a step toward his ultimate downfall, because his treacherous wife gives away the secret. Again, the smaller genre is a miniature of the larger, since Samson the strong is reduced, temporarily, to helplessness.

Another device that looks like hybridization is the switching of channels between speech and song. This is a quite normal habit of **performance** for storytellers in many languages and cultures. Most African and African-derived narrative traditions practice it. In some places, song is the normal channel for communicating with spirits. Plantation tales, from the days of African American slavery, pit the clever slave John against his dupe, Old Marster. In one tale, John takes advantage of Marster's absence to have a party (song: "Turn your partner 'round and 'round, and bring her back home again to me"), only to detect Old Marster there in blackface (song: "Oh, Marster, is that you? Oh, Marster, is that you?"). The clever slave keeps repeating the songs until he makes his escape. No mere decoration, the songs thus are essential to moving the plot forward. Stories such as this include a scene in which singing would be appropriate anyway, like a dance, and the song can be given a double meaning. The switching between speech and song can be called hybrid only within a Eurocentric perspective, which would confine storytelling to the channel of speech. Hence,

European scholars give the hybrid its own name as a genre, **cante fable** (song-story), whereas African or Asian performers would not see any boundary being crossed. To the performer, the hybridization of speech and song yields a range of manipulations of the channel: he or she plays with intonational and vocal possibilities that lie between the extremes of ordinary speech and song.

Since the channel governs the contact between performer and audience, the very writing of an oral tale is another case of channel hybridization, whether it is a verbatim transcript (such as by Katharine M. **Briggs**), an elaboration and revision of an oral tale (for example, by Zora Neale **Hurston**), a literary invention based on oral folklore (such as by Charles **Perrault**), or a **literary fairy tale** based on other literature (such as by Jean de **La Fontaine**).

Hybridization of verbal art gets its theory from Creole linguistics, which studies new languages that have been built from previously existing languages. Hybrid folktales come into existence as part of the exchange of cultural elements between different societies. Hybridization of folktales most often occurs when cultures converge and clash. Narratives are deterritorialized, decontextualized, combined with other narratives, and recontextualized in different settings and places. In the twentieth and early twenty-first centuries, this process most often occurred in colonized or formerly colonized nations, where hybridization meant a kind of reinforcement of inherited tradition. A Jamaican cante fable tells of "Mr. **Bluebeard**" (ATU 312, Maiden-Killer), who "general catch people an' lock up into a room, an' he never let him wife see that room." With her husband away, Mrs. Bluebeard finds out the secret and calls to the cook in song: "Sister Anne, Sister Anne, Ah! You see anyone is coming?" In song, the cook replies, "Oh no, I see no one is coming but the dust that makes the grass so green." When Bluebeard arrives, the wife is rescued by her brothers, who shoot Bluebeard "and kill him 'tiff dead." The song simultaneously advances and retards the action. But another kind of hybridization is at work here. The well-known basic story, which found its way to both East and West Africa, is reinforced in Jamaica by the influence of Africa's most popular story. There, a woman who has wed a beast-man must be rescued from this impossible marriage by a member of her birth family. The brothers in Perrault's version ("La barbe bleue," 1697) do effect the rescue, but their Jamaican characters belong to both European and African traditions, and are therefore hybrids. To call a storyteller, or any person in a Creole society such as Jamaica, a hybrid, however, implies that he or she is a half-breed, a cross-breed, or a mongrel, and therefore an impure representative of the race. Such thinking has long been discredited.

Many hybrid narratives—double-voiced, carrying layers of meanings, valorizing voices from the margins—are products of the domination or subjugation of one group by another. The postmodern fairy tales of Angela **Carter**, for instance, "The Company of Wolves" (1979), build on well-known plots to raise serious questions about the **sex-gender** system, as well as the conventions of fairy-tale narrative. Folk narratives from Madagascar's period of French occupation and Catholic missionary activity (1896–1960) enact the social-political-ideological encounter by fusing traditions. In one, from 1931, lexical hybridization points up the blending of the Bible and Qur'an with older Malagasy mythmaking. Dama and Hova (Arabic translations of Adam and Eve) are expelled by God's son Ratompo (who lives on earth) from the beautiful countryside where they live with their two sons, Farmer and Herdsman. Ratompo says they are spoiling the land. Herdsman reports the sentence to his **father**; they move to where Farmer is working the earth; the **brothers** live harmoniously, both bringing their first fruits to Ratompo. Jealous over the reception of his brother's offering, Herdsman moves away. One day Dama has an eye ailment, so he sends his remaining son to Ratompo, who gives him mankind's first herbal remedy. After living fifty years, Ratompo ascends to heaven, but not before gathering disciples and awarding them the arts of healing, as well as the formula "You are strong, strong, strong, Andrianahary, Ratompo, Ramanitse." The influence of the Christian trinity appears both there and in the names of Farmer's three sons, Babamino (Believer-Father), Makarailo (from the Islamic angel Mika'il and the Christian archangel Michael), and Tsarafailo (from Asrafel, who will sound the trumpet on the day of resurrection). Since *tompo* means "owner" and implies "landowner," the culture hero and the landlord are an intentional hybrid. Indeed, the whole story relies on the intention of its teller. Hybridization requires artistic agency.

Lexical, grammatical, and referential hybridization in folktales and fairy tales are symbolic enactments of the realities of social and cultural conflicts. Hybrid or Creolized folktales and fairy tales are a window into worldwide processes of globalization, often denigrated with the same pejorative terms: mongrelization, mestizaje, pastiche, bricolage, mélange, fusion, or syncretism. After all, orchid growers know more about hybridizing than literary scholars or cultural critics: they create some 800 new species of orchid each year, entirely through deliberate, systematic hybridization. These beautiful plants, like many a tale, exist only through hybridization. *See also* Colonialism; Indian Ocean Tales; Négritude, Créolité, and Folktale.

Further Readings: Bakhtin, M. M. "The Problem of Speech Genres." *Speech Genres and Other Late Essays.* Edited by Caryl Emerson and Michael Holquist. Austin: University of Texas Press, 1986. 60–102; Dorst, John D. "Neck-Riddle as a Dialogue of Genres." *Journal of American Folklore* 96 (1983): 413–33; Kapchan, Deborah A., and Pauline Turner Strong. "Theorizing the Hybrid." *Journal of American Folklore* 112 (1999): 239–53.

Lee Haring

I

Ihimaera, Witi (1944–)

A leading New Zealand writer, librettist, and anthologist, Witi Ihimaera writes fiction that reveals Maori experience and culture. Of Te Aitanga-a-Mahaki descent, Ihimaera was born in Gisborne, educated at the universities of Auckland and Victoria, worked for the Ministry of Foreign Affairs—for some years as a diplomat—and is now a professor of English at the University of Auckland. His fiction often draws on his own experiences, deals with the past and present of Maori life, and is frequently concerned with destiny. Like his fellow Maori writer Patricia **Grace**, he weaves Maori mythology and history into contemporary plots that focus on community, the past, and urban versus rural ways of life. He most overtly draws on modes of Maori **myth** and **storytelling** in his widely beloved book *The Whale Rider* (1987). The book's central character is a girl who disrupts the ancestral tradition of male whale riders by riding a stranded whale out to sea, at the same time fulfilling her destiny and reigniting her village's sense of communal spirit. The award-winning 2002 film **adaptation**, *Whale Rider*, directed by Niki Caro, has brought international attention to Ihimaera's story and by extension has raised wider awareness of Maori myth and culture. ***See also*** Australian and Aotearoan/New Zealand Tales; Pacific Island Tales; *Pear ta ma 'on maf.*

Further Readings: Corballis, Richard, and Simon Garrett. *Introducing Witi Ihimaera.* Auckland: Longman Paul, 1984; "Ihimaera, Witi." New Zealand Book Council. 2005. http://www.bookcouncil.org.nz/writers/ihimaerawiti.html; Ojinmah, Umelo R. *Witi Ihimaera: A Changing Vision.* Dunedin: University of Otago Press, 1993.

Adrienne E. Gavin

Illustration

Two presumptions contributed to the emergence and development of folktale and fairy-tale illustration: that fairy tales are suitable for children, and that children enjoy pictures and need them for a better understanding of verbal stories. Scholars of **children's literature** as well as folklorists have seriously questioned the first of these premises, since the general suitability of folktales for a young audience has always been a controversial issue. The second stance has in fact never been confirmed through empirical research. Naturally, the combination of verbal and visual narratives was known already in the ancient world, for instance,

ILLUSTRATION 469

in Egyptian murals, Greek pottery, and Chinese scrolls. Yet the consistent use of visual images accompanying published folktales and fairy tales is a relatively recent phenomenon, governed by such factors as the improvement of printing techniques, interest in **folklore** from authors and artists during the Romantic era, and, not least of all, the pedagogical ideas about children's perception of stories (see **Pedagogy**).

Illustration by Elsa Beskow in *Swedish Fairy Tales* by F. Berg (New York: Walter Scott Publishing Co., Ltd., 1904), p. 217. [Courtesy of the Eloise Ramsey Collection of Literature for Young People, University Libraries, Wayne State University]

The attraction of illustrating well-known texts again and again, challenging predecessors, and overcoming "the anxiety of influence" lies ostensibly in the enormous freedom of interpretation. Folktales are usually scarce in details concerning settings and the appearance of characters (apart from standard epithets such as "the most beautiful in the world"), which allows a vast spectrum of pictorial solutions. Although we may today perceive some illustrations as standard and the only possible—especially if we have grown up with a particular set—fairy-tale illustrations will likely continue to appear competing with each other and, at best, opening new dimensions of the famous stories.

Naturally, purely commercial reasons cannot be neglected. Illustrated books are attractive for younger age groups and usually sell better than many other book categories. They are also a vital part of children's and school libraries' purchases. Book collectors are yet another important category of consumers.

Brief History

Illustrated books were expensive to produce, and the earliest known books with pictures were usually made in one or a few hand-colored copies to be presented to young princes and sons of nobility. It was habitual to choose one scene from every story, naturally the most exciting and dramatic one. The early European collections of fairy tales, normally addressed to adults rather than children, were rarely if ever illustrated; however, a single illustration could appear on the cover. The first fairy-tale volumes of Hans Christian **Andersen** had no illustrations. Andersen's fairy tales got their first illustrations in 1848 in a German edition; these were done by Vilhelm Pedersen, whom Andersen chose himself and was pleased with, and later by Lorenz Frølich.

Among the nineteenth-century illustrated fairy tales, Gustave **Doré**'s illustrations to Charles **Perrault**'s tales hold a special place. They were first published in a French edition in 1867 and soon became the standard Perrault illustrations in many countries. With their

Illustration by Ivan Bilibin for "Maria Morevna" in *Russian Wonder Tales* by Post Wheeler (New York: The Century Co., 1912).

special seventeenth-century style, grotesque bodies, and daunting details, the pictures were artistically innovative and thus attractive to art lovers, but hardly child-friendly. Today, Doré's illustrations mostly appear in exclusive gift books or in scholarly collections. Yet long before Doré, the British artist George **Cruikshank** illustrated *German Popular Stories* (1823–26), a selection and translation of tales taken mostly from the Brothers **Grimm**; *Italian Tales* (1824), Giambattista **Basile**'s *Pentamerone* (1848), and others. His illustrations contributed to the dissemination of the European folktales and fairy tales in Britain and set frames for many upcoming artists.

By the mid-nineteenth century, children's magazines and Christmas calendars became a vast market for traditional as well as **literary fairy tale**s, and to make the publications more attractive, the stories were illustrated, thus engaging many artists in this particular field. The growing literacy, as a consequence of mandatory primary education in European countries, created the premises and the needs for reading matter for young readers. As literary fairy tales and fantasy became popular genres, many artists, a number of whom were newspaper and magazine cartoonists, produced illustrations to what are now known as fairy-tale classics. John Tenniel's illustrations in *Alice's Adventures in Wonderland* (1865) and *Through the Looking Glass and What Alice Found There* (1872) are perhaps the best known today, appearing in dozens of editions all over the world and successfully competing with many subsequent illustrators of Lewis **Carroll**'s work. From his illustrations, the readers got the memorable portraits of imaginary creatures such as the Gryphon, the Mock Turtle, and the Jabberwocky. Almost as everlasting are the original illustrations of Carlo **Collodi**'s *Le avventure di Pinocchio* (*The Adventures of Pinocchio*, 1883) by Enrico Mazzanti. W. W. Denslow's and John R. Neill's illustrations of L. Frank **Baum**'s Oz books (1900 onward) continued and developed the European trends in the United States. These black-and-white pictures, imaginative as they are, had one trait in common: they were decorative in the sense that they focused on separate characters or episodes in the story, without interpreting or enhancing them. Thus, while illustrations certainly added to the aesthetic experience of

ILLUSTRATION   471

the books and made them more fascinating for the readers, they were not essential for understanding and enjoyment. In fact, many of these classics have also been published without illustrations or with a considerably limited number of original pictures, which does not compromise the flow of the story. This is also true about H. R. Millar's drawings for Rudyard Kipling's and E. **Nesbit**'s fantasy stories, Mabel Lucie Atwell's for Sir James Matthew **Barrie**'s *Peter Pan* (1921), and Ernest Shepard's unforgettable images from A. A. Milne's Pooh books (1926, 1928) and Kenneth Grahame's *The Wind in the Willows* (1931). Most of these illustrations were made at the authors' request and in tight collaboration.

Early illustrations were normally woodcuts, pen, or pencil drawings. Color illustrations could not really emerge before printing techniques had been further developed to allow rela-

Illustration by Walter Crane for *The Frog Prince* (London: George Routledge and Sons, 1874).

tively inexpensive mass production of four-color pictures. By the second half of the nineteenth century, the premises were sufficient to stimulate a number of artists to use color illustrations. Among these, the importance of Randolph Caldecott, Kate Greenaway, and Walter **Crane** cannot be overestimated, the first of the three strongly influencing his successors. Crane's illustrations of "**Beauty and the Beast**," the Brother **Grimm**s' tales, and many British tales were among the first to be published as separate books rather than collections, opening a new chapter in the history of fairy-tale **art**.

British artists had a great impact on the development of fairy-tale illustrations in many countries. In Scandinavia, for instance, Jenny **Nyström**, Ottilia Adelborg, John Bauer, and Elsa **Beskow** were just some of the vast number of fairy-tale artists who worked for children's magazines and the quickly emerging publishers. Foreign impulses notwithstanding, these artists were all highly original in their styles, often focused on the nature and social environment of Nordic countries. They illustrated Scandinavian fairy-tale authors, such as Hans Christian Andersen and Zacharias **Topelius**; they also wrote and illustrated fairy stories of their own, featuring magical **transformation**s or imaginary creatures. Among other outstanding Scandinavian illustrators, we find the Norwegian Theodor **Kittelsen**, with his illustrations to Peter Christen **Asbjørnsen** and Jørgen **Moe**'s tales. Figures of trolls and other magical beings were his trademark; he often conveyed the sense of mankind's confrontation with nature. Yet another famous Scandinavian artist, who won worldwide recognition, was Kay **Nielsen** from Denmark. Nielsen illustrated the Grimms, Asbjørnsen, Andersen, and *Red Magic: A Collection of the World's Best Fairy Tales from All Countries* (1930). The famous Russian artist and illustrator Ivan **Bilibin**, best known for his illustrations of **Russian tales**, was instead inspired by old Russian **chapbook**s in their ornamental detail, as well as by European Jugendstil and Japanese prints. He also created illustrations for Aleksandr **Pushkin**'s fairy tales. By the beginning of the twentieth century, a multitude of styles in illustration had emerged. The tradition of fairy-tale authors illustrating their own stories (or occasionally the other way round, artists providing texts to their illustrations) became firmly established. Beatrix Potter is unquestionably the foremost representative of this trend, followed by such author-illustrators as Wanda **Gág** with her original tale *Millions of Cats* (1928).

Illustrated Collections

Among the most enticing texts for illustrators, European as well as North American, are undoubtedly the classic tales of Perrault, Grimm, and Andersen, frequently a selection of the most popular tales. Perrault's stories have been illustrated in Britain, for example, by W. Heath Robinson, and in the United States by Michael Hague, Susan Jeffers, Sarah Moon (using startling photographs), as well as by many others. Various selections of Grimms' tales were illustrated in Britain by Arthur **Rackham**, Mabel Lucie Attwell, Mervyn Peak, and Michael Foreman; and in the United States by Helen Stratton, John B. Gruelle, Ethel Franklin Betts, Wanda Gág, and many other outstanding artists. Among the first British Andersen illustrators, the Scottish artist Eleanor Vere Boyle can be mentioned, published in 1872. Volumes of Andersen's tales were also illustrated by Atwell, Foreman, and Edward Ardizzone.

The French artist Edmund **Dulac** illustrated *Stories from the **Arabian Nights*** (1907), French and Russian fairy tales, and a volume of Andersen's tales; he also published *Edmund Dulac's Fairy Book* (1916). It has been common for illustrators to collect their various illustrated fairy tales in luxurious volumes, such as *Lucie Attwell's Fairy Book* (1932) and *The Arthur Rackham Fairy Book* (1933). The American artist Gustaf Tenggren, of Scandinavian origin, published *The Tenggren Tell-It-Again Book* (1942), in which he appears a true heir of John Bauer in style and especially in color, inspired by the dark Nordic forests.

In Britain, collections by Joseph **Jacobs** were illustrated by John D. Batten (*English Fairy Tales*, 1890; *Celtic Fairy Tales*, 1892; *Indian Fairy Tales*, 1892; and *Europa's Fairy Tales*, 1916), while the numerous volumes by Andrew **Lang** carried primarily H. J. Ford's and some other artists' illustrations. Lang's collections included, apart from British, also German, French, and Scandinavian folktales, as well as literary fairy tales by Andersen and others. As for individual tales, the famous Pre-Raphaelite painter Edward Burne-Jones illustrated several, including "**Cinderella**" and "**Sleeping Beauty**," in his typical exquisite style.

One of the most successful contemporary fairy-tale illustrators, reaching worldwide fame, was the Danish artist Svend Otto S. (real name Sørensen). His illustrations of the Grimms and Andersen have been used in fairy-tale editions in several countries (in English as *The Best of Grimm's Fairy Tales*, 1979, and *Andersen's Fairytales*, 1990). His illustrations are characterized by a richness of detail, elaborate technique, and warm humor. They also show a clear tendency to counterbalance the Disney style. Unlike many contemporary illustrators of classical fairy tales, S. addressed primarily an audience of children, avoiding adult connotations or allusions. Much of his work has been published as separate books.

Today, many nations have their own standard illustrators for certain fairy tales or sets of fairy tales, not necessarily accepted in other countries. Most contemporary artists have to compete with mass-market editions, not least the **Walt Disney Company**, which has

ILLUSTRATION   473

appropriated many favorite fairy tales and, with its universal and audience-friendly style, supported by merchandise, presents a considerable threat to more sophisticated endeavors.

Fairy-Tale Picture Books

The border between illustrated fairy tales and picture books with supernatural elements is often difficult and perhaps unnecessary to draw. The numerous picture books featuring more or less anthropomorphic animals are, strictly speaking, not fairy tales; rather animals are employed as human beings in disguise. This is true about such titles as Jean de Brunhoff's Babar books, H. A. Rey's Curious George series, or Dr. Seuss's *Cat in the Hat* (1957). As a rule of thumb, it can be said that in illustrated tales, the text can stand on its own, without illustrations, as it once has been written or retold. Picture books offer new dimensions and interpretations that make the images an integral part of the story. Word and pictures in a true picture book are inseparable, and the meaning is created by the synergy of the verbal and the visual art.

By far the most popular among fairy tales has been "**Little Red Riding Hood**." Examples include W. W. Denslow (1903), and, among late-twentieth-century artists, Edward Gorey (1972), Trina Schart Hyman (1983), James Marshall (1987), and Mercer Mayer (1991). Ed Young's *Lon Po Po* (1989) is an inventive story with a Chinese flavor. Other favorite tales are "**Hansel and Gretel**" (Susan Jeffers, 1980; Anthony Browne, 1981; Paul O. Zelinsky, 1984; James Marshall, 1990; and Jane Ray, 1997), "Sleeping Beauty" (Errol Le Cain, 1975, and Hyman, 1977), and "**Snow White**" (Nancy Ekholm Burkert, 1972; Bernadette Watts, 1983; and Hyman, 1974). In many cases, the illustrators also made their own text adaptations. Some of the most remarkable fairy-tale picture books include *The Frog Prince* (1989) by the Swiss artist Binette Schroeder.

American author Shirley Climo has engaged a number of illustrators and produced several ethnic versions of **Cinderella**: *The Egyptian Cinderella* (1989) and *The Korean Cinderella* (1993), both illustrated by Ruth Heller; *The Persian Cinderella* (Robert Florczak, 1999); and *The Irish Cinderlad* (Loretta Krupinski, 1996). Brian Pinkney illustrated *Cendrillon: A Caribbean Cinderella* (1998), and Will Hillenbrand *The Golden Sandal: A Middle Eastern Cinderella Story* (1998). All of these versions naturally strive to emulate national styles.

Among Andersen's tales turned into picture books we frequently find "Thumbelina" (for instance, Susan Jeffers, 1979; Arlene Graston, 1997; Emma Chichester Clark, 1995; and Lithuanian Kestutus Kasparavicius, 2005), followed closely by "The Ugly Duckling" and "The Little Match Girl." Among illustrations of the lesser-known tales, Nancy Ekholm Burkett's soft black-and-white drawings in *The Fir Tree* (1970) deserve mention. Most of these artists do not merely illustrate the texts but bring something radically new into them, by using counterpointing pictures that add or even create a new meaning. For instance, the surrealistic style of Italian Roberto **Innocenti** is quite remarkable. In 2005, commemorating the bicentenary of Andersen's birth, a stream of new illustrated versions appeared throughout the world.

Maurice **Sendak**, who also illustrated fairy tales by Andersen, Wilhelm **Hauff**, Clemens **Brentano**, George **MacDonald**, and Isaak Bashevis **Singer**, is unquestionably the foremost twentieth-century picture-book creator with his imaginative, dreamlike stories *Where the Wild Things Are* (1963), *In the Night Kitchen* (1970), and *Outside over There* (1981). The latter portrays fairy-tale goblins as the main character's adversaries.

Recently, illustrators have appeared who have found inspiration in African, African American, and Native American folklore. Leo and Diane Dillon were among the pioneers. In non-Western countries, where most published children's books are retold local **myth**s and folktales, there is a very strong artistic tradition, often very different from what is familiar to the European and North American audience. Nicky Daly from South Africa and Meshak Asare from Ghana are two notable artists. Artists from Australia, New Zealand, Japan, Korea, Latin America, eastern Europe, the Middle East, and other regions of the world are bringing forward their own styles.

Many contemporary artists work with parodic and fractured fairy tales. Some are, for instance, **gender**-reversed, such as Babette Cole's *Prince Cinders* (1987), whose hero, incidentally, does not lose a slipper but a pair of pants, or role-reversed, such as Ellen Jackson's and Kevin O'Malley's *Cinder Edna* (1994). Others replace fairy-tale woods with equally dangerous large cities. Yet others borrow the main premises of the fairy tale and make something radically new out of them, such as Robert Munsch and Michael Martchenko's *The Paper Bag Princess* (1980) or Cole's *Princess Smartypants* (1986). Allusions to famous fairy tales appear in stories that can primarily be interpreted as a child's imaginative play, such as the Swedish author Pija Lindenbaum's *Bridget and the Gray Wolves* (2000). The most radical metafictive (see **Metafiction**) and intertextual (see **Intertextuality**) versions of fairy tales appear in David Wiesner's *The Three Pigs* (2001), in which the characters walk in and out of their own story; and in Jon Sieczka's three books: *The Stinky Cheese Man and Other Fairly Stupid Tales* (1992), a potpourri of various well-known stories, *The True Story of the Three Little Pigs, by A. Wolf* (1989), both illustrated by Lane Smith, and *The Frog Prince Continued* (1991) with Steve Johnson's pictures. Apart from plot and character distortions, these books employ reversed points of view. The story of the three little **pigs** inspired Eugene Trivizas and Helen Oxenbury in *The Three Little Wolves and the Big Bad Pig* (1993). Janet Perlman's *Cinderella Penguin, or The Little Glass Flipper* (1992) substitutes animals for human beings, naturally with a humorous effect. The German author **Janosch** presented his own ironic versions of Grimm tales in *Janosch erzählt Grimm's Märchen* (1972; translated as *Not Quite as Grimm*, 1974).

Illustrators' Choices

In appreciation of approaches to illustrating fairy tales, several aspects should be taken into consideration. The range of interpretation when the same text is illustrated by different artists is vast. Illustrations enhance certain aspects and tone down others, get adapted to the presumed audience, and address different age groups and tastes. Some illustrations fill in gaps left by the text; others keep strictly to the text as it is. Different illustrators address different aspects of the text. Illustrations reflect not only the individual style of an artist and his or her response to the story, but also a particular period's general style of illustration, the ideology, pedagogical intentions, and the society's views on certain things, such as nudity (for instance in "The Emperor's New Clothes"), **violence**, and sexual connotations present in many folktales. Styles can vary from serious to humorous, romantic to gothic, from realistic to grotesque, from childish and naive to extremely sophisticated. Styles can be medieval and modern, explicitly elaborate and artistic, or kitschy and flat. Contemporary illustrators tend to be quite eclectic. By choosing a particular style, setting, and the appearance and **clothing** of the characters, the artists place the text in a specific historical, social, and literary context. Rachel Isadora's illustrations for *The Little Match Girl* (1987) strive to reproduce authentic settings of nineteenth-century Copenhagen. Not unexpectedly, Lisabeth

ILLUSTRATION   475

Zwerger's *The Nightingale* (1984), based on the Andersen tale, has echoes of Chinese art. The settings can be authentic or anachronistic, fairy-tale-like or naturalistic, idyllic and peaceful, or dangerous and disturbing. They can also be extremely rich in detail or have virtually none, making the characters act in negative space, empty white backgrounds on the page. All of these factors have a strong impact on the reader's appreciation of the story.

The artists can also use special effects, such as vertical perspective, multiple space, optical illusions (similar to M. C. Escher's impossible spaces), framing, mise-en-abyme, and other pictorial contrivances. Further, the details can manipulate the viewer to interpret the text in a certain way. Snow White's stepmother can be presented either as a horrible **witch** or as a beautiful and jealous rival, which enhances one of the themes of the story. The appearance of the **dwarfs** in the various versions of "Snow White" makes them mystical or funny, erotic or asexual. Through anachronistic details of the setting, such as a television set and other attributes of modern times, Anthony Browne's *Hansel and Gretel* (1981) immediately suggests an ironic, postmodern interpretation, which alerts the viewer to more counterpointing details (see **Postmodernism**). Further, Browne's illustrations show a striking likeness between the (step)**mother** and the witch, suggesting—rather, visually enhancing—the interpretation of the story as the child's most forbidden fantasies. The mother is depicted as a fashion-conscious lady with loads of expensive cosmetics on her dressing table, which throws quite a different light on her complaints about the **family**'s poverty. The Oriental setting in Jane Ray's version of the same fairy tale takes the story out of its European context, drawing our attention to its universal nature. In Paul O. Zelinsky's *Hansel and Gretel* (1984), only the first two pictures of the witch's house show it from the children's point of view, that is, a traditional gingerbread house with its roof made of pancakes and windowpanes of candy. As soon as the children are imprisoned, the house loses its enchantment and becomes an ordinary wooden hut, thus suggesting that the gingerbread and sweets were merely an illusion caused by hunger—or else a cunning trick. This transformation makes the many-layered tale still more complex and challenging. Generally Zelinsky's many fairy-tale illustrations are reminiscent of the Flemish school of painting with its rich saturated colors and round, healthy young girls. While his pictures may not appeal to young readers, they are of the highest artistic quality from an art connoisseur's viewpoint.

Significant questions can be raised about artists' choices regarding the number of illustrations and the episodes selected. Many artists decide against including frightening and disturbing scenes, such as cutting open the **wolf**'s stomach in "Little Red Riding Hood," chopping off the giant's daughters' heads in "**Tom Thumb**," or the dead bird in Thumbelina. On the other hand, some artists are explicitly graphic and indulge in scenes that the text merely hints at. Paradoxically, large numbers of images do not necessarily contribute to aesthetic appreciation. Visual density reflects radically opposed approaches to illustration. A larger number of illustrations tends to make them more decorative. Some artists strive to evoke the sense of the text with minimal means, for instance by making pictures dynamic and prefiguring the action, while those with a larger number of illustrations tend to be ornamental instead. Extremely dynamic effects can be conveyed by using whole doublespreads and especially wordless spreads, as can be found, for instance, in Susan Jeffers's *Thumbelina* (1979). Lisbeth Zwerger is extremely scarce in her illustrations; in most cases, they are as few as eight. In contrast, her pictures are in themselves dynamic and highly ironic. Her Thumbelina, for instance, is reminiscent of a healthy, red-cheeked **peasant** girl rather than the elfish magical creature of the original.

It has been pointed out that Sendak, who made just one illustration for each of the Grimm tales in his book *The Juniper Tree and Other Tales from Grimm* (1973), managed to convey the whole story in a single picture, through richness of details and suggestive body postures and facial expressions. Zwerger's illustrated versions of Grimms' and Andersen's tales normally have no more than six to eight full-page pictures, yet their vividness and sequential balance make them quite sufficient to support the text. Artists can also choose between a static scene that conveys a situation and a dynamic scene that suggests movement and the flow of time. The use of conventional graphic devices, such a motion lines and distorted perspectives, simultaneous succession (several images within the same panel, suggesting movement), and a sequence of panels on the same spread enhance the sense of continuity and linearity inherent in the text. Binette Schroeder used the sequential effect to depict the frog's **transformation** into a prince in *The Frog Prince* (1989).

The layout of the doublespread can affect the perception of the story. Surprisingly, many artists use a traditional layout with text and picture on facing pages. This does create a certain rhythm and occasionally can work as a page-turner; yet a clever illustrator uses the many possibilities and variations of the layout to enhance the text. The choice of landscape (horizontal) or portrait (vertical) formats offers different solutions. Pictures that use the whole area of a doublespread are usually more expressive. When the pictures are framed, they create a sense of distance and detachment. Unframed pictures, bleeding, and especially wordless doublespreads invite the viewer into the story. Using contrasting images on facing pages is another powerful artistic process, including the alternation of color and black-and-white illustrations, or of color images and small vignettes on the text page. Facing images often create a causal effect. Layout that varies from spread to spread can be used to underscore the most important episodes of a tale. The varied size of the panel works like a zoom, for instance in Sendak's *Where the Wild Things Are*. It can also convey the different literal points of view. Diagonal movement across the page can be harmonious and disharmonious, affecting the viewer's perception. Round frames in the beginning and the end create a natural opening and closure. Visual page-turners, that is, images in the right bottom corner of the doublespread, contribute to dynamism. Artists can also use the numerous paratexts of the picture-book medium: covers, title pages, and endpapers that can provide additional details and direct the viewer towards new dimensions and interpretations.

Visual characterization can play a significant part in the effect it produces, and the portrayal of the characters allows perhaps the most freedom to artists, since the appearance of the fairy-tale heroes is seldom mentioned in the text. Stereotypical beauties add hardly anything to the story. By contrast, the characters can be presented as small innocent children or sexually mature adolescents; they can be human beings or fairylike creatures. For instance, the various versions of "Thumbelina" portray the tiny character as a chubby baby, a slender **elf**, a robust peasant girl, and even a dangerous, sensual witch. Red Riding Hood is sometimes a very little child, or like the plump heroine in Marshall's version, or sometimes a young lady. Trina Schart Hyman's Wendy from her version of *Peter Pan* is almost in her teens, which naturally changes her relationship with Peter. When visual characterization contradicts the verbal description, new dimensions open up. Hyman gives her version of Hauff's *King Stork* (1973) a feminist touch by using subtle pictorial details. The characters' relative size and mutual position on the page can demonstrate their power. Hyman offers an original interpretation in her *Peter Pan* wherein one picture depicts Peter's face in a close-up, confronted by the dying Tinker Bell. This is a piercing scene, showing, rather

ILLUSTRATION 477

unexpectedly, that the "innocent and heartless" Peter also has feelings. The difference in size emphasizes the impossibility of any relationship between Peter and Tinker Bell and the hopelessness and selflessness of her love. This single picture extracts more meaning from the text than all the rest.

Illustrations can also convey the characters' internal worlds and mental states, such as anxiety, fear, anger, anticipation, loneliness, or desire. In many cases, pictures provide information that the text omits, either for the sake of adaptation to the audience, or simply because folktales and fairy tales are action-oriented rather than character-oriented and thus are rarely focused on the character's inner life. An image or a sequence of images may expand one single phrase of the text, such as "She was very frightened" in Browne's *The Tunnel* (1989).

The portraits of monsters, **ogre**s, dangerous wild animals, and disfigured characters vary both with individual styles and with epochs and cultures. The wolf in "Little Red Riding Hood" can be a hideous wild brute, a **werewolf**, as some of the versions suggest, or a stylish, sexually appealing young man. The beast in "**Beauty and the Beast**" is rarely thoroughly scary and ugly, as the image is supposed to instigate the viewer's compassion, just as it does with Beauty. A genuinely repulsive creature would hardly be suitable. The frog in "The **Frog King**" can be made nice and almost attractive to appeal to the viewer's sympathy despite the princess's aversion. In *Thumbelina* (1997) by Arlene Graston, the tiny girl bears an explicit likeness to the woman in the beginning of the tale. This interpretation suggests that the story reflects a childless woman's longing for a baby, which definitely contradicts the original wherein Andersen easily gets rid of the poor woman. Illustrators also have the choice of omitting certain characters altogether, thus leaving their appearance to the viewer's imagination. This omission, or visual paralipsis, is a very effective device.

Symbols can be integrated into illustrations that point at certain interpretations. The fairy-tale allusions, for instance, in *The Tunnel* (Walter Crane's painting, the gingerbread house, the girl's red hooded cape, and a book of fairy tales) stress the nature of the text as a fairy tale. Some of the most interesting cases are also the most controversial ones. Sendak includes background images of the Holocaust in his picturebook *Dear Mili* (1988), based on a forgotten tale by Wilhelm Grimm.

Finally, artists can add details that provide a metafictional comment, which is either totally absent or only subtly implied in a story. Some versions of "Thumbelina" show Hans Christian Andersen as a response to the ending of the text that refers to the storyteller. Since many of Andersen's fairy tales contain an implicit theme of creativity, such details are congenial to the original. In his illustrations for Andersen's *What the Old Man Does Is Always Right* (2001), the Swedish illustrator Sven Nordqvist includes a parallel plot (a "running story," or syllepsis) featuring tiny animal characters in the foreground, whose adventures comment on the main story and produce a comic effect.

While many original illustrations in such books as *Alice's Adventures in Wonderland* and *The Wizard of Oz* are still used in modern editions, these books have also inspired later artists to offer their own interpretations. Tenniel no longer has exclusive rights to *Alice*, nor Shepard exclusive rights to *Winnie-the-Pooh*. Dozens of artists all over the world have ventured to challenge Tenniel in illustrating the Alice books, among them Arthur Rackham (1907), Mabel Lucie Attwell (1911), Mervyn Peak (1946), Michael Hague (1985), Anthony Browne (1989), Klaus Ensikat (1993), Helen Oxenbury (1999), Lisabeth Zwerger (1999), Jean-Claude Silbermann (2002), and Ralph Steadman (1973). Many contemporary illustrators have transformed Alice into a late-twentieth-century child by means of clothes. Oxenbury's round-faced, happily smiling Alice does not quite fit into the pattern of behavior of the original Alice. Zwerger's pictures strive to affect our visual perception in the same manner the words affect our mind. The distorted perspective, disturbing cut-offs, and other purely visual tricks are congenial to Carroll's verbal games. Of the numerous illustrators of the Alice books, few have ventured to play with images as the text plays with language. Anthony Browne includes many visual allusions, for instance, a portrait of William **Shakespeare**, as well as pictorial quotations from his own books.

When so many different illustrations exist, accompanying folktale, fairy-tale, and fantasy texts, a reasonable question is whether one can speak about classic, or standard, illustrations. We can perhaps intuitively feel that some illustrations are congenial to the texts; some contribute to further interpretations and open new dimensions; some are highly original while still others are derivative, bordering on plagiarism. We can further ask which of the numerous fairy-tale picture books can be counted as unique literary works in which text and image are so integrated that they no longer can exist without each other. *See also* Art; Cartoons and Comics; Graphic Novel.

Further Readings: Barr, John. *Illustrated Children's Books*. London: The British Library, 1986; Cianciolo, Patricia. *Illustrations in Children's Books*. Dubuque: Wm. C. Browne, 1970; Daniels, Morna. *Victorian Book Illustration*. London: The British Library, 1988; Feaver, William. *When We Were Young: Two Centuries of Children's Book Illustrations*. London: Thames and Hudson, 1977; Hürlimann, Bettina. *Picture-Book World: Modern Picture-Books for Children from Twenty-Four Countries*. Translated and edited by Brian W. Alderson. London: Oxford University Press, 1968; Lacy, Lyn Ellen. *Art and Design in Children's Picture Books: An Analysis of Caldecott Award-Winning Illustrations*. Chicago: American Library Association, 1986; Ovenden, Graham, and John Davis. *The Illustrators of Alice in Wonderland and Through the Looking Glass*. London: Academy Editions, 1979; Peppin, Brigid, and Lucy Micklethwait. *Dictionary of British Book Illustrators: The Twentieth Century*. London: Murray, 1983; Schwarcz, Joseph H. *Ways of the Illustrator: Visual Communication in Children's Literature*. Chicago: American Library Association, 1982; Stanton, Joseph. *The Important Books: Children's Picture Books as Art and Literature*. Lanham, MD: Scarecrow Press, 2005; Weinstein, Amy. *Once upon a Time: Illustrations from Fairytales, Fables, Primers, Pop-Ups and Other Children's Books*. New York: Princeton Architectural Press, 2005; Whalley, Joyce Irene, and Tessa Rose Chester. *A History of Children's Book Illustration*. London: John Murray, 1988.

Maria Nikolajeva

Imbriani, Vittorio (1840–1886)

Vittorio Imbriani was one of the most influential nineteenth-century scholars of the Italian **folk** tradition, studying **poetry**, songs, lore, and fairy tales. Imbriani embodied the philological and critical spirit of the new discipline of **folklore**, from his adherence to a rigorous methodology for **collecting** to his endorsement of Romantic ideas concerning folk poetry. He also coined the term "demopsicologia" to describe the new field of the history of folk traditions.

In his compilation *Canti popolari delle province meridionali* (*Popular Songs of the Southern Provinces*, 1871), for instance, Imbriani asserted, like the Brothers **Grimm** and others, that the works studied contained, in mediated form ("on the lips of the folk"), archaic cultural forms that had been created in the "poetic infancy" of Italy. As such, he maintained, their rediscovery and study was an essential ingredient in the informed creation of a modern national identity, which in those years was in the making in Italy.

Other important volumes include several of the first folktale and fairy-tale collections to appear in Italy during this period, *Novellaja fiorentina* (*Florentine Tales*, 1871) and *Novellaja milanese* (*Milanese Tales*, 1872). In these works, Imbriani professed absolute faithfulness to his sources through a methodology based on "stenographic transcription." Imbriani also wrote several original fairy tales, including "Mastr'Impicca" ("Master Hangman," 1871), and was one of the first, in 1875, to dedicate a serious critical study to Giambattista **Basile**'s *Lo cunto de li cunti* (*The Tale of Tales*, 1634–36). *See also* Italian Tales; Nationalism.

Further Reading: Cirese, Alberto Maria. "Paragrafi su Vittorio Imbriani demopsicologo." *Problemi: Periodico Quadrimestrale di Cultura* 80 (1987): 228–57.

Nancy Canepa

Inca Tales

Deeds of gods and old **king**s fill the oral literature of the Incas, much of which was written down at least in outline during the first eighty years following the Spanish conquest of Peru (1533). Complementing this older repertoire are **folktale**s and **legend**s collected in the 1900s in communities still speaking the imperial language, Quechua.

In pre-Conquest times, the official history of the empire, largely legendary, was sung by court poets, or *amautas*. The bundles of knotted strings, called *quipus,* known to have been used for statistical recordkeeping, might have served the poets as mnemonic aids, as did certain "pictures" said to have been stored in a "museum" in the capital, Cuzco.

History begins with the work of the creator, called Viracocha. According to one version, Viracocha appeared after the world flood, created humans, and then made the sun. When the sun, or Inti, rose for the first time, it called out to the newly created man Manco Capac, instructing him to found the Inca dynasty and build an empire. Inti, then, became the special deity of the Inca ruling class. Another version has it that Manco Capac was given a rod of gold and ordered to establish a city wherever the rod could be made to disappear with a single thrust. This important legend, still current, accounts for the founding of Cuzco.

Further legends concern the exploits of Manco Capac's successors. Particularly evocative are the stories of the latter-day kings Huayna Capac (d. 1525) and his son Atahualpa (d. 1533). In one tale, Huayna Capac orders his sepulcher after a messenger in black has brought him a chest filled with moths and butterflies. In another, Viracocha appears to Huayna Capac and instructs him to send to the underworld for a bride; the bride is fetched, but just as she arrives, the earth is aglow, and she and Huayna Capac vanish forever. Still another legend has Atahualpa consulting an oracle and learning that he will be destroyed; in a rage, he incinerates the priest of the oracle and allows the ashes to fly off in the wind.

Two well-developed Inca tales, both love stories, are "The Llama Herder Who Courted a Daughter of the Sun" and a complex narrative that may be called "Coniraya and Cahuillaca." In the first of these, the two principal characters are guilty lovers, who, when their secret is discovered, change into stone. The tale survives in heavily edited Spanish versions in Martín de Murúa's *Historia* (1590) and in the *Relación* (c. 1613) of Juan de Santacruz Pachacuti, who included it in the history of Manco Capac's immediate successor, Sinchi Roca (ruled about 1250). In the second of the two tales, the god Coniraya, also called Coniraya Viracocha, impregnates the goddess Cahuillaca and then, using the excuse that he must urinate, runs away—revealing the deity in his **trickster** aspect. The story survives in a Quechua manuscript from 1608, eventually published in Spanish, German, and English

Moche culture, Peru: Headdress element in the form of a fox head. [Photo by Michael Cavanagh and Kevin Montague, Indiana University Art Museum. Used by permission.]

editions, of which the most recent is Frank Salomon and George Urioste's *The Huarochirí Manuscript: A Testament of Ancient and Colonial Andean Religion* (1991).

Ill-fated love is a repeating theme in modern Quechua folktales. In "The Condor Seeks a Wife," a young shepherdess tires of her condor lover, who brings her only carrion and rotten potatoes, causing her to become foul-smelling; at length, she returns to her weeping **mother**, who cleanses her body with tears. In "The Moth," a jealous husband murders his wife after hearing that a friend sees her at night when he is away; too late he learns that the "friend" had been only a moth that came to her candle flame. "The Mouse Husband" tells of a diminutive bridegroom whose mouse fellows help him devour his catlike mother-in-law. And in "The Boy Who Rose to the Sky," a farmer's son finds a bride in the sky world only to have her abandon him—a tale so affecting that even the storyteller must conclude, "I feel the tears come into my eyes." This last is one of the stories collected by the novelist-ethnographer José María Arguedas (1911–69), one of the most admired of modern Peruvian folklorists. Though modeled in part after the Old World type ATU 550, Bird, Horse and Princess, the story of the boy and his lost bride, with its heavy-heartedness and abundant local color, projects a typical Andean flavor.

Trickster tales are not lacking in modern collections. In these, the central character is often Fox, who brags to Condor that he can outlast him in an endurance contest, but Condor, more quick-witted, wins. Or Fox envies Wren's melodious singing and borrows Wren's flutelike bill, with unfortunate results. Or Fox stuffs his tail into his trousers to court a woman, but the tail bursts out of his tight pants and the woman simply laughs. Each of these little stories has a counterpart in the trickster cycles of the Gran Chaco region of Paraguay and Argentina, indicating a South American origin even if the trickster's name, Fox, happens to coincide with European **Aesop** and **Reynard the Fox** traditions.

Among modern stories that recall the Inca past, the prophetic tale of the figure known as Inkarrí, a generic Inca king, is perhaps the most significant. In milder variants, Inkarrí uses a rod of gold to found the city of Cuzco, as in ancient lore, and then departs leaving footprints that do not disappear. More inflammatory versions have him surviving as a severed head, now growing a new body; when Inkarrí is fully formed he will return to lead a *pachacuti*, "revolution," restoring Peru to native hands. Campaigning in the highlands, modern Peruvian politicians have made symbolic use of this lore, promising a new age of Inkarrí, even a *pachacuti.* ***See also*** Latin American Tales.

Further Readings: Bierhorst, John. *Black Rainbow: Legends of the Incas and Myths of Ancient Peru.* New York: Farrar, Straus and Giroux, 1976; ———. *The Mythology of South America.* 2nd edition, revised. New York: Oxford University Press, 2002; Urton, Gary. *Inca Myths.* Austin: University of Texas Press, 1999.

John Bierhorst

Incantation

Incantations (charms, spells) are magic formulas that are supposed to have an effect on reality due to the supernatural power of spoken words. They are used to influence the weather, to protect oneself from accidents, to cure diseases, to keep predators away from the cattle, to ward off witchcraft, to summon or exorcise spirits, and for many other purposes. The power behind many incantations comes from invoking a mythical precedent in the past—a narrative or an episode that serves as a sacred model of the situation. Thus, a Germanic pagan incantation from the ninth or tenth century—one of the two charms known as the "Merseburger Zaubersprüche" (Merseburg Incantations)—refers to the god Odin healing the broken leg of a horse.

Fairy tales often include incantations as a part of the plot. Because fairy tales do not represent actual belief but depict a fantasy world, the magical effect of incantations gets exaggerated in them. In the **tale type** known as The Suitors Restore the Maiden to Life (ATU 653B), a dead woman is revived with the help of a magic formula. In The Forty **Thieves** (ATU 954), a mountain is opened when the magic words "Open, Sesame" are spoken. Many **legend**s confirm the belief in the power of incantations or give examples warning of their possible dangers. One migratory legend tells of an inexperienced user of a magic black book who summons the **devil** but cannot get rid of him. Later, the true magician returns and exorcises the devil. Johann Wolfgang von **Goethe** used the legend in his poem "Der Zauberlehrling" ("The Sorcerer's Apprentice," 1797), and Walt **Disney**, in the twentieth century, featured Mickey Mouse as the **sorcerer**'s apprentice in an episode in the movie *Fantasia* (1940). *See also* Magic Object.

Further Readings: Roper, Jonathan, ed. *Charms and Charming in Europe*. London: Palgrave, 2004; ———. *English Verbal Charms*. Helsinki: Academia Scientiarum Fennica, 2005.

Ülo Valk

Incest

The definition of incest is culturally variable, as are kinship systems, yet in some form incest figures prominently in many folktales and fairy tales (though it is rarely found in mainstream fairy tales). At its most basic, incest is the sexual union between two **family** members considered too closely related to marry. The **tale type**s characterized by incest tend to deal with sexual relationships within the nuclear family: **mother** and son, **father** and daughter, and sister and brother. The tales are broadly distributed around the world and range from humorous to serious. Four ways to classify tales dealing with incest are accidental incest averted, accidental incest consummated, intended incest averted, and intended incest consummated. These themes can be discussed within multiple analytical frames including psychoanalytic theory and feminist theory depending on whether the incest is interpreted symbolically or literally.

The culturally relative nature of incest leads to some variation in its treatment in folktales and fairy tales. For instance, the endogamous system of Palestinian Arabs encourages a male to marry his parallel first cousin—an arrangement that would be considered incestuous in many European cultures. However, as Ibrahim Muhawi and Sharif Kanaana demonstrate in *Speak, Bird, Speak Again: Palestinian Arab Folktales* (1989), folktales can both validate and critique this kinship arrangement. Because first-cousin **marriage**s are not considered incest within the culture, incest tales instead feature sexual relationships within the nuclear family. These relationships are also subject to variation between cultures. Hasan El-Shamy claims that the relationship between **brothers** and **sisters** in Arab cultures is of special importance within the family unit, whereas North American and European scholarship emphasizes vertical relationships within families.

Some tales that involve incest are humorous; indeed, this is common in **bawdy tale**s. Vance Randolph's *Pissing in the Snow and Other Ozark Folktales* (1976) and Aleksandr **Afanas'ev**'s *Russian Secret Tales: Bawdy Folktales of Old Russia* (1872) both contain humorous incest tales. In fact, Randolph's "Don't Call It Fucking" is cognate with Afanas'ev's "The Hot Cock," in that both feature a girl (perhaps unwittingly) asking her father for **sex**; he then punishes her by another method such that she refuses to have sex in the future unless it is called by an unfamiliar name. Two of Randolph's other tales depict nuclear families wherein the humor derives from the fact that not only are the mother and son and the father and daughter involved in sexual relations, but also the brother and the sister.

The bulk of folktales and fairy tales that treat incest as a topic, however, are serious, and these have received the most scholarly attention. Accidental incest tales function as part of the larger category of incest tales. Tales that depict accidental incest averted are rare. One example is ATU 674, Incest Averted by Talking Animals. Tales with accidental incest consummated have a slightly wider distribution, including ATU 938, Placidas, which has the unwitting incest of brother and sister, and ATU 931, Oedipus. The Oedipus tale is well known for its influence on Sigmund **Freud**'s notion of the Oedipus complex explaining the psychosexual development of male children, including a stage of attraction to the mother and antagonism toward the father.

Tales of intentional incest—both averted and consummated—provide another frame through which to view incest tales. Instances of intentional incest consummated are seen above in some of the bawdy tales, and in tale type ATU 705A, Born from Fruit (Fish), wherein a mother casts out her son's wife and dons the wife's attire to have sex with her son (bear in mind that the accidental/intentional distinction is intended solely as a helpful device for discussion, as this act of incest is intentional from the mother's perspective but accidental for the son).

Interestingly, tales of intentional incest averted tend to cluster along **gender** lines. Tale types ATU 920A* (The Inquisitive King) and 823A* (A Mother Dies of Fright When She Learns that She Was About to Commit Incest with Her Son) both feature a son seeking sexual relations with his mother to test her. In contrast, tale types ATU 510B (The Dress of Gold, of Silver, and of Stars [Cap o' Rushes]) and 706 (The Maiden without Hands) both depict a father seeking to wed his daughter, usually as a replacement for his deceased wife. Another family dynamic is portrayed in ATU 313E*, The Sister's Flight. In all of these cases, it is a male (whether young or old) who makes incestuous overtures to a female. The female character is forced to react, and the male figure is rarely punished despite the consequences his intentions (if not his actions) have on his kinswoman's life. Because the incest is prevented and social order upheld, there is no need to question patriarchal authority.

Interpreting incest in folktales and fairy tales is complicated. One must first determine whether the incest referred to is literal or metaphorical. Psychoanalytic scholars such as Alan **Dundes** read the incest as a manifestation of the Oedipus or Electra complexes in children. Through the device of projective inversion, the son who cannot admit he loves his mother or the daughter who cannot admit she desires her father can enjoy their parents' attention guiltlessly. In this outlook as in other **psychological approaches**, the tales are not about incest per se so much as a desire for connection. In contrast, scholars with a feminist bent view incest as very real and very problematic. Tales such as ATU 510B, "The Dress of Gold, of Silver, and of Stars (Cap o' Rushes)," convey a sexually abused girl's movement from victimhood to empowerment, as when she sheds her animal-skin disguise for a magical dress, signaling that she is ready to marry. The blend of fantastic and realistic elements complicates the interpretation of incest tales, and literal and metaphorical interpretations need not be viewed as mutually exclusive. Rather, the complexity of incest lends itself to multilayered meanings. *See also* Initiation; Trauma and Therapy; Violence.

Further Reading: Ashliman, D. L. *Incest in Indo-European Folktales.* 1997. http://www.pitt.edu/~dash/incest.html.

Jeana Jorgensen

Indian Ocean Tales

The five island groups lying east of Africa, in the southwest Indian Ocean—Madagascar, the Comoros, Mauritius, Réunion, and Seychelles—share a common stock of **folktale** tradition. Madagascar, the first island to be settled, received traditions from both Indonesia and East Africa. Its **epic** *Ibonia* expands the ordinary folktale plot, about a noble hero's search for a wife, by inserting African-style panegyric. The Islamic society of the Comoros, continually exchanging culture with Madagascar, links Arab and African traditions. Mauritius and Réunion (the "Mascarenes") acquired populations and tales from Africa, Europe, and India. In Réunion, today an overseas department of France, a few people remember classic French fairy tales from **oral tradition**—the stories of **Cinderella**, **Sleeping Beauty**, **Bluebeard**, and the Brave Little **Tailor**. The small island of Rodrigues acquired its African-derived population and tales from the abolition of slavery in Mauritius (1835).

African tales are ubiquitous. The two most popular, Hare at the Animals' Well (ATU 175, The Tarbaby and the Rabbit) and the defiant girl who must be rescued from her **marriage** to a **wolf**man, are well known in the southwest Indian Ocean. Seychelles is especially fond of the **trickster** Soungoula, whose name, derived from Kiswahili *sungura*, or hare, is a window into how islands without indigenous populations acquired a common stock of narratives. The trickster figure is central, both as a cultural memory and as a guide for real-life behavior. In a Mauritian version of The Jackal Trapped in the Animal Hide (ATU 68), once Hare has escaped from inside the dead elephant, he joins those who are mourning their **king**, declaring, "No one knows as I do what a good heart, what an excellent heart our king had" (Motif J261, Loudest mourners not greatest sorrowers)—this after he has been gnawing the elephant from the inside. To the mourners, his dialogue conveys his loyalty to the community; to the hearer, it is hilariously ambiguous. In a Mauritian version of Tarbaby, when Tortoise has outwitted the trickster Hare by getting him stuck to his shell with tar, he carries Hare to the king for dinner, where he wisecracks, "Cooked with wine, it's not bad." Through verbal victories, the creole trickster—who may be a human or an animal—both defeats his enemies and cheats his neighbors. In the Madagascar highlands, the trickster is a pair of characters, Wiley and Cheatam, whose every move honors interdependence (they depend on each other) and betrays it (they cheat everybody else). As in East Africa, the Indian Ocean trickster affords the hearer an opportunity to fantasize about escaping the realities of oppression and social restrictions.

Marriage is the most important of themes found in Indian Ocean tales. The defiant girl learns to value her birth **family** over any husband. Especially in the Comoros, reliance on solid relationships between mothers and daughters contrasts with the instability of marriage relations, where the woman is in a man's hands. In some Comoran tales, a young orphan girl is mistreated by another woman to the point of real or symbolic **death**. Then, at her extreme of despair, thanks to the supernatural intervention of her dead **mother**, she is recognized and reelevated to first place.

Imported international story material is adapted to preexisting cultural emphases. One Mauritian tale remodels The Magic Flight (ATU 313). Both Madagascar and Mayotte (in the Comoros) know the tale of The Four Skillful Brothers (ATU 653). Mauritius, Seychelles, and Réunion have the humorous tale, The Smith and the Devil (ATU 330), in which the smith outwits the **devil**; the versions show strong European influence. Madagascar and Mauritius know the story of Midas and the Donkey's Ears (ATU 782), which gives a poor barber more magical power than the king.

Like the region's languages, folktales in these islands are creolized, or syncretic; they combine diverse traditions. Réunionnais *petits blancs*, Mauritian creoles, Seychellois, Comorans, and even Malagasy have inherited multiple cultural repertoires. Mauritius and Mayotte know the Indian tale of "Sabour," which begins in a **riddle**: a daughter says "Sobur" (wait) to her **father** when he asks what to bring from his journey (Motif J1805.2.1). Until he finds Prince Sobur, the father does not know that his daughter will make a rich marriage. The dialogue of genres and the play on his verbal ignorance are especially appropriate in multilingual Mauritius, where jokes often turn on misunderstandings of language. The Seychelles version of the Blind Man and the Hunchback (Motif N886, Blind man carries lame man) most clearly illustrates what happens when different traditions meet. Though at first Blind Man and Hunchback dispute with each other, in the central action they act as loyal to each other as the twin tricksters of Madagascar. They are pitted against *loulou*, "King of the spirits" (from Malagasy *lolo*, a spirit, and French *loup*, wolf). The two hide upstairs in his house and attack him, a **motif** (K1161) that is the key moment of ATU 130, The Animals in Night Quarters (that is, The Bremen Town Musicians). Once they defeat him, they find money and begin arguing again; their fistfight cures their ailments. Blind Man is so thankful to Bondyé (God) that the two stop arguing and decide to cut God in for a share of the money. African, European Christian, and Malagasy elements combine.

Folktale research in the southwest Indian Ocean has been irregular and intermittent. Hundreds of tales are known from Madagascar, and a few dozen from Mauritius, Réunion, and Seychelles. No **collecting** has been done in the Comoran islands of Mohéli or Anjouan. Much remains to be discovered in this region about the nature of cultural mixing. Meanwhile, books of stories are being published for children in local languages. *See also* French Tales; Négritude, Créolité, and Folktale.

Further Readings: Auleear, Dawood, and Lee Haring, trans. and ed. *Indian Folktales from Mauritius.* Chennai, India: National Folklore Support Centre, 2006; Baissac, Charles. *Sirandann, sanpek: Zistwar en kreol; Baissac's l888 collection.* Port Louis, Mauritius: Ledikasyon pu Travayer, 1989. English translation of *Le folk-lore de l'île Maurice.* Paris, 1888; Blanchy, Sophie, and Zaharia Soilihi. *Furukombe et autres contes de Mayotte.* Paris: Éditions Caribéennes, 1991; *Contes, devinettes et jeux de mots des Seychelles: Zistwar ek zedmo sesel.* Paris: Éditions Akpagnon, 1983; Haring, Lee, ed. *Indian Ocean Folktales: Madagascar, Comoros, Mauritius, Réunion, Seychelles.* Chennai, India: National Folklore Support Centre, 2002; Renel, Charles. *Contes de Madagascar.* 3 volumes. Paris: Ernest Leroux, 1910–30.

Lee Haring

Infertility

Many folktales and fairy tales are set against a backdrop of reproductive failure. While often infertility functions as a narrative device to precipitate action unrelated to procreation, it is more commonly developed as a dominant **motif**, one that underscores the implications of childlessness in social, psychological, and religious contexts. The desperation that fuels the characters in these tales is driven by disapproval, jealousy, fear, loneliness, and desire. While modern solutions to infertility rely heavily on science and technology, folktale and fairy-tale heroes and heroines exploit the means available to them: magic, prayer, adoption, folk remedy, and bargaining with the **devil**. Faith in God merits the gift of a long-desired child in the Indian tale "The **Cat** Who Became **Queen**," while the love of an adoptive parent can transform a pumpkin, crab, or **blood** clot into a beloved son or daughter. Selfish child-desire and greed ruin **marriage**s and make insatiable monster-children out of clay, excrement, and even a tree stump in *Otesánek* (*Little Otik*, 2000), a film **adaptation** (directed by Jan Svankmajer) of an old Czech folktale.

The definition of infertility in the context of folktales and fairy tales is broad enough to include couples who have produced daughters but not sons. The Turkish tale "The Magic **Mirror**" makes it clear that a childless **king** must have a male heir; if a female is born, **mother** and child will be executed. **Women** suffer cruelly when they are considered barren. In the African tale "The Guinea Fowl Child," a childless woman is discarded by her husband, scorned by her co-wife, and finally rewarded with the love of a resourceful son. The infertile often seek magic remedies and give **birth** to snakes, snails, pots, apples, twigs, and even a beast of burden in "The Camel Husband" from Palestine. Both spouses utter urgent pleas for a child no matter its condition. In Jacob and Wilhelm **Grimm**'s "Hans My Hedgehog" and Giovan Francesco **Straparola**'s "The **Pig** King," fathers beg for a child; when their careless **wish**es come true, they reject their prickly animal sons. "Tulugaq, Who Was Barren" is an Inuit tale in which a woman wants a child more than anything; unfortunately, she delivers a monster that kills everyone who looks upon it. A pact with an evil magician in the Egyptian tale "The Maghrabi's Apprentice" separates a child from his parents; their son must win his own independence before the **family** is reunited. "The Good Fortune Kettle" from Japan tells of a lonely old man and wife who befriend a wounded fox and are rewarded with riches and a grateful daughter. God, devil, magic, and human ingenuity are the prized weapons in the war against the cruelest of all domestic tragedies—facing the future alone and without heirs.

See also Animal Bride, Animal Groom; Birth; Childhood and Children; Gender.

Further Readings: Beck, Brenda E. F., et al., eds. *Folktales of India*. Chicago: University of Chicago Press, 1987. 59–62; Muhawi, Ibrahim, and Sharif Kanaana. *Speak Bird, Speak Again: Palestinian Folktales*. Berkley: University of California Press, 1989. 81–84, 227–229; Sindiga, Isaac, Chacha Nyaigotti-Chacha, and Mary Peter Kanuanah. *Traditional Medicine in Africa*. Nairobi: East Africa Educational, 1995. 81–84.

Joanna Beall

Informant

An informant is the person from whom a folklorist collects narratives, songs, objects, information, or other folkloric texts and materials during **fieldwork**. In the nineteenth century, when **folklore** began developing as a scholarly discipline, Jacob and Wilhelm **Grimm** were among the first to promote the recording of narratives told by informants. Early folklorists such as the Grimms (who collected tales from both informants and printed sources) did not always clearly identify their informants, although they would typically locate tales regionally or geographically. As fieldwork methods developed, researchers began noting the names of their informants and other sociocultural information about them and the **context** in which the tales were told. However, when it came to recording a narrative, **collectors** and **editors** throughout the nineteenth century often bowdlerized the text to fit their own research or political interests and ethics. For example, one of the most renowned informants of the Brothers Grimm was Dorothea Viehmann, a middle-class French Huguenot from whom the brothers collected a significant number of tales for their ***Kinder- und Hausmärchen*** (*Children's and Household Tales,* 1812–15). Viehmann's tales were subsequently adapted to better fit the German Romantic ideology the Grimms were trying to render through their collection.

Contemporary folklorists are now more careful to make more accurate recordings—frequently using audiovisual technology—and to produce collections that more objectively or accurately reflect the culture being observed. The folklorist will be as specific as possible about the informant, the context of the informant's **performance**, and the informant's cultural environment and background. The transmission of a recorded tale must also be verbatim. With the development of performance theory, some folklorists started to use the word "consultant" instead of "informant" since it better represents the research as a collaborative work in which both the folklorist and the informant become partners.

Further Reading: Jackson, Bruce. *Fieldwork.* Urbana: University of Illinois Press, 1987.

Charlotte Trinquet

Ingelow, Jean (1820–1897)

Jean Ingelow was a Victorian poet and novelist who wrote several fairy tales for children. Early in her career, she wrote a number of **didactic tale**s, which she published in a series of volumes in the 1860s. Later, she also wrote *Mopsa the Fairy* (1869).

Several of Ingelow's children's stories appearing in *Stories Told to a Child* (1865) and other volumes borrowed fairy themes from **folktale**s, presenting them as vehicles for **moral** lessons. Although some stories are presented as allegories, in which fairies represent ideals, many other tales instead embody recognizable fairy **motif**s but are still written to illustrate moral precepts.

However, Ingelow's most noted fairy work, *Mopsa the Fairy,* avoids didacticism entirely. Published in the wake of Lewis **Carroll**'s *Alice in Wonderland* (1865) and Christina **Rossetti**'s "Goblin Market" (1865), *Mopsa* abandons instruction in favor of a fantasy loosely inspired by fairy lore. Honesty and kindness are still important ideals to the characters, but the events of the story are related without moral commentary. The novella begins when a young boy, Jack, finds a nest of fairies in a tree, resembling a nest of baby birds. There is no parent; most fairies in the story consider Fate their mother. The fairies begin to mature before his eyes and instruct him to take them to Fairyland, which he does by riding an albatross. Eventually Jack learns Fairyland is the mortal world, a millennium before the advent of humanity, rather than a separate place.

Mopsa is filled with dreamlike images; for instance, one group of characters spends their days as stones, which resemble living things and come to life only at twilight, when the growing shadows make them appear more lifelike. There are also nightmarish elements; in one scene, an adolescent fairy is eaten by a magpie. When Jack kisses Mopsa, another of the young fairies, she begins to develop human traits, including self-awareness and a mortal physique. A fairy queen tells Jack that the love of mortals changes fairies. Mopsa and Jack travel through Fairyland, which is composed of several countries, and finally arrive in the realm she is fated to rule. With Jack's help, she lifts a curse on the fairies living there and becomes their queen. To allow Jack to leave, Mospa returns his kiss, after which he is shut out of fairy society.

A constant theme of the story is the difference between fairies and mortals; for example, fairies have two forms, one human and the other animal. While fairies naturally create magic and **transformation**, most cannot laugh or cry without a mortal's example. They act and speak, but most cannot think for themselves, and are guided only by instinct. Although they witness day and night, fairies do not experience time as mortals do; therefore, when Jack returns home, his parents have not missed him. Many critics point out that *Mopsa*'s fairies live in an irrational world suggestive of **myth** and the unconscious mind. *See also* Children's Literature; Faerie and Fairy Lore.

Further Reading: Peters, Maureen. *Jean Ingelow: Victorian Poetess.* Totowa, NJ: Rowman and Littlefield, 1972.

Paul James Buczkowski

Initiation

Initiation is both a staple theme and a structural feature of **wonder tale**s. It is a staple insofar as most tales depict, in one form or the other, initiation into adult life; it is a structural feature in light of isomorphism, noted by various researchers, between the pattern of tales and the framework of rites of passage.

When Vladimir **Propp** famously suggested in *Morfologiya skazki* (*Morphology of the Folktale*, 1928) that all wonder tales share a common morphology, he retraced this constant form to the pattern of initiation rites. Jan de Vries, in his *Betrachtungen zum Märchen* (*Observations on the Fairy Tale*, 1954), proposed to explain identity of pattern among wonder tales, **epic** tales, and **myth**s in light of common derivation from initiation rites. Lord Raglan (in 1934) showed a definite hero life pattern in myths, **folktale**s, and **legend**s, which he retraced to ritual; and Alan Dundes (in 1976) recognized in Propp's morphological model the wonder-tale guise of the hero life pattern. Joseph Campbell, in his popular *Hero with a Thousand Faces* (1949), described the hero biography pattern in terms of initiation quest. And as early as 1923, Pierre Saintyves had submitted in *Les contes de Perrault* that tales rewritten by Charles **Perrault** originate in rites of passage, both seasonal and biographic.

Saintyves's association of wonder tales to both biographic rites (which bring about passages in linear **time**, from **birth** to **death**) and seasonal rites (which are cyclic) may appear counterintuitive. Yet, although one's life appears to be a straight line from cradle to grave, biographic rites of passage express cyclic time as much as seasonal rites do. When Arnold van Gennep famously defined rites of passage as ceremonies that accompany changes of place, state, social position, and age (as well as periodic time changes), he pointed out the underlying idea that such transitions involve the proverbial sloughing off of the old skin, along with moon symbolism. In other words, the threefold sequence of separation, margin, and aggregation that, as van Gennep showed, is characteristic of rites of passage implies the notion of cyclic transition through temporary death, **transformation**, and rebirth.

Indeed, the folk view of rites of passage scarcely reflects in the sociological abstraction of persons moving through structural positions in a linear frame. Rather, it is usually about ontological transformation. This is especially conspicuous in initiation ceremonies into social maturity, which hinge on biological mutation. Victor Turner noted that neophytes everywhere are associated with the cyclic symbolism of death and growth. Thus, they are put into huts and tunnels that are at once tombs and wombs, and are stripped naked in reference to both corpses and newborn infants. Importantly, he notes, neophytes during their ontological transformation are supposedly brought into close connection with supernatural power, often expressed by masks. Such symbols of transformation combine features of both sexes, have both animal and human attributes, and generally combine opposites in peculiar configurations, which Turner dubs "the monster or **dragon**."

All this is reminiscent of wonder tales. Remarkably, Propp not only retraced the morphology of tales to the pattern of initiation rites, he also proposed the entire store of wonder tales is a chain of transformations centering on the archetypical theme of the Dragon Slayer. Thus, Propp's contribution implies interconnection between the initiation pattern and the dragon theme at the core of wonder tales. This is relevant insofar as the dragon is one paradigmatic image of cyclic time. Indeed, the dragon image of time forever rewinding itself through periodic death and rebirth is of the essence of disenchantment transitions in wonder tales, as much as of ontological transformation in initiation rituals. Wonder tales express the life thread of heroes and heroines in the transformative perspective of cyclic time, which is why the dragon figure (in its many avatars) is at their core.

Although the authors who recognized isomorphism between wonder tales and initiation rites tended to assume that tales derive from ritual, this remains an unproven claim. Still, wonder tales and initiation rites do share concern for ontological transformations in a cyclic framework. For this reason, death in tales is a prelude to new beginnings—not something terminal. Such is the basis of this genre's celebrated optimism, and why wonder tales depict only the rising part of the hero life pattern.

Indeed, the enchantment/disenchantment leitmotiv is about puberty and initiation into adulthood, which is why wonder tales find their apex in successful **marriage**. Marriage, of course, supposes two life threads; and tales do take a stereoscopic approach to this crucial life passage. Bengt **Holbek** showed that in almost any given tale, there are two interdependent biographic threads from blood ties to marriage. When the bereft hero or heroine passes a maturity test and goes off to another realm, there to set free a secluded youth of the opposite **sex** and achieve a blissful marriage, initiation into adulthood is enacted on the side of the destitute character as well as on the side of the confined persona. This means each of them goes through symbolic death and rebirth (into the otherworld or enchantment) as both pass into adulthood.

This would explain the sheer frequency of **incest, blood,** and **cannibalism** in wonder tales, even up to Jacob and Wilhelm **Grimm**'s collection. In tales as in rites, the watershed passage between youth and adulthood is really a bloodshed. Bloodletting typically marks transitions between confinement in blood relations, rife with incest and cannibal connotations, and a marriage-apt adult life. Overall, death, blood, and strife abound in wonder tales. But, in this optimistic genre, they are means to initiation into a transcending realm of a higher life. *See also* Age.

Further Readings: Dundes, Alan, Lord Raglan, and Otto Rank. *In Quest of the Hero.* Princeton: Princeton University Press, 1990; Gennep, Arnold van. *The Rites of Passage.* Translated by Monika B. Vizedom and Gabrielle L. Caffee. London: Routledge & Kegan Paul, 1960; Holbek, Bengt. *Interpretation of Fairy Tales: Danish Folklore in a European Perspective*. 1987. Helsinki: Academia Scientiarum Fennica, 1998; Turner, Victor W. "Betwixt and Between: The Liminal Period in *Rites de Passage*." *The Forest of Symbols*. Ithaca, NY: Cornell University Press, 1977. 93–111.

Francisco Vaz da Silva

Innocenti, Roberto (1940–)

A masterful Italian illustrator, Roberto Innocenti is known internationally for his exquisite paintings and **illustration**s. Narrating via unforgettable images, Innocenti demonstrates a rare ability to enrich tales through his graphic artwork. Innocenti is a self-taught artist who has illustrated books by E. T. A. **Hoffmann**, Charles **Perrault**, Charles **Dickens**, Oscar **Wilde**, Carlo **Collodi**, and many others. Among Innocenti's most remarkable illustrations are those for ***Cinderella*** (1983), *The Adventures of Pinocchio* (1988), and *Nutcracker* (1996).

In his picture book *Rose Blanche* (1985), written with Christophe Gallaz, Innocenti portrays the sinister Nazi regime and the Holocaust from the perspective of a young German girl. The heroine, Rose Blanche (who shares her name with the German resistance movement Weiße Rose—White Rose), tragically dies while assisting prisoners in a concentration camp near her home. Innocenti's realistic illustrations stand in stark contrast to the simplistic prose of the book, offering young readers a way to discuss the horrors of inconceivable events. Innocenti's collaboration with J. Patrick Lewis on *The Last Resort* (2002) showcased both small, detailed pictures and two-page sweeping panoramic illustrations that bring to life the allegorical tale of an artist who travels to a mysterious seaside resort to recover his lost imagination. In 2002, the *New York Times* lauded Innocenti as one of the world's finest children's illustrators.

Further Reading: O'Sullivan, Emer. "Rose Blanche, Rosa Weiss, Rosa Blanca: A Comparative View of a Controversial Picture Book." *Lion and the Unicorn* 29 (2005): 152–70.

Gina M. Miele

Internet

The digital revolution in the last quarter of the twentieth century gave way to new means of communication, new ways of telling tales, and new dimensions in researching narrative culture, especially since personal computers and local networks became connected to each other in a worldwide web called the Internet. In the 1980s, digital communication took off when a growing number of people were able to afford personal computers and modems and began using e-mail, joining mailing lists, and visiting newsgroups, such as Usenet for example. The 1990s brought many improvements to personal computers, modems, communication software, and Internet service providers. Not only could plain messages be sent by e-mail, but so could larger files with text, pictures, animated gifs (photos with moving details), and animation. Internet browsers such as Mosaic, Netscape, and Explorer were being developed; Web pages gained more visual features and symbols; and hyperlinks led to unprecedented **intertextuality**. Sites with discussion forums also appeared on the Web, and it was in this era that the first **folktale** collections and databases were published on the Internet.

In the twenty-first century, hardware and software became cheaper and faster. Chatting on the Internet became very popular, especially among children and adolescents. At first, conversations in chat rooms consisted of participants typing and sending text to each other, but software such as PalTalk and MSN Messenger made live chat sessions possible with the use of a microphone and a webcam. Meanwhile, mobile phones could function as small computers themselves, sending e-mail by Short Messaging Services (SMS) and mailing pictures and small movies by Multimedia Messaging Services (MMS). These mobile phone messages are good for sending **joke**s, **riddle**s, and funny pictures. A new MSN and SMS language evolved, using abbreviations (for example, lol = laughing out loud; CU l8er = see you later) and emoticons (smileys).

Within a quarter of a century, the possibilities for storing and exchanging folk narratives digitally have expanded dramatically, and technological developments have turned the world into a "global village" where English is the foremost lingua franca. The democratic medium of the Internet has made it possible for many to share their stories with others. Due to the Internet, tales travel faster than ever. A story can now be disseminated around the world in just a few seconds. The exchange of jokes and contemporary or **urban legend**s is a popular pastime among youngsters and inside office culture. The enormous expansion of folkloristic and folk-narrative material on the Internet is making it more difficult to retrieve the information one is looking for, and therefore the importance of search engines like Yahoo and Google is increasing. It seems as if all information can be found on the World Wide Web. More data are added every day, and we sometimes tend to forget that data are changing, moving to other addresses, or even disappearing completely. A joke, a piece of Photoshop lore (a funny, manipulated digital picture), or a discussion on the subject of urban legendry can be here today and gone tomorrow. Google's cache is often a last resort before folkloristic bits and bytes disappear permanently. The Internet even has a patron saint, who is, as far as legend goes, Isidore of Seville (c. 560–636).

Folktale Collections

One of the earliest (1994) and still one of the finest folktale collections is the German Gutenberg Project, which as of 2006 contained some 1,600 **fairy tale**s, 1,200 **fable**s, and 2,500 **legend**s (http://gutenberg.spiegel.de/index.htm). The Gutenberg Web site includes, for instance, the fables of **Aesop**, the fairy tales of Hans Christian **Andersen**, a fairy-tale collection of Ludwig **Bechstein**, the *Decameron* (1349–50) of Giovanni **Boccaccio**, the fables of Jean de **La Fontaine**, the *Kinder- und Hausmärchen* (*Children's and Household Tales*, 1812–15) and the *Deutsche Sagen* (*German Legends*, 1816–18) of Jacob and Wilhelm **Grimm**, the *Volksmärchen der Deutschen* (*Folktales of the Germans*, 1782–86) of Johann Karl August **Musäus**, fairy tales of Charles **Perrault**, and the *Deutsche Hausmärchen* (*German Household Tales*, 1851) of Johann Wilhelm Wolf. The English version of the Gutenberg Project contains several of these works in English, as well as the ***Arabian Nights***, the French *Contes* of Marie-Catherine d'**Aulnoy**, stories from Giambattista **Basile**'s *Lo cunto de li cunti* (*The Tale of Tales*, 1634–36), Geoffrey **Chaucer**'s *Canterbury Tales*, Thomas Malory's *Le Mort d'Arthur* (1485), an edition of the **jest**s of **Nasreddin** Hoca, the *Edda* by Snorri Sturluson, and a collection of slave narratives from Arkansas, Florida, Georgia, Indiana, Kansas, Kentucky, Maryland, Mississippi, and Ohio (http://www.gutenberg.org/wiki/Main_Page). A fine collection of folktales can be found on D. L. Ashliman's site called *Folklore and Mythology: Electronic Texts* (http://www.pitt.edu/~dash/folktexts.html) and on David K. Brown's site, *Folklore, Myth and Legend* (http://www.ucalgary.ca/~dkbrown/

storfolk.html). Of course, there are many Web pages dedicated to a single oeuvre, such as the one containing the works of Hans Christian Andersen (http://hca.gilead.org.il) and the one with a translation of the Latin *Facetiae* (1470) of Gian Francesco Poggio Bracciolini (http://www.elfinspell.com/PoggioTitle.html). The epic of *The Wedding of Mustajbey's Son Bećirbey*, as performed by the Bosnian singer Halil Bajgorić, can be experienced in an original transcript, with an English translation, introduction, and comments and with the authentic audio file (http://www.oraltradition.org/zbm).

Many Web sites around the world present the local legends of a region or town. These sites are built by private persons as a hobby and by local organizations to promote **tourism**.

Modern genres such as urban legends and jokes are collected on the Internet as well. The most famous site on urban legends is the *Urban Legends References Pages*, also known as *Snopes* (http://www.snopes.com), which contains thousands of versions and for every story tries to determine whether it is true or false (or somewhere in between). Apart from this site, there are *Urbanlegends.com* (http://urbanlegends.com), David Emery's pages on *Urban Legends and Folklore* (http://urbanlegends.about.com), the site of *Scambusters* (http://www.scambusters.org/legends.html), and the *Urban Legends & Modern Myths* site (http://www.warphead.com/modules/news/). *Vmyths* is a site that deal particularly with digital chain letters containing virus hoaxes (http://www.vmyths.com). There are so many private sites with collections of jokes and funny pictures that it is impossible to summarize them all. *Jokes Galore* (http://www.jokesgalore.com) and *JokeCenter* (http://www.jokecenter.com) serve as just two examples.

All of these sites provide researchers with a great deal of textual material that can be read, downloaded, and, with the appropriate software, put into databases, indexed, or researched—for example, with respect to word frequencies. To perform comparative research, folklorists still have to do much work themselves. Furthermore, a lot of traditional material constitutes literature, not transcripts of oral transmission; and if sites do present oral material, contextual information is very often lacking. For instance, there is often no indication of when and where the story was told and by whom. Neither do such sites state to which **tale type** the story belongs according to international catalogues by Antti **Aarne**, Stith **Thompson**, and Hans-Jörg Uther. It seems that only small countries such as the Netherlands and Flanders (the northern half of Belgium) are building folktale databases that meet the more specific needs of folk-narrative researchers. Both the *Nederlandse Volksverhalenbank* (*Dutch Folktale Database*, http://www.verhalenbank.nl) and the *Vlaamse Volksverhalenbank* (*Flemish Folktale Database*, http://www.volksverhalenbank.be) allow scholars to search on keywords, names, genres, provinces, places, and dates. Many of the folktales stem from **oral tradition**, are catalogued according to the internationally acknowledged typology, and are contextualized with information about the narrator. These databases take digital archiving and retrievability a step further: they serve as advanced research instruments and can be consulted from all over the world. The single disadvantage is that the databases are available only in Dutch, not in English.

At the moment, folktales from Western cultures are most easily obtained from the Internet. For comparative research there is still a great need for English translations—for example, of traditional Asian folktales such as the Indian **Jātaka**s (third century BCE) and the **Japanese tales** in the *Konjaku monogatari* (*Tales of Times Now Past*, early twelfth century). On the other hand, there is no decent edition of Johannes Pauli's *Schimpf und Ernst* (*Ridiculous and Serious*, 1522) to be found on the Web either.

In addition to these primary sources—that is, texts of folktales and fairy tales—on the Internet, there is also an abundance of Web sites with secondary information about subjects such as folklore and narrativity, mythology, and fairy tales and legends. Examples of these include the *Encyclopedia Mythica* (http://www.pantheon.org), *Myths & Legends* (http://www.myths.com/pub/myths/myth.html), D. L. Ashliman's *Folklinks: Folk and Fairy-Tale Sites* (http://www.pitt.edu/~dash/folklinks.html), and the site on *Irish Literature, Mythology, Folklore, and Drama* (http://www.luminarium.org/mythology/ireland).

Narrating on the Net

In the above cases, the Internet functions more or less as a worldwide digital library. The Internet also can be used as a virtual place to tell stories. For instance, personal narratives or **memorate**s can be found on a variety of weblogs. Riddles, jokes, (urban) legends, and rumors are told on mailing lists and in newsgroups, discussion forums, and chat rooms. When legends are told by someone as being true stories, a discussion often follows with other members of the group on the reliability of the story. There are certain newsgroups specializing in narrative subjects, such as alt.jokes, alt.humor, alt.folklore.ghost-stories, and many more. Some specialized Web sites have their own forums, where narratives can be found on subjects like ethnicity, **fantasy**, the paranormal, hauntings, UFOs, crop circles, and the End of Days. Particularly in newsgroups, mailing lists, and discussion forums, folk- narrative researchers can operate as invisible **fieldwork**ers simply by "lurking" (reading but not participating in the discussion). One of the disadvantages of communication on the Internet, however, is that one can never be sure of the identity of the narrator. Most participants present themselves with a "handle" or nickname and create their own virtual identity through "avatars" (little pictures that are meant to represent some part of their personality) and mottos. One cannot even be sure whether a participant is male or female, or young or old. For this, one needs to follow live chat sessions in which webcams are used. Another way to study human interaction and **storytelling** was facilitated by the (originally Dutch) **television** program *Big Brother*, in which a group of people was voluntarily locked into a house and surrounded by cameras and microphones. All of their actions, pranks, jokes, and memorates could be followed online, twenty-four hours a day, thanks to live video streams on the Internet.

Probably the most popular form of virtual storytelling, especially among youngsters and office workers, is sending textual and visual jokes by e-mail. The oldest visual jokes consisted of ASCII-drawings (http://www.asciiartfarts.com/20060423.html). One of the advantages of virtual joking is that one no longer needs to be a gifted narrator. All that is necessary is the ability to cut and paste or just to forward a funny text. The computer will keep every binary byte in its place, while the sender can still gain prestige as an amusing person. One of the disadvantages is that many jokes no longer show variation, whereas in oral transmission, the narrator would improvise (after all, only a punch line needs to be memorized) and adapt the joke to his or her liking and to that of the audience. Still, there are digital jokes circulated that are altered, reworked, and enhanced—for instance a funny list of differences between men and women.

The digital revolution made another form of visual joking possible: Photoshop lore. Photoshop is one of the most popular computer programs with which images are manipulated. Actually, Photoshop lore is in many ways the successor of the well-known XeroxCopy lore. In the past, people copied funny pictures and **cartoons** and distributed them on paper. The digital distribution of Photoshop lore and the oral transmission of traditional jokes have some features in common: (1) The original maker of the joke remains anonymous most of the time. (2) The joke is transmitted from person to person(s). (3) The joke comments on subjects that—at least according to the narrator and audience—really matter in present-day society. (4) The Photoshop joke deals with the same taboos, frustrations, prejudices, and fantasies as the traditional oral joke. (5) As in traditional joking, Photoshop jokes are recycled every once in a while: lying politicians, for instance, have repeatedly been depicted as Pinocchio with a long nose. The phenomenon of Photoshop lore has existed since the late 1990s, as soon as enough people were able to receive e-mails with attachments. Still, its popularity increased after the terrorist attacks on the World Trade Center and the Pentagon on September 11, 2001. E-mailboxes in the Western world immediately became inundated with Photoshop humor about the Twin Towers, George W. Bush, Osama bin Laden, Afghanistan, al-Qaida, and Muslim terrorism in general. Since then, Photoshop lore has been made on every subject worth joking about; there even exist Internet contests. The visualization of jokes has not stopped at pictures: they are disseminated as PowerPoint presentations, Macromedia animations, and QuickTime movies as well.

As far as narrating on the Internet is concerned, it appears that the telling of jokes, riddles, rumors, and (urban) legends is more popular than telling a traditional fairy tale. Every now and again, fairy-tale parodies (see **Parody**) surface, both as texts and as pictures. Sexual relationships between fairy-tale figures from Disney seem to be especially favored, for instance between **Beauty and the Beast** or **Snow White** and the seven dwarfs.

Another old form of folklore has infested the Internet: the chain letter. The e-mail must be forwarded to multiple persons to avoid (personal) harm and bring about happiness and good fortune. Sometimes it is necessary to forward the e-mail to raise money for a sick child who needs an operation. In other cases, Bill Gates will reward people with a large sum of money for testing his new e-mail tracking software. Of course, these are all hoaxes, as are the many alerts for computer viruses that never come. The first e-mail of this kind started circulating in 1994 as a warning against the (nonexistent) Good Times virus. Many of these virus alerts followed (Irina, Deeyenda, Join the crew, Penpal greetings, It Takes Guts to Say "Jesus," Your friend D@fit, etc.). Most of the time, it is said that opening the e-mail will cause a virus to forward itself to everyone in the address book and to erase all of their hard drives. Companies such as IBM, AOL, Microsoft, and McAfee are mentioned to make the message more believable. In some cases, the e-mail advises recipients to delete a certain file when present, after which the users soon find out they did not erase a virus but a part of the standard Windows software. As a reaction to the virus hoaxes, obvious parodies or antilegends circulated, in which the virus was said to wipe out all of your credit cards, date your girlfriend, and drink all of your beer. Another story that dupes the unwary is the so-called Nigerian Scam. The reader is requested by a very polite, well-educated, and mostly Christian official to help transfer millions of dollars out of the country by opening a trustworthy bank account. The reward will be tremendous, but the reader must first pay a certain amount of money for the associated costs of the transaction. It goes without saying that the victim will never see a penny in return.

A final example of narrating on the Net deals with the neglected genre of the "situation puzzle," also known as the "albatross story" or "kwispel." A "kwispel" is a narrative riddle game in which the narrator or riddler in a few words unveils the mysterious conclusion of a story and asks what happened, whereupon it is up to the audience to unravel the entire plot of the story by asking questions that can only be answered by "yes" or "no." Here is a classic clue the riddler might give: "A man lies dead in his room. On the floor are sawdust and small pieces of wood. What happened?" The game is often played by adolescents, those on vacation, or friends around a campfire. Recently, the game has been played on the Internet by members of a Yahoo mailing list: the contestants were allowed to ask five questions in one e-mail. The solution of the above riddle was: The dead man on the floor was a blind midget and worked in a circus. He was famous for being the shortest man on earth. A jealous competitor secretly sawed small pieces of wood from the blind midget's cane, as well as from the legs of his chairs, his table, and so forth. This made the midget believe that he had started to grow and that, soon, he would no longer be the smallest midget on earth. Finally, in his despair, he committed suicide (and now the competitor is the smallest midget on earth). This is a good example of interactive storytelling in cyberspace.

Playing Tales

Finally, it is not only possible to tell or listen to a tale. Thanks to computer technology, one can also play and experience a tale—at least in virtual reality. Soon after consumers started buying personal computers, the first computer games were developed. Today, the game industry is making more money than the film industry. Many games—especially adventure games—take their themes, **motif**s, and structures from fairy tales, **myth**s, and legends. This applies to early games such as the King's Quest series as well as to later productions such as the Final Fantasy series. Interactivity has been added since computers and game consoles can be plugged into the Internet. Now players can simultaneously play their own roles in folktale-like adventures thanks to the MMORPGs: the Massively Multiplayer Online Role-Playing Games, bearing names such as *Ultima Online*, *EverQuest*, and *World of Warcraft*.

For many people in the early days, the personal computer started out as just another electronic typewriter. The machine with its monochrome screen was mainly used for storing data and texts. Soon it changed from an electronic book into a sort of television due to the addition of audiovisual features: color, icons, illustrations, animations, speech, sound, and so on. Intertextuality was enhanced through hyperlinks, and the computer turned into a multimedia device with unprecedented possibilities, while the Internet greatly expanded the means of storing, retrieving, and exchanging data—including folktales. The Internet did not destroy oral communication or social contact, as pessimists would have it; the Internet just added more and new ways to contact and communicate with people we would probably never otherwise meet. Considering the fact that computer technology and the Internet will become even more audiovisual, we will probably soon use the Internet to tell real-time oral stories to each other once again. In the future, gamelike storytelling may even turn into a "holodeck" experience, in which the tale is lived in 3-D virtual reality. Meanwhile, folktale databases will be filled not only with textual transcripts and photographs but also with movie samples showing storytellers' **performance**s. *See also* Archives; Postmodernism.

Further Readings: Brednich, Rolf W. *www.worldwidewitz.com: Humor im Cyberspace*. Freiburg im Breisgau: Herder, 2005; Brunvand, Erik. "The Heroic Hacker: Legends of the Computer Age." *The Truth Never Stands in the Way of a Good Story*. Urbana: University of Illinois Press, 2000. 170–98; Dégh, Linda. "Collecting Legends Today: Welcome to the Bewildering Maze of the Internet." *Europäische Ethnologie und Folklore im internationalen Kontext: Festschrift für Leander Petzoldt zum 65. Geburtstag*. Edited by Ingo Schneider. Frankfurt a.M.: P. Lang, 1999. 55–66; Ellis, Bill. "Legend/AntiLegend:

Humor as an Integral Part of the Contemporary Legend Process." *Rumor Mills: The Social Impact of Rumor and Legend.* Edited by Gary Alan Fine, Veronique Campion-Vincent, and Chip Heath. New Brunswick: Aldine Transaction 2005. 123–40; Fialkove, Larissa, and Maria N. Yelenevskaya. "Ghosts in the Cyber World: An Analysis of Folklore Sites on the Internet." *Fabula* 42 (2001): 64–89; Foley, John Miles. "Oral Tradition and the Internet: Navigating Pathways." *FF Network* 30 (June 2006): 12–19; Kuipers, Giselinde. "Media Culture and Internet Disaster Jokes: Bin Laden and the Attack on the World Trade Center." *European Journal of Cultural Studies* 5.4 (2002): 451–71; Meder, Theodoor. "Viruspaniek: E-mail-lore van Good Times tot Polleke den Hacker." 2001. http://www.meertens.nl/medewerkers/theo.meder/viruspaniek.html; Murray, Janet H. *Hamlet on the Holodeck: The Future of Narrative in Cyberspace.* 1997. Cambridge, MA: MIT Press, 1998; Pearce, C. "Story as Play Space: Narrative in Games." *Game On: The History and Culture of Video Games.* Edited by Laurence King. London: Laurence King Publishing, 2002. 112–19; Schneider, Ingo. "Erzählen im Internet: Aspekte kommunikativer Kultur im Zeitalter des Computers." *Fabula* 37 (1996): 8–27; Wiebe, Karl. *This Is Not a Hoax: Urban Legends on the Internet.* Baltimore: PublishAmerica, 2003.

Theo Meder

Intertextuality

Intertextuality involves a direct or indirect relation between two or more texts. The antecedents a later text evokes frequently influence our reading. Given their interconnectedness as vital components within a larger cultural continuum, it is probably no exaggeration to say that both oral **folktale**s and **literary fairy tale**s are even more intertextual in nature than most other fictional forms. In his 1697 version of "**Sleeping Beauty**," Charles **Perrault** wittily calls attention to this feature when he has different informants try to satisfy the **prince**'s curiosity about the inhabitants of a castle smothered by dense woods and thickets of brambles and thorns. Some of these informants are convinced that the castle is haunted by ghosts; others contend that it is either the abode of **witch**es or, more likely, of a child-devouring **ogre** who ought to be avoided. Only then does an old **peasant** produce the story he claims to have heard from "my father" more "than fifty years ago" about a dormant **princess** in need of being awakened by a "chosen **king**'s son." Perrault may mock here the notion that it is possible to recover an "original" text—an urtext—through all of its subsequent deformations; yet he also calls attention to his own deliberate modification of earlier Sleeping Beauty narratives such as Giambattista **Basile**'s "Sole, Luna, e Talia" ("Sun, Moon, and Talia," 1836). Perrault's self-consciousness stems from his intense awareness of the intertextuality of his own enterprise: to claim a narrative space of his own, he has to cut through the obstructing brambles of a dense textual growth.

Folklorists and those literary scholars who study fairy tales share a similar task in their own siftings through intertextual thickets. They must trace transmigrations from the Orient to the Near East to the Mediterranean and northern Europe. They must distinguish and individuate texts that have become spliced together by popular culture. Retellings of "**Cinderella**" in children's books or in animated films often result in new amalgams: Perrault's fairy godmother and pumpkin coach may now coexist with the **Grimm**s' grotesque, self-mutilating, and **mother**-dominated stepsisters. The porousness of popular forms such as the Victorian **novel** or modern **film** makes them especially receptive to submerged or overt allusions to well-known fairy tales. Even texts that purport to be firmly anchored in history avail themselves of **folklore** and fairy tale magic. Washington Irving's feminized Rip van Winkle is a hirsute Sleeping Beauty whose enchanted coma allows him to avoid the American War of Independence. Conversely, Rudyard

Kipling's Puck in *Puck of Pookh's Hill* (1906) is a sylvan **fairy** who hauls in real and fictitious figures from English history (Roman soldiers, Picts, Normans, Saxons, Vikings, African natives, a mysterious Chinese sailor, and an exotic Sephardic Jew) to instruct two modern British children about their own multicultural past.

As soon as they were transcribed and codified into printed texts, oral folktales that had been told at different times and in widely varying geographical settings not only invited elaborate comparisons and contrasts but also furnished a fruitful source for a host of literary elaborations. If folklorists and ethnographers mapped out discrepancies and overlaps between, say, an early Chinese and a later Scottish version of an orally transmitted Cinderella story, literary critics and historians were called upon to recognize and interpret the permutations introduced, at different moments in sociopolitical history, by all those adaptors who set out to revise fairy tale "originals" for dissemination among wider and more variegated print cultures. Such literary permutations, however, also raised new questions. Is there a discernible relation between Lucius **Apuleius**'s elaborate mythical romance of "**Cupid and Psyche**" and an African folktale that features a young woman who is startled to discover that her lover is an all-powerful snake-god? If so, is this relation causal? Were African **myth**s given a Greco-Roman patina? Or do the common **motif**s merely suggest the existence of universal, transcultural **archetype**s? And why did, in later French culture, women writers such as Marie-Catherine d'**Aulnoy**, Gabrielle-Suzanne de **Villeneuve**, and Jean-Marie **Leprince de Beaumont** choose to rework the Cupid and Psyche motif into their own moral tales about young **women** and bestial lovers? In what ways have Leprince de Beaumont's nineteenth- and twentieth-century successors from Anne Thackeray **Ritchie** and E. **Nesbit** to Linda Wolverton, the screenwriter for the 1991 animation from the **Walt Disney Company**, continued to revise the story of "**Beauty and the Beast**" for later generations?

There is a difference, however, between the intertextuality of literary fairy tales and the intertextual analogies and distinctions among folktales that folklorists and cultural anthropologists have grouped into "**tale type**s" or "families" with common "themes" or **motif**s. As the example taken from Perrault's "Sleeping Beauty" suggests, the writer of a literary fairy tale is inevitably self-conscious, whether overtly or covertly so. When Louisa May **Alcott** writes "A Modern Cinderella" (1860), she warily Americanizes a European tale. When Henriette-Julie de Castelnau, Comtesse de **Murat** goes out of her way to recast d'Aulnoy's story of "Le prince marcassin" ("The Boar Prince," 1698) in her own "Le roy porc" ("The Pig King," 1699), she wants her readers to recognize her ironic dissociation from her predecessor's text. Irony, so prevalent in literary fairy tales, seems inextricable from their self-conscious intertextuality. In fact, literary fairy tales that rely on burlesque openly parade that intertextuality, since their authors want to make sure that the audience be fully aware of all the common points of reference that the comic narrative playfully invokes and then alters or subverts. *See also* Adaptation; Metafiction; Parody.

Further Reading: Benson, Stephen. "Stories of Love and Death: Reading and Writing the Fairy Tale Romance." *Image and Power: Women in Fiction in the Twentieth Century.* Edited by Darah Sceats and Gail Cunningham. Longman, London, 1996. 103–13.

U. C. Knoepflmacher

Into the Woods

Into the Woods is a musical in two acts, with **music** and lyrics by Stephen Sondheim and book by James Lapine. Premiered in San Diego, California, in 1986, *Into the Woods* weaves together the stories of "Rapunzel," "**Little Red Riding Hood**," "Jack and the Beanstalk," and "**Cinderella.**" Each of the main protagonists enters the woods to pursue their respective needs, and the first part of the musical ends with what appears to be a set of satisfied characters. However, Sondheim and Lapine are primarily interested in the fairy tale as a vehicle for the expression of desire. Accordingly, they use the second half of the musical to take the characters beyond their conventional endings to represent desire as an ongoing condition rather than a one-shot quest. The husbands of Cinderella and Rapunzel are drawn to the new challenge of sleeping beauties. Cinderella's husband even dares to have an extramarital moment in the woods with the Baker's Wife. The woods are not a rite of passage, but a constant possibility. By sending their characters "into the woods," Sondheim and Lapine wittily adapt the morality of the fairy tale to reflect an adult world of temptation and longing, although one in which challenges need not be faced alone. *See also* Theater.

Further Readings: Banfield, Stephen. *Sondheim's Broadway Musicals.* Ann Arbor: University of Michigan Press, 1993; Stoddart, S. F. "'Happily ... Ever ...' NEVER: The Antithetical Romance of *Into the Woods*." *Reading Stephen Sondheim: A Collection of Critical Essays.* Edited by Sandor Goodhart. New York: Garland, 2000. 209–20.

Stephen Benson

Inuit Tales

The native people of the far northern coasts of Alaska, Canada, and Greenland, united by Eskimoan languages (Inuit-Inupiaq and Yupik), share a distinctive repertory of folktales little influenced by "southerners," as the inhabitants of the rest of the world are known. In past times, during the long night from November until mid-January, stories were needed to help pass the winter. In some communities, the narrator droned on in the dark while people settled into their beds. Elsewhere the lamp was lit and the storyteller performed with vivid gestures, creating a kind of **theater**. Accounts of realistic human situations were preferred, though tales of giants, little people, superhuman heroes, and personified animals are well represented in published collections.

Character types recur throughout the stories. A favorite figure is the orphan boy who rises above poverty and ridicule to become a famous hunter. Another is the independent woman, known to Alaskan storytellers as the *uiḷuaqtaq,* "woman who won't take a husband," so adamant in her resistance that she cannot be won except through shamanic power. More resourceful is the independent woman of Canadian and Greenlandic traditions. In "The Woman Who Lived by Herself," a wife proves she can build a house and snare all the game she needs without help from the angry man who has deserted her. In "Two Sisters and Their Caribou Husbands," the heroines slip away from their abusive mates, returning later to harvest their skins.

One of the best-known figures is Kivio, the superhumanly strong and clever hero, who in one of his great adventures paddles his kayak to the Middle of the World, besting all adversaries along the way. In modern Canada, Kivio has appeared in a comic strip. By contrast, the proverbial braggart and bungler, Kasiak, fails in every undertaking, unable even to bring home food for his long-suffering wife.

Sensational stories from Canada and Greenland tell of the baby who ate its parents or the hungry husband who fattened his wife. One of the liveliest of these offers a detailed account of a supposed cannibal village, always some distance away, where the occasional visitor is welcomed with open arms.

Among Inuit **tale type**s known from all three regions is the characteristically poetic tale "The Soul Wanderer," told of both **men** and **women**, in which a human soul completes an odyssey of the natural world, migrating from plant to animal and from animal to animal, finally to be born again as a human. "The Girls Who Wished for Husbands" tells of child brides trapped in frightful marriages but rescued by a compassionate spider woman. In "The Blind Boy and the Loon" a sightless little boy is abused by a cruel stepmother but aided by his sister. Unsurprisingly, the international tale often known as "The Swan Maidens" (Motif D361.1, **Swan Maiden**) has Inuit **variant**s in Alaska, Canada, and Greenland.

Mythological narratives, lacking in some communities, are generally of little importance, especially eastward. As a Netsilik woman of the central Canadian Arctic once remarked to the Danish explorer Knud Rasmussen, "The earth was as it is at the time when our people began to remember." Nevertheless, origin tales have a place in the repertory, especially in Alaska, where the first cause is usually Raven, creator of the world and many of its features. **Etiologic tale**s known from Alaska to Greenland include such typical Inuit **motif**s as the creation of bodies of water by urinating, the origin of fish from wood chips, the descent of humans from a dog ancestor, the production of thunder by two girls rattling a dried skin in the upper world, and the origin of moon and sun from an incestuous brother who still chases his sister across the sky.

An exceptional myth from eastern Canada and Greenland accounts for the activities of the underwater mistress of sea animals. In a version from Baffin Island, recorded by the pioneer anthropologist Franz Boas in the 1880s, the deity's name is Sedna. She and her **father**, it is told, were caught in a storm at sea. To save himself, the father threw his daughter overboard, and as she clutched desperately at the gunwhale, he chopped off her fingers. These bobbed in the water and became seals and walruses, while she herself sank to the underworld. There she still reigns as the woman who provides—or withholds—the sea mammals on which human life in the Arctic depends. Today, though hunting continues, the people of Baffin Island have become Anglicans, and the old rituals in which Sedna was propitiated have been replaced by church services and evening Bible study. (In 2004, Sedna lent her name to a newly discovered planet, or planetlike celestial body, beyond the orbit of Pluto.)

Classic Inuit tales, originally published between 1860 and 1925, were recorded mainly by three investigators: Rasmussen, Boas, and the Danish geographer-turned-folklorist Hinrich Rink. Yet the recent collections of Tom Lowenstein and his Alaskan native collaborators demonstrate that traditional tales of high intensity could still be heard as the twentieth century drew to a close. Sources for the stories mentioned above, including their many variants, may be traced in the three works listed below by Asatchaq and Lowenstein and by Bierhorst.

Further Readings: Asatchaq, Tukummuq, and Tom Lowenstein. *The Things That Were Said of Them: Shaman Stories and Oral Histories of the Tikiġaq People.* Berkeley: University of California Press, 1992; Bierhorst, John. *The Dancing Fox: Arctic Folktales.* New York: William Morrow, 1997; ———. *The Mythology of North America.* 2nd edition. New York: Oxford University Press, 2002; Boas, Franz. *The Eskimo of Baffin Land and Hudson Bay: From Notes Collected by Captain George Comer, Captain James S. Mutch, and Rev. E. J. Peck.* 1907. New York: AMS Press, 1975; Rasmussen, Knud. *Report of the Fifth Thule Expedition, 1921–24.* Vol. 7, no. 1; vol. 7, nos. 2–3; vol. 8, nos. 1–2; vol. 9; vol. 10, no. 2; vol. 10, no. 3. 1929–52. New York: AMS Press, 1976; Rink, Hinrich. *Tales and Traditions of the Eskimo, with a Sketch of Their Habits, Religion, Language and Other Peculiarities.* 1875. New York: AMS Press, 1975.

John Bierhorst

Iranian Tales

While the Persian language is spoken mainly in Iran, Afghanistan, and Tajikistan, the Iranian cultural area is much larger, encompassing parts of Central and South Asia and the areas inhabited by Kurdish peoples in Iran, Iraq, and Turkey. At the same time, most of the present states in the region are multiethnic nations. The state of Iran comprises, besides various Iranian ethnic groups, such as the Bakhtiyari, Lori, Kurds, or Baluch, considerably large ethnic groups of Turkic or Arab origin. This entry is concerned with the Persian folktales of Iran proper, whose characteristics also apply more or less to the folktales of Tajikistan and of Dari-speaking Afghanistan and, to some extent, to Kurdish tradition. (Note that references to **tale type**s in this entry use the names and numbers listed in Ulrich Marzolph's *Typologie des persischen Volksmärchens.*)

Traditional Popular Reading Matter

The great epics of classical Persian literature, such as Ferdousi's *Shah-name* (*Book of Kings*), the anonymous *Eskandar-name* (*Alexander-Romance*), and *Romuz-e Hamze* (*The Secrets of Hamze*), have been appreciated by both the elite and popular strata of Persian society for centuries. Until well into the twentieth century, they were presented to illiterate audiences by professional storytellers. When printing was introduced to Iran in the first decades of the nineteenth century, **epic** literature was gradually adapted to popular reading. Numerous short narrative works published in print were distributed by sidewalk peddlers, bazaar bookstalls, and itinerant merchants. They added decisively to the distribution of popular literature and, hence, to the common knowledge of tales and **motif**s as well as embedded social and moral concepts.

While not necessarily conforming to Western concepts of the "**folktale**," much of the traditional narrative matter in Iran before and up to the beginning of the twentieth century profits from popular tales and motifs. This literature, besides the works quoted above, also includes **legend**s of early Islamic history and the pivotal tragedy of Kerbelâ', when Hosein, the son of 'Ali, and his followers were killed. Collections of **fable**s or **proverb**s contain folktale material, as do numerous short romances focusing on famous lovers such as Leili and Majnun or Shirin and Farhad, or on heroes such as Hosein the Kurd or Rostam, the dominating character of Iran's legendary history. Late in the nineteenth century, versified adaptations of folktales such as *Shangul va Mangul*, a version of AT 123, The Wolf and the Kids, were published. Moreover, an increasing amount of pedagogical and entertaining literature for children, including schoolbooks, contained traditional narrative material that it imparted to its young readers.

Folktales and Fairy Tales

Judging from the volume of publication, folktales and fairy tales in Iran are both highly appreciated in the original context from which they have been recorded and by modern readers. While the impact of modern media and the resulting changes in society certainly have influenced the degree to which folktales and fairy tales are known today, they were, and still are in rural societies, quite popular. Besides nostalgia, the current popularity of folktale and fairy-tale collections in Iran might also demonstrate a sincere human need for this genre of tales.

Terminology.   Folktales and fairy tales are usually denoted by one of the three terms: "*qesse*," "*afsâne*," or "*matal*." *Qesse* retains a relation, albeit somewhat vague, to historical or personal reality, as even characters within a given tale would relate their *qesse*, here meaning their personal history. Fictitious tales of wonder and imagination, all the more so fairy tales relating to sorcery and magic, are usually labeled *afsâne* (including its variants *afsân*, *fasân*, *fasâne*, or the dialect variants *ousun*, *ousâne*). This term demonstrates an etymological and semantic link with words like *fasâ'idan (fasânidan)*, "to charm, fascinate, enchant," or *fosun*, *afsun*, "incantation, fascination." The term *matal* denotes folktales of a formulaic structure.

Language and Formulaic Expression.   Folktales and fairy tales are usually narrated in plain colloquial language, and narrators draw on a large stock of formulaic expressions. Tales of a realistic or historical background, particularly romantic or epic tales in writing, usually begin with the rhymed formula "The tellers of stories and the transmitters of ancient legends (and the sugar-breaking and sweet-talking parrots) have related that. . . ." This formula, by taking recourse to previous authorities, makes the listeners expect a tale whose close connection with reality is at least formally acknowledged.

The standard formula for fairy tales introduces the readers and/or listeners to a world of fantasy and imagination. It reads *yeki bud, yeki nabud*, "There was, and there was not." This phrase at times is supplemented by the mention of *gheir az khodâ hichkas nabud*, "There was nobody but God." In oral **performance**, the storyteller might then even address the audience with the formula "All true believers now say 'O God!' "—to which the audience would respond by exclaiming "O God!" Another, less common formula for the introduction of fairy tales is *ruzi (bud), ruzgâri (bud)*, "(There was) a day, (there was) a time." Only after either one of these formulas does the actual tale begin, most commonly with a sentence like "There was a king (or man, or fox)." Sometimes, the latter is further introduced by specifying "in the old days."

Similar to the introduction into the never-never-land of the fairy tale, closing formulas point out the unreal character of the preceding narrative and make it clear that the fairy-tale action took place in an imaginary world, even though there might have been parallels to the social and historical reality of the narrator's context. Closing formulas, while also structured with simple rhymes, show a greater variety than introductory formulas and are often nonsense rhymes. One of the more common formulas is "Our tale has come to an end, the crow has not reached its home." Another formula clearly demonstrates the fictitious character of the preceding tale: "We went upstairs, there was *mâst* (yoghurt)—our tale was true (*râst*); we went downstairs, there was *dugh* (a drink prepared from yoghurt)—our tale was a lie (*dorugh*)." A more pragmatic version of this formula includes the following variants: "We went upstairs, there was flour, we came downstairs, there was dough/cheese—this was our tale." In romantic tales, particularly in tales about two lovers who finally are united after overcoming a number of obstacles, we find yet another common type of closing formula: "God willing, you [that is, the listeners] will attain your innermost longing in the same way, as they [that is, the characters of the tale] have attained their innermost longing."

Within the tales, narrators can also draw on a large stock of formulas. These formulas often relate to the tale's content and are employed according to the narrator's skill. One of the most common formulas used to structure a tale in its abstract form is: "(Now) leave XY (here), go/come (let us go/come) to YZ (listen about YZ)." In romantic stories, an elaborate formula may be used to demonstrate the process of falling in love: "A pointed arrow made of poplar, its shaft adorned with white feathers, sprang from the young woman's breast and settled deep down in the young man's breast—the young man fell in love with her, not with one, but with a hundred hearts." Finally, the despair the lovers experience while longing for another or when being separated is expressed in the formula "I am completely set on fire, I learned from your love; I was raw and became cooked; oh you shameless and unjust one—I am on fire!"

Categories of Folktales and Fairy Tales.   Persian folktales and fairy tales fit into the general concept of the Indo-European tradition. A total of 351 traditional tales from Persian tradition of the twentieth century submitted to analysis in the early 1980s include fifty **animal tale**s (AT 1–299), eighty-one tales of magic (AT 300–749), nineteen **religious tale**s (AT 750–849), fifty romantic tales (AT 850–999), sixteen tales of the stupid **ogre** (AT 1000–1199), 126 jokes and **anecdote**s (AT 1200–1999), and nine formula tales (AT 2000–2199). The three most frequently published tales are AT 408, The Orange Princess (twenty-three texts); AT 894, The Patient Stone (twenty-two texts); and AT 20D*, The Fox on Pilgrimage. Other often documented tales include AT 123, The Wolf and the Kids; AT *314, The Magic Horse; AT 311A, Namaki and the Div; AT 325, The Magician's Apprentice; AT 613, Good and Evil; and AT 2032, The Mouse That Lost Its Tail.

Characters of Folktales and Fairy Tales.   Persian tales rely on a standard register of protagonists with their stereotypical functions of requisites and actions. The most common hero character is the **prince**, who in the course of the story is often named only "young man." Frequently, the prince is the youngest of three **brothers** and has to make good for the faults or incompetence of his elder brothers. The hero experiences dangerous adventures, fights with demons and monsters, and accomplishes difficult tasks. In the end, he attains his beloved **princess** and inherits the kingdom. A typically Near Eastern hero character is the baldheaded man, often a baldheaded shepherd. At the beginning of the tale, the baldhead is an outcast, a sluggard, or a coward, and always a pauper. During the tale's action and while being challenged, he proves to be clever and witty, courageous and reckless. With these qualities, he masters the most difficult tasks, often wins the favors of the princess, and becomes **king**. Sometimes, as in the tale of "The Magic Horse," the actual prince disguises himself as a baldhead. Another frequent hero character is the wood collector, representing the lowest stratum of society. The wood collector's deep poverty usually goes together with his true belief, helping him to overcome his initial destitution and eventually acquire both wealth and happiness.

While the hero's only standard helper (besides his horse) is the old thinbeard, the range of opponents primarily comprises the female members of his family. Particularly, his mother-in-law, his stepmother, or his aunt is motivated by envy, trying to destroy the hero by calumniating him. His other relatives, including the hero's **father** and older brothers, are no better in agitating against him, and the only close relative whose image is outright positive is his **mother**. Another powerful adversary is the king, who is often depicted as a powerless object of his intriguing ministers.

The role of female characters in Persian folktales is marked by ambivalence. While only girls are pictured outright positively, **women** as active characters are mostly wily and deceitful, often simply just evil. Only when counseling the hero do active women—often in subordinate functions—bear positive traits. As passive characters, women are seldom more than objects the male hero strives to acquire, often motivated by perfunctory external matters:

the hero falls in love with an unseen beauty by seeing one strand of her **hair** float in the water or by listening to someone mentioning her name.

The secondary characters of Persian folktales belong to one of two groups. The first group comprises characters from the real world, such as the shepherd, the wood collector, or the merchant, usually bearing negative traits, or various other professions. Ethnic and/or linguistic minorities are commonly depicted with the usual arrogance of the dominant culture: Jewish merchants, black slaves, and gypsy girls are malevolent characters, while members of the Kurdish or Lori population at best figure as fools. The second group comprises characters from the world beyond. Here, one encounters a strict dichotomy. The demon (*div*), most often male, is usually both malevolent and stupid. His standard role besides fighting the hero is to abduct women to force them into **marriage**. The *div* usually possesses an external soul that he hides in a secret place (most often inside a bottle that has been swallowed by a bird or a fish). He can be vanquished only when the hero discovers and destroys his soul. The **fairy** (*pari*) is a perfect positive character. Most often female, she uses her supernatural capacities, such as magic and the ability to fly, to assist the hero in achieving his tasks. Marriage between a *pari* and a man is quite frequent. But even though the world of the *paris* in its hierarchic organization is similar to the human world, these marriages rarely end happily, as the man is bound to succumb to his human foibles and subsequently loses his fairy wife.

The action in Persian folktales and fairy tales is driven by two forces. The most powerful force within the tale is fate. The pauper trusts in fate and is redeemed. The king challenges fate and is punished. Religion in its official rite does not play any important role. If religious feelings are voiced at all, they are concerned with the popular admiration of venerated saints, such as 'Ali, the prophet Mohammed's cousin and son-in-law, or the mythical character Khezr, most often in asking their intercession so as to be saved from misfortune or to achieve a particular goal. The other force driving Persian tales, to some extent external, is the wishful thinking of both the narrator and the audience. As folktales and fairy tales are often human **wish**es transformed into narrative, they need an upbeat ending, enabling the participants to counter the hardships of their real lives with the attainment of ultimate happiness. The quintessential justice of folktales not only finds its expression in the worthy being redeemed but also makes the exemplary cruel **punishment** of the evil and malevolent adversaries a particular point.

Folk Humor

Persian folk humor offers a jocular treatment of conflicts, be they political, social, economic, moral, or individual. In terms of style, humorous verbal expression is usually short (as in jokes and anecdotes), sometimes interactive (as in humorous **riddle**s or amusing questions), and often arises spontaneously (see **Jest and Joke**). Both the subversive quality of humor and its spontaneity imply severe restrictions on the availability of jocular expression documentation from **oral tradition**.

Persian literature preserves a number of outstanding examples of humor and satire, and although these specimens were produced by members of the literate elite, they often contain elements of popular expression. Even a literary collection of anecdotes such as 'Obeid-e Zâkâni's (died 1371) *Resâle-ye delgoshâ* (*The Exhilarating Treatise*) to some extent might represent contemporary folk humor. On the other hand, the very popularity the collection gained through the process of retelling might have resulted in its jokes and anecdotes eventually becoming elements of folk humor regardless of their origins. Probably the most influential printed collection contributing to the popularization of Persian folk humor is the booklet of anecdotes on Mollâ Nasroddin (see **Nasreddin**), published in countless versions since the end of the nineteenth century.

As for the current dimension of Persian folk humor, the closest one comes to an assessment of jocular expression in contemporary living tradition is on the **Internet** in the form of the California-based Web site *Jokestân* (http://www.jokestan.com), to which Iranian youngsters from all over the world, although supposedly predominantly expatriates residing in the United States, may contribute individually.

Further Readings: Cejpek, Jiri. "Iranian Folk-Literature." *History of Iranian Literature.* Edited by Jan Rypka. Dordrecht: D. Reidel, 1968. 607–709; Lorimer, D. L. R. and E. S. *Persian Tales, Written Down for the First Time in the Original Kermani and Bakhtiari.* London: MacMillan, 1919; Marzolph, Ulrich. *Typologie des persischen Volksmärchens.* Beirut: Deutsche Morgenländische Gesellschaft, 1984; Mills, Margaret A. *Rhetorics and Politics in Afghan Traditional Storytelling.* Philadelphia: University of Pennsylvania Press, 1991; Radhayrapetian, Juliet. *Iranian Folk Narrative: A Survey of Scholarship.* New York: Garland, 1990.

Ulrich Marzolph

Ispirescu, Petre (1830–1887)

The most famous collector of Romanian folktales in the nineteenth century, Petre Ispirescu had little formal education and was largely self-taught. Working as a typesetter, he became director of the State Printing House and the Printing House of the Romanian Academy. In the context of folklore studies, Ispirescu is known as the author of the first great collection of folktales in Walachia: *Legende sau basmele românilor, adunate din gura poporului de ..., culegător–tipograf (Legends or Folktales of the Romanians, Gathered Directly from the People by ..., a Compositor–Printer,* 1882). This collection had been preceded by *Legende sau basmele românilor, ghicitori şi povestiri (Legends or Folktales of the Romanians, Riddles and Stories,* 1872) and *Legende sau basmele românilor, ghicitori şi proverburi (Legends or Folktales of the Romanians, Riddles and Proverbs,* 1874). Still other collections followed.

Most of Ispriescu's collecting occurred in an urban environment—Bucharest at the end of nineteenth century. His

Petre Ispirescu's "The Princess Who Would Be a Prince or Iliane of the Golden Tresses" as illustrated by James D. Powell in *The Foundling Prince and Other Tales,* trans. Julia Collier Harris and Rea Ipcar (Boston: Houghton Mifflin Company; Cambridge: Riverside Press, 1917).

method of **collecting** material was similar to that of his contemporaries: he listened to folk-tales and then reproduced them in written form, sometimes after quite a long while. Consequently, Ispirescu's ultimate contribution as a collector was in transmitting folktales by dint of literary form. Among his best-known tales are "Tinereţe fără bătrâneţe şi viaţă fără de moarte" ("Endless Youth and Everlasting Life"), "Prâslea cel voinic şi merele de aur" ("The Brave Young Son and the Golden Apple"), and "Găinăreasa" ("The Maid Taking Care of Hens"). Ispirescu's tales have been translated and published in Europe and the United States in various editions, including illustrated books for children.

Further Reading: Anghelescu, Mircea. *Introducere în opera lui Petre Ispirescu.* Bucharest: Editura Minerva, 1987.

Nicolae Constantinescu

Italian Tales

In Giambattista **Basile**'s *Lo cunto de li cunti* (*The Tale of Tales*, 1634–36), Italy has the earliest and one of the richest collections of **literary fairy tale**s. Although the influential literary experiments that Basile and Giovan Francesco **Straparola** conducted with the fairy tale as an independent genre during the Renaissance and the baroque period did not give rise in Italy to the "vogue" of literary tales that was to occur in France, from the nineteenth century on, Italy has produced important authors and collections of fairy tales. Even today, Italian folklorists, literary scholars, and writers continue to investigate the constant and fruitful intersections between elite and popular culture and oral and literary narrative forms that characterize Italian tale telling, and to deal with the question of how to integrate the vast storehouse of regional narratives into national culture.

The earliest example of an "Italian" literary fairy tale is the story of "**Cupid and Psyche**," which is embedded in Lucius **Apuleius**'s second-century Latin **novel** *The Golden Ass.* During the millennium that followed, oral tales continued to circulate as they had for hundreds, if not thousands, of years; however, due to various factors, including the absence of a secular literate culture, there were few further experiments with the literary tale. The advent of vernacular culture, especially from the thirteenth century onward, when the **novella** became a predominant genre, marked the point at which the mediation between popular and literary traditions began to manifest itself in the presence of fairy-tale elements in short narrative—in the anonymous *Novellino* (*The Hundred Old Tales*), for example—even if the first integral fairy tales appeared only three centuries later.

It is Giovanni **Boccaccio**'s works that include the most significant early use of fairy-tale **motif**s, as well as what is possibly the first explicit reference to fairy tales (in *Genealogia deorum gentilium* [*The Genealogies of the Gentile Gods*, 1350–75]). His novella collection *Decameron* (1349–50) drew from classical literature, medieval **fabliaux** and chansons de geste, and other popular narratives to relate tales that frequently feature ordinary protagonists who triumph over hardship. Although they are presented as examples of the power of fortune, individual enterprise, and love, a number of tales incorporate fairy-tale structures as well as expressing a fairy-tale-like optimism, especially in day 2, dedicated to the wiles of fortune, and day 5, which features love stories with happy endings.

Fairy-tale motifs are evident in several other fourteenth-century novella collections, such as Ser Giovanni Fiorentino's *Pecorone* (*The Big Sheep*) and Giovanni Sercambi's *Novelle* (*Novellas*). Fairy-tale compositional techniques also informed genres positioned between the oral and literary spheres such as the *cantari*, the **epic** or romantic **ballad**s which in their early forms were recited in town squares by minstrels; and *sacre rappresentazioni*, or religious dramas, which had as their subject biblical stories and **saint's legend**s. The *cantari* were also a signal influence on the Italian chivalric tradition, in which its fairy-tale motifs were transposed to poems such as Luigi Pulci's comic *Morgante* (1483), Matteo Maria Boiardo's *Orlando innamorato* (*Orlando in Love*, 1495), and Ludovico Ariosto's entire *Orlando furioso* (*The Frenzy of Orlando*, 1516–32).

Although a curiosity toward popular and folk culture permeated the Renaissance, until the second half of the sixteenth century, novellas generally favored realistic subjects, often taking up the favorite Boccaccian theme of the *beffa*, or practical joke. There was also an increased interest in this period in moralizing Aesopian **fable**s, which culminated in Giacomo Morlini's Latin *Novellae* (*Novellas*, 1520). It was, however, Giovan Francesco Straparola who for the first time and in undisguised fashion included entire fairy tales in a novella collection. His enormously popular *Le piacevoli notti* (*The Pleasant Nights*, 1550–53) adopts a **frame narrative** similar to that of the *Decameron*, in which, after the ex-bishop of Lodi Ottaviano Maria Sforza leaves Milan for political reasons, he assembles an aristocratic company at his palace near Venice to tell tales over the course of thirteen nights. The tales are an eclectic mix of various genres; of the seventy-four tales, about fifteen are folktales or fairy tales, whose materials were probably gleaned from Oriental tales, animal fables, and **oral tradition**; well-known **tale type**s are found, for example, in "Tebaldo and Doralice," "The **Pig** King," "Crazy Peter," "The Three **Brother**s," and "Costantino Fortunato." Although Straparola's tales are not as innovative as those of Basile a century later, he influenced subsequent fabulists such as Charles **Perrault** and the Brothers **Grimm**.

The spread of print culture, the anthropological interest inspired by geographical discoveries, and the attraction to the marvelous that permeated later Renaissance and baroque culture led to a larger-scale reevaluation of native folkloric traditions and the attempt to transport them into the realm of literature. It is Giambattista Basile's *Lo cunto de li cunti overo lo trattenemiento de peccerille* (*The Tale of Tales, or Entertainment for Little Ones*, 1634–36), the first integral collection of fairy tales in Europe, that most significantly marks the passage from the oral **folktale** to the artful and sophisticated "authored" **fairy tale**. Written in Neapolitan dialect and also known as the *Pentamerone*, *The Tale of Tales* comprises forty-nine fairy tales contained by a fiftieth frame story; these are told over the course of five days by ten grotesque, lower-class old **women**. Despite its subtitle, *The Tale of Tales* is not a work of **children's literature**, but was intended to be read aloud in the "courtly conversations" that were an elite pastime of the period. Basile transformed the materials of oral tradition into highly original tales distinguished by comic verve, rhetorical play, abundant references to the everyday life and popular culture of the time, moral indeterminacy, and a parodic **intertextuality** that targets courtly culture and the canonical literary tradition. *The Tale of Tales* contains the earliest literary versions of many celebrated fairy-tale types—**Cinderella**, **Sleeping Beauty**, Rapunzel, and others—and was both one of the most suggestive expressions of the baroque poetics of the marvelous and an inspiration to later fairy-tale writers.

After the scant five tales of Pompeo **Sarnelli**'s *Posilicheata* (*An Outing to Posillipo*, 1684), it was almost a hundred years before another Italian author wrote a major work based on fairy tales. From 1760 to 1770, Carlo **Gozzi** published his ten *Fiabe teatrali* (*Fairy Tales for the Theatre*), which included *L'amore delle tre melarance* (*The Love of Three Oranges*), *Il corvo* (*The Crow*), *Turandot*, and others. Gozzi's sources included Basile, **French tales**,

Oriental tales such as the recently translated *Arabian Nights*, and popular oral tradition, but the real particularity of his plays lies in their juxtaposition of fairy tales with the conventions and masks of the *commedia dell'arte*, an eclectic mix that often results in a rather cerebral interpretation of the marvelous (see **Theater**). Gozzi's *Fairy Tales* proved to be of great theatrical influence, as is evidenced by their inspiration of **opera**s by Richard Wagner, Busoni, Puccini, and Prokofiev.

The early-nineteenth century Romantic interest in archaic popular traditions, which supposedly most genuinely represented the "spirit of a nation" in Italy, initially expressed itself more in the study of folk songs, oral poetry, and popular customs and beliefs than of fairy tales. Only later in the century, during the period of Italian unification (1860–70), did tales and legends become the focus of positivistic and comparativistic studies and ethnographic collections. Among the first fairy-tale collections were *Novellaja fiorentina* (*Florentine Tales*, 1871) and *Novellaja milanese* (*Milanese Tales*, 1872), both compiled by Vittorio **Imbriani**; and one of the major Italian compilations of the century, the four-volume *Fiabe novelle e racconti popolari siciliani* (*Fairy Tales, Novellas, and Popular Tales of Sicily*, 1875) by Giuseppe **Pitrè**, Italy's foremost nineteenth-century folklorist. These were followed by the publication of countless others, including Domenico Comparetti's *Novelline popolari italiane* (*Italian Popular Tales*, 1875), Gherardo Nerucci's *Sessanta novelle popolari montalesi* (*Sixty Popular Tales from Montale*, 1880), Laura **Gonzenbach**'s *Sicilianische Märchen* (*Sicilian Fairy Tales*, 1870), and Pitré's *Novelle popolari toscane* (*Tuscan Popular Tales*, 1888).

Numerous writers of the time benefited from this huge amount of new material to produce creative elaborations of fairy tales written for young audiences. The best known of these is Carlo **Collodi**'s novel *Le avventure di Pinocchio: Storia di un burattino* (*The Adventures of Pinocchio: Story of a Puppet*, 1883), the tale of a wooden puppet who is induced both by hardship and by his own cheerfully transgressive nature to undergo a series of perilous adventures that eventually lead to his **transformation** into a real boy. Although it shares structural elements with the fairy tale, *Pinocchio* also has much in common with more realistic genres; the society it depicts is colored by privation, **violence**, and indifference, and Collodi's vision is ambivalent and lacking in the "happily-ever-after" optimism of fairy tales. Ultimately, Pinocchio's lasting attraction has less to do with his metamorphosis into a responsible member of society than with the affirmation of the unleashed creativity and vital humanity of **childhood**, which the puppet embodies up until the very last chapter.

The birth of Pinocchio coincided with the publication of the first of Luigi **Capuana**'s many collections of fairy tales, *C'era una volta* (*Once upon a Time*, 1882). Capuana used his familiarity with Sicilian **folklore** to create stories that evoked the oral tales of tradition, although it is his inventive elaboration of these materials through the use of humor, whimsical fantasy, and realistic detail that gives his work its flavor. The prolific experimentations of another children's author, Emma **Perodi**, closed the century; her *Le novelle della nonna* (*Grandmother's Tales*, 1892) interweaves reassuringly domestic scenarios and uncanny fantastic topographies through the use of a realistic frame narrative that in turn contains vividly expressive fairy tales.

Countless other authors of the late nineteenth and early twentieth centuries incorporated the material of local folktales and **legend**s into their non-fairy-tale works. These included Giovanni Verga (Sicily), Grazia **Deledda** (Sardinia), and Gabriele d'Annunzio (Abruzzo).

By the start of World War I, the flurry of compilation of tales had died down somewhat, although it resumed again after World War II. The "rediscovery" of the popular narratives of the various Italian regions in the twentieth century was distinguished, on the one hand, by a more painstakingly philological approach to the source materials and, on the other, by the relatively recent attempt to determine **oicotype**s of tales based on the principal cultural areas of Italy. Furthermore, figures such as Benedetto Croce and Antonio Gramsci significantly redirected folkloric and fairy-tale scholarship in the twentieth century. Croce, above all in his seminal studies of Basile's *The Tale of Tales*, published in the first decades of the twentieth century, maintained that the investigation of folktales as historical and aesthetic entities should supersede questions of origin or comparativistic analysis of motifs, and thus opened the door to a full-fledged literary analysis of fairy tales. Gramsci, in his essay "Osservazioni sul folklore" ("Observations on Folklore," 1935), put forth the idea that popular folklore expresses a "concept of the world" radically different from the "official" worldview, especially in Italy, where due to the particularities of its political and cultural history, an authentically national heritage based on a connection between the "people" and intellectuals had never come to be.

But a "master collection" of Italian tales was not published until Italo **Calvino**'s *Fiabe italiane* (*Italian Folktales*) appeared in 1956. Calvino selected his materials primarily from nineteenth-century tale collections, and by touching up and imposing "stylistic unity" (Calvino, xix), created his own versions of stories that include about fifty major types from all twenty regions of Italy. Calvino motivated his endeavor by maintaining that the narrative potentialities that folktales offer, with their "infinite variety and infinite repetition," make them essential thematic and structural paradigms for all stories; "folktales are real," since they encompass all of human experience in the form of a "catalog of the potential destinies of men and women" (Calvino, xviii).

In this same period, folklorists, ethnologists, and literary scholars (Giuseppe **Cocchiara**, Ernesto de Martino, Franco Fortini, Alberto Cirese, Paolo Toschi, and others) were engaging in discussions on the relation of Italian folklore to national culture. Numerous regional indices, such as G. D'Aronco's *Indice delle fiabe toscane* (1953), facilitated consideration of the geographic specificities of the Italian tale types; other more comprehensive tools, such as Domenic P. Rotunda's *Motif-Index of the Italian Novella in Prose* (1942, revised 1962) and, most recently, Renato Aprile's *Indice delle fiabe popolari italiane di magia* (*Index of Popular Italian Tales of Magic*, 2000), helped to complete the picture. Between the 1960s and 1970s, a region-wide initiative on the part of the State Discoteca also resulted in a vast amount of new material being collected in the field.

In the introduction to his *Folktales*, Calvino exhorted his readers to consult the original sources he used, and encouraged scholars to publish the tales they contain. In recent years, this challenge has been met on multiple fronts: there have been reeditions of the classic nineteenth-century collections, new regional compilations of tales and indices of tale types, and suggestive retellings of traditional tales by well-known contemporary authors. The most ambitious of these projects was a series of sixteen volumes published by Mondadori from 1982 to 1990 dedicated to the fairy tales of the various Italian regions, in which an author and a scholar teamed up to translate and edit the material, with the aim of "stimulating the awakening of consciousness in a subaltern culture whose potentially active role is recognized."

In past decades, there have also been noteworthy experiments in rewriting the classic fairy-tale canon for children. In the case of Gianni **Rodari** this included, in his *Grammatica della fantasia* (*A Grammar of Fantasy*, 1973), a theoretical discussion of how fairy tales could assume a creative and liberating function in the hands of both children and educators.

Rodari's many collections of tales for children, such as *Favole al telefono* (*Tales on the Telephone*, 1962) and *C'era due volte il barone Lamberto* (*Twice upon a Time There Lived Baron Lamberto*, 1978), have often served as models for subsequent authors. These include Beatrice **Solinas Donghi**, Bianca **Pitzorno**, Roberto **Piumini**, and Luigi **Malerba,** who have continued to create innovative works that address contemporary social and political issues within the narrative framework of the fairy tale. Initiatives such as the 1975 anthology *Favole su favole* (*Fairy Tales upon Fairy Tales*), in which well-known contemporary writers and poets offer "free" retellings of fairy tales from their regions, have also been significant.

Further Readings: Aristodemo, Dina, and Pieter de Meijer. "Le fiabe popolari fra cultura regionale e cultura nazionale." *Belfagor* 34 (1979): 711–16; Bronzini, Giovanni Battista. *La letteratura popolare italiana dell'Otto-Novecento: Profilo storico-geografico.* [Novara]: Istituto geografico De Agostini; [Florence]: Le Monnier, 1994; Calvino, Italo. *Italian Folktales.* Translated by George Martin. New York: Pantheon, 1980; Canepa, Nancy. *From Court to Forest: Giambattista Basile's* Lo cunto de li cunti *and the Birth of the Literary Fairy Tale.* Detroit: Wayne State University Press, 1999; ———, ed. *Out of the Woods: The Origins of the Literary Fairy Tale in Italy and France.* Detroit: Wayne State University Press, 1997; Cirese, Alberto M. "Folklore in Italy: A Historical and Systematic Profile and Bibliography." *Journal of the Folklore Institute* 11 (1974): 7–79; Cocchiara, Giuseppe. *Popolo e letteratura in Italia.* Turin: Einaudi, 1959; Petrini, Mario. *La fiaba di magia nella letteratura italiana.* Udine: Del Bianco, 1983.

Nancy Canepa

J

Jack Tales

Jack tales are a substantial heterogeneous group of **folktale**s in the tradition of the British, Scottish, Irish, and North Americans, in which the hero bears the name Jack. Some form of the name John is widespread for a young folktale hero. In Russia, he may be called Ivan, in German Hans, and in Hispanic countries Juan. In the English-speaking world, he is likely to be called Jack, and his **brothers**, if he has any, are usually Will (or Bill) and Tom. The earliest recorded folktale with a Jack hero is an early fifteenth-century rhymed tale, "Jack and His Stepdame." In the twentieth and early twenty-first centuries, Jack tales have been widely collected in Ireland, Scotland (from both settled and traveler storytellers), Newfoundland, and the southern United States, and have been popular as well in the **storytelling** revival.

Although the custom of calling heroes Jack may be ancient and widespread, the term "Jack tales" itself probably did not gain currency until Richard Chase, working for the Works Progress Administration (WPA) in the 1930s, encountered such stories in the Appalachian Mountains of North Carolina and Virginia. He created versions of eighteen of them, and published this collection as *The Jack Tales* in 1943. Such stories, whatever their place of origin, have been called "Jack tales" ever since.

Though storytellers are divided on the question, many consider the Jack who figures in the Jack tales they know to be a single character, one with whom they tend to identify. Throughout the English-language folktale tradition, Jack usually displays a somewhat consistent personality. He starts out as an unlikely hero, the weak youngest brother or an apparent dunce. He proves, however, to be good-hearted, courageous, resourceful, and lucky. Beyond that, he seems to incorporate traits valued in the community and culture where the particular tales are told. Carl Lindahl has shown that Appalachian Jack has a strong individualistic and capitalistic streak and survives more by cleverness and skill than by magic, while English Jack needs his **magic helper**s and devices in a moral struggle that is a microcosm of class struggle (McCarthy, xxvii–xxx). Similarly, Martin Lovelace has shown that Newfoundland Jack models the social survival skills needed by young working men in an economy where livelihood depends on seasonal work at the mercy of sometimes arbitrary employers (Lindahl, 149–70).

As often happens, when a particular personality becomes a popular folktale hero, the personality will attract a wide variety of tales. So, for example, Br'er Rabbit and **Reynard the Fox** figure in local versions of tales otherwise told about quite different heroes. Similarly, the English-language Jack-tale tradition has incorporated a wide range of stories, including **märchen**, **novella**, **trickster** tales, tales of **ogre**s, numbskull tales, humorous tales, formulaic tales, and even **animal tale**s. *See also* Beech Mountain Jack Tale; North American Tales; Simpleton.

Further Readings: Chase, Richard. *The Jack Tales.* Boston: Houghton Mifflin Company, 1943; Lindahl, Carl, ed. *Perspectives on the Jack Tales and Other North American Märchen.* Bloomington: The Folklore Institute, Indiana University, 2001; McCarthy, William Bernard, ed. *Jack in Two Worlds: Contemporary North American Tales and Their Tellers.* Chapel Hill: University of North Carolina Press, 1994; Perdue, Charles L., Jr., ed. *Outwitting the Devil: Jack Tales from Wise County, Virginia.* Santa Fe, NM: Ancient City Press, 1987.

William Bernard McCarthy

Jacobs, Joseph (1854–1916)

Joseph Jacobs was a Victorian folklorist, literary scholar, and historian who edited important collections of fairy tales. Born in Australia, Jacobs immigrated to England in 1872 to study law at Cambridge, but he eventually pursued literature, history, anthropology, and philosophy. Jacobs made significant contributions as a scholar of literature and Jewish history, but he is best known for his work as a folklorist during the golden age of English **folklore** studies. From 1889 to 1900, he was editor of *Folk-Lore,* the journal of the Folk-Lore Society of London, a forum where scholars debated their often-conflicting views of folklore.

Jacobs published numerous editions of traditional texts, but his more enduring and most controversial editions were his fairy-tale collections, which were illustrated by John Batten: *English Fairy Tales* (1890), *Indian Fairy* Tales (1892), *Celtic Fairy Tales* (1892), *More English Fairy Tales* (1894), *More Celtic Fairy Tales* (1894), and *Europa's Fairy Tales* (1916). In prefaces and notes to these editions, Jacobs made it clear that his goal was to produce a scholarly edition that would also provide an entertainment for children. He also admitted openly to revising style and content to make the stories readable for children. Critics objected not only to his practice of rewriting the tales he collected, which blurred the boundary between folklore and literature, but also to his catering to an audience of children, which erased the line between a scholarly edition and **children's literature**.

Jacobs's controversial editorial practices reflected his theories about the creation and dissemination of folktales, especially his theory of folktale **diffusion**, which placed him in opposition to many of his contemporaries. While most folklorists of his time believed that similar folktales found among diverse cultures were created independently of each other due to coincidence or to the universality of human psychology (**polygenesis**), Jacobs argued that each folktale had originated with a unique creator (**monogenesis**) and was spread from place to place through contacts among people and cultures. Because of this view, Jacobs was less interested in what the folktale could reveal about so-called primitive societies and more interested in the relation of each text to the specific time and place in which it was told. Jacobs also acknowledged that folktales could be transmitted through printed texts, so he did not make a strict distinction between folklore (**oral tradition**) and literature (print culture). His interest in the social and historical contexts of individual tales, and his advocacy of literary methods in the study of folklore, turn out to have been very modern ideas that are now widely accepted. *See also* Collecting; Collectors; Context; Editing, Editors; Sociohistorical Approaches.

Further Readings: Fine, Gary Alan. "Joseph Jacobs: A Sociological Folklorist." *Folklore* 98 (1987): 183–93; Haase, Donald, ed. *English Fairy Tales and More English Fairy Tales.* By Joseph Jacobs. Santa Barbara: ABC-CLIO, 2002; Shaner, Mary E. "Joseph Jacobs." *Writers for Children: Critical Studies of Major Authors since the Seventeenth Century.* Edited by Jane Bingham. New York: Scribners, 1987. 309–16.

Donald Haase

Janosch (1931–)

Pseudonym of Horst Eckert, Janosch is the best-selling German author and illustrator of satirical fairy tales and more than sixty children's books, including *Die Maus hat rote Strümpfe an* (*The Mouse Has Red Socks On*, 1978), published in English as *The Big Janosch Book of Fun and Verse* (1980). Janosch made his debut in 1960, and international recognition came when his most famous characters, Bear and Tiger, appeared for the first time in *Oh, wie schön ist Panama* (*The Trip to Panama*, 1978). This book was honored with the Deutscher Jugendliteraturpreis (German Children's Literature Award). Although Janosch's style of writing and illustrating has often been called childlike and naïve, philosophical and existential questions, as well as social criticism, lie at the basis of many of his works.

Most of Janosch's fairy-tale retellings were published in *Janosch erzählt Grimm's Märchen* (*Janosch Tells Grimm's Fairy Tales*, 1972), a selection of which appeared in English as *Not Quite as Grimm* (1974). Many of the tales are relocated to a contemporary setting, which clashes with the **Grimm**s' Romantic style. The Grimm brothers' idealism and bourgeois values seem appropriate only for the fairy-tale realm, whereas Janosch's retellings are inspired by fierce social criticism and anticapitalist and leftist morals. For instance, Janosch turns "The Brave Little **Tailor**" into a critique of the international arms race during the Cold War. The story ends with the tailor sitting in front of a machine that can destroy the whole world—which is considered the supreme proof of his bravery. Only just in time does someone come to disconnect the machine's wires.

Some of Janosch's tales are outright pessimistic. In his version of "**Mother Holle**," the title figure controls the earth's weather and distributes bread and apples. Because Mother Holle has too much work and can no longer guarantee an equal division of wealth, she is held responsible for all the misery in the world. Yet, humankind shares the guilt: people are so lazy that Mother Holle finds no help, the rich are all too eager to exploit the poor, and her apples are used to make schnapps rather than feed those in need.

The parodic effect in Janosch's retellings is often achieved by exaggeration. As in the Grimm tale, Rapunzel's **mother** craves the salad vegetable *rapunzel* during her pregnancy. In Janosch's version, this addiction goes so far that, in the end, she bears not a baby, but a *rapunzel*. Reversal is another frequently used strategy. The **Frog King**, for instance, has to admit an ugly girl to his pond after she has returned his golden ball, and it turns out that she too is a frog that was enchanted by a wicked human being. *See also* Anti-Fairy Tale; Children's Literature; Illustration; Parody.

Further Readings: Wolffheim, Elsbeth. "Demontage der tradierten Märchen-Ideologie." *Jugend und Buch* 26.1 (1977): 25–30; Zipes, Jack. "The Struggle for the Grimms' Throne: The Legacy of the Grimms'

Tales in East and West Germany since 1945." *The Brothers Grimm: From Enchanted Forests to the Modern World.* 2nd edition. New York: Palgrave MacMillan, 2002. 231–69.

Vanessa Joosen

Jansson, Tove (1914–2001)

Finland-Swedish artist, novelist, and children's book author Tove Jansson brought a unique voice to **children's literature**, gaining worldwide popularity with her Moomin books. A painter, illustrator, and author, Jansson was a multifaceted creative artist. She belonged to the Swedish-speaking minority in Finland and grew up in Helsinki in a bohemian family of artists.

Jansson began her Moomin series with *Småtrollen och den stora översvämningen* (*The Little Trolls and the Great Flood*, 1945), followed by a total of twelve books through 1977. The Moomin figure had previously appeared in the late 1930s as a signature in a political cartoon published in the antifascist magazine *Garm*. Jansson's breakthrough came with the **novel**s *Kometen kommer* (*Comet in Moominland*, 1946) and *Trollkarlens Hatt* (*Finn Family Moomintroll*, 1948). Familiar fairy-tale characters such as wizards, **dragon**s, imaginary beasts, or **mermaid**s are used by Jansson in a complex and highly personal manner. Even folktale **motif**s, such as the motif of hidden treasures or magical **transformation**s, are used in a humorous way. *Muminpappans bravader* (*The Exploits of Moominpappa*, 1950) is a cheerful **parody** of the memoir and adventure genre. Jansson continued to parody literary styles in *Farlig midsommar* (*Moominsummer Madness*, 1954), where theater and classical tragedy are used as a setting for carnival and amusing escapades.

The tension between the idyllic and the disordered, between serenity and danger, is a central theme in the Moomin books. Repeated catastrophes function as revitalizing forces that create tension and dynamics in the valley and act as an antithesis to the peaceful bourgeois milieu. *Trollvinter* (*Moominland Midwinter*, 1957) has a more mythical expression. Moomintroll wakes up from hibernation and finds that the valley's appearance has changed and that his family and friends are sleeping. The Moominvalley is covered in snow and surrounded by darkness. The transformation of scenery, from the idyllic and pleasant to the strange and unfamiliar, is characteristic of Jansson's stories.

Det osynliga barnet (*Tales from Moominvalley*, 1962) deviates slightly from the form of the previous books by presenting nine short stories. The final books in the series deal with the theme of departure and change. *Pappan och havet* (*Moominpappa at Sea*, 1965) was followed by *Sent i November* (*Moominvalley in November*, 1970). In this final Moomin novel, the Moomin family has set out on a journey, leaving their home and the valley behind. In their absence, other characters hesitantly step forward as they wait for the family to return.

Jansson also wrote and illustrated three picturebooks. The first one, *Hur gick det sen? Boken om Mymlan, Mumintrollet och lilla My* (*The Book about Moomin, Mymble and Little My*, 1952) conveys radically new expression and indicates a break with earlier narrative principles in the aesthetics of the Nordic picture book. Even *Vem ska trösta Knyttet?* (*Who Will Comfort Toffle?*, 1960) and *Den farliga resan* (*The Dangerous Journey*, 1977) are innovative and original in their appearance. In addition to her own Moomin books, Jansson also illustrated Swedish **translation**s of classics such as J. R. R. **Tolkien**'s *The Hobbit* and Lewis **Carroll**'s *Alice's Adventures in Wonderland*.

Further Readings: Westin, Boel. "Twentieth-Century Swedish Writers after World War II." *Dictionary of Literary Biography*. Edited by Ann-Charlotte Gavel Adams. Volume 257. Detroit: Gale, 2002. 151–66; ———. *Familjen i dalen: Tove Janssons muminvärld*. Stockholm: Bonnier, 1988.

Elina Druker

Japanese Popular Culture

Japan has a rich tradition of tales, which has become the basis of an equally rich narrative popular culture made up of manga (**graphic novel**s) and anime (animated **television** series and movies). These genres derive from the Eastern convention of accompanying oral **storytelling** with painted screens or handwritten booklets illustrating key moments in the story's plot. Storytelling manga were produced in small numbers from the eighteenth century on but became a mass industry after World War II.

Japanese anime at first were imitations of Western **cartoons** until 1963, when the graphic artist Tezuka Osamu, best known for his children's classic *Simba, the White Lion* (1950–), turned to **animation** and began producing series in a distinctively Japanese style. Influenced by Walt **Disney**'s fairy-tale movies, he set his influential manga *Princess Knight* (1953–56), in a Western-style fairy-tale kingdom. Here he introduced many of the standard **motif**s of the **märchen,** notably the **magic helper**, the quest, and the female protagonist who courts a **prince** in disguise. He adapted the story to anime in 1967–68, creating the first *shōjo* (or female-oriented) series in the genre.

But manga/anime series relied on familiarity with Asian folktales as well. The Chinese popular **epic**, *The Journey East*, originally the picaresque journey of a monk with a company of inhuman helpers, proved one early source, and the character types became familiar enough to inspire stories of their own. Son Goku, originally the magical **trickster** monkey of the company, was made into the central figure of the enormously popular manga/anime *Dragonball Z* (1984–). "The Feather Robe," a Japanese version of the **swan maiden** tale, was a universally known children's tale in Japan, and it too formed the basis of a popular manga/anime series *Ah! My Goddess!* (1989–) Recently, the Japanese animator **Miyazaki** Hayao has freely adapted elements from many native Japanese folktales into a series of internationally successful anime movies.

In 1987, Nippon Animation produced a series of fairy-tale **adaptation**s titled *Gurimu meisaku gekijô* (*Grimm Masterpiece Theater*), though in fact the plots were drawn from a variety of European sources. Faithful to the original storylines of these narratives, sometimes disturbingly so, this anime popularized the fairy-tale genre in Japan. The English-language version, broadcast in North America as *Grimm's Fairy Tale Classics*, in turn introduced many viewers on that side of the world to anime. After this, references to classic Western fairy tales became frequent in Japanese popular culture. "**Sleeping Beauty**," being similar to a Japanese folktale about a child cursed at **birth** to die on a future birthday, has proved especially popular, with the core motifs of the birth curse and the magical sleep central in many series, especially *Sailor Moon* (1992–). Other manga and anime series and movies make organic, creative use of fairy-tale plots and motifs, notably "**Beauty and the Beast**" (*Inuyasha*, 1996, and *Fruits Basket*, 1998–) and Pinocchio (*A Tree of Palme*, 2001). *See also* Film and Video; Japanese Tales.

Further Readings: Levi, Antonia. *Samurai from Outer Space: Understanding Japanese Animation.* Chicago: Open Court, 1996; Schodt, Fredrik L. *Dreamland Japan: Writings on Modern Manga.* Berkeley: Stone Bridge Press, 1996.

Bill Ellis

Japanese Tales

There is no single word in Japanese for referring to **folktale**s, though by far the most commonly used term is "mukashi banashi" (tales from long ago), which may arise from the tendency for folktales to begin with the formulaic phrase "mukashi mukashi" (long, long ago).

This usage was first popularized in the late 1800s by scholars such as **Yanagita** Kunio (sometimes rendered Yanagida), who founded the fields of ethnology and **folklore** studies in Japan. Similarly, "minwa" (folktale) and "mingen denshō" (**oral tradition**s of the **folk**) are more patently academic terms that point to familiar notions of tales as (1) particular to preliterate, oral traditions, and (2) hallmarks of "the folk," both of which suggest that the origins of contemporary folklore lie with the nostalgic creations of nineteenth- and twentieth-century scholars. Particularly in the last century, the implicit goal behind such studies was often to identify a national culture or essence that was associated with the rural use of the vernacular, rather than the language and traditions of the urban or proto-urban polyglot. In this, Japan is no exception, and modern folklore studies in that country bear the strong imprint of influence from, most notably, the work of Jacob and Wilhelm **Grimm**.

Though the premodern folkloric tradition in Japan does not use a single, consistent word to refer to folktales, at least one persistent characteristic can be observed. Namely, folktales in Japan are most often related to the project of explaining the meanings behind things such as place names, local traditions, geological features, anomalous occurrences, or meteorological phenomena. We first see this explanatory function of folktales in the earliest written accounts of the mythological creation of the Japanese islands and in early gazetteers.

Myths and Legends

Before the introduction of writing to the Japanese islands (it was imported from the continent sometime between the third and fifth centuries CE), important political and spiritual information was entrusted to the "kataribe" (a clan of hereditary reciters), who were charged with the ritual remembering and narrating of past events. With the advent of the Chinese writing system in Japan, these oral stories were recorded in two separate documents: the *Kojiki* (*Record of Ancient Matters*, 712) and the *Nihon shoki* (*Chronicles of Japan*, c. 720, sometimes rendered *Nihongi*).

Though the two accounts differ in many details, they share the overarching goal of establishing the mythical and divine origins of the Japanese islands, people, and state. According to these sources, the islands of the Japanese archipelago were created by two sibling "kami" (deities) named Izanami and Izanagi. From his place in the sky, Izanagi dipped a long spear into the frothing ocean and stirred up the brine. The white foam dripped from the tip of the spear, creating the first island. The pair descended to dry land and encountered a raised pillar, which they each circled, going in separate directions. When they met on the other side, Izanami spoke to her brother, suggesting that they mate. They did so, but the union produced only deformed offspring who were considered unsatisfactory. After returning to the sky and taking counsel with other deities, the pair repeated the pillar-circling, but this time Izanagi, the male, spoke first. Afterward, the pair mated repeatedly and successfully, producing more islands as well as rivers, mountains, and swamplands, each of which was recognized as a deity in its own right. Upon giving **birth** to fire, however, Izanami sustained critical wounds and died. Izanagi follows her to the land of **death**, is polluted by her corpse, and is forced to use a large rock to separate the world of the living from the world of the dead.

Cleansing himself in a river, Izanagi creates more deities, including Amaterasu (the sun goddess) and Susano-o (the storm god). To Amaterasu, he awards sovereignty over the dry land, and to Susano-o, he gives the sea. Susano-o is unhappy with his lot, and the accounts detail the nature of his feud with Amaterasu before continuing on to chronicle the deeds of

Amaterasu's successors, down to the time of the eighth-century rulers of Yamato, one of the two main population centers of the time. Amaterasu was recognized as the chief deity and forbear of the Yamato people, while her younger brother Susano-o served the same purpose for Izumo, the other major cultural center. Thus, the mythical stories of divine conflict may also be read as a thin gloss on more mundane political strife between Yamato and Izumo, which had been subjugated shortly before the chronicles were recorded.

In addition to this protohistorical compilation of **myth** and **legend**, another of the major undertakings of the Yamato state was the compilation of a series of gazetteers, one for each major geographical area under its rule. Only one of these documents survives: not coincidentally, perhaps, it is the one from Izumo (*Izumo fūdoki*, 733). Like the *Record of Ancient Matters* and *The Chronicle of Japan*, the *Izumo Gazetteer* records oral traditions regarding the origins of place names, the mythical creation of geographical features, and the deeds of local deities.

Medieval and Early Modern Collections

Explanatory Tales. The next major written source of premodern folktales comes largely from the Buddhist tradition. Buddhism was introduced to Japan in the mid-sixth century by an envoy from the Korean peninsula; the new religion was recommended for its abilities to cure disease and protect the state. It remained largely a court religion until the early tenth century, when restrictions on clerical proselytizing were finally loosened. Once monks and, to a lesser extent, nuns were able to travel throughout the countryside, they faced the challenge of explaining abstract religious notions, such as karma and reincarnation, to a rural populace. One of the techniques they used was to draw on local **storytelling** traditions, reshaping folkloric accounts of anomalous events in terms of Buddhist doctrine to create **didactic tale**s.

A number of "setsuwa" (explanatory tale or **etiologic tale**) collections survive, ranging from the ninth to the sixteenth centuries. While many are explicitly Buddhist in orientation, this is not always the case. The most influential of these collections is the *Konjaku monogatari* (*Tales of Times Now Past*, early twelfth century). The multivolume work, divided into thirty-one chapters, follows the expansion of Buddhism eastward, beginning with tales from India, continuing with lore from China and Korea, and concluding with twenty-one chapters of folktales from Japan. Most of the tales in the collection begin with the formulaic "Ima wa mukashi" ("At a time now past"), and end with the phrase, "and so it is handed down," suggesting the tales' origin in oral tradition. The collection provides fascinating glimpses of people from all walks of life; its protagonists hail from all realms of the natural and supernatural, from demons, warring spirits, and human beings to Buddhas, local deities, and even plants. Typical themes include **Jātaka** tales, journeys to hell, encounters with animals disguised as human beings, dreams relating to one's next incarnation, the workings of karma, and daring escapes from demons, robbers, and brigands. As with most premodern collections, the folktales consist mostly of sparsely related plot developments, though the more markedly Buddhist collections will often append a briefly sketched **moral** interpretation.

Companion Tales. Aside from religiously oriented collections, there was also a strong tradition of secular storytelling throughout the late medieval and early modern period (roughly the twelfth through the eighteenth centuries). About 400 examples of these "companion tales" ("otogizōshi"), as they were called, have survived into the modern era.

As with the explanatory tales, when surveyed as a group, the companion tales provide a full commedia of medieval and early modern culture. Many of these folktales, later made famous in children's picture books, are first recorded in the 1300s and 1400s, where they were often accompanied by **illustration**s. One of the characteristics of this period in Japanese history is the development of a plethora of street **performance** genres—many of the companion tales would have been disseminated by traveling performers who kept their audience's interest by accompanying their stories with the well-timed revelation of a new picture.

The stories themselves are much more fleshed-out than those found in explanatory tale collections, though they still consist mostly of plot developments. Rather than tending toward the moralistic, however, these tales are generally humorous, at times even ribald. The popular story "Lazy Tarō" is typical. The tale opens with Tarō, a sort of peasant antihero, sleeping by the ditch that he calls home. A passerby throws Tarō a rice cake, and he decides to save it for later; but the food falls from his hand and rolls a few feet downhill. Too lazy to retrieve it, Tarō tries to cajole the next passerby, the local land steward, into picking it up for him. Amused by Tarō's antics and verbal wit, the land steward decrees that the local townspeople must feed him. Before long, the townspeople hatch a plan to send Tarō to the capital as their required corvée laborer. Though everyone expects the worst, the unwittingly witty Tarō flourishes in the capital, winning both an aristocratic wife and a fortune. He also attracts the attention of the emperor, who discovers that Tarō is, in fact, the long-forgotten son of an aristocratic exile. Other companion tales also tend to focus on themes of social leveling and the unexpected reversal of fortunes, a motif emblematic of much artistic production from this time period.

Folklore and Nation

The late 1600s saw the rise of the nativist school of philosophy, which stressed the importance of reviving Japan's earliest oral traditions and envisioned a recuperation of native Japanese speech patterns which, in the nativists' opinion, had become buried under the weight of Chinese linguistic influence. The earliest generation of nativist scholars focused their attentions on Japan's first poetry anthology, the *Man'yōshū* (*Collection of Ten Thousand Leaves*, 759), which compiled more than 350 years of orally transmitted poetry. Increasingly, however, attention turned to folktales as a potential treasure trove of living oral tradition. Ueda Akinari was one prolific author who, reading this trend correctly, drew extensively on folktales as a major intertextual source for his fiction, in which he tried to capture the nuances of everyday, vernacular language rather than relying on the stilted patterns of formal, literary Japanese. Ueda's *Ugetsu monogatari* (*Tales of Moonlight and Rain*, 1768) mines Chinese and Japanese folkloric tradition for tales of the supernatural, and it was published to quick critical and popular acclaim. It remains an influential work today and was made into a movie by Mizoguchi Kenji (*Ugetsu monogatari*) in 1953.

Another key author to mention in this connection is the émigré Lafcadio Hearn (Japanese name Koizumi Yakumo). Of Greek and Irish parentage, Hearn arrived in Japan in 1890 after having spent time studying Creole and Caribbean folklore in and around New Orleans. He lived the rest of his life in Japan and published a number of works that drew directly on Japanese folktales for their inspiration. His *Japanese Fairy Tales* was first published in 1898, followed by *Ghostly Japan* in 1899, and his most important collection, *Kwaidan: Stories and Studies of Strange Things* in 1903. Kobayashi Masaki adapted four of the stories from this last into movie format in his 1964 film *Kwaidan* (known alternately as *Kaidan [Ghost Stories]*).

Yanagita Kunio is perhaps the single most important figure in terms of the study, collection, and dissemination of Japanese folktales in the modern period. Like many scholars of his time, Yanagita was both inspired by and resistant to the westernization of modern Japanese culture. He envisioned the countryside as a numinous point of connection with Japan's past, and he got his start as a journalist by penning accounts of his travels for the magazine *Tabi to densetsu* (*Travel and Tradition*) and the Asahi newspaper. In the summer of 1909, he journeyed on horseback through the mountainous areas of Iwate Prefecture in northern Japan. In 1910, he published an enormously influential book, *Tōno monogatari* (*Tales of Tōno*), in which he relayed his own experiences in the mountains and recounted local folktales that he had heard primarily from his **informant** Sasaki Kizen (also known as Kyōseki). Representative stories deal with topics such as the appearance of deities of hearth, mountain, and village and encounters with malicious creatures like "kappa" (a sort of water sprite who takes pleasure in drowning the unwary) and "tengu" (goblinlike beings of a martial spirit). Yanagita went on to found the first formal academic society for the study of Japanese folktales and led the movement to institutionalize folklore as a major field of study. **Seki** Keigo built on Yanagita's pioneering work to create a multivolume index of Japanese **tale type**s based on the system originally developed by Antti **Aarne** and Stith **Thompson**.

Contemporary Revisions and Improvisations

A number of contemporary authors have incorporated folktales into their short stories and **novel**s. Akutagawa Ryūnosuke's fiction frequently rehearses material from the medieval *Konjaku monogatari* (*Tales of Times Now Past*), and he is particularly deft at mixing tales together to create psychological tension. Kurosawa Akira reworked two of Akutagawa's short stories, as well as scenes from the *Konjaku monogatari*, in his film *Rashomon* (1950). Izumi Kyōka is another popular author from the early 1900s who weaves folkloric material into his fiction, most commonly picking up on the folktale **motif** of humans who undergo a **transformation** into animals. His **novella** "Kōya Hijiri" ("The Holy Man of Mount Kōya," 1900) is his best-known work.

Beginning in the 1980s, **women** authors in particular began to draw on traditional Japanese folktales in highly critical ways. Ohba Minako's stories frequently feature a "yamamba" (mountain **witch**) as their protagonist, while **Kurahashi** Yumiko's short-story collection *Otona no tame no zankoku dōwa* (*Cruel Fairy Tales for Adults*, 1984) retells tales from collections like the *Konjaku monogatari* from the viewpoint of **feminism**. Other authors such as Tsushima Yūko, Kanai Mieko, and **Tawada** Yōko have frequently reworked folkloric motifs in their fiction. Most notably, this group of women writers has revised the classic theme of an interspecies relationship. In the classic folktale the "Crane Wife," for instance, a woodcutter frees a crane from a trap. A few days later, a beautiful young woman, traveling alone through a snowstorm, asks for shelter. She stays with the man, asking only that he not look at her while she is weaving. As is typical with tales about a **forbidden room**, one day the man peeks in at her working at the loom and discovers that she is actually the crane that he saved. The woman, now free from her obligation to him, flies back to her home in the mountains. While traditional folktales of this type generally revolve around the female's debt of gratitude, modern fiction typically disrupts this economy. In Tawada's stories, it is most frequently the male who is the transforming animal, and in fiction by Kanai and Tsushima, the transformed female is often violent and angry, rather than meek and longsuffering.

From their inception in the legends of the early court through to the contemporary period, Japanese folktales have generally been concerned with mature themes and have not shied away from depictions of **sexuality** or **violence**. From at least the medieval period, folktales have also often taken on critical or moralistic tones. Since the late 1900s, certain anime and manga artists, most notably Tezuka Osamu and **Miyazaki** Hayao, have begun to produce folkloric material that is accessible to a wider age range. *See also* Animal Bride, Animal Groom; Animation; Intertextuality; Japanese Popular Culture; Nationalism.

Further Readings: Aoki Michiko Yamaguchi. *Izumo fūdoki.* Tokyo: Sophia University, 1971; Aston, W. G., trans. *Nihongi: Chronicles of Japan from the Earliest Times to AD 697.* 1896. Tokyo: Tuttle Publishing, 1972; Chamberlain, Basil Hall. *The Kojiki: Records of Ancient Matters.* Tokyo: Tuttle Publishing, 2005; Hearn, Lafcadio. *Kwaidan: Stories and Studies of Strange Things.* Tokyo: Tuttle Publishing, 2005; Koschmann, Victor, ed. *International Perspectives on Yanagita Kunio and Japanese Folklore Studies.* Ithaca, NY: Cornell University East Asia Program, 1985; Seki Keigo. *Folktales of Japan.* Translated by Robert J. Adams. Chicago: University of Chicago Press, 1963; Skord, Virginia. *Tales of Tears and Laughter: Short Fiction of Medieval Japan.* Honolulu: University of Hawaii Press, 1991; Ueda Akinari. *Ugetsu monogatari: Tales of Moonlight and Rain.* Translated by Leon Zolbrod. Tokyo: Charles E. Tuttle Company, 1974; Ury, Marian. *Tales of Times Now Past: 62 Stories from a Medieval Japanese Collection.* Berkeley: University of California Press, 1985.

Charlotte Eubanks

Jarrell, Randall (1914–1965)

Even before he began to translate **Grimm** fairy tales for collections such as *The Golden Bird* (1962) and *The Juniper Tree* (1973), the major American poet and critic Randall Jarrell had published **poetry** that evinced his belief that fairy tales might offer cultural sustenance for a modern psyche traumatized by two catastrophic world wars. In "The **Märchen**" (1948), Jarrell links modernity's postwar paralysis to its willful misreading of the old tales about fishermen, hunters, charcoal-burners, and "soldiers wandering through the country with a crutch." A lust for "power" and a false wishfulness, he hints, led the twentieth-century mind to deny the import of narratives such as "The **Fisherman and His Wife**," for the flounder's hen-pecked petitioner, whom Jarrell calls "Hänsel by the eternal sea," squandered a self-awareness that could have led "to change, to change!"

Jarrell relied on "**Sleeping Beauty**," "**Cinderella**," and "**Hansel and Gretel**" (the latter in another early poem called "A Quilt-Pattern") in verses that reflected his deep interest in the psychologies of both adults and children. In "Children Selecting Books in a Library," he likened youthful readers to foragers whose intuitive selection of "one cure for Everychild's diseases / Beginning: *Once upon a time there was*" can become a therapeutic legacy for later life. It is not surprising, therefore, that Jarrell should have moved from his 1954 novel for adults, *Pictures from an Institution* (into which he had woven references to the Grimms' tale "The Juniper Tree"), to a series of wonder books for children. Three of these, *The Bat-Poet* (1964), *The Animal Family* (1965), and *Fly By Night* (finished before the poet's death in 1965 but not published until 1976), were illustrated by Maurice **Sendak**, who also provided the drawings for Jarrell's Grimm translations in the two-volume *The Juniper Tree.*

Jarrell's *The Animal Family*, though marketed as a children's book, probably ought to be read, like the work of the German Romantic fabulists that he and Sendak so greatly treasured, as an adult **literary fairy tale** rather than as a children's text. The narrative features protagonists whose contrary origins accentuate their **hybridity**: a **mermaid** who has escaped the watery realm of Hans Christian **Andersen**'s famous tale and a shipwrecked hunter who, like Robinson Crusoe, is so swathed in animal furs that he almost seems half-bestial himself. Unable to have children of their own, this odd couple of island dwellers adopts a trio of foundlings: a bear cub, a lynx kitten, and, finally, a little boy who is washed ashore. The child, who identifies himself more with his fantastic **mother**, mends the incompleteness of both surrogate parents. It is the hunter, however, whom Jarrell cures of traumatic memories of an early severance from his own parents. *See also* Childhood and Children.

Further Readings: Flynn, Richard. *Randall Jarrell and the Lost World of Childhood.* Athens: University of Georgia Press. 1990; Griswold, Jerome. *The Children's Books of Randall Jarrell.* Athens: University of Georgia Press. 1988.

U. C. Knoepflmacher

Jātaka

Jātakas are the stories of the Buddha's former births and incarnations. In folktale studies, they are considered to be the oldest known folk narratives. Jātakas have assumed special importance in oral narrative research because they include known **tale type**s and resemble tales found in other Indo-European traditions. Edward B. Cowell's six-volume edition of Jātaka stories, translated from the Pali by a team of scholars, was first published in 1895–1907. Although Cowell's edition is the most exhaustive and scholarly version of the tales, they are also available in other popular formats, including **children's literature**.

Jātaka stories have been popular since the third century BCE. They are believed to have been told by the Buddha himself to his followers at different times. The narrative texts contain the situation in which the story was told. Something in this situation reminds Buddha of one of his previous lives, and he relates an experience that culminates in one of the precepts of Buddhism. The subjects of these narratives include life themes that range from the personal to the political and from animal to human. In previous incarnations, Buddha lived as both human and animal, and at the end of each narrative, Buddha even connects his listeners to their roles in his former lives. The idea of rebirth that pervades all of these stories has its roots in Hindu cosmology and its concept of time. It illustrates the point that an individual's accountability to the world and other people does not end with **death**. *See also* Didactic Tale; Frame Narrative; Religious Tale.

Further Reading: Cowell, Edward B., ed. *The Jātaka or Stories of the Buddha's Former Births.* Translated from the Pali by various hands. 6 volumes in 3. New Delhi: Munshiram Manoharlal Publishers, 1990.

Sadhana Naithani

Jest and Joke

The jest is an idle tale or a mocking speech intended to provoke laughter. The word "joke," used originally in slang or colloquial speech, typically denotes a short narrative constructed around a punch line. As with the jest, jokes are intended to amuse, not to give offense.

Jests are conversational in style and make their point succinctly. Early examples occur in Homer's *Odyssey* and *Iliad*; in the former, we find jests about *things done* (the jest about

Hephaistos told by the blind minstrel) and *things said* (Odysseus's tale about escaping from the Cyclops). Medieval jestbooks were compilations of short, merry prose tales or witty remarks, and were used primarily by preachers as sermon material. In Renaissance Florence, Gian Francesco Poggio Bracciolini's *Liber facetiarum* (*Book of Jests*, 1470) is a good example of jests (Latin *facetiae*) used parodically, without a moralizing intention.

In 1477, Heinrich Steinhöwel compiled a Latin and German collection of **Aesop**ian **fable**s, appending jests from both Poggio and Petrus Alphonsus. This was translated into French by Jules de Machault (1483) and printed in English translation by William Caxton in 1484. Other key examples of English jestbooks are *A Hundred Merry Tales* (1526) by John Rastell; the *Tales and Quick Answers* (1536), translated from Erasmus, Poggio, and Sebastian Brandt, author of the satirical *Narrenshiff* (*Ship of Fools*, 1494); and the *Mirror of Mirth* (1583), wherein jestbook and prose fiction meet.

Jokes may take the form of **riddle**s and **proverb**s, but usually they appear as brief, fictional narratives like the **folktale**. Classical fairy tales are often adapted for use in jokes, where the well-known plots, characters, **motif**s, and morals are given a humorous twist, parodied, or subverted, evoking laughter. *See also* Adaptation; Cartoons and Comics; Iranian Tales; Parody; Trickster.

Further Readings: Jones, Steven Swann. "Joking Transformations of Popular Fairy Tales: A Comparative Analysis of Five Jokes and Their Fairy Tale Sources." *Western Folklore* 44 (1985): 97–114; Oring, Elliot. *Folk Groups and Folklore Genres: An Introduction.* Logan: Utah State University Press, 1986; Preston, Cathy Lynn. "'Cinderella' as a Dirty Joke: Gender, Multivocality, and the Polysemic Text." *Western Folklore* 53 (1994): 27–49; Zall, P. M., ed. *A Hundred Merry Tales and Other English Jestbooks of the Fifteenth and Sixteenth Centuries.* Lincoln: University of Nebraska Press, 1963.

Ana Raquel Fernandes

Jewish Tales

An exceptional feature of the Jewish folktale is that part of the corpus has been preserved in writing since the biblical era. Although these stories—found in the **Bible**, Apocrypha, Rabbinic literature, and medieval texts—have been edited, they are readily identifiable as folktales for a number of reasons: there are frequently multiple versions of the same story; they employ the typical poetics of folk literature; and they belong to folk literary genres.

Ethnographic transcription of Jewish folktales for documentary and scholarly purposes did not begin until the nineteenth century, under the influence of ideological currents in Europe such as Romanticism and nationalism. The fact that these tales have been preserved in writing for so many generations enables in-depth historical research of the Jewish folktale.

The Folktale in the Bible

The Bible encompasses more than 1,000 years of cultural creation. Its stories are full of folk **motif**s. Some of them can be identified as folktales that circulated orally, as indicated by the existence of alternate versions of the same story. The most conspicuous examples of this are the two accounts of the creation of woman (Gen. 1.27 and Gen. 2.21–22); the story of Sarai in Pharaoh's house (Gen. 12.6–20), which is recapitulated when she is abducted by Abimelech, king of Gerar (Genesis 20); and the three versions of Saul's elevation to the kingship (1 Sam. 9.1–10.16; 1 Sam. 10.17–27; and 1 Sam. 11).

Some biblical narratives can also be found in the traditions of the ancient Near East and had international circulation, notably the story of the flood (Gen. 6.9–8.14). The story of Joseph and Potiphar's wife (Genesis 39) is a well-known type about the seduction of a young man by an older woman. The duel between David and Goliath is a version of the prevalent **märchen** or **wonder tale** in which it is always the youngest brother who kills the monster and marries the **princess** (1 Sam. 17–18). Stories of rainmaking and miraculous cures are found in the Elijah and Elisha cycles (1 Kings 17–19; 2 Kings 2.19–22, 4–5).

The most prominent genre in the Bible is the **myth** (the creation stories); however, we also encounter foundation stories, naming stories, and **legend**s, such as those of the patriarchs in Genesis and of the prophets in the book of Kings. There are legendary elements in the book of Jonah and the book of Job. The **parable** is represented by that of Jotham (Judg. 9.6–20), the story of the poor man's ewe lamb (2 Sam. 12.1–4), and Jehoash of Israel's story of the thistle and the cedar (2 Kings 14.8–11; 2 Chron. 25.17–19). There are also **novella**s, including the judgment of Solomon (1 Kings 3.16–27), the Joseph story, and the book of Esther.

The Folktale in the Apocrypha

The Second Temple period covers approximately 500 years of Jewish history, including decisive events such as the return to Zion, the cultural penetration by Hellenism, the Hasmonean revolt, the birth of Christianity, and the establishment of large Jewish centers in Babylonia and Egypt. Many folktales of this period have come down to us in the Apocrypha and Pseudepigrapha, in books that were not admitted to the canon of the Hebrew Bible. Most of this fragmentary material has reached us second and third hand. Many of these books profess to be by or about characters and events known from the Bible. In this respect, there is continuity from the folktales of the biblical period, expressed also in the topics treated, in the materials used, and in the literary genres. Here we can mention stories that expand on biblical accounts and praise-tale cycles (for example, the stories of Daniel). Some of the stories, however, do not have biblical antecedents, although they later became patterns of Jewish folk literature. These include the narratives of coping with life in the Diaspora, which tell of the deliverance of a Jewish community and the doom of those who sought to destroy it. This pattern can be traced back to the book of Esther, but here it is significantly expanded. There are also two stories whose heroines became the **archetype**s for **women** in times of persecution: the story of the **mother** and her seven sons, recounted in two versions in the books of Maccabees (2 Macc. 7 and 4 Macc. 8–15), whose heroine became the archetype of the mother who dies a martyr's death; and Judith, who became the model for female bravery in times of persecution.

The Folktale in Rabbinic Literature

"Rabbinic literature" designates the corpus of texts redacted in the first centuries of the Common Era, which contain traditions that had been transmitted orally and in writing by groups of scholars or sages. This corpus has two main branches—*halakhah* (law) and *aggadah* (lore). These works can be classified by how they relate to the biblical text. They may be divided by their method of arrangement, whether topically, or as a sort of commentary or gloss on the biblical text. Those produced by the *tannaim* (late Second Temple period until c. 220 CE) are found in the Mishnah, Tosefta, and halakhic midrashim (a collection of expositions on biblical verses, usually arranged in the order of verses of a biblical books;

the earliest midrashim are halakhic midrashim). The subsequent period of the *amoraim* (third to fifth centuries) began with the death of Rabbi Judah of the Patriarch. Their traditions, organized as commentaries and expansions on the Mishnah, are recorded in the two Talmuds (the Jerusalem Talmud and the Babylonian Talmud). Not long after the final redaction of the Jerusalem Talmud (late fourth century), several series of homiletic or aggadic midrashim (redacted almost all in Palestine from the transmitted aggadic material of the Amoraic period) were compiled, almost all of them in Eretz Israel.

All of these rabbinic texts are based on the discourses and lectures delivered in the synagogues and houses of study during the Tannaitic and Amoraic periods on Sabbaths and festivals, during lifecycle events (**birth**, **marriage**, and **death**), and on other public occasions. They draw on the link with all strata of the people and incorporate many **folklore** elements, including folktales. Some of the stories told by the sages are expanded biblical narratives. Others are biographical legends about biblical figures, about some of the sages themselves, and about other historical personages canonized by the people. There are also historical legends, **exempla**, animal **fable**s, parables, **ghost stories**, **tall tale**s, and humorous stories. The existence of several **variant**s of the same story in talmudic literature is evidence of their folklore origins, as are the elements of folk-literature poetics that inform them. In some, one can clearly discern the influence of the folk literature of neighboring peoples, and especially Babylonian and Persian motifs.

The Jewish Folktale in the Middle Ages

A number of compositions from the **Middle Ages** contain folktales reworked by authors of that period. Some of them represent continuity with the talmudic tradition, but there are also stories not known to have been written down previously. The earliest of these works is the *Midrash Aseret Hadibrot* (*Midrash of the Ten Commandments*), which dates from the eighth or ninth century. This book continues the earlier midrashic tradition in both its name and its structure (it is ordered by biblical verses, for which it offers homiletic interpretations). In a departure, however, the narrative element is emphasized at the expense of the moralistic element. An important anthology of stories is the ninth-century *Alpha Beta De'Ben Sira* (*Alphabet of Ben Sira*). Its **frame narrative** recounts how the child Ben Sira, summoned to the Babylonian king Nebuchadnezzar, answered each of the king's twenty-two questions (corresponding to the letters of the Hebrew alphabet) with a folktale. Some of these narratives became an integral part of the later Jewish folk tradition, notably those about Lilith, the Queen of Sheba, and the animals in Noah's ark. These two works, produced in the Mesopotamian-Persian cultural sphere, reveal its influence, as well as that of books that circulated in the region and were known also to Jews, such as the *Tales of Kalila and Dimna* and the *Tales of Sindabar* (**Sindbad**).

Other important works are the *Hibbur yafeh meha-yeshuah* (*An Elegant Compilation Concerning Relief After Adversity*) by the outstanding talmudist Rabbi Nissim ben Jacob of Kairouan (eleventh century); *Sefer ha-Ma'asim* (*Book of Deeds*, France, twelfth century), whose tales are based on the European exemplum; and *Sefer ha-Hasidim* (*Book of the Pious*), composed by Rabbi Judah the Pious in Germany in the thirteenth century. This last work, which consists of some 400 stories, is a key document of the German Pietists and of medieval tales in general.

Among the works that include expansions on biblical narratives but frequently go far beyond the biblical text are *Midrash va-Yosha, Toldot Moshe* (*The Chronicles of Moses*),

Sippur Abraham (*The Story of Abraham*), and *Sefer ha-Yashar* (*Book of Pietists*), written in the late Middle Ages. All of them build on a biblical core that serves as the nucleus for a new story that is fully developed and independent of the Bible and whose world and style are in tune with the Middle Ages.

The historical legend is another important medieval genre. Prominent in this category is the *Sefer Josippon* (*Book of Josippon*), written in southern Italy in the tenth century. It is based on the historical works of Josephus Flavius but adds material taken from the talmudic sages and the early Middle Ages to create a sort of historical novel typical of the period. Another historical composition is the *Megilat Ahima'az* (*Scroll of Ahima'az*), a family chronicle written by Ahima'az ben Paltiel in southern Italy in the eleventh century. The *Sefer Ha'Zikhronot* (*Book of Memoirs*), produced in Germany in the early fourteenth century, is a Jewish folk history running from the Creation until the End of Days. *Shalshelet ha-kabbalah* (*The Chain of Tradition*), by Gedaliah ben Joseph Ibn Yahya (Italy, sixteenth century), makes extensive use of hagiographic legends in its presentation of the annals of Torah scholars from the earliest times to the author's own day.

Animal fables and parables were also popular genres in the Middle Ages. They can be found in various works, of which the most important is the *Mishlei shualim* (*Fox Parables*) of Berechiah ben Natronai the Punctuator (thirteenth century).

The Folktale in the Modern Era

The transcription of folktales within Jewish cultures and communities, to preserve and publish them, goes back to the seventeenth century, but no scholarly pretensions were involved. Serious documentation and research had to wait for the nineteenth century. The *Mayse Bukh* (*Mayse Book: Book of Jewish Tales and Legends*), a Yiddish collection of 257 tales compiled by Jacob ben Abraham, was printed in Basel at the start of the seventeenth century. At the end of the century, Eliezer Lieberman translated a collection of historical legends transcribed by his father from Hebrew into Yiddish. This volume was published in Amsterdam in 1696. Another important work, which expresses the cultural identity of the Sephardi Jews, is the Judeo-Spanish *Me'am Lo'ez* (*Me'am Lo'ez—The Torah Anthology*) by Ya'acov Culi.

Folktales were central to Hasidism from its early days in the eighteenth century. In addition to the traditional folktales that Jews had always told, two types emerged to occupy an important role in Hasidic religious practice because they were perceived as a form of divine worship with the potential to rectify the world. The first of these categories is the märchen, which only the *zaddik* (rebbe) himself may tell. Some of these wonder tales are borrowed from the neighboring peoples of eastern Europe. The Hasidim believed that when the rebbe reworked and told them, he was amending both the story and the world. One such book is the *Sefer ha-Ma'assiyot* (*A Book of Tales*), which collects tales told by Rabbi Nahman of Bratslav. The second category is the praise tale, the hagiographic legends that the Hasidim told about their rebbes. The best-known collection of these is the *Shivhei ha-Besht* (*Praises of the Baal Shem Tov*, 1814). The most prominent anthology of Sephardi tales from this period is *Oseh Pele* (*The Miracle Worker*), edited by Joseph Shabbetai Farhi and first published in Livorno in 1864.

As noted, the collection of folktales for documentation and scholarship began in the nineteenth century. In 1897, Dr. Max Grunwald founded the Gesellschaft für jüdische Volkskunde (Society for Jewish Folklore) and edited its periodical, the *Mitteilungen für jüdische Volkskunde,* from 1898 to 1922. In eastern Europe, the collection of folk materials began in the nineteenth century and accelerated in the early twentieth century. Between 1912 and 1914, the first ethnographic expedition, headed by S. An-Ski (Solomon Zainwil Rapaport), traveled through the small towns of Volhynia and Podolia collecting folk materials, including folktales. A group of transcribers led by Noah Prylucki, who was inspired by the author J. L. Peretz, was active in Warsaw. The institution that collected folktales most intensively was YIVO, the Jewish Scientific Institute, established in 1920. Many of its treasures were lost during the Holocaust; some are now housed at the YIVO Institute for Jewish Research in New York City.

In Israel, Dov Noy founded the Israel Folktale **Archives** in Haifa in 1955. Housed today at the University of Haifa, its holdings of 23,000 tales constitute the largest single collection of Jewish folktales in the world.

One of the unusual traits of Jewish folktales is their polyglot existence. Jews generally told their stories in the vernacular of their own community—Yiddish, Judezmo (Ladino), Judeo-Arabic, and so on. Jewish folktales include all of the genres found in the poetics of folk literature. The topics are diverse: there are accounts of the relations between Jews and Gentiles, deliverance from **blood** libels, martyrdom, and so forth; stories about Jewish settlements in various countries and the founding of major Jewish communities there; legends about holy men, ghosts, and demons; ethical principles such as charity, and the ritual precepts between human beings and God and the social precepts governing relations among people; and stories about festivals and life-cycle ceremonies, including circumcision, bar mitzvah, marriage, burial, and the comforting of mourners.

International wonder tales have also penetrated the corpus. The holdings of the Israel Folktale Archives include many of these. Sometimes, distinctly Jewish elements have penetrated these global stories, in the person of King Solomon, the prophet Elijah, and so on. Sometimes the plot format is modified to create a Jewish **oicotype**. Another interesting phenomenon is the alteration that takes place in an international wonder tale when it is transmuted from a märchen into a Jewish legend.

Modern Israel is developing its own ethnic culture. The folktales of the various groups of immigrants draw on the stories they brought with them from their countries of origin, but in Israel they are substantially transformed by the new culture. In addition, new stories of immigration and social integration are created to express the encounter with Israeli landscapes, **food**, other Jewish groups, and Arab society. The emerging myths of Israeli society constitute another important genre. These are the "big" cultural stories that seek to reinforce the glue that holds the new society together. They include stories about the defense of Tel Hai, the Masada narrative, the Tower and Stockade settlements, the submarine Dakar, and others. Place stories have also been created. These focus on the early days of Zionist settlement and are linked with local personalities. Kibbutz stories are central to this category.

Israeli culture also has many humorous stories, **jest**s, and **joke**s. Scholars compare them to the humor of Jews in the Diaspora. The most thoroughly studied form of the Israeli humorous tale is the Palmach *chizbat*. These are humorous tales that are identified with Palmach, the elite military units of the Jewish underground during the last years of the British mandate in Palestine. According to the popular image, the stories were told in the evenings, around the campfire as members of the Palmach entertained themselves. With the publication of a collection of these tales, this genre came to symbolize quintessential Israeli humor. However, the term is borrowed from dialectical Palestinian Arabic, in which it is the feminine plural form of the word *chizba*, a lie. Although the stories include, in addition to original tales, Hebrew versions of Arabic, traditional Jewish tales, and internationally known narratives, they express the symbols and views of Israeli youth in their attempt to distance themselves from the cultural heritage of the Diaspora. The *chizbat* is always associated with Israeli reality, often containing a grain of truth. It deals with real events and real people who are familiar to the narrating society. Its language is Hebrew, interspersed with words in Arabic, Yiddish, Russian, and English. After the establishment of the state of Israel, there was a marked decline in the narration of these tales, although a popularly published additional collection purported to prove the opposite. In the transformation of the genre, the narration situation remained, but its content changed, and the term refers to horror stories told by teenagers around the campfire.

Further Readings: Bar-Itzhak, Haya. *Israeli Folk Narratives: Settlement, Immigration, Ethnicity.* Detroit: Wayne State University Press, 2005; Bar-Itzhak, Haya, and Aliza Shenhar. *Jewish Moroccan Folk Narratives from Israel.* Detroit: Wayne State University Press, 1993; Ben-Amos, Dan. "Jewish Folk Literature." *Oral Tradition* 14.1 (1999): 140–274. http://journal.oraltradition.org/issues/14i/ben-amos; ———, ed. "Jewish Folktales." *Jewish Folklore and Ethnology Review* 14.1–2 (1992): 3–25; Ben-Amos, Dan, and Jerome R. Mintz, ed, and trans. *In Praise of the Baal Shem Tov [Shivḥei ha-Besht]: The Earliest Collection of Legends about the Founder of Hasidism.* Bloomington: Indiana University Press, 1970; Gaster, Moses, trans. and ed. *Ma'asseh Book: Book of Jewish Tales and Legends.* 2 volumes. Philadelphia: Jewish Publication Society of America, 1934; Hasan-Rokem, Galit. *The Web of Life: Folklore and Midrash in Rabbinic Literature.* Translated by Batya Stein. Stanford, CA: Stanford University Press, 2000; Noy, Dov, and Dan Ben-Amos, eds. *The Folktales of Israel.* Translated by Gene Baharav. Chicago: University of Chicago Press, 1963; Oring, Elliott. *Israeli Humor: The Content and Structure of the Chizbat of the Palmah.* Albany: State University of New York Press, 1981; Yassif, Eli. *The Hebrew Folktale: History, Genre, Meaning.* Translated by Jacqueline S. Teitelbaum. Bloomington: Indiana University Press, 1999.

Haya Bar-Itzhak

Joke. *See* Jest and Joke

Jolles, André. *See* Simple Forms

Jones, Diana Wynne (1934–)

Diana Wynne Jones is a British children's **fantasy** author of varied, quirky **novel**s that lend an ironic realism to familiar magical, folkloric, and fairy-tale **motif**s. While many of Jones's novels follow the model of classic children's fantasy, in which the young wielders of magic come to terms with their powers, her often-complex and convoluted narratives rely heavily on recognizable fairy-tale symbols and patterns. Some of her fantasies use mythological rather than fairy-tale elements, most notably the Norse pantheon in *Eight Days of Luke* (1975) and the stars and constellations in *Dogsbody* (1975). Recurring folkloric themes in her work include wicked **witch**es, animal **transformation**s, curses, and magicians' lives hidden in objects. *Archer's Goon* (1984) also features a seventh-son hero. In *Fire and Hemlock* (1985), Jones updates the story of Thomas the Rhymer to a contemporary setting. *Howl's Moving Castle* (1986) and *Castle in the Air* (1990) make playful use of traditional folkloric patterns, such as the failure of the eldest daughter, magical curses, and conditions, and the ***Arabian Nights*** motifs such as flying carpets and genies in bottles. *Black Maria* (1991) offers a particularly interesting investigation of stereotypical **gender** roles within magical narratives, an interest pursued in *The Merlin Conspiracy* (2003). Notably, Jones tends to use the magical elements of her stories as a means of psychological exploration.

She is particularly skilled in her representation of dysfunctional families and relationships, which are understood and transformed through magical experiences.

Jones's best-known works are probably the Chrestomanci series of novels, comprising *Charmed Life* (1977), *The Magicians of Caprona* (1980), *Witch Week* (1982), *The Lives of Christopher Chant* (1988), and *Conrad's Fate* (2005), plus some short stories. These are far more accomplished precursors to the Harry Potter phenomenon and feature multiple parallel universes and matter-of-fact magic subject to government regulation. While these follow the fantasy format of magical heroes, rather than the fairy-tale's example of mundane heroes who are subject to marvelous events, they present the magical as the site of discovery, self-knowledge, and ethical debates about power and responsibility—a common thread throughout Jones's work.

A similar series of debates is reflected in Jones's more adult novels. *Deep Secret* (1997) and its sequel *The Merlin Conspiracy* (2003), together with the stand-alone novel *A Sudden Wild Magic* (1992), play with the notion of cabals of magic users behind our mundane world. While the novels invoke New Age notions of paganism and formalized magic, they also treat them with an irony that becomes actual satire in other adult novels. *The Tough Guide to Fantasyland* (1996) mercilessly attacks the clichés of the modern fantasy romance, the basically commercial underpinning of which is likewise exposed in *The Dark Lord of Derkholm* (1998), where a tour-guide operator from our own universe ruthlessly exploits a standard fantasy world. Jones's obvious affection for the tropes and themes of the fantastic is always ironically self-aware and refreshingly down-to-earth. *See also* Children's Literature; Miyazaki Hayao.

Further Readings: Nikolajeva, Maria. "Fairy Tale and Fantasy: From Archaic to Postmodern." *Marvels & Tales* 17 (2003): 138–56; Rosenberg, Teya, Martha Hixon, Sharon Scapple, and Donna White, eds. *Diana Wynne Jones: An Exciting and Exacting Wisdom.* New York: Peter Lang, 2002.

Jessica Tiffin

Jones, Terry (1942–)

The Welsh scriptwriter, actor, medievalist, and children's writer Terry Jones is most famous for his contributions to the Monty Python **television** series. Most of Jones's considerable scriptwriting output is slanted toward comedy, and a zany humor underpins his children's writing.

Jones's most fairy-tale-like offerings are the two children's collections, *Fairy Tales* (1981) and *Fantastic Tales* (1994), both attractively illustrated by Michael Foreman. Jones makes the most of the classically sparse texture of fairy tales, achieving a comically flat and matter-of-fact statement of the ridiculous. The tales play with classic **motif**s of **king**s, **princess**es, monsters, charms, **fairies**, and **magic object**s; their heroes are mostly children or innocents, and their patterns of symbol and repetition are self-consciously folkloric. Many of these tales border on **fable** in their construction around a straightforward moral lesson—occasionally too much so, in tales that shade into **parable** or allegory.

As with fairy tales, the emphasis in Jones's other children's works is on morality and the growth to self-knowledge of the heroes. *The Saga of Eric the Viking* (1983) is a children's **epic**, a mythological adventure/quest narrative featuring a warrior hero and his companions. Its tone is somewhat different to the later, more adult **film** version (1989). *Nicobobinus* (1985) is a slightly frenetic children's adventure tale, which employs the same incongruity and lateral humor found in Jones's fairy tales. Two medieval stories, *The Knight and the Squire* (1997) and *The Lady and the Squire* (2000), are more straightforward historical adventures.

Jones collaborated on the script of *Labyrinth* (1986), the children's fairy-tale film coproduced by Jim **Henson** and George Lucas in which a child, with the aid of animal and **magic helper**s, must rescue her baby brother from the goblin king. The film led to an association with the artist Brian **Froud**, with whom Jones produced *Lady Cottingdon's Pressed Fairy Book* (1994) and its sequels, which rather nastily parody the Victorian obsession with flower-fairies. The books are a good example of the streak of sadistic cruelty characteristic of Monty Python, which still surfaces occasionally in Jones's work. *See also* Children's Literature; Parody.

Further Reading: Wood, Juliette. "Filming Fairies: Popular Film, Audience Response and Meaning in Contemporary Fairy Lore." *Folklore* 117 (2006): 279–96.

Jessica Tiffin

Jung, Carl Gustav (1875–1961)

Carl Gustav Jung was a depth psychologist most widely known for his theories of the collective unconscious and its **archetype**s. Jung was born in Kesswil, Switzerland, and studied medicine at the University of Basel. He first met Sigmund **Freud** in Vienna in 1907. Initially, Freud regarded Jung as his scientific "son and heir"; however, their disagreements grew intensely bitter and ultimately destroyed their friendship. Jung felt that the unconscious was a creative component of the psyche rather than a storehouse for repressed contents, and he disagreed with Freud's insistence that neuroses originated with sexual fantasies and trauma in childhood. In 1914, Jung officially broke with Freud by resigning as president of the International Psychoanalytic Association. He spent the next seven years in introspective isolation (some scholars consider this a period of mental illness) and emerged with the concept of the archetypes and the collective unconscious.

Jung's only publication devoted explicitly to the fairy tale is "Zur Phänomenologie des Geistes im Märchen" ("The Phenomenology of the Spirit in Fairytales," 1948); however, he considered the fairy tale, like **myth**, to be particularly rich in archetypal content. In Jungian psychology, the unconscious—both collective and personal—is the creative source of dreams as well as literary and artistic expression. In literary works, the contents of the collective unconscious (the archetypes) often find expression through character types. Fairy tales commonly concretize the archetypes through figures such as the hero, the child, the old man, the **witch**, the **trickster**, and others. Jung deals with such figures in works like "Zur Psychologie des Kind-Archetypus" ("The Psychology of the Child Archetype," 1941) and "Zur Psychologie der Schelmenfigur" ("On the Psychology of the Trickster-Figure," 1954).

As in dreams, the manifestation of archetypes in fairy tales signals the existence of psychic content that has been rejected from the self through projection or repression. Such content is typically universal (greed and lust, for example) yet socially unacceptable. Thus fairy tales (as well as dreams, myth, religion, and art) serve a healthy psychological purpose in bringing dissociated psychic content into the light of consciousness. This initiates the process Jung called individuation, whereby externalized or repressed content is reintegrated into the sphere of the self, resulting in a more self-aware and psychically whole individual.

Jungian analysis continues to be practiced in the field of literary criticism. Critics, however, charge that the theoretical foundations of the collective unconscious and the archetypes lack a sound scientific basis. The most serious issues concern definition and falsifiability. The archetypes lack a precise definition that would allow direct observation (they are often vaguely defined as expressions of human instincts); instead, the manifestations of the archetypes (not the archetypes themselves) must be identified and illuminated by the analyst. Further, without the possibility of directly observing the archetypes, the theory cannot truly be falsified. ***See also*** Franz, Marie-Louise von; Psychological Approaches; Trauma and Therapy.

Further Readings: Jung, Carl Gustav. *Memories, Dreams, Reflections*. New York: Pantheon, 1961; ———. "The Phenomenology of the Spirit in Fairytales." *The Archetypes and the Collective Unconscious*. Translated by R. F. C. Hull. Edited by Sir Herbert Read et al. 2nd edition. Volume 9.1. New York: Princeton University Press, 1990. 207–54; Kerr, John. *A Most Dangerous Method: The Story of Jung, Freud, and Sabina Spielrein*. New York: Vintage, 1994.

R. Seth C. Knox

K

Kafka, Franz (1883–1924)

Franz Kafka was an author of **parable**s, short stories, and three fragmentary novels. Born in Prague, Kafka studied law and worked at the Workmen's Accident Insurance Institute until he retired in 1922 due to tuberculosis. While working for the institute, Kafka wrote most of his work, much of it to be published posthumously through the efforts of his close friend Max Brod.

Although Kafka did not write fairy tales, his stories resemble fairy tales because multiple interpretations are possible, and no single analysis seems sufficient. Several of his stories feature the common fairy-tale **motif** of metamorphosis. "Die Verwandlung" ("The Metamorphosis," 1915) opens with the **transformation** of a human being into what seems to be an insect. Metamorphoses are also suggested in "Ein Bericht für eine Akademie" ("A Report to an Academy," 1917), "Forschungen eines Hundes" ("Investigations of a Dog," 1931), and "Die Brücke" ("The Bridge," 1931), in which an ape, a dog, and a bridge are anthropomorphized.

Although **psychological approaches** often treat Kafka's metamorphoses as symbols of mental illness, these changes may also be seen as symbols of exile resulting from an unspecified **transgression**. An interpretation based on the ideas of Carl Gustav **Jung** would likely focus on Kafka's metamorphoses as concretizations of metaphor—a dreamlike phenomenon suggesting the intrusion of unconscious, archetypal content into consciousness (see **Archetype**). Yet, whereas Jungian psychology would view the appearance of previously unconscious content as having the positive potential for individuation, in Kafka's stories it usually has profoundly negative consequences, reversing the path towards personal and social integration typical of the fairy tale.

Further Reading: Bridgwater, Patrick. *Kafka, Gothic and Fairytale*. Amsterdam: Rodopi, 2003.

R. Seth C. Knox

Kalevala

One major milestone in the history of preserving the Finnish national heritage was the founding of the Finnish Literature Society in 1831 by members of educated circles. Elias Lönnrot was the society's first secretary, and he compiled the Finnish national **epic**, the *Kalevala*, on the basis of folk poetry he had collected mainly in the eastern part of Finland. The first edition of the *Kalevala* appeared in 1835; the second and greatly enlarged edition, with a total of 22,795 lines, appeared in 1849. The epic consists of fifty cantos in alliterative, trochaic verse. The main heroes of the epic are the old sage Väinämöinen, the mythic forger Ilmarinen, and the reckless young Lemminkäinen.

Lönnrot had the Romantic vision of a heroic age in history, fragments of which were preserved in tradition. During the compilation work, Lönnrot decided to become a singer himself. By excluding from the poems details related to later Finnish history and to Christianity, he believed that he could create a reliable picture of the poems of the former golden age of epic. The result is actually a mythical epic since Lönnrot succeeded in **collecting** a large amount of mythic epic poetry that, according to him, represented the archaic era. When his work was finished, he was able to recognize that it would have been possible to create at least seven *Kalevala*s from the material he had amassed.

Before the publication of the *Kalevala*, almost all literature published in Finland in Finnish was of a religious nature. The epic's appearance in 1849 gave rise to a Romantic cultural enthusiasm, and the *Kalevala* became a source of themes for literature, painting, music, and drama. It even inspired such important Finnish figures as the composer Jean Sibelius and the artist Akseli Gallén-Kallela in the creation of their masterpieces. Although the crest of national cultural enthusiasm had passed by the beginning of the twentieth century, the *Kalevala* was still used as a source for the arts even in very recent years, in contemporary **film** and **music**, for example.

More than one hundred editions of the *Kalevala* have been published in Finnish, as well as several dozen abridged versions and adaptations. So far, the Finnish national epic has been translated into more than fifty languages.

While all Finns may be familiar with Lönnrot's *Kalevala*, relatively few have studied the original material—that is, the folk poetry in *Kalevala*-meter, of which there are some two million lines recorded in the archives of the Finnish Literature Society. Although the epic does hold great significance as a national symbol and as an artifact that is extensively used in Finnish culture, it nevertheless does not qualify as an item for pure folkloristic research. About two-thirds of the collected poems have been published in the thirty-four-volume *Suomen kansan vanhat runot* (*Ancient Poems of the Finnish People*, 1908–97). The entire published collection of the *Ancient Poems of the Finnish People*, a total of 27,000 pages, has been put into a digitized corpus. *See also* Scandinavian Tales.

Further Readings: Apo, Satu. "Lönnrot's Voice in the *Kalevala*." *Dynamics of Tradition: Perspectives on Oral Poetry and Folk Belief*. Edited by Lotte Tarkka. Helskinki: Finnish Literature Society, 2003. 266–76; ———. "A Singing Scribe or a Nationalist Author? The Making of the Kalevala as Described by Elias Lönnrot." *FF Network* 25 (Dec. 2003): 3–12.

Lauri Harvilahti

Kamiński, Bohdan. *See* Polívka, Jiří

Karadžić, Vuk Stefanović (1787–1864)

Vuk Stefanović Karadžić was a Serbian philologist, reformer of the Serbian language, and ethnographer responsible for recognizing the value of Serbian folk literature. He collected thousands of versions of lyrics, **proverb**s, **riddle**s, songs, heroic **ballad**s, **epic** poems, **folktale**s, and recorded information about the **informant**s and the circumstances under which the material was collected. He also standardized the vernacular language and promoted the language of the people as the literary language.

Karadžić published numerous important collections, including *Mala prostonarodna slaveno-serbska pesnarica* (*A Small Simple Folk Slavonic Serbian Songbook*, 1814); the monumental *Narodne srpske pjesme* (*Serbian Folksongs*, 1823–33); *Srpske narodne priče* (*Serbian Folktales*, 1821), which included 166 riddles; *Narodne srpske poslovice i druge različne, kao one u običaj uzete riječi* (*Serbian Folk Proverbs and Other Common Expressions*, 1834); *Srpske narodne pjesme iz Ercegovine* (*Serbian Folksongs from Herzegovina*, 1866), including a volume devoted to "women's songs." He also translated the New Testament into Serbian for the British and Foreign Bible Society (first partial edition, 1824; first complete edition, 1847).

Karadžić's collections of Serbian folksongs appeared in Europe during the era of Romanticism and became a confirmation of Johann Gottfried Herder's and the Grimms' ideas about **oral tradition**. Jacob **Grimm** began to learn Serbian so that he could read Karadžić's folksongs in the original and write analyses of them. Thanks to Grimm and to the Slovenian scholar Jernej Kopitar, who was the censor for Slavic books and Karadžić's adviser and protector, Serbian folk literature found its place in world literature. Karadžić's collection of folksongs was translated into German, and, on the basis of German translations, his folksongs and folktales were translated into English, French, Swedish, Russian, and other Slavic languages.

Karadžić differentiated narratives from tales. In *Život i običaji naroda srpskoga* (*The Life and Customs of the Serbian Nation*, 1867), he showed an exceptional familiarity with the material and had a feeling for its form and function. He described these categories terminologically. He considered folk prose, like other oral forms, as the expression of the folk spirit; but he also cared about the language, which expresses that spirit and shapes these forms. His life's goal to establish a literary language was based on promoting the vernacular.

Karadžić also inaugurated linguistic reforms and adopted the Serbian vernacular. His introduction of phonetic spellings and invention of new letters to complete the Cyrillic alphabet were major contributions to Serbian linguistics. In reforming the Serbian Cyrillic orthography, he used Johann Christoph Adelung's saying: "Write as you speak and read as it is written," which means one letter per sound.

Among Karadžić's most important lexicographical works are *Početni udžbenik srpskog jezika* (*Primer of Vernacular Serbian Language*, 1814) and *Rječnik srpskog jezika* (*Dictionary of the Serbian Language*, 1818). As early as the *Dictionary* of 1818, Karadžić published more than twenty humorous tales and narratives to explain certain words and show what people think and say about a given word. For him, folksongs, riddles, and folktales were folk literature, which needed a faithful and honest collector who had to place the words carefully in writing the tales—not according to taste, but according to the essence of the Serbian language. In that sense, Karadžić undertook the stylization of stories he had collected. *See also* Collecting, Collectors; Editing, Editors; Slavic Tales.

Further Reading: Milošević-Đorđević, Nada. *The History of Serbian Culture.* Edgware, Middlesex: Porthill Publishers, 1995.

Mojca Ramšak

Kathasaritsagara

The *Kathasaritsagara*, or *Ocean of the Streams of Story*, is an extensive eleventh-century Sanskrit framed tale attributed to Somadeva, a Kashmiri Brahmin. He is said to have composed it for Queen Suryamati (or Suryavati), the wife of a known king of Kashmir, on the basis of previous works. The most important of these is the *Brihatkatha* (the "Great Story") attributed to one Gunadhya, who may well be a mythical figure. Other references to the *Brihatkatha* (by another Sanskrit poet who used the material, and a Nepali Buddhist text) provide evidence that the book did exist, although the Sanskrit form may be lost. In its current incarnation, the *Kathasaritsagara* is a versified work numbering 22,000 shlokas, or couplets, and incorporating a number of other works such as a version of the **Panchatantra** and the *Vetalapanchavinsati*, or *Tales of a Vampire* (which has been translated independently, for example, by Richard Francis **Burton**). The book does not offer an overarching frame on the order of the story of **Sheherazade** in the **Arabian Nights**, although one of the incorporated sections, the story of prince Naravahanadatta, strikes a curious counterpoint with Shahriyar, who beheaded a long series of wives; Naravahanadatta, by contrast, goes through a series of stories in which he marries a long succession of maidens. Instead, the work begins with a mythical narrative of the god Siva and his consort Parvati. To entertain Parvati, Siva tells stories that are overheard and then repeated and finally come to earth to inspire Gunadhya. The work is set in a Hindu context of social categories and beliefs, although Wendy Doniger observes Buddhist elements in the text and notes that eleventh-century Kashmir was an area of religious turmoil.

Kathasaritsagara's **frame narrative** is complex and fluid. The watery metaphor of the title (which is carried into the word used for the different sections of the book, "billows") is a very apt description of the motion of the contents. The framing technique is much closer to that of a work such as Ovid's *Metamorphoses* than to the systematic narratives of the Arabic tradition. A typical method of introducing a new framed story is through **memory** of a past life: the characters in a given situation reach an epiphany that allows them to understand and relate the hidden events that have brought them to the present. The story of the vampire is unusual in the book in offering a regular framing device: a **king** undertakes to carry the vampire without speaking, but the demon offers a series of narratives that lead to a problem requiring judgment, which the king cannot resist giving.

C. H. Tawney produced an English translation of the full text, published in Bengal (1880–84); this text was revised, annotated, and published in ten volumes by N. M. Penzer (1924–28). The text also has been reprinted in India; Arshia Sattar offers a selection of stories in *Tales from the Kathasaritsagara*.

Further Readings: Penzer, N. M., ed. *The Ocean of Story, Being C. H. Tawney's Translation of Somadeva's Kathā Sarit Sāgara*. 10 volumes. 1924–28. Delhi: Motilal Banarsidass, 1968; Somadeva. *Tales from the Kathā-Sarit-Sāgara*. Translated by Arshia Sattar. New York: Penguin Books, 1994.

Stephen Belcher

Keller, Gottfried (1819–1890)

Gottfried Keller, an award-winning Swiss author of essays, poetry, novels, and **novella**s, is best known for his **literary fairy tale**s and novellas that deal with ordinary human foibles and virtues by contrasting the way people are with the way they should be. The majority of his semiautobiographical stories, which are included in numerous fairy-tale anthologies, are set in his native Switzerland. Among the most famous are "Kleider machen Leute" ("Clothes Make the Man"), "Spiegel, das Kätzchen" ("Spiegel the **Cat**"), and "Romeo und Julia auf dem Dorfe" ("Romeo and Juliet of the Village"), a tale that Keller based on a local event, not on William **Shakespeare**'s famous play. These novellas are included in his two-volume work entitled *Die Leute von Seldwyla* (*The People of Seldwyla*, 1856–74), a fictitious Swiss town.

In 1872, Keller, who had rejected his Catholic faith, wrote *Sieben Legenden* (*Seven Legends*; translated as *Legends of Long Ago*), a collection of slightly profane parodies about early Catholic saints and the Virgin Mary, in response to an earlier author's serious tales on the subject. His next work, which appeared in 1878, was *Züricher Novellen* (*Zurich Novellas*), a selection of stories drawn from the city's history. *Das Sinngedicht* (*The Epigram*, 1882), his final book of tales, is a series of novellas based on the Galatea theme.

Further Readings: Hart, Gail K. "Gottfried Keller." *Dictionary of Literary Biography.* Edited by James Hardin and Siegfried Mews. Volume 129. Detroit: Gail Research, 1993. 159–73; Keller, Gottfried. *Legends of Long Ago.* Translated by Charles Hart Handschin. 1911. Freeport, NY: Books for Libraries Press, 1971; Ryder, Frank G., ed. Introduction. *Stories.* By Gottfried Keller. New York: Continuum, 1982. 1–12.

Candace Beutell Gardner

Khemir, Nacer (1948–)

Tunisian-born Nacer Khemir is a storyteller, writer, filmmaker, and visual artist whose work centers on the **Arabian Nights** and specifically the **oral tradition**. Much of his work has its origin in the research Khemir carried out in 1972, when he collected tales from storytellers in the medina of Tunis. His tale collections are written for children and are characterized by a main text in French with some Arabic and Arabic calligraphy. The stories often weave themselves together in the tradition of the *Arabian Nights*, whose authority as a written text frequently comes into question. Khemir's collections include *L'ogresse* (*The Ogress*, 1975), *Le conte des conteurs* (*The Tale of Tellers*, 1984), *J'avale lebébé du voisin* (*I Swallow the Neighbor's Baby*, 2000), *Le livre des génies* (*The Book of Genies*, 2001), and *Le livre des djinns* (*The Book of Djinns*, 2002). Khemir's films, also largely inspired by the *Arabian Nights* and the Oriental tale, have won numerous awards and include *Les baliseurs du désert* (*The Wanderers/Navigators of the Desert*, 1984), in which a young teacher arrives in a village where all the men have left to find the limits of the desert; *Le collier perdu de la colombe* (*The Dove's Lost Necklace*, 1990), which follows a calligraphy student's magical quest for love; and *Bab'Aziz* (2005), whose heroine Ishtar leads her blind grandfather through the desert to the great reunion of dervishes. Andalusia, the desert, and the fantastic figure prominently in his films. **See also** Ogre, Ogress.

Further Reading: Khemir, Nacer. "A Wanderer Seeking the Words of Love in Impossible Cities: Nacer Khemir." Interview by Khemais Khayati. Introduced and translated by Maggie Awadalla. *Alif* 15 (1995): 251–59.

Anne E. Duggan

The Kind and the Unkind Girls

One of the most widely distributed **tale type**s across the globe, the tale of The Kind and the Unkind Girls (ATU 480; also known as The Spinning-Women by the Spring) pits a good, obedient, self-effacing, or kind girl against her opposite, showing how proper behavior will be rewarded and bad behavior punished. Although some **variant**s have male figures, in general this is a tale of and for **women** and girls and has been said to depict the **childhood** crisis of learning to become a self-sufficient adult, both emotionally and materially. Some versions append a **marriage** episode to the end in the form of ATU 510A, **Cinderella**, wherein the heroine moves through the next "childhood crisis" to find sexual love as well.

In the first part of the tale, a girl must leave home. It might be that she bloodies her fingers while **spinning** and falls down a well while trying to clean her spindle; or else a ball of yarn, a piece of cotton, a cake or a cheese, or even animal guts she is washing escape her hand and roll away or are swept away by wind or water. Eventually, she ends up in a realm (generally subterranean) where an old woman or women test her. She may be tested en route as well, showing in every case her modesty, kindness, and generosity. She may perform unbidden tasks, such as taking bread out of an oven before it burns, or shake the apples from overladen branches; often, she must clean a house (or conversely, decline to make a house untidy when instructed to) or comb a person's **hair** or delouse them. She may be asked her opinion of the bed she is allowed to sleep in or the **food** she is given, and she answers graciously and politely. If she is offered a choice among caskets or other containers as a reward, she always chooses the smallest and least ornate. For this, the girl is rewarded with beauty and/or riches: the small casket has jewels and gold in it; roses or gold fall from her mouth when she speaks; a star may appear on her forehead; or she herself may be showered with gold.

Upon her return home, the heroine is envied by a sister or stepsister, and, goaded by a bad **mother** (typically the heroine's stepmother), the envious girl attempts to perform the same sequence of events to be similarly rewarded. In this, she fails as much as the good girl has succeeded: the bad girl allows bread to burn; or she refuses to clean a house, or to delouse a person who needs it; or she chooses the biggest and most ornate box, and so on. The box will be filled with snakes and toads, or else these fall from her mouth when she tries to speak; or a donkey's tail grows from her forehead, or else she is covered in pitch.

The tale most frequently dwells on traditionally female tasks of cooking, cleaning, and caring for others, and on virtues traditionally held to be feminine, such as obedience and modesty. An unfair stepmother has her counterpart in the more just and magically powerful subterranean **witch** or **sorceress**, just as the good and bad girls might be said to be counterparts of one another, representing alternative attitudes rather than two individuals. At the outset, the heroine is beset by a bad mother and bad sister. In the end, she has been rewarded by a good mother-figure and seen the bad sister punished. Initially unable to control the spindle/cheese/swath of cotton or other feminine tool or item, she returns home with her yarn well spun or some other indications of success. Thus it is said that the tale is about a girl successfully growing into her role as a woman. She works through or overcomes feelings of sibling rivalry as well as the antagonism with her (step)mother, reaching an emotional maturity that is lacking at the beginning of the story. Feelings of being unjustly treated dissipate as the girl sees virtue rewarded and vice punished, after all. Her newly won abilities to spin or her success in fulfilling all of the "womanly" duties that have been assigned to her shows her also to be prepared for the physical realities of a woman's life, at least within the social contexts in which this tale has been popular.

The tale's widespread distribution suggests it has links with pubertal rites of passage. Its didactic nature conforms to the reality of many girls' lives, not only in the past but also in some contemporary societies. Though its message may seem out of date to a modern readership, in fact versions in **folklore** and in more literary collections vary widely in their attitudes toward what female "goodness" is taken to mean. This ranges, for example, from a girl's silence and passivity to her reconnecting with the powerful feminine spirit of the well. Moreover, the story does not simply teach obedience and docility as virtues that are supposed to be specifically feminine. The tale also contains the comforting lesson found in many tales of **punishment and reward**—namely, that justice will be done in this life if one only persists in virtue.

Versions of the tale in the European literary tradition include Giambattista **Basile**'s "Le tre fate" ("The Three Fairies," 1634); Charles **Perrault**'s "Les fees" ("The Fairies," 1697); Jacob and Wilhelm **Grimm**'s "Frau Holle" (**Mother Holle**," 1812); Ludwig **Bechstein**'s "Goldmaria und Pechmaria" ("Gold-Mary and Pitch-Mary," 1845); and Benedikte **Naubert**'s "Der kurze Mantel" ("The Cloak," 1789). The motif of the choice among caskets occurs in William **Shakespeare**'s *The Merchant of Venice* (1623). *See also* Didactic Tale; Sisters.

Further Readings: Calame-Griaule, Geneviève. "The Father's Bowl: Analysis of a Dogon Version of AT 480." *Research in African Literatures* 15.2 (1984): 168–84; Freud, Sigmund. "Das Motiv der Kästchenwahl." *Gesammelte Werke.* Volume 10. Frankfurt a.M.: Fischer, 1991, 24–37; Jones, Steven Swann. "Structural and Thematic Applications of the Comparative Method: A Case Study of the 'Kind and Unkind Girls'." *Journal of Folklore Research* 23 (1986): 147–61; Roberts, Warren E. *The Tale of the Kind and the Unkind Girls: AA-TH 480 and Related Titles.* 1958. Detroit: Wayne State University Press, 1994; Thomas, Gerald. "Meaning in Narrative: A Franco-Newfoundland Version of AaTh 480 (*The Spinning Women by the Spring*) and AaTh 510 (*Cinderella* and *Cap O' Rushes*)." *Fabula* 44 (2003): 117–36.

Laura Martin

Kinder- und Hausmärchen

Next to Martin Luther's German translation of the Bible, the fairy-tale collection *Kinder- und Hausmärchen* (*Children's and Household Tales*, 1812–15) by the brothers Jacob and Wilhelm **Grimm** is one of the best-known works in German cultural history. These tales have been translated into more than 160 languages. The Grimms' personal copies of their publication are preserved in the Museum of the Brothers Grimm in Kassel, Germany. Containing numerous notes, corrections, and references written in the Grimms' own hand, these volumes were officially added in 2005 to UNESCO's Memory of the World Registry, which is dedicated to preserving the world's documentary heritage.

Definition and History of Terms

The *Children's and Household Tales* contain a wide variety of genres. There are **wonder tale**s, humorous tales and **jest**s, **etiologic tale**s, **legend**s, **exempla,** moralistic stories, **religious tale**s and legends, and various mixed forms. Despite the collection's title, not all of the tales are meant for children, and children are not always the main characters.

Tales that up to this point had not been considered part of written tradition were now placed equally beside literary texts as an expression of their value. The term *Hausmärchen*—"Household Tales"—in the title, which serves to distinguish this collection from its predecessors, also points to another group of readers, for whom fantasy and entertainment were not the only concerns in literature. *Hausmärlein* ("household tales," a term created by Georg Rollenhagen in 1595) are meant to serve as a guide for Christian upbringing. Therefore, they are tales existing within families as part of the domestic tradition (*fabula domestica*), and they are closely connected to familial norms and values.

This does not apply, however, to all of the stories in the *Children's and Household Tales.* The humorous tales that are spread throughout the collection for the sake of variety contain no moralizing—completely in accord with the tradition of this particular genre. Their purpose was primarily to entertain—by exploiting the dissonance between reality and the protagonist's action, by reducing real situations to absurdity through the breaking of taboos, and by ignoring ethical norms.

At the end of the *Children's and Household Tales*, ten *Kinderlegenden*, or "children's legends," were inserted and reworked in such a way to make them more concrete and vivid for children. The term *Kinderlegende* seems to have been created by Wilhelm Grimm with reference to the older terms *Kinderglaube*, or "childlike faith" (since the sixteenth century), and *Kindermärchen*, or "children's tales" (with its positive connotations since the late eighteenth century).

Background and Genesis of the Collection

It was probably the German writer Clemens **Brentano** who ignited the Grimms' interest in folk literature. Later influences also came also from the writer Achim von Arnim. In their collection of folk songs, *Des Knaben Wunderhorn* (*The Youth's Magic Horn*, 1806–8), Brentano and von Arnim took up the ideas of "**folklore**" (*Volks-Gut*, that is, the cultural wealth or material of the **folk**) from Johann Gottfried Herder and Friedrich Wilhelm Schelling, evaluated printed sources diligently, and complemented them with texts taken from **oral tradition**. The Grimm brothers were included in this creative atmosphere, helped with the collection of folk songs, and were inspired to collect orally transmitted tales and legends as well as ancient literary texts. Starting in 1806, the collection of the Grimm brothers, who were only twenty years old at the time, developed in an environment fed by two cultural trends. On the one hand, there was the influence of the Enlightenment, which held collective tradition to be a reflector of the moral concepts of social and ethnic groups. On the other hand, there was the influence of early German Romanticism, which viewed written texts from the past sentimentally as authentic documentation of a mytho-poetic tradition.

The Grimms' first tales date from the second half of 1807. However, even by 1809 they still had not expressed their intent to publish their own collection. In 1810, they sent their texts in the form of brief summaries to Brentano, who for some time had been planning to publish an edition of fairy tales. However, his project was never realized. In contrast to Brentano, Jacob Grimm was of the opinion that texts could be edited without violating their essential form, but that they should not be embellished with the editor's own poetic interventions. On this point he also differed with his brother Wilhelm, who did not completely rule out literary adaptations. This is evident in the new versions of fairy tales that Wilhelm would later publish.

While the relationship between the Grimm brothers and Brentano came to a halt, their ties to Achim von Arnim grew even closer. It was von Arnim who, in 1812, encouraged the brothers to publish their own collection of tales (based on the material they had sent to Brentano), and it was von Arnim who supported his friends in their search for a suitable publisher. The appearance of the published collection was envisioned for Christmas 1812, so within only a couple of weeks, the Grimms edited the relatively unedited summaries of the tales they had collected and compiled a manuscript ready for printing. But the transfer of the manuscript to the publisher was delayed a few times, and most of the 900 copies of the first volume did not become available for purchase until 1813.

The handwritten versions of the tales sent to Brentano in 1810 (the so-called Ölenberg manuscript) reveal that Jacob had written down most of the tales. He also took part in compiling the first volume of 1812 and contributed considerably to the success of the second volume, which was published in 1815. Correspondence between Jacob and Wilhelm shows how much they consulted each other during the **editing** phase and how hard Wilhelm tried to accelerate the publishing process in agreement with his brother. Wilhelm carried the lion's share of this work since Jacob was repeatedly away on diplomatic missions to Paris or Vienna and was very restricted in the time he could devote to this edition.

As with the *Deutschen Sagen* (*German Legends*, 1816–18), a third volume of fairy tales was originally planned. However, most of the works that were supposed to appear in this third volume found a place in the second edition of 1819, which was edited extensively and expanded through the addition of new tales. Moreover, the volume of scholarly annotations that the Grimms published separately in 1822 contained both summaries and complete versions of additional tales. The reorganization and introduction of new texts in the 1819 edition constituted on the Grimms' part a direct response to criticisms that their first edition had received. Critics had complained about their editorial methods, the fragmentary nature of many tales, the manner of narration, and the fact that the tales were less than appropriate for children.

From 1819 onward, Wilhelm supervised all subsequent editions on his own, even though Jacob frequently expressed his interest in collaborating on the work and brought new tales to Wilhelm's attention. It was not until eighteen years later, in 1837, that the Berlin publisher Georg Reimer was willing to publish a third edition of all of the tales. In the meantime, the Small Editions, a more affordable selection of fifty tales, had been published in 1825, 1833, and 1836.

The success of the *Children's and Household Tales* set in only with the publication of the third edition in 1837, which was now known as the Large Edition (*Große Ausgabe*) to distinguish it from the Small Edition (*Kleine Ausgabe*). At this point, new editions followed quickly one upon the other, always alternating between Large Editions and Small Editions, in roughly three-year intervals. The edition of 1857—the last Large Edition edited by Wilhelm Grimms' own hand—contained 200 tales and ten children's legends and was most likely viewed by Wilhelm as the culmination of his work on fairy tales. After a decades-long interruption, he saw to it in 1856 that the third volume of annotations and commentary was revised and that its survey of international fairy tale editions was expanded. The ongoing process of updating and developing the *Children's and Household Tales* continued until the final edition of 1857. In various passages throughout the last several editions of the collection, Wilhelm incorporated allusions to previous tales to accord the whole work a greater unity and coherence.

The more affordable Small Editions helped considerably to make the *Children's and Household Tales* well known. The number of texts in these editions remained constant—fifty tales, the same number as in Giambattista **Basile**'s *Lo cunto de li cunti* (*The Tale of Tales*, 1634–36), a work that was highly valued by the Brothers Grimm. Although the tales in the Small Edition also appeared in the Large Edition, they were still subjected to critical scrutiny—being embellished with additional details or rewritten. For this reason, the tales in the Small Editions constitute important intermediate stages in the ongoing process of editing the tales.

Structure

The *Children's and Household Tales* give the impression that the sequence in which the tales appear is completely random. However, the order of the texts (which are numbered as well as titled) is not arbitrary. Sometimes the tales are ordered thematically. For example, tales about foxes are grouped together (nos. 72–75), as are tales of redemption (nos. 92–93).

Pedagogical considerations probably also played a role in the ordering of texts. The tale "Sterntaler" ("The Star Coins"), in which a kind and merciful child is rewarded, is followed by a tale in which a child is punished for stealing alms. This child finds peace in its grave only after the parents have found and passed on the money that had been intended for a poor person but was hidden by the child.

Editing

Contrary to their own claims, the Grimm brothers edited the tales continuously (except for the stories in dialect). However, this editing took various forms. It started already before the publication of the second edition of 1819. Wilhelm's remarks in the annotated volume of 1856—that a given text was "rewritten in our own way" ("in unsere Weise umgeschrieben"), "interpreted according to my understanding" ("nach meiner Weise aufgefaßt"), or "composed" ("ausgearbeitet")—sounded quite harmless. But these remarks always meant that there had been significant revision in terms of language and, in particular, content. Later editions reveal a tendency to harmonize inconsistencies and different strands of the plot, as well as efforts to replace concrete expressions with euphemisms (for example, in nos. 122 and 186).

Beginning with the first edition, there were tales that were especially suited for children, which was not a matter of course in those days. These include well-known stories such as "Rotkäppchen" ("**Little Red Riding Hood**"), "Der Wolf und die sieben jungen Geißlein" ("The **Wolf** and the Seven Young Kids"), and "Daumerlings Wanderschaft" ("**Thumbling**'s Travels"). In addition, the children's tales—in the truest sense of the term—encompass **nonsense tale**s (nos. 131 and 140), the story of the animal funeral procession (no. 80), the travels of animals and objects (no. 41), and numerous texts containing children's rhymes, such as "Das Lämmchen und das Fischchen" ("The Little Lamb and the Little Fish"). After the publication of the first edition of 1812–15, sexual allusions in the *Children's and Household Tales* were played down.

As with their *German Legends*, different levels of editing can be discerned in the Grimms' fairy-tale collection. These range from the adoption of passages verbatim to extensive reformulations of a tale's language and content, to the merging of several different versions of the same tale. On the structural level, the editorial interventions included creating a strong motific coherence among individual sections while retaining the tale's basic plot structure, as well as emphasizing structural symmetries and reinforcing dynamic elements (although from the 1830s onward, revisions of a tale's structure tended to become more liberal). Editorial revisions also focused on breaking up the structure of the plot into several phases, creating brief beginnings, and avoiding abrupt transitions. On the level of style, editing tended to be concerned with producing a more literary language, polishing the syntax of complicated sentences, and establishing logical connections. It also enhanced the clarity of a tale's narration by making its wording more precise and introducing direct speech, proverbs, idiomatic expressions, and other elements of orality. Additional editorial strategies included incorporating lessons of Christian morality, replacing foreign terms and loan words with German expressions, and providing greater psychological motivation for the behavior of characters.

Thematic and Pedagogical Issues

The *Children's and Household Tales* are replete with moral lessons and pedagogical concerns. Drawing on Herder's idea of *Naturpoesie* ("natural poetry"), the preface to the 1812 volume of tales describes the fairy tale's essential characteristic and then states: "In these features we can see the basis for the moral precept or for the relevant object lesson that can be derived so readily from these tales" (trans. Tatar, 255). The preface to the volume of 1815 describes more precisely the effect of the poetry inherent in the tales and the function of the collection, which was to "bring pleasure wherever it could, and that it therefore become a manual of manners [*eigentliches Erziehungsbuch*]" (trans. Tatar, 262).

With each further edition, there were more and more additions that depicted heroes and especially heroines as pious and god-fearing. Characters who were portrayed positively were obedient and unconditionally prepared to do their duty. In many fairy tales, the heroine is the embodiment of diligence and beauty—although her beauty does not always reveal itself from the very start. Sometimes the heroine may be inconspicuous. She comes from modest means but has everything required to advance socially: she works hard, knows how to keep house, and shows compassion for animals and nature. Virtue is rewarded when the heroine's rise in status is made possible. However, it is not intellect or practical skills that are being promoted; rather, the good fortune of the heroine or hero comes about through chance and favorable circumstances. Readers learn how to understand and evaluate the deeds and behaviors of characters with the help of numerous monologues that are spread throughout the tales.

Most of the middle-class norms promoted in the *Children's and Household Tales* mirror the world of Biedermeier. However, the virtues propagated in the Grimms' collection, such as diligence, cleanliness, and a strong work ethic, transcend time and are valued highly, whereas laziness and idleness are branded as vices.

Children behave the way good children are expected to behave. They play, learn, sing, go for walks, work, cook, wash, spin, eat, drink, tend to the animals, make music, pick flowers, and are self-sufficient. They are described on the basis of aesthetic comparisons, and their personal character is labeled according to moral categories, such as bad, good, greedy, disobedient, lazy, diligent, pious, good-natured, obedient, or demure. Their intellectual abilities, such as intelligence and prudence, are outlined concisely. Most of the time, the social milieu is also mentioned. A tale will tell of a child who comes from a poor family. Children are raised according to general principles of education and catechistic teachings—in particular the fourth commandment—which demands children's strict obedience to their parents. Thus, the tales paint clear images of the protagonists, which readers can embellish with their own imagination. Only the humorous tale—the *Schwank*—with its tendency to reverse moral values, allows for deviations from the norm.

Since Grimms' collection of fairy tales possesses an educational function, it can be directly linked to *Hausväterliteratur*—a genre of German literature that offered advice to landowners about running their affairs and families, and that left its mark especially in Lutheran teachings concerning the home and household. In this concept of the household and how it should be run, everyone from master to servant is actively involved. The household is structured hierarchically: The husband has power over his wife, children, and servants. All members of the household have a responsibility to work. Their duty to work is founded on the religious justification that couples the sanctity of marriage with the sanctity of work and on the principle that every Christian is obligated to toil in the service of his neighbor. Understood in this way, the Grimm's tales can be considered a book of virtues for the members of a household and a set of guidelines for their behavior in all possible situations. This makes the fairy tales comparable to so-called moral tales, whereas books of legends, with their historical and heroic narratives, were supposed to promote patriotic upbringing. That this view of the tales as a book of virtues is of great import cannot be deduced only from the Grimms' own statements and from the prefaces to their editions; it can also be recognized most clearly in the various stages of editing that the tales underwent. Christian values were embedded in the tales during the editorial process, right up to the very last editions.

Oral and Print Traditions

Printed collections and older literature were not the only sources for the *Children's and Household Tales*. Far more heavily than their predecessors, the Grimm brothers also relied on oral traditions. But contrary to what is commonly thought, they did not wander about the countryside with a pad and a pencil to collect oral **folktales** from **informant**s. Much of their material came to them in written form or stemmed from diverse literary sources. It is conceivable that Jacob and Wilhelm Grimm ascribed the term "oral" to their tales to increase the quantity of folk poetry that they held in such high esteem. In reality, they most likely obtained their fairy tales in written form—rarely with reference to an informant but sometimes with reference to another written original or with the assurance that this tale was still told in a specific region.

In their efforts to collect fairy tales for their first editions, the Grimm brothers were assisted by their aristocratic and bourgeois friends and relatives, who also provided materials for the *German Legends,* which was taking shape at almost the same time. Most of the tales that are based undoubtedly on a written original appeared in the editions published from 1819 onward. Among the newly added texts, there were thirty-five pieces that can be traced back to literary sources of the sixteenth and seventeenth centuries. Others were taken from periodicals (for example, nos. 130 and 183) or from contemporary fairy-tale collections. For only eight of the tales does the information provided about their origins point to oral tradition.

Popular Reception

Shortly after the appearance of the *Children's and Household Tales*, **translation**s of individual stories appeared in Denmark (1816), the Netherlands (1820), and—with **illustration**s by George **Cruikshank**—in England (1823–26). More early editions appeared in Sweden (1824), France (1830), Hungary (1860), Russia (1862), and other countries.

The Grimms' tales were an integral part of popular printmaking in the nineteenth century. After all, the primary consumers for the fairy tales were ostensibly children. The **broadside** foundries in Munich, Stuttgart, and Vienna produced fairy-tale broadsides of stories such as such as "**Cinderella**," "Little Red Riding Hood," "**Snow White**," "**Hansel and Gretel**," and "The Goose Girl," sometimes in a printing of several hundred thousand. These broadsheets were not only produced for the national market but were also exported in significant volume to the Netherlands, Scandinavia, France, and England.

There were also early reprints of the Grimm tales in storybooks, calendars, and magazines. Some publishers added the Grimms' tales to their anthologies, and although they frequently altered the texts, the connection to the *Children's and Household Tales* remained obvious. In fact, Wilhelm Grimm used some of these transformed and expanded versions in later editions by incorporating them to some degree back into his original version (for example, "Hansel and Gretel"). Many tales also served Ludwig **Bechstein** as the basis for his popular fairy-tale collections, which had been appearing since 1845.

Throughout Europe and ultimately the whole world, the *Children's and Household Tales* met with unique approval. In the course of the nineteenth and twentieth centuries, the tales were adapted for every significant new medium, and at the beginning of the twenty-first century, they still topped the list—along with the stories of Hans Christian **Andersen** and Charles **Perrault**—as the most popular of all fairy tales.

Pedagogues draw on the *Children's and Household Tales* as a model of traditional **storytelling**. Moreover, in the field of international narrative research, scholars discuss the particular aspects of the *Buchmärchen*, or "book tale," on the basis of the Grimms' *Children's and Household Tales*—to the disadvantage of other collections. The Grimms' tales are also pervasive in a metaphoric-symbolic way as allusions to or in connection with proverbial expressions, especially in visual and print media. Sometimes Grimms' fairy tales appear in a defamiliarized form—for example, in the depiction of a key scene that presupposes knowledge of the tale's content, reverses the tale's message into its opposite, and thus creates a humorous contradiction between reality and the magic of the fairy tale, in the process reducing the story's **moral** to an absurdity.

In creating the *Children's and Household Tales*, the Brothers Grimm did not blaze new territory, nor did they develop fresh ideas. However, they did realize in a rigorous way what some of their contemporaries had already anticipated in their published collections. By adding detailed annotations and commentaries to the texts they had collected, Jacob and Wilhelm Grimm laid the cornerstone for the exploration and study of fairy tales. To think that the value of Grimms' tales lies in their ostensible relation to Germanic myth is an outdated point of view that cannot be supported by scholarship. The Grimms' work had an indisputable international influence on the collecting of fairy tales and on generations of **collectors** and editors. The norms and desires conveyed in these texts appear to coincide to a great extent with universal needs and wishes. In Germany, throughout Europe, and eventually overseas, comparable collections came into being, all modeled not only on the concept and style of the *Children's and Household Tales*, but also on the diversity of narrative genres that were brought together there under the German term **Märchen**. *See also* Advertising; Aphorisms; Brothers Grimm in Biopics; Cartoons and Comics; Mythological Approaches; Proverbs.

Further Readings: Bolte, Johannes, and Georg Polívka. *Anmerkungen zu den Kinder- und Hausmärchen der Brüder Grimm.* 5 volumes. 1913–32. Hildesheim: Olms, 1963; Bottigheimer, Ruth B. *Grimms' Bad Girls and Bold Boys: The Moral and Social Vision of the Tales.* New Haven, CT: Yale University Press, 1987; Denecke, Ludwig. *Jacob Grimm und sein Bruder Wilhelm.* Stuttgart: Metzler, 1971; Grimm, Jacob and Wilhelm. *The Complete Fairy Tales of the Brothers Grimm.* Translated by Jack Zipes. 3rd expanded edition. New York: Bantam, 2003; ———. *Kinder- und Hausmärchen: Nach der Großen Ausgabe von 1857, textkritisch revidiert, kommentiert und durch Register erschlossen.* Edited by Hans-Jörg Uther. 4 volumes. Munich: Diederichs, 1996; Haase, Donald, ed. *The Reception of Grimm's Fairy Tales: Responses, Reactions, Revisions.* Detroit: Wayne State University Press, 1993; Kamenetsky, Christa. *The Brothers Grimm and Their Critics: Folktales and the Quest for Meaning.* Athens: Ohio University Press, 1992; McGlathery, James M. *Grimm's Fairy Tales: A History of Criticism on a Popular Classic.* Columbia, SC: Camden House, 1993; Monk, Craig. *Parody as an Interpretive Response to Grimms' "Kinder- und Hausmärchen."* Dunedin: University of Otago, 1998; Murayama, Isamitsu: *Poesie–Natur–Kinder: Die Brüder Grimm und ihre Idee einer "natürlichen Bildung" in den "Kinder- und Hausmärchen."* Heidelberg: Winter, 2005; Tatar, Maria. *The Hard Fact of the Grimms' Fairy Tales.* 2nd edition. Princeton, NJ: Princeton University Press, 2003; Uther, Hans-Jörg. "Die Brüder Grimm als Sammler von Märchen und Sagen." *Kultur und Politik: Die Grimms.* Edited by Bernd Heidenreich and Ewald Grothe. Frankfurt a.M.: Societätsverlag, 2003. 67–107; Zipes, Jack. *The Brothers Grimm: From Enchanted Forests to the Modern World.* 2nd edition. New York: Palgrave MacMillan, 2002.

Hans-Jörg Uther

King

Kings are vital to folktales and fairy tales. While the individual characters may vary, they can be divided into three categories: kings as protagonists, kings as villains, and kings as helpers. As with most royal figures, the king's high social status and wielding of power—whether for good or evil—account for his prominent role in folktales and fairy tales.

The King as Protagonist

In the category involving the king as protagonist, one of the most important aspects is the status of kingship as a goal. This is especially significant in the genre of the **fairy tale**. In *Morfologiya skazki* (*Morphology of the Folktale*, 1928), Vladimir **Propp** summarized the final **function** in the fairy tale with the phrase "The Hero Is Married and Ascends the Throne." Accordingly, attaining kingly status is to some degree the ultimate sign of success for fairy-tale protagonists, who would typically start out not as kings but as characters on a lower rung in the social hierarchy.

Nonetheless, kings also serve as protagonists in fairy tales. Sometimes kings have specific names, such as Polycrates, the king who throws his ring away to avoid divine jealousy in tales of the type ATU 736A (The Ring of Polycrates); or King Thrushbeard, the eponymous humiliated king of international folktale type ATU 900. More often these kings are nameless, standing only as a symbol of kingship. This is the case in ATU 924, Discussion in Sign Language, in which a nameless king and an anonymous **peasant** exchange confused hand signals. Similarly, the stranger who is made king and then banished in the **tale type** called King for a Year (ATU 944) is not known by name. In The King and the Robber (ATU 951A), the king even goes about in disguise, joining a robber in his crime. The theme of the ruler in disguise transcends cultures and is not limited to those societies that use the specific term "king." For example, a disguised sultan features prominently in a number of tales from the *Arabian Nights*.

Many kingly protagonists are marked by folly and suffer from foolish decisions. In The **Princess** in the Coffin (ATU 307), a royal couple wishes for a child but finds their desire turned around on them when the **queen** gives **birth** to a diabolic child. In The King and the Lamia (ATU 411), an unmarried king finds a wife in a snake woman and begins to suffer from poor health. One especially famous foolish king is King Midas, the hero of Midas' Short-Sighted Wish (ATU 775). In this well-known tale, King Midas acquires the ability to turn things to gold, but the power becomes a curse when everything he touches, including his food and drink, is transformed. Similarly, in the tale type known as Midas and the Donkey's Ears (ATU 782), the king interferes in a divine **music** contest and is cursed with a donkey's ears.

The King as Villain

Kings also frequently play the role of villain, acting against the protagonist. One of the most common forms of kingly villainy is the unwilling **marriage**. Sometimes the king wants to marry the wife of the protagonist, as in Life Dependent on a Sword (ATU 302B) or The Man Persecuted because of His Beautiful Wife (ATU 465). Sometimes it is his own daughter, as in Peau d'Asne (ATU 510B) and The Princess in the Chest (510B*), where the king's desire raises the threat of **incest**. One recurring version of the villain king is the serial wife murderer, a character who appears frequently in foundational stories from the fairy-tale tradition, in **literary fairy tale**s, and in film. This threatening serial killer is at the heart of the **Bluebeard** or Maiden-Killer tale type (ATU 312), which may be taken as a warning about the dangers of arranged marriages. The king as serial murderer also stands at the center of The Clever Girl and the King (ATU 875B), which is the tale of Scheherazade and how she avoids execution at the hands of her husband.

Other tales feature myriad kingly villainies. In The Three Stolen Princesses (ATU 301), the story opens with a king banishing his daughters. In The Faithless Wife (ATU 318), a king orders the **death** of his castrated son-in-law. This villainy often backfires. For example, in both The Magic Flight (ATU 313) and The Donkey (ATU 430), a king's wickedness cures the protagonists—in the former, of leprosy; in the latter, of being a donkey.

The King as Helper

The third category of kingly roles in folktales and fairy tales involves the helper king, the ruler whose actions advance the story's plot in a nonvillainous way. The most common form is the rewarding king, who validates the actions of the hero in some way. The archetypal character in this category is the king who rewards the hero for rescuing a princess, as in The Dragon-Slayer (ATU 300), The Princess's Ring (ATU 301D), and The Shepherd and the Three Giants (ATU 314A), among other tale types.

Kings also reward heroes for services other than the rescue of a princess. The hero who cures a king of illness by magical means receives his due reward from his royal patient in The Dragon's Heart-Blood as Remedy (ATU 305) and Water of Life (ATU 551). In Hans My Hedgehog (ATU 441), the protagonist gives directions to lost kings and is rewarded for it. In The King and the Soldier (ATU 952), a **soldier** is rewarded for rescuing a disguised king.

Another key role of the helper king is that of mission giver. Frequently in folktales, a king will present a task to be accomplished, often with an attached reward. In one variation of the King Lindorm tale (ATU 433B), the tasks set by the king are impossible, a common theme. However, in tales such as The Danced-Out Shoes (ATU 306) and The Diver (ATU 434*), the tasks prescribed by the king are more reasonable, involving, respectively, the investigation of the short life of his daughter's footwear and the retrieval of objects from the water.

Marriage also plays a part in tales about helper kings. Many of the realistic tales, or **novella**s—especially those that appear between number 850 and 899 in Hans-Jörg Uther's *The Types of International Folktales* (2004)—involve a king searching for a marriage partner either for himself or for a daughter. Interesting variations on this theme occur in The Maiden without Hands (ATU 706), where a kindly king marries a handless girl; and in The Black and the White Bride (ATU 403) and The Blinded Bride (ATU 404), both of which entail a king attempting to marry a girl for whom the evil stepmother substitutes her own daughter.

Finally, folktales and fairy tales frequently deal with the subject of animal kings. In the tales about **Reynard the Fox**, the character Noble the Lion serves in the role of king of the animals; but he is not alone. In The Mice Choose Cat as King (ATU 113), The Election of King of Birds (ATU 221), and The King of the Frogs (ATU 277), groups of animals choose their rulers—selecting respectively, a **cat**, a wren, and a log, soon followed by a crane after the log proves to be an unfit ruler. *See also* Politics; Prince; Punishment and Reward.

Further Readings: Heindrichs, Ursula, Albert Heinz, and Harlinda Lox, eds. *Als es noch Könige gab: For-schungsberichte aus der Welt der Märchen*. Munich: Diederichs, 2001; Röhrich, Lutz. "The Social

Milieu." *Folktales and Reality*. Translated by Peter Tokofsky. Bloomington: Indiana University Press, 1991. 184–98; Walsh, Elizabeth. "The King in Disguise." *Folklore* 86 (1975): 3–24.

B. Grantham Aldred

The King and Mr. Bird. See Le roi et l'oiseau

Kirikou et la sorcière (1998)

Kirikou et la sorcière (*Kirikou and the Sorceress*, 1998) is an animated feature film written and directed by French animator Michel Ocelot. Kirikou, the main character, is a newborn West African boy. By keeping his young hero only twenty-seven centimeters tall, Ocelot reminds viewers of Tom Thumb from the **Grimm** stories and Thumbelina from Hans Christian **Andersen**. Ocelot's inspiration, however, was not Grimm or Andersen but a three-volume book of indigenous tales from West Africa, originally published in 1913–16 and collected by François-Victor Equilbecq, a colonial administrator. Having spent six years as a child in Conakry, Guinea, Ocelot was well attuned to the stories he found in Equilbecq's collection.

Ocelot liked a section of one tale so much that he used it in the first Kirikou film as the opening dialogue. A tiny voice from inside the womb of a pregnant woman says, "Mother, give **birth** to me." To this the woman replies calmly, "A child who can speak from his mother's womb can give birth to himself." And so a little boy delivers himself, cuts his umbilical cord, and declares: "My name is Kirikou." He then bathes himself and rushes off to help his uncle, the last man alive in their village, in a confrontation with the evil **sorceress** Karaba. Through all subsequent adventures, he remains as confident and resourceful as in the opening scene.

Ocelot's use of Equilbecq's collection ended there. Whereas in the source tale, the hero grows up and acquires magical power equal to that of the sorceress, Ocelot found it more dramatic to have Kirikou remain a newborn and oppose Karabar with wit and courage rather than through wizardry. Ocelot also rejected the original ending, in which the hero kills the sorceress. Instead, Ocelot invented a way for Kirikou to redeem and marry her. From these two structural changes flowed all of the new characters (such as the wise grandfather, who alone knows the cause of Karaba's malevolence) and incidents (the dried-up water source threatening the village) that went into the creation of *Kirkou and*

A scene from the 2005 French animated film *Kirikou et les bêtes sauvages* (*Kirikou and the Wild Beasts*). [Gébéka Films/Photofest]

the Sorceress. The tale the film tells thus invokes the West African oral tradition as filtered through an early twentieth-century colonial folktale collection and refracts it through the lens of a late twentieth-century European animator.

As such, the film enjoyed critical and audience success, not only in the cinema and on DVD but also with merchandising in many countries—though not the anglophone market, where major distributors refused to handle it because the women are shown going about their normal business bare-breasted.

So great was the public response that Ocelot agreed to make another Kirikou movie. It could not exactly be a sequel, though, because at the end of the first film, a kiss from Karaba sends little Kirikou shooting up to maturity—and a two-meter-tall, married Kirikou was not the hero audiences wanted to see. Therefore *Kirikou et les bêtes sauvages* (*Kirikou and the Wild Beasts*, 2005) goes back to a pre-kiss situation and shows the twenty-seven-centimeter Kirikou using his wits to help his village overcome various problems caused by wild animals. *See also* Animation; Colonialism; Film and Video; Thumbling, Tom Thumb.

Further Readings: Equilbecq, François-Victor. *Contes populaire d'Afrique occidentale: Précédés d'un essai sur la littérature merveilleuse des noirs.* New edition. Paris: G.-P. Maisonneuve et Larose, 1972; Gudin, Christine. "'J'utilise les contes comme un minerai avec lequel j'essaie de faire des bijoux': Entretien avec Michel Ocelot." *Contes et légendes à l'écran.* Special issue of *CinémAction* 116 (2005): 267–74.

Terry Staples

Kittelsen, Theodor (1857–1914)

Theodor Kittelsen was the Norwegian artist whose drawings and watercolors of trolls formed the concept of these creatures in popular imagination. Born in Kragerø, Kittelsen began studying **art** in Christiania (now Oslo) when he was seventeen. He also studied in Paris and Munich, where he became a good friend of another famous Norwegian artist, Erik Werenskiold.

It was Werenskiold, who earlier had provided illustrations for Peter Christen **Asbjørnsen** and Jørgen **Moe**'s *Norske folkeeventyr (Norwegian Folktales,* 1841–44), who recommended Kittelsen to Asbjørnsen as an artist possessing a sense for the fantastic. Some of Kittelsen's earliest drawings for Asbjørnsen and Moe's collection included the imaginative illustration of a troll hag bearing her head under her arm for the story "Butterball," and a drawing for "The Boy Who Had an Eating Contest with the Troll." Kittelsen continued to add illustrations to *Norwegian Folktales* throughout his life. Some of the most memorable include the drawing of the princess riding on the white bear in "White Bear King Valemon" and illustrations for "The Ashlad and His Good Helpers." Other famous drawings include "Troll Wondering How Old He Is" and "The Troll on Karl Johan."

In addition to his many drawings for *Norwegian Folktales,* Kittelsen painted figures from Norwegian **folklore,** such as *nøkken* (nix, water sprite), images of Soria Moria castle, and a striking and disturbing black-and-white series illustrating **motif**s from **legend**s of the Black Plague. Kittelsen struggled with poverty and illness but continued working until his death in 1914. *See also* Illustration.

Further Readings: Ketilsson, Eli. *Troll i Norge.* Oslo: J. M. Stenersens Forlag, 1989; Ostby, Leif. *Theodor Kittelsen.* Oslo: Dreyers Forlag, 1976.

Marte Hult

Köhler, Reinhold (1830–1892)

Reinhold Köhler, literary historian and folklorist, was an outstanding contributor to comparative research. Educated academically in **classical antiquity**, Romance and Germanic languages and literatures, comparative linguistics, Sanskrit and Middle Eastern studies, Köhler spent his whole life in Weimar, the home of German classsical literature. There, in 1856, he became an enthusiastic and impassioned librarian at the Großherzogliche Bibliothek. Although he rarely traveled, he corresponded with many European folklorists (for example, he received some fifty letters from the Italian folklorist Giuseppe **Pitrè**). He was considered an unselfish **informant** and authority on **folktale**s worldwide.

Köhler's exclusive interest was themes and **motif**s. He considered texts from classical, medieval, and modern literature as well as **oral tradition**s of his own time, including **chapbook**s and genres such as songs, sayings, **riddle**s, and **proverbs**. His wide comparative annotations of fairy tales are particularly important for international **folklore** studies. They can be found integrated into the collections of **Estonian tales** by Friedrich Reinhold **Kreutzwald,** Sicilian tales by Laura **Gonzenbach,** or **French tales** by Jean-Francois Bladé, or published separately in short articles, commentaries, and reviews in numerous periodicals—for example, his comments on the collections of Gaelic tales by John Francis Campbell, Breton tales by Francois-Marie Luzel, and Swahili tales by Edward Steere. Köhler continually documented the interrelationship between written and oral traditions.

Further Readings: Köhler, Reinhold. *Aufsätze über Märchen und Volkslieder: Aus seinem handschriftlichen Nachlaß.* Edited by Johannes Bolte and Erich Schmidt. Berlin: Weidmannsche Buchhandlung, 1894; ———. *Kleinere Schriften.* Edited by Johannes Bolte. 3 vols. Weimar: Emil Felber, 1898–1900.

Ines Köhler-Zülch

Konjaku monogatari. See Japanese Tales

Korean Tales

While the term "**folktale**" may be broadly applied to the traditional stories of the Korean peninsula, and while numerous **tale type**s exist that correspond to international types, the diverse origins and orientations of the tales render the corpus distinct from most other national traditions. Furthermore, unlike classical Greek or Norse mythology, Korean mythology does not present a unified system, but a multiplicity. Because Korea is a peninsular country, bordered by Manchuria and Russia to the north, China to the west, and Japan to the east and south, it was long a strategic site in which philosophies and religions from the surrounding countries mixed and mingled with native traditions, such as animism. This admixture is evident in Korean tales, which grow out of the influence of four major religions and belief systems: Shamanism, Buddhism, Confucianism, and Taoism. While modern Korean societies have been influenced by Christianity, this has not inspired a new body of tales.

The oldest of these shaping systems, Shamanism, attributes spirits, which affect the lives of the living, to all natural forces (such as wind or rain) and inanimate objects (such as rocks or trees). Lord over all is Hananim, the celestial emperor of the heavenly kingdom. After **death**, decent people are believed to become good spirits and reside in the heavenly kingdom, while bad people are believed to become evil spirits and reside in the kingdom of darkness or the underworld. Shamanism long permeated the spiritual culture of Korea, and all other religions and beliefs developed within its formative spiritual climate. The "Princess Pari" story, in which the heroine successfully completes a dangerous quest to save the lives of her parents, is an excellent example of confluence. While the story pivots on filial piety, the cardinal virtue in Confucianism, and Pari completes her quest by performing designated female roles for nine years (drawing water, tending the fire, and cutting firewood) followed by **marriage** and the bearing of seven sons, the journey she makes to another world is essentially shamanistic. According to the tale, after her death Pari attains the position of a shamanistic goddess, and a recital of her story is instrumental in ensuring a safe passage of the souls of the dead into the other world. Numerous Korean ghost stories that turn on the release of a wandering ghost into the other world show shamanistic origins (see **Ghost Story**). Historically, Shamanism has enabled **women** to exert influence in Korean society, a possibility explored in recent times in *Comfort Woman* (1997) by Korean American novelist Nora Okja Keller.

Buddhism, introduced to Korea in the late fourth century CE, flourished in compatibility with Shamanism. Its grounding premise that one's present life is determined by the past and the future is shaped by actions in this life are reflected in tales such as "The Curse on the Only Son" (Zŏng, no. 30) which tells how for nine generations the only son of a **family** was fated to be eaten by a tiger, but the son in the tale finds help to avert that doom and lives a happy life "and had many children." By the fourteenth century CE, Buddhism had fallen into disrepute because of the worldliness of many monks, and, consequently, tales often depict monks as lecherous and violent, like the monk of "The Tiger Priest," who murders a family who refuse to give him their daughter.

Confucianism dominated religious life and social practice throughout the Yi Dynasty (1392–1910). Because the *kwagŏ*, or civil service examinations, which determined position and wealth in Korean society, were focused on the Confucian classics, orthodox Confucian teachings permeated social life. Korean tales thus reflect Confucianism in themes that express loyalty to family, veneration of ancestors, privileging of sons over daughters, education, self-discipline, and considerate social behavior. In "Gift from the Mountain Spirit," a couple willing to cook their only child to make a soup to cure the man's elderly **father** are rewarded when a ginseng root is substituted for the child in the soup pot, and the old man recovers. Conversely, in the well-known tale of "The Green Frog," a son who fails to respect and obey his **mother** is doomed to a life of grief and regret after her death. Although in the Confucian scheme of things, social mobility was almost impossible, "The Value of Salt" (Han) shows that considerate behavior may override social hierarchy, wherein a bride's wealthy parents learn to embrace the family of their lower-class son-in-law.

Finally, Taoism, which came to Korea from China, contributed numerous **motif**s and plot elements, such as fortune-telling and prophecy, and a bundle of symbols and ideas related to longevity and superhuman powers. "The Curse on the Only Son," for example, brings a Taoist dimension to a Buddhist tale in that the hero saves himself by following a fortune-teller's advice. "The Legend of Zŏn U-Czi" (Zŏng, no. 99) is a compendium of Taoist motifs, especially in the powers of the eponymous hero to transform himself into other forms, change his size, and fly through the air. His powers are devoted to other activities, however, such as helping the poor, humbling the proud, and bringing justice upon wrongdoers.

International classifications such as **myth**, **legend**, folktale, animal **fable**, **etiologic tale**, and **anecdote** may be applied to Korean tales. There are a substantial number of national-foundation myths in the corpus, and this, together with the dominance of Confucian patriarchal assumptions, has contributed to a sustained interest in them in modern times. Korean folktales and legendary tales play a new role in the cultures of the Korean Diaspora. On the one hand, they are promulgated as part of the cultural heritage of generations born outside of Korea but possessed of a distinctive "hyphenated" Korean culture. The U.S. journal *Koream*, for example, includes in each monthly issue a folktale (often abridged) from Zŏng In-Sŏb's definitive collection (1952), and there are numerous publications for children available to diasporan communities. In contrast, contemporary fiction in English by writers such as Nora Okja Keller or Mia Yun use stories such as the misogynistic "Fox Girl" tales more deconstructively to explore a contemporary diasporan society's break with the past.

Further Readings: Ha, Tae Hung. *Folk Tales of Old Korea.* 1959. Seoul: Yonsei University Press, 1970; Han, Suzanne Crowder. *Korean Folk and Fairy Tales.* Elizabeth, NJ: Hollym, 1991; Kim, So-Un. *The Story Bag: A Collection of Korean Folk Tales.* Translated by Setsu Higashi. Rutland, VT: Charles E. Tuttle, 1955; Riordan, James. *Korean Folk-Tales.* Oxford: Oxford University Press, 1994; Zŏng In-Sŏb, ed. and trans. *Folk Tales from Korea.* 1952. Elizabeth, NJ: Hollym, 1982.

John Stephens

Korneichukov, Nikolai. *See* Chukovsky, Kornei

Kreutzwald, Friedrich Reinhold (1803–1882)

Friedrich Reinhold Kreutzwald was the author of the Estonian national **epic** *Kalevipoeg* (*Kalev's Son*, 1857–1861) and of the first collection of fairy tales in the Estonian language based on **folk** tradition (1866). Kreutzwald, who after graduating with a medical degree from the university worked as a physician in a small town throughout his professional life, was a prolific writer who published a number of popular books. His major literary effort, which followed the example of Estonian traditional folk songs, is the epic *Kalevipoeg*, bearing the subtitle *Eine estnische Sage* (*An Ancient Estonian Tale*). The epic is based largely on **motif**s of Estonian giant **legend**s.

The best-known of all Kreutzwald's popular editions is the collection of fairy tales and legends *Eesti rahva ennemuistsed jutud* (*Old Estonian Fairy Tales*, 1866). The **adaptation**s in the collection use local and international plot elements known in Estonia, which in some tales have been mixed with the literary influence of Charles **Perrault**, Ludwig **Tieck**, Johann Karl August **Musäus**, and others. Thanks to the folksy style of storytelling, many of the adaptations reentered oral **folklore** and were later collected to be held in folklore **archives**.

Kreutzwald retold traditional fairy tales in his other works, for example in the collection *Reinuvader rebane* (***Reynard the Fox***, 1848–51), which consists of adaptations of **animal tale**s based on folktales and Johann Wolfgang von **Goethe**'s *Reineke Fuchs* (1794), and in his adaptations of German numskull (*Schildbürger*) stories, *Kilplaste imevärklikud ... jutud ja teud* (*The Odd Tales and Deeds of the Numskull*, 1857). *See also* Estonian Tales.

Further Readings: Jaago, Tiiu. "Friedrich Reinhold Kreutzwald and the Cultural Bridge." *Studies in Estonian folkloristics and Ethnology: A Reader and Reflexive History.* Edited by Kristin Kuutma and Tiiu Jaago. Tartu: Tartu University Press, 2005. 19–64; Valk, Ülo. "Authorship and Textuality: The *Kalevipoeg* as Epic Landscape." *Kalevala and the World's Traditional Epics.* Edited by Lauri Honko. Helsinki: Finnish Literature Society, 2002. 407–19.

Risto Järv

Kurahashi Yumiko (1935–2005)

Japanese author Kurahashi Yumiko is considered to be one of the most innovative and original writers of her generation. Best known for her political satire, experimental novels, and fantastic short stories, Kurahashi was also the author of two notable collections of fairy tales. Born in Kōchi Prefecture in Shikoku, Kurahashi defied her father's wish for her to become a dentist and instead entered Meiji University in Tokyo, where she studied French literature. Kurahashi first attracted critical attention in 1960, when her short story "Parutai" ("Party") won the Meiji University President's Prize. During the 1960s, Kurahashi wrote many controversial but critically acclaimed short stories and novels, which make little attempt at realistic representation. In fact, Kurahashi stated in numerous essays that she had no interest in realism or in expressing herself through autobiographical confessions. She was also deeply skeptical about the privileged position accorded to the author; she described her own writings as pastiche and preferred to respect her literary antecedents by borrowing openly from their work. For Kurahashi, all texts were produced by reworking and retelling previous writings.

Kurahashi first turned her attention to the fairy-tale genre in 1984 with *Otona no tame no zankoku dōwa* (*Cruel Fairy Tales for Adults*), a collection of twenty-six short stories that exemplify the principles of **intertextualty**. In *Cruel Fairy Tales for Adults*, tales by Hans Christian **Andersen** and the **Grimm** brothers were rewritten and juxtaposed with retold classics from *Konjaku monogatari* (*Tales of Times Now Past*, early twelfth century); Franz **Kafka**'s *Die Verwandlung* (*The Metamorphosis*, 1915) was conflated with an English folktale; and tales by Charles **Perrault**, Tanizaki Junichirō, and Oscar **Wilde** were interwoven with Greek **myth**s. Citing G. K. Chesterton in the afterword, Kurahashi described fairy tales as perfectly logical and rational. She also praised the genre's clear narrative style and its avoidance of superfluous psychological and emotional descriptions. Kurahashi's fairy tales are similarly based on reason rather than emotion; they are *cruel*, she wrote, because they are governed by standards of retributive justice and didactic morals, and *for adults* because their erotic nature might be considered too poisonous for children.

In 2003, Kurahashi published a second collection of fairy tales: *Rōjin no tame no zankoku dōwa* (*Cruel Fairy Tales for Old Folks*). Although the stories in this second collection draw less heavily on overt literary sources, Kurahashi continued to employ fairy-tale themes and **motif**s alongside fragments of Buddhist and Chinese mythology and Japanese **legend**s. The protagonists are predominantly the elderly: a childless old woman, a woman whose body seems to be unaffected by the aging process, an old man practicing to be a wizard, and one elderly person who gets lost while attempting to read all the books in a Borgesian library.

Two years after the publication of *Cruel Fairy Tales for Old Folks*, Kurahashi completed a new translation of French author Antoine de Saint-Exupéry's *Le petit prince* (1943). The translation, *Hoshi no ōjisama*, was published posthumously in July 2005. *See also* Japanese Tales.

Further Readings: Kleeman, Faye Yuan. "Sexual Politics and Sexual Poetics in Kurahashi Yumiko's *Cruel Fairy Tales for Adults*." *Literary Studies East and West* 12 (1996): 150–58; Sakaki Atsuko. "(Re)Canonizing Kurahashi Yumiko: Toward Alternative Perspectives for 'Modern' 'Japanese' 'Literature.' "*Ōe and Beyond: Fiction in Contemporary Japan*. Edited by Stephen Snyder and Philip Gabriel. Honolulu: University of Hawaii Press, 1999. 153–76.

Marc Sebastian-Jones

Kushner, Ellen (1955–)

Ellen Kushner is an American writer of literary **fantasy** with roots in folktale and fairy tale. She also scripts and hosts *Sound & Spirit*, a nationally broadcast public radio show that often contains folkloric content, including one show devoted to fairy tales. Her work with fairy tales is part of a larger project, the interstitial arts movement, dedicated to crossing genre boundaries, and Kushner crosses both genres and boundaries with grace.

Kushner's first **novel**, *Swordspoint* (1987), begins with a fairy-tale image: a drop of ruby **blood** upon ivory snow. It then breaks with expectations to focus instead on the underside of human motivations that drive the plot of the novel. Similarly, *The Fall of the Kings* (2002), coauthored with Delia **Sherman**, employs fairy-tale imagery without adhering to any fairy-tale plot. Kushner's novel *The Privilege of the Sword* (2006) plays subversively with the plot of "**Beauty and the Beast**."

Kushner has edited two anthologies, *Basilisk* (1980) and *The Horns of Elfland* (1997, with Donald Keller and Delia Sherman), that touch on fairy-tale themes but more generally draw on narrative folklore. The same is true of Kushner's novel *Thomas the Rhymer* (1990), which is based on a **ballad** and fueled by ballad themes. Kushner's work, including her short fiction and **poetry**, synthesizes fairy tales, related folk narrative genres, and **folklore** in general, in order to reshape stories and their meanings. She explores fantastic yet familiar settings and alternative sexualities with a feeling for **music** and magic, two common fairy-tale themes. *See also* Gay and Lesbian Tales.

Further Readings: Kushner, Ellen. *The Privilege of the Sword.* Northampton, MA: Small Beer Press, 2006; ———. *Thomas the Rhymer.* New York: W. Morrow, 1990; *Sound & Spirit.* http://www.wgbh.org/pages/pri/spirit/.

Jeana Jorgensen

L

La Fontaine, Jean de (1621–1695)

The seventeenth-century French author of **fable**s and tales Jean de La Fontaine did not begin writing intensively until his late thirties. Born and raised in the Champagne region, he first studied theology before deciding on a law degree. In 1652, La Fontaine purchased the office of Maître des Eaux et Forêts (Regional Water and Forest Board), a post that afforded him much spare time to study a vast number of literary works, especially Greek and Roman classics. After settling in Paris in 1658, he eventually found various patrons who enabled him to devote the rest of his life to his literary activities.

La Fontaine's work spans a wide range of genres, such as poetry, short stories, tales, and fables. Representative of seventeenth-century classicism, almost all of his fables follow classical models. In accordance with the literary convention of his time, La Fontaine considered the originality of a literary work as residing less in its subject matter than in its form. While very few fables are of his invention, he transformed the texts of his predecessors, such as **Aesop**, Horace, and Pilpay, into very concise short narratives written in verse with a skillfully constructed simplicity. Most often presenting animal characters endowed with human traits, La Fontaine sought to reveal his contemporaries' shortcomings while humorously exposing the absurdities of human nature. Several of his tales also constitute carefully disguised satirical comments on French society of the time.

THE·WOLF·TURNED·SHEPHERD.

Jean de La Fontaine's "The Wolf Turned Shepherd," *A Hundred Fables of La Fontaine*, illustrated by Percy J. Billinghurst (London and New York: Ballantyne Press, 1900).

Before publishing his first fables, La Fontaine tried his hand at writing tales. Just as his fables were inspired by ancient models, his *Contes et nouvelles en vers* (*Tales and Short Stories in Verse*, 1664) drew from various sources, including medieval French **fabliaux**, François Rabelais's stories, Italian tales by Giovanni **Boccacio** and Ludovico Ariosto, as well as texts by the Greek authors Anacreon and Petronius. La Fontaine thus elaborated on themes already well known at the time, although generally presented in an attenuated fashion in seventeenth-century novels. His favorite topics include the questionable virtue of **women**, the naïveté of girls, misadventures of nuns, and foibles of the **clergy**. Dealing with matters of love in a farcical and derisive fashion, considered vulgar by many of his contemporary and later readers, La Fontaine's stories constitute risqué **erotic tales** written in decasyllabic or octosyllabic verse. Some of the tales he published in 1674 were even judged to be licentious and seized by the police.

Combining poetics with sexual innuendo presented in a burlesque style often relying on prosaic expressions, La Fontaine's tales initially met with some success. Yet, although they pertained to a long Gallic narrative tradition, his tales became increasingly less popular with seventeenth-century readers and were eventually overshadowed by his fables, for which, to this day, he remains best known. *See also* French Tales; Moral; Sex, Sexuality.

Further Readings: Duchêne, Roger. *La Fontaine*. Paris: Fayard, 1990; Grise, Catherine M. *Cognitive Spaces and Patterns of Deceit in La Fontaine's Contes*. Charlottesville: Rockwood Press, 1998; Orieux, Jean. *La Fontaine, ou La vie est un conte*. Paris: Flammarion, 1976.

Harold Neemann

La Force, Charlotte-Rose de Caumont de (c. 1650–1724)

The French author of fairy tales and historical novels Charlotte-Rose de Caumont de La Force was originally from a Protestant family. Her conversion to Catholicism in1686 enabled La Force to gain access to the highest aristocratic circles. She was appointed lady-in-waiting to the Dauphine and even awarded a pension by Louis XIV. Yet, after being implicated in scandals resulting from love affairs and an unauthorized marriage, which was subsequently annulled, she had to retire temporarily to a convent.

La Force reportedly wrote several novels and eight fairy tales, published under the title *Les contes des contes* (*The Tales of Tales*, 1697), during her confinement in the convent. Shorter than most seventeenth-century **literary fairy tale**s, La Force's stories play on contemporary novelistic and narrative conventions. Her physical and often erotic depictions of love ran counter to prevailing moral and social values. La Force broke social and sexual taboos by refuting strictly defined **gender** roles and portraying sensuality as an integral part of the feminine nature.

Modeled after an episode of the *Perceval* romance (1530), her fairy tale "L'enchanteur" ("The **Sorcerer**") delineates how a woman subjected to an arranged **marriage** with the **king** deceives him on their wedding day. The heroine enjoys spending the night with her lover, the sorcerer, who dupes her husband by putting a female slave in his bed. In "Plus belle que fée" ("More Beautiful than a **Fairy**"), the narrator describes the **princess** hastily undressing before literally mounting her lover, transformed into an eagle, who gently lifts her up into the clouds. Although she uses veiled language, La Force clearly relates the sexual act from a female perspective as a pleasurable experience enjoyed without fear of punishment. In "Vert et bleu" ("Green and Blue"), she depicts the heroine bathing nude while clearly enjoying the gaze of a man admiring her beautiful body. Although La Force limited this erotic passage to visual and verbal exchanges, she seems to valorize **women**'s sensual experiences.

Based on the **tale type** ATU 310 (The Maiden in the Tower), La Force's "Persinette" features a young woman who becomes pregnant without knowing how and whose secret marriage to the **prince** was not approved by the church. While initially subjecting the protagonists to a **punishment**, the author seems to empathize particularly with the heroine. La Force ultimately has the fairy forgive the couple, thus allowing for a happy ending.

"La puissance d'amour" ("The Power of Love") and "Tourbillon" ("Whirlwind") constitute fairy tales interspersed with mythological **motif**s. "La bonne femme" ("The Good Woman") and "Le pays des délices" ("The Land of Delights") are tales informed by pastoral novels.

La Force intelligently exploited the narrative freedom of the fairy-tale genre in asserting women's identity. Her tales can be read as written in reaction to the constraints she experienced as a seventeenth-century French woman. *See also* Erotic Tales; French Tales; Sex, Sexuality.

Further Readings: Vellenga, Carolyn. "Rapunzel's Desire: A Reading of Mlle de La Force." *Merveilles et contes* 6 (1992): 59–73; Welch, Marcelle Maistre. "L'Éros féminin dans les contes de fées de Mlle de La Force." *Papers on French Seventeenth-Century Literature* 60 (1991): 217–23.

Harold Neemann

La Llorona

Best described as a twentieth-century Mexican **urban legend**, "La Llorona"—"The Weeping Woman"—has an apparent connection to ancient Aztec lore. The typical modern story, or report, tells of a woman who wails eerily at night in a certain district as she searches for her lost children. Usually it is said that she has murdered them, and often she wears white.

The related Aztec traditions are well documented in sixteenth-century manuscripts widely published in the 1800s and 1900s. According to one version of the Aztec creation **myth**, the goddess from whose body the earth was formed used to weep at night, crying out for human **blood**. Another of the Aztec stories told how the deity Cihuacoatl, "Serpent Woman," dressed in white, wailing, carried a cradle on her back as if it held a child—though it contained the flint knife used to extract hearts in the ritual of human sacrifice. The underlying idea, still vivid if less bloody, survives in a modern Indian tale, "Why the Earth Eats the Dead," known from Mexico, Guatemala, Honduras, Costa Rica, and Panama. The story explains that because we work the earth and therefore "wound" her, she takes payment by reclaiming our bodies when we die.

"La Llorona" as it circulates in the general population, however, is basically a spook story. As such, it combines with other lore, especially tales of a sirenlike temptress who wails in desolate places, luring men to their destruction. In its pure form, the story of the dangerous temptress—called *xtabay* in the Yucatec Maya language—is best known in southeast Mexico. Less often the tale is fused with the widespread belief in an **ogress** called Tzitzimitl, or Sesimite, who descends from the sky or lurks in the woods. In some versions, expanding upon **folklore**, the weeper is identified with the historical Malinche, the native woman who assisted Hernán Cortés in the conquest of Mexico, becoming his interpreter and mistress. As she bore him a son and was later married off to one of his lieutenants, Malinche's life story fits with the weeping-woman motif.

An elaborate fairy-tale version has it that the woman was a seamstress who fell in love with a **prince** and bore him two sons. He abandoned her for a **princess**, sending the poor seamstress some gold coins. Furious, she threw away the coins, took a dagger, and then killed the two boys and herself. Her wailing ghost now wanders along riverbanks. This version, collected orally in 1961, coincides in part with a poem by the Mexican writer Vicente Riva Palacio (1832–96), paraphrased in Thomas A. Janvier's *Legends of the City of Mexico* (1910).

The most recent interpretation, as in Sandra Cisneros' *Woman Hollering Creek and Other Stories* (1991), recasts La Llorona as a woman of strength—not unlike the old native goddess or earth spirit—who, though wounded, fights back. *See also* Ghost Story.

Further Readings: Bierhorst, John. *The Mythology of Mexico and Central America.* 2nd edition, revised. New York: Oxford University Press, 2002; Cypress, Sandra M. *La Malinche in Mexican Literature: From History to Myth.* Austin: University of Texas Press, 1991; Horcasitas, Fernando, and Douglas Butterworth. "La Llorona." *Tlalocan* 4 (1963): 177–209.

John Bierhorst

Laforet, Carmen (1921–2004)

Spanish author Carmen Laforet called upon her childhood experiences to write about the folktales of the Canary Islands, where she lived from the age of two to eighteen. In her work entitled *Gran Canaria* (*Grand Canary*, 1961), Laforet discusses the diverse **myth**s that authors of **classical antiquity** wrote about the islands, which were referred to as the remains of Atlantis, the Garden of Hesperides, the Fortunate Isles, and the site of the Elysian Fields. Laforet also includes details about her islands' history, landscape, and gastronomy in this book, which is essentially a travel guide.

Perhaps the unhappy relationship with her stepmother stirred Laforet to incorporate fairy-tale elements in her first and most successful **novel**, *Nada* (*Nothing*, 1945), which won two literary prizes, the Premio Nadal and the Premio Fastenrath. In this work, the protagonist Andrea is a modern-day **Cinderella** figure: she has two **sisters** who bully her and a grandmother who fills the role of her **fairy** godmother. At one point in the novel, like Cinderella, Andrea is able to forget her travails for one brief moment as she looks forward to a special event.

Known for her short stories, novelettes, and semiautobiographical novels that reflect life in post-Civil War Spain, Laforet was her country's first important postwar female author, thus paving the way for other female Spanish novelists such as Ana María **Matute** and Carmen **Martín Gaite**. *See also* Spanish Tales.

Further Reading: Rosenvinge, Teresa, and Benjamín Prado. *Carmen Laforet Díaz.* Barcelona: Ediciones Omega, 2004.

Candace Beutell Gardner

Lagerkvist, Pär (1891–1974)

Sweden's foremost modernist and exponent of existential angst, Pär Lagerkvist was born in Växjö in Småland to pietistic religious parents. His entire oeuvre reflects questions about God's existence, the nature of good and evil, and the meaning of life. Although he wrote drama, poetry, essays, and short stories, he is probably best known internationally as the author of the **novel**s *Dvärgen* (*The **Dwarf***, 1944) and *Barabbas* (1950). Lagerkvist won the 1951 Nobel Prize in Literature.

Influenced by cubism, medieval literature, the **Bible**, and texts of Eastern religions, Lagerkvist's style is deceptively simple but rife with intertextual allusions. Fairy-tale elements appear in some of Lagerkvist's bleak modernist texts wherein happy endings are rare. In his **novella** *Det eviga leendet* (*The Eternal Smile*, 1920), based on the **motif**involving conversations between the dead (Motif E545.1), a number of deceased talk about their lives and deaths. In one vignette, a young man arrives at an old mill in the forest where he is welcomed by an old miller and his bizarre and **ogress**like wife, who plies him with enormous amounts of food before joining him in his bed. He later plunges to his **death** in the mill wheel. In *Onda sagor* (*Evil Tales*, 1924) a timeless quality and lack of localization in many of the short stories contribute to a sense of "once upon a time" even in those stories that lack this formulaic beginning.

Lagerkvist was an intensely private man, but he left a large collection of private writings to the Royal Library of Sweden at his death in 1974.

Further Readings: Fabreus, Karin. *Sagan, myten och modernismen i Pär Lagerkvists Tidigaste prosa och Onda Sagor.* Stockholm: Stockholm Studies in History of Literature XLV, 2002; Schöier, Ingrid. *Pär Lagerkvist: En biografi.* Stockholm: Bonniers, 1987.

Marte Hult

Lagerlöf, Selma (1858–1940)

Selma Lagerlöf was the first woman to win the Nobel Prize for Literature (1909) and the first female member of the Swedish Academy. She is considered one of the finest authors in Swedish literature.

Born on her family's ancestral estate, Mårbacka in Värmland, in 1858, Lagerlöf, whose first efforts were in verse, realized early on that she wanted to write. Perhaps more than any other Swedish author, Lagerlöf utilized traditional **motif**s as inspiration for her creativity, and when she realized that she could find insight in the stories and **legend**s of her childhood, she turned to them again and again. Because of economic conditions, Mårbacka had to be sold in 1890, and the loss of the ancestral home shattered Lagerlöf. The motif of young **women** leaving home appears in many of her **novel**s in various guises. In 1907, she was able to buy back Mårbacka, and over the next few years had it renovated. Later, she bought the surrounding farmland and moved permanently to Mårbacka, running the estate.

Lagerlöf is the master of a poetic storytelling style that sometimes is reminiscent of oral narrative, with the directness of spoken speech, and much of her best work is found in her short stories and **novella**s. Her first book, the classic neo-Romantic prose epic *Gösta Berlings saga* (*The Story of Gösta Berling*, 1891) is episodic, as is much of her work. Several of her novels first appeared as serials in periodicals. A work rich in **fantasy** and hyperbole, with archetypal characters and romanticized heroes and landscapes, the stories of Gösta and the twelve cavaliers at Ekeby are represented through acts of both depravity and heroism, with a chilling sense of fatalism, supernaturalism, and the demonic. No one who has read it will forget the chill that runs up the spine when old Ulrika turns from playing the polka, the only tune she knows, to see sitting behind her in the rocking chair: "the one little children don't dare name." *The Story of Gösta Berling* has been called the most remarkable first novel to have been published in Sweden, but at the time of its publication, the story received generally poor reviews, even though five chapters had previously appeared in the periodical *Idun* and won a literary prize. Criticized for being loosely composed, it wasn't until the next year when the Danish translation was praised by Georg Brandes that Lagerlöf began to make a name for herself.

Trips to Italy and the Middle East with Sophie Elkan inspired *Antikrists mirakler* (*The Miracles of Antichrist*, 1897), a novel of Christianity and socialism set in Sicily and influenced by the work of Guiseppe **Pitré**, and the two-volume best seller *Jerusalem* (1901–2), her international breakthrough, which is a story of a Swedish farming family and their emigration from Sweden to the American Colony in Jerusalem. *Jerusalem*, as well as several other Lagerlöf works, became films by Victor Sjöström.

After ten years of teaching elementary school in Skåne, Lagerlöf moved to Falun in 1897. Many believe that *En herrgårdssägen* (*The Tale of a Manor*, 1899), a story with a **Beauty and the Beast** motif, is Lagerlöf's masterpiece. Legend was Lagerlöf's genre, and from fragments she embellished and created characters with realistic psychological depth in situations of life and death, sin and redemption, and good and evil. Recurring themes in her work are familial relationships: the patriarchal **father** and his daughter, the **mother** and her son, and the fairy-tale motif of the evil stepmother (mother-in-law). The collection *Drottningar i Kongahälla* (*Queens of Kungahalla*, 1899) was inspired by **saga**s from the *Heimskringla*, Snorri Sturleson's medieval chronicle of the Norwegian kings, among other sources. In 1903, Lagerlöf published *Herr Arnes penningar* (*Herr Arne's Hoard*), a novel of murder and retribution with supernatural elements. It has been called the first thriller in Swedish literature. Religious themes are reflected in the short stories in *Kristuslegender* (*Christ Legends*, 1904). Included in this collection is the charming **etiologic tale** "Fågel Rödbröst" ("Robin Redbreast"), which purports to explain why the robin has a red breast.

Best known internationally is *Nils Holgerssons underbara resa genom Sverige* (*The Wonderful Adventures of Nils* and *The Further Adventures of Nils Holgersson*, 1906–7). For this commissioned work for the National Teachers Association of Sweden, Lagerlöf utilized the fairy-tale genre to describe Swedish geography, **folklore**, and nature. Nils, a fourteen-year-old boy who is inconsiderate and cruel to animals, becomes transformed to **Thumbling** size, is able to understand the speech of animals, and must pass a series of tests through which he undergoes a spiritual redemption. On his travels through Sweden with wild geese and his mentor, the wise old Akka from Kebnekaise, Nils rescues baby squirrels, saves an old castle from invading rats, and rescues a little boy from drowning, among other feats. Poetic natural descriptions are blended with local legends to describe the defining character of each Swedish province. Lagerlöf also expressed her belief in conservation and the interdependence of human and animals in this text, and includes a plea against emigration in her story of an old woman, dying alone, because all of her children have gone to America. As in *The Story of Gösta Berling*, each chapter can be read as a separate narrative.

A character introduced in *The Story of Gösta Berling* reappears in the fairy tale *Liljecronas hem* (*Liljecrona's Home*, 1911), in which Raklitz, the classic evil stepmother, comes between a loving **father** and his daughter. The masterful *Kejsarn av Portugallien* (*The Emperor of Portugallia*), which Lagerlöf herself called a "Swedish King Lear," appeared in 1914. One of her finest stories, "Bortbytingen" ("The Changeling"), was published in *Troll och människor* (*Trolls and People*) in 1915. In this story, Lagerlöf changes the legendary dynamic of misuse toward **changeling**s into a story of love and compassion. Other work inspired by Värmland legends and the stories of her childhood includes a historical trilogy translated as *The Ring of the Löwensköld* (1925–28).

Selma Lagerlöf wrote three volumes of childhood memoirs, published in 1922, 1930, and 1932. She died at her beloved Mårbacka in 1940. ***See also*** Scandinavian Tales.

Further Readings: Edström, Vivi. *Selma Lagerlöf: Livets vågspel*. Stockholm: Natur og Kultur, 2002; Rahn, Suzanne. *Rediscoveries in Children's Literature*. New York: Garland, 1995. 39–50.

Marte Hult

The Land Has Eyes. See Pear ta ma 'on maf

Lane, Edward W. (1801–1876)

The first to translate the **Arabian Nights** into English from Arabic (rather than from Antoine **Galland**'s eighteenth-century French edition), British scholar Edward W. Lane contributed significantly to the popularity of the *Nights* as English **children's literature** and to nineteenth-century British visions of the Arab world.

Commissioned by the Society for the Diffusion of Useful Knowledge in London, Lane's annotated and illustrated *Arabian Nights* was published in thirty-two periodic installments (1838–40), a three-volume format (1839–41), and, subsequently, in multiple abridged editions. Lane's express goal was to translate both the text and the source culture of the *Arabian Nights*—which, he argued, was Egyptian. To accommodate the tastes and sensibilities of a Victorian family readership, Lane reshaped the content and form of his source material. For example, he purged the text of many explicitly sexual and violent passages and rearranged the 271 nights of **storytelling** into a more familiar format, to resemble a fairy-tale collection or chapter book.

Despite criticism of Lane's textual choices, his *Arabian Nights* was considered the standard English edition for at least half a century, serving as a point of comparison for later Victorian translations by John Payne and Richard Francis **Burton**. ***See also*** Translation.

Further Readings: Ahmed, Leila. *Edward W. Lane: A Study of His Life and Works and of British Ideas of the Middle East in the Nineteenth Century*. London: Longman, 1978; Schacker, Jennifer. "Otherness and Otherworldliness: Edward W. Lane's Ethnographic Treatment of the *Arabian Nights*." *Journal of American Folklore* 113 (2000): 164–84.

Jennifer Schacker

Lang, Andrew (1844–1912)

Scottish-born poet, novelist, historian, and classicist, Andrew Lang is remembered primarily for his publications on mythology, **folklore**, and especially for the Color Fairy Book series. Born in Selkirk, he was brought up on the history, **ballad**s, tales, and **legend**s of the Scottish Borders and, as a precocious student, was later schooled in the classics at St. Andrews, Glasgow, and finally at Oxford, where he was subsequently elected as a Fellow of Merton College. Leaving his position as an academic for that of a journalist, he arrived in London in 1875, where he proceeded to make a name for himself as a prominent man of letters.

Versed in the mythologies of Greece as well as those of his native Scotland, Lang began to research the **myth**s and legends of other cultures with the keen interest and scientific care of an anthropologist. He wrote a piece on the Finnish ***Kalevala***, another on Kaffir folktales, and numerous other periodical articles that tracked his growing interest in the field of linguistic and literary anthropology. Among his most important early articles for folklore studies, "Mythology and Fairy Tales" (published 1873 in the *Fortnightly Review*) asserted the anthropological value of studying myth comparatively. In *Custom and Myth* (1884), he tested his theory that seemingly irrational customs were based on practices that originally had a rational basis. In the same year, Lang wrote a long introduction to the first complete English translation of Jacob and Wilhelm **Grimm**'s *Kinder- und Hausmärchen* (*Children's and Household Tales*, 1812–15). Lang was fascinated with cultural artifacts and practices, but his attention was always drawn back to folklore, to the orally produced records of cultural learning. In the course of this work, he developed theories that were seminal in folklore studies, as he is often credited with being the first to advocate and to sustain an anthropological study of myth. *Myth, Ritual and Religion* (1887) ran counter to the time's prevailing belief that myth had developed into religion. Lang argued instead that spirituality could be tracked to the earliest humans. Lang also famously disputed the theories advanced by two notable scholars working in the related fields of linguistics and mythology— Friedrich Max **Müller** and James Frazer. While Müller contended that myth had developed relatively late and did so out of errors in transmission and understanding, Lang held that myth derived from a primitive inability to distinguish between human events and natural phenomena. And, while Frazer (*The Golden Bough*) contended that primitive humans practiced magic, not religion, Lang refuted this claim at length in his 1901 *Magic and Religion*, finding again that spiritual elements were evident in the folklore and cultural practices of the earliest people.

But it is with fairy tales that Lang's name is now inextricably aligned. A comparative mythologist from early on, he saw particularly in the history of fairy tales the intersection of conscious art and unconscious cultural transmission. In his introduction to the English version of Grimms' tales, Lang observed that the tales featured relatively few incidents and situations occurring in many different combinations. He also noted that the **tale type**s were distributed across a wide geographic area. Along with other scholars of his time, George Cox and the Grimm brothers among them, Lang faced the question of what accounted for this cross-cultural existence of tales and just what it might have to do with evolutionary theory. Eventually, by the time he penned the definitive article on folklore for the eleventh edition of the *Encyclopaedia Britannica*, Lang rejected the idea of a spontaneous genesis of similar tales across cultures and emphasized instead the likelihood of cross-fertilization and cultural **diffusion** of tales. As such, he stood in clear opposition to the single-origin Aryan theory espoused by both Cox and the Grimms.

Lang's **collecting** and **editing** of tales for children came relatively late in his career. His *Blue Fairy Book* (1889) was a beautifully produced and illustrated edition of fairy tales that has become a classic, as have—to a lesser degree—the eleven collections of fairy tales that followed (the *Red Fairy Book* in 1890, the *Green* in 1892, the *Yellow* in 1894, on up to the *Lilac* in 1910). Generally, as the series progressed, Lang moved toward lesser-known tales. While the *Blue Fairy Book* included traditional European tales and ventured into the *Arabian Nights*, by the close of the series, he had also represented tales whose sources were African, Celtic, Native American, Japanese, Brazilian, and Australian. Even in Lang's own time, his name became so closely associated with these collections, which appealed to adult tastes as much as to children's, that he was often mistakenly taken to be the author of the tales he collected, an error that vexed him and drew more than one surly response from him. Indeed, many others translated and rewrote the included tales—prime among them his wife Leonora. Still, although Lang was mainly a collector of the tales in this series, as he repeatedly emphasized in the preface to each book, he did have a hand in refashioning some of the stories. The *Blue* book, for instance, contains Lang's own retelling of the Perseus and Gorgon story. His selection and editing process was also informed by his own experience in writing fairy stories, at which he had tried his hand years before. In 1884, he had written *The Princess Nobody*, and later also wrote *Princess Prince Prigio* (1889) and *Prince Ricardo* (1893), each marked with a sense of the anthropological but tinged also with burlesque. Most agree that Lang's finest original fairy story written during this period is *The Gold of Fairnilee* (1888), which derives from the Border ballads of his native Scotland and features the countryside as well as the human-stealing **fairies** familiar from Lang's youth. *See also* Anthropological Approaches; Monogenesis; Polygenesis.

Further Readings: Burne, Glenn S. "Andrew Lang's *The Blue Fairy Book*: Changing the Course of History." *Touchstones: Reflections on the Best in Children's Literature.* Volume 2. West Lafayette: Children's Literature Association, 1987. 140–50; Dorson, Richard M. *The British Folklorists: A History.* Chicago: University of Chicago Press, 1968; Green, Roger Lancelyn. *Andrew Lang: A Critical Biography.* Leicester: E. Ward, 1946.

Lori Schroeder Haslem

Latin American Tales

During the course of twentieth-century folktale **collecting**, the region embracing South America, Central America, Mexico, and the Spanish-speaking Caribbean was revealed as a storehouse of traditional Iberian tales, many reaching back through Europe or North Africa to the Middle East and India. At the same time, a seemingly inexhaustible supply of unacculturated American Indian lore came to light, especially in South America, while along the western, or Cordilleran, rim of the entire region, notably in Mexico, a mixed lore combining Old and New World elements was found to have developed in the majority of Indian communities.

For the purposes of this article, folktales from the old Hispanic settlements of the North American Southwest will be taken as belonging to Latin America (whereas Southwest Indian lore is treated under **Native American Tales**); and it is to be understood that the content of Brazilian **Portuguese tales** is essentially the same as that of the much more fully documented New World Spanish versions.

Folklore documentation in the western hemisphere begins no later than 1496, when Columbus, to facilitate the business of conquest, had his chaplain record the

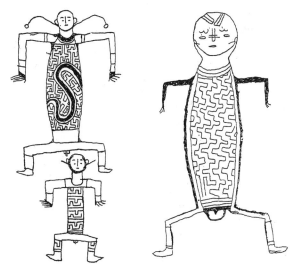

The two heroes of the South American Twin Myth (left) with their father; Shipaya drawing, Brazil, 1917. Reproduced from Curt Nimuendajú, "Bruchstücke aus Religion und Überlieferung der Šipaia-Indianer," *Athropos* 14–15 (1919–20): 1017.

beliefs and traditions of the Taino of Hispaniola. The project immediately yielded such typical Latin American Indian motifs as the ocean trapped in a gourd, the origin of **women** from trees, and the emergence of ancestors from inside the earth (Motif A1631, Emergence of tribe from lower world). Through the 1500s, following the conquest of Mexico and Peru, **Aztec tales** and **Inca tales** were recorded. These, principally, are stories of world origins and the doings of Native gods and kings. Evidence that **folktale**s in the usual sense of the term were already being imported from Spain may be seen in an Aztec-language manuscript from the late 1500s, which preserves forty-seven of **Aesop**'s fables, several with **Coyote** replacing the European **trickster** Fox. Other evidence of folkloric importation can be seen in a Peruvian Quechua manuscript from 1608, which includes the medical remedy overheard in a conversation of animals (Motif N452), found also in the seventeenth-century *Pentamerone* of Giambattista **Basile** and traceable to the ***Panchatantra***.

After the early 1600s, there is a hiatus of some 250 years, when traditional tales, whether Amerindian or Iberian, virtually ceased to be recorded. The Romantic stirrings in Europe and North America that produced the landmark collections of Jacob and Wilhelm **Grimm** and Henry Rowe Schoolcraft were not felt in Latin America until the last quarter of the nineteenth century; and while no single contribution ever achieved the reach of the Grimms' ***Kinder- und Hausmärchen*** (*Children's and Household Tales*, 1812–15) or Schoolcraft's *Algic Researches* (1836; adapted by the poet Henry Longfellow as *The Song of Hiawatha*), major Latin American collections began to appear in print shortly after 1900. By mid-century, the whole corpus, still growing, had achieved a critical mass, ushering in Terrence Leslie Hansen's *Types of the Folktale in Cuba, Puerto Rico, the Dominican Republic, and Spanish South America* (1957) and Stanley L. Robe's *Index of Mexican Folktales* (1973), which systematized the Hispanic tales, and, in the field of Indian lore, Claude Lévi-Strauss's four-volume *Mythologiques* (*Introduction to a Science of Mythology*, 1969–81). A further development was the twenty-four volume series Folk Literature of South American Indians, with its comprehensive **motif** index, supervised by Johannes Wilbert and Karin Simoneau.

The Iberian Tradition

Spanish-speaking storytellers in Latin America deliver the standard repertory of **Spanish tales** whether in Mexico, Chile, or Puerto Rico. These, as expected, range from the comic and the anecdotal to the heroic, the moralizing, and the religious.

Among the most popular are "**Cinderella**" and two closely related rags-to-riches tales, "The Three Gowns" (ATU 510B, Peau d'Asne) and "The Horse of Seven Colors" (ATU 530, The Princess on the Glass Mountain). The helpful horse of ATU 530 appears throughout the folktale's range, but that it must be of "seven colors" is a Latin American requirement. Another well-known story is The Basil Maiden (ATU 879), in which a clever young woman, often a **princess**, outwits the **king** and becomes his bride—though, typically, the princess of European versions is a poor girl in the Latin American examples. Still another is "The **Bear's Son**," notably Latin American in a gritty Honduran version in which Old World motifs are adapted to a plotline built around New World slash-and-burn agriculture and the exploitation of native labor. In these few examples, two characteristics emerge: a fondness for the baroque, on the one hand; and on the other, a pull toward the plain and earthborn. The former belongs to non-Indian communities; the latter to Indian communities that have internalized Iberian lore.

Storytelling may occur in work camps, where men take up residence during a harvest season; or on Sunday mornings at the grocery store while other people are at church; or at home in the evening where a mother, perhaps, will lie in her hammock with a young daughter and tell *cuentos*, "folktales." Up through the middle of the twentieth century, at least, the typical occasion for public storytelling was the *velorio*, "wake," the vigil that begins at the first nightfall following a death and ends with burial the next morning. In some communities, the vigil continues for eight more nights, becoming a *novena*, with storytelling on the first and ninth nights or, rarely, on each of the nine nights (though not beyond midnight after the first night). As soon as a death has occurred, the family will take care to notify a recognized storyteller to ensure her or his attendance. The Costa Rican writer Carmen Lyra (pseudonym of María Isabel Carvajal), herself a sometime folklorist, recalls that her aunt, an outstandingly gifted narrator, was "always dressed in black."

From India and the Middle East. Not unexpectedly, Latin America preserves tales that have become rare in Europe or may even have been forgotten. Two stories of presumed Indic origin may be considered in this light. The first is the tale of the seven blinded **queen**s (ATU 462, The Outcast Queens and the **Ogress** Queen), recorded for Chile, widespread in South Asia, but virtually unknown in Europe outside of Spain. The second, apparently missing from Spain as well as from the rest of southern Europe, is the still-rarer item known in a Quechua version from Peru as "The Pongo's Dream" (ATU 1572M*, The Apprentice's Dream). In this story, an Amerindian menial, a *pongo*, employed on a great hacienda is cruelly harassed by the owner, or *patrón*. Suddenly stepping out of character, the meek *pongo* informs the self-satisfied *patrón* of a dream he has had in which the *patrón* is covered in honey, the *pongo* in excrement—the two of them condemned by St. Francis to lick each other perpetually. In a twentieth-century version from South India, the self-satisfied antagonist is the king, and his challenger, the court jester.

Here, incidentally, we observe a rule, or at least a tendency, in the transmission of Old World folktales told in Latin American Indian communities: the ubiquitous king is now changed into an overseer, a landlord, or a *patrón*—a much less appealing figure—as the enchanting realm of palaces and courtiers dissolves into the reality of New World plantation life.

As has often been remarked, tales of Indic, Persian, and Arabic origin are a hallmark of Hispanic lore, told and retold with their Asian roots habitually covered up. Sometimes, however, a literary source may be suspected, and on occasion the storyteller consciously transports the listener to the Orient, as in a Chilean version of "The Seven Blinded Queens," which begins, "In a faraway country...." Or in an Ecuadorean telling of the **Sheherazade** story, the framing tale of the ***Arabian Nights,*** set in "the far-distant city called *Benjuí*," referring to the aromatic gum benzoin (also known as benjamin), as though a fragrance were wafting from the East.

Piety and Skepticism. The **religious tale**s of Iberian tradition persist in Latin America, and in stories of nearly every description, a saint such as Francis, Peter, Theresa, or the Virgin Mother, often with her "little boy," may appear briefly to reward virtue, ward off danger, or pronounce a judgment. Perhaps the most popular of the sacred helpers is St. Anthony (of Padua), who enables women to find husbands. Yet St. Anthony himself does not escape rough treatment if he fails to deliver.

Prayers, paradise, purgatory, the rosary, and the Sacred Heart of Jesus all find their way into folktales. Yet the traditional storytellers and their audiences remain firmly anticlerical. It may be said that in stories the role of the priest or monk is to extort money.

Associated with the **clergy**, in life if not in folktales, is the institution of *compadrazgo*, which helps create social order by linking families in lifelong relationships based on the baptism of children. Although the bond that ties *compadres*, "coparents," is a sacred trust, it is often strained by social and economic inequalities between the partners. In folktales, the mere mention of the word *compadre* is enough to alert the listener that a story of betrayal is about to unfold. In a New Mexico variant of "The Twelve Truths of the World" (based on Motif S224, Child promised to devil for acting as godfather), a poor man in a fit of rage cries that he will invite the **devil** to be his *compadre*—and gets his wish. In a version from Guatemala of the tale known as "The Bad Compadre" (ATU 531, The Clever Horse), the treacherous partner is killed in the forest by jaguars. In folktales, if not in life, justice prevails over social order.

Role Reversals. Quite aside from the universal tendency of male storytellers to inject a male point of view, and female tellers to do the opposite, certain folktale types can be augmented to accommodate a full reversal of **gender** roles. Among the most noteworthy is the female dragon-slayer who rescues a **prince** in distress. This in a Mexican variant of ATU 300, The Dragon-Slayer, collected from an unidentified narrator before 1943. Another is the New Mexican tale of a widow who liberates three princesses and becomes the general of the king's armies, a variant of ATU 301, The Three Stolen Princesses, collected from a male narrator before 1937.

In a reversal of the Cinderella theme, a Venezuelan story tells of a put-upon hero obliged to stay home and wash the dishes while his two **brothers** go off to a tournament. The vanity of the hero, who finally gets the chance to wear a fancy suit and join the tournament himself, combined with the swaggering dialogue of his contemptuous brothers, amounts to a commentary on machismo. The full story, a variant of ATU 530, The Princess on the Glass Mountain, was collected from a female narrator before 1953.

In the present context, a pair of contrasting tales, distinctly New World, may be mentioned. One is the story of the **witch** wife who leaves the house each night having removed her head or her skin (or changed her skin); this tale is known from Mexico, El Salvador, Honduras, and Puerto Rico. The reverse is "The Buzzard Husband," from Mexico and Guatemala, the tale of a worthless man who leaves the house each morning but never actually works. The former seems to have African as well as Hispanic roots; the latter apparently is Amerindian.

Levity and Nonsense. A vein of levity, essential to the art of the folktale, may be detected not only in the sing-song rhymes and **riddle**s that interrupt the narrative flow but in the opening and closing formulas that frame the tale, inviting listeners into a make-believe realm or, in conclusion, releasing them from the spell. In Latin America, these little devices often appear in baroque configurations.

Instead of the familiar "Once upon a time ...," narrators in Puerto Rico may begin, "Once and twice makes thrice upon a time...." And in place of the closing formula "... lived happily ever after," a tale from Argentina can end, "They were happy as the dickens / And ate chickens" (*Así vivieron felices / y comieron perdices*, literally, "Thus they lived happily / And ate partridges"). In Panama, more elaborately, one may say, "They all lived happily till the day they died—and here we are, still waiting for our luck to change; my tale is done, and the wind blows it off, when the wind brings it back I'll tell it again." Examples from Chile are more playful, as in the opening formula, "If you learn it you'll know it, so listen and learn how to tell it; now, don't pick the fig until it's big; if you want a pear, you'll need a ladder; and if you'd like a melon, marry a man with a big nose." Such features are in contrast to the direct style of Native storytelling in communities that have been historically isolated from Old World lore.

The Native Traditions

American Indian, or Native, tales, strictly defined, comprise the oral literature of whole cultures, not a compartmentalized "folk." In general, they lack the element of nonsense, the preoccupation with money, and the happy endings (whether sentimental or vindictive) that one associates with the term "folktale." Yet child protagonists, tricksters, dangerous parental figures, talking animals, supernatural interventions, and episodic (often reiterative) plotting are common in both spheres, even if anthropologists prefer to call the Native examples **"myth"** (in the broad sense of Greek *mythos*, "story"), saving "folktale" for the imported Old World material.

Native tales throughout Latin America exhibit a pronounced identification with the natural world, including **marriage**s between humans and animals (or plants) and a particular interest in astral bodies (especially the sun and moon). Etiologic—that is, explanatory or "just so"—motifs are reflexive features of the Native style, much as the moralizing element, if not the overt **moral**, serves to round off the telling of many a European tale. And, again in contrast to European traditions (where the feature is present but not typical), protagonists are frequently **twins**.

Areal Characteristics.   For the purposes of an overview, the approximately 200 cultures whose oral traditions have been investigated may be grouped by geographical area, since Native tale types tend to cluster accordingly.

The richest of the areas can be designated as Greater Brazil, including border areas of Colombia, Peru, Bolivia, and Paraguay (but excluding both northeast Brazil north of the Amazon River and the Brazilian Highlands of east-central Brazil). Tupian languages predominate in this South American heartland. Typical tales include "The Twin Myth" (a hero cycle that pits two boys against an ogre jaguar), "Moon and His Sister" (an **incest** story), and "The Origin of Night" (a Pandora-like **etiologic** tale). The so-called "Yurupary Myth," common to many tribes in the area, accounts for the origin of male domination. The equally well-known "Amazon Myth" tells of a **woman warrior** band always on the march in the forest. Early reports of this Greek-like story, often in the form of a plausible rumor, led to the naming of the Amazon River.

Both the "Amazon Myth" and "The Twin Myth" (but with the **ogre** jaguar replaced by a fire-spitting toad) may also be found in the Guiana area, centering on Venezuela. Arawakan and Cariban languages are spoken in this largely coastal territory, which extends into the Caribbean and eastward through French Guiana and northeast Brazil north of the Amazon. In addition to the two stories that have been mentioned, typical tales include "The Vulture Wife" (whose father sorely tests his human son-in-law), "The Underwater Woman" (who takes a human husband and eventually reveals herself to be a fish or an anaconda), and "The Tree and the Flood" (in which the ocean, trapped in a tree or a gourd, is suddenly released, creating the world as we know it today).

In the Ge-speaking Brazilian Highlands, home to cultures with a flair for entertainment, the darkly novelistic "Twin Myth" is lacking, replaced by the adventures of the witty tricksters Sun and Moon.

Southward, in the Gran Chaco of western Paraguay and adjacent borderlands, the trickster is either Carancho (a kind of hawk) or the native Fox, a world-transforming scapegrace who is part dupe, part hero, and part devil. More than any other figure in Latin American mythology, the Gran Chaco trickster recalls the well-known Coyote of North American lore.

A thinly populated Far South area, including Tierra del Fuego, gives rise to highly original stories, defying the rule that oral tales are built on recurring plots. An exception may be made for the standard Fuegian tale, or at least theme, of the men's revolt against the women—who in the ancient days held the secret of domination until their husbands wrested it from them.

A Northwest area of South America, centering on Colombia, may be identified where Chibchan languages are dominant. Again, "The Twin Myth" can be found, as well as "Moon and His Sister" and "The Tree and the Flood." The myths of a female creator, known from both highland and lowland cultures, and a curious lore involving giants and little people, are distinctive. A typical tale is "The Food-Inhaler Bride," in which a man marries into a race of not-quite humans who, since they lack anuses, must nourish themselves by inhaling odors. Correspondence with an Old World motif, F529.2, People without anuses, would appear to be coincidental. In at least one version, from northwest Ecuador, the food inhalers are **dwarf**-sized. In the realm of **legend**, highland Colombia may be cited as the home territory of the lore of **El Dorado.**

Highland and eastern Ecuador joined with highland Peru and highland Bolivia form the Andean area once controlled by the Incas and still dominated by the Inca language, Quechua. Indigenous tales in this region are best preserved along the heavily forested eastern flank of the highlands, known as the *montaña*, where versions of "The Underwater Woman" (mentioned above for the Guiana area) and "The Twin Myth"—the single most characteristic tale of South America—are still told. A much-attenuated variant of "The Twin Myth," but still recognizable, is preserved in a manuscript dating from the early 1600s from the western Peruvian highlands. Also recorded for both the high country and the *montaña*, and from both the seventeenth and the twentieth centuries, is "The Parrot Brides," the story of a bachelor who chooses the lesser of two available parrot women and thus institutes marriage—with its shortcomings. In Quechua-speaking communities, mainly in the high country, Hispanic lore has been substantially integrated, much less so in the non-Quechua forest settlements of the *montaña*.

Middle America, comprising Mexico and Central America west of the Panama Canal, combines a rich heritage of old Aztec and Maya lore with a surviving repertory of Native tales. The more-or-less unmingled indigenous lore belongs especially to the remoter cultures such as the Huichol and the Lacandon of Mexico or the Bribri and the Cabécar of Costa Rica. Among the apparently Native stories found throughout this vast area are "The Loss of the Ancients" (an early race disappears), "Why the Earth Eats the Dead" (the earth "wounded" by cultivation takes payment in human lives), "The Visit to the Animal Master" (a careless hunter is scolded by the supernatural keeper of animals), and "The Dead Wife" (a Middle American subtype of the Native [North] American Orpheus tale, in which a widower—like the Greek Orpheus—seeks his wife in the afterworld). Important tales confined to Mexico include "Corn Woman's Marriage" (the corn bride is abused by her human husband's mother and flees to safety) and "The Childhood of Sun and Moon" (mischievous twin orphans rebel against an old woman who has protected them and rise into the sky as the sun and the moon). Mexico is also the principal locale of the legend of **La Llorona**, "The Weeping Woman." A tale confined to the Bribri, the Cabécar, and the other tribes of Lower Central America is "The Seeds of Humanity," in which the human race grows from corn kernels planted by a deity or hero.

Various New World cultures have produced foundational **epic**s such as the Hebrew **Bible** or the *Kalevala*, or at least the tales that are waiting to be organized into such epics. An outstanding example of the finished product is the sixteenth-century *Popol Vuh* of the Quiché Maya of Guatemala. A modern example is the anthropologist Marc de Civrieux's *Watunna* (1970; English version by David M. Guss, 1980), a cycle of the traditional tales of the Yekuana, or Makiritare, of Venezuela. In the manner of Elias Lönnrot, author-compiler of the *Kalevala*, de Civrieux became as adept as his Yekuana teachers and thus claimed the authority to fashion the Yekuana national epic.

Mixed Lore.   Generally, Latin American tales travel in one direction only: from the Hispanic or neo-Brazilian to the Indian community. The reverse rarely occurs within **oral tradition**. In other words, Ibero-American storytellers do not adopt Indian tales (but see comments on non-oral fiction and poetry, below).

In a typical replacement, as noted above in the case of an Indic tale recurring in Peru, the stock character of the king becomes the hacienda owner in the Native version. Meanwhile, in Middle America and the Andes, the old Amerindian king survives in a completely different sort of story, a modern legend in which it is said that Montezuma, for instance, is now in hiding or has been captured and may yet return. In highland Peru, the millenarian tale is of Inkarrí (a neologism composed of *Inca* and the Spanish word *rey,* "king"). Inkarrí is in hiding but will return to lead a Native revolution.

In another kind of replacement, the Iberian trickster Pedro de Urdemalas loses his name, though his exploits may survive, as in a Huichol version of "The Gold-Dung Donkey" (Motif K111.1, Alleged gold-dropping animal sold) assigned to the Huichol trickster, Kauyumari.

Though Pedro de Urdemalas has continued to be popular in Hispanic and neo-Brazilian communities, neither he nor even many of his adventures have made the transition to the Native repertory. At the same time, a different kind of Old World trickster tale, the animal **anecdote**, has become widespread in the Native setting while showing signs of decline in the Hispanic sphere. Monkey, Jaguar, and various other personified animals fill the principal roles, yet the Old World **tale type**s are easily recognizable: ATU 34, The Wolf Dives into the Water for Reflected Cheese; ATU 1530, Holding up the Rock (in which the trickster escapes after persuading his enemy to hold up the roof of a cave); and many others.

In Mexico and Guatemala and to a lesser extent in the Andes, **Bible tale**s are told in Native communities either as isolated stories or as a cycle. Inspired by the catechism of early missionaries, the full cycle begins with Adam and Eve, proceeding to their expulsion from Eden, the Great Flood, and the life, death, and resurrection of Christ. More than simply Bible miscellany, these stories illustrate the Catholic doctrine of original sin, the failed attempt to wash it away by means of the Flood, and humanity's eventual salvation through

Christ. No longer a part of the Hispanic oral repertory, the cycle as preserved in American Indian tellings is rich in medieval, nonscriptural details. Not surprisingly, the theme of sin and redemption has been lost, replaced by an emphasis on persecution. Especially favored are those tales that tell of Christ's flight from his pursuers and the clever tricks by which he temporarily eludes them.

In various stories, whether of Old or New World origin, syncretism may be detected. In a Colombian variant of **Cupid and Psyche** (ATU 425B, Son of the Witch), to take a basically Old World example, the Virgin Mother appears at a critical moment, advising the heroine to obtain a hair from "the mother of all the animals." Thus Christian lore is combined with a reference to the female creator, the old mother deity of Native Colombia. A basically New World example is the tale of the wise hero who comes out of the east, teaches the arts of civilization, then disappears into the sky. Quetzalcoatl of the Aztecs and Votan of the Tzeltal Maya fit into this pattern, which often accommodates details from the life of Christ.

Influence

Traditional tales have helped to project the image of Latin America onto the international stage with results that are artistic, scholarly, and political. In this regard, it is the Native (not the imported Iberian) tale that conveys the spirit of the region and its constituent cultures.

Latin American fiction and **poetry**, which began to expand its global audience in the 1960s, has drawn freely on Amerindian lore. Native tales per se have added color to the sympathetic portrayal of Indian life in novels by Mexican and Central American writers, as in Rosario Castellanos' tribute to Mayan tradition in her *Balún-Canán* (*The Nine Guardians*, 1958). An exception to the rule stated in the previous paragraph, favoring indigenous over imported tales, is the Venezuelan novelist Ramón Díaz Sánchez's *Cumboto* (1950; English edition, 1969), which incorporates the lore of Pedro de Urdemalas. Breaking away from folklore, other writers have developed a modern fairy-tale genre that has been identified with **magical realism.** Still others have used the Indian tale as an artistic model in its own right, notably the Brazilian novelist-anthropologist Darcy Ribeiro, whose *Maira* (1978; English edition, 1984) is a modern reworking of "The Twin Myth"—in Native tellings, Maira is either the father of the twins or the senior twin himself. A sign of the movement's maturity is that it became ripe for parody. The North American novelist John Updike's *Brazil* (1994) is a tongue-in-cheek exercise in magical realism, in which the lore of the Native hero-deity Maira makes an extended appearance.

Also beginning in the 1960s, responding to the accumulation of Native tales, the academic sector spawned a variety of scholarly enterprises that have been widely influential. Lévi-Strauss made South American Indian tales the proving ground for **structuralism** as the theory applies to myth. Ethnopoetics, another new approach to myth, based on oral patterning, would make **Maya tales**, with their tendency to resolve into couplets, a showcase for the translation of narrative as poetry—a way of understanding myth that culminated in Gary Gossen's 1,000-page presentation of Tzotzil Maya tales, *Four Creations* (2002). Recognizing the sheer wealth of data contained in the South American repertory, Wilbert and Simoneau turned their twenty-four volume Folk Literature series into a massive resource that has attracted scholars in anthropology, comparative literature, medicine, and zoology.

Meanwhile, Native communities throughout the region began acting on their political aspirations, often using or adapting traditional tales in a manner that linked up with international currents. In 2000, taking advantage of environmentalism and late twentieth-century calls for religious freedom, the Huichol, with help from the World Wildlife Fund, succeeded in doubling the size of the Huiricuta Natural and Cultural State Reserve in central Mexico. A refuge for endangered species, Huiricuta is also a "religious use" area, recognized as the place of origin for the Huichol trickster Kauyumari and, according to one version of the story, the homeland of the tragic heroine of "Corn Woman's Marriage."

A similar development in Colombia matched the Kogi tribe with The Nature Conservancy. The result is that the Kogi, with their impressive female creator and associated earth-centered lore, became the indigenous owners and custodians of a national park in the Sierra Nevada de Santa Marta.

In yet another development, a new version of "The Seeds of Humanity," published by the Bribri and Cabécar of Costa Rica in cooperation with the North American-based organization Cultural Survival, prefigured late-twentieth-century multiculturalism, explaining that in ancient times, the seeds that gave rise to humans were of different colors. Additional new tales from the same source explained that forests are "the lungs of the earth" and that "there are sacred places in the forest that must not be touched." The stories were published in small books during the 1980s and 1990s and helped to stimulate charitable giving in Europe and North America for the purpose of buying inholdings in the Native reserves.

As the twentieth century drew to a close, the so-called Zapatista rebellion among the Tzeltal and Tzotzil Maya of southern Mexico became highly newsworthy. Identifying the movement with democracy and cultural pluralism, the mysterious non-Indian Zapatista leader, known to television audiences worldwide as Subcomandante Marcos, issued a stream of **parable**-like press releases and even a modern folktale entitled *La historia de colores* (1994), thematically related to the new Bribri and Cabécar version of "The Seeds of Humanity." Released in the United States as *The Story of Colors* (1999) with illustrations, the tale as published in book form was to have been funded by the National Endowment for the Arts. However, the project was suddenly considered too political, and the funding was cancelled. This merely drew more attention to the Zapatista cause. In fact, Marcos had promised, in one of his communiqués, a messianic return of the old Tzeltal hero Votan, who had been "dying" and had now come to life. (Primary sources for information in this article may be traced in the works listed below, especially the first three.) *See also* African American Tales; Espinosa, Aurelio M.; Virgin of Guadalupe.

Further Readings: Bierhorst, John. *Latin American Folktales: Stories from Hispanic and Indian Traditions.* New York: Pantheon, 2002; ———. *The Mythology of Mexico and Central America.* 2nd revised edition. New York: Oxford University Press, 2002; ———. *The Mythology of South America.* 2nd revised edition. New York: Oxford University Press, 2002; Gossen, Gary H., ed. and trans. *Four Creations: An Epic Story of the Chiapas Mayas.* Norman: University of Oklahoma Press, 2002; Hansen, Terrence Leslie. *The Types of the Folktale in Cuba, Puerto Rico, the Dominican Republic, and Spanish South America.* Berkeley: University of California Press, 1957; Lévi-Strauss, Claude. *The Raw and the Cooked.* Volume 1 of *Introduction to a Science of Mythology.* New York: Harper, 1969; Robe, Stanley L. *Index of Mexican Folktales.* Berkeley: University of California Press, 1973; Wilbert, Johannes, and Karin Simoneau, series eds. *The Folk Literature of South American Indians.* 24 volumes. Los Angeles: UCLA Latin American Center, 1970–92.

John Bierhorst

Le Guin, Ursula K. (1929–)

Ursula K. Le Guin is a leading writer and critic in the field of American science fiction and **fantasy**, whose award-winning fiction and criticism alike are characteristically rigorous and intelligent. The daughter of anthropologist Theodora Kroeber and historian Alfred Kroeber, she demonstrates an anthropological and sociological approach to speculative writing. Her young adult Earthsea series of books (1968–2001) are fantasy **novel**s that combine the usual formula of the magical hero-quest with sophisticated thematic explorations, being particularly concerned with naming, **death**, and **dragon**s; the fourth and fifth novels reflect Le Guin's strong feminist awareness, repositioning the female figure as the heroic/mythic agent in the quest. Other works, which use the framework of the magical quest, include *The Beginning Place* (1980) and *Rocannon's World* (1966), as well as short stories, which play with fairy-tale **motif**s. Her several children's books are attractively simplified fantasies, which work to reconcile children with magical creatures. Many of her more prolific science-fiction narratives, including the Hainish cycle based in the multiplanetary union of the Ecumen, also tend to a mythic, often Jungian or Taoist resonance that gives them symbolic shape.

There is a strong awareness of folkloric themes and oral **storytelling** in Le Guin's writing, and she has a recurring interest in **Native American tales**, particularly the **trickster** figure of **Coyote**. The importance of **oral tradition**s is explored particularly in the pastoral **utopia** *Always Coming Home* (1985). The short stories and poems in *Buffalo Gals and Other Animal Presences* (1987) likewise offer tales about talking animals, using a magical framework to explore notions of otherness. She is a spare, controlled stylist whose reserve of tone captures some of the flatness of the fairy-tale voice, although she is also capable of vivid flights of language. Her critical writings in particular, collected in *The Language of the Night* (1979, 1989) and *Dancing on the Edge of the World* (1989), demonstrate her self-consciousness about narrative and her sense of the cultural importance of story and orality. *See also* Children's Literature; Feminist Tales.

Further Reading: Rochelle, Warren G. *Communities of the Heart: The Rhetoric of Myth in the Fiction of Ursula K. Le Guin.* Liverpool: Liverpool University Press, 2001.

Jessica Tiffin

Lee, Tanith (1947–)

A prolific and popular English writer of **fantasy**, horror, and science fiction, Tanith Lee also demonstrates a recurring interest in fairy tales. While her narratives are often at the pulp end of the fantasy/science-fiction spectrum, offering sword-and-sorcery epics and various self-consciously dark horror narratives, she is capable of dramatic and interesting structural and ideological play. Her writing also betrays an interest in **gender** issues, particularly the nature of power and sexuality for **women**; she writes powerfully, unabashedly, and often disturbingly about **sex**. In the context of her fairy-tale writing, this makes her something of a popular shadow to Angela **Carter**, her characters likewise exploring female selfhood through symbol and narrative. Her more realist lesbian fiction, written under the pen name Esther Garber, reflects her somewhat shifting sense of female identity. Lee's writing tends toward an obsession with otherness, expressed through recurring motifs such as vampires, the animal, shape-changing, sex change, and the demonic. Her use of the clichés of magical symbol is, however, often unreflecting and does not always deconstruct patriarchal notions of the idealized or demonized feminine.

Lee's career began with young adult and children's fantasy novels, which tend to employ fantasy quest **motif**s somewhat predictably in the service of adolescent discovery. Concern with fairy-tale structures, however, is seen in her early novel *The Dragon Hoard* (1971), whose Jason-style quest undercuts fairy-tale expectations for comic effect. Likewise, her collection *Princess Hynchatti and Some Other Surprises* (1972) is notable for its playful address to the familiar tropes of the form, its various protagonists (alternating **prince**s and **princess**es) completing moral as well as physical quests with the assistance of charms, **magic object**s, and animal helpers. While there is a wry, parodic element to her children's stories, they are somewhat simplistic in comparison to her later, adult fairy-tale collection, *Red as Blood or Tales from the Sisters Grimmer* (1983), which shows a self-conscious reinfusion of the fairy tale with its darker, more violent, and erotic roots. In *Red as Blood*, Lee clearly intends to shock the reader out of complacent acceptance of the classic tales through twists, inversions, and distortions. Particularly interesting stories include the Nebula Award-nominated "Red as Blood," a vampiric **Snow White**; "Wolfland," a Victorian Gothic version of "**Little Red Riding Hood**"; and "Beauty," a flawed but compelling retelling of "**Beauty and the Beast**" as science fiction. Lee's full-length fairy-tale novel, *White as Snow* (2000), part of Terri **Windling**'s Fairy Tale Series, is less successful, being a scattered and somewhat awkward interplay of the Snow White story with the Persephone **myth**.

Although Lee has written comparatively few actual fairy-tale narratives, a strong awareness of mythic structures and the expectations of magical narrative underpin much of her writing. This is seen particularly in her short stories, collected in volumes such as *The Gorgon and Other Beastly Tales* (1985), *Women as Demons* (1989), and *The Forests of the Night* (1989). *See also* Erotic Tales; Feminist Tales.

Further Readings: Haut, Mavis. *The Hidden Library of Tanith Lee: Themes and Subtexts from Dionysos to the Immortal Gene.* Jefferson, NC: McFarland & Company, 2001; Lefanu, Sarah. "Robots and Romance: The Science Fiction and Fantasy of Tanith Lee." *Sweet Dreams: Sexuality, Gender and Science Fiction.* Edited by Susannah Radstone. London: Lawrence & Wishart, 1988. 121–36.

Jessica Tiffin

Legend

The legend is a genre of folk narrative that is not easily defined. The term "legend," coming from the Latin verb *legere* (to read), once referred specifically to stories about the lives of the saints read aloud in sermons or other religious settings from at least the twelfth century in the Christian Western world. The term expanded by the eighteenth century to include any story, written or oral, based on folk beliefs that were seen as unofficial knowledge, more positively by the Romantics than by Enlightenment scholars.

Although the German term *Legende* retains the narrower sense of **saint's legend**, the broader definition of legend corresponds to the German term *Sage*, especially as it was used in Jacob and Wilhelm **Grimm**'s pioneering nineteenth-century work, *Deutsche Sagen* (*German Legends*, 1816–18). Better known for their collection of **folktale**s and **fairy tale**s, *Kinder- und Hausmärchen* (*Children's and Household Tales*, 1812–15), the Grimms were also interested in stories that they saw as less international and more local, as less fantastic and more realistic. Their famous statement in the foreword to the first volume of *German Legends* that "The fairy tale is more poetic; the legend is more historical" (Grimm 1: 1) set the groundwork for defining the legend by contrasting it to the fairy tale through the twentieth century.

In comparing the two genres' styles, Swiss folklorist Max **Lüthi** characterized the fairy tale as an art form, symbolized by an image of a castle in its abstract, timeless aesthetic and exemplified in its formulaic opening, "Once upon a time." Lüthi characterized the legend as a less artful form, symbolized by an image of a cave in its realistic, almost journalistic, depictions of people caught in unusual situations that are not always resolved. Accounts of the dead returning, of sunken cities and lost treasures revealed, and of individuals encountering giants, **dwarf**s, the **devil**, and other creatures as well as narratives about local events, famous individuals, and place-name origins indicate these legendary qualities.

A common twentieth-century definition of the legend as a story, set in the recent or historical past, that is believed to be true by those by whom and to whom it is told, grows out of these generic distinctions. Scholars have not agreed upon a universal classification system for the legend as they have for the folktale and fairy tale; some scholars even question the cross-cultural application of a European term to non-European narratives. American folklorist Jan Harold Brunvand, however, has identified broad subcategories that correspond to, or extend, the kinds of legends that the Grimms had documented. Religious legend includes saints' legends but also stories about blessings, miracles, and interactions between the human and the divine in world religions. Supernatural legend, once believed by scholars to have died out at the end of the nineteenth century, appears to be one of the most viable of narratives in both developing and modern, postindustrial societies.

Local legend, seen by the Grimms as location specific, often about the supernatural, and distinct from historical legends that could be traced to ancient mythologies (in their case Teutonic), is now conceived as both place oriented and historical. Personal legend is about famous persons and local characters as it was for the Grimms, but it is also now about the personal experiences of the tellers, one of the newer areas in folk narrative studies (see **Memorate**). **Urban legend**, a twentieth-century category, deals with modern situations and contemporary events.

Current criticism of this definition and classification of the legend redefines the genre to some extent. One thread picks up the Grimms' recognition that distinctions between the fairy tale and the legend can be overdrawn because both genres "intermingle with one another in infinite combinations and intertwinings, often resembling one another to a greater or lesser degree" (Grimm 1: 2). A legend may not be so much local and historical as a localized and historicized **oicotype** or **variant** of a migrating story. The supernatural legend of "The Vanishing Hitchhiker," which tells of a driver of a car picking up a ghost of a young girl or a prophetic religious figure who later disappears, has as global a distribution as the international fairy tale, although each version of the legend is grounded in a specific region or location. The local legend "The Pied Piper of Hamelin," although based on a possible historic event in the medieval German city that fails to pay its rat catcher and so loses its children, has since taken on the patina of folktale in many of its retellings worldwide. Scholars now recognize a **storytelling** continuum that ties legends not only to fairy tales, but also to **anecdote**s, rumors, jokes, and other transitional narrative forms (see **Jest and Joke**).

Another related critical thread addresses the issue that not all participants necessarily believe the legends that they tell and hear to be true. Taking account of legend as more than text but as a conversational **performance** within a specific **context** allows analysis of different participants' responses to, and comments about, the veracity of the subject of the story under discussion. Folklorist Linda **Dégh** has noted that most legend-telling sessions are debates in which participants take different positions such as believers, debunkers, or those undecided, based on their cultural belief systems and personal life experiences. What Dégh labels "legend dialectics," or arguments about reality, then, define the genre from this perspective. However legend will be defined in the future, it appears that scholars' debates mirror the very narratives that they are studying. *See also* Conduit Theory; Religious Tale; Time and Place.

Further Readings: Brunvand, Jan Harold. "Legends and Anecdotes." *The Study of American Folklore: An Introduction.* 4th edition. New York: Norton, 1998. 196–228; Dégh, Linda. *Legend and Belief: Dialectics of a Genre.* Bloomington: Indiana University Press, 2001; Grimm, Jacob and Wilhelm. *The German Legends of the Brothers Grimm.* Edited and translated by Donald Ward. 2 volumes. Philadelphia: Institute for the Study of Human Issues, 1981; Lüthi, Max. "Aspects of the *Märchen* and the Legend." *Folklore Genres.* Edited by Dan Ben-Amos. Austin: University of Texas Press, 1976. 17–33.

Janet L. Langlois

Leprince de Beaumont, Jeanne-Marie (1711–1780)

Writing in the second half of the eighteenth century, during the period known as the Enlightenment, Jeanne-Marie Leprince de Beaumont was a prolific author of fairy tales and other works for women and children, as well as one of the first French women magazine editors. Although she published seventy volumes in her lifetime, she is best known today for her classic rendition of "La belle et la bête" ("**Beauty and the Beast**," 1756), which gave rise in turn to many nineteenth- and twentieth-century rewritings of the tale, and which formed the basis of the famous **film** versions by Jean Cocteau (*La Belle et la Bête*, 1946) and the **Walt Disney Company** (*Beauty and the Beast*, 1991).

Born in Rouen, France, to an artistic family of modest means, Beaumont was educated at a convent school, but left before taking her vows. Married in 1743 and mother of an only child, Elizabeth, she had her marriage annulled in 1745. Her literary debut occurred in 1748 with the publication of a novel, *Le triomphe de la vérité* (*The Triumph of Truth*), followed the same year by her feminist rebuttal of the abbé Coyer's notorious satire against women. Despite this auspicious beginning, however, she moved to England, where she worked as a governess for fifteen years to support herself and her daughter. In 1750, Beaumont began editing a monthly French magazine, *Le nouveau magasin français* (*The New French Magazine*), which appeared for three years and offered its primarily female readership a range of both lighthearted and instructive topics. The contents included **fable**s, fairy tales, poems, feminist essays, and articles on education and scientific subjects, frequently contributed by famous Enlightenment authors and prominent scientists. *The New French Magazine* reflected Beaumont's view, already expressed in her rebuttal of Coyer's satire, that women are perfectly capable of sound reasoning if given the opportunity to learn to think for themselves. Similar progressive ideas underlie many other works by Beaumont, including *L'education complete* (1752); *Le magasin des enfants* (1756; translated into English as *The Young Misses' Magazine* in 1759), a compendium of **didactic tale**s for children that was reprinted for more than a century in various languages and established her reputation abroad; *Le magasin des adolescentes* (1760); *Le mentor moderne* (1772–73); the *Contes moraux* (*Moral Tales*, 1773); and the *Nouveaux contes moraux* (*New Moral Tales*, 1776). Her widely disseminated pedagogical reflections and didactic stories made her a pioneer in the education of girls and in the field of **children's literature**.

Beaumont's "Beauty and the Beast" was first published in her original *Magasin des enfants* in 1756 and has been reprinted continuously ever since, both alone and in fairy-tale anthologies. The story belonged to the **oral tradition** and had already appeared in print in 1740 in the original novel by Gabrielle-Suzanne de **Villeneuve**. Beaumont shortened Villeneuve's work considerably, eliminating a number of characters, multiple references to **sex**, and three fantastic episodes that may have seemed to her digressive or out of date. The result is a concise and pointed tale that retains only the most basic plot elements of Villeneuve's novel.

Beaumont's "Beauty" stresses the moral lessons she wishes to impart to her target readership, girls aged five to thirteen. Beauty is the dominant character in the tale. She is presented as a kind, hardworking, patient and, above all, self-sacrificing young lady, who has cheerfully adapted to her wealthy merchant **father**'s business failure and the **family**'s new, arduous life in the country. Even more than her beauty, it is her superior character that wins praise from others, especially in contrast to the demeanor of her envious and hypocritical older **sisters**, who are vain social climbers. Furthermore, Beauty rises to heroic standing when she insists on taking her father's place in the castle of the terrifying beast, although she believes that she will die at the Beast's hands. Her courage and generosity are rewarded when the Beast turns out to be a similarly kind and docile being, and ultimately a handsome **prince**. In the end, the malicious sisters are turned into statues, symbolizing the impossibility of redeeming their hard hearts, and Beauty and the Beast enjoy an enduring marriage, representing the ideal of "perfect happiness founded on virtue," to quote the last words of the tale.

Despite this emphasis on the story's moral elements, and although Beaumont insisted that youngsters can learn to reason and become virtuous through exposure to pleasurable narratives, the author took the precaution of inserting "Beauty and the Beast" into a dialogue between a governess and her wards, which allows her to praise and draw out the moral reasoning of the children who comment on the tale. Through the use of this device, Beaumont encourages children to think about what they have just read or heard, while at the same time providing an example for tutors and governesses who may be using the book to instruct their own charges.

For all of the author's efforts to make her message clear, there is no consensus among critics as to the tale's meaning. Beaumont's "Beauty" has been subjected to **psychological approaches**, **sociohistorical approaches**, and feminist commentaries, resulting in widely divergent interpretations of the story. Even feminist critics do not agree about the intended impact of the tale on its young readers. Some believe that, notwithstanding Beaumont's demonstrated feminist leanings, she has written a story encouraging **women**'s self-sacrifice and submissiveness to **men**. Others, noting that Beauty exercises her free will when she goes to the Beast's castle and when she repeatedly refuses to marry him, argue that Beauty is an example of women's power and assertiveness. Still others read Beaumont's "Beauty and the Beast" as the subtle story of a good girl's erotic attraction to a mysterious or dangerous male. ***See also*** Childhood and Children; Feminism; French Tales; Pedagogy.

Further Readings: Griswold, Jerry. *The Meanings of "Beauty and the Beast": A Handbook.* Peterborough, Ontario: Broadview Press, 2004; Kaltz, Barbara, ed. *Jeanne Marie Le Prince de Beaumont: Contes et autres écrits.* Oxford: Voltaire Foundation, 2000.

Virginia E. Swain

Lesbian Tales. *See* Gay and Lesbian Tales

Lewis, C. S. (1898–1963)

Clive Staples Lewis was born in Ireland, but spent much of his life in England. Like his friend and contemporary J. R. R. **Tolkien,** he lectured at Oxford, where he was a member of the Inklings literary group. Lewis is an iconic figure of Christian writing but is probably best known for Narnia, a children's **fantasy** series. His other writing includes many works of Christian philosophy and apology, as well as a science-fiction trilogy and other novels and stories using allegory and **myth**. His Irish heritage can be seen in his fondness for Celtic myth and writers such as William Butler **Yeats**, but he shared with Tolkien an interest in Norse mythology, Greek and Roman myths, and the Christian fantasies of George **MacDonald**.

Lewis's fervent Christianity could be seen to sit somewhat uneasily with his preoccupation with the marvelous, but in fact both seem rooted in the same impulses: a desire for the magical and numinous and a recognition of the power of symbol. While he rejected Christianity as a young man, it is possible that Lewis reembraced the religion later in his life precisely because he recognized and needed its mythological intensity. Much of his Christian writing defends the importance of the imagination in Christian belief. He makes full use of a somewhat whimsical fabulation in the corrupting demons of *The Screwtape Letters* (1942). Essays in his collection *Of Other Worlds* (1966) also argue that fairy tale and fantasy are important and necessary for children.

Lewis's one foray into science fiction supports his tendency toward mythologizing: his Space trilogy of *Out of the Silent Planet* (1938), *Perelandra* (1943), and *That Hideous Strength* (1945) was in some ways a deliberate rebuttal of the rationality of early twentieth-century science fiction. The novels replace science fiction's outward voyage of discovery with a more inward, mysterious, and symbolic sense of meaning. The first two novels, set respectively on Mars and Venus, read like fantasy, their alien races not unlike the talking creatures of fairy tale. The trilogy also has Christian allegorical elements, including angelic beings in charge of each planet, and the corruption of Earth's own guardian into clearly satanic evil. Ransom, the hero of the first two books, becomes an everyman figure grappling with evil. On the beautiful floating islands of *Perelandra*, he defeats a satanic tempter in a reenactment of the Adam and Eve myth. *That Hideous Strength*, set on a grimly near-future Earth, offers a profoundly dystopian view of science and technology and makes overt use of Arthurian mythology in the figure of an awakened Merlin, and in its identification of Ransom as the Pendragon and a wounded king **archetype**.

It is the Narnia series for which Lewis is best remembered, and his fantasy otherworld is a classic of **children's literature**, although its innate Christian allegory remains problematic for many readers. The world of Narnia is a medieval **utopia**, inhabited by the magical and mythological entities of many folkloric traditions: talking animals, animate trees, giants, **dwarves**, and the centaurs, fauns, nymphs, and even gods of Greek myth. Narnia's construction betrays not only Lewis's mythological interests, but his early fondness for beast-fable, seen in his childhood love for the works of Beatrix Potter and Kenneth Graham, and in his own childhood fantasies about Boxen, the land of talking animals. *The Magician's Nephew* (1955) provides a Victorian evil magician as well as a creation myth in which the lion Aslan brings Narnia into being, and the child-heroes protect it against an evil **witch**. The adventures of *The Lion, the Witch and the Wardrobe* (1950) test the moral worth and courage of the four children who are elevated to rule Narnia after defeating the White Witch, an evil enchantress in the fairy-tale mold. In the figure of Aslan, the book also enacts an analogy of Christ's crucifixion, complete with a traitor, a redemptive sacrifice, and a resurrection, although Aslan himself is a complex and resonant figure with pagan implications of strength and rulership overlaying the Christian symbolism. *The Horse and His Boy* (1954) is set in the neighboring Calormen empire, which has a decadent exoticism that owes a great deal to the *Arabian Nights*. *Prince Caspian* (1951) pits the gentle magic of Narnia against the mundane and heartless rationality of colonizing humans; its hero returns in *The Voyage of the Dawn Treader* (1952), a voyage of adventure whose quest after the seven missing lords of Narnia is satisfyingly patterned and occasionally haunting. *The Silver Chair* (1953) has resonances of Arthurian **legend**, with a seductive shape-shifting enchantress and a deluded young knight and the pattern of signs the rescuing children must recognize to complete the quest. The concluding book of the series, *The Last Battle* (1956), sees the destruction of Narnia, but makes most explicitly the connections between the fantasy otherworld and the tenets of Christianity, notably in the conflation of the idealized "inner" Narnia with the Christian heaven.

The successful release of *The Chronicles of Narnia: The Lion, the Witch and the Wardrobe* (2005), a big-budget film version of the book, has underlined both the popularity of the series and the uneasy duality with which it speaks both to the current wave of fantasy popularity and to contemporary Christian markets. Lewis was drawn to allegory as a form, most notably in *The Pilgrim's Regress* (1933), his response to John Bunyan; and critics from Tolkien onward have been troubled by Narnia's allegorical elements, which channel and compromise its fantasy function instead of allowing it to stand alone as an imaginative act. Children and adult readers may well be alienated by the realization that an absorbing fantasy world is in fact the vehicle for religious polemic, a problem that also applies to the Space trilogy. Lewis's other writing seems more content to include tangential Christian meaning, in the manner of writers such as MacDonald. His adult myth *Till We Have Faces* (1956), a version of the **Cupid and Psyche** story, maintains an interest in spirituality that is less overt than in Narnia. *See also* English Tales; Film and Video; Religious Tale.

Further Readings: Manlove, Colin. *The Chronicles of Narnia: The Patterning of a Fantastic World.* Woodbridge, CT: Twayne, 1993; Riga, Frank P. "Mortals Call Their History Fable: Narnia and the Use of Fairy Tale." *Children's Literature Association Quarterly* 14 (1989): 26–30.

Jessica Tiffin

Lhéritier de Villandon, Marie-Jeanne (1664–1734)

Although not as well known today as her uncle, Charles **Perrault**, Marie-Jeanne Lhéritier de Villandon published the first collection of **literary fairy tale**s in France. Born to Nicolas Lhéritier de Nouvellon, royal historiographer and poet under Louis XIV, she was highly educated and remained unmarried until her death just shy of her seventieth birthday. Lhéritier is said to have inherited the **salon** of her famous friend and author, Madeleine de Scudéry. A single woman of relatively modest means, she depended on two illustrious patrons to support her life and literary career: Marie d'Orléans de Longueville, the Duchess of Nemours; and, after the duchess's death, Germain Louis Chauvelin, Chancellor of France.

Lhéritier's literary corpus includes fairy tales as well as poetry, essays, and translations. *Les oeuvres meslées* (*Miscellaneous Works*, 1695; reprint, 1696), a potpourri of genres, contains the first French literary fairy tales published outside of a **frame narrative**:

"Marmoisan, ou L'innocente tromperie" ("Marmoisan, or the Innocent Imposture"), "L'avare puni" ("The Miser's Punishment"), "Les enchantemens de l'éloquence, ou Les effets de la douceurs" ("Eloquent Enchantment, or the Effects of Sweetness"), and "L'adroite princesse, ou Les avantures de Finette" ("The Subtle Princess, or the Adventures of Finessa"). A second edition of these stories appeared as *Les bigarrures ingénieuses* (*Ingenious Medley*, 1696). With *La tour ténébreuse et les jours luminuex* (*The Dark Tower and Bright Days*, 1705), Lhéritier embedded two new fairy tales into a frame story about Richard the Lionhearted. Having achieved notoriety through fairy tales, she edited the memoirs of the Duchess de Nemours before returning to tales and miscellany with *Les caprices du destin* (*The Whims of Destiny*, 1717). Several of her fairy tales were reprinted in **Le cabinet des fées** (*The Fairies' Cabinet*, 1785–89).

Many of Lhéritier's tales feature intelligent women who triumph over adversity through their ingenuity. "The Subtle Princess" is her most important tale and exemplifies her eclectic style, alternatively precious and modern, dry and funny. In this story, the heroine Finessa outwits a villainous prince who threatens her virtue and that of her two sisters. Although fairies are present, they perform little magic. When Finessa doubts her ability to fight the scheming prince, she requests help from a fairy only to be told she does not need magic and should simply trust herself. The narrative is also replete with proverbial wisdom and commentary by the narrator. These philosophical reflections and the **moral** at the end of the tale—mistrust is the mother of safety—serve a didactic purpose by encouraging young women to depend upon their own ingenuity and resourcefulness.

Following the publication of *Les oeuvres meslées*, Lhéritier was admitted to two literary academies. In the year of her death, the *Journal des sçavans* (*Scholars' Journal*) published a eulogy to honor her lifelong commitment to the literary arts. *See also* French Tales.

Further Readings: Francillon, Roger. "Une théorie du folklore à la fin du XVIIème siècle: Mlle L'Héritier." *Hören, Sagen, Lesen, Lernen: Bausteine zu einer Geschichte der Kommunikativen Kultur.* Edited by Ursula Brunold-Bigler and Hermann Bausinger. New York: Peter Lang, 1995. 205–17; Seifert, Lewis C. "The Rhetoric of 'invraisemblance': *Les Enchantements de l'éloquence.*" *Cahier du Dix-Septième* 3.1 (1989): 121–39.

Christine A. Jones

Lindgren, Astrid (1907–2002)

Astrid Lindgren, the world-famous creator of Pippi Longstocking, is Sweden's most famous and celebrated children's writer. She wrote in many genres, including the fairy tale. In all of her works, Lindgren spoke to and for children, and the experiences of her young protagonists reflect both the reality and fantasy of childhood. Lindgren was a master at revitalizing all of the established genres of **children's literature** in which she wrote while simultaneously writing poetic prose of stunning clarity, with an **intertextuality** that appeals to readers of all ages.

Born in Vimmerby, Småland, Lindgren moved to Stockholm at nineteen and became a secretary. She married, and when her daughter was born in 1934, she became a full-time homemaker. Her first books, *Britt-Mari lättar sitt hjärta* (*Confidences of Britt-Mari*, 1944) and *Kerstin och jag* (*Kerstin and I*, 1945), follow in the tradition of the girls' book, a genre with which she was very familiar. From childhood she had loved *Anne of Green Gables* (1908) and other classics of this genre. Among her other influences were Tom Sawyer and Huckleberry Finn, who helped inspire the very popular children's detective story trilogy *Mästerdetektiven*

Blomkvist (*Bill Bergson, Master Detective*, 1946), *Mästerdetektiven Blomkvist lever farligt* (*Bill Bergson lives dangerously*, 1951), and *Kalle Blomkvist och Rasmus* (*Bill Bergson and the White Rose*, 1953). In these stories, Lindgren does not shy away from dark subjects and villainous characters, themes that later reappear forcefully in the great heroic quest **novel**s.

From the time *Pippi Långstrump* (*Pippi Longstocking*) was published in 1945, the young heroine attracted both praise and censure. Pippi—with her red hair and freckles, superhuman strength, and parentless paradise—played havoc with the established generic heroine of the girls' book. Pippi has variously been called a child of nature, a mythical figure, a Peter Pan, a strange and alien child, an anarchist, and even a somewhat diabolic monster or **witch**. The first Pippi book and the sequels, *Pippi Längstrump går ombord* (*Pippi Goes on Board*, 1946) and *Pippi Längstrump i Söderhavet* (*Pippi in the South Seas*, 1948), reflected societal discussions on child-rearing practices and pedagogy. Pippi's antics are often absurd, and reflect wide-ranging literary fore-bearers. For example, Pippi's "discovery" of the new word *stump* is a nod to Knut Hamsun's nameless hero in *Sult* (*Hunger*, 1890).

Lindgren revitalized the **tall-tale** genre in the Emil stories, which also reflect her childhood memories of growing up in rural Småland, and incorporates memories of her father. In *Emil i Lönneberga* (*Emil in the Soup Tureen*, 1963), *Nya hyss av Emil i Lönneberga* (*Emil's Pranks*, 1966), and *Än lever Emil i Lönneberga* (*Emil and His Clever Pig*, 1970), little five-year-old Emil's incorrigible pranks are the talk of the town. At one point, there is even a discussion of taking up a collection to send him away to America. Especially popular in the countries of Eastern Europe is the fairy-tale-like Karlsson-on-the-roof, who flies with a propeller on his back and is the selfish friend of a lonely little boy (*Lillebror och Karlsson på taket* [1955] and subsequent books in 1962 and 1968). Lindgren published a collection of short fairy tales, *Nils Karlsson-Pyssling: Sagor* (*Nils Karlsson-Pyssling: Fairy Tales*, 1949), for which she won the Nils Holgersson Medal, and she drew on tradition and **legend**s in the collection *Sunnanäng* (*South Wind Meadow*, 1959).

Prevalent in all of Lindgren's books is the empowerment of the child. The young protagonists are sometimes lonely or neglected but find consolation and compensation in the world of **fantasy**. In *Mio, min Mio* (*Mio, My Son*, 1954), the young hero of this modern **literary fairy tale** retreats, with the help of a genie in a bottle, into the world of Farawayland, where he is welcomed as the beloved missing son of the **king**. Faced with a dangerous quest to combat the evil Sir Kato, little Mio does what must be done, although he is often afraid. Elements of his actual world become transformed through imagination into the marvelous elements that aid him in his quest and allow the wish-fulfillment ending so typical of fairy tales. Like her other great novels, *Bröderna lejonhjärta* (*The Brothers Lionheart*, 1973) and *Ronja rövardotter* (*Ronia, the Robber's Daughter*, 1981), *Mio, My Mio* lends itself to multiple readings and functions on several levels.

Mio, My Mio was hailed as a brilliant renewal within the fairy-tale genre, and *The Brothers Lionheart* continues in this tradition. Dying in real life, young Rusky is reunited with his older brother Jonathan in the pastoral Cherry Tree Valley in his imaginary other-worldly Nangiyala, where idyllic peace is threatened by the tyrant Tengil, who has conquered neighboring Wild Rose Valley. Like Mio, Rusky is often afraid, but is inspired to courage by his brother, a pacifist, who nevertheless is involved in the resistance movement against Tengil and his **dragon**, Katla. The ending of the book, when Rusky conquers his fear and jumps into Nangilima (the next world beyond) with Jonathan on his back, has been criticized for giving children a positive portrayal of suicide.

Lindgren's last great fairy tale is *Ronia, the Robber's Daughter*, which is a story of **family** relationships and female maturation. Ronia continues Lindgren's long line of child heroes who cope with reality in creative and successful ways.

Lindgren was the recipient of many literary awards and decorations, and she was a cultural icon in Sweden, where she also worked for animal rights. Many people felt that she should have been awarded the Nobel Prize in Literature. In many ways, she can be considered Selma **Lagerlöf**'s successor within Swedish literature, her best work dealing with eternal existential questions of life and **death**, war and peace, love and hate, and familial relationships. *See also* Scandinavian Tales.

Further Readings: Edström, Vivi. *Astrid Lindgren: A Critical Study*. Translated by Eivor Cormack. Stockholm: Rabén & Sjögren, 2000; Metcalf, Eva-Maria. *Astrid Lindgren*. New York: Twayne, 1995; Strömstedt, Margareta. *Astrid Lindgren: En levnadsteckning*. 2nd edition. Stockholm: Rabén & Sjögren, 1999.

Marte Hult

Linguistic Approaches

Linguistic approaches to the study of folktales and fairy tales can be traced back to the nineteenth century. Early **collectors** and **editors** of folktales were driven in part by their interest in language and in folktale texts as expressions of **oral tradition**. The work of pioneering philologists such as Jacob and Wilhelm **Grimm** was based on their belief that the essence of culture was linguistic—that is, that a people's language was the expression of its culture. In the wake of the Grimms and in the context of nineteenth-century philological studies, Friedrich Max **Müller** used techniques of comparative philology to establish the relationship between Vedic **myth**s (from Sanskrit texts) and European folktales that forms the basis of his theory of solar mythology.

In the twentieth century, formalism and **structuralism** adapted the ideas and techniques of linguistics in their approach to the study of folktales and fairy tales. Vladimir **Propp**'s syntagmatic structuralism, for example, took the concepts of morphology, the study of word formation, from linguistics and adapted it for use in folktales, replacing the concept of lexeme (a meaningful linguistic unit that is an item in the vocabulary of a language) with that of **function** to develop a syntax-based approach to folktales. This adaptation was furthered by Alan **Dundes**'s *The Morphology of North American Indian Folktales* (1980). Dundes adapted linguistic techniques to folktale study, using the concept of **motifeme**, adapted by Kenneth Pike from the linguistic concept morpheme, the smallest sound-part of a word, and applying it to the study of **Native American tales**. Dundes's morphology also adapted the concept of allomorphs, various words formed from individual morphemes, into allomotifs, various tale models formed from individual motifemes, for use in folktale analysis.

In the 1960s and 1970s, the turn toward the study of **context** and **performance** and the development of ethnopoetics also relied on linguistic ideas and methods of investigation. In the linguistic analysis of folktale performances, scholars examine what Alan Dundes referred to as the examination of texture. Specifically, this approach examines the linguistic features of a folktale; and, to paraphrase Dell Hymes, the study of the structure of language is joined with the study of its use. One especially important example of this approach is evident in Hymes's book *"In Vain I Tried to Tell You"* (first published in 1981). In this work, Hymes attempts to reconstruct linguistic features of written texts and undertakes a linguistic analysis of folkloric texts to examine Native American culture. In this approach, sociolinguistics and ethnopoetics work toward the goal of understanding the relationship among language, narrative artistry, and culture. Hymes argues that the linguistic analysis of folkloric texts allows a greater understanding of the culture that produced them and helps to explain, for example, social conceptions of gender and kinship.

In performance studies, the concept of "narrative framing" derives in part from the concept of "markedness," which was developed by the Prague Linguistic Circle. Combined with theoretical examination of participant roles from linguistics, these approaches have moved the focus of the study of folktales from the text alone to its performance, thereby stressing the process of communication. Prominent work in this field has come from John McDowell, who has examined paralinguistic features in Bolivian Quechua narrative, and Dennis Tedlock, who has focused on **fieldwork** techniques for linguistic study of Zuni narrative.

In recent scholarship, linguistic tools and perspectives have been put to use in studying the relation between language and gender in classic fairy tales such as "**Little Red Riding Hood**" and in considering the role of dialect in Grimms' *Kinder- und Hausmärchen* (*Children's and Household Tales*, 1812–15). *See also* Anthropological Approaches; Ethnographic Approaches; Translation.

Further Readings: Dundes, Alan. *The Morphology of North American Indian Folktales.* Helsinki: Academia Scientiarium Fennica, 1980; Hymes, Dell. *"In Vain I Tried to Tell You": Essays in Native American Ethnopoetics.* New edition. Lincoln: University of Nebraska Press, 2004; Levorato, Alessandra. *Language and Gender in the Fairy Tale Tradition: A Linguistic Analysis of Old and New Story-Telling.* London: Palgrave Macmillan, 2003; Robinson, Orrin W. "Rhymes and Reasons in the Grimms' *Kinder- und Hausmärchen*." *German Quarterly* 77 (2004): 47–58.

B. Grantham Aldred

Literary Fairy Tale

Literary fairy tales are tales written by an individual, usually identifiable author. Though these writers usually draw on preexisting published material for some or all of their characters and plot, they put them together in a new way. Unlike many folktales, literary fairy tales exist in only one version, fixed in print.

The English term "literary fairy tale" is a translation of the German compound *Kunstmärchen* (artistic tales) that distinguishes original tales written by a single, educated writer from "folktales," or *Volksmärchen*, tales thought to have been transmitted orally by the uneducated, often illiterate "**folk**." The Romantics hoped to revive the culture of the German "Volk" by **collecting** traditional songs, as in Clemens **Brentano** and Achim von Arnim's *Des Knaben Wunderhorn* (*The Boy's Magic Horn*, 1805–8), or by collecting traditional fairy tales, as in the **Grimm** brothers' *Kinder- und Hausmärchen* (*Children's and Household Tales*, 1812–15.) The term *Kunstmärchen* reflects the distinction some German Romantics wanted to make between *Volkspoesie* (the poetry of the folk) or *Naturpoesie* (legendary and mythical collective poetry) and *Kunstpoesie* (poetry that is the result of an individual creative act), though it seems to have been used first in 1868 by German author Theodor Storm in a letter to the novelist Theodor Fontane.

The English term "literary fairy tale" is still more complex than its German counterpart, *Kunstmärchen*. "Fairy tale" is actually a translation of the French *conte de fées* or *contes des fées*, terms used interchangeably for the long, involved tales written in the 1690s by a group of highly educated and sophisticated writers (the **women** among them often were called the *conteuses*, or the storytellers). Their tales often included powerful fairies, but the English term "fairy tale" simply refers to any tale that involves real people in an unrealistic, marvelous world. Though English speakers tend to use "fairy tale" interchangeably with "folktale," the fairy tale comes from an intensely literary tradition. Even the word "literary" has its complexities and evolving meanings. "Literature" once referred to anything written, including history, scientific accounts, and so on. Only during the eighteenth century did it come to mean exclusively what the French would call *belles lettres*, writings that are fictional or personal.

Literary fairy tales are still usually distinguished from folktales. Some scholars believe, however, that the distinction can often be misleading. The Grimms, for example, found many of their tales in written sources, and they extensively edited the ones they collected orally, rarely from members of the "folk." Sometimes their tales are called *Buchmärchen*, or book tales, a term that suggests a mixture of written and oral. Many tales collected orally by folklorists in the nineteenth and twentieth centuries derive at least in part from written sources. Cheap **chapbook** reprints of written tales were often sold and read aloud in peasant or worker communities. The strict line we tend to draw between the oral and the written, the authentic and the created, the traditional and the invented, and folk literature and high culture has begun to blur.

History of Literary Fairy Tales

Folktales are often said to be "timeless," existing throughout the ages without change. Jacob Grimm wrote to Achim von Arnim, for example, that he was convinced that "all the tales in our collection were told centuries ago" (from a letter dated October 29, 1812). Many people still believe that folktales can give us access to the traditions, customs, hopes, and fears of illiterate people in earlier times.

Literary fairy tales, on the other hand, have a long history that can be traced back at least to the **Middle Ages**. Many scholars believe that they began as medieval **wonder tale**s, tales that stressed marvelous **transformation**s and change (unlike other early genres, such as the religious **exemplum**, **fable**s, **legend**s, **anecdote**s, and **myth**s). Some compilations, such as the ***Gesta Romanorum*** (*Deeds of the Romans*, late thirteenth century) or Noël du Fail's *Propos rustiques* (*Rustic Chats*, 1549), and other collections of French *contes* (stories) contain many **motif**s that later appeared in literary fairy tales. While these wonder tales were usually included in longer narratives and romances, the first discrete literary fairy tales began to be published in early Italian framed collections: Giovan Francesco **Straparola**'s *Le piacevoli notte* (*The Pleasant Night*s, 1550–53) and Giambattista **Basile**'s *Lo cunto de li cunti*, or *Pentamerone* (*The Tale of Tales*, 1634–36). Following their countryman Giovanni **Boccaccio**, both of these writers invented a tale-telling situation in which various characters told stories to each other. (In Straparola's case, the noble characters are escaping political unrest on an island off Venice; in Basile's, a group of ancient, lower-class crones known for their narrative talent tell their tales in an attempt to make a princess laugh.) Although Straparola's tales are not all considered fairy tales, many became crucial sources for later fairy-tale writers, including the French *conteuses* and the Brothers Grimm. Basile's tales, though not translated from a difficult Neapolitan dialect until the eighteenth century, also influenced many later authors.

Perhaps the liveliest period in the history of the literary fairy tale, however, was the end of the seventeenth and beginning of the eighteenth century in France. Starting in 1690, with the publication of the tale "L'isle de la félicité" ("The Island of Happiness") by Marie-Catherine d'**Aulnoy** in one of her **novel**s, many French writers—from the well-known Academician Charles **Perrault** to the group of women known as the *conteuses*, including d'Aulnoy, Catherine **Bernard**, Marie-Jeanne **Lhéritier de Villandon**, and Henriette-Julie de Castelnau, Comtesse de **Murat**—suddenly began to publish fairy tales, or *contes de fées*. These writers seem to have worked collectively, sometimes even collaboratively, telling their tales in the literary **salon**s of the period, borrowing themes and plots from each other (as well as from Straparola and Basile), and dedicating stories and whole collections to each other. While Perrault's tales are generally concise and quite laconic, closer to the form we now expect fairy tales to take, the *conteuses'* tales tend to be long, digressive, and elaborate, focusing on the trials of a separated noble couple and the magic powers of fairies, both beneficent and malign. In fact, their tales often seem to be short versions of earlier romances, from episodes in Ludovico Ariosto's *Orlando furioso* (1516) to the endless mid-seventeenth-century novels of the *précieuses* like Madeleine de Scudéry.

French writers continued to write and publish fairy tales in the first half of the eighteenth century, though often these later tales were parodic, tongue-in-cheek, or even pornographic. The publication of Antoine **Galland**'s translation of the *Arabian Nights* (1704–17) led to a proliferation of Oriental tales in France, England, and Germany, as well as of letters supposedly from the "Orient," like Montesquieu's satirical *Lettres persanes* (*Persian Letters*, 1721). Late in the century, Charles-Joseph Chevalier de **Mayer** put together a forty-volume collection of French tales written since the 1690s, *Le cabinet des fées* (1785–89). This collection, in addition to the simplified versions of the tales in chapbooks from *La bibliothèque bleue* (*The Blue Library*) published throughout the eighteenth century, made them easily available to readers all over Europe.

English and German writers certainly were aware of the French fairy-tale fashion almost immediately. In England, translations of d'Aulnoy's work appeared in 1699, and Perrault's in 1729. A German *Cabinet der Feen*, edited by Friedrich Immanuel Bierling, appeared from 1761 to 1765, with seventy-two translated tales; Christoph Martin **Wieland**'s novel *Don Sylvio* (1764) both echoes and parodies d'Aulnoy's work. Germans also began to publish volumes that they claimed were collections of folktales, like Johann Karl August **Musäus**'s *Volksmärchen der Deutschen* (*Folktales of the Germans*, 1782–86), though their tales usually were based on French models or other European sources. Following Perrault and the *conteuses*, they often mischievously claimed that their tales came from oral folk tradition, that they had heard them from grandmothers or nurses.

Inspired by the theories of Johann Gottfried Herder and Bishop Percy's collection *Reliques of Ancient English Poesie* (1765), writers such as Achim von Arnim, Clemens Brentano, and the Brothers Grimm also began to emphasize the supposed German origin of the tales and songs they collected, in part as a reaction to the French invasions of Germany in 1795–96 and, under Napoleon, in 1806–13. Johann Wolfgang von **Goethe**'s "Das Märchen" ("The Fairy Tale") is part of a framed collection entitled *Unterhaltungen deutscher Ausgewanderten* (*Conversations of German Refugees*, 1795), whose characters have taken refuge from the French armies on the east side of the Rhine. Many German Romantic writers, from Ludwig **Tieck** to **Novalis** to E. T. A. **Hoffmann**, made original fairy tales the centerpiece of their work. Their tales, often dark and mysterious, have become the models for many later literary tales.

During the later eighteenth and nineteenth century, fairy tales gradually became known primarily as **children's literature**. Jeanne-Marie **Leprince de Beaumont**'s abridged tales in her didactic *Le magasin des enfants* (1756; translated into English as *The Young Misses' Magazine* in 1759), notably "**Beauty and the Beast**," were among the first designed specifically for the moral education of children. The *Kleine Ausgabe* (Small Edition, 1825) of the Grimms' tales, unlike the earlier editions, was primarily intended for children; it was probably inspired by Edgar **Taylor**'s successful translation of selected Grimm tales for children as *German Popular Stories* in 1823. Throughout the nineteenth century, writers like Hans Christian **Andersen** in Denmark, Ludwig **Bechstein** in Germany, Sophie, Comtesse de **Ségur** in France, and Oscar **Wilde** in England wrote and adapted tales to amuse and to educate children. Many collections of fairy tales designed for children and for reading aloud also appeared, for example Andrew **Lang**'s many colored volumes (1889–1910). The literary fairy tale, once a genre that had permitted freedom and experimentation, became steadily more regimented and more commercialized, a trend that culminated in Walt **Disney**'s fairy-tale film **adaptation**s in the twentieth century and in the repetitive republication of the best-known tales, often one-by-one in expensive picture books.

At the same time, however, many writers, often women, began creating stories and **poetry** that question and reimagine some of the best-known tales. A group of German women, known as the *Kaffeterkreis* (Coffee Circle), published the *Kaffeterzeitung* (*Coffee Circle News*) from 1843 to 1848 that included many unusual fairy tales and fairy-tale plays. In England, Christina Georgina **Rossetti**'s poem "Goblin Market" (1862) turns on the encounters of two young **sisters** with seductive and threatening creatures who exist on the border between the real world and a sinister realm; some motifs, like eating dangerous magic fruit or the sacrifice of a lock of **hair**, suggest themes of sexual guilt and redemption. Anne Thackeray **Ritchie** in her *Five Old Friends and a Young Prince* (published in the United States as *Fairy Tales for Grown Folks*, 1868) and *Bluebeard's Keys and Other Stories* (1874) transformed the setting of tales like "Beauty and the Beast" and "**Sleeping Beauty**" from a magic-filled world to everyday Victorian life, emphasizing the psychological truths behind these traditional plots. Some believe that Lewis **Carroll**'s *Alice's Adventures in Wonderland* (1865) and *Through the Looking-Glass* (1871) are anarchic dream versions of traditional fairy-tale motifs like the descent underground.

Such rewritings multiplied toward the end of the twentieth century. Both Donald **Barthelme,** in his novel *Snow White* (1967), and Robert **Coover,** in stories like "The Gingerbread House" (in *Pricksongs and Descants*, 1969) and in his novel *Briar Rose* (1996), gave tales a postmodern, wryly experimental twist. Following the second wave of **feminism** in the 1970s, collections like Anne **Sexton**'s volume of poems *Transformations* (1971) and Angela **Carter**'s *The Bloody Chamber and Other Stories* (1979) offered new versions of "classic" tales, often retelling them from a woman's perspective. Other writers, such as Olga **Broumas,** in her volume *Beginning with O* (1977), and Emma **Donoghue**, in her linked collection of stories *Kissing the Witch* (1997), recast tales from a lesbian perspective, rejecting the usual fairy-tale patterns of heterosexual desire. Many other recent poets and fiction writers have based some of their work on fairy tales. The collection *The Poets' Grimm* (2003), edited by Jeanne Marie Beaumont and Claudia Carlson, for example, includes about 100 twentieth-century poems in English based on the Grimms' versions of the tales. Ellen Datlow and Terri **Windling** edited several volumes of stories that reimagine well-known tales.

In the early twenty-first century, many literary fairy tales are still being produced, by writers like Margaret **Atwood**, Salman **Rushdie**, Michel Tournier, and Jeannette Winterson. Cartoonists and advertisers also continue to publish many texts and visual images that depend on the familiarity of certain "classic" tales (like "**Snow White**" and "The **Frog King**"). Collections of fairy-tale parodies are also popular. As knowledge of **Bible tale**s and Greek myths wanes, fairy tales increasingly have become an important cultural reservoir to draw on, question, and reshape.

Approaches to the Literary Fairy Tale

Many scholars since the later nineteenth century have studied literary fairy tales. The earliest studies were often attempts to demonstrate their origins in Indo-European **folklore**. The culmination of this tradition was the indexing and analysis of **tale type**s and motifs by members of the "Finnish" or historical-geographic school (Stith **Thompson** and Antii **Aarne**, with recent revisions by Hans-Jörg Uther). Other scholars, however, following the work of the structuralist Vladimir **Propp** in Russia, attempted to show that all tales have the same basic structure: a sequence of events and **function**s that must proceed in the same way.

Scholars interested in psychoanalysis have also turned to fairy tales. Freudians such as Bruno **Bettelheim** in his influential book *The Uses of Enchantment* (1976) have stressed their function in helping children to understand and repress their uncivilized impulses; Jungians such as Erich Fromm and Marie-Louise von **Franz** stress the way fairy tales reveal universal **archetype**s and "collective unconscious psychic processes."

Other historians and cultural critics have tried to show that folktales and fairy tales are not "timeless," that they change in response to changing social conditions and ideologies. Many feminist critics in the 1970s thought fairy tales reproduced patriarchal social forms, with passive or sleeping heroines and active heroes; others focused on stories that had active, intelligent heroines. Recently, however, feminists have adopted more nuanced and more eclectic methods, relying less on the study of "images of women" and more on the combination of **gender** analysis with attention to social and literary history.

Though all of these methods are primarily based on the study of folktales, they have influenced both the analysis and the interpretation of literary fairy tales as well. Many scholars now believe that the techniques of close textual analysis, often thought unsuitable for understanding tales, can in fact reveal the sources and the possible meanings of literary fairy tales. *See also* Advertising; Cartoons and Comics; Erotic Tales; Fairy Tale; Folktale; French Tales; Gay and Lesbian Tales; German Tales; Italian Tales; Postmodernism.

Further Readings: Canepa, Nancy. *From Court to Forest: Giambattista Basile's* Lo cunto de li cunti *and the Birth of the Literary Fairy Tale.* Detroit: Wayne State University Press, 1999; Grätz, Manfred. *Das Märchen in der deutschen Aufklärung: Vom Feenmärchen zum Volksmärchen.* Stuttgart: Metzler, 1988; Hannon, Patricia. *Fabulous Identities: Women's Fairy Tales in Seventeenth-Century France.* Amsterdam: Rodopi, 1998; Harries, Elizabeth Wanning. *Twice upon a Time: Women Writers and the History of the Fairy Tale.* Princeton, NJ: Princeton University Press, 2001; Lampart, Fabian. "The Turn to History and the *Volk*: Brentano, Arnim, and the Grimm Brothers." *The Literature of German Romanticism.* Edited by Dennis Mahoney. Rochester, NY: Camden House, 2004. 168–89; Schenda, Rudolph. "Semiliterate and Semi-Oral Processes." *Marvels & Tales* 21 (2007): 127–40; Seifert, Lewis C. *Fairy Tales, Sexuality, and Gender in France, 1690–1715: Nostalgic Utopias.* New York: Cambridge University Press, 1996; Soriano, Marc. *Les contes de Perrault: Culture savante et traditions populaires.* Paris: Gallimard, 1968; Tatar, Maria. *The Hard Facts of the Grimms' Fairy Tales.* 2nd edition. Princeton, NJ: Princeton University Press, 2003; Tismar, Jens. *Kunstmärchen.* 2nd revised, expanded edition. Stuttgart:

Metzler, 1983; Zipes, Jack. "Introduction: Towards a Definition of the Literary Fairy Tale." *The Oxford Companion to Fairy Tale*. Edited by Jack Zipes. Oxford: Oxford University Press, 2000. xv–xxxii.

Elizabeth Wanning Harries

Little Red Riding Hood

"Little Red Riding Hood" is one of the world's best-known fairy tales and provides the name for the tale type classified as ATU 333 in Hans-Jörg Uther's *The Types of International Folktales* (2004). The first literary version of this tale, "Le petit chaperon rouge," was published in 1697 in Charles **Perrault**'s *Histoires ou contes du temps passé* (*Stories or Tales of Times Past*). Prior to Perrault's literary **adaptation**, however, the story probably existed in the **oral tradition**.

The Oral Tale

Since Perrault's time, elements of the literary tale have influenced some oral versions. It is generally agreed, however, that the "Conte de la mère-grand" ("The Grandmother's Tale"), which was collected in Nièvre about 1885 and published by the French folklorist Paul **Delarue** in 1951, illustrates how the story was told before Perrault penned his tale. In this folktale, a **peasant** girl is sent to her grandmother's with a hot loaf of bread and a bottle of milk. At a fork in the path, she meets a *bzou*, or **werewolf**, who, after learning where she is going, asks whether she is taking the path of needles or the path of pins. In this version, the girl chooses needles, but in some tales she prefers pins. Whereas pins seem to be a symbol of coming of age, needles seem to signify the **sexuality** of an older woman. The werewolf takes the other path and arrives first at the grandmother's house, where he kills the old woman and puts some of her flesh in the pantry and some of her **blood** in a bottle. When the girl arrives, the werewolf invites her to have some meat and wine. During this cannibal repast, the girl is warned by one or more animals, in this version by a **cat**, that she is eating the flesh and drinking the blood of her grandmother. The ritual meal seems to symbolize a physical incorporation of the old lady, who is replaced by the younger generation. When the werewolf invites the little girl to undress and join him in bed, a lengthy striptease follows. As she removes her **clothing** one piece at a time, she asks the werewolf what to do with her apron, bodice, skirt, petticoat, and stockings. She is told each time to throw the item into the fire as she won't need it any longer. The dramatic dialogue about the werewolf's physical features is lengthier and includes his hairy body.

In this version of the tale, the heroine is a courageous and resourceful young girl who tricks the wolf and escapes unharmed, without any male assistance. When the werewolf prepares to eat her, the little girl convinces him to let her go outdoors to relieve herself. The werewolf ties a woolen thread to her foot, but the girl ties the thread to a plum tree and escapes. Most oral tales have a variation of this scatalogical happy ending, but sometimes the heroine kills the wolf and sometimes he is killed with the assistance of others. In one variant, laundresses spread a sheet over the river to help the escaping girl cross, but later release the bridge of cloth to drown the wolf.

Variants of "The Grandmother's Tale" have been collected in the Loire basin, the Forez, the Velay, the Morvan, and the Hautes-Alpes, as well as in other parts of Europe. Italo **Calvino** included "La finta nonna" ("The False Grandmother"), a tale from Abruzzo, in his collection *Fiabe italiane* (*Italian Folktales*, 1956). The protagonist of this tale encounters an **ogress**, is invited to eat her grandmother's teeth and ears, and ties the rope to a nanny goat, but the story is essentially the same. Some oral versions of the tale present several girls rather than one, as in "Il lupo e le tre ragazze" ("The Wolf and the Three Girls"), also included in Calvino's collection.

Asian variants of the story include the 241 versions of "Grandaunt Tiger" collected in Taiwan by Wolfram Eberhard. In this tale, a tiger poses as the **mother**, grandmother, or grandaunt. The tiger gobbles up the girl's younger sibling(s), and in some versions gives her a finger to chew on. In the Chinese tale "Lon Po Po," the wolf, disguised as the grandmother, visits the children at home while the mother goes through the woods. Ed Young's picture book *Lon Po Po: A Red Riding Hood Story from China* (1989) won the Caldecott Medal in 1990.

Perrault's Tale

The initiatory tale of the oral tradition became a **cautionary tale** when Perrault adapted it for the French court of Louis XIV. Perrault gives his heroine, a pretty, naive little village girl, a red *chaperon* (hood) that provides her nickname. For many scholars and psychoanalysts, the red hood has sexual connotations, symbolizing the onset of menstruation, precocious sexuality, and/or sin. When the girl's mother sends her to her sick grandmother with a cake and a little pot of butter, she meets the wolf in the woods and naively tells him where she is going. As she dawdles along the longer path, the wolf hurries to the grandmother's and devours the old lady. Perrault eliminates the cannibal meal and the detailed striptease, but the little girl obligingly undresses and gets into bed with the wolf, whose astonishing appearance provokes the climactic dialogue. Perrault's version ends with the little girl being eaten by the wolf. The author's lesson is explicitly expressed at the end of the tale in the witty and sexually suggestive verse **moral** that warns young ladies to beware of genteel two-legged wolves. Perrault's popular tale was translated into many European languages in the eighteenth century, appearing in English in 1729.

The Grimms' Tale

When Wilhelm and Jacob **Grimm** published "Rotkäppchen" ("Little Red Cap") in the first edition of their collection ***Kinder- und Hausmärchen*** (*Children's and Household Tales*) in 1812, it was presented as part of the German oral folk tradition. In fact, the Brothers Grimm collected the tale from Marie Hassenpflug, an educated woman of French Huguenot ancestry, and then adapted it. They would continue to revise it in subsequent editions that were increasingly aimed at children. Their heroine wears a red velvet cap and takes cake and wine to her grandmother. The Grimms introduce an admonitory scene in which the mother warns her daughter not to stray from the path. Thus the story becomes a cautionary tale warning little girls of the perils of disobedience. The Grimms add a happy ending, in which Little Red Cap and her grandmother are rescued by a hunter. He cuts open the sleeping wolf's belly and the girl and her grandmother emerge unharmed. The wolf's belly is then filled with large stones, resulting in his **death**. The Grimms append another, anticlimactic tale that resembles an epilogue or a sequel, in which Little Red Cap is accosted by a different wolf when she returns to her grandmother's. This time, Little Red Cap goes straight to her grandmother's and together they outsmart the wolf, who is drowned in a big trough.

From Children's Story to Crossover Tale

In the nineteenth century, developments in printing methods led to the rise of the children's book publishing industry and the tale was further altered to adapt it for children. The Perrault and Grimm versions often were blended together. In many cases, the result was a generic, sanitized tale. For a time, "Little Red Riding Hood" was relegated to the children's library. Today, however, the tale is generally considered as appropriate for all age groups. Contemporary revisions of the fairy tale often appeal to a crossover audience.

Literary Retellings

Over the centuries, "Little Red Riding Hood" has been interpreted and retold according to the social and literary preoccupations of the time. Nineteenth-century revisions include Ludwig **Tieck**'s play "Leben und Tod des kleinen Rotkäppchens: eine Tragödie" ("The Life and Death of Little Red Riding Hood: A Tragedy," 1800), Alphonse **Daudet**'s "Le roman du chaperon rouge" ("The Romance of Red Riding Hood," 1862), Léo Lespès's "Le Petit Chaperon Rouge après sa mort" ("Little Red Riding Hood after Her Death," 1865), Harriet Childe-Pemberton's "All My Doing, or Little Red-Riding Hood Over Again" (1882), and Emilie Mathieu's *Le nouveau petit chaperon rouge* (The New Little Red Riding Hood, 1893).

In the twentieth century there was an explosion of revisions of the tale for both children and adults. These retellings address such contemporary subjects as technology, ecology, animal rights, seniors, sexuality, **gender** issues, **violence**, and war. The story has been recast to deal with psychological and metaphysical issues such as solitude, fear, freedom, love, and **death**. It has been told in modes from comic to tragic, and following the conventions of every literary genre.

Short Stories. Marcel Aymé's witty **parody** "Le loup" ("The Wolf") appeared in 1934. Gianni **Rodari** published his fractured tale "A sbagliare le storie" ("Telling Stories Wrong") in 1962. Jacques Ferron's risqué version "Le petit chaperon rouge" (1968) and João Guimarães Rosa's existentialist retelling "Fita verde no cabelo" ("Green Ribbon in the Hair," 1970) appeared in collections for adults. **Janosch**'s "Das elektrische Rotkäppchen" ("The Electrical Little Red Cap," 1972) and Tomi **Ungerer**'s "Little Red Riding Hood" (1974) are satirical parodies published in collections for children. Philippe **Dumas** and Boris Moissard turn the tale upside down in "Le petit chaperon bleu marine" ("Little Navy Blue Riding Hood," 1977).

Angela **Carter**'s "The Werewolf" and "The Company of Wolves" (1979) are complex, multilayered tales. "Wolfland" (1983) by Tanith **Lee** is a dark, gothic tale. Pierrette Fleutiaux blends two tales in "Petit Pantalon Rouge, Barbe-Bleue et Notules" ("Little Red Pants, Bluebeard, and Notules," 1984). Annie Riis's "Ulven og Rødhette" ("The Wolf and Little Red Riding Hood," 1986) and Luisa **Valenzuela**'s "Si esto es la vida, yo soy Caperucita Roja" ("If This Is Life, I'm Red Riding Hood," 1993) are sensual retellings for adults. James Finn Garner casts his "Little Red Riding Hood" (1994) as a politically correct tale. Priscilla Galloway's "The Good Mother" (1995) is a futuristic, postapocalyptic science-fiction version. Pierre Léon included three politically correct versions in *Le mariage politiquement correct du petit chaperon rouge* (*Little Red Riding Hood's Politically Correct Marriage*, 1996), whereas David Fisher's "Little Red Riding Hood v. Regal Pictures, Inc.," is one of his *Legally Correct Fairy Tales* (1996). Nalo **Hopkinson**'s "Riding the Red" (1997) is a powerful tale about female sexuality, whereas Francesca Lia **Block**'s "Wolf" (2000) is a grim tale of sexual abuse. A version circulating on the Internet throughout the Hispanic world, "Cyber Kaperucita" ("Cyber Little Riding Hood," 2003), retells the story in computer jargon.

Novels. Hernán Rodríguez Castello's *Caperucita azul* (*Little Blue Riding Hood*, 1975) is a children's novel that constitutes a defense of the fairy tale. Manlio Argueta's *Caperucita en la zona roja* (*Little Red Riding Hood in the Red Light District*, 1977) is a violent, political novel set in El Salvador. Märta Tikkanen uses the tale to examine her own life in the autobiographical novel *Rödluvan* (*Little Red Riding Hood*, 1986). Viviane Julien's *Bye Bye Chaperon Rouge* (1989) and Carmen **Martín Gaite**'s *Caperucita en Manhattan* (*Little Red Riding Hood in Manhattan*, 1990)combine **fantasy** and realism to address the theme of growing up. Gillian Cross deals with fear, terrorism, and **family** relationships in her multi-layered novel *Wolf* (1990). Anthony Schmitz's *Darkest Desire: The Wolf's Own Tale* (1998) is a short novel in which the Grimms' tale is viewed from the wolf's perspective.

Poetry. Reworkings of the tale in **poetry** are numerous and varied. Gabriela Mistral's "Caperucita Roja" (1924) and Francisco Villaespesa's two "Caperucita" poems (1954) underscore the innocence of the child victim. Anne **Sexton**'s "Red Riding Hood" (1971) uses the story to discuss deception, whereas Olga **Broumas** explores mother-daughter relationships in her "Little Red Riding Hood" (1977). Roald **Dahl**'s "Little Red Riding Hood and the Wolf" (1982) is a witty, satirical retelling. Agha Shahid Ali's "The Wolf's Postscript to 'Little Red Riding Hood'" (1987) is told from the wolf's perspective, as is Gwen Strauss's "The Waiting Wolf" (1990). Pierre **Gripari** devotes a poem to "Le loup" and another to "Le petit chaperon malin" ("Little Cunning Riding Hood," 1996).

Illustrated Books and Picture Books. Over the centuries, "Little Red Riding Hood" has been illustrated by countless artists. The most famous **illustration**s are Gustave **Doré**'s powerful engravings. The memorable works by illustrators such as Doré, Walter **Crane**, and Arthur **Rackham** continue to influence current artists. Beni Montresor's *Little Red Riding Hood* (1991) is an homage to Doré, and Anthony **Browne** parodies Walter Crane in *The Tunnel* (1989). The classic fairy tale has inspired many major contemporary illustrators, including Éric Battut, Klaus Ensikat, Trina Schart Hyman, Nikolaus Heidelbach, Kazuyoshi Iino, Roberto **Innocenti**, Susanne Janssen, Binette Schroeder, Svend Otto **S.**, and Lisbeth Zwerger.

Illustrators of "Little Red Riding Hood" often offer highly original retellings in their visual narratives. Kelek transplants the tale into a Vittore Carpaccio painting in *Contes de Charles Perrault* (1986). Jean Ache recasts the story in the manner of seven famous twentieth-century artists in his series "Le petit chaperon rouge" (1973). Warja Lavater's *Imageries* "Le petit chaperon rouge" (1965) tells the tale in visual code, as does Jean Ache's version in *Le monde des ronds et des carrés* (*The World of Circles and Squares*, 1975). Sarah Moon's dramatic black-and-white photographs cast Perrault's tale in a dark, disturbing light, whereas William Wegman's Polaroid photographs of his Weimaraners turn the Grimms' version into a light-hearted, witty tale.

Picture book retellings exist for all ages. Bruno Munari published multiple versions of the tale: *Cappuccetto verde* (*Little Green Riding Hood*, 1972), *Cappuccetto giallo* (*Little Yellow*

Riding Hood, 1972), and *Cappuccetto bianco* (*Little White Riding Hood*, 1999). Paul Biegel adopts a psychoanalytical approach in his lengthy tale *Wie je droomt ben je zelf* (*You Are Who You Dream About*, 1977), illustrated by Carl Hollander. Chico Buarque's *Chapeuzinho amarelo* (*Little Yellow Riding Hood*, 1979) is a poetic, playful examination of fear. Both Fam **Ekman**'s *Rødhatten og Ulven* (*Red Hat and the Wolf*, 1985) and Makiko Satou's *Itazura Akazukin-chan* (*Mischievous Little Red Riding Hood*, 1989) cast a boy in the title role. *Mina, je t'aime* (*Mina, I love you*, 1991), by Patricia Joiret and Xavier Bruyère, is a cautionary tale for little boys about a girl/wolf.

Yvan Pommaux's *John Chatterton détective* (1993) recasts the tale as a whodunit in comics style. Anne Bertier's *Mon loup* (*My Wolf*, 1995) is a charming love story illustrated with black silhouettes. Elise Fagerli uses woodcuts to tell the story of a heroine who gobbles up a wolf in *Ulvehunger* (*Wolfhunger*, 1995). Christian Bruel and Nicole Claveloux's *Petits chaperons loups* (*Little Riding Hood Wolves*, 1997) is a versatile, wordless book that invites multiple readings. *Mon chaperon rouge* (*My Red Riding Hood*, 1998), by Anne Ikhlef and Alain Gauthier, is a sensual, sophisticated picture book for older readers. *Un petit chaperon rouge* (*A Little Red Riding Hood*, 2000), by Claude Clément and Isabelle Forestier, is a poetic retelling that deals with the theme of sexual abuse.

Comics. The tale has been retold in comics for all ages. Japanese manga versions range from Shotaro Ishinomori's "Akazukin-chan" ("Little Red Riding Hood," 1962) for young girls to Shouko Hamada's "Akazukin ha ookami otoko no yume wo miru" ("Little Red Riding Hood Dreams of Werewolf," 1993), a romance for young women. In the 1970s and early 1980s, the famous French artists Gotlib and F'Murr published multiple comics inspired by the tale.

Film and Theater

Walt **Disney**'s adaptations include an early animated silent black-and-white short *Little Red Riding Hood* (1922), as well as the Silly Symphony cartoon short *The Big Bad Wolf* (1934) and *Redux Riding Hood* (1998). Animated cartoons range from Frederick "Tex" **Avery**'s *Little Red Walking Hood* (1937), *Red Hot Riding Hood* (1943), and *Little Rural Riding Hood* (1949), to the Bugs Bunny cartoon *Little Red Riding Rabbit* (1944). The computer animated, full-length feature film *Hoodwinked* (2005) turns the story into a whodunit. The anime feature film *Jin-Roh: The Wolf Brigade* (1998) is a science fiction fairy tale. A number of films offer sensual, multilayered interpretations, including Neil Jordan's ***The Company of Wolves*** (1984), based on Carter's short story, Anne Ikhlef's *La véritable histoire du Chaperon Rouge* (*The True Story of Red Riding Hood*, 1985), Marta Meszaros's *Bye Bye Red Riding Hood* (also known as ***Bye Bye Chaperon Rouge***, 1989), and David Kaplan's *Little Red Riding Hood* (1997). The tale has inspired a number of thrillers, including Matthew Bright's ***Freeway*** (1996), *Promenons-nous dans les bois*, released in English as *Deep in the Woods* (2000), *Cappuccetto rosso* (*Red Riding Hood*, 2003), and *A Wicked Tale* (2005).

Dramatic adaptations include Shelley **Duvall**'s *Little Red Riding Hood* (1983) in her television series *Shelley Duvall's Faerie Tale Theatre*, Stephen Sondheim and James Lapine's musical ***Into the Woods*** (1987), and a Japanese *kyogen*, by Man-no-jo Nomura, that was produced at the National Noh Theater.

The classic fairy tale "Little Red Riding Hood" continues to inspire creative works in many genres and media. *See also* Cannibalism; Cartoons and Comics; Food; Initiation.

Further Readings: Beckett, Sandra L. *Recycling Red Riding Hood.* New York: Routledge, 2002; Dundes, Alan, ed. *Little Red Riding Hood: A Casebook.* Madison: University of Wisconsin Press, 1989; Genardière, Claude de la. *Encore un conte? Le petit chaperon rouge à l'usage des adultes.* Nancy: Presses Universitaires de Nancy, 1993; Mieder, Wolfgang. "Survival Forms of 'Little Red Riding Hood' in Modern Society." *International Folklore Review* 2 (1982): 23–40; Orenstein, Catherine. *Little Red Riding Hood Uncloaked: Sex, Morality, and the Evolution of a Fairy Tale.* New York: Basic Books, 2002; Zipes, Jack, ed. *The Trials and Tribulations of Little Red Riding Hood.* 2nd revised edition. New York: Routledge, 1993.

Sandra L. Beckett

Lochhead, Liz (1947–)

The work of Scottish poet, playwright, and performer Liz Lochhead is characterized by her lyric use of the working-class idiom and the manner in which this voice of the people represents marginalized identity. While Lochhead is concerned with Scottish identity as a whole, her writing demonstrates a specific interest in female identity. One way Lochhead explores the concept of female self-representation in a male domain is to transform conventional dramas, **myth**s, **ballad**s, and fairy tales into fresh and often darkly comic feminist revisions.

In her poetry collection *The Grimm Sisters* (1979), Lochhead subverts stereotypical **gender** roles present in the classic fairy tales by giving traditionally silent or one-dimensional female characters a voice. By allowing stock female characters such as "the spinster" and "the harridan" to speak from their own point of view, Lochhead revises these characters into a position of literary power and authority that ultimately allows them to transcend their conventional female roles. The poem "Rapunzstiltskin," for example, features a self-sufficient heroine, happy in her tower, and the hapless would-be hero who comes to her "rescue." In this case, the combination and ironic revision of the two classic fairy tales, "Rapunzel" and "Rumplestiltskin," evinces Lochhead's desire to subvert not only the traditional male and female roles within the original tales but the conventional form of the tales themselves. *See also* Feminism; Feminist Tales; Postmodernism.

Further Reading: Crawford, Robert, and Anne Varty, eds. *Liz Lochhead's Voices.* Edinburgh: Edinburgh University Press, 1993.

Barbara Tannert-Smith

Loorits, Oskar (1900–1961)

The Estonian folklorist Oskar Loorits contributed significantly to spreading awareness about Estonian **folklore** and folktales both within Estonia and beyond. His German-language edition of Estonian folktales, *Estnische Volkserzählungen*, (*Estonian Folk Narratives*, 1959), remains important as the only comprehensive anthology of **Estonian tales** available to readers and scholars not fluent in Estonian. As the first director of the Estonian Folklore Archives, which was founded in 1927, Loorits and his collaborators undertook to replenish the folk treasury based on Jakob Hurt's folklore collection. His early interest in **collecting** and studying Livonian folklore provided materials for a multivolume monograph on folk beliefs, *Liivi rahva usund* (*The Folk Religion of the Livonians*, vols. 1–3 [1926–28], vols. 4–5 [2000]), and for a catalogue of folktales and legends, *Livische Märchen- und Sagenvarianten* (*Livonian Variants of Tales and Legends*, 1926).

Upon emigrating from Estonia after World War II, Loorits continued his research in Sweden and published his major work, *Grundzüge des estnischen Volksglaubens* (*The Essential Features of Estonian Folk Belief*, 3 vols., 1949–57), which includes not only research on folk beliefs but also an analysis of religious motifs in fairy tales and legends. Fairy tales received special attention in his article "Some Notes on the Repertoire of the Estonian Folk-Tale" (1937) and in "Das Märchen vom gestohlenen Donnerinstrument bei Esten" (1930), which deals with Estonian variants of **tale type** ATU 1148B, Thunder's Instruments. Loorits published many shorter articles characterized by a colorful style and frequent emphasis on national consciousness. These articles include an abundance of sample texts because Loorits thought it essential that the folklore **archives** be accessible not only to researchers but also to the wider public.

Further Reading: Västrik, Ergo-Hart. "Oskar Loorits: Byzantine Cultural Relations and Practical Application of Folklore Archives." *Studies in Estonian Folkloristics and Ethnology: A Reader and Reflexive History*. Edited by Kristin Kuutma and Tiiu Jaago. Tartu: Tartu University Press, 2005. 203–15.

Risto Järv

The Lord of the Rings Trilogy (2001–2003)

Director Peter Jackson's film versions of J. R. R. **Tolkien**'s famous **fantasy** novels have probably been the most successful cinematic **adaptation**s of literary fantasy ever, setting new standards for the visual realization of magical landscapes and heroic adventure. The films are generally faithful to Tolkien's novel and gracefully perform the necessary task of slimming down the dense pages of the **epic** into more cinematic narratives. Despite their excessive length in theatrical terms, they are successful action films as well as skillful adaptations.

The use of New Zealand's landscapes in the three films allows a particularly powerful representation of the magical realm, allowing, for the non-New Zealanders who comprise

Elijah Wood plays Frodo Baggins in Rivendell in the 2001 film *The Lord of the Rings: The Fellowship of the Ring*. [New Line Cinema/Photofest]

the bulk of the cinema-going audience, both for grandeur and for the necessary degree of unfamiliarity that persuades the viewer that they have transcended the mundane world. The live-action format is certainly more successful than the low-budget animation of Ralph Bakshi's earlier adaptation (1978). While Tolkien himself resisted the notion of fantasy films, or even **illustration**s to fairy tales, few viewers seem to feel that the visual version limits their imaginative engagement as he feared. What has been lost, perhaps, is inevitable given the translation of nonhuman characters into human actors: some aspect of the danger underlying the magical in Middle-earth, the notion of the Elves as akin to the inhabitants of **faerie**, beautiful but also dangerously enthralling. At times, the gritty earthiness of the action also works directly against Tolkien's characteristically idealized prose.

The action-movie format translates well the heroic framework of the story, with its sword-wielding heroes and terrifying monsters. It also visually underlines the smallness of the hobbit heroes against the landscape and the importance of their quest. Interestingly, the stripped-down cinema version of the story is, in its essentialist function, perhaps closer to the economy of fairy-tale narrative than is the sprawling literary epic of the novel: the films effectively compress time and action to focus on vital moments and events. The story becomes two essentialist quests, those of Aragorn's restoration to his throne and Frodo's journey to destroy the Ring of Power. What the film also loses, however, is much of the folkloric framework of Middle-earth, the background of **legend**, song, and poetry, which lends such depth and texture to Tolkien's writing. Indeed, it is hard to imagine this translating well to the expectations of modern cinema. Jackson's film attempts to retain some aspects of this background in his deliberate framing of the narrative with both the history of the Ring and the story's existence as narrative in Bilbo's Red Book, although the mythology of the Valar is largely absent. Where the legendary framework and the notion of an oral mythology are partially restored, however, is in the extended versions of the films, released on DVD. These reinstate details omitted from the theatrical versions and make for more wandering and textured stories, which are less successful as cinematic narratives but perhaps closer to Tolkien's literary vision and sense of folkloric depth. *See also* Elf, Elves; Film and Video.

Further Reading: Croft, Janet Brennan, ed. *Tolkien on Film: Essays on Peter Jackson's The Lord of the Rings*. Altadena, CA: Mythopoeic, 2004.

Jessica Tiffin

Lorenzini, Carlo. *See* Collodi, Carlo

Lubert, Marguerite de. *See* Lubert, Marie-Madeleine de

Lubert, Marie-Madeleine de (c. 1710–c. 1779)

Marie-Madeleine de Lubert (also referred to as Marguerite de Lubert) was a prolific prose writer whose work includes **novel**s, **novella**s, poetry, and unconventional fairy tales. The daughter of the general treasurer of the French Marine Infantry from Bourges, Lubert moved to Paris with her family at a very young age. What little we know about her life comes primarily from references in correspondence to her friendships with some of the most-prominent cultural and literary figures of the time. In 1732, Voltaire addressed a letter to Lubert, calling her his "muse and grace," and later dedicated his gallant Épîtres 35 and 50 to her. The prominent *salonnière* (female **salon** participant) Madame de Graffigny mentions Lubert frequently in her letters and describes the immediate affection she and Lubert had for each other from the moment they met on February 26, 1739. They continued a close friendship over the course of their lives. There is also good reason to conclude that Lubert knew the influential natural philosopher Jean-Louis Moreau de Maupertuis, author of the *Vénus Physique* (*The Earthly Venus*, 1745) and also an acquaintance of both Voltaire and Graffigny.

Lubert has been attributed as the author of more than a dozen tales, most published between 1743 and 1756. In *La Princesse Sensible et le Prince Typhon* (*Princess Sensible and Prince Typhon*, 1743), Lubert offers up a **didactic tale** in which two **fairies** raise a young child. However, this tale deviates substantially from Lubert's typical parodic rewritings of the noble themes and personages that dominated earlier French **literary fairy tale**s. Her tales are humorous and, at times, irreverent. Her characters are often exaggerated and scatological, with ludic names to match their unusual behaviors: Croquinolet (King Sweet), BonBec (Good Beak), and Prince Coquerico (Prince Cockadoodledoo). Representative of the dreamlike, parodic turn seen in eighteenth-century **French tales**, Lubert's protagonists are frequently hybrids who move across animal, human, plant, and mechanical boundaries. *La Princesse Camion* (*Princess Camion*, 1743), for example, describes the adventures of female protagonist who, after forgetting to take a bath, is transformed into a half-whale, half-human creature. Kind **fairies** take pity on her and agree to transform her into a mechanical, talking doll who can slip easily into the pocket of her beloved. Of her corpus, "La Princesse Coque d'Oeuf et le Prince Bonbon" ("Princess Eggshell and Prince Bonbon," 1745) is the most direct **parody** of earlier French tales. It has been attributed to both Lubert and Michelet-Dubocage de Bléville, a shipping merchant. The title page's reference to "M. Debgacobub," an anagram of Dubocage, does lend some support to this. However, *Le cabinet des fées* (*The Fairies' Cabinet*) assigns the tale to Lubert, and its delirious story of a young princess hatched from an egg is consistent with Lubert's highly imaginative writing style.

Further Readings: La Harpe, Jacqueline de. "La 'Muse et Grâce' de Voltaire. (Le conte de fées en France vers 1750)." *PMLA* 54 (1939): 454–66; Tucker, Holly. "The Chicken and the Egg." *Pregnant Fictions: Childbirth and the Fairy Tale in Early-Modern France*. Detroit: Wayne State University Press, 2003. 119–39.

Holly Tucker

Lüthi, Max (1909–1991)

The Swiss folktale scholar and professor of European folk literature Max Lüthi significantly influenced the study of the **folktale**'s style. His starting point was the literary text, and his primary goal was to establish the essential laws of the folktale that account for its stylistic consistency. In method and objective, his work most closely resembles that of the Danish folklorist Axel Olrik. Whereas Olrik's "epic laws" comprise formal traits such as opening and closing formulas, repetition, and the pattern of three, Lüthi held that the uniquely "abstract" style of the folktale derives as much from a particular worldview as from specific narrative traits. Like the Dutch literary scholar Andre Jolles, Lüthi assumed that the folktale, as with other **simple forms** of folk narrative, is the expression of a particular mental or spiritual activity. However, in contrast to Jolles, he attributed the style of the folktale to conditions of oral transmission and to a psychological attitude distinguishing it from other forms of folk narrative.

In major works, including *Das europäische Volksmärchen* (1947; translated as *The European Folktale: Form and Nature*, 1982) and *Das Volksmärchen als Dichtung: Ästhetik und Anthropologie* (1975; translated as *The Fairytale as Art Form and Portrait of Man*, 1984), Lüthi delineated the formal traits that characterize the folktale and give it its abstract style. According to Lüthi, the folktale is hero-centered and action-driven. Its story line is linear and its style partial to sharp contrasts and clearly formed characters and objects. *The European Folktale* proposed to do for the style of the folktale what Vladmir **Propp**'s *Morfologiya skazki* (*Morphology of the Folktale*, 1928) had done for its structure. Focusing mainly on the European **wonder tale** (ATU 300–749), Lüthi identified its principal formal traits: one-dimensionality, depthlessness, abstract style, isolation and interconnection, and sublimation and all-inclusiveness. Variation in **tale types** and versions notwithstanding, these traits comprise the basic style to which the folktale as a genre aspires. While recognizing that some of these traits are found in other genres of folk narrative, Lüthi nonetheless held that they are exhibited most consistently in the folktale and give it its particular style.

The Fairy Tale as Art Form and Portrait of Man moves beyond narrowly formal considerations to explore the interrelationship among narrative technique, its artistic effect, and its anthropological message. The aesthetics of the folktale and its portrait of humanity are seen in relation to one another, with beauty constituting both an absolute ideal and a moving force in the plot. In keeping with the folktale's abstract style, characters are types, and beauty is general in nature. The folktale prefers to describe the effect of beauty on its characters rather than beauty itself.

Lüthi, who taught at the University of Zürich from 1968 until his retirement in 1979, is also well known for his book *Es war einmal: Vom Wesen des Volksmärchens* (1962), which was translated into English as *Once upon a Time: On the Nature of Fairy Tales* and has become a popular introduction to the study of folktales and fairy tales.

Further Readings: Lüthi, Max. *The European Folktale: Form and Nature*. Translated by John D. Niles. Bloomington: Indiana University Press, 1982; ———. *The Fairytale as Art Form and Portrait of Man*. Translated by Jon Erickson. Bloomington: Indiana University Press, 1984; ———. *Once upon a Time: On the Nature of Fairy Tales*. Translated by Lee Chadeayne and Paul Gottwald. Bloomington: Indiana University Press, 1976.

Mary Beth Stein

M

MacDonald, George (1824–1905)

Scottish writer George MacDonald is one of the most powerful Victorian precursors to modern **fantasy**, particularly Christian fantasy. While he was a prolific writer of realist Scottish fiction, it was his fantasy novels and fairy tales that were a profound influence on writers such as J. R. R. **Tolkien** and C. S. **Lewis**, and he was a close friend and literary confidante of Lewis **Carroll**. Despite MacDonald's training as a minister in the Congregational church, his semiallegorical fantasies demonstrate Christian mysticism and independent theology. He was himself a follower of German thinkers such as **Novalis**, and in later life he rejected Calvinist doctrine in favor of a gentler, more all-embracing Christianity. Despite their religious content his fantasies remain more generally resonant, moving, and mysterious, offering symbolic figurations of unconscious processes that often repay analysis in Jungian terms (see **Jung, Carl Gustav**).

MacDonald is particularly self-conscious about the process of creating magical narrative. His collection *A Dish of Orts* (1893) contains various discussions of the imagination and its importance. In particular, "The Fantastic Imagination," an introduction to *The Light Princess and Other Fairy Tales* (1893), is a thoughtful analysis of fantasy and its difference from allegory. Like Tolkien, MacDonald uses the term "fairy tale" to describe fantastic writing generally and argues eloquently for the necessity of its structured operation, specifically according to moral laws. While demanding that the created world exist in harmony with moral truths of the real world, however, he denies the strict one-to-one equivalences of classical allegory, arguing that genuine fantastic creation, mirroring divine creation, must be capable of multiple meanings and complex resonance.

MacDonald's fantasy writing is clearly divided between adult and children's fantasies, although he insisted that his writing generally appealed to a childlike quality rather than a specific age group. The children's fantasies include the much-loved classics *The Princess and the Goblin* (1872) and *The Princess and Curdie* (1883), in which the young protagonists must overcome magical and mundane horrors, including mountain goblins and the corruption of the **king**'s court. *The Princess and Curdie* is notable for a sustained **motif** of animal **transformation**, linked to a pervasive moral message. Both stories revolve around the **fairy**-godmother-like figure of Princess Irene's great-grandmother, who, in her beauty, power, and constant transmutation from **age** to youth, exemplifies the strong, magical

mother-figures that are particularly characteristic of MacDonald's fantasy. *At the Back of the North Wind* (1871) includes a similarly powerful figure in the North Wind herself. This more overtly moralistic **fable** features a somewhat oversentimentalized child-hero whose particular sensitivity and moral maturity allow him temporary access to the country at the back of the North Wind, an ideal realm that conflates notions of **faerie** and heaven.

MacDonald's two full-length adult fantasies, *Phantastes: A Faerie Romance for Men and Women* (1858) and *Lilith: A Romance* (1895), both entail the hero navigating a magical otherworld filled with complex, mysterious symbols and challenges relating to his moral quest. They show, in their rich texture and occasionally wandering plotlines, the influence of German Romantic fairy-tale writers such as Ludwig **Tieck**, E. T. A. **Hoffmann**, and Frei-drich de la Motte **Fouqué**. *Phantastes* is identified as "A Faerie Romance" in its subtitle, and the world explored by Anodos is explicitly Fairy Land, holding miniature fairy creatures as well as motifs such as magical trees, a woman transformed to marble, Arthurian knights on quest, **ogre**s, goblins, and enchanted palaces. The novel is notable for an intense, suppressed thread of **sexuality** running through its imagery, and for its use of the motif of a shadow-self. *Lilith* returns to more overtly biblical symbolism, taking as its central character Adam's first wife, a beautiful woman who can assume the form of a leopard, and who represents Edenic fall and the stain of sin. The novel is integrally concerned with the exploration of **death**. Its symbols include ghostly figures, children, underground monsters, and the importance of water. A similar moral quest through fairyland, although a more compact and childlike one, is found in "The Golden Key" (*Dealings with the Fairies*, 1867).

It is in MacDonald's stand-alone fairy tales that he shows the most overt awareness of issues of form and tradition. Many of his tales were originally published in longer works, most notably in *Adela Cathcart* (1864). Of these, a large proportion are folkloric in feel, often orally transmitted in the novel, and are concerned with the landscape and **folk** traditions of Scotland, including ghosts, the second sight, and encounters with fey folk. Examples include "The Portent" (serialized in 1860), "The Carasoyne," and "The Grey Wolf" (both in *Works of Fancy and Imagination*, 1871). MacDonald's most playful and self-aware fairy tales are "Little Daylight," which occurs in the text of *At the Back of the North Wind*, and "The Light Princess," first published as part of *Adela Cathcart*. Both tales deal with christening curses, although their terms are comic inversions of traditional scenarios. Little Daylight is cursed to sleep all day and wake all night, while the Light Princess is inflicted with a lack of gravity, a pun which works on both the physical, comic level—she floats in the air—and on the moral, in that she is unable to be serious. The christening curses conform to fairy-tale expectations: the wicked fairy's work is partially undone, and an eventual escape is provided by the intervention of a good fairy. In "Little Daylight," however, this is playfully exaggerated so that two good fairies keep themselves back from giving gifts, recognizing that the wicked fairy has an equal knowledge of tradition. The curse thus takes on a curiously disjointed and multi-layered effect. MacDonald's awareness of fairy-tale tradition allows him to comment on and invert expected structures not only for comic effect but to effective moral and symbolic purpose. The function of symbol is considerably heightened in "The Romance of Photogen and Nycteris," sometimes entitled "The Day Boy and the Night Girl" (1879), in which a wicked **witch** raises a girl as a gentle night-only creature and a boy as a daylight sun-god figure. Despite its rampant **gender** stereotypes, the story is an effective and powerful investigation of the interaction between opposing symbols in overcoming evil. ***See also*** Children's Literature; English Tales; Psychological Approaches; Religious Tale.

Further Readings: Prickett, Stephen. "Adults in Allegory Land: Kingsley and MacDonald." *Victorian Fantasy.* Bloomington: Indiana University Press, 1979. 150–97; Raeper, William, ed. *The Gold Thread: Essays on George MacDonald.* Edinburgh: Edinburgh University Press, 1990.

Jessica Tiffin

Machado y Alvarez, Antonio (1848–1892)

Known by the pseudonym Demófilo (Lover of People), Antonio Machado y Alvarez, a lawyer, judge, translator and author, was the greatest Spanish folklorist of his time. Deeply concerned about the preservation of Spanish folk culture, he was the driving force behind the establishment of Spain's regional **folklore** societies, such as Folklore Andaluz (Andalusian Folkore), Folklore Extremeño (Extremaduran Folklore), and Folklore Castellano (Castillian Folklore), among others. The goal of these organizations was to further interest in the Iberian Peninsula's tales, songs, **proverb**s, poems, customs, superstitions, and so on, which were all considered indispensable parts of Spanish and Portuguese culture.

Machado is also the author of *Bases del folklore español* (*The Background of Spanish Folklore*, 1881) and the editor of the eleven-volume periodical *Biblioteca de las tradiciones populares españolas* (*Library of Spanish Folk Traditions*, 1883–86), to which he personally contributed volume 5, entitled *Estudios sobre literatura popular* (*Studies on Folk Literature*, 1884). This collection of his country's customs, beliefs, and folklore also includes many centuries-old tales, which are Spanish versions of older Arabic tales (the **Arabian Nights**, among others).

Machado's interest in Spain's folklore spurred him to publish the renowned *Colección de cantes flamencos* (*Collection of Flamenco Songs*, 1881), a work in which he not only gathers, for the first time, the lyrics to almost 900 flamenco songs, but also includes the origins of numerous song forms. Due to this work's importance, Spain considers him the nation's first flamencologist. *See also* Spanish Tales.

Further Readings: Alonso Montero, Xesús. "Antonio Machado y Alvarez ('Demófilo') e a cultura popular galega." *Senara: Revista de Filoloxia* 1 (1979): 127–50; Higgin, L., and Eugène E. Street. *Spanish Life in Town and Country.* New York: Putnam, 1904.

Candace Beutell Gardner

Maeterlinck, Maurice (1862–1949)

A Belgian writer who revolutionized French **theater** by bringing symbolism to the stage, Maurice Maeterlinck launched his career with *Serres chaudes* (*Hothouses*, 1889), a collection of poems that paved the way for surrealism. That same year appeared Maeterlinck's first play, *La Princesse Maleine* (1889), which brought him critical acclaim. This was the first of several plays in which Maeterlinck combined chivalric tales set in the **Middle Ages** with a looming sense of dread most explicitly expressed in his acclaimed play written in a minimalist style, *L'intruse* (*The Intruder*, 1890). *Les septs princesses* (*The Seven Princesses*, 1891), *Pelléas et Mélisande* (1892), *Alladine et Palomides* (1894), and *La mort de Tintagiles* (*The Death of Tintagiles*, 1894) all follow in the wake of *La Princesse Maleine* with their gothic settings, their love triangles, and their preoccupation with **death**.

In 1901, Maeterlinck published a symbolist version of "**Bluebeard**" entitled *Ariane et Barbe-bleue*. Blending the well-known tale by Charles **Perrault** with the **myth** of Ariadne, the daughter of Minos who helps Theseus find his way out of the Minotaur's labyrinth, Maeterlinck transforms the significance and function of Bluebeard's wife in his play. As Ariane, Bluebeard's wife represents a free spirit who attempts to liberate the other wives, who are imprisoned in body as well as in mind. In his play *L'oiseau bleu* (*The Blue Bird*, 1908), the brother and sister pair Tyltyl and Mytyl set out on a quest on behalf of the **fairy** Bérylune to find the blue bird of happiness to cure her sick and unhappy daughter. The quest, however, really has to do with the pair seeing their world with different eyes.

Several of Maeterlinck's plays have been adapted to other media. Both *Pelléas et Mélisande* and *Ariane et Barbe-bleue* were made into **opera**s in 1902 and 1907, with **music** by Claude Debussy and Paul Dukas, respectively. Several filmic versions of *The Blue Bird* have been produced, including a 1918 silent film directed by Maurice Tourneur; a 1940 film directed by Walter Lang and starring Shirley Temple as Mytyl; and a 1976 version directed by George Cukor and starring Elizabeth Taylor, Jane Fonda, Cicely Tyson, and Ava Gardner. In 1980, Fuji TV released twenty-six episodes of the Japanese anime *Maeterlinck no aoi no tori: Tyltyl Mytyl no bouken ryokou* (*Maeterlinck's Blue Bird: Tyltyl and Mytyl's Adventurous Journey*). Referred to as the "Belgian Shakespeare," Maeterlinck received the Nobel Prize in Literature in 1911. *See also* Film and Video; French Tales; Japanese Popular Culture; Silent Films and Fairy Tales.

Further Readings: Goehr, Lydia. "Radical Modernism and the Failure of Style: Philosophical Reflections on Maeterlinck-Debussy's *Pelléas et Mélisande*." *Representations* 74 (Spring 2001): 55–82; Suschitzky, Anya. "*Ariane et Barbe-Bleue*: Dukas, the Light and the Well." *Cambridge Opera Journal* 9.2 (1997): 133–61.

Anne E. Duggan

Magic Helper

A magic helper is a character, whether supernatural, human, or animal, who renders an extraordinary kind of assistance to heroes or heroines in **folktales** and other related narrative forms. The role played by magic helpers is a favorite building block in many fantastic oral stories.

The popularity of magic helpers in folklore over most of the world and in much of old literature indicates that this **motif** is of great antiquity. Although the fanciful notion that help could be forthcoming from extraordinary and unexpected sources is perennial in human thought, and the contemplation of animal behavior gives rise to natural fancies that they are aware of human problems, it may be suggested that the actual magic helpers originated in primeval religious rituals. In such rituals, figures such as shamans represented themselves as visiting the otherworld and being assisted there by helpful spirits. These spirits could be unspecified or could be either anthropomorphic or theriomorphic. Indeed, the shaman himself or herself, while in a trance or another detached state, behaved like a magician and sometimes claimed to go about in the form of animals. The allotted function of such a person in a community was to undertake quests in the otherworld by way of helping members of the community to solve their problems, thus focusing on the issue of magical help.

Although the parallels in function between such ancient rituals and the marvelous tales of magic helpers is clear, the lack of ancient evidence makes it difficult to prove a direct chronological connection. It may be assumed, however, that the well-known process of ritual imagery being transformed into romantic narrative was at work. It is likely that the earliest development of such ideas into an entertaining narrative concerned the helpers as animals. The basic form of this is that a hero performs kind deeds for a number of animals. He may, for instance, save an ant, duck, bee, fish, fox, raven, or eagle from danger or starvation. As a result, he is assisted in a very difficult task by these creatures, each using its own special ability. This narrative unit has come to be used in many far-flung folktales, including **tale type**s ATU 302–3, 313, 329, 400, 551, 554, and 566. Closely related to this format is another, which has the hero being given the power by animals to assume their shape and thus perform the necessary deeds (for example, ATU 316, 665), or even animals taking on human shape when necessary to assist the hero (ATU 552). In addition, many folktales have animals such as a horse, a bull, or a dog assisting the hero, and often these are self-transformed or enchanted humans who regain their proper shapes after the task is completed.

The setting into story format of the idea that a person may be helped by a kind of supernatural human must be of comparable antiquity. This is expressed in a type of narrative which has a hero being assisted by a number of characters who each possess a distinctive superhuman ability. In ancient Greek tradition, the magic helpers appear as the Argonauts, a series of men with various astounding abilities who assist the hero Jason in his quests. The portrayal of the Argonauts is thought to have been inherited from stories told by the prehistoric Mycenaeans, who in turn would appear to have received it from the Middle East. Its ultimate origin is believed to have been in India, where one may suppose that some shamanic-type lore was the source. The plot is present in ATU 513, The Extraordinary Companions, which has a hero being fortunate in gaining the assistance of several strange companions—examples might be a man so strong that he pulls trees up by their roots, another man who can shoot the eye out of a fly's head at a great distance, a man with superhuman hearing ability, a stupendous runner, an extraordinarily adept thief, and so on.

This plot became very popular in medieval literature, and fine examples of it exist in the Welsh story of Culhwch and Olwen and in Irish stories of Fionn mac Cumhaill. Notable examples are found also in the Renaissance literature of Italy, such as in the works of Giovanni Sercambi and Giambattista **Basile**. One of the principal tasks performed by these helpers may be the gaining of the hand of a beautiful **princess** for the hero. She also has great abilities—such as archery, wrestling, and running—and will agree to marry only the man who can overcome her in these pursuits. The helpers, disguised as the hero, accomplish this. In that form, the plot lies behind various texts in old literature, such as the medieval German account of the wooing of Brunhild in the *Nibelungenlied*. A further variant of the plot was developed in Europe in the **Middle Ages**. This is listed as ATU 653, The Four Skillful Brothers; it concerns a group of **brothers** with extraordinary skills who combine to rescue a princess who has been stolen away to a rock on a distant sea. They then argue as to which of them is more deserving of her.

In folk belief, the idea is widespread that help can be obtained from a spiritual community inhabiting the landscape but remaining apart from, and generally invisible to, the human community. The idea that such a community exists is in itself of great antiquity, and may also owe its origin, at least in part, to shamanic-type practices. Usually this local supernatural community is thought of as comprising beings in the nature of spirits, **fairies**, or **dwarf**s, but sometimes it may also be a kind of secret communal life practiced by animals. In folk **legend**, assistance from such exotic sources can vary from cures for ailments to knowledge of hidden treasure or magical talent for some art or skill. The value of these gifts depends, however, on continuing good relations between the source and the receiver. In

European folklore in general, for instance, money received from the fairies can only too easily change into withered leaves or dross of some other kind. ***See also*** Magic Object.

Further Readings: Thompson, Stith. "Supernatural Helpers." *The Folktale.* 1946. Berkeley: University of California Press, 1977. 47–67; Uther, Hans-Jörg. *The Types of International Folktales.* Volume 1. Helsinki: Academia Scientiarum Fennica, 2004. 180–83, 231–396.

Dáithí Ó hÓgáin

Magic Object

The belief in objects and substances endowed with supernatural powers touches all human cultures. Talismans, sacred relics, and good-luck tokens are found everywhere. These sometimes belong to formal belief systems; in other instances, their reputed magic powers emanate from beyond the sphere of traditional religion. Rationalized and trivialized, such objects may become little more than decorative pieces, for example, "charms" worn on a bracelet; but to true believers, they can serve as material links to superhuman powers and thus be worth any cost to acquire and hold.

The wondrous events common to fairy tales everywhere often rely on physical artifacts. To cultures accepting the efficacy of such magic items, depictions of their miraculous effects belong more to reality—albeit an otherworldly reality—than to **fantasy** and fiction. Numerous **tale type**s (ATU 560–649) are built around the acquisition and use of specific magic objects. Furthermore, **folktale**s, **myth**s, and **legend**s of many different types include **motif**s featuring such items. Stith **Thompson**, in his monumental *Motif-Index of Folk-Literature*, catalogues hundreds of magic items (Motifs D800–D1600 plus numerous subcategories).

Many well-known fairy tales feature magic items. "Jack and the Beanstalk" (ATU 328A) opens when magic beans create a ladder to a kingdom in the sky. **Cinderella** (ATU 510A), robed in magic (or magically acquired) **clothing** and transported by a magic carriage, escapes from her bleak domestic environment. Seven-league boots and flying carpets transport heroes and villains alike in tales of many different types. **Snow White**'s stepmother learns unwelcome truths about herself from a magic **mirror**. Similarly, in **Beauty and the Beast** tales (ATU 425C) from Jeanne-Marie **Leprince de Beaumont** to Walt **Disney**, a looking glass provides miraculous communication between the heroine and her **father**. Clothing that renders the wearer invisible appears in many tales, for example, type ATU 306, The Danced-Out Shoes. A purse that continuously replenishes its supply of money plays a central role in tales of type ATU 566, The Three Magic Objects and the Wonderful Fruits, among many others. The list goes on, seemingly without end.

Magic plays such an important role in fairy tales that a more accurate designation for the genre might be "magic tale," especially given the fact that **fairies** themselves appear in a relatively small number of such stories. Legends, a genre marked by claims of credibility, also often feature miracle-producing objects. These include naturally occurring substances such as salt and iron; herbs such as garlic, mandrake root, and rowan leaves; magic weapons and impenetrable armor; and religious talismans.

Arguably the most famous tale built around a magic object is the story of **Aladdin** (ATU 561) from the ***Arabian Nights***. Its basic plot forms an outline followed by numerous tales from various lands: A poor youth acquires an apparently ordinary item that controls a superhuman power (here a genie), through which he gains wealth and happiness. Complications arise with the theft of the magic item, but in the end the hero recovers it, and the tale concludes with the expected **punishment and reward** for all concerned.

Many additional folktale plots are built around the acquisition, loss, and recovery of magic objects. Prominent among these are tales of type ATU 563, The Table, the Donkey, and the Stick. An exemplary version of this internationally distributed tale is Giambattista **Basile**'s "Lo cunto dell'uerco" ("The Tale of the Ogre," 1634). In this story, a poor boy named Antuono enters into service for an **ogre** and in payment receives a donkey that voids precious stones. A dishonest innkeeper steals the magic donkey. Following a second period of service, Antuono receives a napkin that, when unfolded, yields costly things of all kinds, but this too is stolen by the innkeeper. After a final period of service, Antuono receives a magic stick. When the innkeeper attempts to learn its secret, it begins to beat him. Antuono calls off the stick only after the **thief** returns to him the previously stolen items.

As suggested in the above tale, the ability to control a magic item is as important as its possession. In the famous story of "**Ali Baba** and the Forty **Thieves**" (ATU 954) from the *Arabian Nights*, the hero correctly remembers the formula "Open, Sesame" that controls the magic cave, and he enriches himself from its treasures. However, his selfish brother forgets the magic word and is trapped inside the cave.

Similarly, in tales of type ATU 565, The Magic Mill, the inability to control a magic item turns potentially good fortune into tragedy. The *Prose Edda* of Snorri Sturluson, an important sourcebook for Norse mythology, contains an example. A mill called Grotti can produce whatever its owner requires. A Viking named Mysing steals the mill and orders it to make salt. However, he does not know how to make it stop, and it produces so much salt that it sinks his ship. At the bottom of the ocean, it continues to grind out salt, and that is why the sea is salty. This tale, with appropriate local variations, is told around the world.

"The **Sorcerer**'s Apprentice" (ATU 325*), because of its treatment in different artistic forms, is one of the world's best-known tales dealing with the failure to control a magic item. This title applies to a family of folktales as well as to a **ballad** by Johann Wolfgang von **Goethe** ("Der Zauberlehrling," 1797) and to a symphonic poem by Paul Dukas (*L'apprenti sorcier*, 1897). The story, accompanied by Dukas's music, is famously retold in Walt Disney's animated film *Fantasia* (1940) and its revision (2000). The apprentice, played in the Disney version by Mickey Mouse, endows a broom with magic and orders it to carry water. However, he does not know how to reverse the charm, and the broom causes a flood. The desperate apprentice attacks the broom with an axe, but each of the fragments produces a bucket and continues to carry water. In the end, the master returns and breaks the spell.
See also Incantation; Magic Helper; Shoe; Wonder Tale.
Further Reading: Thompson, Stith. "Magic and Marvels." *The Folktale*. 1946. Berkeley: University of California Press, 1977. 67–87.

D. L. Ashliman

Magic Tale. *See* Wonder Tale

Magical Realism

Structures and **motif**s derived from **myth** and **folktale** are frequently strategic components of magical realism, a mode of writing that seamlessly fuses a realistic representation of everyday phenomena and events with fantastic or magical elements. Where representations of time, place, and space in realist narrative normally conform to mimetic versions of actual world-consensus reality, magical realism subverts realist settings and rational cause-and-effect relationships, and problematizes the marvelous: Is the marvelous something that already inheres in reality, a product of a way of perceiving, or an irruption of the improbable or supernatural into the text?

Myths and folktales are drawn into magical realist narratives from three principal sources—classical mythology, Christian myth (narratives and motifs), and local or indigenous traditions—and have a range of functions. When five characters from Greek myth (Sisyphus, Prometheus, Odysseus, Orpheus, and Jason) are included in Alejo Carpentier's *Los pasos perdidos* (*The Lost Steps*, 1953), they can be seen as offering parallels with the **novel**'s modern characters. An effect of this parallel might be to suggest that certain human behaviors are endemic or that the contrast between mythic and modern offers hope for change. Classical myth can also be used less overtly as a deep structuring device for a narrative, as when the myth of Actaeon shapes John Fowles's **novella**, *The Ebony Tower* (1974). The story of how the hunter Actaeon was transformed into a stag and torn apart by his own dogs is evoked by allusions to paintings and the name of a character (Diana), and then structures the downfall of the would-be art critic Williams, guilty (like Actaeon) of unwittingly violating an interdiction on certain activities. Myth thus functions as a vehicle for interpreting the structure and significance of the narrative. Myth may also act as a vehicle for commentary, as with Jorge Luis **Borges**'s use of the Minotaur in his story "La casa de Asterión" ("The House of Asterion," 1947) to comment on a life implicated in evil.

Classical myths, such as myths of metamorphosis, introduce elements of inexplicable, mysterious magic that contrast to the text's grounding realism and disrupt the logic of cause and effect (punishment for seeing a goddess bathing is metamorphosis into a stag). A consequent effect is that apparently everyday events and objects take on a magical reality.

Christian myth performs similar functions in enabling magical, sacred, premodern and non-Western constructions of reality. Toni Morrison's *Paradise* (1997), for example, is shaped by images of the Paradise myth of Eden and the covenant of the biblical Book of Exodus, and includes a magical resurgence of the women whose deaths were described in the opening chapter. There, however, the biblical motif is already transformed into another, magical discourse: "Bodacious black Eves unredeemed by Mary, they are like panicked does leaping toward a sun that has finished burning off the mist and now pours its holy oil over the hides of game. / God at their side, the men take aim." A notable use of a mythic motif appears on the final page, which depicts a mythic isomorphism of a pietà: by placing two women, a modern and cross-racial couple, within the frame of a pietà, the text resonates with possibilities of signification. This ontological disruption well illustrates how in magical realism the marvelous functions as a corrective that disrupts what may be taken for granted politically and culturally.

The practice of drawing upon local or indigenous folk traditions in magical realist texts may be a source of controversy. Erik Camayd-Freixas argues that magical realism is a particular form of "primitivism" and is to be defined by a narrative viewpoint positioned within a "primitive" perspective such as the magical worldview of indigenous people or of rural **folk**, as in Gabriel **García Márquez**'s *Cien años de soledad* (*One Hundred Years of Solitude*, 1967). Such a narrative viewpoint assumes non-Western reality norms that establish an alternative referential context for verisimilitude. A narrative grounded in folk traditions will thus assume that tradition itself is normative. Time is mythical, not linear, and the empirical chain of cause and effect is undermined by magical forces, the power of nature, or the effects of taboo **transgression**s. The boundary disappears between the visible world and the invisible, between the divine and the human, and between the living and the dead. The supernatural is immanent in all actions and experiences, just as human existence participates in the form and substance of other beings, and is thus subject to ontological fluidity and **transformation**.

Such an account applies to a limited number of works, and when magical realism is considered more widely, as an international genre, it can be viewed as constituting either a productive form of cultural **hybridity**, whose culturally heterogeneous texts and radically different voices encourage toleration of dissonance and hence are harbingers of improved literary and social relations, or else it slides into a primitivist colonial appropriation of voices and traditions, in which the indigenous and the folk are commodified and romanticized.

Isabel Allende's young-adult novel, *La ciudad de las bestias* (*City of the Beasts*, 2002), is susceptible to all three understandings of magical realism. Drawing on myth (the **legend** of **El Dorado**) as well as indigenous belief (the shamanistic transformation of self into totem animal, for instance), it hybridizes magical realism both with the coming-of-age narrative for younger readers (as English author David Almond also has done in several novels since 2001) and with the very recent genre of the eco-thriller. Hence, it employs a familiar quest structure to take Alex, its protagonist, from the "First World" to the heart of the Amazon jungle, where "the rules he was used to didn't count" and where, "in the hazy territory of dreams, intuition and magic," he encounters a tribe of mysterious indigenous people and even more mysterious beasts. Alex's narrative focalization of the People of the Mist shifts from a rational view to an understanding that entails an alternative perspective on the world. He learns, for example, to see and accept that the shaman, Walimai, has a spirit "angel wife." While *City of the Beasts* is a political novel about the destruction of the Amazon forest and its indigenous peoples, it is also about the rationalism and individualism that in the modern capitalist West erases human and spiritual values. Thus, as in the best magical realism, Allende's novel espouses epistemological diversity as a cultural corrective and interrogates realistic conventions of materiality and motivation in the quest for a better way of life.

See also Colonialism; Fantasy; Rushdie, Salman; Time and Place; Young Adult Fiction.

Further Readings: Camayd-Freixas, Erik. "Magical Realism as Primitivism: An Alternate Verisimilitude." *Romance Languages Annual* 9 (1998): 414–23; Faris, Wendy B. *Ordinary Enchantments: Magical Realism and the Remystification of Narrative*. Nashville: Vanderbilt University Press, 2004; Zamora, Lois Parkinson, and Wendy B. Faris, eds. *Magical Realism: Theory, History, Community*. Durham, NC: Duke University Press, 1995.

John Stephens

Maguire, Gregory (1954–)

Born in Albany, New York, Gregory Maguire is an author of **novel**s for adults, young adults, and children. He is best-known among adult readers for his best-selling novel *Wicked: The Life and Times of the Wicked Witch of the West* (1995). After receiving his Bachelor of Arts from the State University of New York, Albany, in 1976, Maguire taught English at Vincentian Grade School in Albany. He received a Master's degree from Simmons College in 1978 and a PhD in English and American literature from Tufts University in 1990. From 1979 to 1986, he taught at Simmons College Center for the Study of Children's Literature. Since 1987, Maguire has been a founding board member and codirector of Children's Literature New England, Inc., a nonprofit educational charity exploring the significance of **children's literature**.

Maguire has written more than a dozen novels for children and young adults. Many of them, such as *The Lightning Time* (1978) and *The Daughter of the Moon* (1980), feature magical elements and fairy-tale **motif**s, such as absent **mother**s. Set in Russia, *The Dream Stealer* (1983) consciously draws on traditional **Russian tales** and their motifs, including **Baba Yaga**, the Firebird, and Vasilissa the Beautiful. In 2004, Maguire published a collection of fractured fairy tales, *Leaping Beauty and Other Animal Fairy Tales*. These eight short stories are humorous retellings of popular fairy tales such as "**Sleeping Beauty**" ("Leaping Beauty"), "**Little Red Riding Hood**" ("Little Red Robin Hood"), and "**Rumplestiltskin**" ("Rumplesnakeskin")—but with animal protagonists. The Hamlet Chronicles series—which includes *Seven Sisters Spinning* (1994), *Six Haunted Hairdos* (1997), and *A Couple of April Fools* (2004)—features the unpredictable antics of a fifth-grade class in Hamlet, Vermont.

Like much of his work for children, Maguire's adult **fantasy** fiction also draws on elements from **literary fairy tale**s and oral **folktale**s. To date, Maguire has published five novels for adults, including the best-selling *Wicked*, which is an alternate backstory to L. Frank **Baum**'s classic novel, *The Wonderful Wizard of Oz* (1900). Told from the perspective of Elphaba, the green Munchkinlander who becomes the Wicked **Witch** of the West, it is a different take on Baum's Oz in which Elphaba defends the animals and attempts to unseat the tyrannical Wizard of Oz. In 2003, the novel was adapted into a Tony Award-winning Broadway musical by the same name, with music by Stephen Schwartz and lyrics by Winnie Holzman. Maguire's other novels for adults include *Confessions of an Ugly Stepsister* (1999), which tells the story of one of **Cinderella**'s stepsisters and which was adapted for American **television** (2002); *Mirror, Mirror* (2003), which is a retelling of **Snow White**; and *Lost* (2001), which combines motifs from classic literary tales such as Charles **Dickens**'s *A Christmas Carol* (1843) and **legend**s about Jack the Ripper. His most recent novel for adults is *Son of a Witch* (2005), the sequel to *Wicked*, which is set a decade later and tells the story of Liir, who might be the son of Elphaba. *See also* Adaptation; Young Adult Fiction.

Further Reading: "Maguire, Gregory." *Contemporary Authors.* Volume 226. Farmington Hills, MI: Thomson Gale, 2004. 227–60.

Linda J. Lee

Mailly, Jean, Chevalier de (c. 1724)

Jean, Chevalier de Mailly, was one of the few male authors who contributed to the wave of fairy-tale writing that swept France in the 1690s and the early years of the eighteenth century. His most important books in this vein were *Les illustres fées, contes galans dédiés aux dames (The Famous Fairies, Gallant Tales Dedicated to the Ladies*, 1698) and *Le voyage et les aventures des trois princes de Sarendip (The Voyage and Adventures of the Three Princes of Serendip*, 1719), a free translation of a pseudo-Persian tale by the little-known Italian writer Cristoforo Armenio (1557), later adapted by Voltaire for his *Zadig* (1747). A prolific writer, Mailly also published many books in other genres, including works on hunting and on natural history.

Mailly's *The Famous Fairies* is a collection of eleven tales drawn from many sources. Some tales conform in part to known folktale types, but Mailly probably encountered them in written form or possibly in the **salon**s. Significantly, this volume is "dedicated to the ladies," perhaps a subtle acknowledgment that he is entering a field then dominated by women writers; it is not surprising that his anonymous collection was at first misattributed to one of them. Like Marie-

Catherine d'**Aulnoy** and Henriette-Julie de Castelnau, Comtesse de **Murat**, French fairy-tale writers of the same period, Mailly clearly knew Giovan Francesco **Straparola**'s *Le piacevole notte* (*The Pleasant Nights*, 1550–53), which was translated and widely reprinted in France. At least three of his tales—"Fortunio," "Blanche-Belle" ("White Beauty"), and "Le Prince Guerini"—are based on that collection. He also drew on an episode in the same story by Cristoforo Armenio for his tale "Le bienfaisant ou Quiribini" ("The Good Man, or Quiribirini").

"La reine de l'isle des fleurs" ("The Queen of the Island of Flowers") is one of Mailly's most distinctive tales. He economically combines various **motif**s familiar from earlier sources and other contemporary tales: female rivalry between the aging and vindictive **queen** of the islands and a beautiful young **princess**; the ground opening up in front of the princess, as in the two versions of "Riquet à la houppe" ("Ricky with the Tuft") by Charles **Perrault** and Catherine **Bernard**; and the malign **transformation** of a young prince into a little dog and then his release from animal form, as in various tales by d'Aulnoy. (Some of his other tales contain even more magical transformations than those of his contemporaries, particularly "The Good Man, or Quiribirini.") The prince and princess are saved and united by the intervention of a beneficent **fairy**, a figure in many tales, who deprives the queen of the islands of her powers. In "Blanche-Belle," however, Mailly introduces a male sylph whose powers are greater than any fairy's.

A godson of Louis XIV, Mailly also included a long homage to a "great king" in the last tale of the collection, "L'isle inaccessible" ("The Inaccessible Island'), as well as a representation of the glittering entertainments at Versailles. *See also* French Tales.

Further Reading: Hannon, Patricia. "Feminine Voice and Motivated Text: Madame d'Aulnoy and the Chevalier de Mailly." *Merveilles et contes* 2 (1988): 13–24.

Elizabeth Wanning Harries

Malerba, Luigi (1927–)

Luigi Malerba, the pen name of the writer and journalist Luigi Bonardi, was born near Parma, Italy, and has throughout his career written fictional works for both children and adults. The fantastic and surreal figure prominently in his corpus, often taking expression in transgressive "modern **fable**s" that incorporate icons of our times, such as highways, skyscrapers, and computers, to comment on the solitude and difficulty of communication that permeates everyday reality. For example, in the early collection *La scoperta dell'alfabeto* (*The Discovery of the Alphabet*, 1963), one protagonist throws his house and then the window itself out of the window in a fit of anger, after which he begins a new, freer existence under the bridges of the Tiber.

Malerba's later children's works, *Mozziconi* (*Butts*, 1975) and *Storie dell'Anno Mille* (*Stories of the Year One Thousand*, 1977), also highlight the search for fresh ways of envisioning the past and the present. *Le galline pensieriose* (*Pensive Hens*, 1980) are short aphoristic fables in the vein of **Aesop**, whereas *Storiette tascabili* (*Little Pocket Tales*, 1984) are absurdist **parable**s on the paradoxes of modern consumerist society. The work most indebted to the fairy tale, whose marvelous dimension does not, in general, lure Malerba as much as the more realistic fable, is *Pinocchio con gli stivali* (*Pinocchio in Boots*, 1977). In this pastiche, Pinocchio's adventures are interlaced with those of other classic fairy-tale characters, such as **Little Red Riding Hood** and **Cinderella**, after he decides that he no longer wants to become a boy and escapes from his own story. Malerba uses the tale not only to poke fun at the original Pinocchio's "noble" aspiration but also to contest fixed narrative roles and functions. *See also* Italian Tales.

Further Reading: Accardo, Giovanni. "Le avventure della fantasia: I libri per bambini e per ragazzi di Luigi Malerba." *Studi novecenteschi* 23 (1996): 403–16.

Nancy Canepa

Märchen

Märchen is the internationally established German term for the genre broadly referred to in English as "**fairy tale**." In German, the word "Märchen" has existed since the Middle Ages and is the diminutive form of *Mär* or *Märe*. Originally, "Märchen" meant "news," "message," or "tidings." Gradually it acquired, in popular parlance, a pejorative connotation suggesting false news or rumor, a meaning that is still evident in the German expression "Erzähl mir keine Märchen" ("Don't tell me any fairy tales"; that is, "Don't tell me lies"). In the late eighteenth century, the word "Märchen" came to denote oral stories or **folktale**s.

Since the Renaissance, the genre signified by the term "märchen" (today adopted for use in English and not necessarily capitalized as in German) has had a remarkable literary development in western Europe that gave rise to the *Kunstmärchen*, or **literary fairy tale**. This literary phase of the genre's history can be traced in the works of the Italian authors Giovanni **Boccacio**, Giovan Francesco **Straparola,** and Giambattista **Basile**, in the *contes de fées* of seventeenth- and eighteenth-century French authors, and in the literary tales of many well-known German authors of the Enlightenment and Romantic eras, including Johann Wolfgang von **Goethe**, **Novalis**, Ludwig **Tieck**, Clemens **Brentano**, and E. T. A. **Hoffmann**.

It was, however, the German brothers Jacob and Wilhelm **Grimm** who played the most important role in establishing the märchen as a genre and concept. Their influential *Kinder-und Hausmärchen* (*Children's and Household Tales*, 1812–15) is effectively the most representative book of märchen worldwide, a landmark work that initiated countless collections of oral material in the years and decades following its publication. The Grimms' collection consists not only of fairy tales but also of diverse stories that have been adapted and transformed with morals suited especially for children. The Grimm brothers gave no concrete definition of the term "märchen." However, Jacob Grimm—in the preface to the 1816 edition of their German **legend**s (*Deutsche Sagen*)—did attempt to distinguish the märchen from the legend by writing, "The märchen is more poetic, the legend [*Sage*] more historical." In the wake of the Grimms, there have been many definitions of märchen; their common element refers to the genre's imaginary and poetic nature.

Further Readings: Lüthi, Max. *Märchen*. 9th expanded edition. Edited by Heinz Rölleke. Stuttgart: Metzler, 1996. 1–5; Thompson, Stith. *The Folktale*. 1946. Berkeley: University of California Press, 1977. 7–10.

Maria Kaliambou

Mardrus, Joseph Charles (1868–1949)

With his publication of a new French **translation** of *Les milles et une nuits* (*The Thousand and One Nights*, 1899–1904), Joseph Charles Mardrus was applauded by the literary avant-garde of the period. Born in Cairo, Mardrus studied medicine in Lebanon and then in

Paris, after which he traveled as a doctor on shipping lines in the Middle East and Asia until 1899, when he returned to Paris. While studying in Paris, Mardrus already was frequenting the circle of the symbolist poet Stéphane Mallarmé, who may have encouraged him to retranslate the *Nights*, and to whom the first volume is dedicated, along with the poet Paul Valéry. Volume five was dedicated to his wife, Lucie Delarue-Mardrus, a notable writer herself. Other volumes also were dedicated to prominent writers such as André Gide, Anatole France, Maurice **Maeterlinck**, and Marcel Schwob.

Mardrus clearly was familiar with Antoine **Galland**'s translation (based on a fourteenth-century Syrian manuscript), but the sources for his rendition of the *Nights* were the Egyptian Bulaq I edition of 1835 and the four-volume Calcutta II edition of 1839–42. Critical of Galland's editorial decisions, Mardrus claimed to carry out a more faithful and unexpurgated rendition of the *Nights*, notably retaining the poetry and religious language that Galland had edited out. Mardrus did not seek to "Frenchify" the *Nights* but rather attempted to maintain (and perhaps enhance) the text's "otherness" with his truly fin-de-siècle translation. *See also* Arabian Nights.
Further Reading: Larzul, Sylvette. *Les traductions françaises des Mille et une nuits: Étude des versions Galland, Trébutien et Mardrus.* Paris: L'Harmattan, 1996.

Anne E. Duggan

Marie de France (fl. 1160–1190)

Marie de France is a twelfth-century French author of **fable**s and lays (short narrative romances in verse), whose life is virtually unknown. All that is known about her is that, in her collection of fables, *Isopet*, she states: "My name is Marie and I am from France," thus emphasizing that, though she lived at the court of Henry II in England, she was a Frenchwoman. Experts have placed her work between 1160 and 1190 and dated her lays prior to 1170. In drawing from Celtic **folklore**, she composed her lays in the form of short narratives written in octosyllabic verse.

In accordance with storytelling convention, Marie de France claims to have merely written down the stories told to her. Varying in length between 118 and 184 lines, several of her twelve lays feature magical elements and **fairies**. All of her lays deal with the moral and social conflicts created by courtly love.

Focusing less on the events than on the characters' psychology, Marie de France presents love as a natural and spontaneous emotion that escapes convention. Although she subtly analyzes love as an irresistible force that provides an excuse for transgressing social laws, she lucidly depicts the high price the male protagonists especially must pay for character faults such as ingratitude and perfidy. While situated in the realm of medieval court society, her lays preserve the enchantment and magic of the original folk narratives. *See also* French Tales.
Further Readings: Burgess, Glyn S., and Keith Busby, trans. and ed. *The Lais of Marie de France.* Harmondsworth: Penguin, 1986; Harf-Lancer, Laurence, ed. *Lais de Marie de France.* Paris: Librairie Générale Française, 1990.

Harold Neemann

Marriage

Folktales and fairy tales present a mixed view of marriage. On the positive side, marriage (especially to a **prince** or **princess**) is the expected outcome of countless stories, the ultimate fairy-tale reward. However, marital conflicts also feature prominently in tales of many types, providing a sometimes-sordid catalog of infidelity, jealousy, and spousal abuse. Most traditional tales reflect the patriarchal values of the cultures in which they evolved, with authoritarian husbands and submissive wives. In a small but important subset of tales about marriage, the woman is in charge, often with positive results.

Unquestioned loyalty is a wife's first obligation toward her husband in many fairy tales. This allegiance is often tested through the conflict arising from a young bride's visit to her parents. "Østenfor sol og vestenfor måne" ("East of the Sun and West of the Moon"; ATU 425A, The Animal as Bridegroom) from *Norske Folkeeventyr* (*Norwegian Folktales*, 1841–44) by Peter Christen **Asbjørnsen** and Jørgen **Moe** offers an excellent example. A young woman whose spouse has the form of a bear by day but a man by night seeks permission to visit her parents. The husband consents, but warns her to not speak alone with her **mother**. She violates this requirement, with consequences that nearly lead to a permanent separation between the bride and her husband, who in truth is an enchanted prince.

The **tale type** generically titled Taming of the Shrew (ATU 901), famously dramatized by William **Shakespeare**, illustrates some of the extreme measures taken by folktale husbands to preserve their authority. Known internationally, this story still circulates as a **jest** or joke. In its simplest form, a man is riding home with his new bride when his horse stumbles. "That's once!" he shouts. It stumbles again, and he shouts "That's twice!" It stumbles a third time, and the man shoots it dead. "Wasn't that too strict?" asks the bride. "That's once!" replies the husband. Now knowing the consequences of displeasing her husband, she becomes a perfect wife.

The abuse demonstrated in type 901 tales is typically psychological and emotional but not physical. However, many folktales describe—even prescribe—wife beating. Foremost among these are tales of type ATU 670, The Man Who Understands Animal Languages. "The Bull and the Ass" from the **frame narrative** of the ***Arabian Nights*** is typical of **variant**s told around the world. A farmer is magically granted the ability to understand animal languages under the condition that he reveal this gift to no one. A conversation between a bull and an ass causes him to laugh out loud. His wife asks him why he is laughing. He refuses to tell her, but she persists. Nearly prepared to accede to her nagging, he overhears a rooster complaining that the master cannot control a single wife whereas he, the rooster, rules over fifty hens. Inspired by this message, the farmer beats his wife with a stick until she repents of her curiosity.

Not all tales about married couples are so misogynistic. In an important (albeit minority) group of tales, a berated or threatened wife takes control of her husband with a positive outcome. A dramatic example is "The Wife Who Would Not Be Beaten" (ATU 888A) from India, as recorded in *Folklore of the Santal Parganas* (1909) by Cecil Henry Bompas. A recently married man insists that his wife submit to a daily beating. She consents, but only on condition that he first prove himself a man by completing a successful trading expedition. The inept husband's journey is a disaster; he loses all of his merchandise and as a pauper is forced into slavery. The wife seeks out his place of servitude and through clever trickery recovers his lost fortune and restores his freedom. Recognizing his debt to her, the husband abandons all plans to beat her.

Adultery—actual or suspected—plays a role in many folktales. A famous example is the tale type called The Wager on the Wife's Chastity (ATU 882), known in folkloric and literary versions around the world, including Shakespeare's *Cymbeline* and Giovanni **Boccaccio**'s *Decameron* (2.9). As typically told, a man bets a merchant that he can seduce the latter's wife. To win the wager, the unprincipled bettor hides in a chest and has himself smuggled into the wife's bedroom. From this hiding place, he learns the location of a birthmark on the woman and thus convinces the merchant that his wife has been unfaithful. The angered husband orders his wife killed, but she escapes, disguised as a man. With time the truth comes to light, and the husband and wife are reunited.

Folktales originating in cultures accepting polygamous marriages often feature conflicts among co-wives. For example, in "The Story of Appayya" from Georgiana Kingscote's *Tales of the Sun; or, Folklore of Southern India* (1890), a Brahman's barren and jealous older wife attempts to poison a younger co-wife, now some seven months pregnant. However, through a stroke of good luck, a band of robbers eats the poisoned **food**; all perish, the credit for their demise going to the Brahman. The **king** rewards him with the hand of the princess for this supposed act of valor. The tale ends happily for all. The Brahman forgives his first wife for her jealousy, and the husband and his three wives live together in peace.

Less dramatic is the well-known Turkish tale, variously titled "The Favorite Wife" or "The Blue Beads" and featuring **Nasreddin** Hodja. Included in many anthologies, this jest tells how Nasreddin's two wives are jealous of one another until he secretly gives each a blue bead, privately instructing each woman that she should tell no one of the gift. Then he announces that his favorite wife is the one to whom he gave the blue bead, and all are satisfied. *See also* Animal Bride, Animal Groom; False Bride; Family; Father; Punishment and Reward; Sex, Sexuality.

Further Reading: Warner, Marina. "Reluctant Brides." *From the Beast to the Blonde: On Fairy Tales and Their Tellers.* New York: Farrar, Straus, and Giroux, 1994. 273–97.

D. L. Ashliman

Martín Gaite, Carmen (1925–2000)

Fairy tales play an important role in the works of the Spanish author Carmen Martín Gaite, the first woman to win Spain's Premio Nacional de Literatura in 1978. References to fairy tales occur in both her fiction and nonfiction. She appropriates the titles of two tales by Charles **Perrault** for essays in *El cuento de nunca acabar* (*The Never-Ending Tale*, 1983), an important reflection on narrative that she wrote after rereading Perrault's *Histoires ou contes du temps passé* (*Stories or Tales of Times Past*, 1697) for a **translation** of French fairy tales. All three of her works published for children are fairy tales. *El castillo de las tres murallas* (*The Three-Walled Castle*, 1981), a prize-winning novel illustrated by Juan Carlos Eguillor and considered by some critics to be her best work, was followed by *El pastel del diablo* (*The Devil's Cake*, 1985). *Caperucita en Manhattan* (**Little Red Riding Hood** *in Manhattan*, 1990) is a fairy-tale **novel** for readers of all ages, illustrated with thirteen childlike black-and-white drawings by the author herself. Dissatisfied with the passive characters of classic fairy tales, the author set out to rewrite Perrault's famous tale by presenting a courageous, confident heroine in contemporary New York City. In 1994, she published *La Reina de la Nieves* (*The Snow Queen*), a novel for adults inspired by Hans Christian **Andersen**'s "Snedronningen" ("The Snow Queen," 1845). *See also* Spanish Tales.

Further Readings: Beckett, Sandra L. *Recycling Red Riding Hood.* New York: Routledge, 2002. 308–31; Brown, Joan Lipman. *Secrets from the Back Room: The Fiction of Carmen Martín Gaite.* University, MS: Romance Monographs, 1987.

Sandra L. Beckett

Matičetov, Milko (1919–)

Milko Matičetov is a Slovene philologist and folklorist whose research focused on folk literature and religion. He collected folk narratives, especially **animal tale**s, from western Slovenia, Austria, Italy, and Hungary, documented the repertoire of tradition bearers, conducted **fieldwork**, and established a folk-narrative **archive**. His studies of literary **folklore** are based on the **historic-geographic method**.

Matičetov studied philology in Padua from 1938 to 1943 and received his doctorate in Ljubljana in 1955 with a study of a European story—little known at the time—about a man who is burned alive and reborn. That dissertation was published in 1961 as *Sežgani in prerojeni človek* (*Burned and Reborn Man*). From 1945 to 1952, Matičetov worked in the Ethnographic Museum and then, from 1952 to 1985, in the Institute of Slovene Ethnology in Ljubljana.

Among Matičetov's important works is the monograph *Umita in v prt zavita lobanja pri Slovencih* (*The Washed and Shrouded Skull among Slovenes*, 1955), a study of the burial of corpses and the washing of the skulls. His research culminated in collections from the Resian literary tradition with its characteristic traditional elements. These collections include *Rožice iz Rezije* (*Little Flowers from Resia*, 1972), dedicated to lyric poetry; and *Zverinice iz Rezije* (*Little Wild Animals from Resia*, 1973), a collection of animal tales in which the wild mammals (fox, bear, **wolf**, etc.) act and speak as human beings.

Matičetov was the editor of all Slovene ethnographic periodicals and was one of the founders of the free study group Alpes Orientales, which was established in 1956 and included ethnologists representing all nationalities in the eastern Alps. His scholarship includes research published in German, Italian, and other languages; and he received several international folklore awards. *See also* Slavic Tales.

Further Reading: Smerdel, Inja. "Etnološki krotilec zverinic: Milko Matičetov, raziskovalec ustnega slovstva." (With English summary: "An Ethnological Tamer of 'Little Creatures': Milko Matičetov, Researcher of Oral Literature.") *Etnolog: Bulletin of the Slovene Ethnographic Museum* 13 (2003): 133–64. http://www.etno-muzej.si/pdf/0354-0316_13_Smerdel_Etnoloski.pdf.

Mojca Ramšak

Matute, Ana María (1926–)

Famous for her semiautobiographical novels and short stories, Ana María Matute is also known for her parodic, some would say subversive, revisions of fairy tales that imitate the plots of and incorporate prominent intertextual links to classic works of children's fiction (see **Intertextuality**). Therefore, in her award-winning stories, the reader finds familiar elements from the works of authors such as Hans Christian **Andersen**, whom she credits for her career as a writer, Sir James Matthew **Barrie**, Lewis **Carroll**, and Charles **Perrault**. Like the Little Mermaid, Wendy, Alice, and **Cinderella**, the protagonists of Matute's *Primera memoria* (*First Memory*, 1959), *La trampa* (*The Trap*, 1969), *Sólo un pie descalzo* (*Only One Bare Foot*, 1983), and other works also develop without a mother's love. However, in contrast to these typically submissive female figures, Matute's strong-willed heroines make the reader rethink the codes of social indoctrination found in traditional stories.

Through her **feminist tales**, Matute, along with contemporaries such as Carmen **Martín Gaite**, challenged Spain's conservative literary establishment and thereby helped transform it into one that is now willing to accept diverse portrayals of female characters. A child during the Spanish Civil War, Matute also used these works to protest, in a way that successfully escaped censorship, stereotypical female roles promoted by Franco's postwar regime.

Further Readings: Anderson, Christopher L., and Lynne Vespe Sheay. "Ana María Matute's *Primera memoria*: A Fairy Tale Gone Awry." *Revista Canadiense de estudios Hispánicos* 14 (1989): 1–14; Soliño, María Elena. *Women and Children First: Spanish Women Writers and the Fairy Tale Tradition.* Potomac, MD: Scripta Humanística, 2002.

Candace Beutell Gardner

Maya Tales

The modern Maya are the descendants of the creators of the ancient Maya civilizations of southern Mexico, Guatemala, Honduras, and Belize, which flourished around 250–1500 CE. The ancient Maya erected great cities characterized by monumental architecture and possessed a highly developed economic, political, and religious organization. They utilized a complex, extremely precise calendar and wrote with a hieroglyphic system based on a combination of logographic and phonetic signs, preserved principally on buildings, monuments, and utensils. After the Spanish invasion, the Catholic clergy ordered the destruction of the numerous folded books (codices) in which the Maya had recorded historical and astronomical events, as well as scientific and other information. Only four survived this intellectual devastation.

During the last two decades of the twentieth century, knowledge of pre-Hispanic Maya culture greatly expanded, and more than half of all existing inscriptions have now been translated. In remote areas, the Cuchumatán Mountains of northwest Guatemala or among the Lacandón Maya of the Chiapas rainforest of Mexico for example, much of the ancient Maya culture has survived, either in relatively pure or syncretistic form. At the beginning of the twenty-first century, many contemporary Maya communities still reckoned time according to the ancient 260-day ceremonial calendar *(tzolkin),* which has been in uninterrupted use for more than 1,500 years.

During the colonial period, the Maya learned to use the Spanish alphabet and wrote down many of their most important **oral tradition**s in various Mayan languages. The *Books of Chilam Balam* from the seventeenth and eighteenth centuries contain information on religion, astronomy, rituals, and literature. Texts dealing with land rights and mythological and historical traditions have been preserved in various Mayan languages, especially K'iche' and Kaqchikel.

The most valuable preserved work, the *Popol Wuj (The Book of Counsel)* is at the same time the most extensive work of pre-Hispanic literature. Often referred to as the Bible of the K'iche' Maya, it was apparently transcribed from a sixteenth-century hieroglyphic text. It recounts the origin of the earth and humanity, as well as the migrations and history of the K'iche' Maya before the Spanish invasion. Many of the themes of the *Book of Counsel* turn up in the **folktale**s of the contemporary Maya. Another work preserved in K'iche' is the tragic dance-drama, *Rabinal Achi (The Lord of Rabinal),* which recounts the capture and ritual execution of a K'iche' warrior.

For a long time, the very existence of Maya folktales was in doubt, mainly because many groups of Maya opposed sharing their traditions with outsiders since their cultures had been despised for centuries and had been subject to disrespect and ridicule. Nevertheless, it has become clear that the modern Maya know and tell thousands of traditional folktales. Since the late nineteenth century, scholars, missionaries, and others have been collecting the oral traditions of the Maya. In many cases, the results are to be found in private and public

archives, and a number of collections have been published. However, there have been few serious studies of these materials, for folktales generally have been collected only as a by-product of the activities of specialists in other disciplines.

About 150 **tale type**s of European or African origin included in the Aarne-Thompson-Uther index may be found in Maya folktales: for example, ATU 1310A, Briar-Patch Punishment for Rabbit; ATU 313, The Magic Flight; and ATU 554, The Grateful Animals. There is little or nothing in the style of these tales that would lead one to suspect their nonindigenous origin, as they have been thoroughly adapted to Maya culture. For example, in Maya versions of ATU 327A, **Hansel and Gretel**, the children drop grains of corn, not bread crumbs, to mark the way home. On the other hand, many folktales, **epic**s, **legend**s, and **myth**s are obviously of native origin, particularly the numerous etiological myths (see **Etiologic Tale**) about the origins of maize, which is so important in Maya culture. In addition, numerous legends describe the origin of certain towns and their patron saints or protectors. Some native tales are extremely widely distributed, such as "The Man and the Buzzard," in which a man changes into a buzzard and vice versa. This tale has been recorded in sixteen of the thirty living Mayan languages. There is also a wide variety of indigenous tales of the supernatural, such as those dealing with the Lord of the Animals (who punishes abusive hunters), **witch**es who shed their skins, and assorted frightful monsters.

Many Maya folktales manifest elements both of indigenous and Old World origins. A noteworthy syncretistic example of the diverse origins of the folktales is the Q'anjob'al Maya folktale "Naj txonwom yetoj yistil" ("The Merchant and his Wife"), in which we can identify Motif F529.2, People without anuses (also attested among the K'iche' Maya and some South American Indian tribes); ATU 882, The Wager on the Wife's Chastity; Joseph's interpretation of Pharaoh's dream (Gen. 45:1–40); and the contemporary theme of a man who drinks to drown his sorrows.

Many Maya folktales tell of a weak but clever animal, usually a rabbit, who outwits a strong, stupid animal like a **coyote**. There are also a large number of stories about a human **trickster**, such as the notorious Pedro Rimares, who bests a Ladino (non-Maya), often a priest or merchant. Some scholars have conjectured that the popularity of these stories is based on the inability of the Maya to confront directly their Hispanic oppressors, so they like to hear stories of the weak vanquishing the strong.

The contemporary Maya not only continue to retell and publish their oral literature but have also expanded into the field of written literature, including **novel**s, short stories, and **poetry**, based on traditional themes.

Further Readings: Peñalosa, Fernando. *The Mayan Folktale: An Introduction.* Rancho Palos Verdes, CA: Yax Te' Press, 1996; _____. *Tales and Legends of the Q'anjob'al Maya.* Rancho Palos Verdes, CA: Yax Te' Foundation, 1999.

Fernando Peñalosa

Mayer, Charles-Joseph, Chevalier de (1751–1825)

Charles-Joseph, Chevalier de Mayer was an essayist, romance writer, and editor who compiled a monumental collection of French fairy tales between 1785 and 1789, the forty-one volume *Le cabinet des fées* (*The Fairies' Cabinet*). Born in Toulon, France, Mayer in his twenties wrote on a wide range of learned topics. Beginning in 1775, he collaborated with the Marquis de Paulmy d'Argenson on the latter's literary encyclopedia, *La bibliothèque universelle des romans* (*The Universal Library of Novels*), which featured excerpts of fiction and biographical notices of authors. Among the works Paulmy included were several fairy tales.

Mayer left the *Bibliothèque* in 1785 to undertake his own encyclopedic and ambitious collection of French fairy tales. By that time, the creation of literary tales, which had begun almost a century earlier with Charles **Perrault** and Marie-Catherine d'**Aulnoy**, not only had almost ceased, but many hard-to-find old tales were in danger of being forgotten. Mayer hoped to save what he considered the best fairy tales. He regarded them as sophisticated treatments of humanity's oldest stories. As he later expressed in his "Discours préliminaire," he believed that the central plots and themes of fairy tales were universal and served as the basis of both early literature and **myth**. Further, he explained that these essential ideas were developed characteristically by each culture. He felt special satisfaction with the artistic and moral refinement he found in **French tale**s.

Mayer judged that, after the initial outpouring of **literary fairy tale**s, much later work proved inferior, so he chose only from the tales he most esteemed for his collection. However, unable to include all he admired, he omitted tales that would survive on their own, such as those of Voltaire. He ruled out the **bawdy tale** as not representing the delicacy he believed essential to the *conte des fées*. Finally, Mayer arranged the stories according to his perception of their literary merit, for instance putting Perrault first and d'Aulnoy second among his authors.

As in the *Bibliothèque*, he also provided biographical information on 100 authors of fairy tales (many more than were represented by works in the *Cabinet*). Gathering the information was a major undertaking, since many writers had published anonymously or under pseudonyms. Mayer's notes range from one-sentence remarks that he could identify nothing except the name of an author to lengthy discussions of the work of others. He even included a facetious third-person notice of himself.

Mayer is credited with saving both tales and records of authors that might otherwise have been lost and bringing them to the attention of later readers, some of whom (as he hoped) discovered in the *Cabinet* inspirations for their own imaginative literature. *See also* Salon.

Further Reading: Mayer, Charles-Joseph de. "Discours préliminaire." Volume 18. *Le Nouveau cabinet des Fées.* Edited by Jacques Barchilon. Geneva: Slatkine Reprints, 1978.

Paul James Buczkowski

McKillip, Patricia A. (1948–)

Patricia McKillip is a successful American **fantasy** author notable for dense, evocative prose and richly imagined descriptions, often with a self-reflexive element that uses magic as a metaphor for narrative itself. Fairy-tale elements are a recurring thread in her writing, particularly talking beasts, fairy realms, and the effects of spells and curses, perhaps most vividly in the wise magical beasts of *The Forgotten Beasts of Eld* (1974) or the **witch**'s curse of *In the Forests of Serre* (2003). Her earlier **novel**s include the Riddle-Master trilogy (1976–79), a more conventional fantasy series centering on the encapsulation of both **legend** and history into ritualized **riddle**s, revealing a precise and powerful awareness of the interrelation of structure and meaning. *The **Sorceress** and the Cygnet* (1991) depicts magical figures who are simultaneously constellations, heraldic signs, and compelling figures at the heart of folkloric narratives that must be understood and reenacted before the novel's conflicts can be resolved.

The other recurring element in McKillip's writing is the realm of **faerie**, particularly the difficult, heartbreaking transition between fairyland and the real world. *Winter Rose* (1996) is a fairy bride story with echoes of "Tam Lin," while in *The Book of Atrix Wolfe* (1995), an exile from the fairy realm struggles with her identity. *The Tower at Stony Wood* (2000) self-consciously recreates and represents the knightly romance but also includes **false bride** and selkie **motif**s and a magical **mirror**. *See also* Young Adult Fiction.

Further Reading: Greenlee, Jessica. "No Longer Divided: Wholeness in *Winter Rose*." *Extrapolation: A Journal of Science Fiction and Fantasy* 42 (2001): 75–86.

Jessica Tiffin

McKinley, Robin (1952–)

Robin McKinley is an American writer of **fantasy** and fairy tale who lives in England with her husband, fantasy novelist Peter Dickinson. She is notable for novel-length expansions of fairy tales that lend depth, texture, and characterization to classic forms without compromising their flavor. She has also published short-story collections and more mainstream fantasy **novel**s. Her work is pitched mostly at the young-adult market and tends to feature resourceful, practical heroines overcoming marginalization and psychological crises on the way to completing more external quests, often with the assistance of animal companions such as dogs or horses. She has considerable sensitivity to the workings of fairy tale and of symbolic fantasy, but her writing, while effective, is at times emotionally overwrought, and her style can shift uneasily between the pragmatic and the overly elevated. She is better in tales with a darker edge, which balances her tendency toward romanticism.

Almost all of McKinley's work relies to some extent on fairy tale or folkloric patterns. Novels such as *The Blue Sword* (1982) and its companion tale, the Newbury Medal-winning *The Hero and the Crown* (1984), are fantasies in the sword-and-sorcery vein but rely on a similarly essentialist story shapes. *The Blue Sword*'s heroine finds and reclaims her heritage as both warrior and **sorcerer**; Lady Aerin of *The Hero and the Crown* is a **dragon**-slayer in a particularly gritty and realistic mode. Tales in McKinley's shared collection with Peter Dickinson, *Elementals: Water* (2002), and her own short-story collection, *A Knot in the Grain* (1994), continue to explore the world of Damar established in *The Blue Sword*, although their heroines are wielders of magic rather than warriors. McKinley has also edited an anthology of fantasy short stories, several with folkloric themes. *Imaginary Lands* (1985) includes tales by Dickinson, Patricia **McKillip**, and Jane **Yolen**, and won the World Fantasy Award.

McKinley's interest in the field of fairy tale is broad, as seen in her 1988 retelling of George **MacDonald**'s *The Light Princess* (1893), packaged as a children's picture book. Generally, however, her technique is to lend realism and detail to the bare bones of recognizable plots, which is particularly effective in her novel-length fairy tales. The earliest of these is *Beauty* (1978), a retelling of "**Beauty and the Beast**." It presents an essentially undisrupted version of the tale but with attractive, appealing details and rounded characterization. The "Beauty and the Beast" story appears to be central to McKinley's personal mythology, as she has subsequently written a second retelling, *Rose Daughter* (1997), which explores and expands the motif of the rose in Jeanne-Marie **Leprince de Beaumont**'s tale. She constructs an interesting magical framework around the significance of roses, but the story is otherwise rushed and somewhat tangled. *The Door in the Hedge* (1981) contains a selection of rewritten fairy tales, including a particularly effective retelling of "The **Frog**

King" infused with considerable menace and a version of "The Twelve Dancing Princesses" that adds substance and appeal to the figure of the **soldier**. The other tales are more generally folkloric: one story of an enchanted deer and a story about the **faerie** realm and the stealing of mortal children whose conclusion is somewhat overly utopian.

Perhaps the best of McKinley's adaptations are *Deerskin* (1993) and *Spindle's End* (2000), dealing respectively with the "Donkey Skin" tale and "**Sleeping Beauty**." *Deerskin* is very much darker than *Beauty*, a development of the incestuous implications in the original tale; the **princess** is not only desired by her mad, enchanted **father** but also brutally raped by him before fleeing. The intervention of a moon-goddess figure and McKinley's characteristic reliance on friendly pets as a source of healing and identity allow a realistically partial redemption of the traumatized princess. *Spindle's End* similarly demonstrates McKinley's ability to highlight and develop significant **motif**s in the fairy tale; its magic-saturated kingdom is whimsical and charming, providing considerable background logic in explaining the importance of christening blessings. The novel's most effective aspect is its restructuring of the Sleeping Beauty story to allow the princess to be brought up outside the curse, oblivious to her true identity, with obvious emotional repercussions for her parents and for her when she discovers the truth. The character-switching that attempts to neutralize the christening curse is, again, slightly confused, but ultimately effective; the motif of the friendly **animal helper** is taken here to somewhat excessive extremes.

Folkloric elements recur in much of McKinley's fantasy, even when she is not explicitly rewriting a fairy tale. Most obviously, she has written a young-adult version of the Robin Hood story, *The Outlaws of Sherwood* (1988). This again works to add depth of characterization and to some extent historicization. Like many of her novels, it is enjoyable without being a significantly original adaptation. *The Stone Fey* (1998), a reissue of McKinley's own contribution to *Imaginary Lands* as an illustrated children's book, is more innovative. Its analysis of the faerie-lover motif is evocative, focusing mostly on its effect on the young girl who falls in love with the fey. The tension between the real and the faerie realms is beautifully drawn. This contrast is common to many of McKinley's strongest tales, notably "A Knot in the Grain" from the collection of the same title and "A Pool in the Desert" in *Elementals*. Both stories derive strength from their situation in the real, mundane world and their exploration of the magical as an alternative, whether it is ultimately rejected or embraced. A similar pattern underlies McKinley's most recent work, *Sunshine* (2003), a strong, intelligent, and original version of vampire mythology set in an urban alternative universe with many points in common with our own. This could be read as yet another version of "Beauty and the Beast" in its focus on the heroine's relationship with the monstrous "other" of the vampire. *See also* Bachelier, Anne; Incest; Woman Warrior; Young Adult Fiction.

Further Readings: Hains, Maryellen. "Beauty and the Beast: 20th Century Romance?" *Merveilles et contes* 3 (1989): 75–83; Rutledge, Amelia A. "Robin McKinley's *Deerskin*: Challenging Narcissisms." *Marvels & Tales* 15 (2001): 168–82.

Jessica Tiffin

Megas, Georgios A. (1893–1976)

Greek folklorist and academician Georgios A. Megas made significant contributions to **folklore** and **folktale** studies in Greece. His special contribution to folktale studies was framed by the European movement in the early twentieth century to collect, archive, and classify folktales. Megas used primarily the **historic-geographic method** in his research. In 1910, he was charged by Nikolaos Politis, the founder of folklore studies in Greece, with compiling a catalogue of Greek folktales according to the Aarne-Thompson classification system. This task turned into a lifetime project due to the continuous process of **collecting** and classifying new Greek **variant**s. Megas left some 20,000 summaries of classified folktale variants and introduced 509 **oicotype**s to fit the Greek corpus into the Aarne-Thompson classification. Most parts of his catalogue remain unpublished. Himself a fieldworker, Megas encouraged the collection of folktales by any means, and his work has been responsible for increasing the number of Greek folktale variants that have been transcribed. Megas's scholarship has had an international impact and consists of more than 200 essays, monographs, and collections, especially in Greek and German. *See also* Aarne, Antti; Archives; Fieldwork; Greek Tales; Tale Type; Thompson, Stith.

Further Readings: Megas, Georgios A. *Das Märchen von Amor und Psyche in der griechischen Volksüberlieferung.* Athens: Academy of Athens Publications, 1971; Puchner, Walter. "Der unveröffentlichte Zettelkasten eines Katalogs der griechischen Märchentypen nach dem System von Aarne-Thompson von Georgios A. Megas." *Die heutige Bedeutung oraler Traditionen: Ihre Archivierung, Publikation und Index-Erschliessung.* Edited by Walther Heissig and Rüdiger Schott. Opladen: Westdeutscher Verlag, 1998. 87–105.

Marilena Papachristophorou

Méliès, Georges (1861–1938)

One of the founding fathers of cinema, the French director, producer, and actor Georges Méliès began his career as a magician, running the Robert-Houdin Theater, a background that clearly had an impact on his approach to the new medium. Whereas the Lumière brothers would be considered the originators of the realist film, Méliès set the stage for the fantastic on screen. He accidentally discovered stop-action technique, and his work was groundbreaking in the history of special effects. Along with fairy, magic, and Orientalist films, Méliès also produced the first science-fiction film in cinema history, *Le voyage dans la lune* (*A Trip to the Moon*, 1902).

To create his films, Méliès drew heavily from vaudeville *féeries*, or fairy plays, that were popular from the beginning of the nineteenth century well into the Second Empire. Writers such as Marc-Antoine Désaugiers and the brothers Cogniard adapted for the stage fairy tales, Oriental tales, stories about demons, and even science-fiction stories aimed at a largely lower-class audience who marveled at the spectacles created by theatrical machines. Méliès used the new technology of film to continue to improve upon well-established theatrical conventions of appearance, disappearance, **transformation**, and change of scenes developed for the vaudeville *féerie*. Even the apotheosis concluding many of Méliès's films comes from the *féerie* tradition.

The impact of the *féerie* is evident not just in the form of Méliès's films, but also in the choice of subjects. Méliès produced three films derived from tales by Charles **Perrault** that have vaudeville antecedents: the now-lost 1899 version of *Cendrillon* (**Cinderella**), remade in 1912; *Le petit chaperon rouge* (**Little Red Riding Hood**, 1901); and *Barbe-bleue* (**Bluebeard**, 1901). *Le royaume des fées* (*The Kingdom of the Fairies*, 1903) takes its inspiration from the Cogniards' *La biche au bois, ou Le royaume des fées* (*The Doe in the Woods, or the Kingdom of the Fairies*, 1853), whose title recalls a tale by Marie-Catherine d'**Aulnoy**.

Like *The Kingdom of the Fairies, Le palais des mille et une nuits* (*The Palace of the Thousand and One Nights*/**Arabian Nights**, 1905), *La fée carabosse ou le poignard fatal* (*The Witch*, 1906), and *Le chevalier des neiges* (*The Knight of the Snows*, 1912) all concern a lover who, separated from his **princess**, must perform marvelous feats to be reunited with her, a stock plot that underpinned the vaudeville *féerie*.

Méliès was a prolific filmmaker, producing movies with Orientalist flavor, such as *Tchin-Chao, le thaumaturge chinois* (*The Chinese Conjurer*, 1904). Others had fantastic creatures, such as *La sirène* (*The Mermaid*, 1904); **magic object**s, such as *Les cartes vivantes* (*The Living Playing Cards*, 1905); and fanciful characters, such as *Le baron de Munchhausen* (1911). Through his use of special effects that supported his fantastic vision of cinema, Georges Méliès was one of the most important pioneers of early cinema. *See also* Arabian *Nights* Films; Film and Video; French Tales; Silent Films and Fairy Tales; Theater.

Further Readings: Frazer, John. *Artificially Arranged Scenes: The Films of Georges Méliès*. Boston: G. K. Hall, 1979; Kovacs, Katherine Singer. "Georges Méliès and the 'Féerie.'" *Cinema Journal* 16.1 (Autumn 1976): 1–13; Sadoul, Georges. *Georges Méliès*. Paris: Seghers, 1961.

Anne E. Duggan

Memorate

Swedish folklorist Carl Wilhelm von Sydow coined the term "memorate" in 1934 to refer to a first-person story about a personal supernatural experience to distinguish it from what he called a "fabulate," a traditional folk story told in the third person that is well known and shared in and across communities, the **legend** being a prime example. Von Sydow argued that recognizing generic distinctions between these story forms allowed scholars more accurate understandings of underlying folk beliefs.

Other scholars, however, have seen the relationship between first-person and third-person folk narratives as an intricate, overlapping one. A narrator's personal story about encountering a ghost, for example, may become what folklorists Linda **Dégh** and Andrew Vázsonyi have called a "proto-memorate" at the core of many a **ghost story**. Storytellers may personalize traditional narratives by making themselves protagonists and so turn legends into memorates, or they may frame their memorates as if they were **folktale**s or **fairy tale**s.

Folklorist Sandra Dolby Stahl has argued that any personal narrative might be considered a secular memorate. Currently, "memorate" is often generalized to refer to all personal experience narratives, not only to those about the supernatural, and so connects folk narratives to autobiography and memoir. *See also* Memory.

Further Readings: Honko, Lauri. "Memorates and the Study of Folk Belief." 1965. *Nordic Folklore: Recent Studies*. Edited by Reimund Kvideland and Henning K. Sehmsdorf. Bloomington: Indiana University Press, 1989. 100–09; Stahl, Sandra Dobly. *Literary Folkloristics and the Personal Narrative*. Bloomington: Indiana University Press, 1989.

Janet L. Langlois

Memory

The processes by which storytellers and their audiences can store the materials of **folklore** in their minds largely determines the forms in which these materials exist. The processes have to do with mental images, with the manner in which they are relayed through words, and with the culturally conditioned conventions. In such terms, folklore is dependent on the multiple interactions among imagination, language, and social context. The individual memory is also conditioned by issues of taste, emotion, and choice; again, the individual storyteller influences, and is influenced by, the community that is his or her audience.

Folklore, like memory understood psychologically, depends greatly on **context**. It is very difficult to gain reliable insights into the transmission of narrative through experiment, as the conditions of a particular experiment can hardly be taken as representative of real life. The procedure followed in the "method of repeated reproduction," as carried out by F. C. Bartlett, for instance, was to note the developments and contractions in a story as told at different stages by one person, and as it passed from one person to another. He selected twenty university students, gave a story to each of them to read, and had each student write it down at intervals over a long period. He also gave a story to read to one student only and arranged that the story would be relayed individually from one student to the next in a series and written down by each.

Though these experiments showed a great deal about how stories are preserved, the individuals were acting in isolation, and the procedure did not take into account the multiple transmission in all directions within an actual community and the multifarious influences and re-influences that can occur at all sorts of intervals in a real cultural context. Also, the stories used were of a particular type—one a Native American tale and the other an African tale—and these would not necessarily be the kinds of lore that would be relayed in their own cultural context by the English university students employed in the experiments. The use of writing rather than oral delivery could also be misleading, as the basic aspect of the transmission of folklore is from the mouth to the ear rather than in set form on a page for the eye. Notwithstanding these reservations, Bartlett's experiments, and research carried out by others on similar lines, are of value in that they reveal certain alterations at work. These are enumerated by Bartlett himself as familiarization (allowing the story to be influenced by previously known material), rationalization (making it acceptable to previously known patterns of thinking), and dominance (selecting some aspects of the story and placing extra stress on them).

One clear benefit of such "laboratory" experiments is that they emphasize that the memorization of narrative material is greatly indebted to the individual mind. In this sense, we may speak of the internal transmission of lore or even of "personal tradition." The term "**memorate**" is usually employed to denote a specifically supernatural experience as described by the individual who experienced it, but the concept of a "memorate" may be extended to include an account of any especially dramatic personal experience. In the telling of such memorates, a person may be influenced by, or be recalling, a previous telling rather than the original experience itself; so the question of transmission is internalized. A similar process often can be noted for the relaying of other more developed and complicated kinds of narrative—such as oral **legend**s, **folktale**s, or even **epic** stories. In all of these cases, traits may be identified as belonging to particular tellers.

The particular traits become clearer and more lasting as plot variations within communal tradition. Here, variations, and resultant development, are due to the contributions of many individuals, both tellers and hearers. It should be noted, however, that the very number of tradition-bearers increases the influence of an opposing tendency, that of standardization. Again, as with the individual, the community does not easily tolerate radical breaks with received tradition, and any unwarranted or dislocating deviation from either imagery or plot will soon be corrected. Furthermore, the very process of verbal-aural transmission requires that the plot communicates easily, and for this reason, it must be reasonably familiar and in the context rational.

Since folklore can be defined basically as the preservation of information by oral and customary means, its basic stages of development must follow the pattern of interaction between thought and speech. Folklorists will therefore differentiate between initial material and material that has become full-fledged folklore. The use of speech in ordinary conversation clearly does not come under the heading of folklore, as it is fleeting and "spontaneous" by nature. A more preserved form of speech is rumor, or information that lasts for a while and can therefore be described as "current." Folklore, however, goes beyond this again, attaining to a kind of permanence that we call "traditional"—it takes on a life of its own, and in its import need not directly relate to any particular social circumstance. A direct result of this is that a special kind of creativity is evinced by the folk narrative, a process that the psychologist Ian M. L. Hunter described as a largely unconscious recreating of the narrative from fragmentary recall. The folklorist Alan Bruford has described the telling of a tale as the skilled verbal representation of a series of mental tableaux. In the whole process, individual bearers of tradition vary in terms of the received structure, the style, and the aptness of improvisation.

In studying the workings of memory in folklore, it is most desirable to be able to observe the preservation of data within an oral community over a prolonged period. It is not easy to find the ideal situation for this in the contemporary world, given the prevalence of information gained through literacy and mass communications. Good insights have, however, been gained where a definite starting point for a narrative can be identified, such as a manuscript or rare literary source. Where reintroduction at some intermediary stage may be ruled out for the relevant purposes, the **variant**s that have developed from such a unique source can be compared. Much can thereby be learned about how **folk** "memory" is dependent on, and susceptible to, factors such as social structure and values, personal fancy, geographical location, and above all the strength of folklore itself in the particular heritage. *See also* Oral Theory; Oral Tradition.

Further Readings: Bartlett, F. C. "Some Experiments on the Reproduction of Folk Stories." 1920. *The Study of Folklore.* Edited by Alan Dundes. Englewood Cliffs, NJ: Prentice-Hall, 1965. 243–58; Bruford, Alan. *Gaelic Folk-Tales and Mediaeval Romances.* Dublin: The Folklore of Ireland Society, 1969. 210–49; Dégh, Linda. "The Memorate and Protomemorate" *Journal of American Folklore* 87 (1974): 225–39; Hunter, Ian M. L. *Memory.* Middlesex: Penguin Books, 1964; Stahl, Sandra Dolby. *Literary Folkloristics and the Personal Narrative.* Bloomington: Indiana University Press, 1989.

Dáithí Ó hÓgáin

Men

Men have figured prominently in fairy tales and folktales as well as in fairy-tale and folktale scholarship. Much of our understanding of the ways in which men are represented and the roles they have played in shaping, transmitting, performing, collecting, and organizing tales grows out of feminist scholarship begun in the 1970s. For instance, feminist critiques of the representation of **women** and girls in fairy tales and folktales also focus attention on the representation of men and boys, particularly in the European tradition. Feminist scholars point out that men and boys are more often active participants in determining their fates and are heroes in their own stories; they are mobile, free to roam the world—not to mention the underworld and other nether-kingdoms—in pursuit of their quests, often overcoming great odds through the assistance of **magic helper**s, animals, and women and girls. Whereas female characters are typically punished for pursuing their curiosity, male characters often strike out on new adventures and make their way in the world. Similarly, within the European fairy-tale and folktale tradition, men are also more likely to be active speakers. In a study of Jacob and Wilhelm **Grimm**'s *Kinder- und Hausmärchen* (*Children's and Household Tales*, 1812–15), Ruth B. Bottigheimer points out that through a combination of the Grimms' editorial decisions and the tales' plot elements, men are active speakers—often presented as using direct speech and active verbs, for instance—whereas women are consigned to silence. For both male and female characters, the gendered relationship to speech reflects the dominant social values of the time as well as the Grimms' attempts to perpetuate hegemonic **gender** identities.

Within European fairy tales and folktales, men are also frequently represented by beasts and animals; not only are they the enchanted beasts of such tales as "Beauty and the Beast" (ATU 425C), but they might also be transformed into beastly worms and snakes as well as more common animals such as lions, stags, geese, swine, frogs, and even hedgehogs. In East Asian tales, by comparison, **transformation**s often occur in the opposite direction, whereby animals become men, and even more commonly, women; thus, **Japanese tales**, for example, offer examples of young men who unknowingly marry *kitsune* (foxes) who have taken the shape of beautiful women. After years of domestic bliss, the husband discovers that his wife is a *kitsune*, and he forces her to leave; in some tales, the husband awakens disoriented and far from home and must return in shame.

Scholars with an interest in psychoanalysis as well as practicing psychoanalysts have mined fairy tales and folktales for precisely these sorts of representations and symbols. Jungian psychoanalysts and their scholarly counterparts have argued that such representations of men are part of a larger set of universal **archetype**s for masculinity, while Freudian psychoanalysts and their scholarly counterparts have suggested that such transformations are means by which storytellers address and negotiate their own and/or others' anxieties about masculine **sexuality**.

Outside the world of the tales themselves, men have also played active, leading roles in the **performance, collecting, editing,** and organization of tales. As storytellers, men have shaped individual tales according to their own life experiences, goals, and struggles. Male fairy-tale and folktale collectors and editors are also largely responsible for establishing some of our most widely known anthologies and national **archives**: Jacob and Wilhelm Grimm in Germany, Peter Christen **Asbjørnsen** and Jorgen **Møe** in Norway, Aleksandr **Afanes'ev** in Russia, and Andrew **Lang** in England. Even if many of the storytellers who provided tales for these collections were women, it was the male collectors and editors who most fully shaped those tales for public consumption, often encoding their own social values into the collections through editorial decisions of the sort described above. Men also wrote **literary fairy tale**s, much as their female counterparts did, and some of the most famous literary tales we have today—the ones that have long been considered canonical—were penned by men, including Giambattista **Basile**, Charles **Perrault**, and Hans Christian **Andersen**. In addition, their tales often provide the foundation for the cinematic versions created by one of the greatest storytellers of our time, Walt **Disney**, who further shaped fairy tales according to dominant American ideas about gender as well as his own. Beyond fairy-tale and folktale performing, collecting, and editing, men were also crucial in determining the course of fairy-tale and folktale scholarship. As feminist scholars such as Torborg Lundell have pointed out, even the seemingly objective tools we use in studying fairy tales and folktales are marked by the men who created them. In her study of Antti **Aarne** and Stith **Thompson**'s *The Types of the Folktale* and Thompson's *Motif-Index of Folk-Literature*, Lundell demonstrates the ways in which these indexes replicate the dominant view of the tales themselves, presenting women as little more than passive beauties.

Beyond the academic realm, Robert **Bly** has focused on the Grimms' tale "Iron Hans" (also known as "Iron John," ATU 502), together with **legend**s and **myth**s from many different cultural areas, to structure his vision for a contemporary men's movement. In his 1990 book *Iron John: A Book about Men*, Bly offers a detailed reading of "Iron John" through the lens of psychoanalytic theories of Carl Gustav **Jung** to explain why American men are largely dissatisfied and emotionally underdeveloped. What Bly finds most appealing about "Iron John" is the wild-man helper who "mentors" the young boy on his quest; for Bly, reviving (or inventing) rites of passage to mark boys' transition to manhood such as he finds in this tale and creating a tradition of male mentoring would help men understand how to be masculine (in the traditional sense) while also holding on to feminist values. Bly's use of "Iron John" in the service of the men's movement underscores the many ways in which fairy tales and folktales continue to resonate with men's lives and the diverse ways in which men continue to perform, shape, and transmit them. *See also* Feminism.

Further Readings: Bernheimer, Kate, ed. *Brothers and Beasts: An Anthology of Men on Fairy Tales.* Detroit: Wayne State University Press, 2007; Bly, Robert. *Iron John: A Book about Men.* New York: Vintage Books, 1990; Bottigheimer, Ruth B. "Silenced Women in the Grimms' Tales: The 'Fit' Between Fairy Tales and Society in Their Historical Context." *Fairy Tales and Society: Illusion, Allusion, and Paradigm.* Edited by Ruth B. Bottigheimer. Philadelphia: University of Pennsylvania Press, 1986. 115–31; Lundell, Torborg. "Gender-Related Biases in the Type and Motif Indexes of Aarne and Thompson." *Fairy Tales and Society: Illusion, Allusion, and Paradigm.* Edited by Ruth B. Bottigheimer. Philadelphia: University of Pennsylvania Press, 1986. 149–63; Taggart, James. *The Bear and His Sons: Masculinity in Spanish and Mexican Folktales.* Austin: University of Texas Press, 1997; Tatar, Maria. "Born Yesterday: The Spear Side." *The Hard Fact of the Grimms' Fairy Tales.* 2nd edition. Princeton, NJ: Princeton University Press, 2003. 85–105; Zipes, Jack. "Spreading Myths about Iron John." *Fairy Tale as Myth/Myth as Fairy Tale.* Lexington: University Press of Kentucky, 1994. 96–118.

Kimberly J. Lau

Mermaid

A mermaid—half human, half fish—is said to be an especially beguiling water creature whose beautiful voice lures seafarers to their deaths. Inhabiting an underwater world otherwise identical to that of humans, a mermaid may surface to sit on rocks while admiring her blue eyes in a **mirror** and combing her golden or greenish locks of hair. The mermaid possesses no immortal soul, casts no shadow, and cannot shed tears. These characteristics appear in **folklore** and fairy tales of mermaids as seductresses, protectresses, or the incarnations of woman's sacrifice in patriarchy.

The mermaid known today is of mixed ancestry and a somewhat confusing lineage. Many scholars suggest the classical mermaid developed her physical attributes from various semi-zoomorphic figures, such as the Babylonian sea god Oannes (the half-man, half-fish principal deity of the Sumerian creation **epic**) and the Semitic fertility/moon goddess Atergatis/Derceto. Mermaids also trace their ancestry to various Greek sea creatures (the Nereides, Tritons, and Tritonids), with their most important ancestors being the alluring Sirens of

"The Little Mermaid" illustrated by Linley Sambourne in *Three Tales of Hans Andersen* (London: Macmillan and Co., Ltd., 1910), p. 55. [Courtesy of the Eloise Ramsey Collection of Literature for Young People, University Libraries, Wayne State University]

Homer's *Odyssey*. Those woman-faced birds, themselves descended from the ancient Egyptian Ba (demons of death sent to capture souls), account for the mermaid's captivating, often-fatal song and her preoccupation with the human soul. Physiologus's early Christian bestiary (second-fourth century) provided her first description: "a beast of the sea wonderfully shapen as a maid from the navel upward and a fish from the navel downward, and this beast is glad and merry in tempest and sad and heavy in fair weather." Later medieval bestiaries cemented her accoutrements (comb and mirror) and her image as a siren-songed, vain, and beautiful temptress dangerous to the human soul. Paracelsus's treatise on the elementary spirits, *Liber de nymphis, sylphis, pygmaeis et salamandris et de ceteris spiritibus* (*Book of Nymphs, Sylphs, Pygmies and Salamanders and Other Spirits*, 1566), introduced the idea of the mermaid's longing for an immortal soul she could gain through marriage to a human; his opining precipitated the mermaid's shift from seductress to a water creature in need of Christian help—a shift that would inform many later literary reworkings.

In maritime folklore, a mermaid was a harbinger of storms and sea disasters, or a mariner's protectress. She could be helpful—bestowing gold, silver, cattle, great shipbuilding skills, bountiful catches, or healing powers—or vengeful—her captor might be drowned and whole towns washed away. At sea, a sighted mermaid was carefully watched: if she followed a ship, sailors feared disaster; good fortune ensued if she turned away. Her tossing of fish (a symbol of the abducted Christian soul) toward the ship portended some crewmembers' doom; tossing fish away from the ship signaled deliverance. For centuries, respected seafarers, historians, and scientists—from Pliny the Elder to Alexander the Great, Christopher Columbus, and Henry Hudson—confirmed the existence of mermaids, based on sightings or captures (and dissections) from Ceylon to the Arctic Ocean. There have been reports of a mermaid washed ashore as recently as the 2004 Indian Ocean tsunami.

Mermaid tales are known around the world, often transmitted through maritime influences. In Asia, the Javanese mermaid goddess Loro Kidul aids men collecting birds' nests from cliffs. In west-coastal Sumatra, the **legend** of the mermaid Sikambang has impacted local **storytelling**, **dance**, and **music** traditions. Ma, the creation goddess in many African **myth**s, inspired numerous tales in the black and mixed-race communities of the Cape Verde Islands; Black Portuguese immigrants brought them to North America, where they circulate in the West Indies, the Sea Islands, and along the coast to Cape Cod. **Native American tales** tell of mermaid worship along the Pascagoula River in Louisiana and Lake Mashapang in Connecticut. Mermaid tales are also common in Iceland and the Faeroe Islands, Norway, Denmark, Scotland, and among the Lapps, the Orkneys, and Shetland Islanders, with the greatest concentration in nearly all-coastal areas of Ireland. It is this northern group of tales that accounts for many of the numerous mermaid **motif**s in Stith **Thompson**'s *Motif-Index of Folk-Literature:* namely, Motif B81.2 (Mermaid marries man); D1410.4 (Possession of mermaid's belt gives power over her); F611.1.14 (Strong hero son of woman of the sea); F611.2.2 (Strong hero suckled by mermaid); and R138.1 (Mermaid rescues hero [boy] from shipwreck). Accounts of mer-lineage among financially and politically powerful families are still an active belief in contemporary Ireland and Greece.

Mermaid lore found its way into **literary fairy tale**s (another case of mixed ancestry), where mermaids, **Undine**s, Melusines, nixies, selkies, nymphs, water sprites, and kelpies often merged. The mermaid shifted from a powerful, siren-voiced temptress to a mute, shadowless, soulless creature in need of human aid for her eternal redemption. Many Elizabethan writers, including William **Shakespeare** and John Milton, made reference to mer-

The famous statue of The Little Mermaid in Copenhagen, Denmark. [Courtesy of Shutterstock]

maids, but the most influential literary interpretations began with German writer Friedrich de la Motte **Fouqué**'s 1811 "Undine" (drawing on the Romantics' interest in Paracelsus), which in turn inspired Hans Christian **Andersen**'s "Den lille havfrue" ("The Little Mermaid," 1837), the best-known literary mermaid tale (due in part to the animated film **adaptation** by the **Walt Disney Company**). Andersen's and subsequent tales have become a site of feminist critique. The mermaid's plight in the patriarchal world—her glorified female masochism, her self-mutilation in her transformation, and the willing silencing of her once-powerful voice—have all been problematized. Some of the most interesting reworkings are by female writers who explore the disaster for the mermaid through human contact. Many twentieth-century feminist writers shift the voice of the siren song to **men**, luring **women** to subjugation and subservience in the patriarchy. Interestingly, in Thompson's *Motif-Index of Folk-Literature,* there are far fewer motifs associated with the merman, the mermaid's male counterpart, than with the mermaid herself, suggesting the very **gender**-based issues in folktales that feminist writers seem to address with their rewritings.

The mermaid has had a rich tradition in the visual and performing arts, with four centuries of ballets, numerous **opera**s, stage plays, and a century of feature and animated films. Portrayals of mermaids appeared in medieval **art** in wall paintings, carvings, roof bosses, and other architectural features. The mermaid has also been an important image in **advertising** and in **cartoons and comics**. *See also* Animation; Feminism; Film and Video; *The Secret of Roan Inish*; *Splash*; Swan Maiden.

Further Readings: Benwell, Gwen, and Arthur Waugh. *Sea Enchantress: The Tale of the Mermaid and Her Kin.* London: Hutchinson and Co, 1961; Phillpotts, Beatrice. *Mermaids.* New York: Ballantine, 1980.

Shawn C. Jarvis

Metafiction

A favored technique of postmodernists, metafiction is literally fiction *about* fiction, writing that is self-conscious and self-reflexive, setting out to expose its own nature as fiction rather than as reality. Given the extent to which fairy tale presents itself self-consciously as a fictional construct, and given fairy tale's conscious intertextuality with its own traditions and highly recognizable structures, metafiction as a technique has particular relevance to classic fairy tales and especially to their more complex modern and postmodern retellings. It could be argued that, to a greater or lesser extent, *all* fiction has metafictional qualities. If this is so, then on the spectrum of possibility, fairy tale in any form is inherently more metafictional than many other literary traditions.

Seminal critics writing on the subject of metafiction include Roland Barthes, Linda Hutcheon, and Patricia Waugh. Robert Scholes is also particularly relevant because of his specific interest in the intersections between metafiction and nonrealist narrative. The basis of metafictional criticism can be found in **structuralism**, specifically Saussaurean semiotics, which begins to problematize the relationship between fiction and reality by its awareness of language as an arbitrary system that shapes as well as describes the world. The importance of **context** for the creation of meaning in textual utterance highlights the role of the producer and thus the nature of the production as artifact. Literary realism is revealed as a deception and a paradox. These concepts are central to the pursuit of literary self-consciousness in the work of Barthes. His line of argument, which hinges on the activity rather than passivity of the reader in constructing the literary production, is developed further by Jacques Derrida and the poststructuralists and becomes a central argument in the theories of **postmodernism**. Hutcheon's focus on historiographic metafiction highlights self-conscious narrative's necessary dialogue with its own structural traditions and past, insisting that it must situate itself in history and discourse. Waugh's definition of metafiction is particularly useful for the study of fairy tale, because it centers not only on self-consciousness but also on the notion of text as proffered artifact whose self-aware construction destabilizes notions of both text and reality.

The parallels between fairy tale and metafictional writing can be seen most clearly in the notion of self-conscious structure, intertextual dialogue with a body of literary tradition, and manufacture of literary artifact that makes no gesture at mimesis, or imitation of reality. Classic fairy tale and its folkloric antecedents generally lack the elements of explicit commentary, **parody**, and deliberate framebreak that characterize much metafictional writing. However, these elements are found liberally in the work of writers of more modern **literary fairy tale**s from the Victorians onwards, both in original fairy tales, which parody the form, and in self-conscious retellings that highlight construction and structural play. Postmodern writers, among them Donald **Barthelme**, A. S. **Byatt**, Angela **Carter,** and Robert **Coover,** demonstrate a particular affection for the fairy-tale form, using its rigid and recognizable structures for complex metafictional play. ***See also*** Frame Narrative; Intertextuality.

Further Readings: Curry, Mark, ed. *Metafiction.* London: Longman, 1995; Hutcheon, Linda. *Narcissistic Narrative: The Metafictional Paradox.* New York: Methuen, 1984; Scholes, Robert. *Fabulation and Metafiction.* Urbana: University of Illinois Press, 1979; Waugh, Patricia. *Metafiction: The Theory and Practice of Self-Conscious Fiction.* London: Routledge, 1984.

Jessica Tiffin

Metamorphosis. *See* Transformation

Metaxa-Krontera, Antigone (1905–1972)

Antigone Metaxa-Krontera, well known under the pseudonym Theia Lena (Aunt Lena), was a Greek author of **children's literature**. She also created the first radio programs for children and the first children's **theater** in Greece. After studying theater, she worked initially as an actress, and in 1932 she founded the first Greek theater for children. Later, she worked in Greek radio and established the first weekly children's radio programs. Her famous morning radio broadcast, *Kalimera paidakia* (*Good Morning, Children*), which took to the airwaves in the late 1930s, was widely anticipated and achieved high ratings. Later, she also worked in Greek **television** on the show *Kalispera paidakia* (*Good Evening, Children*). For these radio and television programs, she cooperated with renowned Greek authors and artists.

In the realm of children's literature, Metaxa-Krontera published some 200 books, fifty of which she wrote herself. Her books are directed at children of all ages. One landmark publication was *He enkyklopaideia tou paidiou* (*Children's Encyclopedia*), the first of its kind in Greek, which she edited and which received enthusiastic reviews. Equally famous are her books about Greek mythology (for example, *Mythologiko lexiko* [*Mythological Lexikon*]) and her children's travel books that appeared under the title *Elate na taxidepsoume* (*Let's Travel*) and were intended to teach children about Greek archaeology. She was also the editor of the children's newspaper *He efimeridoula tis theias Lenas* (*Aunt Lena's Little Newspaper*), which was published twice a month and enjoyed great popularity in Greece in the 1950s. During this same period, she wrote many tales for children, including *Ta paramythia tis theias Lenas* (*The Tales of Aunt Lena*), *Akouse me, Maria* (*Hear me, Maria*), and many others, as well as books for children's theater. For her significant contribution to children's literature, she received numerous awards in Greece. *See also* Greek Tales.

Further Reading: Hatzifotis, Ioannis M. "He Antigoni Metaxa, 'Theia Lena,' kai he logotechnia yia ta pedia." *Pneumatike Kypros* 16 (1975): 18–22.

Maria Kaliambou

Mhlophe, Gcina (1958–)

A key figure in the revival and preservation of **African tales** and traditional oral **storytelling**, Gcina Mhlophe is a dynamic performer who uses language, **music**, and movement to bring tales alive onstage in her native South Africa and on international tours. Born in Hammarsdale, near Durban, and educated in the Transkei, she was inspired toward storytelling through her grandmother's tale-telling abilities and through being asked to tell stories of Africa while working as an actor in Chicago. Now established in Johannesburg, she recounts traditional South African folktales and creates her own tales, which have a political edge in dealing with racial and tribal identity, apartheid, and preserving history through story.

Mhlophe is also an actor, director, musician, poet, writer, and storyteller on children's **television**. Her play *Have You Seen Zandile?* (1989) is based on her childhood, and she has written several books for children which draw on her passion for folktales, including *The Snake with Seven Heads* (1989), *Queen of the Tortoises* (1990), and *Stories of Africa* (2003). Her award-winning storytelling CD *Fudukazi's Magic* was produced in 2000, and, in connection with her promotion of reading in rural schools, she produced *Nozincwadi Mother of Books* (2001). She is also actively involved in encouraging young oral storytellers through the Zanendaba ("Bring me a story") Storytellers program. *See also* Children's Literature; Performance; Politics.

Further Reading: Killam, Douglas, and Ruth Rowe. "Gcina Mhlope: Profiles." *Contemporary Africa Database*. 2003. http://people.africadatabase.org/en/profile/11741.html.

Adrienne E. Gavin

Middle Ages

The Brothers **Grimm** were students of the Middle Ages who held that a typically German culture constituted in the medieval period had endured to their day among the humble and less educated. Accordingly, they sought to distill in their ***Kinder- und Hausmärchen*** (*Children's and Household Tales*, 1812–15) the narrative heritage of **märchen** that they imagined they could recover and preserve. Thus, the medieval-seeming paraphernalia of castles, **princess**es, knights, and so forth that persist even in the **animation** of Walt **Disney** have been associated with fairy tales at least since the Brothers Grimm. But were the Brothers right? Did folktales and fairy tales exist, or even arise, in the Middle Ages? If they were found then, who told them, and to whom? And which types of tales circulated in which type of media?

In western Europe, the sum of late antiquity and the Middle Ages spans roughly a millennium, from about 400 to 1400 CE. The first half of these years saw the transformation of Roman antiquity, under the impact initially of incursions by non-Romans (both European and non-European) and then of a Christianization (and Latinization) that swept northward. These long processes brought into ever-closer contact and combination a richly Mediterranean culture, in which ancient Rome participated with the very different cultures of Germanic, Celtic, and Slavic peoples, to name just a few. Simultaneously, a manuscript culture, which entailed practical skills of reading and writing, a distinctive intellectual outlook, and moral values, took root nearly everywhere on the continent. With it arrived not only the **Bible** with its many genres (such as **parable**s) and **religious tale**s, but also texts that were stock in the teaching of Latin, among which **fable**s ascribed to **Aesop** and **riddle**s were perennial favorites.

The relationship between such standards of the grammar school and what could be literary reflexes of the **oral tradition** is hard to assess. Latin riddles are akin to riddles in Old English and other Germanic languages, but it is debatable whether they are direct sources of inspiration or merely analogues. Apart from the superficial resemblance of their names, the fable and **fabliau** have little in common, but fables could have helped prepare the ground for the later cycle of **trickster** tales about **Reynard the Fox**. From the twelfth century, such **animal tale**s are attested first in Latin and later in Old French and other literature (for example, in Geoffrey **Chaucer**'s "Nun's Priest's Tale"). Reynard enjoyed so mighty a vogue that his name drove out the previous French word for fox. (Imagine if in English, "rabbit" were displaced by "Bugs.") **Motif**s from Reynard the Fox can be detected seven centuries later in the **Uncle Remus** stories of Joel Chandler **Harris**.

The second half of the medieval millennium witnessed an outward projection of Christianity and European political and economic interests that culminated in the expulsion of Muslims and Jews from Spain, and in the exploration of new lands to colonize, a complication of religion that set the stage for the Reformation, and a gradual shift from parchment and manuscripts to paper and printed books. With the establishment of print culture in the early modern period, many medieval tales lived on to circulate more widely than ever before. Some were published in the late fifteenth and early sixteenth centuries with woodprints and anticipated seventeenth- and eighteenth-century **chapbook**s, which made some such stories available cheaply and outfitted them with **illustration**s.

Medieval cultures were discussed throughout much of the twentieth century as if they could be viewed usefully in terms of sharp polarities. Among the most common dichotomies have been orality and literacy, popular and learned, secular and Christian, lay and clerical, and vernacular and Latin. In all of these pairings, the first elements have often been presumed to belong together in one group, the second in another. In recent decades, perspectives have grown more nuanced, with recognition both that the vernaculars could be literate, learned, and Christian, and that Latin could have oral traits, could be devoted to popular lore, and could qualify as secular. Equally relevant, all of the terms have acquired shadings of meanings that have made them less antithetical. The opposition of high and low culture has yielded to an appreciation that almost no one would have been excluded even largely from exposure to popular culture.

Compounding the difficulties of evaluating any medieval texts that relate to folktales and fairy tales is that what we have is not even unmediated oral folktales put into writing but instead reworked into literary form. In other words, what survives of medieval tale telling takes the form of texts and not of recordings, audio, video, or both, which would allow immediate access to the words and techniques of the performers. If we seek from medieval literature documents on a par with verbatim transcriptions of tale telling, we will be disappointed. Then again, no texts from any time period before the late nineteenth century can meet such a standard. The medieval millennium carried forward the long and complicated transition from cultures governed by oral traditions to ones pervaded by literary and especially scriptural authorities. Yet, even as written authorities became entrenched, people, and their words, persisted in shuttling back and forth between the oral and the written. Oral tradition lost none of its strength.

The expression "book tale" has been applied to differentiate between what the Brothers Grimm wrote, as distinguished on the one hand from oral folktales and on the other from **literary fairy tale**s that are intended more overtly to comply with literary aesthetics. From the Middle Ages, we have mainly the medieval equivalents of literary fairy tales, but sometimes also what could be termed "manuscript tales."

Looking in a different direction, whether we regard as foundational the literary fairy tales of such postmedieval authors as Giovan Francesco **Straparola**, Giambattista **Basile**, Charles **Perrault**, or the Brothers Grimm, we will of course not unearth in the Middle Ages texts that coincide exactly with the usages of these later collections. Perhaps not surprisingly, what we can find are tales that are alleged to have emerged from popular tellings, that sometimes correspond closely to tales presented later as folktales or fairy tales, and that are written down according to the generic and stylistic conventions that made sense to the medieval authors on the basis of the literature they knew. The stories may be longer or shorter than what we regard as typical **folktale**s or **fairy tale**s, and they may differ stylistically from what authors of the sixteenth century or later would have penned, but they contain motifs and narrative structures that have fairy tale written all over them.

From the early eleventh century, there is a short tale in Latin verse entitled "De puella a lupellis seruata" ("About a Girl Saved from Wolfcubs") that has been argued to be a prototype—the earliest extant—for part of Perrault's "Le petit chaperon rouge" ("**Little Red Riding Hood**," 1697) and the Grimms' "Rotkäppchen" ("Little Red Cap"). Egbert of Liège, a schoolmaster who included the tale in his textbook the *Fecunda ratis* (*Richly Laden Ship*, between 1022 and 1024), acknowledges that he drew it along with other materials from peasant **informant**s, who may have recounted it as a **cautionary tale**. *Unibos* (*One-Ox*), from the later eleventh century, is a poem in Latin verse that ties together three tales about a **peasant** trickster. The poem resembles the Grimms' "Das Bürle" ("Little Farmer") somewhat, and Hans Christian **Andersen**'s "Lille Claus og store Claus" ("Little Claus and Big Claus") even more closely. In a different category fall the late twelfth-century or early thirteenth-century *Asinarius* (*The Donkey Tale*) and *Rapularius* (*The Turnip Tale*). In these cases, the Medieval Latin poems, which are sometimes classified generically as *comoediae*, were mined directly by the Brothers Grimm to produce "Das Eselein" ("The Donkey"), which relates a **wonder tale** of an **animal groom**, and "Die Rübe" ("The Turnip"), which tells of an impoverished **soldier** who has been reduced to working the soil but who wins riches through cleverness and the luck of growing a gigantic turnip.

Medieval references to taletelling, tale tellers, and tales afford many insights into the groups that were deemed to be preeminent in transmitting oral traditions. These descriptions point consistently to the activity of groups that have been identified often since the Brothers Grimm and other Romantics as being significant bearers of tradition. Those credited include the elderly, especially old **women**; peasants and other common people, particularly country **folk**; travelers; and professional entertainers. Of the many Latin names by which the last group went, one that exemplifies the range of their activities is *ioculator* (French *jongleur*), cognate with the English *juggler*, *joker*, and *jocular*. How much responsibility these professionals hold for the **jest**s **and joke**s that survive in medieval literary forms remains disputed. Humorous tales known in Latin as *ridicula* (laughable tales) in the eleventh century (in the so-called *Cambridge Songs*) and **bawdy tale**s designated as *comoediae* (comedies) in the twelfth century receive ever-greater currency in Old French as *fabliaux* and in Italian as *novelle* (see **Novella**).

The rate at which tales passed from one group to another must have varied considerably, depending on the movements of people in war, trade, religion, and other processes that led to engagement. In the twelfth century, Welsh traditions about King Arthur entered the Anglo-Norman cultural axis and spread rapidly throughout Europe through courtly romance and other related shorter genres. Another long form of literature, which sometimes incorporated folktales and motifs, was the Old French **epic**, *chanson de geste* (song of deeds). In the thirteenth century, Old Norse **saga**s, colored by both continental Latin and Old French literature but heavily reliant on native materials, proliferated. The subcategory known as *fornaldarsögur* (sagas of antiquity) abounds in folktale and fairy-tale elements.

Tales also percolated into Europe from outside through those who were not Latin Christians. These others included, among others, Greek Christians, Jews, and Muslims. Jews often lived in close proximity to medieval Christians but also engaged with coreligionists throughout the Mediterranean. Despite **anti-Semitism**, Jews shared with Christians much of their Bible, as a result of which Jewish extrascriptural traditions seeped into Christian writings and arts. Muslims occupied large swaths of Spain and Italy as well as regions of the Middle East that for centuries fell under the domination of the crusaders. Both Jews and Muslims had connections that led to the Far East, and both served, along with merchants and others, as intermediaries for bodies of tales that radiated along the Silk Road from India, China, and elsewhere. Emblematic of the fascination that counterbalanced the frequent hostility toward Muslims among Christians is the *chantefable* (or **cante fable**, singtale, in alternating prose and verse) of *Aucassin et Nicolette*, written in Old French in the thirteenth century, which narrates the love of the young French nobleman Aucassin for the Saracen captive girl Nicolette.

Particularly after the Crusades began, new materials entered Europe in abundance. Along with them arrived a new vehicle for short fiction, the **frame narrative**. The only real example from antiquity (aside from **Ovid**'s *Metamorphoses*) is Lucius **Apuleius**'s *The Golden Ass* or *Metamorphoses*, containing the **Beauty-and-the-Beast**-like tale of **Cupid and Psyche**, which had a highly restricted circulation in the Middle Ages. In the twelfth century, we encounter the *Dolopathos* by John of Alta Silva (Hauteseille). Loosely related to the *Arabian Nights* and much more tightly to the so-called Seven Sages cycle, John's prose frame tale features sages who (like **Sheherazade**) tell tales on a daily basis so as to stave off **death**, in this case of the hero at the instigation of his wicked stepmother. This kind of structure finds celebrated expressions in Giovanni **Boccaccio**'s *Decameron* (1349–50) and Geoffrey **Chaucer**'s *Canterbury Tales* (begun around 1387). The form allowed authors to coordinate large numbers of the short narratives known in Italian as novellas, the very name of which looks ultimately toward the **novel**. The two works contain too many **tale type**s and motifs for a listing here to be feasible, but it is worth singling out Chaucer's treatment of the Loathly Lady in "The Wife of Bath's Tale."

Even without **Jewish tales** preserved outside of the Scriptures, exegesis and popular culture appropriated many beliefs that were not attested in the canonical Christian Bible. The Book of Jonah mentions not a whale but a great fish. The harrowing of hell, in which Jesus descends to hell, contends with the devil, and releases souls imprisoned there, is barely implied in the New Testament. Even the accepted books of the medieval Bible relate incidents that conform closely to folktales. Many other motifs reminiscent of folktales and fairy tales appear in the apocrypha, texts in the periphery of the Bible that helped to fill its many gaps.

Another place where folktales and fairy tales, or at least motifs from them, could come to lodge and would find justification was in the **saint's legend**. Literature about saints encompasses several genres, of which the most important are biographies, known as saints' lives; accounts of their martyrdoms, called passions; and enumerations of their posthumous feats and miracles. A famous collection of such material is the *Legenda aurea* (*The Golden Legend*, thirteenth century).

In the early Middle Ages, systematic amassing of folktales and fairy tales took place almost solely in connection with saints' legends. From the twelfth century, the number and variety of such legends exploded, as for example in conjunction with the Virgin Mary. At the same time, changes in the church motivated preachers to compile and consult large collections of short **anecdote**s, religious tales, and other stories with which they enlivened sermons. These narratives are called **exempla**. The best known of such compendia is the *Gesta Romanorum* (*Deeds of the Romans*), an anonymous composition of the late thirteenth or early fourteenth century that was copied widely in manuscripts and later printed repeatedly in both Latin and translations. Despite its title, the *Gesta Romanorum* is not restricted to narratives of the Romans but absorbs all manner of other material, including stories of Eastern origin.

Preaching that relied upon such collections caused a very efficient exchange of tales among different groups, since it prompted preachers to tap what was available popularly, and in turn disseminated among the people what preachers drew from written sources. The same could be said for many other agglomerations of narratives, such as those made for courts and schools. As a result, there is often little point in seeking to determine whether a given story was fundamentally oral or written, popular or learned, folk or clerical, or the like. The Middle Ages was an era, perhaps the preeminent one, of transitions and interchanges, between cultures and social classes, and especially between orality and literacy. As such, it gave long and warm hospitality to folktales and fairy tales, of which the surviving written records are but the smallest fraction. *See also* Classical Antiquity.

Further Readings: Berlioz, Jacques, Claude Bremond, and Catherine Velay-Vallantin. *Formes médiévales du conte merveilleux.* Paris: Éditions Stock, 1989; Clausen-Stolzenburg, Maren. *Märchen und mittelalterliche Literaturtradition.* Heidelberg: Universitätsverlag Carl Winter, 1995; Ogilvy, J. D. A. "*Mimi, Scurrae, Histriones:* Entertainers of the Early Middle Ages." *Speculum* 38 (1963): 603–19; Rosenberg, Bruce A. *Folklore and Literature: Rival Siblings.* Knoxville: University of Tennessee Press, 1991; Wesselski, Albert. *Märchen des Mittelalters.* Berlin: H. Stubenrauch, 1925; Wolterbeek, Marc. *Comic Tales of the Middle Ages: An Anthology and Commentary.* Westport, CT: Greenwood Press, 1991; Ziolkowski, Jan M. *Fairy Tales from Before Fairy Tales: The Medieval Latin Past of Wonderful Lies.* Ann Arbor: University of Michigan Press, 2007.

Jan M. Ziolkowski

Mirror

The mirror has been an object of fascination for more than 3,000 years. From the earliest recorded discovery of its optical effects in China (c. 1200 BCE), the mirror, along with related concepts such as the shadow and the double, became a primary image in the traditions, art, and literatures of countless cultures. Appearing in the form of a looking glass, windowpane, or reflective pool, the mirror was familiar both at home and in nature. Yet its seemingly magical ability to capture the semblance of a thing and reflect it led to the view of the mirror as a mystical, supernatural, and often demonic object. As such, it became a stock **motif** of folktales and fairy tales throughout the world.

Despite longstanding scientific theories of reflection, the function of the mirror was shrouded in mystery for centuries. Ancient misunderstandings about the mirror's physical properties quickly secured it a prominent position in folk superstition. As mirrors became customary in households across Europe, they also became more prevalent in **literary fairy tale**s, assuming various uncanny qualities. Stith Thompson's *Motif-Index of Folk-Literature* cites virtually innumerable instances of mirrors, some with clairvoyant and transforming abilities, others that serve as doorways to fantastic realms, or those that are directly linked to the soul. The diversity of these motifs chronicles the ever malleable and mysterious essence of the mirror.

In ancient civilizations from South America to Asia, the reflection, like the shadow, was believed to be a manifestation of the soul. Mirror images gave form to the souls of sacred human beings and divine figures as well as those of the dead. Similarly, those without a soul, such as vampires, saw no reflection in a mirror when standing before it because they were soulless. The dynamic nature of the looking glass rendered it a portal through which spirits left this world and crossed over to the next; similarly, it served as the gateway through which the **devil** entered the world and seized the souls of the unwitting. For this reason, folk belief, as noted in the entry for "Spiegel" (mirror) in **Grimm**s' *Deutsches Wörterbuch (German Dictionary)*, directed children not to gaze into the mirror after dusk and advised that all reflective surfaces be covered after death to prevent the soul of the deceased from returning to haunt the living.

The German Romantic writer E. T. A. **Hoffmann** draws on the link between the mirror and the soul in "The Story of the Lost Reflection" (1815), in which an enlivened mirror image serves as the focus. In a Faustian scenario, the protagonist Spikher exchanges his mirror reflection for the love of an evil temptress, Giulietta. When he refuses to surrender his soul entirely to the devil, Spikher must relinquish forever his reflection, which continues to live independently of him with Giulietta. Adalbert von **Chamisso**, who inspired Hoffmann, likewise makes use of the connection between the soul, reflection, and the shadow in his famous **novella** *The Wonderful History of Peter Schlemihl* (1814). Chamisso's hero surrenders his shadow to the devil's representative in return for material fortune. Like Spikher, he retains his soul, but his shadow, just as the former's mirror image, wanders about in an eternal state of limbo.

Based on the mirror's ability to replicate pictures of objects placed before it with visual accuracy, it became known by the nineteenth century for its impartial cognitive aptitude. The mirror provided truths about objective reality, both present and displaced. In Jeanne-Marie **Leprince de Beaumont**'s "Beauty and the Beast" (1757), Beauty views the mirror in her room to learn of the fate of her family at home, and in Friedrich de la Motte **Fouqué**'s "The Magic Ring" (1813), the cognitive mirror reveals to the viewer the pleasures of far-away lands. In the Grimms' "**Snow White**" (1812), the evil stepmother consults the omniscient mirror, which conveys to her unpleasant truths based on its obligation to reflect reality. The emperor in Hans Christian **Andersen**'s "The Emperor's New Clothes" (1837) seeks from the mirror a confirmation of the reality that has been given him. In both tales, the characters seek the mirror's truths, yet they ultimately reject them. When the mirror does not reflect the idealized image the protagonists imagine, they change themselves or their outside circumstances to match the ideal they wish to see.

During the nineteenth century, the mirror changed from a primarily magical entity to an object with psychological dimensions. Living reflections, broken mirrors, and the doppelgänger—the double—acquired negative connotations as their physical forms were used to embody morality, angst, and the troubled subconscious of the protagonist. While at times the mirror still revealed magical powers and served as an entrance into fantastic worlds, as in works such as Hoffmann's *The Golden Pot* (1814) and Lewis **Carroll**'s *Through the Looking Glass* (1871), the mirror was more often used to reflect the modern individual's divided existence between the waking world and the torments of the psyche (not surprisingly, a full-length decorative mirror in France was called a *psyché*).

While the doppelgänger dates back to the early nineteenth century, when it was a physical being that often possessed comical qualities, the mirror image later became a projection of the subject's fraught psychological state and posed a threat to the protagonist's sanity. In particular, the double was a fitting symbol for the inner struggle of the artist, who, out of place in the bourgeois world, crosses into the ethically suspect realm of art. Many modernist texts linked to the fairy-tale tradition, such as Fyodor Dostoevsky's *The Double* (1846), Hugo von **Hofmannsthal**'s *The Cavalier's Tale* (1899), Franz Werfel's *Mirror Man* (1920), Hermann **Hesse**'s *Steppenwolf* (1927), and Ingeborg Bachmann's *Malina* (1971), employ the animate mirror image or the double to represent the rift between subject and object worlds and to reveal the protagonist's self-scrutiny and criticism of the artist's calling. *See also* Magic Object.

Further Readings: Melchior-Bonnet, Sabine. *The Mirror: A History.* Translated by Katharine H. Jewett. New York: Routledge, 2001; Ziolkowski, Theodore. *Disenchanted Images: A Literary Iconology.* Princeton, NJ: Princeton University Press, 1977.

Cynthia Chalupa

Miyazaki Hayao (1941–)

Writer, artist, animator, and director of Japanese **animation**, or anime, Miyazaki Hayao's work reaches international audiences with its complex plots and stunning visuals. Many of

Miyazaki's films contain references to characters and **motif**s from folktales, both Japanese and Western. Miyazaki established the animation studio, Studio Ghibli, with colleagues such as Takahata Isao, who, alone and in conjunction with Miyazaki, have released numerous films. Miyazaki also writes and draws manga (Japanese comics or **graphic novel**s), which inform some of his films. One of the ways in which Miyazaki uses folktales and fairy tales is to incorporate specific characters as well as general themes, sometimes altering them to address larger social issues.

Miyazaki's main characters tend to be female, and many of them exhibit folktale and fairy-tale influences. Nausicaä, the title character of *Kaze no tani no Naushika* (*Nausicaä of the Valley of the Wind*, 1984), resonates with a thirteenth-century character from a Japanese tale titled "The Princess Who Loved Insects." Nausicaä, too, loves insects, even the dangerous ones that populate her postapocalyptic world. Kiki of *Majo no takkyūbin* (*Kiki's Delivery Service*, 1989) is a **witch** in the Western sense. She rides a broomstick, can work magic, and has a black **cat**. Unlike most of the witches that appear in Western folktales and fairy tales, however, she is a benevolent witch who uses her powers to aid the people in the community where she has settled. The witch in *Hauru no ugoku shiro* (*Howl's Moving Castle*, 2004) curses a few of the main characters, one of whom is also a wizard. This film follows more closely the Western stereotype that witches are dangerous. Possibly this is because it is adapted from the **novel** *Howl's Moving Castle* (1986) by Diana Wynne **Jones**. *Gedo Senki* (*Tales from Earthsea*, 2006)—Studio Ghibli's adaptation of Ursula K. **Le Guin**'s Earthsea series of books (1968–2001)—follows a similar pattern.

Some of Miyazaki's characters are more generally tied to folktale traditions in their familial relationships. Just as folktale and fairy-tale characters tend to be separated from their families, the circumstances of Miyazaki's plots often assume or introduce departures and **death**s. Kiki, mentioned above, must establish herself independently in a new town because it is the witches' way of doing things. Sen, the female lead in *Mononoke-hime* (*Princess*

Miyazaki Hayao. [Haruyoshi Yamaguchi/Corbis]

Mononoke, 1997), was abandoned by her human parents and raised by the wolf spirit Moro. Sheeta and Pazu, the main characters in *Tenkû no shiro Rapyuta* (*Laputa: Castle in the Sky*, 1986), are both orphans, though in another fairy-tale twist, Sheeta is revealed to be heir to the throne of Laputa. *Nausicaä of the Valley of the Wind* is also a **princess**, though her kingdom is invaded and occupied. Chihiro, main character of *Sen to Chihiro no kamikakushi* (*Spirited Away*, 2001), has both her parents when the film begins, but when they all stumble into a supernatural realm, her parents are transformed into **pig**s, and Chihiro alone must free them. The adolescent girl Sophie of *Howl's Moving Castle* also has a **family**, but she must leave them when a witch curses her, forcibly aging her body until she resembles an ancient woman.

The relationships between humans and animals in Miyazaki's films are also reminiscent of those in folktales and fairy tales. *Princess Mononoke* and *Spirited Away* feature talking animals, and the main character of *Kurenai no buta* (*Porco Rosso*, 1992) is himself an animal—he is a fighter pilot whose head turns into a pig's head. Animals also serve as guides and friends in Miyazaki's films. The two young sisters in *Tonari no Totoro* (*My Neighbor Totoro*, 1988) go live in the countryside while their mother is ill, and there they encounter friendly forest spirits called *totoro*. Kiki and Nausicaä each have pets; Ashitaka of *Princess Mononoke* has a special relationship with the red elk he rides; and Sophie adopts the dog that once belonged to the witch who cursed her.

Transformation and flight are also important themes in Miyazaki's work that correlate to folktales and fairy tales. Many of Miyazaki's characters are placed under transformative curses—from Sophie in *Howl's Moving Castle*, who is trapped in an old woman's body, to Ashitaka in *Princess Mononoke*, who is cursed by a dying boar god, to Chihiro in *Spirited Away*, whose parents are turned into pigs for their greed. Flight is so prevalent in Miyazaki's work that of the films mentioned above, only *Princess Mononoke* does not explicitly involve it. As in folktales and fairy tales, flight can be a convenient method of transportation as well as a transformative experience. For instance, Kiki's ability to fly is both a part of her identity as a witch that allows her to travel, and a part of her psychology that falters when she loses confidence in herself.

One final connection—though there are many—between Miyazaki's work and folktales and fairy tales is the coming-of-age story. Just as many folktales and fairy tales deal with young people grappling with experiences that lead them to greater maturity, so do Miyazaki's protagonists learn and gain valuable knowledge about life. One of the clearest examples is Chihiro's adventure in *Spirited Away*. The plot begins when her family is moving to a new town; however, when her entire family is transported to a realm of spirits, Chihiro must change from a disheartened and cynical girl into a courageous young woman with the wits and compassion to set free not only her parents, but other denizens of the spirit world who need rescue.

Miyazaki's art, writing, and animation are all interesting for their connections to folklore in general, both Japanese and Western, but his storytelling techniques especially mirror many of those found in folktales and fairy tales. He has been compared to Walt **Disney** in his scope and enormous output, yet Miyazaki's tales tend to value diversity. He destabilizes rather than homogenizes through the use of fantasy, which is perhaps one reason for the popularity of his films. ***See also*** Film and Video; Japanese Popular Culture; Japanese Tales; Women.

Further Readings: Drazen, Patrick. "Flying with Ghibli: The Animation of Hayao Miyazaki and Company." *Anime Explosion: The What? Why? & Wow! of Japanese Animation.* Berkeley: Stone Bridge

Press, 2003. 253–79; Osmond, Andrew. "Nausicaa and the Fantasy of Hayao Miyazaki." *Foundation: The International Review of Science Fiction* 72 (Spring 1998): 57–80; Team Ghiblink. *The Hayao Miyazaki Web.* 1995–2007. http://www.nausicaa.net/miyazaki/.

Jeana Jorgensen

Miyazawa Kenji (1896–1933)

Poet, essayist, and writer of children's tales, Japanese author Miyazawa Kenji published only two books during his short life. The first, a volume of poetry, appeared in April 1924, and was followed in December of the same year by a collection of fairy tales, *Chūmon no ōi ryōriten* (*The Restaurant of Many Orders*). Although neglected during his lifetime, Miyazawa is now recognized as one of Japan's foremost storytellers.

Born in Hanamaki, in the rural northern prefecture of Iwate, Miyazawa was the oldest of five children. He graduated in agricultural science in 1918, and three years later left for Tokyo, where he intended to pursue his literary ambitions. After just eight months, he returned to Iwate because of his sister's ill health and took a position in a local agricultural school. Miyazawa gave up teaching in 1926 and, while continuing to write prolifically, spent his remaining years utilizing his skills as an agriculturalist to advise local farmers.

Many of Miyazawa's tales, including "Shishi-odori no hajimari" ("The First Deer Dance"), are inspired by the folk traditions and natural beauty of his native Iwate. Other tales and **fable**s, like "Donguri to yamaneko" ("Wildcat and the Acorns") and "Yomata no yuri" ("A Stem of Lilies"), are influenced by his deep devotion to Nichiren Buddhism. The influence of Buddhism also can be seen in Miyazawa's most popular and enduring work: *Ginga Tetsudō no yoru* (*Night Train to the Stars*, 1927). *See also* Japanese Tales.

Further Readings: Bester, John, trans. *Once and Forever: The Tales of Kenji Miyazawa.* Tokyo: Kodansha International, 1997; Colligan-Taylor, Karen. "Miyazawa Kenji: The Seeds of a Land Ethic." *The Emergence of Environmental Literature in Japan.* New York: Garland, 1990. 34–68.

Marc Sebastian-Jones

Mizuno Junko (1973–)

One of Japan's leading young manga artists, Tokyo-born Mizuno Junko gained international acclaim in 2002 with the publication, in English translation, of *Junko Mizuno's Cinderalla*, the first part of her "fractured fairy tales" trilogy. Mizuno first received recognition in Japan in 1998 with the publication of her first book-length manga, *Pyua toransu* (*Pure Trance*). Originally serialized in CD booklets for the techno music label Avex Trax, *Pure Trance* appeared in English in 2005. Mizuno's work, which is noted for its striking and instantly recognizable visual style, has also appeared in *Pulp: The Manga Magazine* and *Secret Comics Japan* (2000). It is frequently described by commentators as adorable, attractive, and erotic, while at the same time being disturbing, repulsive, and vulgar. This perceived ambiguity has led to its being labeled "cute-grotesque." Mizuno, however, insists that the presence of both attractive and repulsive elements in her work is natural because they coexist in real life.

Mizuno's engagement with the fairy-tale genre came at the behest of her publisher, who asked her to consider creating a work by utilizing preexisting material. The result, based very loosely on the fairy-tale classic "**Cinderella**," was *Mizuno Junko no Shinderāra-chan* (*Junko Mizuno's Cinderalla*, 2000). In Mizuno's ironic and darkly humorous retelling of the traditional tale, the voluptuous and scantily clad heroine, Cinderalla, works as a waitress in a *yakitori* (bite-sized pieces of grilled chicken on a skewer) restaurant; she has a stepmother and two stepsisters, but in a nightmarish twist, they are undead. At the same time, Cinderalla's "prince" is a zombie pop star called The Prince, and it is only after she too has been transformed into a zombie that she is allowed to go to his show. In an ending that echoes the harmonious conclusion of Charles **Perrault**'s version of the tale, Cinderalla forgives her troublesome stepsisters and marries The Prince.

Mizuno followed the success of *Cinderalla* with retellings of fairy tales by the **Grimm** brothers and Hans Christian **Andersen**. *Henzeru to Gurēteru* (***Hansel and Gretel***, 2000) tells the story of two high school students whose parents own a supermarket; they face starvation when their suppliers stop selling to them. Hansel and Gretel discover that the cause of their distress is the witchlike Queen Marilyn, who has everybody under her **spell**. They break the magic spell and discover Marilyn's true identity. Unlike the children in the Grimms' tale, Hansel and Gretel are not rewarded with jewels, but the end nevertheless brings a return to happiness. The darkest of Mizuno's retold tales, *Ningyohime den* (*Princess **Mermaid***, 2001), focuses on the brutality and cruelty implicit in Andersen's "The Little Mermaid." Mizuno's mermaids are bloodthirsty prostitutes bent on killing and eating humans to avenge their mother's death. One of the mermaids dies after being imprisoned by a wealthy prince, while her sister, who falls in love with a fisherman, is deceived by the Dragon King, who has promised to transform her into a human. Mizuno's "fractured fairy tales" continue to attract a growing international audience, most recently in France, where the three titles in the trilogy appeared in French translation from 2004 to 2006. ***See also*** Graphic Novel; Japanese Popular Culture; Japanese Tales.

Further Readings: Mizuno Junko. *Junko Mizuno's Cinderalla*. English adaptation by Yuji Oniki. San Francisco: Viz Communications, 2002; _____. *Junko Mizuno's Hansel & Gretel*. English adaptation by Yuji Oniki. San Francisco: Viz Communications, 2003; _____. *Junko Mizuno's Princess Mermaid*. English adaptation by Yuji Oniki. San Francisco: Viz Comics, 2003.

Marc Sebastian-Jones

Moe, Jørgen (1813–1882)

Norwegian Jørgen Moe was a clergyman, poet, and folklorist best known for **collecting** and publishing *Norske folkeeventyr* (*Norwegian Folktales*, 1841–44) with Peter Christen **Asbjørnsen**. Moe became acquainted with Asbjørnsen when they were both students at the Støren brothers' preparatory school at Norderhov in Ringerike in 1827. Ten years later, the two young friends decided to collect and publish Norwegian folktales as Jacob and Wilhelm **Grimm** had done in Germany. It is not clear which of the friends suggested the project, but many believe that it was Moe, and he is also considered to have had the best grasp of stylistics, at least initially. He had studied aesthetics, German and Danish literature, and was influenced early on by Adam **Oehlenschläger**, Christian Winther, and Johan Welhaven.

The first small pamphlet of *Norwegian Folktales* appeared in 1841 amid some controversy, since Asbjørnsen and Moe made a special effort to use Norwegian vocabulary and forms of

Portrait of Jørgen Moe from *The Fairy World: Folk and Fairy Tales*, trans. H. L. Braekstad (Boston: D Wolfe, Fiske and Co., 1900), p. xv. [Courtesy of the Eloise Ramsey Collection of Literature for Young People, University Libraries, Wayne State University]

speech that were considered too "raw" by some readers. Their use of uniquely Norwegian forms, as opposed to the Danish, which was the literary language at the time, was of seminal importance in the development of the modern Norwegian written language. Asbjørnsen and Moe believed, in the reigning spirit of Romantic nationalism, that by collecting the tales and developing a lively and natural style in which to render them, they were helping to conserve an important element of Norwegian cultural heritage, the voice of "the **folk**." Additional collections of tales were published in 1842, 1843, and 1844. *Norwegian Folktales* contained primarily **wonder tale**s, humorous **anecdote**s, and some **fable**s. In 1852, Moe wrote an influential introduction to the second edition of *Norwegian Folktales*, in which he noted that Norwegian tales are characterized by a form of humor than can be developed only in a country where people live in a harsh natural environment. To Moe, this humor had much in common with the intrepid humor found in Icelandic **saga**s. Moe saw the Norwegian folktale as a continuation of saga poetics in some respects, with the same directness and simplicity of expression.

Although Moe had taken his theological exam in 1839, he did not become a clergyman until 1853, following a religious crisis. Moe became increasingly occupied with the duties of his calling; in 1865, he gave his fairy-tale and **legend** collections to Asbjørnsen and his folk song collections to Sophus Bugge. Subsequent editions of *Norske folkeeventyr* were published by Asbjørnsen alone, who continued revising both spelling and syntax to conform to the changing language. Moe became the bishop in Kristiansand in 1875. In addition to his work on the folktale collections, he published *Digte* (*Poems*, 1849) and what is considered Norway's first children's classic, *I brønnen og i tjernet* (*In the Well and in the Pond*, 1851). *See also* Kittelsen, Theodor; Nationalism; Scandinavian Tales.

Further Readings: Christiansen, Reidar T., ed. *Folktales of Norway*. Translated by Pat Shaw Iversen. Chicago: University of Chicago Press, 1964; Krogvig, Anders, ed. *Fra det Nationale Gjennembruds Tid: Breve fra Jørgen Moe til P. Chr. Asbjørnsen og andre*. Kristiania: H. Aschehoug & Co. (W. Nygaard), 1915.

Marte Hult

Molesworth, Mary Louisa (1839–1921)

An English novelist and prolific children's writer, Mary Louisa Molesworth was born in Rotterdam, raised in Manchester, and, in 1861, married Richard Molesworth, from whom she separated in 1879. Predominately a writer of domestic realism, she also produced fairy tales, many of which were illustrated by Walter **Crane**. Her work often depicts **fairies** as kind godmotherly figures who improve children's behavior. *The Cuckoo Clock* (1877) tells of a girl who is discontented with the rules in her great-aunts' house and finds escape through adventures on which she is taken by a clock's magical cuckoo. *The Tapestry Room* (1879) recounts the magical experiences of two children who find themselves within a tapestry, where they hear the interpolated folktale "The Brown Bull of Norrowa." The influence of George **MacDonald** is shown in *Christmas-Tree Land* (1884), *Four Winds Farm* (1887), and *The Children of the Castle* (1890). A magic ring in *The Ruby Ring* (1904) reforms a spoiled child, and in "The Groaning Clock" from *Fairies—of Sorts* (1908), a clock-dwelling brownie growls when children behave badly. Molesworth moved away from the godmother trope in the shorter fairy tales of *An Enchanted Garden* (1892) and *Fairies Afield* (1911). *See also* Children's Literature; English Tales.

Further Readings: Avery, Gillian. "Molesworth, Mary Louisa (1839–1921)." *Oxford Dictionary of National Biography.* Edited by H. C. G. Matthew and Brian Harrison. Oxford: Oxford University Press, 2004; Cooper, Jane. *Mrs. Molesworth: A Biography.* Crowborough, East Sussex: Pratts Folly Press, 2002.

Adrienne E. Gavin

Momaday, N. Scott (1934–)

N. Scott Momaday is a Native American (Kiowa) writer, born in Lawton, Oklahoma, to the writer Natachee Scott Momaday and the painter Al Momaday. Momaday's **novel** *House Made of Dawn* (1968) tells the story of a young Native American man who, upon his return from war, is torn between the beauty of his native land and the lure of industrial America. The novel won the Pulitzer Prize for fiction in 1969 and led to a surge in interest in Native American fiction.

Momaday's *The Journey of Tai-Me* (1967) is a collection of narratives that are blended with Kiowa history. *The Way to Rainy Mountain*, first published in 1976, recounts the **oral tradition**s of the Kiowa and are reflective of the stories told to Momaday by his father when he was a child. The book tells of the journey of Momaday's ancestors from their initial phase in Montana, through hostilities with the United States. The last segment, which depicts the tribe's relocation to Oklahoma, recollects the golden age of the Kiowa, and mourns the imminent death of Kiowa culture.

Due to his profound portrayal of native Kiowa **legend**s and history, Momaday was featured in the documentary *The West* (1996) by Ken Burns and Stephen Ives. Momaday's other works include *The Gourd Dancer* (1976), *The Names: A Memoir* (1976), *The Ancient Child* (1989), *Circle of Wonder: A Native American Christmas Story* (1994), *The Man Made of Words: Essays, Stories, Passages* (1997), and *In the Bear's House* (1999). *See also* Native American Tales.

Further Reading: Woodward, Charles L. *Ancestral Voice: Conversations with N. Scott Momaday.* Lincoln: University of Nebraska Press, 1989.

Helen J. Callow

N. Scott Momaday at the Saint Malo Book Fair in France, 2001. [Getty Images]

Monogenesis

The term "monogenesis" ("single origin") refers to the theory that a certain narrative, song, or other item of **folklore** was created once by an individual and was then spread over time and space. As a theory, monogenesis explains the similarities among different performances and recordings of folktales through the genetic affinity of these texts. They all are supposed to have derived from one primary form (**urform**), of which they are later variations. The opposite view, **polygenesis,** claims that similar items of folklore originated from multiple sources. The **historic-geographic method** has relied on the idea of monogenesis and has tried to track the routes by which folktales were distributed geographically and over time, with the aim of identifying their primary form. Several folklorists have connected tales of magic (ATU 300–749) with Indo-European cultures and sought their origin among these peoples. An example of a tale that belongs to Indo-European inheritance is The Search for the Lost Husband (ATU 425).

The concept of monogenesis also is supported by the morphological approach of Vladimir **Propp**. According to his work, the tale of The Dragon-Slayer (ATU 300), in which a hero rescues a **princess** from the **dragon**, is the urform that has been developed into many versions whose common core appears on the deep structural level. Most researchers agree that simple plots can be created many times in different cultures without any contact between them. In contrast, complex plots that are widely spread across cultures support the theory of monogenesis—that is, of a single origin. Their origin from multiple sources does not seem likely. *See also* Structuralism.

Further Reading: Swahn, Jan-Öjvind. *The Tale of Cupid and Psyche (Aarne-Thompson 425 & 428).* Lund: CWK Gleerup, 1955.

Ülo Valk

Moral

A moral is a lesson to be learned about right and wrong, and good and evil, especially as it applies to human character or behavior. The moral of a given story can be stated in the form of maxim (typically at the end of the narrative) or may be implicit, so that it is inferred by the listener, reader, or viewer. In general, a moral—whether explicit or implicit—is meant to influence and shape a person's character or conduct.

Moral lessons may be offered in a variety of genres, from epics such as the *Iliad* and *Odyssey* to drama. In classical drama or Greek **theater**, the chorus is used to make comments on the events and to convey a moral message to the audience. However, morals are most closely identified with short narrative forms such as the **fable**. **Aesop**'s fables are especially well known because of the morals they express, and they are frequently directed by adults at children because of the role they are believed to play in a child's moral education. The popular medieval **fabliaux**, distinct in content and intention from the Aesopian fable tradition, were also often used to convey valuable moral lessons. Similarly, **jest**s—idle tales intended to provoke not only laughter but serious reflection—also were very popular in the **Middle Ages**. The medieval and early Renaissance jestbooks compiled short merry prose tales or witty remarks, used with a moralizing intention, as in Gian Francesco Poggio Bracciolini's *Liber Facetiarum* (*Book of Jests*, 1470).

Morals are often evident in fairy tales, especially because of their role in **children's literature** and in the civilizing process. In the case of Charles **Perrault**'s seventeenth-century French tales, each story's moral (sometimes accompanied by a second moral and sometimes with a good dose of irony) is set in verse and pronounced explicitly at the end of the tale. In Germany, Jacob and Wilhelm **Grimm**'s ***Kinder- und Hausmärchen*** (*Children's and Household Tales*, 1812–15) is a collection replete with **didactic tale**s; and although Grimms' stories may not have explicit morals like Perrault's tales, the moral messages are no less obvious. Similarly, the tales of Hans Christian **Andersen**—for example, "The Little Match Girl," "The Red Shoes," "The Ugly Duckling," and "The Emperor's New Clothes," among many others—abound in moral lessons to be inferred by the reader.

Contemporary fairy tales and fairy-tale **adaptation**s often **parody** or subvert traditional morals, in works both for adults and for children. Such ironic play is characteristic of books such as James **Thurber**'s *Fables for Our Time* (1940), Roald **Dahl**'s *Revolting Rhymes* (1982), and Jon Sciescka's *The Stinky Cheese Man and Other Fairly Stupid Tales* (1992).

Further Readings: Anderson, Graham. *Fairytale in the Ancient World.* New York: Routledge, 2000; Bottigheimer, Ruth B. *Grimm's Bad Girls and Bold Boys: The Moral and Social Vision of the Tales.* New Haven, CT: Yale University Press, 1987; Zipes, Jack. *Fairy Tales and the Art of Subversion: The Classical Genre for Children and the Process of Civilization.* New York: Wildman, 1983.

Ana Raquel Fernandes

Mother

Many folktales and fairy tales, especially **wonder tale**s and romantic **novella**s, begin with an initial situation that is related to motherhood, such as a childless couple that wishes for a child (as in ATU 410, **Sleeping Beauty**), or a mother dies and is replaced with a monstrous stepmother who mistreats the hero (as in ATU 720, The Juniper Tree) or heroine (as in ATU 510A, **Cinderella**; and ATU 709, **Snow White**). The absent mother who is replaced with a wicked stepmother (Motif S31, Cruel stepmother) is a common **motif**. Mothers frequently figure prominently in the central conflicts of folktales and fairy tales, with the role of the villain being a mother or substitute mother (such as a stepmother or mother-in-law). Good mothers or substitute mothers (such as **fairy** godmothers, **magic helper**s, and donor figures) test the protagonist and offer advice and magical assistance. Author Jane **Yolen** and her daughter, Heidi E. Y. Stemple, have published *Mirror, Mirror* (2000), a collection (with commentary) of forty folktales from around the world about both good and bad mothers. Mothers also play a prominent role in **jokes** and **anecdotes** from certain ethnic, religious, and cultural groups; for instance, the doting

Cinderella and her fairy godmother in *Nimmo's Juvenile Tales: Cinderella* (Edinburgh: William P. Nimmo, 1889), p. 2. [Courtesy of the Eloise Ramsey Collection of Literature for Young People, University Libraries, Wayne State University]

and domineering Jewish mother is a cultural stereotype who appears in many types of jokes.

Many folktale and fairy-tale scholars put all older, female characters into a broadly defined "mother" category, suggesting that any older woman symbolizes a mother figure. Negative mother figures such as evil stepmothers and **witch**es become manifestations of the "bad" mother that preserves the fantasy of the "good" mother. Scholars such as Heinz Rölleke and Marina **Warner** have discussed how the Brothers **Grimm** changed the mothers in their *Kinder- und Hausmärchen* (*Children's and Household Tales*, 1812–15) to step-mothers in an effort to preserve ideals of German motherhood. In *The Uses of Enchantment* (1976), Bruno **Bettelheim** suggests that the transformation of good mothers into negative characters displaces a child's guilt for feeling angry at his parents. Andreas Johns investigates the ambiguity of **Baba Yaga**, the witch/grandmother figure from Russian folklore in *Baba Yaga: The Ambiguous Mother and Witch of the Russian Folktale* (2004). In *The Absent Mother, or Women against Women in the 'Old Wives' Tale* (1991), Marina Warner offers perhaps the most extensive folkloristic consideration of bad mothers, absent mothers, stepmothers, and mothers-in-law, and she argues that wonder tales reflect the lived circumstances of their tellers and audiences. She describes three types of mothers that commonly replace absent natal mothers in folktales and fairy tales: the wicked stepmother and other monsters, the absent mother, and the mother-in-law.

Natal Mothers

Natal mothers are often absent from folktales and fairy tales, but when they are present, they may be either benign or hostile figures. When present in the introduction, they are usually presented as desperately wanting a child. Wishing for a daughter as white as snow, red as **blood**, and black as ebony is a typical motif in the opening of many versions of "Snow White." Often, these future mothers resort to magical remedies to conceive, such as eating special **food** (Motif T511.1, Conception from eating a fruit; and Motif T511.1.1, Conception from eating apple), beverages, flowers (Motif T511.4, Conception from eating flower), or fish (Motif T511.5.1, Conception from eating fish), usually obtained from a witch. A common beginning of ATU 303, The **Twins** or Blood-Brothers, includes conception after eating a magical fish. Often, these **women** fail to follow instructions properly (by eating both the red and the white flower, rather than just one, for example) and consequently give **birth** to monstrous children (Motif T550, Monstrous births). For example, in ATU 711, The Beautiful and the Ugly Twinsisters, the mother violates a condition for magical conception and gives birth to twin daughters, one of whom is deformed or monstrous. Other magical pregnancies that result in monstrous births occur due to a **wish** or a prayer (Motif T510, Miraculous conception; Motif T513, Conception from wish; and Motif T548.1, Child born in answer to prayer). For example, ATU 433B, King Lindorm, frequently begins with a magical pregnancy that results in the monstrous birth of an animal son. By contrast, in Jewish folktales, childless mothers who become pregnant as a result of prayer usually give birth to very spiritual children. Hasty curses may harm living or unborn children. For example, in ATU 451, The Maiden Who Seeks Her Brothers, the female protagonist searches for her six **brothers** who have been transformed into ravens or swans after their mother curses them because there is not enough food. These motifs also appear in **legend** tradition; for instance, most versions of the Jersey **Devil** legend begin with a mother who has too many children cursing her unborn baby by saying she would rather have a devil than another child.

During pregnancy, expectant mothers in fairy tales are often subject to intense cravings, and indulging or denying these cravings usually results in harm to their unborn children. For example, in many versions of ATU 310, The Maiden in the Tower, a pregnant woman steals herbs or fruit from a witch's garden. When caught, she promises to give the witch her unborn child. Additionally, female protagonists may also promise to give up their firstborn in exchange for aid from donor figures, as in ATU 500, The Name of the Supernatural Helper. Mothers-to-be may also harm their unborn children because of things they see, smell, or eat (for example, Motif T550.4, Monstrous birth because mother sees horrible sight).

Dead mothers may render help or harm to their children (usually daughters). Some absent or dead mothers may function as donor figures, providing assistance to their daughters from beyond the grave. Perhaps the most common example is some versions of "Cinderella," in which the donor figure is the deceased mother who aids her daughter via a tree that grows from her grave (Motif N819.2.1, Transformed mother as helper). The tree provides the dresses and slippers that Cinderella wears to the ball (Motif D815.1, **Magic object** received from mother). Alternately, dead mothers may also unwittingly instigate the villainy of a tale. For example, some versions of ATU 706, The Maiden without Hands, includes the **father**'s deathbed promise to his wife to remarry only when he finds a woman exactly like her; this promise results in the father's desire to marry his daughter.

A minority of folktales and fairy tales feature villainous actions perpetrated by the birth mother, as seen in Motif S322.2, Jealous mother casts daughter forth, and Motif H491.1, In large family father unwilling but mother willing to sell children. Frequently, the villain role in these narratives may be filled by either the mother or stepmother. In early editions of Jacob and Wilhelm Grimm's *Children's and Household Tales*, it is the mother rather than the stepmother who persuades the father to abandon the children in the forest in "**Hansel and Gretel**." In the first edition of the Grimms' collection, it is the mother (rather than the stepmother) who abandons Snow White or orders the hunter to kill her in the woods.

Female Protagonists as Mothers

In some folktales and fairy tales, the female protagonist becomes a mother during the course of the narrative. In some versions of "Sleeping Beauty," the heroine is disenchanted when, after giving birth to twins, one of them sucks the spindle splinter out of her finger. Frequently, the heroine's pregnancy instigates a crisis that results in the separation of the male and female protagonists. For example, in The Maiden in the Tower **tale type**, the witch who imprisons Rapunzel sometimes discovers that the **prince** has been visiting when the pregnant female protagonist asks why her clothes are becoming too tight. After escaping from the tower, she wanders alone for years with her twin children until she is reunited with the prince. In the second episode of ATU 883A, The Innocent Slandered Maiden, the female protagonist gives birth to twins and is slandered a second time when her mother-in-law or her rejected seducer tells her husband that she gave birth to puppies or murdered her children.

Substitute Mothers

If the birth mother is absent from a folktale, usually because of **death**, her role in the **family** is often filled by a substitute mother, who may be a stepmother, a grandmother, a godmother, or a foster mother. Marina Warner interprets the regularity of the absent mother in folktales and fairy tales as a reflection of the lived circumstance of storytellers and their audiences. Until the twentieth century, many women died in childbirth, making the absent mother a hard fact of life rather than a convenient plot device. Most widowers remarried, making stepmothers a real concern for many. In circumstances when a father was absent or deceased, children were raised by grandparents or other relatives, which could be reflected in the range of substitute mother figures in folktales and fairy tales.

The substitute mother may be a benign or a hostile figure, depending on whether she fills the tale role of donor/helper or villain. In an Indian tale called "The Serpent Mother," the female protagonist, who has no family, is tormented by all of her in-laws. After offering blessings rather than curses to a serpent who steals her food while she is bathing, she gains the serpent's family as a surrogate family. Typically, traditional folktales will include two older female characters, a hostile, female villain (usually the stepmother) and a benign or beneficent older female helper, who is a mother substitute. For instance, in ATU 480, **The Kind and the Unkind Girls**, the heroine is mistreated by her stepmother and, after falling into a well or being carried off by a river, encounters an old woman (or **ogress** or **Mother Holle**) who tests and rewards her. In many modern written and cinematic versions of fairy tales, the deceased or absent mother as a donor figure is replaced by the fairy godmother figure, as in the Walt **Disney** version of *Cinderella* (1950) (by contrast, this role is filled by Leonardo da Vinci in the film *Ever After*, 1998). A minority of tale types feature both a living mother and godmother figure (for example, Sleeping Beauty).

Stepmothers

Wicked stepmothers are perhaps the most ubiquitous powerful female characters in folktales and fairy tales. The open hostility they show toward their stepchildren is a common feature of narratives in many parts of the world, and it is present in traditional oral versions, **literary fairy tale**s, **adaptation**s, and **films**. Stepmothers exemplify the "bad" mother who allows the fantasy of the "good" mother to remain; she is cruel, greedy, malicious, and jealous. The stepmother is one of the most common villainous characters, and she is closely aligned with other hostile female characters, including witches, ogresses, enchantresses, and the like. Stith **Thompson**'s *Motif-Index of Folk-Literature* lists numerous motifs related to the stepmother's cruelty: Motif S31, Cruel stepmother; Motif G205, Witch stepmother; Motif L55.1, Abused stepdaughter; Motif M411.1.1, Curse by stepmother; and Motif S31.4, Cruel stepmother feeds children with fish spines (thorns) to kill them.

Numerous traditional tale types include wicked stepmothers who seek to hurt their husband's children. Stepmothers may overwork, starve, kill, or eat them. These acts of villainy are perpetrated against both male and female protagonists. For example, in ATU 720, The Juniper Tree, the stepmother kills her stepson and serves him to his father, who unknowingly eats him. The boy's bones are placed under a tree, and a bird (or a bone) sings to the family about what happened, after which the stepmother is killed. In the opening of tale type ATU 450, Little Brother and Little Sister, the children run away because their stepmother wants to eat them. A key element of the most widely distributed versions of ATU 327A, Hansel and Gretel, is the cruel stepmother, who is responsible for abandoning the children in the forest.

If a tale includes the stepmother's natural children, she almost always works toward their promotion while abusing her stepchild(ren). For instance, in many versions of The Kind and the Unkind Girls, the stepmother shoves the female protagonist into a well, where she encounters the donor figure who tests and rewards her. After the heroine's return home, the stepmother then sends her own daughter on the same quest. In Cinderella tales, the stepmother gives the heroine impossible tasks to complete before going to the ball, intending that only her natural daughters will go. When the prince arrives with the recognition token (the **shoe**), the stepmother schemes to have her daughters try on the shoe before allowing the heroine to try. Jealousy is another typical motivation for the stepmother's villainy, as in "Snow White," wherein she is jealous of the heroine's beauty.

Mothers-in-Law

Often overlooked in favor of evil stepmothers, witches, and other female villains, mothers-in-law are important, traditional hostile mother figures in folktales and fairy tales from Europe, the Mediterranean, the Middle East, India, and much of Asia. The mother-in-law also appears as a cultural stereotype in many jokes, anecdotes, and personal narratives across many Indo-European and Asian cultures. Typically depicted as a source of tension or conflict within a **marriage**, the mother-in-law can be a controlling, domineering woman. Mothers-in-law and stepmothers have much in common in folktales and fairy tales. Warner identifies a linguistic connection between these figures: The French word for both stepmother and mother-in-law is *belle-mere*, literally "beautiful mother." Additionally, until the mid-nineteenth century, the English term "mother-in-law" was also used to refer to stepmothers. The *Motif-Index* lists several traditional motifs indicating the conflict between mothers-in-law and daughters-in-law: Motif P262.1, Bad relations of mother-in-law and daughter-in-law; Motif S51, Cruel mother-in-law; Motif S51.1, Cruel mother-in-law plans death of daughter-in-law; and Motif S322.6, Jealous mother-in-law and sisters cast woman's children forth.

Warner suggests that the tension between the mother-in-law and daughter-in-law may be another reflection of lived circumstances in folktales and fairy tales. The presence of a son's wife in the household meant that the mother had a rival for her son's affections. In strongly patriarchal societies, the mother's security in old **age** depended on her son's loyalty. This situation nearly institutionalizes a rivalry between these women that is expressed in many folktales and fairy tales, and pregnancy often precipitates the crisis between the women. In many narratives with mothers-in-law as adversaries, the acts of villainy harm the children, question whether the children are the husband's through accusations of adultery, or accuse the female protagonist of killing her children (for example, Motif K2117, The calumniated wife: substituted letter; Motif K2112, Woman slandered as adulteress; Motif K2115, Animal-birth slander; and Motif K2116.1.1.1, Innocent woman accused of killing her new-born children). Many of these motifs appear in the second episodes of ATU 883A, The Innocent Slandered Maiden, in which the female protagonist undergoes a second slandering when (usually) the mother-in-law accuses the heroine of adultery, casts her out, or attempts to murder her children. There are also many traditional tales depicting this adversarial relationship found in Arabic and Asian countries that do not appear in international tale types. *See also* Childhood and Children; Infertility.

Further Readings: Barker, Adele Marie. *The Mother Syndrome in the Russian Folk Imagination.* Columbus: Slavica, 1986; Birkhäuser-Oeri, Sibylle. *The Mother: Archetypal Image in Fairy Tales.* Translated by Michael Mitchell. Toronto: Inner City Books, 1988; Hirsch, Marianne. *The Mother/Daughter Plot: Narrative, Psychoanalysis, Feminism.* Bloomington: Indiana University Press, 1989; Johns, Andreas. *Baba Yaga: The Ambiguous Mother and Witch of the Russian Folktale.* New York: Peter Lang, 2004; Tucker, Holly. *Pregnant Fictions: Childbirth and the Fairy Tale in Early-Modern France.* Detroit:

Wayne State University Press, 2003; Warner, Marina. *The Absent Mother, or Women against Women in the 'Old Wives' Tale*. Hilversum [Netherlands]: Verloren, 1991; _____. *From the Beast to the Blonde: On Fairy Tales and Their Tellers*. New York: Farrar, Straus and Giroux, 1994; Yolen, Jane, and Heidi E. Y. Stemple, eds. *Mirror, Mirror: Forty Folktales for Mothers and Daughters to Share*. New York: Viking, 2000.

Linda J. Lee

Mother Goose

Although various explanations have been proposed for the term "Mother Goose," its origins remain mysterious nonetheless. Expressions such as "old wives' tales" or "tales of wise **women**" abound in seventeenth-century England and France, and epithets of this kind refer to tales belonging to the popular and **oral tradition**, in times when old women were often tending to geese in the pasture.

French author Charles **Perrault** was the first to link the French expression "Ma Mère l'Oye"—Mother Goose—with a collection of fairy tales. His influential *Histoires ou contes du temps passé* (*Stories or Tales of Times Past*, 1697) includes a frontispiece that depicts an old woman **spinning** by the hearth while telling stories to children under a sign that reads "Contes de ma mère l'oye." As a consequence, Perrault's tales are often known and published in France under the title *Contes de ma mère l'oye* (*Tales of Mother Goose*).

The term "Mother Goose" came to England in 1729 when Robert Samber translated Perrault's stories for the first time into English. Like Perrault's original French edition, Samber's translation, *Histories or Tales of Past Times*, includes its own engraved illustration of a woman telling tales to children beneath a sign bearing the words "Mother Goose's Tales." Since then, Mother Goose has become a familiar and beloved fixture in English **children's literature**. In the Victorian era, she had the appearance of an actual goose dressed like an old lady and became one of the favorite themes of countless nursery rhymes and tales.

Further Readings: Barchilon, Jacques, and Henry Pettit. *The Authentic Mother Goose Fairy Tales and Nursery Rhymes*. Denver: Alan Swallow, 1960; Warner, Marina. *From the Beast to the Blonde: On Fairy Tales and Their Tellers*. New York: Farrar, Straus and Giroux, 1994.

Claire L. Malarte-Feldman

Mother Holle

The tale known as "Mother Holle"—"Frau Holle" in Jacob and Wilhelm **Grimm**'s *Kinder- und Hausmärchen* (*Children's and Household Tales*, 1812–15)—is about a good girl who is rewarded and a bad one who is punished. It belongs to the **tale type** called **The Kind and the Unkind Girls** (ATU 480), which focuses attention on the good/bad girls as a main **motif**, rather than on Mother Holle, the goddesslike title figure in her subterranean realm.

In this tale, an abused stepdaughter falls into a well while cleaning a distaff she has bloodied while **spinning** diligently. She lands in a magical realm, where she unquestioningly performs various duties: for example, propping up heavily laden apple tree branches and removing bread from the oven before it burns. For her docility and obedience, she is rewarded by the old woman with a shower of gold. The lazy stepsister attempts to win the same favors from Mother Holle, but she fails to do the work and is rewarded with a shower of pitch. The double nature of the girls is indicated by the names they are referred to in the later version by Ludwig **Bechstein**: "Goldmaria und Pechmaria" ("Gold-Mary and Pitch-Mary," 1845).

In the wake of late-twentieth-century **feminism**, the Grimms in particular have been criticized for characterizing **women** and girls as either "beautiful and diligent" or "ugly and lazy" and for rewarding female characters for their unquestioning obedience. This tendency in the portrayal of female figures shows them to be a part of a wider trend in nineteenth-century literature, which evinces any number of good blondes and bad brunettes. Whereas "kindness versus unkindness" forms a motif in many tales of **punishment and reward**, what distinguishes the Grimms' version is the excessive passivity of the "good" girl.

Whatever mythical significance Mother Holle herself may have had has been almost entirely lost in the Grimms' version; however, she is clearly related to other **fairies** who reward and punish. In Jacob Grimm's *Deutsche Mythologie* (1835; translated as *Teutonic Mythology*, 1883), Mother Holle is mentioned as a lake or well spirit who rewards good housework, and she is particularly associated with spinning and snowfall. Despite her hideous appearance—she has long teeth and wild **hair**—she is generally good to humans. In her older pagan form, Holle (sometimes spelled Hulla or Holde) may have been a fertility goddess, although sometimes her connection with flax and spinning make her more of an earth goddess. She is also associated with Frau Perchta, another figure from German mythology, and with the **legend** of the *wütendes Heer* (literally "Raging Army," also known as the "Wild Hunt"), in which she is said to take the souls of children who have died unbaptised.

The Grimms' "Mother Holle" is related to other tales in their collection, such as "Die weiße und die schwarze Braut" ("The White Bride and the Black Bride") and "Der arme und der Reiche" ("The Poor Man and the Rich Man"). Other versions of "Mother Holle" include not only Bechstein's "Goldmaria und Pechmaria" but also Benedikte **Naubert**'s "Der kurze Mantel" ("The Cloak," 1789). The tale's punishment-and-reward motif has precursors in Giambattista **Basile**'s "Le tre fate" ("Three Fairies," 1634) and Charles **Perrault**'s "Les fées" ("The Fairies," 1697). Naubert's German version foregrounds the economic independence spinning gives to women; her Mother Hulla is a benign a guiding feminine spirit who aids well-intended women, even when they make mistakes. In Bechstein, on the other hand, the supernatural figure is an old man instead of an old woman. The good girl distinguishes herself by always choosing the worse of two options, and is rewarded with the better; her bad stepsister demands the better and gets the worse. *See also* Cinderella; False Bride; Mother; Sisters.

Further Readings: Bottigheimer, Ruth B. *Grimms' Bad Girls and Bold Boys: The Moral and Social Vision of the Tales*. New Haven, CT: Yale University Press, 1987; Grimm, Jacob, *Deutsche Mythologie*. 2nd edition. Göttingen: Dieterische Buchhandlung, 1844; Naubert, Benedikte. "The Cloak." *Bitter Healing: German Women Authors, 1700–1840*. Edited by Jeannine Blackwell and Susanne Zantop. Lincoln: University of Nebraska Press, 1990. 207–77; Thiel, Anne. "From Woman to Woman: Benedikte Naubert's 'Der kurze Mantel.'" *Harmony in Discord: German Women Writers in the Eighteenth and Nineteenth Centuries*. Edited by Laura Martin. Berne: Lang, 2002. 125–44.

Laura Martin

Motif

In literature, "motif" refers to a recurring element that accrues significance through repetition. Motifs can occur within a given piece or throughout the works of a specific author. The emphasis is on meaning and effect. In **folklore** and fairy-tale studies, however, begat during the vogue of historicism, comparativism, and diffusionism, "motif" has acquired a more typological and comparative sense. Here, "motif" has come to mean specific recognized characters, themes, concepts, actions, and topoi, none of which, in isolation, constitute a complete narrative, but, in mix-and-match combinations, are narrative building blocks—"those details out of which full-fledged narratives are composed" (Thompson, *Motif-Index* 1: 10).

Due to the efforts of Stith **Thompson**, first in his collaboration with Antti **Aarne** on *The Types of the Folktale* (1928; revised 1961), and subsequently in his own six-volume *Motif-Index of Folk-Literature*, specific combinations of motifs that retained remarkable consistency over time and space were identified and designated as "**tale types**" in Aarne's classificatory system. These tale types were considered to be cognate, that is, historically related and products of **monogenesis** and **diffusion**, and were analyzed using the comparative **historic-geographic method**, which ultimately sought the origin of individual tale types. As the Eurocentric limitations of the tale-type system of classification became apparent, Thompson increasingly turned to the motif as the preferred unit of comparison. Because motifs are partial, however, and explicitly combinatory and generative, they provide a model of innovation rather than stasis; thus, motifs sharing the same motif number are not considered to be cognate. Neither does the *Motif-Index* organize motifs by country of origin or genre; instead, motifs are disassembled and reorganized into a system of twenty-three categories, loosely progressing from the more supernatural to "reality-based" motifs, designated by letter headings: A. Mythological Motifs; B. Animals; C. Tabu; D. Magic; E. The Dead; F. Marvels; G. Ogres; H. Tests; J. The Wise and the Foolish; K. Deceptions; L. Reversal of Fortune; M. Ordaining the Future; N. Chance and Fate; P. Society; Q. Rewards and Punishments; R. Captives and Fugitives; S. Unnatural Cruelty; T. Sex; U. The Nature of Life; V. Religion; W. Traits of Character; X. Humor; Z. Miscellaneous Groups of Motifs. These general headings are then broken down further into discrete and specific motifs, so that, for example, F. Marvels is followed by F. 200 Fairies and F. 200.1 Pixies. Occasionally, a single motif coincides with a tale type, but this is due to the ad hoc nature of these indexes.

In the twentieth century, as a result of the intellectual rejection of both positivism and the evolutionary theory that undergirded the comparative method, motif analysis became gradually supplanted by more synchronic methods, such as **structuralism**, **performance** theory, and psychoanalytic applications. Structuralism, particularly that attributed to Valdimir **Propp** in his *Morfologiya skazki* (*Morphology of the Folktale*, 1928), was understood to be antithetical to a motif-based analysis of tales. Structuralism emphasized narrative patterns, relationships, and the processes by which plots progressed, and the basic Proppian unit, the **function**, was fundamentally a plot motivator, fulfilling a structural role. Motifs, in their specificity, were seen as too subjective, or irrelevant to the underlying unity. Propp's system, a combination of the Finnish method and Russian formalism, was not, however, really antithetical to motif analysis, since it too broke down tales into their component parts, albeit more abstract in form. Nevertheless, the concepts of motif and function are not synonymous, a claim that is sometimes made. Alan **Dundes**, embracing structuralism in the 1960s, sought to reconcile the two systems in his articulation of the "**motifeme**." But this methodology, which he further developed to achieve a psychoanalytic approach to tales, has, for the most part, not been adopted.

Regardless of the methodological flaws and ideological premises inherent in the *Motif-Index*, it is a powerful resource for cross-cultural source material. In addition, each motif is cross-referenced with similar or corresponding motifs, allowing for an expanded structural and symbolic analysis. The *Motif-Index* is available online (through most university databases) and is also available on CD-ROM. *See also* Folktale.

Further Readings: Thompson, Stith. *Motif-Index of Folk-Literature: A Classification of Narrative Elements in Folktales, Ballads, Myths, Fables, Mediaeval Romances, Exempla, Fabliaux, Jest-Books, and Local Legends.* Revised and enlarged edition. 6 volumes. Bloomington: Indiana University Press, 1955–58. CD-ROM. 1993; _____. *Narrative Motif-Analysis as Folklore Method.* Helsinki: Suomalainen Teideakatemia, 1955.

JoAnn Conrad

Motifeme

Commonly attributed to Alan **Dundes**'s structural approach to folktales and fairy tales, the term "motifeme" signifies a minimal structural unit. Influenced by *Morphology of the Folktale*—the 1958 English translation of Vladimir **Propp**'s *Morfologiya skazki* (1928)—Dundes's methodology called for a revision of the **historic-geographic method**, which had used **motif**s to define and determine the typology of tales (**tale type**). Instead, Dundes argued for a fundamental structural paradigm. Expanding and modifying Propp's notion of "**function**," Dundes proposed substituting in its place the more abstracted form of the motif—the "motifeme." By incorporating it into the previously antithetical, syntagmatic structural approach, Dundes rehabilitated the motif, which had previously not taken into account the structural patterns of tales. In this way, he also merged the structuralist and typological approaches.

The abstracted motifeme could be filled by any number of motifs, and this array of motifs, termed "allomotifs," could both fulfill a given function or "motifemic slot" and be used interchangeably. Allomotifs are thus paradigmatic equivalents used in differing contexts to fill a "motifemic slot." Dundes's method consisted of assembling many versions of a tale and identifying the structures common to them and the allomotifs used in these functions. This kind of comparison made it possible to determine allomotif equivalents, which ultimately were not only structurally but also symbolically equivalent. *See also* Comparative Method; Structuralism.

Further Readings: Dundes, Alan. "From Etic to Emic Units in the Structural Study of Folktales." *Journal of American Folklore* 75 (1962): 95–105; _____. "The Symbolic Equivalence of Allomotifs: Towards a Method of Analyzing Folktales." *Le conte: Pourquoi? Comment?* Edited by Genevieève Calame-Griaule, Veronika Görög-Karady, and Micheèle Chiche. Paris: Éditions du Centre National de la Recherche Scientifique, 1984. 187–97.

JoAnn Conrad

Müller, Friedrich Max (1823–1900)

Born in Dessau, Germany, in 1823, Friedrich Max Müller attended Leipzig University, training under linguist Franz Bopp, before moving to England, and Oxford University, in 1846. Like his former professor, Müller is best known as a philologist, Indo-Europeanist, and scholar of Sanskrit, but his interests also led him into the fields of comparative religion and mythology. **Myth**, Müller suggested, was the result of what he called the disease of language—the personification and narrativization of abstract concepts by primitive peoples. In part, the abstract concept that Indo-European myths expressed in narrative was the pattern by which the sun traveled across the sky.

This theory—solar mythology, as it has become known—came under fire even in its own time. Noted scholar and social critic Andrew **Lang** treated it harshly in his writings, calling instead for an approach to myth more closely aligned with E. B. Tylor's unilinear evolutionary theory. Bronislaw Malinowski, in his essay "Myth in Primitive Psychology" (1926), called the theory extravagant and self-indulgent, while Richard M. **Dorson**, in 1955, referred to it as little more than a historical curiosity. Although solar mythology has largely faded into obscurity today, Müller's place in the history of folk narrative studies cannot be ignored. *See also* Anthropological Approaches; Linguistic Approaches; Mythological Approaches.

Further Readings: Dorson, Richard M. "The Eclipse of Solar Mythology." *Journal of American Folklore* 68 (1955): 393–416; Schrempp, Gregory. "The Re-Education of Friedrich Max Müller: Intellectual Appropriation and Epistemological Antinomy in Mid-Victorian Evolutionary Thought." *Man* ns 18 (1983): 90–110.

Adam Zolkover

Munro, Alice (1931–)

The acclaimed Canadian writer of short fiction, widely regarded as having equaled or surpassed such predecessors as Anton Chekhov and James Joyce, Alice Munro has published story collections at regular intervals since *Dance of the Happy Shades* (1968). Later volumes include *Open Secrets* (1994) and *Runaway* (2004). Her life experience—two marriages and two places of residence, Ontario and British Columbia—forms the basis of her fiction. Rich in subplots and tales within tales, her stories often involve coincidences, parallelism, twinlike characters, or characters who are storytellers.

The effects she achieves are heightened by allusions to **ballad**s, traditional tales, and literary **folklore**, especially in her later stories. A tour de force laced with intimations about men's **sexuality**, "Wenlock Edge" (*New Yorker*, December 5, 2005) refashions the fourteenth-century romance *Sir Gawain and the Green Knight*. In *The Love of a Good Woman* (1998), "The Children Stay" presents an adulterous affair modeled after Jean Anouilh's *Eurydice*, which in turn recalls the Greek **myth** of Orpheus and Eurydice. Among other stories in the same volume, "Save the Reaper" takes its title from Alfred Lord **Tennyson**'s "The Lady of Shalott"; "Before the Change" incorporates W. B. **Yeats**'s "The Song of Wandering Aengus"; and the ghostly tale "My Mother's Dream" suggests an English ballad, "The Cruel Mother," as well as **folktale** type ATU 769, The Child's Grave. *See also* Bear's Son.

Further Readings: Edemariam, Aida. "Riches of a Double Life." *The Guardian* October 4, 2003. http://books.guardian.co.uk/review/story/0,12084,1054206,00.html; Thacker, Robert. *Alice Munro: Writing Her Lives: A Biography*. Toronto: McClelland and Stewart, 2005.

John Bierhorst

Murat, Henriette-Julie de Castelnau, Comtesse de (1670–1716)

Henriette-Julie de Castelnau, Comtesse de Murat was the daughter of the prominent Castelnau family of Britanny, France. She moved to Paris at the age of fifteen or sixteen and married the Comte de Murat shortly afterward. Of the late seventeenth-century French *conteuses* (female tale tellers), Murat has perhaps one of the most detailed biographical records—which is primarily the result of her high-profile and highly controversial personality in what was an increasingly conventionalized late seventeenth-century French society.

Both during her adult life and in the centuries following, Murat's name was consistently associated with scandal and sexuality. In 1695, Murat's *Mémoires de Madame le Comtesse de *** avant sa retraite, ou La défense des dames* (*Memoirs of Madame the Countess of*

*** *before Her Retirement, or The Defense of Women*) described the events leading up to the author's exile, at the urging of Madame de Maintenon, by Louis XIV. She described the unhappy circumstances of her marriage and associated attempts to separate from her husband, and she worked to reclaim her reputation at court following claims of sexual impropriety. In a second wave of scandal, Parisian police records between 1699 and 1702 alleged unruly behavior and made claims of Murat's love affairs with men and women alike and resultant fits of jealous rage. Officially denounced by the king, Murat remained in exile in the city of Loches until 1715, just one year before her death.

The majority of Murat's texts were published just before the second scandal: *Contes de fées* (*Fairy Tales*, 1698); *Nouveaux contes de fées* (*New Fairy Tales*, 1698); and *Histoires sublimes et allégoriques* (*Sublime and Allegorical Stories*, 1699). Many tales in these collections present **marriage** and constraints on female desire in ways that are similar to those depicted in the *Mémoires.* "Palais de la vengeance," ("Palace of Vengeance"), for example, ends with the male and female protagonists being granted their wish to spend their lives together; however, their fate is not the happy one hoped for, but rather a miserable eternity of literal imprisonment together. "Heureuse peine" ("Happy Labor") contains a similarly unhappy ending and the narratorial warning that "a wedding is almost always a sad occasion." Murat's *Voyage de campagne* (*Trip to the Country*, 1699) is a collection of stories told by a group of acquaintances on a holiday in the country. While not a collection of fairy tales per se, *Trip to the Country* is suggestive of the type of **salon** conversation and literary creativity that is understood to underlie the genesis of the early French *contes de fées*. Moreover, Murat's inclusion of the genre of the **ghost story** (including an account of the well-known *salonnière* [female salon participant] Madame Deshoulières's own ghost hunt) offer a preview of sorts for Murat's later, otherworldly *Les lutins du château de Kermosy* (*The Goblins of the Kermosy Chateau*, 1710).

Murat's *Sublime and Allegorical Stories* is of particular interest to scholars of the **literary fairy tale** in France. In her preface, Murat dedicates her volume to her fellow "fées modernes" (modern **fairies**) and contrasts their noble work to that of their more domesticated and rudimentary predecessors: servants and wet-nurses. In this work, Murat directly engages Charles **Perrault** and presents her tales in such a way that would revalorize not only the *conte de fées* as a genre but also female authorship more generally. *See also* French Tales; Women.

Further Readings: Robinson, David Michael. "The Abominable Madame de Murat." *Journal of Homosexuality* 41 (2001): 53–67; Storer, Mary Elizabeth. "Madame de Murat." *Un épisode littéraire de la fin du XVIIe siècle: La mode des contes de fées (1685–1700).* Paris: Honoré Champion, 1928. 140–59; Tucker, Holly, and Melanie R. Siemens, trans. "Perrault's Preface to *Griselda* and Murat's 'To Modern Fairies.'" *Marvels & Tales* 19 (2005): 125–30.

Holly Tucker

Musäus, Johann Karl August (1735–1787)

With his *Volksmärchen der Deutschen* (*Folktales of the Germans*, 1782–86), Johann Karl August Musäus cashed in on the growing popularity of tales of the marvelous, a trend that had been apparent in Germany since the beginning of the eighteenth century and that now included (supposedly) homegrown German tales as opposed to translations from the French. Like Christoph Martin **Wieland**, Musäus had no interest in trying to retain the **folk** tone of the material. On the contrary, he created rococo masterpieces of wit and erudition, with a slyly knowing narrator and many topical allusions to the contemporary literary world. Musäus's work fell out of favor with the generation of German Romantics, who either, like the Brothers **Grimm**, desired a closer attention to **authenticity** or, like Achim von Arnim and Clemens **Brentano**, felt that the modern author should follow the spirit of the folk tradition in writing new, more personal tales. For these later writers, Musäus failed by maintaining an arrogant and "Enlightened" superiority over his material. However, in his fourteen tales, Musäus may well have kept some stories and traditions from falling into obscurity. Among his most popular tales are the ones about the mountain spirit Rübezahl, the bigamist Graf (Count) von Gleichen, and the Czech amazon Libussa. *See also* Folktale; German Tales; Literary Fairy Tale.

Further Readings: Berger, Dorothea. "*Die Volksmärchen der Deutschen* von Musäus, ein Meisterwerk der Rokokodichtung." *PMLA* 69 (1954): 1200–12; Grätz, Manfred. *Das Märchen in der deutschen Aufklärung: Vom Feenmärchen zum Volksmärchen.* Stuttgart: Metzler, 1988; Miller, Norbert. Afterword. *Volksmärchen der Deutschen.* By Johann Karl August Musäus. Munich: Winkler, 1976. 876–906.

Laura Martin

Music

Music is at once an ally of folktales and fairy tales and a decidedly strange bedfellow. The distinct characters, colors and, in some cases, fantastical environments of tales tend to evoke a quite particular mood, and so lend themselves readily to the emotional facilities of music. Conversely, folktales and fairy tales are, above all other things, stories; to tell a story via music alone presents a particular challenge to the composer, hence the number of folktale and fairy-tale musical works in which the story is carried by words, as in **opera** and song, or dramatic enactment, as in **dance**. Music written in response to these tales thus tends to be oriented around either narrative or mood, although the two are far from mutually exclusive.

The most obvious example of music used to accompany the telling of tales comes in the form of the ever-popular fairy-tale ballet. Russian works predominate here, most notably those written in the late nineteenth century by Pyotr Il'ich **Tchaikovsky**: *Swan Lake* (1877), *The Sleeping Beauty* (1890), and *The Nutcracker* (1892). The most successful of these, *The Sleeping Beauty*, went on to serve as inspiration for what is surely one of the stranger fairy-tale ballets: Igor Stravinsky's *Le baiser de la fée* (*The Fairy's Kiss*, 1928). The influential Russian critic Alexandre Benois suggested to the composer the idea of a ballet based on the relatively minor piano pieces of Tchaikovsky, with the story taken loosely from Hans Christian **Andersen**'s "Iisjomfruen" ("The Ice Maiden," 1862). It was Stravinsky himself who selected the tale, conceiving it as an allegory of the life of his beloved compatriot composer. What makes the endeavor puzzling is the sheer gusto with which Stravinsky set about writing unashamedly conventional music—brilliantly conventional, no doubt—with little sign of irony or satire. The ballet is flagrantly anachronistic, not only in its music—including the sections written by Stravinsky alone—but also in its affectionate staging of an old world markedly at odds with the events of the first decades of the twentieth century. Yet it is precisely this pervasive anachronism that serves the fairy-tale subject so well.

Stravinsky's earlier stage works are more characteristically modern in their mix of folktale and musical innovation. Among them are *L'oiseau de feu* (*The Firebird*, 1910), the composer's first collaboration with Sergey Diaghilev of the Ballets Russes. It was Diaghilev who suggested a ballet score based around the Russian legend of "The Firebird," or phoenix, an idea to which Stravinsky responded with music of startling harmonic and rhythmic originality. Later folk-inspired works include two dramatic stagings of tales from the collections of Alesandr **Afanas'ev**: *Renard* (1915–16; first performed in 1922) and *Histoire du soldat* (*The Soldier's Tale*, 1918).

Along with Léo Delibes' *Coppélia* (1870), based on E. T. A. **Hoffmann**'s "Der Sandmann" ("The Sandman," 1816), the other staple of the fairy-tale ballet world is Sergey Prokofiev's **Cinderella** (1945), a late work striking in its disillusioned portrayal of the court of the **prince**. One final ballet of Russian origin is **Sheherazade**, presented by Diaghilev in the same year as *The Firebird* (1910). This is in fact an adaptation of a preexisting orchestral work by Nikolai **Rimsky-Korsakov** (1888), composed in just a few weeks in the wake of a reading of the **Arabian Nights**. The voice of the heroine is carried over the four movements of the music by a windingly rhapsodic violin solo set against washes of brilliant orchestration. The individual movements were originally titled, but Rimsky-Korsakov opted to play down direct correlations with specific tales, preferring to present the work as a nonprogrammatic symphonic poem.

Another orchestral work inspired by the *Arabain Nights* is Maurice Ravel's *Shéhérazade* (1898), the overture to a projected but never-realized opera on the subject. The composer went on to write an orchestral song cycle with the same title (1903), a work that in fact has nothing to do with the eponymous heroine, being instead a setting of three exoticist poems by Tristan Klingsor. Ravel was quietly attracted to an idealized child's world of tales and toys, as demonstrated in the opera *L'enfant et les sortilèges* (*The Child and the Spells*, 1925), with its naughty boy, loving Maman, and cast of miraculously singing objects. Yet it is in *Ma mère l'oye* (**Mother Goose**, 1908–10) that the composer's interest specifically in the environment of the fairy tale is most strikingly captured. A set of five pieces written originally for piano duet, Ravel orchestrated the work in 1911 and then expanded it further a year later in the form of a ballet based around the figure of Sleeping Beauty. The music is inspired by the golden age of the French fairy tale. In its final manifestation, as ballet, it begins with the "Dance of the Spinning Wheel" and the "Pavane of the Sleeping Beauty." Then follow a waltzing **Beauty and the Beast** and **Tom Thumb**. The work ends with the beautiful scene of "The Fairy Garden," the encapsulation of a very particular compositional sensibility. In its singular mix of sophistication and simplicity, Ravel's suite is perhaps the most successful purely musical fairy-tale work.

Just as Ravel's music and literary inspiration are decidedly French, so the set of four orchestral ballads by the Czech composer, Antonín **Dvořák**, are in a recognizable national tradition. Of all the orchestral works on folktale or fairy-tale themes, Dvořák's symphonic poems are the most closely tied to the path of the individual stories. The stories themselves— *The Water Goblin*, *The Noon Witch*, *The Golden Wheel*, and *The Wild Dove* (all 1896)—are taken from a collection of folktales and ballads compiled by the poet and folklorist Karel Jaromír Erben.

Beyond works based clearly on a specific tale or character, musical traditions are of course littered with broad allusions to folktales and fairy tales. In this category falls Russian composer Nikolai Medtner's various sets of "Fairy Tale" piano pieces, composed throughout the first half of the twentieth century, and the *Fairy Tale* suite (1917), again for piano, by the British composer Frank Bridge. One striking instance of the evocation in music of a fairy-tale ambience can be found in the late chamber music miniatures of Robert Schumann, in particular *Märchenbilder*, op. 113, for piano and viola, and *Märchenerzählungen*, op. 132, for piano, clarinet, and viola. The works are entirely devoid of programs, opting instead to conjure images in music. The music ranges from rhapsodic to epic, melancholy to nostalgic, with the listener left free to establish the nature of the relationship between such music and the fairy tale. It is perhaps in this stimulation of the imagination, coupled with the mercurial quality of the music, that we can locate Schumann's own attraction to the tales.

Music such as this raises the question of just what it means to call a musical work a fairy tale. It may be that the initial attraction of the tales for composers lies not in the content of the narratives but rather in the mood they create, a mood the very indistinctness of which not only invokes music, but could itself be said to be somehow musical. Of course, folktales and fairy tales enjoy a healthy afterlife in the far-from-indistinct world of popular music—from the songs that accompany Walt **Disney**'s fairy-tale films to the Cinderella of Bob Dylan's "Desolation Row" (1965) and beyond. Yet such music tends towards the illustrative rather than the evocative. The question of whether fairy tales could be said to be *like* music was raised briefly toward the end of the eighteenth century, in the early years of German Romanticism. Responding to the Kantian notion that, left free to roam, the imagination produces only nonsense, authors such as **Novalis** and Ludwig **Tieck** explored the idea of a mode of imaginative writing unconstrained by the demand to make sense. The fairy tale seemed fit for the purpose because of its lack of conventional characterization, disregard for motivation, and uncannily repetitive plots. It was in the perceived dreamy incoherence of the fairy tale that a link could be established with music, not least because music, according to Kant, is the art form that escapes rational reflection (and is thus, for Kant, of secondary importance). Whether or not music and the fairy tale really are alike in their frustration of conventional ideas of coherence and sense, the historical relationship between the two forms suggests that music, more than words or images, has a particular gift for capturing something essential in folktales and fairy tales. *See also* Music and Musical Instruments.

Further Reading: Harwell Celenza, Anna. *Hans Christian Andersen and Music: The Nightingale Revealed.* Aldershot: Ashgate, 2005.

Stephen Benson

Music and Musical Instruments

Many folktales and fairy tales feature **music**, not as a sung part of the text as in the case of **ballads**, but as a significant motif in the story. Music and musical instruments tend to appear in folktales and fairy tales in three major ways. First, music is frequently referenced in relation to animals. Second, characters in folktales are often known by musical practice or abilities. Third, music and musical instruments sometimes play a role directly in folktale plots.

Music in folktales frequently has magical effects on animals. Perhaps the most obvious and best-known example is the tale of The Rat-Catcher (ATU 570*), popularly known as the "Pied Piper of Hamelin" in Jacob and Wilhelm **Grimm**'s collection of *Deutsche Sagen* (*German Legends*, 1816–18). In the Grimms' version of the story, the main character—the Piper—uses his flute to lead rats from the town of Hamelin. Similar situations exist in the **tale type** known as The Rabbit-Herd (ATU 570), where a man has a magic whistle that can summon rabbits, and in The Birthmarks of the Princess (ATU 850), which tells of a swineherd with a magic flute that can make his hogs dance.

In addition to being enchanted by music, animals in folktales also make music on their own, though rarely to good effect. In The Wolf Is Caught Because of His Singing (ATU 100), a **wolf** is tricked into singing and is thrashed or killed; and the tale of the Singing Donkey and Dancing Camel (ATU 214A) features a donkey whose music gets the two in trouble. Music produced by animals, however, does not invariably disadvantage the music makers. The popular tale of "The Bremen Town Musicians" (ATU 130, The Animals in Night Quarters) offers the best example. In this story, a band of old and poorly treated animals—a donkey, dog, cat, and rooster—leave their owners and set out on their way to earn a living in the free town of Bremen by performing as a musical band. On their way, they encounter **thieves**, whom they frighten off with their cacophonous chorus of animal sounds. With the loot the thieves have left behind, the animals live out their days in comfort. The power of music here is quite the opposite of the notion of the human idea of "music that soothes the savage beast." In fact, the exploited animals' power lies less in the music per se than in their acting in unison.

Music in folktales also is linked to individual folktale characters. There are tales specifically about musicians, such as some versions of ATU 1536B, The Three Hunchback Brothers Drowned, in which the **brothers** are musicians. Moreover, some versions of ATU 1656, How the Jews Were Lured Out of Heaven, feature noisy violinists as those expelled from Heaven (see **Anti-Semitism**).

Musical talent tends to be rewarded in folktales, although in "Easy Come, Easy Go!" (ATU 944*), a musician and his little house are swept out to sea while he fiddles. Tales of the type ATU 677* (Below the Sea) feature a musician who entertains the **king** of the sea and wins a bride. Other tales describe the consequences of lacking musical talent, such as St. Peter with the Fiddle (ATU 774F), in which Peter receives a beating for being unable to play the fiddle in a bar. An especially interesting example of the relationship between music and the theme of **punishment and reward** comes in the tale type known as St. Wilgefortis and Her Beard (ATU 706D). In versions of this tale, a musician plays for the crucified Wilgefortis, who gives him a shoe in payment. Accused of theft, the musician is about to be punished until he plays in the church and a picture of Wilgefortis drops another shoe to prove his innocence.

Other characters stand in yet another relationship to music. In The Fleeing Pancake (ATU 2025), well known for the variation featuring a gingerbread man, the main character sings a song as he escapes from things wanting to eat him. Many versions of Jack and the Beanstalk (ATU 328A) feature a talking harp as part of the story. **Variant**s of The Flatulent Girl (ATU 1453****) have some versions in which a flatulent girl who is plugged up with tar and leather leads to the invention of wind instruments. King Midas tales relating to Midas and the Donkey's Ears (ATU 782) include music and musical instruments in two places. First, Midas is cursed with donkey ears for interfering in a divine musical challenge; then, when his barber whispers the secret into a hole in the ground, a musical instrument made from reeds growing nearby reveals the secret when it is played.

Music and musical instruments also serve various functions in folktale plots. For example, musical instruments serve as objects of value or power. Some versions of The Animal as Bridegroom (ATU 425A) include a musical rose. In versions of The Dance among Thorns (ATU 592), a man receives a fiddle that compels people to dance. Variants of The Three Magic Objects and the Wonderful Fruits (ATU 566) include as one of the magic objects a horn or whistle that furnishes the blower with soldiers or power. According to the tale type Thunder's Instruments (ATU 1148B), thunderstorms are made by the thunder god playing a musical instrument of some sort, generally bagpipes or horns, a fact made known when an **ogre** steals the instruments.

Music in folktales often is associated with trickery. In stories that feature a Singing Contest (ATU 1082A), a man and **devil** agree that they will carry each other for the length of a song. While the devil sings a short song, the man sings a song that does not end, forcing the devil to keep carrying him. Versions of The Ogre Caught in the Cleft (ATU 1159) involve an ogre who wants to learn to play a musical instrument and kidnaps a musician to teach him. The musician tells the ogre he needs to straighten his fingers and traps the ogre's hand in a cleft of rock. In both tale types ATU 425E (The Enchanted Husband Sings Lullaby) and ATU 1419H (Woman Warns Lover of Husband by Singing Song), music is used to communicate surreptitiously. In the first case, the husband's song gives a clue to his disenchantment. In the second, the woman's song lets her lover know that her husband is home, preventing them from being caught. ***See also*** Music.

Further Reading: Tari, Lujza. "Musical Instruments and Music in Hungarian Folk Tales." *Artes Populares* 16–17 (1995): 767–83.

B. Grantham Aldred

Myth

Folklorists see myths as stories about grand events in ancient times, often discussing the origin of the present world, of its order and of different objects, phenomena, and creatures. Common characters in myths are gods, goddesses, demons, heroes, and other beings with superhuman qualities and powers. Myths are held to be true in the culture where they belong. As sacred narratives, they are included in religious canons and acted out in rituals; as a prominent genre of folklore, they have spread worldwide at different time periods from the Stone Age to the present day. Myths do not come as single texts; instead, they usually belong to an identifiable textual tradition, a set of interrelated myths that is called "mythology." The word "mythology" also refers to the study of myths and encompasses a broad range of theoretical and methodological approaches.

The contemporary colloquial meaning of "myth" as a false belief reflects the changed attitude toward its value. Myths of one's own culture tend to be understood as fundamental truths, whereas the myths of others—those of different religious and ethnic groups and of past times—are easily recognized as untrue poetic fantasies. This negative connotation has a long history. The original meaning of the Greek word *mûthos* was "tale" or "narrative," but, beginning in the fifth century BCE, some authors, such as Plato, started to imply that not all stories about gods and heroes should be taken seriously. Thus, a distinction was made between *lógos* and *myth*. *Lógos* ("word") began to denote positive knowledge—true stories and rational ideas, while myth referred to **fable**s, **tall tale**s, and lies that some people erroneously believe.

Euhemerus was among the early theoreticians of myth and formulated his views about the origin of gods and mythical events around 320 BCE. He interpreted gods as former human heroes who have been uplifted to a divine status, and he understood grand events in myths as a reflection of real history. Such a historical explanation of myths is known as "euhemerism." The spread of Christianity reinforced negative attitudes toward the ancient heritage and pagan gods, who were interpreted as demons or manifestations of the **devil**. One of the first thinkers to rehabilitate myths was the Italian philosopher Giambattista Vico (1688–1744), who interpreted them as expressions of poetic imagination and a positive force in the history of humankind. Jacob **Grimm** (1785–1863) published his comparative philological monograph *Deutsche Mythologie* (*German Mythology*) in 1835. He believed that the **oral tradition**s of the illiterate people preserved essential information about old Germanic myths. On the basis of these fragments, he tried to reconstruct the lost whole—the mythology of pre-Christian times. During the nineteenth century, the study of myths became a systematic scholarly discipline. Thus, James G. Frazer (1854–1941) published a great comparative monograph *The Golden Bough* in twelve volumes (1890–1915), which is based on the belief in the unilinear evolution of cultures from savagery to civilization, from irrational belief in magic and myths toward scientific rationalism. Bronislaw Malinowski (1884–1942), who lived for several years in the Trobriand Islands, was one of the first scholars to study myths as parts of living oral traditions. Malinowski was interested in the function of myths and saw them as powerful tools that uphold culture and society and strengthen their traditions by endowing them with value and prestige.

Claude Lévi-Strauss (1908–) applied to myths the principles of linguistic analysis and came to the conclusion that they are based on binary oppositions, such as raw and cooked, wet and dry, and life and death. According to Lévi-Strauss, myths represent and mediate conflicts between such basic oppositions. To understand the meaning of myths, one has to find these underlying patterns, hidden in the plot of narratives. The school established and inspired by Lévi-Strauss is known as **structuralism**. An early predecessor of this approach was Vladimir **Propp** (1895–1970), whose *Morfologiya skazki* (*Morphology of the Folktale*, 1928) delineated the basic sequence of events in Russian **wonder tale**s. Propp discovered that the underlying structure of these tales is "lack/lack liquidated," which was later found in myths as well (for example, nonexistence-creation of the world).

Most folklorists have studied myths as a narrative genre of folklore. William Bascom (1912–81) compared them to **fairy tale**s and **legend**s and drew attention to their basic differences. Whereas fairy tales are fictional and profane narratives whose events take place in a fantasy world that is regarded as unreal by the teller and the audience, myths are believed to be true. Legends discuss human encounters with the supernatural powers in the present world. Mythical events take place in the distant past and do not focus on human experience as legends do, but instead on the life of deities. This contrastive approach to myths, fairy tales, and legends does not mean that the three genres have no connection. Many fairy-tale **motif**s, such as the fight with the **dragon** or a trip to the other world, derive historically from myths. Also, legends generally confirm the reality of the mythical world and the power of gods over minor supernatural beings, such as nature spirits, ghosts, and the devil. Alan **Dundes** (1934–2005) has noted that the number of myths in each culture is finite if compared to the abundance of other prose narrative genres, such as fairy tales and legends.

Although limited in number, myths form a fundamental genre that establishes worldviews and supports the stability and functioning of whole societies. Creation or the birth of the cosmos is one of the most important topics of myths all over the world. Such myths are called "cosmogonic," and in them we can find a large variety of views about how the world came into being. According to the **Bible**, God first created heaven and earth, and then he made light, followed by other objects, phenomena, and beings. God also established order in the world that he created by separating the light and the darkness, dividing the waters, and making all other arrangements to render the world suitable for life. The ancient Indian collection of religious hymns *Rig Veda* presents a variety of myths—the world is born from a cosmic sacrifice, from desire (*kāma*), heat (*tapas*), the divine word (*vāc*), or some other underlying power. In some Rig Vedic hymns, the personal demiurge Prajāpati ("lord of generations") appears and gives shape to the world. According to Karelian and Estonian mythical songs, the cosmos is born from the eggs of an eagle, a swallow, or some other divine bird. Topics of cosmogonic myths vary greatly but most of them see our world as the center of the universe, differently from contemporary cosmology, which has dislocated Earth from being the center of cosmos. Another common trait in myths is the search for a single origin, an underlying power, or a demiurge who created the cosmos and established its order.

In most mythologies, the world is not eternal but will eventually be destroyed. Myths that discuss the "ultimate" topics are called "eschatological" (the Greek *eschatos* meaning "last, furthest"). Sometimes hope is expressed in a new creation and in a better world after life on earth has been destroyed in huge catastrophes. The mythical concept of time thus tends to be cyclical. In the Old Testament, we find the myth of flood that was meant to punish the sinful men who had been corrupted by the fallen angels. Before the deluge, murderous evil giants lived on earth—the children of angels and mortal women. Whereas God destroyed the seed of evil, he had mercy on the righteous Noah, who built the ark that saved humankind and animals from extinction. In ancient Indian myths, the savior of humankind from flood and the forefather of later generations is Manu, who once saved a little fish. The fish warned him of the coming flood and told him to build a boat.

Other myths tell about the destruction of world through fire. Some Native American visions of the future, such as the Hopi prophecies, foretell a "Great Purification" and fiery cataclysm. According to old Germanic sources, the demonic **wolf** Fenrir finally devours the Sun and the evil god Loki, and giants start a battle against the gods. In the cosmic catastrophe, called Ragnarök ("fate of gods"), flames seize heaven and earth, and the world is destroyed. However, in this myth we also find the motif of the renewal of earth, which will grow plants again. The great destruction will be followed by a happy age of love and harmony.

In addition to discussing the beginning and end of the world, myths also provide humans with the mental map of the universe. Mircea Eliade (1907–86) has shown that many mythologies fix the sacred center of the world or its axis (*axis mundi*). The center can be a mythical world mountain, such as Meru in India, but also a temple, a palace, or a huge tree such as Yggdrasil in Germanic mythology. Many peoples in North Eurasia believed in the existence of such a world tree, whose roots lie in the underworld and whose branches reach the sky. Such a cosmic tree corresponds to the tripartite division of the world in North Eurasia: heaven was believed to be inhabited by deities, earth was the realm of human beings, and the underworld was for demonic creatures and the dead. These three layers of the universe are paralleled by heaven, earth, and hell in Christian traditions.

Besides such vertical models, several mythologies conceptualize the world horizontally. Peoples who live on the banks of the great Siberian rivers that flow from south to north have seen them as world rivers that link the land of gods in the south with the realm of death in the far north. The mundane geography of these peoples has a celestial parallel in the constellations, stars, and planets. Thus, among the Finno-Ugric peoples, the Milky Way is known as "birds' way." The migratory birds that fly south in the fall and then back north in the spring represent the souls of the dead—divine ancestors and deities who appear in birdlike forms.

One of the underlying mythical patterns in the horizontal conception of the world are the borders drawn between human society and the dangerous outside realm of chaos and disorder. Societies tend to see themselves as consisting of "normal" humans who have civilization, laws, morals, and proper habits. The outside world is believed to be governed by demonic or inhuman forces and inhabited by "others"—strange peoples and demonic powers who are viewed with suspicion and fear. Thus, myths also define the status of humans in their relationship with various groups of "others," such as gods, goddesses, demons, and animals.

The main characters of myths are gods—supernatural creatures with extraordinary powers. They are usually immortal, but some die at an astronomically old age, as in Hinduism, while others can be resurrected from the dead. Human beings are mortal, and their fate depends on gods, whom they try to appease with sacrifices, offerings, prayers, and rituals. Myths thus depict humans as a part of a broad hierarchical system of classification. Their lower status is confirmed by narratives that tell about their creation by god. We find these beliefs in many religious traditions, such as Christianity, Islam, and Mesopotamian myths, where Marduk creates the first man from clay. In other mythologies, human beings appear long after the universe has existed together with the divine and demonic powers. In Tibetan mythology, the first people appear as the offspring of a divine ape (later identified with the Buddhist embodiment of compassion, Avalokiteshvara) and a mountain **sorceress**.

Very often, gods are classified into different groups. In ancient India, there were two types of gods: *devas* and *asuras*. Whereas *devas* hold power over the world, *asuras* lack power and are hostile towards *devas*. They were not worshipped by the Aryan people of India and were transformed into demons. Many myths tell about the wars between the *devas* and the *asuras*, who are eager to assume power. Both classes complement each other as they are necessary for the stability of the world. In Germanic mythology, gods are grouped into *aesir*, such as Odin, and *vanir*, such as the goddess Freya. Both groups of gods were opposed to giants and other forces of evil.

Some religions are dominated by patriarchal male figures, such as the Heavenly Father in Christianity. In other belief systems, goddesses have a prominent role to play. In Hindu mythology, goddesses are often interpreted as various forms of the one divine Devi (Sanskrit for "goddess"), who represents the female creative energy *shakti*. In some Indian texts, Devi is glorified as the true demiurge who is more powerful than the great male gods Brahmā, Vishnu, and Shiva. In other myths, Devi is the brave warrior who defeats the *asuras* in a cosmic battle.

Religion and ritual have always served as the basic context of mythologies. In many contemporary Western societies, the growing power of the scientific worldview and of secularization has weakened the explanatory function of myths. It is possible to identify a movement of demythologization that rejects myths, explains them away, or looks for new, rational interpretations of myths, including those of Christianity. However, myths have maintained their poetic attraction and powerful symbolic meanings and still play an important role in the contemporary world. Demythologization is supplemented by other tendencies, such as the revival of old myths and the emergence of new in literature, arts, and other fields of culture. Myths continue to appear in many contexts and forms, including the **Internet**, **art**, **film**, **novels**, **poetry**, **politics**, and ideology, such as **nationalism**. As a productive concept, myth has not exhausted its potential to inspire new theoretical approaches to human existence and culture. Although myths have gained much more attention than any other folklore genre, research in mythology is constantly expanding and new perspectives are emerging. ***See also*** Classical Antiquity; Epic; Etiologic Tale; Mythological Approaches; Religious Tale; Saint's Legend.

Further Readings: Coupe, Laurence. *Myth: The New Critical Idiom.* London: Routledge, 1997; Dundes, Alan, ed. *Sacred Narrative: Readings in the Theory of Myth.* Berkeley: University of California Press, 1984; Eliade, Mircea. *The Myth of the Eternal Return or, Cosmos and History.* Princeton, NJ: Princeton University Press, 1991; O'Flaherty, Wendy Doniger. *Other Peoples' Myths.* New York: Macmillan, 1988; Puhvel, Jaan. *Comparative Mythology.* Baltimore: Johns Hopkins University Press, 1987; Sebeok, Thomas E., ed. *Myth: A Symposium.* 1965. Bloomington: Indiana University Press, 1971; Schrempp, Gregory, and Hansen, William, eds. *Myth: A New Symposium.* Bloomington: Indiana University Press, 2002; Thury, Eva M., and Margaret K. Devinney. *Introduction to Mythology: Contemporary Approaches to Classical and World Myths.* New York: Oxford University Press, 2005.

Ülo Valk

Mythological Approaches

Mythological approaches to fairy tales and folktales are based on a loosely connected set of theories that look for the historical roots of folktales and fairy tales in obsolete **myth**s. In a broad sense, these approaches include **structuralism** and **psychological approaches**, as well as other views that regard myths as the dominant verbal genre, that interpret different kinds of expressive art as forms of mythology, or that otherwise emphasize the centrality of myth.

Scholars have explained the fairy tale's development as a genre by arguing that it is an offshoot of myth whose plots have been elaborated by storytellers. According to this generally held theory, myths began as sacred narratives but were ultimately transformed into entertaining stories about adventures in a fantasy world. Theories of the fairy tale's genesis out of myth have persisted since the beginnings of folk-narrative research in the nineteenth century, when Jacob and Wilhelm **Grimm** advanced the idea that the magical elements in fairy tales were remnants of ancient Indo-European mythology, which had declined in tandem with the Christianization of Europe. Nineteenth-century solar mythologists such as Friedrich Max **Müller** went so far as to reduce the symbolism of fairy tales to a set of ancient nature myths. According to the interpretation of the solar mythologists, the fairy-tale hero's slaying of a **dragon** constituted the sun's victory over night. Other scholars concluded that rites and rituals, which they studied as phenomena parallel to myth, were also preserved as archaic **motif**s in fairy tales. When Lord Raglan studied the "hero pattern" in narratives about the birth of the hero who later becomes a **king** and finally dies, he understood these folktale events as reflections of the main rites of passage connected with **birth, initiation,** and **death**. Russian formalist scholar Vladimir **Propp** studied myths and fairy tales in his monograph *Istoricheskie korni volshebnoi skazki* (*Historical Roots of the Wondertale*, 1946). Like the Grimm brothers, he maintained that fairy tales had emerged from myths when belief in the myths themselves had begun to decline. Propp explained the narrative plot of fairy tales on the basis of two basic sets of myths—those related to the initiation of young people, as reflected in the various tests to which heroes are subjected, and those related to the shaman's imagined trip to the otherworld. According to Propp, these mythical journeys are reflected in the dangerous trips to faraway lands that heroes make in fairy tales. Propp and other scholars who have studied the cultural development of civilization have claimed that some fairy tales reflect the ancient myths and rites of a matriarchal stage in human history.

Some **legend**s also have been explained as survivals of ancient mythology, and the supernatural beings who figure in them have been interpreted as diminished deities. In European folklore, there is a widespread migratory legend known as "Fairies Send a Message" (ATU 113A, Pan Is Dead). In many versions of this story, a traveler is asked by a stranger to deliver a message about the death of a supernatural being. Scholars have connected these legends with myths of dying and resurrected gods in Near Eastern religions and with vegetation deities that guard the annual cycle of nature in pre-Christian beliefs. North European folklore is rich in legends about natural locations that are said to be haunted by spirits or demonic creatures, and pose a danger to people. According to historical studies, many of these legends tell about former cult places, such as holy groves, that had been dedicated to pre-Christian gods who had lost their divine status. **Werewolf** legends have been explained as echoes of myths about totemistic deities who had the ability to appear in animal form.

Research has shown that many events in heroic **epic**s are ancient myths that have been historicized. Thus, in the Indian epic *Mahābhārata*, the huge battle at the field of Kurukshetra has been explained as a reflection of ancient Indo-European eschatological myths about the cosmic conflict between good and evil powers who fight at the end of the world. In Germanic mythology, the battle is known as Ragnarök ("fate of gods"), and in the **Bible** it is called Armageddon. Thus, mythological studies also seek to clarify the relationship between mythology and history.

Alan **Dundes** and Eleazar M. Meletinsky developed the structuralist methodology of Propp's study *Morfologiya skazki* (*Morphology of the Folktale*, 1928) and showed that many fairy tales and myths share the basic structure of "lack/lack liquidated." The plot begins with a deficiency of something (for example, an old couple has no children, or there is no land, and the world consists of water only) and ends with a balanced situation, wherein the original trouble, or "lack," is liquidated and the outcome is positive. According to Meletinsky, the basic distinction between the two genres is that myth discusses collective values and the fate of a group, whereas the fairy tale focuses on the life of an individual who rises from a low position to a high status by **marriage** to a member of the royal family. Similarities in the plot structure of the two genres support the theory that fairy tales emerged from myths whose plots have been elaborated into a more complex sequence of episodes.

Some scholars have seen myths as the main form of culture and interpreted different artistic forms through the mythical paradigm. One of the greatest popularizers of mythology and the mythological approach to understanding culture was Joseph Campbell, the author of the widely read book *The Hero with a Thousand Faces* (1949). Campbell's work is based on his observation that there is a single archetypal pattern of heroic monomyth found in cultures worldwide. Throughout his mythological studies, Campbell relied on Carl Gustav **Jung**'s ideas about the collective unconscious and universal **archetype**s. In instances such as this, psychological approaches merge with mythological theories as they try to explain the varieties of folktales by reducing their richness to a single underlying pattern, such as a universal theory of human psychology or an omnipresent monomyth. *See also* Anthropological Approaches.

Further Readings: Dundes, Alan, ed. *Sacred Narrative: Readings in the Theory of Myth.* Berkeley: University of California Press, 1984; Holbek, Bengt. *Interpretation of Fairy Tales: Danish Folklore in a*

European Perspective. 1987. Helsinki: Academia Scientiarum Fennica, 1998; Meletinsky, Eleazar. *The Poetics of Myth.* Translated by Guy Lanoue and Aleksandre Sadetsky. 1998. New York: Routledge, 2000; Propp, Vladimir. *Theory and History of Folklore.* Translated by Ariadna Y. Martin and Richard P. Martin. Minneapolis: University of Minnesota Press, 1984; Thompson, Stith. "Myth and Folktales." *Myth: A Symposium.* Edited by Thomas E. Sebeok. 1965. Bloomington: Indiana University Press, 1971. 169–80; Zipes, Jack. Introduction. *Fairy Tale as Myth/Myth as Fairy Tale.* Lexington: University Press of Kentucky, 1994. 1–16.

Ülo Valk

N

Namjoshi, Suniti (1941–)

Born in India and currently living in England, Suniti Namjoshi is a writer of **poetry**, **fable**s, fiction, and **children's literature**. She also has published articles in anthologies and literary and women's studies journals in India, Canada, the United States, and Britain. In 1968, she left India and began a series of journeys that were to enrich her literary career.

During a sabbatical from the University of Toronto in 1978–79, Namjoshi went to England and was influenced by the evolving feminist and gay liberation movements. Back in Toronto, she wrote the widely acclaimed *Feminist Fables* (1981), a collection of very short stories that are rewrites of **fairy tale**s, stories from Greek and Indian mythology, and texts from the English literary canon. *The Blue Donkey Fables* (1988) is a collection of fables and poems in which Namjoshi explores feminist ideas and stereotypical notions of identity and **gender** while revisiting well-known stories from diverse sources, the Western fairy-tale tradition included.

Namjoshi's work is celebrated for its experimentation with classical genres and the transgressive appeal of her revisionist mythmaking. The blend of Eastern and Western influences that inform her writing make it a good example of the diasporic experience; moreover, her constant commitment to defending women's and minorities' rights transforms her texts into pleas for tolerance and respect. *See also* Feminism; Feminist Tales; Gay and Lesbian Fairy Tales; Myth.

Further Reading: Vijayasree, C. *Suniti Namjoshi: The Artful Transgressor*. New Delhi: Rawat Publications, 2001.

Carolina Fernández-Rodríguez

Napoli, Donna Jo (1948–)

Donna Jo Napoli is professor of linguistics at Swarthmore College and acclaimed author of **children's literature** and **young adult fiction** that draws on folktale, fairy tale, and folkloric materials in general. Some of her **novel**s inspired explicitly by folktales and fairy tales are *The Prince of the Pond, Otherwise Known as De Fawg Pin* (1992), *The Magic Circle* (1993), *Jimmy, the Pickpocket of the Palace* (1995), *Zel* (1996), *Sirena* (1998), *Spinners* (1999, coauthored with Richard Tchen), *Crazy Jack* (1999), *Beast* (2000), *Bound* (2004), and *Gracie, the*

Pixie of the Puddle (2004). Napoli's sophisticated retellings depart from oral and canonized versions of tales in two notable ways: in their contextual and descriptive specificity and in their attention to previously silent or absent but sometimes-implied characters.

Napoli's attention to specifics in her retellings manifests in several ways. She often sets them in specific locations. For instance, *Beast*, a retelling of **Beauty and the Beast**, begins in Persia. Napoli draws on Persian **folklore** and Islamic traditions to give verisimilitude to the son of the shah, who, when cursed, becomes the beast of the book's title. Similarly, *Bound*, a retelling of **Cinderella**, is set in Ming China; and *Zel*, a retelling of Rapunzel, is set in Switzerland in the mid-1500s.

Others of Napoli's retellings do not focus on a precise historical period so much as they evoke a general milieu. *Sirena*, which incorporates Greek mythology, **mermaid** lore, and elements of Hans Christian **Andersen**'s "The Little Mermaid," takes place in the Mediterranean during the Trojan War. Less mythical but still evocative, *The Magic Circle* and *Spinners* both take place in medieval Europe. *The Magic Circle*, a retelling of **Hansel and Gretel**, is especially immersed in religious beliefs surrounding **witch**es. Also notable for their rich settings are *Breath* (2003), a retelling of the Pied Piper **legend**, and *The Great God Pan* (2003), a love story involving many characters from Greek mythology.

In addition to lending specificity to her tales' settings, Napoli infuses her characters with complex traits and desires, often privileging previously unheard voices. One of the most striking examples of this peopling occurs in *The Magic Circle*, which is narrated entirely from the perspective of the witch, alternately named Ugly One, Mother, and Old Woman. Ugly One is a midwife-turned-sorceress who calls upon **devil**s only to heal, yet she falls under the power of these same devils, whom she thought to control for material gain to improve her daughter's life. Exiled, the witch seeks to live in solitude and harm none. The details of her personal development occupy the majority of the novel; it is not until the last third of the book that Hansel and Gretel encounter her candy-covered cottage (which is a monument to her absent daughter's sweet tooth). Even then, the witch fights the devils that control her and tries to mother the starving children. In the end, the witch manages to shake the devils' control and sacrifice her own life by allowing Gretel to push her into the oven.

Zel also contains the perspective of the tale's usual antagonist, the witch, though it shares the novel's pages with the perspectives of Zel (Rapunzel) as well as the **prince** (in this case a count), Konrad. This witch, who is named only Mother, bargains for her powers with dark forces such as the witch in *The Magic Circle*. She, too, acts out of concern for her daughter— the daughter she does not yet have, since she is barren. Mother uses her magic to obtain Rapunzel with trickery and desire as in the classic tale, and it is from love that she locks away her daughter, to keep them together until Zel is mature enough to choose life with her **mother** over life with a lover. The isolation in fact drives Zel mad, which is the final twist Napoli adds to the tale, for its denouement is standard: Zel bears the count's twin children in a foreign land while he wanders, blinded by thorns at the tower's base; and finally they are reunited, his eyes healed by her tears.

Like *Zel*, *Spinners* uses a split perspective, telling the story from the points of view of the spinner who becomes Rumpelstiltskin, and his estranged daughter Saskia, who is forced to weave straw into gold and then marry the **king**. This is a complex and tragic tale. One character not found in the traditonal tales, Elke, works in the palace and serves as a liaison between Rumpelstiltskin and the outside world. She comes to love him, but due to his obsession with obtaining his grandchild through the bargain he made with Saskia while

spinning straw into gold, their love can never be realized. Indeed, she betrays his whereabouts to Saskia, who then sends spies to learn the spinner's true name. The tale also does not end happily for Saskia, whose marriage to the king is joyless. Unlike *Zel* with its happy ending, *Spinners* concludes without hope. Love fails to conquer power relations and unfairness multiple times, making *Spinners* in one sense an inversion of a fairy tale.

One last example of Napoli's consideration of minor, even absent, characters can be found in her The Prince of the Pond trilogy. In the first book, *The Prince of the Pond, Otherwise Known as De Fawg Pin*, the story is told entirely from the perspective of a female frog who befriends the befuddled **prince** in frog shape. The next two books, *Jimmy, the Pickpocket of the Palace* and *Gracie, the Pixie of the Puddle*, also have frogs as main characters. Napoli's creation of culture among frogs supports the assumptions in tales such as "The **Frog King**," by literalizing the confusion a human must feel when transformed into an animal (and vice versa).

Napoli's incorporation of cultural contexts and her expansion of tale roles formerly seen as one-dimensional or negligible help make her retellings complex and interesting to read for fairy-tale enthusiasts of all ages.

Further Readings: Bryant, Jen. "A Conversation with Donna Jo Napoli, Eileen and Jerry Spinelli." *Image: A Journal of the Arts and Religion* 28 (2000): 79–92; Earthman, Elise. "Instructions for Survival—Or Plans for Disaster? Young Adult Novels with Mythological Themes." *He Said, She Says: An RSVP to the Male Text.* Edited by Mica Howe and Sarah Appleton Aguiar. Madison, NJ: Fairleigh Dickinson University Press, 2001. 161–75.

Jeana Jorgensen

Nasreddin

Known under various names—most of which derive from Nasreddin Hoca (Turkish), Juha (Arabic), or (Nasreddin) Efendi (Middle Asian and Chinese)—Nasreddin is the most popular protagonist of short jocular prose narratives in the Islamic world.

Whether or not Nasreddin was a historical character is still being debated. Popular tradition imagines him as a preacher or minor cleric living in southern Anatolia (present-day Turkey) toward the end of the thirteenth century. Several tales link him to the Mongol emperor Timur (Tamerlan; died 1405). Nasreddin's alleged tombstone in Akşehir bears the date 386 of the Islamic era. According to a popular interpretation, this date has to be read backward as 683, corresponding to 1284 of the Common Era.

The earliest preserved manuscripts containing tales of Nasreddin are Turkish and date from the sixteenth century. In an ensuing process that to some extent had already been effective previously, the repertoire of jocular narratives focusing on Nasreddin mingled with that of the equally popular Juha, an Arabic **trickster** character first found in Arabic literature in the ninth century. Nineteenth-century Arabic editions that were soon translated into Turkish and Persian succeeded in amalgamating those two characters while also integrating into the narrative repertoire numerous jocular tales from various sources that had previously never been linked to either one of them. Nowadays, Nasreddin/Juha is popular all over the large area that was or still is under Islamic influence. This includes not only Turkey and the areas of Turkic-speaking peoples in the Caucasus and in Central Asia, but also the Arab world from Morocco to Iraq; the Iranian sphere of influence, including Afghan and Tajik tradition; and the **oral traditions** of southern Italy, Sicily, Malta, various ethnic groups in the Balkans, and the Sephardic Jews. By way of **translation**, mostly from modern Turkish sources, Nasreddin has more recently become known worldwide, particularly as a goodwill ambassador of the Republic of Turkey, in which capacity he was also celebrated in 1996, a commemorative year acknowledged by UNESCO.

Most of the tales linked to Nasreddin are short jocular narratives. While the early repertoire contained a considerable percentage of sexually aggressive, scatological, or otherwise provocative narratives, Nasreddin over the centuries has been "domesticated," particularly in editions aimed at a young audience published since the beginning of the twentieth century. Today, he is mostly portrayed as a lovable trickster with an inclination for a strikingly simple kind of philosophy that often mirrors the absurdities of social conventions. In one of the most famous tales, he ponders God's wisdom for having large melons grow from feeble plants in the fields, while the large walnut tree only bears small fruit. As soon as one of the nuts falls on his head, he praises God's wisdom, since a falling melon would have crushed his skull. *See also* Jest and Joke; Simpleton.

Further Readings: Başgöz, İlhan, and Pertev N. Boratav. *I, Hoca Nasreddin, Never Shall I Die*. Bloomington: Indiana University Press, 1998; Marzolph, Ulrich. "Adab in Transition: Creative Compilation in Nineteenth Century Print Tradition." *Israel Oriental Studies* 19 (1999): 161–72; ———. "Mollâ Nasroddîn in Persia." *Iranian Studies* 28.3–4 (1995): 157–74.

Ulrich Marzolph

Nationalism

Folktale and fairy-tale studies have their roots in the study of **folklore**, and the development of folklore studies is closely tied to the rise of Romantic nationalism. Based on the premise that nationhood is founded on a people's shared cultural past, Romantic nationalism emerged in late eighteenth- and early nineteenth-century Europe and fueled interest in collecting and publishing the lore of the **folk** as a means of defining national identity and laying the groundwork for nation-states.

The most significant impulses came from late eighteenth-century Germany, where interest in questions of cultural identity and cultural tradition was especially robust. Unlike the English and French, the German-speaking people were unified neither politically nor culturally. Disturbed by the Germans' vulnerability to the political, military, literary, cultural, and even linguistic power of France, German writers and philosophers undertook to recover and cultivate a unique German identity based on a common German culture, embodied ultimately in a shared language.

The most influential voice was that of Johann Gottfried Herder, who elaborated ideas about folk culture that would ultimately serve the cause of nationalism and provide the early theoretical foundation for the study of folklore. In searching for the spirit or soul of a people, Herder looked to the past—to the origins of the Germans—and to the folk, who were the true bearers of authentic tradition. According to Herder, the most authentic expressions of a people's character, beliefs, and customs could be found in their most traditional forms, which were transmitted by those living close to nature and speaking in a natural voice unspoiled by artifice. These were the folk, uncorrupted by modern civilization and linked directly to the past by the unbroken, unsullied chain of **oral tradition**. According to this idealized vision, the "poetry of the folk" (*Volkspoesie*) preserved the past and embodied the purest, most natural expression of a people's character or spirit. Herder's idea of the folk spirit was easily translated into the idea of national identity, which meant that oral tradition assumed a privileged place in the emerging discourse of Romantic nationalism.

The idea of searching for national identity in the poetry of the people resonated among Germans, whose nationalistic fervor increased between 1792 and 1815 with the Wars of the French Revolution and the ensuing Napoleonic Wars. This was epitomized in the work of Jacob and Wilhelm **Grimm**, who undertook a lifelong project to preserve the heritage of the German people as it was expressed in the language and oral traditions of the "common folk." That the Grimms' *Kinder- und Hausmärchen* (*Children's and Household Tales*, 1812–15) was first published while they lived under French occupation speaks clearly to the role that the **collecting** and **editing** of folktales played in the German quest for national identity. Moreover, the Grimms' editorial practices reveal their investment in shaping a collection representative of German culture. For example, tales of obviously French provenance were excised from the collection (for example, "**Bluebeard**" and "**Puss in Boots**"); and French loanwords were replaced with German equivalents (for example, *Prinz* was changed to *Königssohn* [king's son]). It would be 1871 before a unified German nation was realized, but Grimms' work and other collections of **German tales** played a significant role in establishing the shared cultural tradition and sense of national identity that were critical to the process of nation building.

Fueled by Herder's ideas and Grimms' work as collectors and editors, Romantic nationalism spread throughout nineteenth-century Europe. From Italy and Spain to the Nordic and Slavic lands, the collection and study of folktales became a strategy to assert national identity and establish or reestablish a basis of nationhood. This was eventually true worldwide and has forged a nearly unbreakable link between folklore and nationalism.

The symbiotic relation between folklore and nationalism has sometimes compromised folklore scholarship. For example, the occurrence of **fakelore** has been attributed to the nationalistic agenda of the collector or editor who reshapes texts to fit a cultural ideal or creates texts to supply a cultural need. Suggesting that such fabrications take place in response to nationalistic inferiority complexes, Alan **Dundes** considered whether the Grimms' editorial practices in the *Kinder- und Hausmärchen* and Elias Lönnrot's editing of the Finnish national **epic** the *Kalevala* (1835) constitute the creation of fakelore in the service of nationalism. There are also serious political implications in the alignment of folklore studies with nationalism. The most obvious and notorious example is from the Third Reich, where folklore and folklorists were pressed into the service of National Socialist propaganda. On the other hand, in the postcolonial and post-Soviet eras, Romantic nationalism has served as a model for cultural and ethnic groups seeking to reestablish their identities and independence. *See also* Authenticity; Colonialism; Négritude, Créolité, and Folktale; Pedagogy; Politics; Race and Ethnicity.

Further Readings: Abrahams, Roger D. "Phantoms of Romantic Nationalism in Folkloristics." *Journal of American Folklore* 106 (1993): 3–37; Cocchiara, Giuseppe. *The History of Folklore in Europe.* Translated by John N. McDaniel. Philadelphia: Institute for the Study of Human Issues, 1981; Dundes, Alan. "The Fabrication of Faklore." *Folklore Matters.* Knoxville: University of Tennessee Press, 1989. 40–56; Schacker, Jennifer. *National Dreams: The Remaking of Fairy Tales in Nineteenth-Century England.* Philadelphia: University of Pennsylvania Press, 2003; Snyder, Louis L. "Cultural Nationalism: The Grimm Brothers' Fairy Tales." *Roots of German Nationalism.* Bloomington: Indiana University Press, 1978. 35–54; Williams, Raymond. "Nationalist." *Keywords: A Vocabulary of Culture and Society.* Revised edition. New York: Oxford University Press, 1983. 213–14; Wilson, S. W. A. "Herder, Folklore, and Romantic Nationalism." *Journal of Popular Culture* 6 (1973): 819–35.

Donald Haase

Native American Tales

By the time Christopher Columbus reached what Europeans came to perceive as a "New World" in the late fifteenth century, hundreds of distinct culture groups existed in North America. Even five centuries after the beginnings of the contact with European societies, which led to the decimation and, in some cases, extermination of many Native American populations, primarily through virgin soil epidemics, the U.S. federal government today still recognizes more than 300 different American Indian groups in the forty-eight contiguous states. In addition, many communities see themselves as "Native American" without official federal or state recognition. Meanwhile, almost 600 separate groups of First Nations people maintain their identities in Canada. While many of these groups, both recognized and unrecognized, are culturally related and may have overlapping literary heritages, nevertheless wide diversities in narrative traditions that may not always correspond precisely to the Western genre concepts of **folktale** and **fairy tale** have flourished.

Genres

Nevertheless, generic distinctions among Native American narrative traditions generally reflect the same differentiating criteria that William Bascom identified in his international survey of prose folk narratives. Though the differences may not be as definite as they are in the conventional European model of **myth**, **legend**, and folktale, story categories usually can be defined in varying permutations of the contrasts between true and fictional, sacred and nonsacred, and whether they are set in the remote past or in the recent past. In some communities, these may represent continua more than oppositions, and some story types may straddle what seem to be contrasting features from a Western perspective. Furthermore, some traditions ignore one or more of the continua when defining narrative genres. Among the Arikara, a group whose traditional homeland was the Northern Plains, for example, two fundamental categories of story have existed: "true stories" and "tales" (now called "fairy tales" by contemporary Arikara). The indigenous term for the latter category is *naa'iikáWIš*. No indigenous term exists for true stories, so unless a narrative is assigned to a generic category, it is assumed to be true. The true (unmarked) story category includes sacred narratives analogous to myths in the Western sense (which deal with the genesis of sacred medicine bundles and recount events that occurred before the earth assumed its present form and before human institutions developed) as well as "historical legends," many etiological, which tell of dreams and supernatural encounters. Nonsacred true stories may deal with exploits during warfare, recent historical events, or personal experiences. *Naa'iikáWIš* include stories about the **Coyote** Trickster, other **animal tale**s, and children's stories. However, these tales often have the same characters as the true stories, so the basis of distinction may be nebulous. Moreover, different tellers of the same story may disagree on its genre identity.

Currently, the Choctaw, traditional inhabitants of the southeast—some of whom live in their ancestral homeland in Mississippi and others of whom live in Oklahoma—use only one native-language term for narrative. *Shukha anumpa* literally means "hog talk" (perhaps "hogwash" would be an idiomatic English equivalent) and refers to jokes, **tall tale**s, and animal stories. Choctaws also recognize another genre of stories, for which they use the English phrase "talk of the elders": creation stories and myths, historical legends, supernatural legends, and prophecy. They also make a temporal distinction between stories that have been passed along from earlier generations of tellers and narratives that describe events that have occurred recently. The latter kind of stories may also be categorized according to their truth value. Among the Dene Nhaa, who live in the Canadian Subarctic, *tonhat'onh wodihé* encompasses all traditional stories (or "stories of long ago"). Subclasses of narrative include *wodih* (primarily stories about culture heroes and animal people, though also used for accounts of recent events, hunting stories, moral lectures, and prophecies), *nóghe wodihé* (stories about the Wolverine Trickster), and *Mbetsun Yendéhshéhi wodihé* (stories about "The Boy Raised by His Grandmother," a frequent protagonist in Northern Plains and Subarctic narrative traditions). In the southwestern United States, storytellers at Zuni Pueblo in New Mexico may relate *telapnaawe* ("tales," which are regarded as fiction) and *chimiky'a-na'kowa* (stories about the Beginning, which are told as true).

Some of these story genres from various culture groups (and those of the scores of other Native American narrative traditions still being told) correspond more or less to the European-derived concept of folktale and, in some cases, may even share some of the features of fairy tales. Ideally, though, they should be considered first within the indigenous inventory of narrative genres of which they are a part. **Trickster** stories, almost universal in Native North America, are usually told as fictions, though their principal purpose may be more to teach moral lessons than simply to entertain. Since he transgresses the norms of a society and often suffers discomfiture for doing so, Trickster can remind a storyteller's audience of what they should avoid doing to remain accepted members of their communities. Trickster assumes various guises: the familiar Coyote of the Southern Plains, the Southwest, and California, but also Raven and Crow on the Northwest Coast, Rabbit in the Southeast, Spider among some Plains groups, and anthropomophic figures such as Saynday among the Kiowa of the Southern Plains and Nanabozho among the Ojibwe, traditional inhabitants of the Great Lakes area, and among other speakers of Algonquian languages. Frequently, Trickster stories from various Indian traditions end with etiological tags, which purport to explain the origins of some aspect of culture or nature. Often, though, these tags serve more to ground the stories in an observable reality than to offer definitive explanations about origins. The indigenous stories with the most similarity to European fairy tales are those that depict the adventures of an unprepossessing central character, often an orphan who lives on the margins of a community, sometimes with a grandparent. Through his or her personal efforts and talents, the assistance of spiritual beings or forces, or luck, the protagonist attains power, prestige, and occasionally material wealth. Like Trickster stories, these narratives often have didactic purposes and, particularly when they are set in the mythic past, may be regarded as having some truth.

Despite the inappropriateness of doing so, many early **collectors** and commentators on American Indian narrative traditions compared them to European fairy tales. One of these collectors was Henry Rowe Schoolcraft, whose *Algic Researches* (1839) was the first important collection of Native American oral literature. Some collectors documented fairy tales that had apparently entered various Native American narrative repertoires from European sources. For example, Stith **Thompson**'s anthology *Tales of the North American Indians* (1929) concludes with a section entitled "Tales Borrowed from Europeans." Included are versions of "The Seven-Headed **Dragon**" from an Ojibwe source, an Assiniboine version of "John the Bear," a Zuni retelling of "**Cinderella**," and a text of the "The Clever Numskull" from the Micmac. Linguist Anthony Mattina translated and published a tape-recorded performance of "The Golden Woman" (1985), a European fairy tale from the repertoire of a Colville storyteller.

Performance Styles

The generic differences and similarities that have manifested themselves in American Indian **storytelling** are paralleled by differences and similarities associated with narrative **performance**. In some societies, performance of all narrative genres might be the province of anyone with no particular restrictions on where or when stories might be told. In other communities, though, certain individuals, often cultural elders, might emerge as storytelling specialists, and some performers might have more or less exclusive rights, based perhaps on lineage or clan membership, to particular stories. For example, Edward W. Gifford, an anthropologist, reported that among the Kamia, a California group, what he called "myths" were told on winter nights only by **men**, who adopted a particular storytelling stance while performing. Storytellers would stand with hands at their sides and sway their bodies slowly from side to side as they narrated. William Jones noted that among the Meskwaki (a Midwestern group formerly known as the Sauk and Fox), storytellers would sit in a circle and take turns delivering their tales in a pace so rapid and elliptical that outsiders would be unable to follow the thread of narration. The literary style of the Maidu of California has been marked by repetition of words, parallelism, and alternation of prose and poetry. The most successful Clackamas storytellers reminded anthropologist Melville Jacobs of Western actors giving solo readings of plays. Paralinguistic manipulations characterized the performance styles of many Native American narrative traditions. Raconteurs might, for example, adopt different vocal timbres to represent dialogue spoken by a tale's characters. The character Skunk in stories of the Alsea, another California group, would speak in a whining tone. Gestures also played an important role in the delivery of many tales. Some traditions also placed restrictions on when storytelling might occur. Some genres, for instance, were intended exclusively for winter performance, and a narrator who performed a tale in one of these genres in the inappropriate season might face supernatural retribution for doing so. In fact, some societies believed that telling stories might invoke the presence of the creatures whose deeds the tales related. Telling the stories in winter, when beings such as snakes and bears were in hibernation, could prevent that from happening.

Collection and Translation

American Indian storytelling came to the attention of Europeans during the early years of contact. The annual reports filed by the Jesuit missionaries in New France, for example, occasionally mention and summarize stories told in the various groups with whom they came in contact. While the Puritans in New England paid little attention to American Indian verbal art of any sort, explorers and travelers in the middle and southern colonies that eventually became the original thirteen states sometimes included synopses of tales they had heard from Native storytellers in their memoirs and journals. Fuller "texts"—retellings in English—of Native American stories appear in the journals kept by the Corps of Discovery led by Lewis and Clark, as well as in the works of missionaries such as David Zeisberger and John Heckewelder in the early nineteenth century. The first important collection of stories from an American Indian **oral tradition** was published by Indian agent Henry Rowe Schoolcraft. His *Algic Researches* includes rewritten versions of stories that he had heard from his Ojibwe charges at Sault Ste. Marie and which had been translated by his wife Jane Johnston, who was part Ojibwe. An influential feature of Schoolcraft's collection was the way in which he reworked the Ojibwe stories so that they resembled the **literary fairy tale**s of the Brothers **Grimm** and other European publications during the first half of the nineteenth century. Not attempting at all to represent the manner in which the stories were told, Schoolcraft recast the Ojibwe tales in an ornamented literary style and expurgated materials that he deemed offensive or indecent. While Schoolcraft's collection bore only a slight resemblance to what the Ojibwe storytellers had related, he deserves credit for recognizing that the stories were indeed works of literary art. His approach to presenting these Ojibwe stories (from which the poet Henry Wadsworth Longfellow borrowed for his epic poem, *The Song of Hiawatha*) set the standard for published reworkings of narratives from various Native American groups that appeared during the 1800s and well into the twentieth century (and which continues in some popularly oriented publications even into the twenty-first century).

Not until the founding of the Bureau of American Ethnology (BAE) in the Smithsonian Institution in 1879 and the contemporaneous **fieldwork** of Franz Boas and his students in anthropology did a more "scientific" approach to publishing American Indian tales emerge. For the most part, though, the BAE scientists as well as the Boasians viewed recording stories primarily as a way to gather information on other features of Native cultures, especially language. Typically, a Boasian anthropologist would have an Indian storyteller dictate a story in the indigenous language. Sometimes the anthropologist might not even have understood what was being said, but would capture the sounds of the speaker by writing them out phonetically. This laborious process yielded scrupulously exact linguistic texts, which might be published with a literal **translation** that matched the Native-language words and morphemes with English equivalents. Perhaps a "free" translation would also appear, but it would most likely reflect only the content of the story and nothing of its Native artistry, some of which would have disappeared anyway because of the exigencies of the dictation situation. Literally thousands of stories were collected in this way during the early twentieth century, and many of them were published in highly specialized forums such as museum publications and scholarly journals. Although they could not represent Native American verbal art either accurately or comprehensively, their sheer number make them a valuable resource, to which more recent linguists and translators have returned with considerable success.

The published and archived corpus of Native American tales is vast, but not until the last third of the twentieth century did an approach develop to making this material accessible as indigenous verbal art. During the 1960s and 1970s, several methods for presenting American Indian verbal art in print emerged under the general rubric of "ethnopoetics," a movement that while not exclusively associated with American Indian materials nevertheless found most of its adherents among those anthropologists, literary scholars, translators, and creative writers whose interests were primarily in Native Americana. The goal of ethnopoetics is to preserve the indigenous aesthetic in translations into English and other European languages, usually from literary traditions that are largely oral. Consequently, it involves not only language-to-language translation but also the transformation of orally performed art into written or printed versions. As far as American Indian oral narratives are concerned, the two most influential ethnopoetic approaches have been the "verse analysis" of Dell Hymes and the "pause phrasing" of Dennis Tedlock. Though both approaches begin with the assumption that oral narration can better be represented on the printed page as poetry than as prose, they differ in the kinds of source material they use and in their perception of what constitutes the aesthetic essence of verbal art.

Using verse analysis, Hymes has effectively shown how the many indigenous-language texts punctiliously documented by BAE researchers and Boasian anthropologists using the esthetically inhospitable dictation technique nevertheless retain elements of the original artistry that can be recovered by careful linguistic investigation. Hymes's approach suggests that tales printed as prose in original-language texts can be recast in poetic lines by noting the recurrence of grammatical markers such as particles. Lines then can be organized into verses and stanzas using such cues as the pattern number of the culture from which the stories come (three or five in most of the Northwest Coast groups whose oral literature Hymes has studied). These, then, form scenes and acts to result in final products structured as dramatic poetry. Since verse analysis often works with previously recorded material and frequently has only written versions of the words used in the performances, it cannot represent the totality of oral performance, including paralinguistic and kinesic devices used by the storytellers. But it does, according to its advocates, allow some of the verbal art to emerge out of material whose provenance did not encourage art.

While verse analysis seems to suggest that the art of storytelling can transcend the particulars of a performance situation, pause phrasing situates that art precisely in those particulars. Developed by Dennis Tedlock as he worked with storytellers from Zuñi Pueblo in the 1960s, this approach to representing orally expressed verbal art in print relies upon tape recordings of specific performances. The verbal component of these performances is cast in lines based upon pauses made by the narrator, many of which correspond to the same kinds of grammatical markers that verse analysis uses to define lines. Since Tedlock worked with tape recordings, he was also able to reflect paralinguistic features such as changes in volume, tempo, and vocal quality. These he represented with typographic manipulation to produce what he called "scores," which a reader might articulate aloud to recreate something very similar to what might be heard on the tape recording of the story. Pause phrasing thus captures many of the precise details of a specific telling of a story, and many of those details would change each time the story was told.

While these two approaches to presenting Native American tales in print have become prominent among serious students of those tales, some translators have continued to opt for prose, though they are likely to take care to meet the goals of ethnopoetics more scrupulously than did their predecessors. Popular presentations of Native American tales, however, often continue to represent the stories using an esthetic that reflects the influence more of Euro-American printed literature than of American Indian oral literature.

Interpretations

Just as there have been a variety of ways to represent Native American tales in print throughout the history of European and Euro-American interest in them, a number of approaches to analyzing and understanding them have also emerged. As early as the seventeenth century, commentators viewed oral literature as a source of data about other aspects of Native American cultures. Stories were cited as reflections of a generalized American Indian worldview or of the specific mindset of a particular group. For example, the Jesuits in New France as well as later missionaries in other parts of North America cited the stories they heard as evidence of the benighted perspective of Indians and, more positively, as evidence of a collective intelligence that could be receptive to the tenets of Christianity. Lewis Cass, who represented the U.S. federal government to Indians in the Old Northwest during the early nineteenth century, encouraged his agents——one of whom was Schoolcraft——to gather information on oral literature for what it could tell them about how to manage their charges most effectively. Using tales as an information source was an important data-gathering technique among anthropologists in the late nineteenth century. Franz Boas and his students systematically collected stories not only as sources for language information but for the general cultural data they might preserve. In many cases—particularly on the Northwest Coast and later in California—Boasians might collect stories from the few remaining speakers of a language whose cultural base had been supplanted. They would then attempt to reconstruct that culture using descriptions of kinship organization, **marriage** practices, rituals, and material culture preserved in the stories. Arguing that **folklore** in general and tales in particular "mirror" culture, some anthropologists continue to view the primary significance of oral literature in what it can reveal about a society's way of life.

A predominant approach to studying folktales in Europe during the first half of the twentieth century, the **historic-geographic method** did not enjoy similar popularity among students of American Indian tales. However, the American folklorist Stith Thompson used a Native American narrative, "The Star Husband Tale," to demonstrate how this method might be applied in "laboratory" conditions. The purpose of the historic-geographic method was to trace tales to their time and point of origin, to define routes of **diffusion** from that point, to reconstruct the original form of the story, and to identify subtypes that may have developed. European storytelling traditions had, according to critics of the method, been corrupted by printed versions of tales, which might nullify attempts to delineate the processes of oral transmission over time and space.

Thompson suggested that looking at an American Indian story would pose no such problem. What Thompson defined as the original form of "The Star Husband Tale" has two young **women** wishing to marry stars. Each has her **wish** granted and finds herself in the "upper world." They are warned against digging there but disobey and make a hole in the sky. They can see their earthly home below and long to return there. They successfully return home using a long rope. Thompson worked with eighty-six versions of this story that he located, for the most part, in academic and museum publications. An examination of these yielded what he took to be the story's original form, which he believed to have originated in the Central Plains. He was not at all successful in dating the tale's origin, though he noted that the earliest publications of the original form occurred in the 1890s. Thompson also identified two subtypes of the story—one involving a porcupine which the young women follow into the upper world, and the other having the young women dependent on a series of animal trickster figures when they become trapped in a treetop upon their return to earth. While he was able to plot the original form and the subtypes on maps, he could not clearly define routes of diffusion.

The use of tales for ethnographic information and the historic-geographic method came under criticism because both ignored the stories as verbal art. Other attempts to understand American Indian storytelling have often been just as unsuccessful in revealing their artistry. For example, the morphological approach that Alan **Dundes** borrowed from Russian folklorist Vladimir **Propp** to study Native American tales did effectively counter critics of those stories, who believed them to be formless, episodic hodgepodges. For example, Dundes noted a movement from the lack of something desirable to a liquidation of that lack as a recurrent formula. Another frequent pattern has a tale's protagonist being given a warning, his or her not heeding that warning, and the consequences of such irresponsibility. A range of **motif**s might flesh out these formulaic outlines, which Dundes perceived as transcending cultural and linguistic boundaries. Few analysts followed up on Dundes's preliminary work, though, and he himself did not go beyond identifying formulaic patterns to examining how those patterns were realized in actual story performances. More influential has been the work of French anthropologist Claude Lévi-Strauss, who brought his investigations into the fundamental structures of human thought processes to bear on Native American tales. Lévi-Strauss has repeatedly identified a structural mediation of binary opposition underlying narratives from throughout the Americas, including the origin account from Zuni Pueblo and a number of stories recorded from narrators on the Northwest Coast. Pursuing **psychological approaches,** analysts have also used the theories and methods of depth psychology to interpret the significance of American Indian tales. The work of Sigmund **Freud** has informed readings of Mescalero Apache narratives and Mohave Coyote tales, while Carl Gustav **Jung** has often been invoked to explain such material as the cycle of stories about the Winnebago Trickster.

Literary Redactions

Retellings of Native American oral narratives have been a staple of **children's literature** since the nineteenth century. Many of the period's anthropologists and other students of indigenous cultures believed they were examining people whose way of life represented an immature stage of development—maturity being represented by European and Euro-American civilization. Since Native Americans were considered childlike, it seemed reasonable that their stories were suitable for children, though only after objectionable scatological and sexual elements had been expurgated. Consequently, children's magazines such as *St. Nicholas* often included American Indian stories retold for young readers. Some early Native American writers, such as the Santee physician Charles Alexander Eastman, explored the potential of marketing their culture's narrative traditions for an audience familiar with European fairy tales. *Smokey Day's Wigwam Evenings* (1909), which Eastman prepared in collaboration with his wife Elaine Goodale Eastman, exemplifies this trend, as do some of the collections published by Zitkala-Sa (Getrude Bonnin), a Yankton. The practice of retelling Native American tales for children has continued with work by the writer-illustrator Paul Goble providing particularly attractive examples. Contemporary Native American writers such as Ojibwe novelist and poet Louise **Erdrich** have also written children's books based upon oral narrative traditions.

Erdrich is only one of several modern Native American writers who perceive their work as continuing the traditional storytelling practices of their communities. Some, such as N. Scott **Momaday**, have used those practices as a way of exploring their cultural identity. His book *The Way to Rainy Mountain* (1969) recounts a multidimensional pilgrimage that he made in search of his identity following the death of his Kiowa grandmother. In addition to physically retracing the route which his ancestors followed as they migrated from the Plateau of western Montana to the Southern Plains, Momaday uses the stories told by his grandmother and other raconteurs as a way of discovering that identity. In presenting these stories, he also ensures that they will endure more securely and reach a wider audience than would be the case had they depended entirely on oral transmission. Meanwhile, Leslie Marmon **Silko** from Laguna Pueblo in New Mexico has emphasized her identity as storyteller in the tradition of her female ancestors and relatives and has stressed the continuing significance of traditional narrative motifs and patterns in contemporary life. Her novel *Ceremony* (1977), for example, depicts a Laguna World War II veteran who can reintegrate into his community only by following the patterns of traditional story. Silko has also updated such figures as the Coyote Trickster, showing how the techniques and values that he represents are more than appropriate for survival in the twentieth century. The continuing valence of Trickster provides a dominant theme in the fiction and culture commentary of Ojibwe novelist and scholar Gerald Vizenor, who insists that "tricksterism" provides the only method by which American Indians can survive in the modern era.

Meanwhile, a number of recent anthologies of Native American tales have helped to make this material accessible to the general public. Some of these are essentially collections of rewritten materials, but others include texts that attempt to represent original performances faithfully. Perhaps the best-known recent anthology is Richard Erdoes and Alfonso Ortiz's *American Indian Myths and Legends* (1984). However, while some of the material in the volume was collected from storytellers by the authors themselves, much of it comes from previously published sources that the **editors** have rewritten without returning to original-language texts. More successful are several anthologies edited by Brian Swann, especially *Coming to Light* (1994) and *Voices from Four Directions* (2004), both subtitled *Contemporary Translations of the Native Literatures of North America*. These volumes include texts translated (or retranslated) from either oral performances or earlier published versions that use the principles of ethnopoetics to capture both the original storytelling aesthetic and to represent some of the features of oral performance. Moreover, each example is accompanied by a thorough introduction that provides the reader with essential information about the cultural context. These anthologies have been faulted for not including Native-language texts, an absence which Swann himself has lamented. But thriving programs for publishing such texts have emerged in several Native American communities, especially in Alaska and on the Northwest Coast. Concurrently, storytellers have begun using English in their performances, so that even in situations where the original language may not be available, the storytelling tradition flourishes.

Since the beginnings of Euro-American interest in American Indian narrative traditions, two perceptions have colored collection, publication, and analysis. One of these is the commonplace belief that oral literature and storytelling are bound to disappear under the influence of literacy and the mass media. While this idea has been a motivation for collecting and studying oral literature in a range of contexts since the inception of such scholarship, the Native American situation has also been affected by the trope of the "vanishing American," central to views of Indian life since colonial days and a principal influence on government policies regarding Indians. The assumption has been that "primitive" Indian cultures will inevitably give way to the advance of Western civilization. Native American tales, hence, have been affected not only by the threat of literacy but by the demise of their cultural matrices. The late twentieth-century revival of interest in Native American verbal art, termed the "Native American Renaissance" by critic Kenneth Lincoln, indicates that concerns about the survival of Indian cultures and their literatures either were unfounded or contributed to attempts by scholars and by communities to ensure that they did not disappear. In the twenty-first century, narrative and other verbal art traditions of Native Americans continue to thrive both orally and as an influence on written literature. *See also* Anthropological Approaches; Ethnographic Approaches.

Further Readings: Boas, Franz. *Race, Language, and Culture.* Chicago: University of Chicago Press, 1940; Erdoes, Richard, and Alfonso Ortiz, eds. *American Indian Myths and Legends.* New York: Pantheon, 1984; Hymes, Dell. *"In Vain I Tried to Tell You": Essays in Native American Ethnopoetics.* New edition. Lincoln: University of Nebraska Press, 2004; Jacobs, Melville. *The Content and Style of an*

Oral Literature: Clackamas Chinook Myths and Tales. Chicago: University of Chicago Press, 1959; Mattina, Anthony. *The Golden Woman: The Colville Narrative of Peter J. Seymour.* Tucson: University of Arizona Press, 1985; Momaday, N. Scott. *The Way to Rainy Mountain.* Albuquerque: University of New Mexico Press, 1969; Schoolcraft, Henry Rowe. *Algic Researches: Indian Tales and Legends.* 1839. Baltimore: Clearfield, 1992; Swann, Brian, ed. *On the Translation of Native American Literatures.* Washington, D.C.: Smithsonian Institution Press, 1992; ———, ed. *Coming to Light: Contemporary Translations of the Native Literatures of North America.* New York: Random House, 1994; ———, ed. *Voices from Four Directions: Contemporary Translations of the Native Literatures of North America.* Lincoln: University of Nebraska Press, 2004; Tedlock, Dennis. *Finding the Center: Narrative Poetry of the Zuñi Indians.* New York: Dial Press, 1972; ———. *The Spoken Word and the Work of Interpretation.* Philadelphia: University of Pennsylvania Press, 1983; Thompson, Stith. *Tales of the North American Indians.* Cambridge, MA: Harvard University Press, 1929.

William M. Clements

Naubert, Benedikte (1756–1819)

Author of more than fifty **novel**s and numerous fairy tales and **novella**s, Benedikte Naubert was the most prolific German writer of the Age of Goethe. Often using chronicles and **legend**s from ancient and medieval Germanic history as sources, she successfully combined the **family** romance with fairy-tale and mythic **motif**s. Her works influenced the German and English Romantics and the development of the historical, gothic, and detective novel; her tales anticipated many of the themes and motifs of later German **women**'s fairy tales.

In the midst of her novel production, Naubert anonymously began publishing fairy tales: *Neue Volksmährchen der Deutschen* (*New German Folktales*, 5 volumes, 1789–93); *Alme, oder ägyptische Mährchen* (*Alme, or Egyptian Fairy Tales*, 5 volumes, 1793–1797); and *Velleda, ein Zauberroman* (*Velleda, a Magical Novel*, 1803). Her *New German Folktales*, set in the tenth to fifteenth centuries, was an attempt to heed Johann Gottfried Herder's call to document the cultural history of the **Middle Ages** and the roots of the German way of thinking. Two of the tales in the collection, "Erlkönigs Tochter" ("The Erl-King's Daughter") and "Der kurze Mantel" ("The Short Cloak"; translated as "The Cloak"), hark back to **ballad**s and songs Herder had recorded; and although the plan was never realized, Jacob **Grimm** had hoped to include "Ottilie" in a German legend collection.

Naubert's fairy tales typically have a **frame narrative** with a clear female narrator who actively shapes the story. Recurring themes include female communities outside traditional society; the teaching of skills for intellectual and material independence; the interactions within female triads (magical wise woman, biological **mother**, and daughter); and most importantly, the mediation of the female's rite of passage by a wise woman and through reading. Naubert's tales suggest the story is not "universal" but rather a subjective experiencing and rendering of events.

Naubert's critical reception has varied over time. Her contemporaries initially praised her and then criticized that she did not follow Johann Karl August **Musäus**'s model in the *Volksmärchen der Deutschen* (*Folktales of the Germans*, 1782–86). The German Romantics embraced and often emulated her work, and scholars have traced her influence on writers from Walter Scott to Thomas Mann. Naubert has also become an important focus for recent feminist research, and that scholarship has led to the recovery of other women (Friederike Helene Unger, Sophie Albrecht, Therese Huber, Caroline de la Motte-Fouqué, Dorothea Schlegel, and Sophie Tieck-Bernhardi) who published individual fairy tales and **saga** reworkings before 1810. Feminist research has also shown how Naubert influenced and informed her female successors. *See also* Feminism; Feminist Tales; German Tales; Goethe, Johann Wolfgang von.

Further Readings: Jarvis, Shawn C. "The Vanished Woman of Great Influence: Benedikte Naubert's Legacy and German Women's Fairy Tales." *In the Shadow of Olympus: German Women Writers Around 1800.* Edited by Katherine R. Goodman and Edith Waldstein. Albany: SUNY Press, 1992. 191–209; Martin, Laura. "The Rübezahl Legend in Benedikte Naubert and Johann Karl August Musäus." *Marvels & Tales* 17 (2003): 197–211; Naubert, Benedikte. "Boadicea and Velleda." *The Queen's Mirror: Fairy Tales by German Women, 1780–1900.* Edited by Shawn C. Jarvis and Jeannine Blackwell. Lincoln: University of Nebraska, 2001. 35–74; ———. "The Cloak." *Bitter Healing: German Women Writers, 1700–1830.* Edited by Jeannine Blackwell and Susanne Zantop. Lincoln: University of Nebraska Press, 1990. 207–77.

Shawn C. Jarvis

Négritude, Créolité, and Folktale

Négritude and créolité are two related yet distinct political and aesthetic movements, promoted especially by French-speaking writers, that place particular value on the **oral traditions** of sub-Saharan Africa and the African diaspora. Although the term was actually coined later, négritude was conceived by three students who met in Paris during the 1930s: Aimé Césaire, Léon-Gontran Damas, and Leopold Sédar Senghor. Hailing from different French colonies—Martinique, Guyana, and Senegal, respectively—these three were confronted firsthand with an oppressive educational system that strove to assimilate colonized populations by erasing any cultural heritage other than France's. Négritude was not only a cry of protest against this system and racism in general, but also a valorization of a collective black identity that traced its roots to African history and cultures. As such, négritude demanded the recognition of Africa's contributions to human civilization and the end of economic and political exploitation of the continent. Although Césaire, Damas, and Senghor pursued political activities (Césaire as a member of the French National Assembly and Senghor as the first president of Senegal), all three became well known as poets. Indeed, **poetry** became the primary means of expression for proponents of négritude. Its impact came to be felt not only among colonized intellectuals and writers, but also among prominent figures in France, such as André Breton and Jean-Paul Sartre. This support notwithstanding, négritude was attacked as being an essentialist idealization of black identity and for being too inclusive to speak on behalf of the diverse black populations of the world.

Créolité was born from a dialectical relationship with négritude, building on many of its goals while affirming the specificity of Creole cultures in the Caribbean basin. With roots in Europe, Africa, and Asia, these cultures are nonetheless distinct, créolité maintains, and there are more differences than similarities between them. Above all, créolité is a celebration of the cultural *métissage* that is so prominent in the Caribbean and visible in the cultures and languages of that region. Consequently, créolité rejects what is seen as the emphasis on "purity" in négritude. But like that movement, it aspires to political autonomy (specifically from France, since many of the theorists in this movement are from Francophone islands). Paradoxically, in spite of the valorization of Creole cultures and languages, most of the spokespersons for créolité, such as Jean Bernabé, Raphaël Confiant, and Patrick **Chamoiseau**, write in European languages, especially French.

Folklore plays important but different roles in each of these two movements. To promote African cultures of the continent and the diaspora, négritude necessarily had to rely on the oral traditions that were so vital before the arrival of writing with European colonists. Much of the literary output inspired by négritude takes as its point of reference the **proverbs**, tales, and **epic**s of traditional African societies. More often than not, though, such references are oblique and, when present, are not motivated by a desire to preserve traditional aspects of African cultures, but rather by the necessity of addressing the social and political exigencies of colonial and postcolonial realities. Négritude did not explicitly call for the recovery of oral traditions in sub-Saharan Africa, work that has a long tradition of its own going back to early colonial times. Still, the literary versions of West African folktales and **fable**s by Birago **Diop** revealed the influence of négritude. Like Senghor, Diop sought to confront African and European perspectives, remaining faithful to the dominant spirit and style of West African oral narratives all the while using the resources of Western literary traditions to "translate" them into French. Unlike other proponents of négritude, Diop only rarely used his tales to make an explicit denunciation of racism and colonial oppression. But fully congruent with the aims of this movement were his efforts to put into new forms traditional narratives that were rapidly disappearing due to the colonial and postcolonial modernization of Africa.

Compared to négritude, créolité devotes considerable attention to oral traditions and oral **storytelling**, first and foremost for theoretical reasons. Patrick Chamoiseau and Edouard Glissant have urged Creole intellectuals to seek inspiration in traditional storytelling not so much to "preserve" it as to unleash its potential for resistance and self-realization. For them, the historical figure of the slave storyteller is a model for postcolonial Caribbean writers. Forced to obscure the subversive message of his stories under the watchful eye of the slave master and resigned to the futility of outright resistance, this archetypal storyteller prefigures the tactics that Creole intellectuals could adopt in the face of Western hegemony. He shows them how to affirm the counter-values of créolité while recognizing the complexities of resistance. In addition, the orality of Creole folklore is used to forestall the fixity and predictability of writing and to signify the fluidity of philosophical and political self-reflection in this movement.

Unlike writers inspired by négritude, those connected directly and indirectly with créolité have frequently reworked characters, **motif**s, and plots from oral traditions. Some, such as Simone Schwarz-Bart in her **novel** *Ti Jean l'horizon* (1979; translated as *Between Two Worlds*, 1981), have used folkloric heroes to capture the dreamlike struggles and aspirations of Creole peoples. Others—most notably Chamoiseau in *Au temps de l'antan* (1988; translated as *Creole Folktales*, 1994) and *Emerveilles* (*Marvels*, 1998)—have written literary adaptations of Creole folktales, aiming not only to recover oral traditions of the past but also to rework literary forms and language inherited from the West. Still others, such as Raphaël Confiant in *Les maîtres de la parole créole* (*Creole Storytellers*, 1995), have actively promoted contemporary storytelling in the French Caribbean. All in all, the Creole folktale, itself a dynamic reworking of (mostly) African stories, continues to recast itself in fruitful ways. *See also* African Tales; Colonialism; Hopkinson, Nalo; Hybridity, Hybridization; Race and Ethnicity.

Further Readings: Kane, Mohamadou. *Les contes d'Amadou Coumba: Du conte traditionnel au conte moderne d'expression française*. Dakar: Université de Dakar, 1968; Ludwig, Ralph, ed. *Ecrire la "parole de nuit": La nouvelle littérature antillaise*. Paris: Gallimard, 1994; Seifert, Lewis C. "Orality, History, and 'Creoleness' in Patrick Chamoiseau's *Creole Folktales*." *Marvels & Tales* 16 (2002): 214–30.

Lewis C. Seifert

Nesbit, E. (1858–1924)

E. Nesbit is the androgynous pen name for Edith Bland, née Edith Nesbit, a prolific Edwardian writer of children's books, including **fantasy** and realist stories as well as **poetry**, adult **novel**s, and journalism. Her writing career started in the need to support her family and somewhat unsteady husband, Hubert Bland. She was a colorful figure, an anachronistically strong woman and self-consciously bohemian character who shared with her husband a commitment to socialism, a founding interest in the Fabian Society (a British socialist intellectual movement), and a tendency to have extramarital affairs. As a children's writer, she demonstrates a strong, empathetic sense of exuberant, self-willed **childhood**, and of the divide between children's and adults' perspectives. Her female characters are particularly active and emancipated, and across her work, girls are more likely to be practical and effective adventurers than are boys. Her writing is intelligent, witty, and humorous, very aware of its contemporary world despite her frequent forays into fantasy.

Nesbit's realist children's novels are perhaps her best known, including *The Railway Children* (1906) and the three chronicles of the ebullient Bastable children, *The Story of the Treasure Seekers* (1899), *The Wouldbegoods* (1901), and *The New Treasure Seekers* (1904). These exemplify the new generation of Victorian children's writing, sympathetic portrayals of childhood on its own terms, without overt didacticism. While Nesbit's characters do learn moral and psychological lessons, she also frequently mocks the moralistic tendencies of earlier children's writing, refusing to provide an overt **moral** and pillorying adult characters who seek to censor children's behavior. This down-to-earth, realist setting remains the basis of much of her fantasy writing, and the source of its success. She could be said to have originated the subgenre, later developed by writers such as Edward Eager, Diana Wynne **Jones**, and even J. K. **Rowling**, in which secondary fantastic realms are abandoned in favor of infusing with magic the mundane, familiar world of children's lives.

Many of Nesbit's best-known fantasies are not strictly fairy tale, although they tend to focus on a pivotal **magic object** such as the amulet of *The Story of the Amulet* (1906) or a **magic helper**, often mundane or mythical animals. In this latter category belong the Phoenix of *The Phoenix and the Carpet* (1904), the Psammead of *Five Children and It* (1902) and *The Story of the Amulet*, and the Mouldiwarp of *The House of Arden* (1908) and *Harding's Luck* (1909). Characteristically, these creatures are wry, down-to-earth, and often scathing to the children they assist, requiring high standards of initiative and honor: adventures and magic must be earned, and their results negotiated with care and logic. The initiatory scenarios and continual testing of fairy tale are thus updated and expanded.

Nesbit is not entirely free from the secondary-world obsessions of Victorian writers such as Lewis **Carroll** and George **MacDonald**, and she develops this theme explicitly in *The Magic City* (1910); however, her personal concerns are more with time, time travel, and the access to history it provides. Her socialist beliefs can be seen in elements such as the **utopia**n future of *The Story of the Amulet*, or the recurring theme of the lost civilization of Atlantis, which is constructed as an ideal society; even historical periods offer some idyllic elements in contrast to the realities of her own time. A particularly innovative aspect of her treatment of secondary worlds is in her frequent literalization of children's games: the miniature city of "The Town in the Library in The Town in The Library" (in *Nine Unlikely Tales for Children*, 1901), and the hideously animated Ugly-Wuglies of *The Enchanted Castle* (1907).

Nesbit's fairy tales are among the most delightful products of the Victorian obsession with the form and allow free reign to her playful, witty, and somewhat iconoclastic intelligence. Her numerous short fairy tales tinker self-consciously with the familiar elements of the tale, mining a strong vein of comedy from inversions, incongruities, and anachronisms; these were frequently published in *Strand* magazine, but also were collected in *The Book of Dragons* (1900), *Nine Unlikely Tales for Children,* and *The Magic World* (1912). Many of her stories feature practical, rational **prince**s and **princess**es thrown into horrible illogic by the imposition of such fairy-tale clichés as christening curses, evil magicians, or the need to slay **dragon**s. Nesbit's christening curses are particularly delightful: princesses are turned into apples ("Fortunatus Rex & Co."), or cursed to be increasingly ugly on one day of the week ("Belinda and Bellamant"), or afflicted with ever-growing **hair** ("Melisande, or Long and Short Division"). Other stories feature the updating of fairy tales with contemporary **motif**s that neatly substitute for the traditional magical item: the elevator in "The Charmed Life," or the employment office for royalty and the dragon-slaying Lee Enfield rifle in "Billy the King." These tales seamlessly meld the traditional with the modern, resulting in a knowing, tongue-in-cheek humor and a simultaneous illumination of fairy tale's characteristics and purposes. They are also relentlessly logical, in many cases simply exploring the implications of fairy-tale structures taken to their furthest extreme. Thus, in "Melisande," the hapless **king** and **queen** try to avoid offending **fairies** by not inviting *any* to the christening of the princess, with the inevitable result that they offend all of them; however, since fairy-tale tradition insists that only *one* fairy is ever offended, only one christening curse is applied. *The Book of Dragons* plays similar games with notions of the monstrous and with innovative means of dragon-slaying; often the monster is shrunk, transformed, trapped, or simply tamed.

Given the whimsy and innocence of Nesbit's children's tales, it is worth noting that she also published numerous short horror stories, featuring ghosts, hauntings, and other supernatural elements. ***See also*** Children's Literature; English Tales.

Further Readings: Knoepflmacher, U. C. "Of Babylands and Babylons: E. Nesbit and the Reclamation of the Fairy Tale." *Tulsa Studies in Women's Literature* 6 (1987): 299–325; Prickett, Stephen. *Victorian Fantasy*. Bloomington: Indiana University Press, 1979; Sircar, Sanjay. "The Generic Decorum of the Burlesque Kunstmärchen: E. Nesbit's 'The Magician's Heart.'" *Folklore* 110 (1999): 75–91.

Jessica Tiffin

The NeverEnding Story (1984)

Directed by Wolfgang Petersen, the **film** *Die unendliche Geschichte* (1984)—known in English as *The NeverEnding Story*—is an **adaptation** of German author Michael **Ende**'s eponymous **novel** of 1979. Both the book and the movie use thematic and structural elements from fairy-tale sources and incorporate themes prominent in modern fairy-tale adaptations.

The basic plot of the film involves a **frame narrative** featuring a boy named Bastian who steals a book and spends a day in his school's attic reading. In the book, a hero named Atreyu is summoned to assist the Childlike Empress in saving the world of Fantasia from the Nothing, a force that threatens to devour everything. On his quest, Atreyu encounters helper figures in the form of a giant turtle and a luck **dragon**, is tested and aided by the Southern Oracle, and fights the lupine villain G'mork. The climax of the book involves the destruction

Noah Hathaway as Atreyu rides Falkor the luck dragon in the 1984 film *The NeverEnding Story*. [Warner Bros./Photofest]

of the world of Fantasia and the incorporation of Bastian from the frame tale into the narrative he is reading to reinfuse the world with creativity by naming the Childlike Empress.

While not an adaptation of a specific **tale type**, *The NeverEnding Story* incorporates a number of elements from fairy-tale sources. The clearest aspect of this comes in the structure of the book's plot. The heroic journey of Atreyu is similar to the morphology described by Vladimir **Propp** in his *Morfologiya skazki* (*Morphology of the Folktale*, 1928). A key example of this comes in the Southern Oracle sequence. The Southern Oracle acts as a donor figure in the story, first testing Atreyu before giving him the information necessary to defeat the villainy that motivated the journey. In addition, the incorporation of Bastian involves a false-hero sequence. Atreyu is revealed as a false hero, and Bastian and the Childlike Empress are brought together.

In addition to structural similarities, the movie bears stylistic similarities to fairy tales. Within the story are such regular fairy-tale figures as talking animals and miniature people. Additionally, thematic elements such as the "rule of three" (that is, the prevalence of structures based on three) appear within the film. In addition to these traditional elements, *The NeverEnding Story* includes elements from modern fairy-tale adaptations. One of the key elements is the use of a pastiche world, in which subjects of unrelated stories coexist in one cosmology, in this case Fantasia. Another element is the thematic linkage between folktales and **childhood** creativity. Within the story, the Nothing is representative of Bastian's disbelief, destroying the world of the story. This is similar to elements in works such as the stage adaptation of Sir James Matthew **Barrie**'s *Peter Pan* (1904), in which the audience is called upon to save the character of Tinker Bell from disbelief.

While Petersen's film adaptation only incorporates half of the book, two additional feature films have adapted the later parts of the book: *The NeverEnding Story II: The Next Chapter* (directed by George Miller, 1990) and *The NeverEnding Story III* (directed by Peter MacDonald, 1994). Additionally, the book has been adapted for American **television** (*Tales from the NeverEnding Story*, 2001) and into other media, including both an **opera** and a ballet by Siegfried Matthus (2004).

Further Readings: Ende, Michael. *The Neverending Story*. Translated by Roswitha Quadflieg. New York: Doubleday, 1983; *The NeverEnding Story*. Directed by Wolfgang Petersen. 1984. DVD. Warner Home Video, 2001.

B. Grantham Aldred

New Zealand. *See* Australian and Aotearoan/New Zealand Tales

Nielsen, Kay (1886–1957)

As an illustrator of folktales and fairy tales, Kay Nielsen created a richly decorative style inspired by the early twentieth-century artistic movements of Jugendstil and art deco. Born in Copenhagen, Nielsen was a cosmopolitan figure, spending most of his working life outside of Denmark. Following his education in Paris from 1904 to 1910 at Académie Julian and Académie Colarossi, Nielsen lived in London until 1917. During this period, he drew illustrations in modern style of fairy-tale collections, such as *East of the Sun and West of the Moon: Old Tales from the North* (1914). Participating in the late nineteenth-century boom in fairy-tale **illustration**, the style of this collection is characterized by sinuous, ornamental lines and an emphasis on the image as formalized surface.

From 1917 to 1936, Nielsen lived in Denmark, where he gained experience as a scenographer. Extending a lifelong interest in fairy tales to encompass the dramatic form, Nielsen's scenographic works for the Royal Danish Theatre included "Aladdin" (1917) and "Stormen" ("The Storm," 1926). Among Nielsen's fairy-tale illustrations from this period are the ***Arabian Nights*** (1917–20) and illustrations of tales from Hans Christian **Andersen** (1924) and from Jacob and Wilhelm **Grimm** (1925). In *Fairy Tales* (1924) by Andersen, Nielsen employs a detailed, decorative style with an emphasis on the image as stylized tableau. In 1936, Nielsen moved to Hollywood, and from 1937 to 1941, worked for the Walt Disney Studios, where his insights into different media were combined when he contributed to *Fantasia* (1940). *See also* Disney, Walt; Walt Disney Company.

Further Reading: Dal, Erik. *Danske H. C. Andersen-illustrationer, 1835–1975.* Copenhagen: Forening for Boghaandværk, 1975.

Helene Høyrup

Nodier, Charles (1780–1844)

Often neglected in handbooks of literature, French author Charles Nodier was an influential figure in his time. Born in Besançon, he was a precocious intellectual who started his career as a writer at the age of ten with Jacobin speeches. However, he was quickly disappointed with the French Revolution and the Reign of Terror and became an ultraroyalist. Deeply involved in secret societies since the age of ten, when he associated himself with the secret group Les Philadelphes, he created in 1793 another group that allegedly included a number of individuals who plotted against Napoleon. Author of *La Napoléone* (1803), a satire against the Prime Consul of France, Nodier denounced himself to Bonaparte and asked to be sent to jail. In 1815, he published anonymously *Histoire des sociétés secrètes dans l'armée: Napoléon et ses constitutions* (*A History of Secret Societies in Napoleon's Army*), in which he develops allegorically the philosophy of secret societies. Nodier is supposed to have been grand master of the Prieuré de Sion—the Priory of Scion—from 1801 until his death, upon which he was succeeded by his pupil and close friend Victor Hugo.

Following the path opened by Jacques **Cazotte** in the eighteenth century, Nodier's involvement with the occult was a major influence on his literary and professional career. This is evident in his famous tales *Smarra, ou Les démons de la nuit* (*Smarra, or The Demons of the Night*, 1821) and *Trilby, ou Le lutin d'Argail*, 1822 (*Trilby, or The Fairy of*

Argail), in which Nodier explored the realms of dreams and nightmares. In examining the frontier of the conscious and unconscious, he anticipated Sigmund **Freud.** Nodier's influence on subsequent generations of authors culminated in the surrealist movement.

In 1824, Nodier was appointed the chief librarian at the Arsenal Library, which had an extensive collection of medieval texts, manuscripts, and occult books. By cataloguing and exploring these texts, Nodier and his collaborators Jean-Baptiste Pitois and Eliphas Levy stimulated the nineteenth-century French revival of the occult and the vogue in fantastic literature.

During his tenure at the Arsenal, for three years Nodier hosted a **salon** that had a significant influence on the French Romantic movement. Among his circle were literary personalities such as François-René de Chateaubriand, Honoré de Balzac, Alphonse de Lamartine, Alfred de Musset, Théophile **Gautier**, Gérard de Nerval, Alfred de Vigny, and Hugo, as well as painters like Eugène Delacroix, all of whom frequently drew on esoteric and Hermetic traditions in their works.

After 1830, a time of political and personal disenchantments in his life, Nodier became increasingly interested in fairy tales and their fantastic worlds, which he could mold to his own imagination. Going beyond his predecessors in the genre, he celebrated lunacy, which he referred to as wisdom rather than madness. His masterpiece, *La fée aux miettes* (*The Crumb Fairy*, 1832), is a story told by the protagonist Michel about his life. Early on, he befriended an old hag surnamed the Crumb **Fairy**, who flattered herself and claimed to be Belkiss, the Queen of Saba. They became engaged and later married. Michel lived a laborious life during the day with the Crumb Fairy but was visited at night in his dreams by Belkiss, thus existing in perfect equilibrium between the constraints of reality and the enchantments of the dreams. However, the Crumb Fairy asked Michel to find a miraculous plant, the singing mandrake, to regain her youth and beauty. While attempting to buy it from a herbalist, he was recognized as a lunatic and sent to an asylum. This fairy tale mixes the land of ghosts (Scotland) with reality (Normandy) through a touch of Oriental decorum reminiscent of the *Arabian Nights*.

Nodier wrote more than twenty stories during the last fifteen years of his life, including one fairy tale for children, *Trésor des fèves et fleur des pois* (*Treasure of Broad Beans and Flower of Peas*) in 1833, the year he became a member of the Académie Française. *See also* Fantasy; French Tales.

Further Reading: Vodoz, Jules. *La fée aux miettes: Essai sur le rôle du subconscient dans l'oeuvre de Charles Nodier*. Paris: Honoré Champion, 1925.

Charlotte Trinquet

Nonsense Tale

Storytellers everywhere have created tales in which the irrational is used not as a means to an end but in its own right. In the nonsense tale, mutually inconsistent elements do not advance the plot but rather revel in their own absurdity. A case in point is "Sir Gammer Gans" (ATU 2335, Tales Filled with Contradictions), as recorded by Joseph **Jacobs** in *More English Fairy Tales* (1894). This story consists entirely of sentences that are both internally self-contradictory and senseless in their broader context. For example: "Could they tell me whether the little old woman was dead yet who was hanged last Saturday week for drowning herself in a shower of feathers?"

Some nonsense tales are called "lying tales" because of the storyteller's flagrant disregard for truth. One example is type ATU 1965, The Disabled Comrades, which is known worldwide. Characteristically, the story features three hunters: one blind, one lame, and the other naked. Coming upon a hare, the lame one runs after it, the blind one shoots it, and the naked one puts it in his pocket.

Nonsense tales often are presented in verse and thus have a close affinity to **Mother-Goose** rhymes and other forms of **children's literature**. Here are the opening lines of a rhyme still widely known throughout the English-speaking world:

> One dark night in the middle of the day
> Two dead boys came out to play.
> Back to back they faced each other,
> Drew their swords and shot each other.

See also Tall Tale; Unfinished Tale.

Further Reading: Thompson, Stith. "Formula Tales." *The Folktale.* 1946. Berkeley: University of California Press, 1977. 229–34.

D. L. Ashliman

North American Tales

Tales from North America north of Mexico fall into three categories: (1) tales from the **oral tradition**; (2) semiliterary tales circulated in **chapbook**s, **broadside**s, and cheap publications; and (3) **literary fairy tale**s inspired by earlier European fairy tales or by tales from the oral tradition.

Folktales from Oral Tradition

Although the full range of **folktale**s in North American oral tradition also includes the **jest and joke**, **anecdote**, **memorate**, **tall tale**, and **legend**, this entry will focus on folktales in the narrower sense, that is, on a single complex of tales that embraces **wonder tale**s or **märchen**, **novella**s, **animal tale**s, humorous tales including stories of the **simpleton** and the stupid **ogre**, and formulaic tales. The North American stories in this repertoire have their roots in the Old World, specifically in that part that extends from Ireland in the west to Russia and Armenia in the east, and from Scandinavia in the north to the Mediterranean countries in the south. This largely Indo-European world possesses as part of its traditional culture a single repertoire of tales and tale genres found throughout its length and breadth. Although no single part of this region has had the whole repertoire, the various subregions have possessed traditional tale repertoires that, while distinctive to the particular subregion, are also representative of the whole repertoire. This broad complex of tales is united by a generally European sensibility, worldview, aesthetic, and value system that distinguish it even from closely related tale repertoires such as those of India or the Muslim Middle East, to say nothing of more distant repertoires such as those of the Far East, sub-Saharan Africa, or from Native American cultures. These tales came to North America with immigrants and bond servants from Europe, western parts of Asia, and parts of Africa that had close contact with Europe.

These tales are generally treated by storytellers in a given region as all the same kind of story. So in a **storytelling** context, a märchen might be followed by an animal tale or a formulaic tale, for example. But a joke or personal experience memorate would be out of place. Contrariwise, in a context of jokes or legends, a märchen or formulaic story would not ordinarily be told. The culturally established occasions for telling tales from the tale complex are quite distinct from the culturally established occasions for jokes, tall tales, or legends. The point of these tales also defines them. Jokes exist to evoke a laugh, tall tales are usually competitive, and legends seek to draw in the listener to respond with a frisson or a comment about belief. But tales from this repertoire exist principally for the joy of narrative: they exist for the sake of the story. A final indication that, despite the various subgenres included, this repertoire is regarded as of a piece is the fact that cycles of tales can include stories from any of the subgenres. So Jack, Br'er Rabbit, or Juan Bobo might figure as the hero of a märchen, novella, animal story, humorous tale, or formulaic tale.

What is known about folktales in the North American oral tradition reflects, more than one would like, the vagaries of folktale **collecting** in the United States and Canada since colonial days. A number of factors have affected what stories have entered the record. First, the largest ethnic groups, those with roots in Spain, France, the British Isles, and Africa, are, as might be expected, the best collected. Second, the definition of "**folk**" fashionable at the time of the founding of the American Folklore Society (in 1888) and the establishment of **folklore** as a field of enquiry pointed to certain groups, such as rural southern African Americans. This impression was strengthened by Joel Chandler **Harris**'s discovery and publication of Br'er Rabbit tales, and by the subsequent cottage industry of gathering and setting down Br'er Rabbit and other **African American tales**. Native Americans, or First People, also seemed "folk," as that word was understood 100 years ago, and some extraordinary scholarship has been devoted to **Native American tales**.

Third, fashion also dictated, to some extent, which regions of the continent were suitable for collecting folklore. Obviously, the Southern Appalachians and indeed the entire South from the Virginia Tidewater to the Texas Plains featured picturesque rural populations from whom to gather tales. The Pennsylvania Germans were another obvious choice. The Pine Barrens of New Jersey and the rocky coasts of Maine offered good picking conveniently close to home—if home was one of the eastern U.S. colleges and universities where the study of folklore first took root. But early New England collectors did not have much respect for French Canadians, Irish, and Poles, and the collected record of their folktale traditions is quite skimpy. For Canadian folklorists, the obvious choices were the rural communities of French Canadian Quebec and the farming and fishing communities of what are now the Maritime Provinces. But whole sections of the continent were relatively neglected, including most of Canada north or west of Quebec, and the U.S. urban Northeast, the Midwest, and the West Coast. This neglect has been corrected to some extent in the last fifty years, but in the same period, much of the continent has industrialized, and the collected folklore reflects this industrialized culture more than it reflects the Old-World roots of the people.

Fourth, fashion of another sort was a negative factor influencing what got collected. The trend of collecting music in the Southern Appalachians almost led to overlooking the regional tale tradition. The fashion of collecting foodways, crafts, and customs—especially Christmas customs—from Swedish Americans led to the neglect of Swedish narrative tradition and of all Norwegian tradition. Similarly, Pennsylvania German folklife and material culture is much better documented than the corresponding narrative tradition.

A fifth reason why folktales go uncollected is that they often constitute what Carl Lindahl has called a "shy tradition." Storytellers who see tales as suitable for telling only to children or within the family circle may be embarrassed or even unable to perform them in other circumstances, and consequently may well disclaim any knowledge of these tales.

Sometimes, too, an ethnic group was simply too small or isolated to call attention to itself. In addition, some ethnicities worked hard to assimilate, shedding their language and the tales that were a part of it. And it is indeed true, as scholars have been claiming for a century, that daily life in the United States often does not make room for telling long, leisurely stories. Many tales doubtlessly died out because immigrants or their children could not find a place for them in their daily lives.

Fortunately, however, a surprisingly large number of folktales, now numbering in the thousands, have been collected in North America since the very late eighteenth century. In each of the three main traditions, tales have been gathered not only from descendants of the original immigrants but also from particular groups of Native Americans or First People and of black Americans or Canadians.

The earliest to arrive of these three sets of folktale traditions in North America is the Iberian. Ponce de Leon established the first Spanish settlement in Puerto Rico in 1508, and the island has been occupied continuously for five centuries. The major collection of Puerto Rican tales is that of J. Alden Mason, published in various issues of the *Journal of American Folklore* in the 1920s. Other early collectors are Rafael Ramirez De Arellano and Ralph Boggs. In the twentieth century, outmigration brought Puerto Ricans in large numbers to mainland North America, especially to New York. Recent collection in New York has provided educational material for schools that aim to promote the education of ghettoized children. In the southwestern United States, continuous occupation by the Hispanic population dates from approximately 1690 as, presumably, does the folktale tradition. Southwestern tales were collected by Juan B. Rael, Aurelio M. **Espinosa,** and José Manuel Espinosa, and folklorists continue to mine this field. The Isleño community of coastal Louisiana, which came from the Canary Islands in 1799, likewise retained a store of folktales, collected by Junor O. Claudel and Raymond R. MacCurdy. Native Americans living in close proximity to Hispanics in the southwestern United States, including Pueblo groups and tribes of Southern California, have absorbed many Hispanic folktales into their own traditional storytelling repertoires. A mixed African and Portuguese population from the Cape Verde Islands also brought a strongly Iberian folktale tradition to southern New England. Elsie Clews Parson published an early collection and **translation** of Cape Verde stories. Recent **fieldwork** in New England suggests that these tales are now as likely to be told in English as in Cape Verde Creole.

The several regional folktale traditions that derive from the richly romantic Iberian tradition show great consistency. Many of the same tales are found in Puerto Rico, in the Hispanic Southwest, in Louisiana, and among the Cape Verdeans of New England. These include the popular märchen such as The Magic Flight (ATU 313), and **The Kind and the Unkind Girls** (ATU 480), often fused with **Cinderella** (ATU 510). More distinctive to the tradition are tales such as The Basil Maiden (ATU 879), "The Bird of Truth" (ATU 707, The Three Golden Children), and "Mousie Perez" (ATU 2023, Little Ant Marries), many variations on the theme of Juan del Oso (John the **Bear's Son**), an Iberian **oicotype** of The Three Stolen Princesses (ATU 301), märchen with extremely long-suffering heroines such as The Maiden without Hands (ATU 706), and wisdom tales such as The Observance of the Master's Precepts (ATU 910B). Märchen often have a religious slant, with the Virgin Mary or St. Joseph becoming the **magic helper** or donor and the **devil** becoming the villain. Tale types from all across the spectrum, including märchen and animal tales, are refashioned into humorous tales that feature the loveable simpleton Juan Bobo or the cunning **trickster** Pedro de Urdemales. African elements often penetrate the tradition, and the tar baby story is almost ubiquitous. The Cape Verde tradition is distinctive for tales from the *Arabian Nights* that probably entered oral tradition from eighteenth-century translations. In addition, the trickster character in this tradition is Brother Wolf ('Nho Lhob), and the tales are often strongly Africanized.

The second major set of documented folktale traditions in North America is the French. The French presence in the New World began in southeastern Canada in the sixteenth century. Missionaries led the way, followed by merchants and the *voyageurs* or *coureurs des bois*, who extended their travels as far as the Rocky Mountains on both sides of the present international border. True settlement began after 1600 with the Acadians in Nova Scotia, followed by the *habitants* of the St. Lawrence Valley. To this day, the provinces of Nova Scotia and Quebec are the centers of two distinctive French cultures in Canada. In 1682, La Salle claimed the land drained by the Mississippi for France and named it Louisiana. French cities in the present states of Louisiana and Missouri followed. The original language brought by French settlers to Louisiana was reinforced and modified by French-speaking Caribbean immigrants and merchants and by Creole-speaking black slaves likewise imported from the Caribbean. In 1755, when the English governor ordered that the Acadians be deported from Nova Scotia, the Louisiana Territory was one of the places to which refugees dispersed, bringing with them their distinctive version of French language and culture. The French language survived in Missouri up until the twentieth century, still survives marginally in New Orleans and vigorously in rural southern Louisiana, and is one of the two official languages of Canada.

Collected Canadian French folktale texts number in the many thousands, documenting vigorous folktale traditions among Acadians, Quebecois, Ontarians, Newfoundlanders, and Metis from Manitoba. The first great collector was Marius Berbeau, who published Quebecois tales in seven issues of the *Journal of American Folklore*. Helen Crichton and Gerald Pocius collected in the Maritime Provinces. In the United States, Joseph Médard Carrière and Ward Allison Dorrance collected in the Old Mines area of Missouri. Alcée Fortier and Lafayette Jarreau both collected Louisiana black (Creole) folktales. Acadian folktales were collected in the 1930s by Calvin Claudel and again in the 1970s by various folklorists publishing in the journal *Louisiana Folklore Miscellany*. Barry Ancelet's *Cajun and Creole Folktales* (1994), containing recently collected texts, demonstrates that rural Louisiana traditions, Acadian and Creole, are still strong. Indirect evidence exists for vigorous traditions among French Canadians in the United States and among French-speaking inhabitants of New Orleans, but apparently neither group was ever the subject of extensive folktale research. In addition, the folktale traditions of many Native American or First Nation peoples show **motif**s and whole tales from the French tradition. Apparently, the *voyageurs* were good storytellers.

The French repertoire has much in common with the Spanish repertoire, sharing many core märchen. The generic hero is often called 'Tit Jean, and the simpleton is Jean Sot (Stupid John), while the trickster is often a figure called Roclore (variously spelled), a name derived, perhaps, from the family name of the Baron de Roquelaure and his son and grandson, all of whom were known for wit. Tales from Charles **Perrault**'s collection of 1697 have reentered the tradition, especially "Les fées" ("The Fairies"; ATU 480, The Kind and the Unkind Girls) and "Le petit poucet" ("Little **Thumbling**"; ATU 327B, The **Brothers** and the Ogre). In Louisiana and Missouri, the repertoire is also spiced with tales of Bouqui and Lapin. These are related to southern black Br'er Rabbit stories, but the rabbit's foil is Bouqui rather than a fox.

The name "Bouqui" generally goes unexplained, and storytellers seem to imagine Bouqui variously; but etymologically, the word is derived from the Woloof word for "hyena."

The third large set of traditions in North America has roots in the British Isles. British settlement of North America began in Virginia in 1607. Other southern colonies soon followed, with settlement at first in coastal areas. By the mid-eighteenth century, settlement had moved into the Piedmont and Appalachia, and from there it spread to the Ozarks and across the lowland South as far as Texas. The first settlers were English, but the Jacobite wars, the Highland Clearances, agricultural enclosure in the Scottish Lowlands, and dissatisfaction with the Ulster plantations encouraged immigration from Scotland and from Ulster (the Scotch-Irish). In addition, immigration of French Huguenots and of German speakers ensured that the folk culture would not be purely English. In the 1930s, the Works Progress Administration (WPA) gathered English-language folktales in various southern states. The southern tradition dominates Carl Lindahl's anthology of tales from the U.S. Library of Congress. Leonard Roberts collected Appalachian tales and Vance Randolph gathered the related Ozark traditions. Appalachia is also home to the large Hicks-Harmon family of storytellers and singers. Richard Chase's *The Jack Tales* (1943) was the first book growing out of this family's tradition, but succumbs to the temptation to rewrite the tales according to Chase's own notions and aesthetic. Later collectors do better by the family. No single collector of lowland Southern tales stands out, but John Burrison's anthology *Storytellers* (1989) presents a good cross section. Other excellent tales appear in Annuals of the Texas Folklore Society. Outside the South, white British-Isles folktales are documented only sporadically, most notably in Emelyn E. Gardner's *Folklore from the Hills of Schoharie County, New York State* (1935).

English settlement in Canada began in Newfoundland in the early seventeenth century, and the Treaty of Utrecht (1713) conceded Newfoundland and Nova Scotia to Britain. In the late eighteenth century, conditions in Scotland and Ulster brought waves of Scottish immigrants into Newfoundland and Nova Scotia as into the United States. And the mid-nineteenth-century potato famine spurred similar immigration from Ireland. *Folktales of Newfoundland* (1996) by Herbert Halpert and J. D. A. Widdowson presents English, Scots, and Irish folktales from Newfoundland, and is superbly annotated. Howard Kennedy and Cyrus Macmillan published English Canadian folktales early in the twentieth century. Helen Crichton also collected in Atlantic Canada. The Cape Breton Scottish Gaelic repertoires of Hector Campbell, Joe Neil MacNeil, and others have been collected by Margaret MacDonnell and John Shaw.

The black population of the southern United States came largely from West Africa via the slave trade. Folktales of British origin, variously modified by African influence, form a significant element in the folklore of the Gullah of the Carolina and Georgia coastal areas and of southern U.S. African Americans and their descendants who migrated into northern U.S. cities. In *Folk-Lore of the Sea Islands, South Carolina* (1923)—an early volume from the American Folklore Society—Elsie Clews Parsons documents Gullah traditions. Joel Chandler Harris's **Uncle Remus** tales about Br'er Rabbit represent a more broadly southern black tradition. Richard M. **Dorson** has published a good survey of African American folktales from both the rural South and the urban North. In Canada, the early black population reflects immigration from the United States by British sympathizers after the American Revolution and the War of 1812. The Fugitive Slave Laws of the 1850s, which denied asylum to runaways in northern states, also led to immigration of fugitive slaves who had come to the Canadian border via the Underground Railroad. The opening of mines in Nova Scotia in the early twentieth century attracted Afro-Caribbean immigrants from the West Indies, along with their folktales of a strong English flavor. Arthur Hauf Fauset's *Folklore from Nova Scotia* (1931), representing mostly black traditions, shows this English influence mediated by recent immigrants from the West Indians. The volume's animal tales feature Brother Nancy (see **Anansi**) rather than Br'er Rabbit.

Folktales of British origin have also filtered into the folktale repertoires of Creek, Cherokee, and other southeastern U.S. Native American tribes. When the newly founded American Folklore Society began publishing its journal in 1888, the editor, William Wells Newell, made discovery of folktales a major focus. American versions of English folktales appeared in the very first issue, inspiring efforts over the next years by both collectors and correspondents.

British folktale traditions in North America are probably dominated by tales of Scots origin. Among popular tales are the ever-present Kind and the Unkind Girls and Cinderella, including versions of "Catskins" and of "The Golden Horse" (both ATU 510B, Peau d'Asne). Other popular stories are The Three Stolen Princesses (ATU 301), The Devil's Daughter (ATU 313, The Magic Flight), The Children and the Ogre (ATU 327), The Smith and the Devil (ATU 330), and the **Bluebeard-riddle** tale of "Mr. Fox" (ATU 955, The Robber Bridegroom). Nursery stories include "The Three **Pig**s" (ATU 124, Blowing the House In) and the formulaic tales of The Mouse Regains Its Tail (ATU 2034) and The Old Woman and Her Pig (ATU 2030). The **Jack tale** is characteristic of this repertoire, with the generally good-hearted but plain Jack figuring in both simpleton and trickster tales as well as in märchen and novellas. The English branch of this set of traditions is short on magical tales but long on humor, especially on tales of simpletons and tricksters. The Scots and Irish branches include many magical tales. In the southern United States, these repertoires may well reflect a German element, too. Certainly, the popular tales from the Brothers **Grimm** have entered oral tradition. These repertoires also incorporate African elements, especially the element of the hero escaping up a tree and being rescued by dogs with strange names, which occurs widely, often in tales of the **Hansel and Gretel** type (ATU 327A). In the South, too, European tales often become Br'er Rabbit Tales. These tales, more typically told among African Americans, seem to amalgamate a basically African idea of the trickster tale, a Native American trickster (who may be either the female Old Molly Hare or the male Br'er Rabbit), and plots drawn from both European and African traditions.

Of course, tales came to North America from many nations and traditions, and many ethnic groups are represented by only a few tales or by the work of just one collector. Ukrainian Canadians, however, long the fourth-largest ethnic group in the country, have been more fortunate. Robert Klymasz's collection of tales from Ukrainians settled on the Prairie for eighty years or more at the time (1973) is one of several collections. Edith Fowke and Kay Stone have published collections that include tales from a fairly wide selection of Canadian ethnicities. The Canadian Museum of Civilization has sponsored the collection of folktales from various ethnic groups, including the old Chinese community in Montreal and Jewish communities, but much of this material has not been published. Tale collection in western Canada has focused on tall tales. In the United States, several excellent collections document stories from the immigrant generation, including Carla Bianco's *The Two Rosetos* (1974), with Italian tales from Roseto, Pennsylvania, and Susie Hoogasian-Villa's *100 Armenian Tales and Their Folkloristic Relevance* (1966), with tales from Detroit. Research by Linda **Dégh** and others further documents Armenian traditions in California, including **Nasreddin** stories. Richard M. Dorson, doing fieldwork in the Upper Peninsula of Michigan, discovered good immigrant Polish and Finnish storytellers as well as a settled-in French Canadian tale tradition. Over the years, folklore journals have published Italian, Polish, Syrian, Portuguese, Lithuanian, Gypsy, Czech, Hungarian, and other tales from the immigrant generation.

The Subliterary Tradition in Chapbooks and Cheap Publications

Serious folktale collecting in North America did not begin until the 1880s. Nevertheless, using indirect means, it is possible to have some idea of the English-language tradition on the eastern seaboard in the colonial and postcolonial period. While no one wrote down the tales that the first settlers brought to soothe children and intrigue adults, there were printers putting out one-page broadsides and small chapbooks and almanacs that included stories of various kinds. These printers usually reprinted stories from each other or from English (or German) sources. But many of the stories they reprinted were the sort that easily passed back and forth when people met at the crossroad, emporium, tavern, or hearth. These almanac and chapbook versions of popular tales can give some idea of tales and taletelling in the United States in those early years. Since almanacs were the standard calendars of early America, they were in constant demand. The layout of an almanac usually left room for filler, frequently historical or humorous. Typical reprinted stories include "Clever Crispin" (a version of The Master **Thief**, ATU 1525D), "The Fortune Teller" (a version of The King and the Abbot, ATU 922), and "The Three **Wish**es" (The Devil Is to Fulfill Three Wishes, ATU 1173A). Chapbooks usually reprinted popular English titles, including "Cinderella," the English Cinderella stories "Catskins" and "The Golden Bull" (or sometimes in North America, "The Golden Horse"), the *Arabian Nights* stories, and "Jack the Giant Killer." The more romantic tales were often versified and sometimes sold as broadsides instead of chapbooks. Whether drawn from almanacs and chapbooks or from memory, stories were precious commodities, shared and shared again from colony to colony, state to state, province to province, up and down the seaboard and across the mountains into the frontier.

Stories recorded in early chapbooks and almanacs continue to show up in North American oral tradition, suggesting that such publications tend to reinforce oral tradition. Three great European fairy-tale collections, Perrault's tales (1697), Antoine **Galland**'s French translation of the *Arabian Nights* (1704–17), and the **Grimm**s' *Kinder- und Hausmärchen* (*Children's and Household Tales*, 1812–15), all frequently translated or retranslated into other languages including English, have likewise influenced oral tradition in varying ways. The Creole stories collected in Louisiana by Alcée Fortier include versions of Perrault's stories. The *Arabian Nights* stories, especially The Forty Thieves (ATU 954), are characteristic of the Cape Verde repertoire, but also appear in Nova Scotia black storytelling. And the influence of the Grimms is pervasive. Subliterary influences also continue to affect the oral tradition. Cheap illustrated versions of the more popular fairy tales, with texts often printed from one another, have been available since sometime in the late nineteenth century, and sold in candy stores, variety stores, ten-cent stores, and now dollar stores. Bright pictures and low prices have guaranteed high sales of such titles as "Cinderella," "**Beauty and the Beast**," "**Puss in Boots**," "**Little Red Riding Hood**," "The Three Little Pigs," and "The Three Billy Goats Gruff" in editions from Big Little Books, Golden Books, Pan Books, Ideal Books, and others. Walt **Disney**'s films and the books based on them have also influenced how people imagine and retell these stories. There is a whole semi-oral tradition, confined largely to urban and middle-class families, fed by these subliterary versions, sometimes isolated from any other oral tradition.

Folktales and Fairy Tales in North American Popular and Literary Culture

When literary authors draw on folktale themes to serve their various agendas, scholars today usually call the consciously literary products "**fairy tale**s" to distinguish them from folktales with variable texts that circulate in oral tradition. Since the early nineteenth century, American authors have created a wide variety of fairy tales. Apparently inspired by German models, Washington Irving created two tales that have proved enduring: "The Legend of Sleepy Hollow," a combination ghost story and trickster tale, and "Rip Van Winkle," a variation on the theme of a seemingly brief visit to **faerie** that turns out to have lasted a long time. These stories—published in *The Sketch Book of Geoffrey Crayon* (1819–20)—situated a world of fantasy in the Hudson River Valley of the author's own lifetime. Nathaniel **Hawthorne**'s "Feathertop" (1846) set in colonial Massachusetts, is really more of a fantasy **fable**, but the retellings of Greek **myth** in *A Wonder Book for Boys and Girls* (1851) and *Tanglewood Tales for Boys and Girls* (1853) do capture the style of fairy tales. Indeed, "The Golden Touch," his version of the myth of King Midas, has achieved canonical status as a fairy tale. For the Christmas annuals popular after the U.S. Civil War and for children's magazines such as *St. Nicholas*, Louisa May **Alcott**, Frank Stockton, Howard Pyle, and other authors created a wide variety of fantasy fiction, some more like short stories, and some more closely modeled on European folktales and fairy tales. Alcott's first fairy stories, published when she was eighteen (1854), are didactic fables, but the heroine in Alcott's "Rosy's Journey" is a thoroughly independent young lass, and the realm of make-believe through which she journeys in search of her gold-miner father, despite its camels, monkeys, and lion, feels like Alcott's own United States. L. Frank **Baum** brought **fantasy** to the Midwest when he situated *The Wonderful Wizard of Oz* (1900) in Kansas and the *American Fairy Tales* (1901) in a Chicago-like urban setting. The Oz that he created has been capable of supporting contradictory images of North America, to which it is related as anti-type to type. In Baum's series of novels, Dorothy and her aunt and uncle eventually leave Kansas to settle permanently in Oz. In the 1939 film based on the novel (and on stage dramatizations of it), however, Dorothy becomes convinced that she does not want to live in Oz because "there's no place like home." Philip José Farmer's *A Barnstormer in Oz* (1982) focuses on Oz to fashion a critique of the United States and its environmental, military, and foreign policies. Indeed, political and satirical treatment of fairy-tale themes has remained popular among North America writers since Baum's time. The list of such writers is long, but among the more recent are feminists such as Jane **Yolen** and Margaret **Atwood**.

One exception to the trend toward the political, however, was the work of Carl **Sandburg** in *Rootabaga Stories* (1922) and two further volumes. Written explicitly to give American children American tales, the stories incorporate fairy-tale elements alongside trains, sidewalks, and even skyscrapers. But the tales have not aged well: the wordplay and nonsense can seem tedious and heavy-handed today. James **Thurber** wrote satirically in *Fables for Our Time* (1940). But his children's books, such as *Many Moons* (1943) and *The Thirteen Clocks* (1950), though aiming at wisdom as well as humor, seem to eschew both old-fashioned moral didacticism and more adult social satire. And their nonsense has aged well (see **Nonsense Tale**). Tomie dePaola, in his eight Strega Nona books, is an example of a contemporary children's book creator in the Thurber vein, combining broadly human wisdom and humor with adult appeal in tales that are modeled on or echo traditional folktale themes.

American **poetry** too, since James Whitcomb Riley, has recast fairy tales for the poet's contemporaries. Wolfgang Mieder's *Disenchantments: An Anthology of Modern Fairy Tale*

Poetry (1985) includes such poets as Randall **Jarrell**, Sara Henderson **Hay**, and Olga **Broumas**. Especially influential has been Anne **Sexton**'s *Transformations* (1971), which takes a feminist and modernist tack in retelling classic tales, usually from an unexpected perspective.

North American **film and video** has also embraced the fairy tale. Baum made silent Oz movies, now lost. Douglas Fairbanks created *Arabian Nights* adventures in the first of the **Thief of Bagdad films** (1924), a series much borrowed from by the **Walt Disney Company** in *Aladdin* (1992). Disney's **Snow White** *and the Seven Dwarfs* (1937) showed how capable **animation** was of engrossing its audience. Disney and the company he founded have continued to make musical animations of classic fantasy and fairy tales, but Disney's domination of the animation market has been challenged by DreamWorks Animation in **Shrek**, a 2001 fairy-tale **parody**. Perhaps the most influential live-action fantasy film has been *The Wizard of Oz* (1939), whose songs, images, and language have become part of the American imagination, especially since it began showing on **television** in the 1950s. But North American cinema includes many styles of fairy-tale film, including straight (*The Glass Slipper*, 1955), revisionist (*The Princess Bride*, 1987), and updated (*Pretty Woman*, 1990). Tom **Davenport** moved fairy tales to the southern United States in a series of short films. And Shelley **Duvall** presented twenty-six tales on her television series *Faerie Tale Theatre* (1982–87), remarkable for the décor of each production and for the casts and directors.

Fairy tales have also been a staple of live children's **theater**. Charlotte Chorpenning's imaginative versions written for the Goodman Theatre (1932–52) have been produced all over the United States. Chorpenning's *The Emperor's New Clothes* reached Broadway in 1935. New York had already seen Baum's version of *The Wonderful Wizard of Oz* in 1903, and *Alice in Wonderland* by Eva La Gallienne and Florida Friebus in 1932 (more memorably revived with star Bambi Lynn and new music in 1947). Oz returned to New York often, notably in 1975 with the African American updating *The Wiz*, and in Stephen Schwartz's *Wicked* (2003), based on the novel by Gregory **Maguire**. Sir James Matthew **Barrie**'s *Peter Pan* first played in New York in 1905, with Maude Adams, and has returned often, more recently in the American musical version created by Jerome Robbins (1954). *Once upon a Mattress* (1959) has proved a staple in the regional theater. Stephen Sondheim's **Into the Woods** (1986) asks what happens to fairy-tale protagonists after "happily ever after." And with *Beauty and the Beast* (1994) and *The Lion King* (1997), Disney has mounted long-running stage versions of popular animated films from 1991 and 1994, respectively.

Storytelling

Formal storytelling events have figured in North America for more than a century. Librarians and teachers were trained to tell stories even in the early 1900s. But a storytelling revival, with festivals, "concerts," street performances, and a storytelling circuit, got underway in the 1960s. Both Kay Stone and Joseph Daniel Sobol have written histories of this movement. Stone (*Burning Brightly*, 1998) emphasizes the Toronto Storyteller's School, founded in 1979, while Sobol (*The Storytellers' Journey*, 1999) emphasizes the National Storytelling Association, growing out of the National Storytelling Festival in Jonesborough, Tennessee (the first festival was in 1973), organized by Jimmy Neal Smith. This revival started on a wave of wonder tales, but issues of copyright and ethnic property have edged the revival over into stories that are more commonly the property of individual storytellers.

Contemporary Criticism of Folktales and Fairy Tales

The storytelling revival grew out of the 1960s concern with all things natural. Study of the tale in **performance** has become an important critical approach. Critical scrutiny from the point of view of **feminism** dates from a 1970s controversy between Alison Lurie and Marcia R. Lieberman as to whether fairy tales are liberating or oppressive. Many in this era, including conservative Christians, sought to recapture fairy tales for their own agendas. Those who found the tales liberating or ideologically compatible, or sought to make them so, usually followed one of several tactics: (1) group tales perceived as acceptable into anthologies; (2) refashion tales or invent new ones with outcomes compatible with the desired ideology, including **utopia**n revisions of tales and motifs; (3) parody; (4) postmodern experiments; and (5) reinterpretation of tales through psychoanalytic or Jungian interpretation. Included among important feminist scholars and anthologists since the late twentieth century, in addition to Lurie and Lieberman, are Rosemary Minard, Ethel Johnson Phelps, Kay Stone, and Marina **Warner**. Other critics of fairy tales include Christina Bacchilega, Ruth B. Bottigheimer, Christine Goldberg, Donald Haase, William McCarthy, Maria Tatar, and Jack **Zipes**. **Psychological approaches** include the Jungian in Robert **Bly**'s *Iron John: A Book about Men* (1990) and Clarissa Pinkola Estes's *Women Who Run With the Wolves: Myths and Stories of the Wild Woman Archetype* (1992), books for and about **men** and **women**, respectively. Bruno **Bettelheim**'s popularized Sigmund **Freund**'s psychoanalytic approach in *The Uses of Enchantment: The Meaning and Importance of Fairy Tales*, published in 1976 in the wake of cultural, social, and political change in the United States. And all folktale criticism owes a debt to North American folklorist Stith **Thompson,** who updated and expanded Antti **Aarne**'s system for classifying **tale type**s and added the *Motif-Index of Folk-Literature* (1932–36; revised edition 1955–58). ***See also*** Beech Mountain Jack Tale; English Tales; French Canadian Tales; Postmodernism.

Further Readings: Bascom, William. *African Folktales in the New World.* 1976. Bloomington: Indiana University Press, 1992; Burrison, John A., ed. *Storytellers: Folktales and Legends from the South.* Athens: University of Georgia Press, 1991; Fowke, Edith. *Canadian Folklore.* Toronto: Oxford University Press, 1988; ———, comp. and trans. *Folktales of French Canada.* Toronto: NC Press, 1979; Lindahl, Carl, ed. *American Folktales from the Collections of the Library of Congress.* 2 volumes. Armonk, NY: M. E. Sharpe, 2004; McCarthy, William Bernard, ed. *Jack in Two Worlds: Contemporary North American Tales and Their Tellers.* Chapel Hill: University of North Carolina Press, 1994; MacNeil, Joe Neil. *Tales until Dawn: The World of a Cape Breton Gaelic Story-Teller.* Translated and edited by John Shaw. Kingston: McGill-Queen's University Press, 1987; Zipes, Jack. *Fairy Tale as Myth/Myth as Fairy Tale.* Lexington: University Press of Kentucky, 1994. 72–161.

William Bernard McCarthy

Novalis (1772–1801)

Friedrich von Hardenberg, who adopted the pen name "Novalis," was central to the early Romantic school in Germany. He was involved in collaboration and discussion with many key figures of the period such as Ludwig **Tieck** and the brothers August Wilhelm and Friedrich Schlegel, and made original and distinctive contributions to both the theory and practice of the *Kunstmärchen*—the **literary fairy tale**.

Hardenberg was the eldest son of a minor aristocratic family from Oberwiederstedt in central Germany. His father had been involved with the Pietist movement, the mystical

An 1845 engraving of German writer Baron Friedrich von Hardenberg, known as Novalis. [Roger Viollet Collection/Getty Images]

aspect of whose teachings probably influenced the writings of Novalis. As a law student at Jena, Leipzig, and Wittenberg between 1790 and 1794, Novalis became acquainted with Friedrich Schiller, Friedrich Schlegel, and Johann Gottlieb Fichte, and he developed a strong interest in philosophy (especially aesthetics), cultural theory, and literature. After graduation, Novalis took a legal position at Tennstedt in Thuringia, where, in the course of a business trip, he met and fell in love with a young girl, Sophie von Kühn, to whom he became secretly engaged in 1795, two days before her thirteenth birthday. His father's position as director of the Saxon saltworks gave Novalis the opportunity for a career in the mining industry. At the Freiberg Mining Academy, he developed a fascination for mining and mineralogy that was reflected in his writing. This interest was arguably bequeathed to Tieck ("Rune Mountain," 1804), E. T. A. **Hoffmann** ("The Mines at Falun," 1819), and George **MacDonald** (*The Princess and the Goblin*, 1872). In 1797, Novalis was shattered by the death of Sophie from tuberculosis. Particularly after her death, Sophie came to dominate Novalis's writings; she figures as the character Mathilda in the fairy-tale **novel** *Heinrich von Ofterdingen* (1802), where she is closely associated with "the blue flower," the object of Heinrich's mystical quest. Following the deaths of Sophie and his brother Erasmus, Novalis too developed tuberculosis. He began a series of mystical meditations on **death** entitled *Hymnen an die Nacht* (*Hymns to the Night*, 1800), where Sophie seems to be conflated with the figure of Wisdom (Sophia in Greek) and the Virgin Mother, a process that can also be seen in Novalis's fairy tales. Most of Novalis's work was published in an incomplete or fragmentary form after his death in 1801.

The name "Novalis" means something like "someone who opens up new land," and Hardenberg's choice of pseudonym is appropriate. His approach to the **märchen** in both theory and practice was revolutionary. Novalis made extremely high claims for the fairy tale. Far from being relegated to the nursery, the märchen was for Novalis the condition to which all the arts—and indeed life itself—should aspire. In a famous fragment (which MacDonald cites as the epigraph to his *Phantastes* [1858]), Novalis suggested a **utopia**n function for the fairy tale. The true fairy tale is a prophetic representation, he claimed; it does not represent the order of things as they are but rather the disorder, the chaos, the freedom, of primeval nature, which is "a strange picture of the eternal kingdom." History itself will in time become a fairy tale, according to Novalis, and be once more what it was in the beginning: "All fairy tales are only dreams of that familiar world of home which is everywhere and nowhere." The märchen is about turning reality into **poetry**, a project that Novalis called "magical idealism." As he put it in another famous aphorism, again much quoted by MacDonald: "Our life is no dream, but it should, and perhaps will, become one."

These ideas appear in Novalis's own fairy tales, which are dominated by the Romantic idea that our way leads "always homewards" ("immer nach Hause"), in the words of the mysterious young girl in the second part of *Heinrich von Ofterdingen*. In the fairy tale "Hyazinth und Rosenblütchen" ("Hyacinth and Roseblossom"), recounted in Novalis's philosophical novel *Die Lehrlinge zu Sais* (*The Novices of Sais*, 1802), the protagonist Hyacinth embarks on a quest for the goddess Isis, who in the end, at the moment of unveiling, turns out to be Roseblossom. Like other German Romantics, Novalis was fascinated by Johan Wolfgang von **Goethe**'s classic Bildungsroman (novel of development), *Wilhelm Meisters Lehrjahre* (*Wilhelm Meister's Apprenticeship*, 1795–96), though he came to see it as anti-Romantic and destructive of poetry, and he wrote *Heinrich von Ofterdingen* as a kind of counterblast. Novalis sought in the very form of this work to destabilize the distinction between novel and fairy tale. *Heinrich von Ofterdingen* is in effect a long (and unfinished) fairy tale about Heinrich's quest for the blue flower and his beloved Mathilda. It contains three smaller märchen. The first of these alludes to the classical Greek **myth** of Arion and is about the power of music to communicate with nature and overcome base materialism. The second, also recounted by one of the merchants accompanying Heinrich on his journey to Augsburg, is revealed at the end to be about Atlantis and concerns the power of love, poetry, and a true knowledge of nature to establish a golden age against the constraints of hierarchy and prejudice. The third is told by Klingsohr, the great poet of Augsburg. Klingsohr is not only reputedly modelled on Goethe; his fairy tale is a radicalization of Goethe's elaborate fairy tale entitled simply "Das Märchen" ("The Fairy Tale," 1795). Like the latter, Klingsor's fairy tale is extremely complex and in a sense allegorical. It tells how the characters Fabel (Poetry), Ginnistan (Imagination), and Eros defeat the power of the Scribe (Enlightenment rationalism) to found "the kingdom of eternity" under Arcturus and Sophie (Wisdom).

Novalis has had considerable literary influence, not only on later German writers such as Hermann **Hesse** but also via Thomas Carlyle and MacDonald on British writers of fairy tales. Novalis also influenced the French literary tradition running through symbolism to surrealism. His writings, especially those featuring dreams, are susceptible of Freudian readings, and may arguably prefigure Sigmund **Freud**'s work. *See also* Fantasy; German Tales; Magical Realism.

Further Readings: Novalis. *Henry von Ofterdingen*. Translated by Palmer Hilty. 1964. Long Grove: Waveland, 1990; ———. *The Novices of Sais*. Translated by Ralph Manheim. Illustrated by Paul Klee. Brooklyn: Archipelago, 2005; ———. *Philosophical Writings*. Translated by Margaret Mahoney Stoljar. Albany: SUNY Press, 1997; Calhoon, Kenneth S., *Novalis, Freud, and the Discipline of Romance*. Detroit: Wayne State University Press, 1992.

William Gray

Novel

Vladimir Nabokov once wrote, "All great novels are great fairy tales." Taking its inspiration from Nabokov's quotation, this entry provides a broad survey of the relationship between the novel and the **fairy tale**. Such great diversity reveals itself in the novels cited below that one may begin to sense that fairy tales must influence *all* novels, as Nabokov's assertion strongly suggests. The novels discussed here share an indisputably strong, uniquely apparent relationship to fairy tales, which invites new critical scrutiny.

Fairy-tale novels work from fairy tales in diverse ways. This may be because a novel is a long prose work while a literary fairy tale is a short prose work; so using the short form to create a long form inevitably causes new things to happen. Some novels base their plots and primary **motif**s on particular fairy tales. These could accurately be called retellings. Some novelists invent new fairy tales. Other novelists weave together multiple fairy tales to create a newly unified whole. Still other novelists, through tale-like language, motifs, and structural devices, evoke a fairy-tale-like aesthetic right to their core. Victorian, modernist, surrealist, feminist, and postmodern novels have all revealed fascination with fairy tales.

Early Examples

Perhaps the earliest example of the relationship between the novel and fairy tales is Lucien **Apuleius**'s second-century Roman novel *The Golden Ass*. In fairy-tale studies, Apuleius's novel is best known for its inclusion of the story of **Cupid and Psyche**, which is the earliest literary version of the tale of **Beauty and the Beast**. However, Apuleius's work also is important because it prefigures the integration of discrete fairy tales into the plot of the novel. Embedding fairy tales in novels was a strategy employed by numerous fairy-tale authors in the seventeenth and eighteenth centuries, especially during the so-called fairy-tale vogue in France. Marie-Catherine d'**Aulnoy**, Anthony **Hamilton**, Gabrielle-Suzanne Barbot de **Villeneuve**, and other writers introduced literary fairy tales of their own within their novelistic works.

Some scholars consider the *Arabian Nights*—or *Thousand and One Nights*—the greatest influence on all fairy-tale novels. While debatable, this consideration has weight: the book is at the very least a very early example of a long prose narrative that explicitly incorporates numerous fairy tales and a tale-like structure deeply into its form. *Thousand and One Nights*—which entered the European literary tradition in 1704 by way of Antoine **Galland**'s French translation—utilizes a **frame narrative** for shape and incorporates multiple narratives into a long whole. Thus, it can be considered the prototype for a certain kind of fairy-tale novel, discussed later: that which draws distinctly from fairy-tale devices and motifs to create original novel forms, as opposed to what might be called "retellings," novels which take fairy tales and recast them in novel form. *Thousand and One Nights* also predicts inventive uses of fairy tales by many modernist and postmodernist writers; interestingly, such later works are often deemed "experimental" in nature, when in fact they may be among our most-traditional works. One clear example of a later novel deeply informed by *Thousand and One Nights* is *Se una notte d'inverno un viaggiatore* (*If on a Winter's Night a Traveler*, 1979) by Italo **Calvino**, a novel that has a self-referential, mirroring structure and is full of interruptions and incompletion. In fact, the consideration of fairy-tale novels as experimental is a theme that runs through their reception in literary circles.

Romantic and Victorian Novels

In the Romantic tradition, one also sees fairy tales deeply at work. The German Romantic writer **Novalis**, who considered the fairy tale the poetic genre par excellence, integrated fairy tales into his novels *Die Lehrlinge zu Sais* (*The Disciples of Sais*, 1802) and *Heinrich von Ofterdingen* (1802). This was for Novalis a conscious and sophisticated literary strategy. By having his characters tell fairy tales to other characters, Novalis was not only using the novel as a vehicle for his tales, but was also creating a profound thematic and structural resonance between the tales and the frame narrative. In the reciprocal mirroring that took place between the novel's frame story and the tales told within it, the novel itself was revealed as a fairy tale.

French scholar Marthe Robert has argued that the fairy tale is a condensed novel—that the utopian progress of the fairy-tale protagonist toward the happy ending expresses the desire to overcome the circumstances of his or her birth, which is at the heart of many classical novels. This take on the relationship between the novel and the fairy tale helps to explain the **Cinderella**-type plot that scholars have identified in eighteenth- and nineteenth-century European novels. Huang Mei has read eighteenth- and nineteenth-century British novels by **women** in particular as a response to the Cinderella-motif embodied in Samuel Richardson's novel *Pamela* (1740). In this view, it is not only **intertextuality** that creates an association between the novel and fairy tale but a certain generic identity as well.

Wuthering Heights by Emily Brontë and *Jane Eyre* by Charlotte Brontë (both published in 1847) have a fantastic fairy-tale feel, even as their literary mode is a heightened, gothic realism. These novels are good examples of how novelists may work from fairy tales even in a so-called realist mode. In their themes of work, bondage, freedom, and love, *Wuthering Heights* and *Jane Eyre* also relate to fairy tales. Formally speaking, both novels employ nested plot elements (stories within stories), offering readers one of the aesthetic effects of fairy tales. Scholars have written about both novels' relationships to particular fairy tales, including **Bluebeard** and Cinderella **variant**s, among others. The fixity, the fated sensation, of the novels' characters' romances and losses deeply entrench them in fairy tales. Particularly with *Wuthering Heights*, a dark suggestiveness combines with a deceptively childlike tone, making the path to interpretation through fairy tales a readily accessible one.

George Eliot's novel *Silas Marner* (1861), while also lacking overt magical elements, qualifies here as an interesting example as well. The story of an isolated weaver whose life is transformed by a young girl who appears in his home quite suddenly, this novel reads as a fairy tale with ease. Its taut, deeply patterned structure and theme of goodness qualify it compellingly as a fairy-tale novel. The novel's essentially realist mode makes it an interesting example of how fairy-tale novels do not fall into the easy category of "novels with magic in them." Rather, these novels' syntactic arrangement (language + form) evokes fairy tales.

Lewis **Carroll**'s *Alice's Adventures in Wonderland* (1865) represents one of the most inventive fairy-tale novels ever to have been written; as its naïve but cheeky hero explores Wonderland, the book's complex structure, many-layered interpretive values, magical-everyday qualities, and eccentric cast of characters reveal multitudes of fairy-tale tropes.

Early Twentieth Century

Peter Pan, or The Boy Who Would Not Grow Up by Sir James Matthew **Barrie** (1904) creates a new fairy tale drawn from the motifs of multiple earlier fairy tales, particularly those stories about **childhood** and **death**. Another of its primary themes—banishment from home and the quest to return—clearly places it in the fairy-tale mode. A fascinating, ambivalent work, *Peter Pan* reveals itself as much more complex in novel form than, generally speaking, its **adaptation**s to **theater**, film, and **animation**.

Franz **Kafka**'s *Die Verwandlung* (*The Metamorphosis*, 1915) and *Das Schloß* (*The Castle*, 1926) are also extraordinary fairy-tale novels. *The Metamorphosis* reads with the contained-world intensity of a short story though it is of novel (or **novella**) length. In it, the protagonist Gregor Samsa awakens to discover himself transformed into some insectlike form.

Strikingly, this **transformation** is not treated as an extraordinary magical event; the real and the unreal in the story collapse as in fairy tales. In *The Castle*, Kafka offers a different use of the fairy-tale form. *The Castle*'s flatly drawn protagonist, known only as K., strives to gain access to a castle that may or may not exist. Many aspects of K.'s quest closely mirror classic fairy-tale tropes (encounters with strangers, sudden changes of weather and circumstance, and character types).

Like Kafka's *Metamorphosis,* Henry James's *The Turn of the Screw* (1898) may be considered a novella by many, as it is a slim volume. However, it is a substantial narrative and warrants consideration as a fairy-tale novel. One may, indeed, consider novellas a short form of fairy-tale novels; novellas bear more relation to novels as a form than to short stories or tales. James himself called *The Turn of the Screw* a fairy tale in the preface to the 1908 U.S. edition. He wrote that *The Turn of The Screw* is "a fairy-tale pure and simple—save indeed as to its springing not from an artless and measureless, but from a conscious and cultivated credulity." This supernatural novel owes so much to fairy tales that it is impossible to list all of the elements here, but for some brief examples consider its framing device, childhood domain, supernatural fixation, and plot similarity to many stories of the Brothers **Grimm**.

James went on, in his preface, to say something of deep relevance to the topic of fairy tales and novels: "[T]he fairy-tale belongs mainly to either of two classes, the short and sharp and single, charged more or less with the compactness of **anecdote** (as to which let the familiars of our childhood, Cinderella and Blue-Beard and Hop o' my Thumb and **Little Red Riding Hood** and many of the gems of the Brothers Grimm directly testify), or else the long and loose, the copious, the various, the endless, where, dramatically speaking, roundness is quite sacrificed—sacrificed to fullness, sacrificed to exuberance, if one will: witness at hazard almost any one of the Arabian Nights." This latter form defines the novels described herein, and this quotation serves as an excellent description of many books not included here. Unfortunately, few studies to date have inspected the fairy-tale aspects of James's work in particular, just as few studies have analyzed fairy-tale novels in general.

Surrealism and Modernism

Though there is not much scholarship yet on fairy tales and modernism, modernist authors reveal a great fascination with fairy tales, frequently incorporating fairy-tale references into their books. Such authors include James Joyce and Virginia **Woolf**, whose refracted narratives, lyric language, and collapsing uses of **time** bear strong relation to these effects in fairy tales. Joyce's *Ulysses* (1922) contains many direct fairy-tale references, and its poetic language—striving through new syntax to make new meaning—is fairy-tale-like in tone. Strikingly, in Woolf's *To the Lighthouse* (1927), the protagonist Mrs. Ramsey reads the Grimms' fairy tale "The Fisherman and His Wife" to her son and then compares fairy stories to "the bass accompanying a tune, which now and then ran up unexpectedly into the melody." This sentence beautifully describes how fairy tales often work as the subtle background to many novels throughout the ages.

In 1936, Djuna Barnes published the poetic novel *Nightwood*, which, in addition to containing overt fairy-tale references ("children know something they can't tell: They like Little Red Riding Hood in bed with the wolf"), employs surreal, perverse language to shape its classic plot. (Barnes's style seems to be a strong influence on the remarkable, encyclopedic high style of the late twentieth-century British author Angela **Carter**, discussed later in this entry.)

Though primarily known for her paintings (particularly the dreamlike "birthday series" produced in the 1940s), surrealist Dorothea Tanning also published a supernatural novel called *Chasm* (2004). Set in a mysterious mansion in the desert and revolving around a fantastical cast of characters, the novel recalls fairy tales, gothic realism, and early modernism.

Postwar Novels

Beginning in the early mid-twentieth century, fairy tales seem to have begun an inexorable influence on the novel tradition, one that seems to have grown stronger with each decade. The magnitude of this trend defies summary.

Of Eudora **Welty**'s 1942 novel *The Robber Bride*, Marianne Hauser wrote in the *New York Times*, the "story is a fairy tale from beginning to end, and to call it simply fiction would be throwing our traditional conception of the word quite out of balance." Welty's novel, which is based on the Grimms' tale "The Robber Bridegroom," as well as "The Goose Girl" and "Snow White," is a lovely, funny, and exquisitely arranged novel that draws from the western European fairy-tale tradition while also forging a distinctly American style.

Though considered a children's novel, and not currently widely read, Rumer Godden's slender book *The Doll's House* (1947) reads like a disquieting adult fairy tale. The sudden appearance of the malevolent doll Marchpane has drastic effects on a simple family, particularly the mother who burns alive—reminding readers perhaps of the violent, strange, popular German children's book *Der Struwwelpeter* (1845) by Heinrich Hoffman. Peculiarly, Godden's *The Doll's House* has not been of interest to fairy-tale scholars, along with its literary precursors outside the form of the novel, *A Doll's House* (1879) Henrik Ibsen's play about **marriage** and transformation, centering on the strikingly depthless heroine Nora; and "The Doll's House" (1921), a haunting short story by Katherine Mansfield. Interestingly, a dollhouse becomes very significant in contemporary author Kathryn Davis's book *Hell* (1998), a novel in three modes, one of which devotes itself to the lives of a doll family. Davis's entire body of work reveals remarkable incorporation of fairy-tale themes and motifs.

Other postwar novels with fairy-tale intertexts include Brazilian-Jewish author Clarice Lispector's *Perto do coração selvagem* (*Near to the Wild Heart*, 1944) and *A hora da estrela* (*The Hour of the Star*, 1977); New Zealand author Janet Frame's *Owls Do Cry* (1957), with its poetic language and a childhood landscape of fear and mistaken identity; Barbara Comyns's fairy-tale retelling *The Juniper Tree* (1985); East German writer Christa Wolf's *Nachdenken über Christa T.* (*The Quest for Christa T.*, 1968); and many others.

Mid- to Late Twentieth Century

The twentieth century continued to see fairy tales flourish as a point of embarkation for novelists. Angela Carter's body of work contributes an entirely new, intrinsic fairy-tale structure. Two of her novels stand out: *The Magic Toy Shop* (1967) and *Nights at the Circus* (1984)—although in fairy-tale studies, her collection of shorter fairy-tale rewritings, *The Company of Wolves* (1979), has monopolized critical attention. Margaret **Atwood**'s novels drawing on the fairy tale—such as *The Handmaid's Tale* (1985) and *The Robber Bride* (1993)—have received their fair share of acclaim and critical commentary, especially in the context of **feminism**. The late twentieth century also generated postmodern adventures in fairy tales, such as Donald

Barthelme's *Snow White* (1967), John Barth's *Lost in the Funhouse* (1968), Thomas Pynchon's *Gravity's Rainbow* (1973), and Robert **Coover**'s various novelistic experiments. It is striking to note that reviews and articles about these novels often take note of the fairy-tale references without delving more stridently into their formal debt to fairy tales.

Even with the rising interest in fairy-tale studies, scholars have been hard pressed to keep pace with the steady stream of twentieth- and twenty-first century fairy-tale novels. Even a sampling of the authors and titles conveys the fierce impact on the novel form that fairy tales have had for the past fifty years especially. Among the many novels deserving further attention are the following: *Hitsuji o meguru bōken* (*A Wild Sheep Chase*, 1982), *Sekai no owari to hādo-boirudo wandārando* (*Hardboiled Wonderland and the End of the World*, 1985), and *Nejimaki-dōri kuronikuru* (*The Wind-up Bird Chronicle: A Novel*, 1994) by Murakami Haruki; Kathryn Davis's *Labrador* (1988), with a nested-doll plot and beautiful, frightening tale-telling device; A. S. **Byatt**'s *Possession* (1990); Rikki Ducornet's *The Jade Cabinet* (1993); *Kitchin* (*Kitchen*, 1988) by Yoshimoto Banana, which contains not only subtle, supernatural devices but also parsed-down plots; Salman **Rushdie**'s numerous novels, whose books belong more to the magical-realist tradition than to that of fairy tales, but whose imagery owes much to fairy tales; Joyce Carol Oates's novels, especially *Beasts* (2002); Lynda Barry, whose **graphic novel** *Cruddy: An Illustrated Novel* (1997) offers grotesque imagery and **violence** to shockingly poignant effect; Gaetan Soucy's *La petite fille qui aimait trop les allumettes* (*The Little Girl Who Was Too Fond of Matches*, 1998), perhaps one of the most cruel and enchanting novels of our time; Mary Gaitskill's *Veronica* (2005), a realist novel with classic fairy-tale tropes; and Kate Bernheimer's *roman-fleuve* about the Gold family sisters, the first two installments of which have been published (out of a series of ten), *The Complete Tales of Ketzia Gold* (2001) and *The Complete Tales of Merry Gold* (2006), which brings together fairy-tale history, aesthetics, and motifs to create a new kind of novel, one obsessed with isolation and told in separate installments. Fairy-tale novels are multiple in form, wild in their differences, and an area of study that requires renewed attention by fairy-tale scholars. *See also* Fantasy; Magical Realism; Metafiction; Postmodernism; Young Adult Fiction.

Further Readings: Bacchilega, Cristina. *Postmodern Fairy Tales: Gender and Narrative Strategies*. Philadelphia: University of Pennsylvania Press, 1997; Benson, Stephen. *Cycles of Influence: Fiction, Folktale, and Theory*. Detroit: Wayne State University Press, 2003; Huang Mei. *Transforming the Cinderella Dream: From Francis Burney to Charlotte Brontë*. New Brunswick, NJ: Rutgers University Press, 1990; Jones, Steven Swann. "Folklore in Henry James's Fiction: Turning of the Screw." *Western Folklore* 60 (2001): 1–24; Martin, Ann. *Red Riding Hood and the Wolf in Bed: Modernism's Fairy Tales*. Toronto: University of Toronto Press, 2006; Robert, Marthe. "Castles in the Air." *Origins of the Novel*. Translated by Sacha Rabinovitch. Bloomington: Indiana University Press, 1980. 49–63.

Kate Bernheimer

Novella

In a discussion of the **fairy tale**, the most pertinent definition of "novella" is also the oldest: the kind of tale Giovanni **Boccaccio** wrote in his collection, the *Decameron* (1349–50), and which can be said to have influenced works such as Marguerite de Navarre's *Heptaméron* (1559) and Miguel de Cervantes Saavedra's *Noveljas ejemplares* (*Moral or*

Instructive Novellas, 1613). These are short narratives generally describing a single incident (having a simple plot) about events that may be true or fictional (but which are said to be true), and which may contain a **moral** or lesson, but also are meant to entertain. The various tales are held together by a "cornice" or **frame narrative**, in which the setting of the tale telling itself is foregrounded. For example, in the *Decameron*, a group of people are escaping plague-ridden Florence; in Geoffrey **Chaucer**'s *Canterbury Tales* (begun c. 1387), all of the participants meet on a pilgrimage. Although the term "novella" also means "news" and implies that something "new" is being recounted, this is not in regard to the plots, which are often openly borrowed from medieval or classical oral and written sources. Instead, it pertains to the new telling of an old tale, to the unusual or unexpected twists in the outcome of the plots, and simply to the "newsiness" of the genre—its relationship to gossip.

The novellas of the **Middle Ages** and the Renaissance innovated by giving written, literary form to tales of entertainment. Usually written in prose and in the vernacular, and highlighting the act of narration itself, they form a bridge between the orally transmitted folktale or fairy tale and the literary genres, not least through their sharing of plots, **motif**s, and subject matter. In general, this link is taken to constitute the difference between the novella and the fairy tale. Whereas the **fairy tale** relates events occurring in a fantastic realm of magic and monsters, the novella approaches literary realism—although, as in the folk genres, there is a lack of "rounding" or psychological depth to the characters, who remain very much stereotyped. The novella shares plots and motifs with a variety of other genres: the **fabliau**, **fable**, **legend**, **saint's legend**, chivalric romance, the **Bible**, and Greco-Roman and Oriental sources, among others.

Sometimes the term "novella" has been used to describe any short narrative, but such imprecision does not help the student of narratology. In the late eighteenth and early nineteenth centuries, a new genre developed in Germany that reached its peak in the nineteenth century: the German *Novelle* was a highly stylized tale of short-to-medium length, usually describing a single plot, often the occurrence of some "unheard-of event" (as noted by Johann Wolfgang von **Goethe**) and its fallout. Theoreticians worked out elaborate descriptions of the genre, including its "turning point" (*Wendepunkt*), the strict unity of the plot, and its tendency to have a unifying symbolism. Despite a continued debt to folktale traditions, this highly honed genre also largely grew out of a tendency to reject less refined narratives of the uneducated as well as the more verbose literary productions of, for example, many contemporary **women** fiction writers.

More recently, the term has come to mean a short novel or a long short story, particularly in reference to works of the nineteenth and twentieth centuries. However, this takes us far away from the folk-narrative origins and results primarily from the use of the English term "**novel**" to refer to what most European languages call a *roman* (or its cognates). *See also* Classical Antiquity; Literary Fairy Tale; Middle Ages.

Further Readings: Caporello-Szykman, Corradina. *The Boccaccian Novella: Creation and Waning of a Genre*. Bern: Lang, 1990; Cholakian, Patricia Francis, and Rouben Charles Cholakian, eds. and trans. *The Early French Novella: An Anthology of Fifteenth- and Sixteenth-Century Tales*. Albany: SUNY Press, 1972; Clements, Robert J., and Jospeh Gibaldi. *Anatomy of the Novella: The European Tale Collection from Boccaccio and Chaucer to Cervantes*. New York: New York University Press, 1977; Rabell, Carmen. *Rewriting the Italian Novella in Counter-Reformation Spain*. Woodbridge: Tamesis, 2003; Wiese, Benno von. *Novelle*. Stuttgart: Metzler, 1963.

Laura Martin

Numbers

Numbers play an important role in the aesthetic and formal dimensions of folktales and fairy tales. Stith **Thompson**'s *Motif-Index of Folk-Literature* lists dozens of specific **motifs** related to individual formulistic numbers. Pattern numbers are culturally specific and guide the aesthetic, formal, and symbolic aspects of folktales and fairy tales. Although the number three drives the most important pattern in Indo-European and Euro-American culture, the numbers two, seven, and twelve are also significant (Motifs Z71.1, Formulistic number: three; Z71.5, Formulistic number: seven; Z71.8, Formulistic number: twelve). For most Native American peoples, four is the ritual and pattern number (Motif Z71.2, Formulistic number: four), whereas in many Asian countries, including China, the governing pattern number is five (Motif Z71.3, Formulistic number: five).

Pattern numbers function at multiple levels within folktales and fairy tales. Numbers may be explicitly named in the manifest content of a narrative. For example, there may be two or three **brothers**, a maiden wearing seven veils, or forty **thieves**. Pattern numbers may also implicitly appear through the repetition of words, motifs, actions, or tale moves—for example, when the hero completes the third task or kills the third **ogre**. At the level of a tale's formal structure, there may be repetition of entire narrative moves rather than simply shorter incidents or specific motifs. For example, in some versions of ATU 300, The Dragon-Slayer, there are three brothers, horses, and dogs; after the first two sets are turned into statues, the youngest brother, horse, and dog succeed.

Scholars have identified the importance of pattern numbers, especially the numbers two and three, in folktales and fairy tales. The centrality of two and three in Indo-European folk and fairy tales is underscored by several of Axel Olrik's Epic Laws of Folk Narratives, including the Law of Repetition (generally of three), the Law of Three, the Law of Two to a Scene, the Law of Contrast (between two oppositions, such as a good and an evil character), and the Law of Twins. These laws contribute to the tales' internal logic and aid narrators in transmission. Few scholars, however, have speculated about the meanings behind the use of these numbers. In *The Fairytale as Art Form and Portrait of Man*, Max **Lüthi** examines the role of numbers in fairy tales. He argues that the number two represents both the pair and the possibility of polarity between pairs. Tripling, he contends, is a concentrated form of perfectionism in fairy tales, and as a sequence it is marked by repetition, variation, and contrast.

There are several systems of number symbolism that are helpful for understanding the meanings of pattern numbers in folktales and fairy tales, including elementary, astrological, and Pythagorean number systems. Elementary number symbolism is based on the belief that numbers have concrete associations with the physical world. It is characterized by the distinction between the concepts of one and many. Two represents diversity, antithetical pairs, and the dualities of nature (such as male/female and day/night). Characters in folktales and fairy tales often come in such pairs: the hero and the antihero, the male and female protagonists, the hero and the villain. Greater than a pair, three represents the concept of many and, by extension, all. Three is also associated with the superlative. Folktales are characterized by the success of the third sibling, the hero's success on third attempt, and the third task that wins the bride. In ATU 923, Love Like Salt, it is the youngest (third) daughter who loves her **father** most. Ten represents finality and completeness, while nine is almost complete.

Astrological number symbolism is closely related to the passage of time, with an emphasis on the numbers four (weeks in a month), seven (days in a week), and twelve (months in a year). Seven has multiple associations in astrological number symbolism: it represents the original act of creation, the balance between good and evil, and a traditional number of sacrifice. Seven is frequently used to mark the passage of time, as in Motif Z72.2, Seven years, seven months, seven days. In many versions of ATU 425, The Search for the Lost Husband, the female protagonist wanders for seven years or seven days, or must fill seven bottles with tears or wear out seven pairs of iron shoes before finding her husband. In versions of ATU 310, The Maiden in the Tower, the mother promises to give her child to the **witch** when she is seven years old. The hero of ATU 361, Bear-Skin, gives up his soul to the **devil** in exchange for wealth; his soul can be released only after not washing for seven years. Seven is also used to characterize both positive and negative characters. For example, the female protagonist of ATU 408, The Three Oranges, is sometimes called the Beauty with the Seven Veils. Alternately, in some versions of ATU 300, The **Dragon**-Slayer, the hero must kill a seven-headed monster or a seven-headed witch.

Pythagorean number theory is attributed to the Greek philosopher Pythagoras of the fifth century BCE. This numerical system posits a connection between abstract numbers and concrete reality. A point represents one, a line (between two points) represents two, a triad (a plane figure created by joining three points) represents three, and a solid represents four. In this system, one is the Monad, which embodies unity and divinity. The Duad represents diversity and a breaking away from unity. Three, a Triad, is the first real number and signifies perfect unity. This meaning of three appears in folktales and fairy tales where the tripling signifies a whole rather than intensification. For example, in some variants of The Dragon-Slayer **tale type**, a fisherman gives part of a magic fish to his wife, dog, and horse, and each gives **birth** to three offspring. There is an implied unity among the triplets that may be articulated through a life token, a sympathetic object that indicates when one of the triplets is in mortal danger.

Further Readings: Dundes, Alan. "The Number Three in American Culture." *Every Man His Way: Readings in Cultural Anthropology.* Englewood Cliffs, NJ: Prentice-Hall, 1968. 401–24; Hopper, Vincent Foster. *Medieval Number Symbolism: Its Sources, Meaning, and Influence on Thought and Expression.* 1938. Mineola, NY: Dover Publications, 2000; Lorenz, Bernd. "Notizen zu Zwölf und Dreihundert im Märchen: Ausdruck bedeutungsvoller Größe und abgegrenzter Bereiche." *Fabula* 27 (1986): 42–45; Lüthi, Max. *The Fairytale as Art Form and Portrait of Man.* Translated by Jon Erickson. Bloomington: Indiana University Press, 1984; Olrik, Axel. *Principles for Oral Narrative Research.* Translated by Kirsten Wolf. Bloomington: Indiana University Press, 1992; Röllcke, Heinz. "Nochmals zu den Zahlen Zwölf und Dreihundert im Märchen." *Fabula* 28 (1987): 106–09.

Linda J. Lee

Numskull. *See* Simpleton

Nursery and Household Tales. See Kinder- und Hausmärchen

Nyblom, Helena (1843–1926)

Along with Anna Wahlenberg and Anna Maria Roos, Helena Nyblom was one of the most prominent writers of the **literary fairy tale** in Sweden in the late nineteenth and early twentieth centuries. Born in Copenhagen, Denmark, she received a classical education and met her future husband, Carl Rupert Nyblom, on a trip to Rome with her father, the painter

Jørgen Roed. Settled in Uppsala, Sweden, after her marriage, Nyblom bore seven children, established a flourishing cultural center in her home (she was a fine pianist, and a lyrical quality is evident in her prose), and published her first literary work in 1875. She wrote essays and short stories and also established herself as a literary critic before publishing her first fairy-tale collection, *Der var en gang: Aeventyr for smaa og store* (*Once upon a Time: Fairy Tales for Young and Old*) in 1897. As a genre, the fairy tale gave Nyblom the perfect vehicle for expressing the dilemma that was at the center of her work: how can duty toward others be reconciled with developing fully as an artist? This theme is treated symbolically in two of her allegorical stories, "Alla hafvets vilda vågor" ("The Wild Waves of the Sea" in *Der var en gang*) and "Flickan, som dansade förbi alla" ("The Girl Who Danced past Everyone" in *Der var en gang II*, 1898). Between 1896 and 1920, she wrote about eighty tales, including a version of "**Beauty and the Beast**," as well as stories based on legendary **motif**s such as **changeling**s and being taken into the mountain. *See also* Scandinavian Tales.

Further Reading: Nordlinder, Eva. *Sekelskiftets svenska konstsaga och sagodiktaren Helena Nyblom.* Stockholm: Bonniers Junior Förlag, 1991.

Marte Hult

Nyström, Jenny (1854–1946)

Jenny Nyström was a gifted portrait painter who is best known for her **illustration**s of the benevolent Swedish Christmas "tomten" (gnome) and the happy idyllic children that appeared (and continue to be reproduced) on thousands of postcards, in Christmas periodicals, and in children's books. Enormously prolific, Nyström produced about 10,000 images over a seventy-year period, including illustrations for adult literature in various genres, religious publications, serials, and newspapers.

Nyström's talent was discovered and encouraged early, and when Viktor Rydberg's pioneering **literary fairy tale** *Lille Viggs äventyr på julafton* (*Little Viggs' Adventure on Christmas Eve*) appeared in book form in 1875, the illustrations were Nyström's. She later illustrated his famous poem "Tomten" ("The Gnome," 1881). Nyström studied at the Royal Academy in Stockholm for eight years and in 1881 received the Royal Medal, which enabled her to study in Paris. In 1887, she married Daniel Stoopendaal, and some of her works are modeled on her son Curt.

In 1882, the classic *Barnkammarens bok* (*The Nursery Book*) was published, and the same year Nyström contributed six drawings to *Svenska Folksägner* (*Swedish Folktales*). She contributed for many years to the children's periodical *Saga* which published classic fairy tales and folktales, as well as to *Jultomten* and other children's periodicals. Her work includes illustrations of the fairy tales of Jacob and Wilhelm **Grimm** and many other fairy tales, folktales, and themes from mythology. *See also* Scandinavian Tales.

Further Readings: Jäder, Karl and Astrid. *Jenny Nyström—den folkkära.* Stockholm: Gummessons, 1975; Lindholm, Stig. *Med penseln som trollspö.* Stockholm: CKM: Föreningen Jenny Nyströms Vänner, 2004.

Marte Hult

O

Ocampo, Silvina (1903–1993)

As a child, the Argentinean short-story writer and poet Silvina Ocampo was fascinated with Hans Christian **Andersen** and the Brothers **Grimm**. Ocampo used **motif**s from folktales and fairy tales—such as metamorphosis or **punishment and reward**—as the basis for new tales. She also used animals in a manner evoking the **fable** and incorporated into her works elements of **fantasy**, **parable**, science fiction, and Greek **myth**.

Her most obvious use of a folktale source is in "Jardín de infierno" ("Garden of Hell," 1988), which rewrites "**Bluebeard**," reversing **gender** roles and making Bluebeard (*barba azul*) into a woman (Bárbara). Its tone characterizes Ocampo's ambiguous attitude to **feminism**, suggesting both a feminist appropriation of the story and a backlash against caricatured role reversals. Ocampo's quizzical approach to fairy-tale notions of happiness is summed up in her unpublished text in English, entitled "In Fairy Tales." In it, a magic wand will change the cook to a **queen** (alluding to "**Cinderella**"), but the narrator asks the reader, "Would you want to change?"

Other examples of fairy-tale elements can be found in "El verdugo" ("The Executioner," 1959) and "El progreso de la ciencia" ("The Progress of Science," 1961), both featuring rulers who, out of vanity, impose certain conditions on their subjects, reminding us of "The Emperor's New Clothes." Ocampo's new fairy tales include those of a science fiction tendency, such as "Las ondas" ("The Waves," 1959) or the parablelike "Éxodo" ("Exodus," 1961). *See also* Feminist Tales.

Further Readings: Mackintosh, Fiona. "Babes in the *Bosque:* Fairy Tales in Twentieth-Century Argentine Women's Writing." *Fairy Tales and Feminism: New Approaches.* Edited by Donald Haase. Detroit: Wayne State University Press, 2004. 149–67; Ocampo, Silvina. *Leopoldina's Dream.* Translated by Daniel Balderston. New York: Penguin Books, 1988.

Fiona J. Mackintosh

Oehlenschläger, Adam (1779–1850)

As the first translator of tales by Jacob and Wilhelm **Grimm** into Danish, Adam Oehlenschläger helped introduce the fairy tale into the literary tradition during the era of Romanticism. A leading national poet, Oehlenschläger considered fairy tales part of what the German Romantic theorist Friedrich Schlegel had called "universal poetry," and in the preface to his *Eventyr af forskiellige digtere* (*Fairy Tales from Several Writers*, 1816), Oehlenschläger argued that the genre represents the possibility of a common aesthetic that appeals to children and adults alike. *Fairy Tales from Several Writers* includes six tales by Grimm, of which three are specifically designated as "**children's literature**." Oehlenschläger recommended fairy tales as the ideal reading matter for children because tales are not overtly pedagogical but, blending the plasticity of **myth** with the circumscription of poetry, "connect the individual to the whole of nature." In contrast to Jean-Jacques Rousseau, Oehlenschläger advocated for a full-fledged literature for children based on fairy tales.

Among his notable creative works are ***Aladdin*** (1805; English translation, 1857), a seminal work in Danish literature. In this dramatic play, inspired by the ***Arabian Nights*** and the German Romantic tales of Ludwig **Tieck**, "nature's light-hearted son" develops into a mature hero deserving happiness through a fairy-tale-like plot. *Aladdin* was later deconstructed humorously in Hans Christian **Andersen**'s fairy tale "Fyrtøjet" ("The Tinderbox," 1835). In *Vaulundurs Saga* (1805), Oehlenschläger introduces Old Norse mythology in a Romantic style related to Tieck's tales. ***See also*** Scandinavian Tales; Theater.

Further Reading: Rossel, Sven H., ed. *A History of Danish Literature*. Lincoln: University of Nebraska Press, 1992.

Helene Høyrup

Ogre, Ogress

An ogre is a bizarre and dangerous antagonist whose main ambition is to catch and devour humans. The English term "ogre" (feminine "ogress") was borrowed in the eighteenth century from the French *ogre* (feminine *ogresse*). Famous ogre types are represented in Charles **Perrault**'s classic French tales of 1697: "La belle au bois dormant" ("**Sleeping Beauty**"; ATU 410), "Le maître chat ou le chat botté" ("**Puss in Boots**"; ATU 545B), and "Le petit poucet" ("Little **Thumbling**"; ATU 327B). According to Jacob **Grimm**'s etymology, *ogre* is derived from Latin *Orcus*, the God of the Underworld.

Although the terminology varies from language to language, the concept of the "ogre" is known in many of the world's narrative traditions. An impression of the large variety of **motif**s, traits, and plots can be gained from Stith **Thompson**'s *Motif-Index of Folk-Literature*, where an entire chapter (chapter G) is devoted solely to ogres. The traits associated with ogres that are described in this entry are culled from a comparative examination of Perrault's French tales, selected **Chinese tales** and **Japanese tales**, and a larger number of **African tales**, in which the ogre is frequently connected with ancestral spirits.

A monstrous giant being beaten by Tom Hickathrift as illustrated by John D. Batten in Joseph Jacobs' *More English Fairy Tales* (London: David Nutt, 1894).

Outright descriptions of the ogre's qualities are rare in **oral tradition**, in contrast to written narratives, where descriptions are more explicit. An ogre is therefore characterized primarily by his malicious behavior toward his human counterparts, from whom he differs by species. Sometimes the ogre is a loner, but typically he has a **family**. Certain traditions (for example, those of Berber and Somali) specifically employ the ogress. An ogre usually dwells in a dark unpopulated forest, where he behaves like its owner. His habitation is usually a special kind of house—for instance, a dark castle. Other ogres dwell in enormous old trees or large bodies of water.

Ogres usually appear as humans and are frequently depicted as giants. In Oriental tales, the ogre's skin may be black, in Chinese tales blue, and in Namibian tales white. His hair is unkempt. Berber ogresses have very long breasts, which they constantly have to throw back over their shoulders. Some ogres have reversed feet. Typically, ogres speak the language of humans, although their speech is coarse and corrupt. An ogre may be one-eyed, three-eyed, or cross-eyed; and sometimes his gaze is penetrating and spellbinding. The ogre's ability to detect human flesh by sense of smell is especially threatening to fairy-tale protagonists, as conveyed in the now almost-proverbial refrain from "Jack and the Beanstalk": "Fee-fi-fo-fum, I smell the blood of an Englishman." Consonant with this ruling passion for devouring humans, the ogre is depicted with long fingernails, arms that can extend to any distance, and a mouth that goes from ear to ear and is filled with razorblade teeth. His strength is signaled when he arrives on the scene in blasts and whirlwinds. On the one hand, an ogre can be tricky when it comes to capturing humans (for example, by disguising his voice); on the other hand, he can be stupid and lose his advantage if he feels too confident about his superiority. An ogre typically possesses riches or valuable goods such as medicine or **food**.

Some ogres are half alive and half decayed. Others can transform themselves into predatory animals, sometimes with multiple heads. In many cases, the ogre first appears as a human until the hero or heroine recognizes him as strange and dangerous. Certain ogres take the shape of an animal from the beginning—a lion, leopard, crocodile, giant snake, or **wolf**. African traditions also tell of ogres who transform themselves into monstrous "swallowing pumpkins" that devour people.

Typically, the ogre acts as the adversary of human heroes or heroines, who are often small children, despised youngest siblings, or young adults. Humans fall under the ogre's domination while they are hunting or searching for food or medicine in the bush, or when they are seeking a **marriage** partner in a strange land. One frequent motif involves the marriage of a human female to an ogre, especially when she rejects the average type of man. Conversely, a human male may marry an ogress who eventually assimilates into human society. In many cases, the ogre has an advantage over the human because he already knows in advance the specific problem confronting the distressed protagonist. Certain stories tell of children who are promised to an ogre in return for some advantage. More-aggressive forms of capture occur when ogres take humans by brute force. For example, ogre hordes may launch a terrifying attack on a village and carry off the victims in a bag.

An ogre's main objective is to devour human beings, who are generally swallowed whole. Sophisticated ogres fatten their victims and later season them for consumption. The ogre's voracious greed is a vulnerability that the hero can exploit for his own benefit and to initiate the story's dramatic turning point. Humans resist ogres by fighting, usually with peculiar weapons, or by fleeing at just the right moment, often with the aid of **magic object**s. Disappointed ogres resort to swallowing their comrades, then dismembering themselves. To overcome an ogre, a human has to be alert, socially adjusted (especially toward elders and potential allies), resourceful, clever, and audacious. Humans who succeed in defeating an ogre return home with essential experiences, personal maturity (inherently lacking at the beginning of the story), and the qualities needed to lead a successful life. Sometimes humans rescue not only themselves but also their family members, if not humanity itself.

Ogre stories can be regarded as traditional thrillers full of gruesome and shocking details, but also spiced with the comical and satirical elements of caricature. In their relation to each other, ogres and humans clearly express the binary oppositions of bad and good, stupid and clever, ugly and beautiful, and nature and culture. Stories of ogres can also be interpreted as depicting the protagonist's **initiation** into adolescence, based on the typical tripartite structure involving: (1) a displacement from home and an ensuing quest/journey; (2) painful development among weird and life-threatening forces in a liminal space; and (3) a return home and humble reintegration into society. In the course of the story, the strange and dangerous ogre acts as a therapeutic catalyst. This is particularly evident in ogre-tale traditions from societies with ancestral cults, where, on a surface level, spirits may be experienced as malevolent, but ultimately are believed to have benevolent motives. *See also* Cannibalism.

Further Readings: Calame-Griaule, Geneviève. "Les chemins de l'autre monde: Contes initiatiques africains." *Cahiers de Littérature Orale* 39–40 (1996): 29–59; Foust, R. E. "Monstrous Image: Theory of Fantasy Antagonists." *Genre* 13 (1980): 441–53; Geider, Thomas. *Die Figur des Oger in der traditionellen Literatur und Lebenswelt der Pokomo in Ost-Kenya.* 2 volumes. Cologne: Koeppe, 1990; Jobling, Ian. "The Psychological Foundations of the Hero-Ogre Story: A Cross-Cultural Study." *Human Nature* 12 (2001): 247–72; Revel, Jacques, and Jean-Claude Schmitt, eds. *L'ogre historien: Autour de Jacques Le Goff.* Paris: Gallimard, 1998. 303–33; Thompson, Stith. "Ogres and Witches." *The Folktale.* 1946. Berkeley: University of California Press, 1977. 35–40; Turner, Victor W. "Social Dramas and Stories about Them." *On Narrative.* Edited by W. J. T. Mitchell. Chicago: University of Chicago Press, 1981. 137–64; Warner, Marina. "Fee Fie Fo Fum: The Child in the Jaws of the Story." *Cannibalism and the Colonial World.* Edited by Francis Barker, Peter Hulme, and Margaret Iversen. Cambridge: Cambridge University Press, 1997. 158–82.

Thomas Geider

Oicotype

In folktale studies, an oicotype (also spelled "oikotype" and "ecotype") is a localized form of a **tale type** that diverges from the widespread plot or pattern considered to be the primary form (**urform**). In the context of **folklore** studies more generally, the term "oicotype" may be applied not only to oral narratives but also to customs and beliefs. The Swedish philologist and folklore scholar Carl Wilhelm von Sydow introduced "oicotype" in 1934, when he borrowed it from the biological sciences to stress the fact that an isolated local culture could shape the reception of a tale in a new environment and social **context**. In advancing this idea, von Sydow provided an explanation for the **diffusion** of folktales: a tale's migration to a new geographical or sociocultural environment occurs when it is adapted to reflect and become part of the new context. Although oicotypification is very common in oral narratives, research on oicotypes is not frequently undertaken in folklore studies. To be sure, scholars have revealed the importance of such studies as a way of depicting and analyzing the social and cultural values of specific groups. The American folklorist Roger D. Abrahams pointed out that the transgression of **gender** borders played a role in the process of oicotypification, whereas the Finnish folklorist Lauri **Honko** expanded von Sydow's concept by identifying several forms of such **adaptation**s that depend largely on cultural, social, and economic systems.

Further Readings: Abrahams, Roger D. *Deep Down in the Jungle: Negro Narrative Folklore from the Streets of Philadelphia.* 1963. Chicago: Aldine, 1974; Honko, Lauri. "The Formation of Ecotypes." *Folklore on Two Continents: Essays in Honor of Linda Dégh.* Edited by N. Burlakoff and C. Lindahl. Bloomington: Trickster Press, 1980. 280–85; Sydow, Carl Wilhelm von. "Geography and Folktale Oikotypes." *Selected Papers on Folklore.* Copenhagen: Rosenkilde & Bagger, 1948. 44–59.

Marilena Papachristophorou

Once upon a Mattress

The American musical *Once upon a Mattress*—with music by Mary Rodgers, lyrics by Marshall Barer, and book by Jay Thompson, Dean Fuller, and Marshall Barer—adapts the tale "The Princess on the Pea," especially the well-known version by Hans Christian **Andersen**. As with many twentieth-century fairy-tale **adaptation**s, this version is notable for the reflexivity of its characters and the inclusion of modern elements such as class tensions and premarital **sex**.

The plot of the musical is an expansion of the tale and is narrated by a minstrel. King Septimus is cursed with silence and his evil wife Aggravaine has declared that nobody may wed before her son, Dauntless the Drab. Meanwhile, Sir Harry, a knight with a pregnant girlfriend named Lady Larken, sets out to find the last eligible **princess** in the land to wed Dauntless. Sir Harry brings back Winnifred the Woebegone, an uncouth marshland princess. After some comic mishaps, Queen Aggravaine declares that Winnifred must be tested with a pea beneath a number of mattresses, as in the tale. Winnifred passes the test, the **king** is uncursed, the **queen** is punished, and Dauntless and Winnifred are engaged, as are Harry and Larken, though it is revealed later that Winnifred had help in her test from the king, the jester, and the minstrel.

Once upon a Mattress premiered on Broadway in 1959 with Carol Burnett as Winnifred and ran for 460 performances. It has been revived several times and adapted for **television** three times (in 1964, 1972, and 2005). It is also a popular high-school musical. *See also* Theater.

Further Readings: *Once upon a Mattress.* Directed by Kathleen Marshall. DVD. Buena Vista Home Entertainment/Disney, 2005; *Once upon a Mattress.* Original Broadway cast recording. 1959. Audio CD. Decca US, 1993.

B. Grantham Aldred

Opera

Opera and the folktale are in one sense diametrically opposed. Beginning in late sixteenth-century Italy, opera originated in an alliance of mythological subject matter, imagined classical modes of dramatic performance, and the milieu of the court. Yet opera is also an essentially fantastical form of **theater**, as much multimedia spectacle as philosophical forum. It is therefore not surprising that folktales and fairy tales have served frequently, if intermittently, as source material for operas. The fusion of high and low, the learned and the popular, is demonstrated most famously in Wolfgang Amadeus Mozart's *Die Zauberflöte* (*The Magic Flute*, 1791), with libretto by Emanuel Schikaneder. The work is a fusion of Masonic ritual and symbolism, Enlightenment philosophizing and folkloric high jinks, taken

Duke Bluebeard's Castle, as performed by the Scottish Opera.
[Robbie Jack/Corbis]

from a disparate range of sources that includes the fairy tale "Lulu, oder Die Zauberflöte" ("Lulu, or The Magic Flute") from Christoph Martin **Wieland**'s collection, *Dschinnistan* (1786–89).

Gioacchino Rossini's *La Cenerentola* (*Cinderella*, 1817), with libretto by Jacopo Ferretti adapted from Charles **Perrault**, is the most famous of the many operas based on **Cinderella** and one of the first identifiably fairy-tale operas. As this suggests, it is with the advent of Romanticism that the folktale and fairy tale came into their own as operatic subjects, beginning in particular with Carl Maria von Weber's hugely successful *Der Freischütz* (*The Freeshooter*, 1821), a self-styled "romantic opera" with libretto by Friedrich Kind. This tale of magic bullets and devilish pacts, set against a backdrop of the Bohemian Forest, is rich with folkloric resonance. *Der Freischütz* played a key role in the establishment of a self-consciously German operatic form, which reached its controversial apogee in the work of Richard Wagner, particularly in *Der Ring des Nibelungen* (*The Ring of the Nibelung*, 1852–54). Although based primarily on **myth** and **legend**, Wagner's mature work aspires to the archetypal and has thus been read as including a wide range of folktale **motif**s. It is perhaps indicative of the two strands that run through the history of opera—the mythical and the folkloric, the learned and the popular—that the death of Wagner was soon followed by the premiere of perhaps the most important, certainly the most successful, fairy-tale opera in the German tradition, Engelbert **Humperdinck**'s *Hänsel und Gretel* (1893) (see **Hansel and Gretel**). Humperdinck had worked for Wagner at Bayreuth, and *Hänsel und Gretel* represents an **adaptation** of distinctly Wagnerian compositional techniques to a more folk-oriented musical idiom. Humperdinck went on to write several other fairy-tale operas, including *Königskinder* (*The Royal Children*, 1897).

As indicated by the rise of German Romantic opera, composers of opera in the nineteenth and early twentieth centuries were motivated in part by **nationalism** in turning to indigenous folktale and fairy-tale material. In Russia, Mikhail **Glinka** worked toward the establishment of a national operatic style, most notably in his second opera, *Ruslan i Lyudmila* (*Ruslan and Lyudmila*, 1842), based on a Russian folktale as adapted in verse by Aleksandr **Pushkin**. In the wake of Glinka, and building on the alliance of a Russian musical mode with folk narrative, came Nikolai **Rimsky-Korsakov**'s *Snegurochka* (*The Snow Maiden*, 1882), based on a tale by Alexander Ostrovsky. While Igor Stravinsky's interest in the folktale was channeled predominantly into ballet, his early and most explicitly Russian work includes the first part of the opera *La rossignol* (*The Nightingale*), based on the tale by Hans Christian **Andersen**. Having abandoned the opera in 1908, he returned to it several years later, and the completed work had its full premiere in 1914. In what was Czechoslovakia, operas inspired by local legend and fairy tale include Antonín **Dvořák**'s *Čert a Káča* (*The Devil and Kate*, 1899) and *Rusalka* (1901), and Leoš Janáček's *Příhody lišky bystroušky* (*The Cunning Little Vixen*, 1924).

The early decades of the twentieth century witnessed several significant fairy-tale operas. The symbolist aesthetic gave rise to two singular adaptations of the **Bluebeard** narrative: Paul Dukas's *Ariane et Barbe-bleue* (*Ariadne and Blue Beard*, 1907), which sets Maurice **Maeterlinck**'s play of the same name; and, using a distinctly Hungarian vocal idiom, Béla **Bartók**'s *Kékszakállú herceg vára* (*Duke Bluebeard's Castle*, 1918), after the play by Béla **Balázs**. Giacomo Puccini's *Turandot* (1926) is based on Carlo **Gozzi**'s play of 1761, itself adapted in part from the *Arabian Nights*. Gozzi's fantastical theatrical works—his *Fiabe teatrali* (*Fairy Tales for the Theatre*, 1761–70)—take inspiration from Giambattista **Basile**'s *Lo cunto de li cunti* (*The Tale of Tales*, 1634–36) and have inspired several other operas, including Sergey Prokofiev's *Liubov' k trem apel'sinam* (*The Love for Three Oranges*, 1921) and Hans Werner Henze's *König Hirsch* (*The Stag King*, 1956; revised in 1963 as *Il re cervo*). Other notable works include *Die Frau ohne Schatten* (*The Woman without a Shadow*, 1919), the only fairy-tale opera by composer Richard Strauss and librettist Hugo von **Hofmannsthal**, with an original story modeled in part after *The Magic Flute*; and Alexander Zemlinsky's *Es war einmal* (*Once upon a Time*, 1900), a fairy-tale comedy.

Contemporary opera is a disparate field, with the form itself increasingly under threat from more populist modes of music theater and from cuts in state subsidies for what is an expensive medium. Significant work is still being written, however, and the folktale and fairy tale continue to attract composers and librettists. Along with Hans Werner Henze's *Pollicino* (1980), a "Märchen für Musik" ("fairy tale for music") based on an amalgamation of Charles Perrault, the Brothers **Grimm**, and Carlo **Collodi**'s *Pinocchio*, and Philip Glass's *La Belle et la Bête: An Opera for Ensemble and Film* (1994), an adaptation of Jean **Cocteau**'s film of 1946, the fairy tale has given rise to two strikingly innovative works: Swiss composer Heinz Holliger's *Schneewittchen* (*Snow White*, 1998), a disquieting setting of Robert Walser's enigmatic 1901 "dramolett" of the same name; and perhaps most startling, Helmut Lachenmann's *Das Mädchen mit den Schwefelhölzern* (*The Little Match Girl*, 2000). Lachenmann, a politically committed composer working at the far edges of the European modernist tradition, pairs the girl of Andersen's tale with texts by Leonardo da Vinci and Gudrun Ensslin, a member of the Baader-Meinhof Gang, the German terrorist group of the 1960s and 1970s. Unlikely as it may seem, the alliance of polemically avant-garde musical theater and the fairy tale suggests an interesting future for this particular genre of opera. *See also* Dance; Music; Tchaikovsky, Pyotr Il'ich.

Further Readings: Bendix, Regina. "Folk Narrative, Opera and the Expression of Cultural Identity." *Fabula* 31 (1990): 297–303; Benson, Stephen. "'Something's missing': Towards a Listening Space for Fairy-Tale Opera." *New Comparison* 31 (2001): 112–29; Taruskin, Richard. "From Fairy Tale to Opera in Four Moves (not so simple)." *Opera and the Enlightenment*. Edited by Thomas Bauman and Marita Petzoldt McClymonds. Cambridge: Cambridge University Press, 1995. 299–307.

Stephen Benson

Opie, Iona (1923–) and Opie, Peter (1918–1982)

Peter and Iona Opie are British collectors and scholars of children's **folklore** and anthologists of fairy tales and **children's literature**. In the decades after World War II, Iona and Peter Opie pioneered modern childlore studies by **collecting** modern orally transmitted rhymes, stories, and playground games among schoolchildren. The Opies' combination of primary **fieldwork** and literary research revealed children's culture to be a world rich in communication, by which "the people of the playground" appropriate and transcend the cultural structures in play. In *The Lore and Language of Schoolchildren* (1959) and *Children's Games in Street and Playground* (1969), previously uncharted territory of play cultures emerged, providing material for the study of children's folklore as an interdisciplinary venue.

Another important strand in the Opies' work is the effort to recover early or alternative traditions, such as nursery rhymes, **poetry**, and early fairy-tale versions. *The Oxford Dictionary of Nursery Rhymes* (1951) reflects the collectors' consciousness of competing variations and an awareness of the problems of turning oral literature into booklore. In *The Oxford Nursery Rhyme Book* (1955), historic rhymes were made accessible to modern children. *The Classic Fairy Tales* (1974), containing the earliest published English versions of the tales selected with notes on the history and analogues of stories, bears further witness to the Opies' textual criticism. *See also* Childhood and Children.

Further Reading: Avery, Gillian, and Briggs, Julia, eds. *Children and Their Books: A Celebration of the Work of Iona and Peter Opie*. Milton Keynes: The Open University Press, 1990.

Helene Høyrup

Oral Theory

Oral theory provides a framework for understanding how and within what conventions traditional stories, including folktales and fairy tales, were (and are) created and transmitted orally. It also provides a way of ascertaining the oral-traditional meaning of key narrative elements, even after they have been "frozen" in written form. The development of oral theory parallels and often converges with advancements in folktale theory, such as the work of Axel Olrik (1909) on epic laws and Vladimir **Propp** (1928) on functional and ordered slots in Russian fairy tales. The origins of oral theory, however, began with research on Homeric **epic**.

While questions about the nature of the Homeric texts had been asked since the classical period, in the modern period, "Analyst" scholars such as Friedrich Wolf (1795) and Karl Lachmann (1816) considered the Homeric poems to be the result of written, layered redaction of smaller and more primitive poems (in contrast with the so-called Unitarians, who championed single authorship). The quest for the "original" layers was seen as necessary, since any inherited unity was perceived as subsequent, mechanical, literary, and interpolated. Although inadequate, Analyst theory did ask researchers to consider the "Homeric Question"—how the Homeric epics came to be (their composition, authorship, and dates). It would be this same question, considered by Milman Parry in the late 1920s, that would itself inspire the quest leading to the first comprehensive oral theory.

Parry, influenced by the work of the philologist Antoine Meillet and the anthropologist Vasily V. Radlov, had recognized the need to study formulaic phraseology and oral **performance** in the field. So Parry, along with his assistant Albert B. Lord, conducted research in various parts of the former Yugoslavia, recording and analyzing living oral epics sung by the South Slavic *gulsari* (epic bards). They observed that these epics were created in performance by bards who composed their stories according to strict metrical rules, with traditional formulas (or formulaic systems), themes, and story patterns. Tradition was seen as controlling both the type of material and the way it was presented. In fact, Lord would later note that "oral poets who are not traditional do not exist" (Lord, 155). The living South Slavic performances were then used as a comparative analogue for the manuscript-bound poetry of Homer.

Parry and Lord's findings proved revolutionary for their day. They demonstrated that such epithets as "swift-footed Achilles" and "much-suffering Odysseus" were formulaic and had an "aura of meaning" that adhered from all past contexts. Further, they also concluded that larger themes (somewhat comparable to Walter Arend's "type scenes") and story patterns also followed established traditional pathways as a particular singer navigated his tale's telling. For the South Slavic *guslar*, the plot of his tale might be a traditional wedding song; for Homer, a traditional tale of a war or a returning hero. In either case, Parry and Lord realized that it was the singer's familiarity with the traditional formulas, themes, and story patterns—the known tradition—that provided both performer and audience with a fixed point of reference for the story being told. Consequently, in place of the analyst's disjointed, textual, cut-and-paste approach, Parry and Lord created a unified theory of oral poetic composition.

The basic premise established by Parry and Lord—that the study of living **oral tradition**s can help explicate the formation and meaning of other oral traditions, living or existing only in written form—was the impetus for subsequent research in many fields. Furthermore, their initial oral theory eventually led other researchers, such as John Miles Foley, to suggest that the difference between "oral-derived" literatures that exist only in and through inscribed media (such as the ***Gilgamesh Epic***, the book of Judges, or the *Odyssey*) and living oral performance tradition (such as the South Slavic) is only a matter of degree. As a result of the **fieldwork** of Parry, Lord, and many subsequent researchers, investigation of living oral traditions and oral-derived texts began vigorously and continues with an established methodology in more than 100 different language areas, including Old English, Old French, medieval German, Russian, Japanese, Chinese, Irish, and Native American, to name just a few.

The initial purpose of studying living oral tradition, that of providing comparisons for oral-derived literature, remains a priority for scholars, although research has modified and expanded the initial findings, particularly regarding the actual history, creation, identification, and immanent meaning of formulas, themes, and story patterns. It is now generally recognized that the foregoing structural elements reach out (metonymically) to the entire tradition and access a larger world of shared meaning (traditional referentiality) for both storyteller and audience. Unlike the modern **novel,** which has meaning conferred through the agency of a single author, in oral-derived "texts" (as in actual oral performance), the traditional referents themselves are stable elements that provide profound inherent meaning for the narrative at all levels.

Since the initial discoveries of Parry and Lord, progress has also been made on the related questions of traditional characterization and type scenes. Further, intensive research on additional instances of living oral traditions has continued to influence the evolution of oral theory and has initiated more careful treatment of important subjects, such as the inevitable differences among oral traditions and genre types as well as the significance of the performance arena and features of reception. Interdisciplinary perspectives have been key.

Oral theory is similar to comparatively oriented folktale research in that it has provided important tools for the study of indigenous, inherited stories via other disciplines within the humanities and social sciences. A fortunate corollary to the rise of oral theory has been an increased interest in the study and preservation of the living oral traditions themselves. *See also* Memory.

Further Readings: Center for Studies in Oral Tradition. http://www.oraltradition.org; Foley, John M. *Immanent Art: From Structure to Meaning in Traditional Oral Epic*. Bloomington: Indiana University Press, 1991; Lord, Albert B. *The Singer of Tales*. 2nd edition. Edited by Stephen Mitchell and Gregory Nagy. Cambridge, MA: Harvard University Press, 2000; Zumwalt, Rosemary Lévy. "A Historical

Glossary of Critical Approaches." *Teaching Oral Traditions*. Edited by John Miles Foley. New York: Modern Language Association, 1998. 75–94.

Andrew E. Porter

Oral Tradition

A Brief Definition

Whether we define the utterances of an oral tradition broadly, as any customary oral expression, or more specifically, as verbal arts using a "poetic" form of spoken language unlike everyday speech, it is generally recognized that oral traditions may encompass a wealth of verbal genres of enduring value to their communities. The scope of oral-traditional expressions extends from oral histories and **folktale**s to **epic** poetry; from stylized, lengthy greeting ceremonies to religious invocations, mourning songs, medical recipes, and many other genres. To understand as accurately as possible each oral-traditional expression, we—ideally—learn the language in which it is spoken and the special idioms of that culture's oral tradition, and we listen to what the tradition-bearers have to say about it.

The term "oral tradition" underscores two important aspects of these specialized expressions: their orality and their connection to a tradition. The "oral" half of the label "oral tradition" points to the use of vocal cords (versus pen and paper, keyboard and monitor, etc.) and also the demands upon the narrator or "tradition-bearer" that accompany the act of composing "in real time," without the option to erase, shuffle paragraphs, or cut and paste. An oral **performance** places demands upon an audience, which participates by listening and, often, by responding. Orality shapes the composition and dissemination of the many forms of performed verbal expressions and art—both narrative and non-narrative.

The "tradition" half of the term "oral tradition" balances out the emphasis, implied by the word "oral," upon the present moment of the utterance, which is shaped by the oral-aural dynamic between the "tradition-bearer" and the other participants, by the sound of a voice, by attentive listening, and by people being present to each other. "Tradition" calls to mind, as far as **memory** reaches, all of the previous performances of a particular story or song. It also calls to mind the interrelationships between many different genres of oral expression, which, within a particular community, may share a set of related themes, ideals, characters, **proverb**s, and story patterns, including those appearing in folktales and fairy tales. "Tradition" may also be carried in the register of language that tradition-bearers draw upon to recollect and reinvent verbal expressions in performance. Often this register can easily be differentiated from everyday speech. Like "once upon a time," it sets the stage for a specialized form of communication. The mere intonation of "once upon a time" may invoke the generic expectations intrinsic to fairy tales and the narrative content of those stories known to a community where these tales form a vital part of its culture.

Those who study oral traditions may work with ancient and medieval manuscripts, with the records of anthropologists, folklorists, and linguists, or with living performers and their communities.

Oral Traditions and Folklore

Studies in the twin fields of **folklore** and oral tradition inevitably converge. The oral performance of a poet, shaman, matriarch, healer, or any other sort of tradition-bearer helps to create and re-create the knowledge of a community (its "folklore"). A sophisticated verbal technology, oral traditions encode historical **legend**s, place names, detailed medical, botanical, and agricultural information, moral and ethical teachings, games, mourning songs, proverbs, **myth**s, epics, praise songs, and wisdom sayings. The foregoing—and far from comprehensive—list reveals that oral traditions encode highly diverse types of information. It should also be stressed, however, that oral traditions often privilege the performative power of language: sometimes saying is doing. A medical charm incanted by a South Slavic *bajalica* ("conjurer") may heal the suffering patient, just as the recitation of a genealogy placates ancestors, or Baul devotional songs of mystic minstrels enact the sacred. Thus, the *process* of an oral-traditional performance may bear as heavily upon its significance as the *product*—and we would be mistaken to equate an oral tradition with knowledge that may be distilled into discrete, paraphrasable (written) concepts. Oral-traditional lore is both particle and wave, never solely one or the other.

Although oral-traditional lore may be frozen in writing or recorded by other media, it is usually executed in real-time enactments. Just as *saying* cannot always be parted from *doing*, the lexical content (what is said) during such performances may not be separated from its physicality (how it is said). Such physicality includes the emergent and ephemeral medium of the tradition-bearer's voice (for instance, vocal tone, rhythm, and silence punctuating sound) and, depending on the tradition, his or her gestures, stance, facial expressions, and use of props. Furthermore, oral traditions depend largely upon the face-to-face relationships shared by performer and audience. An audience's attentive comprehension and feedback vitally contribute to the oral-traditional performance; in turn, a skilled verbal artist adapts his or her performance to the context and the responses of those present. The people's lore—neither solely process nor product—thus emerges within the community and potentially transforms or maintains it.

Diversity and Fluidity in Oral Traditions

The term "oral tradition" does not indicate a homogenous entity—a static and monolithic collection of stories and sayings to which speakers subserviently give voice. Rather, from one culture's traditional practices to the next, we find that oral traditions are, in fact, highly diverse in terms of function, genre, style, and transmission. A single oral tradition may include a wide variety of important genres, whose tradition-specific parameters will shift from culture to culture and from language to language.

Even the recounting of a single narrative or epic song within one language group's tradition reveals that there is enormous room for creative expression as well as continual retailoring to fit the demands of the performance context. For example, the Tibetan epic *Gesar* (also known as *Geser*, *Gesar of Ling*, and *King Gesar*) may be sung by a traveling bard for a household for the twofold purpose of entertainment and moral instruction or, at the other end of the spectrum, by a solitary Buddhist as he traverses a mountainside chanting *Gesar* "hymns" that are believed to manifest purificatory and protective powers. In the former case, an audience in the typical sense is present, while in the latter, a virtual audience composed of "all sentient beings" witnesses and receives the benefits of *Gesar* prayers. The *Gesar* epic has shown remarkable adaptability in response to both oral and written media, traveling fluidly between the two. Over the past two centuries, literary poems and written rituals (*pujas*) have emerged that reframe *Gesar* for aristocratic and monastic audiences, resulting in more diverse renderings of this oral epic.

Oral Traditions and the Literary Arts

The study of oral traditions has shed light on important features that differentiate them from literary works. Expectations associated with the literary arts do not adequately take into consideration how oral traditions work and may even obscure their aesthetic vitality. The following list, while neither complete nor universally applicable to all oral traditions, provides an overview of key contrasts between oral and literary compositions.

1. Oral traditions do not supply the crude, "primitive" prototype of a written literature; they are a sophisticated form of communication in their own right.

2. In place of the literary tradition's "original" poem produced by a single author, we find many versions of a well-known narrative, song, or other instances of oral expression that has no **urform**. Each evanescent version may differ according to the talent of a performer and the context of the performance. Even a single storyteller may re-create many versions of "the same" fairy tale or folktale.

3. From a literary perspective, the reuse of a common phrase runs the risk of sounding flat and clichéd. Conversely, recurring traditional "formulas" (phrases and verses that sometimes vary little from telling to telling) resonate idiomatically with far greater meaning than would, say, the same number of words utilized in everyday, nontraditional conversation. The same holds true for images, **motif**s, type-scenes, and story patterns. Consider, for example, such tale types as the **Cinderella** story or the narrative etiologies that recur in folktales. Rather than being trite, the ongoing reframing of a tale draws its power from a simultaneous responsiveness to the newness of the immediate situation and the traditional weight of a narrative that resonates with prior instances of its telling and reception.

4. While we think of words as units delimited by white space upon the page, a traditional poet or storyteller often conceives of whole units of acoustically encoded information as "words," whether this means a line of verse, a scene, or an entire story. Each "word," long or short, forms a part of the performer's repertoire. Thus, to understand oral expressions properly, we need to learn the working vocabulary, the "words," of the tradition.

5. A "great divide" was once imagined to exist between oral-folkloric and written-literary works, but the actual practices of tradition-bearers have debunked this myth. Artists (among others) negotiate ongoing alliances between the literary and the oral in their creation of verbal expressions. Hybrid compositions in written form—the Middle English *Pearl* and *Sir Gawain and the Green Knight*, for instance—employ an oral poetics. Literate tradition-bearers and their audiences could (and can) use resources provided by both the oral-traditional and literary paradigms, much the same way that communities of bi- and trilingual speakers may switch languages multiple times within a single conversation.

6. The following "media morphology" (Foley, 39–53) addresses the adaptability of oral traditions with respect to writing: "voices from the past" (for example, Homeric epics, the medieval Japanese *Tale of the Heike*, and the Old French *chansons de geste*), "voiced texts" (slam poetry), "written oral poems" (*Pjevannija*, Finnish **Kalevala**, and the works of Lydia Cabrera), and "oral performance" (Tenore Song, Mongolian Long Song [*Urtiin Duu*], Palestinian Hikaye, and Tibetan *Gesar*). "Oral performance" contains by far the most diverse species of oral traditions, and the features of oral traditions in the foregoing section derive mainly from the study of oral performances. Due to their various relationships with the technology of writing, performances and works in the other categories—"voices from the past" and "written oral poems"—may be mistakenly treated as literary. Recognition that these pieces rely upon oral-traditional modes of composition helps audiences reframe their expectations, avoid depending too heavily on the wrong set of interpretive tools (that is, the literary), and learn a new set (the oral).

The Study of Oral Traditions

From the eighteenth century, when oral tales first became the object of enduring scholarly interest, to the present, scholars have attempted to describe the products (and, to some extent, the process) of oral-traditional expression (primarily **storytelling**, folktales, and oral histories) in light of a growing appreciation for their aesthetic and cultural value. Along the way, as certain ethnocentric prejudices and literary expectations have been recognized, scholarship in this field has gradually paid more attention to what communities and tradition-bearers have to say about what they say. There has been a general transition from the appropriation of folktales, epics, and songs for literary collections or ideological agendas toward the study (and perpetuation) of living traditions within their own contexts and according to their own rules. The following survey of approaches to the study of oral traditions is informed by Rosemary Lévy Zumwalt's in-depth article on the subject, "A Historical Glossary of Critical Approaches."

During the eighteenth and nineteenth centuries, solar mythology (Friedrich Max **Müller**), cultural evolutionary studies (Edward B. Tylor, Andrew **Lang**), and, the most far-reaching of these, Romantic **nationalism** (Jacob and Wilhelm **Grimm**, Johann Gottfried Herder) treated oral tales as newfound objects of serious study. The nineteenth century witnessed a burgeoning interest in oral traditions for the purpose of defining national identity—an interest that resulted in **fieldwork** within national boundaries and the transplanting of oral expressions from indigenous habitats to the more prestigious realm of literature. At their worst, solar mythology, cultural evolutionary studies, and Romantic nationalism problematically stripped agency from the **folk**, failed to assess the dynamic relationship between performer and audience, and assumed an urtext—an original text—that could be rediscovered through redaction and **editing**.

Two fruits of the Romantic-nationalist movement in Europe are the Grimm brothers' German ***Kinder- und Hausmärchen*** (*Children's and Household Tales*, 1812–15) and Elias Lönnrot's Finnish epic, *Kalevala* (1835, 1849). The Grimms' early editions of their folktales and fairy tales treated oral storytelling as *Naturpoesie* ("natural poetry") that ought to be collected and published in a relatively unmodified form. However, due to the poor reception of these early editions and their emerging expectations for the **märchen**, the Grimms gradually replaced many of the tales with either those that were told by more talented storytellers or their own rewritten versions that blended texts or added content and structure of a more literary style. The result is that the final 1857 edition shines with the polish of literary stories recounted for an audience with literary expectations. The Grimms' careful notes on their collections and their attempts at classification inspired later motif and tale-type indices. Like the Grimm brothers, Elias Lönnrot performed fieldwork to gather oral **Finnish tales** (these recounted in verse), which he then prepared according to the rubric of literary standards. However, Lönnrot was fluent in the traditional oral register of Karelia, and, using the poems he had collected, he both compiled *and* composed the *Kalevala*, which is now considered the Finnish national epic. Lönnrot became the first secretary of the Finnish Literature Society, which to this day promotes the study of Finnish and international folktales and publishes such indices as those set in motion by the Grimm brothers' annotations.

The excesses of Romantic nationalism were countered by twentieth-century "mechanical" approaches: the Finnish **historic-geographic method** (Antti **Aarne** and Stith **Thompson**), where extensive catalogs of geographically dispersed folklore themes served to deflate

Eurocentrism, and the age-area hypothesis approach (Franz Boas), which sought to map the migrations of cultures and their traditions, paying little heed to national boundaries. Cultural approaches—culture reflector (Boas), culture and personality (Ruth Benedict, Edward Sapir), and functionalism (William Bascom)—analyzed the relationship between the content of oral-traditional performances and the needs of communities, thereby attempting to bridge the gap that the previous approaches introduced between folk and folkways. The mechanical and cultural approaches could, however, be criticized for not heeding the artistry of oral traditions.

The issue of aesthetics was initially addressed by approaches that explored the patterning of text: epic laws (Axel Olrik), myth-ritual approach (Lord Raglan), morphological approach (Vladimir **Propp**), and oral-formulaic theory (Albert Lord and Milman Parry). For the aesthetic interpretation of oral expressions, the first three of these approaches have proven to be rather blunt instruments: "epic laws," mythic features, and morphological functions describe commonalities among epics and folktales irrespective of their tradition-specific differences. Their generalizations, largely imposed from the outside, often risk being reductive. However, the work of Milman Parry and his assistant Albert Lord transformed the study of oral traditions by generating the first **oral theory**—*oral-formulaic theory*—that truly took into account the role of oral performance in the process of composition.

Parry, whose dissertation demonstrated that a large percentage of the *Iliad* and the *Odyssey* (nearly 27,000 lines of ancient Greek hexameter combined) relied upon oral-formulaic phrases, decided to record and interview living epic poets in the former Yugoslavia who maintained a tradition similar to that of the ancient Greeks. With Lord as his assistant, Parry sought to understand the role of memory in the recitation of epic-length poems. Without Parry and Lord's discoveries, we would still have very little insight into the complexities of surviving records of ancient epic poetry and the practices of oral poets and other tradition-bearers to this day. They found that, rather than a feat of superhuman memory, a narrative oral poem is composed *in situ* using a repertoire of templates: stories, passages, and lines (also called story patterns, themes, and formulas). To meet the demands of improvisation, a bard re-creates entire stories by expanding or compressing these templates of various duration—as long as they remain recognizable to their audience (Foley's concept of "variation within limits" in *The Traditional Oral Epic*). Furthermore, an oral poet draws upon a virtual cultural repository ("the tradition") of shared stories, characters, and idioms familiar to his or her audience. These findings switched attention from the generic patterns common to stories in many languages (patterns perceived by a scholar in isolation from the actual communities that use such tales) to specific traditions, a community's commentary on the tradition (if possible), and the poet's process of composition.

Alongside oral-formulaic theory, other approaches have been brought to bear upon the study of oral traditions: **structuralism** (Claude Lévi-Strauss), the symbolic-interpretive (Richard Geertz), psychoanalysis (Alan **Dundes**), **feminism** (Susan Tower Hollis, Susan Slymovics), **authenticity** (Regina Bendix), ethnopoetics (Dennis Tedlock, Dell Hymes), performance theory (Richard Bauman), and immanent art (John Miles Foley) (for more information, see Zumwalt). Ethnopoetics, performance theory, and immanent art examine the nexus of performance, tradition, and the specialized, idiomatic registers of language that form oral traditions. Proponents of ethnopoetics ask how oral performances may be recorded in writing and read (or re-performed) on their own terms. Dell Hymes has searched for those structural units within a poem that are constitutive of its meaning, working to rediscover the effaced poetic structures of **Native American tales** recorded in writing by anthropologists and linguists who paid little attention to their artistic value. In contrast, Dennis Tedlock seeks to graphically represent paralinguistic performative traits—such as volume, rising and falling tones, pauses, and so on—by modifying typefaces and spacing. In performance theory, Richard Bauman and others have argued that performance plays an integral role in the meaning of an oral "text." Bauman's "keys to performance" (special codes, figurative language, parallelism, appeals to tradition, special formulae, disclaimers of performance, and others) all call attention to performance per se. Immanent art, developed by John Miles Foley, builds upon Parry and Lord's oral-formulaic theory by exploring examples of the agency and creativity of oral-traditional bards. Foley demonstrates how a verbal artist may modulate and even recombine traditional "words"—individual words, phrases, lines, half-lines, themes, type-scenes, and story patterns—for special effect. His research on ancient Greek, South Slavic, and Anglo-Saxon oral traditions also incorporates the findings of performance theory and ethnopoetics to investigate performance, traditional idioms, and translation practices.

At present, scholars and policy makers are concerned about safeguarding traditional cultures threatened by globalization, cataloging "intangible heritages" worldwide, and giving communities the opportunity to define their own traditions and choose the best means to safeguard them. For example, in 2001, a transnational association was founded for the preservation of oral epics: Mezhdunarodnaya Assotsiatsia "Eposy Narodov Mira" (MAEN)/International Association "Epics of the World's Peoples" (IAEWP). The majority of participants hail from central Asia (Turkey, Iran, Mongolia, Kyrgyzstan, and Kazakhstan, but also Germany and Armenia), where tradition-bearers continue to recompose epics in performance. This association addresses those factors that threaten to undermine the ongoing existence of epic traditions. On a global scale, UNESCO's 2003 Convention for the Safeguarding of the Intangible Cultural Heritage (ICH) seeks to support and bring recognition to such cultural heritages as oral tradition, ritual and social practices, traditional knowledge, performing arts, and traditional craftsmanship—domains that inevitably overlap. The UNESCO 2003 Convention asks member nations to amass inventories of their communities' ICHs, while promoting community-based (versus scholarly) definitions of ICH.

Future directions for the study of oral traditions include preserving the conditions that allow for the continued existence of oral traditions; defining and translating the idiomatic vocabulary ("words" such as phrases, poetic lines and line segments, type-scenes, story patterns, and so on) of a tradition for a reader or listener outside that tradition; the relationship between performance **context** and genre, and the issue of "genrification" in folklore studies; hybrid oral and literary works of verbal art; contributions from cognitive science concerning memory and performance; cultural studies approaches that question the relationship between tradition and political authority; and many more. Volume 18 of the journal *Oral Tradition* offers a collection of short articles written by more than eighty scholars addressing the state of the field with respect to individual traditions worldwide. ***See also*** Collecting, Collectors; Ethnographic Approaches; Literary Fairy Tale.

Further Readings: Amodio, Mark C. *Writing the Oral Tradition: Oral Poetics and Literate Culture in Medieval England.* Notre Dame, IN: University of Notre Dame Press, 2004; Fine, Elizabeth C. *The Folklore Text: From Performance to Print.* 1984. Bloomington: Indiana University Press, 1994; Foley, John Miles. *How to Read an Oral Poem.* Urbana: University of Illinois Press, 2002. eCompanion at http://www.oraltradition.org/hrop; ———. *Traditional Oral Epic: The Odyssey,* Beowulf, *and the*

Serbo-Croatian Return Song. Berkeley: University of California Press, 1990; Folklore Fellows, Finnish Academy of Science and Letters, University of Helsinki. http://www.folklorefellows.fi; Honko, Lauri. *Textualising the Siri Epic*. Helsinki: Suomalainen Tiedeakatemia, 1998; Lord, Albert Bates. *The Singer of Tales*. Revised edition. Cambridge, MA: Harvard University Press, 2000; *Oral Tradition: An Interdisciplinary Academic Journal*. http://www.oraltradition.org for free electronic editions of the journal and eCompanions (audio, video, photographs, and text) accompanying journal articles; UNESCO Culture Sector. Intangible Heritage. http://www.unesco.org/culture/; Zumwalt, Rosemary Lévy. "A Historical Glossary of Critical Approaches." *Teaching Oral Traditions*. Edited by John Miles Foley. New York: Modern Language Association, 1998. 75–94.

Heather Maring

Ovid (43 BCE–17 CE)

Ovid (Publius Ovidius Naso) is one of the best-known and widely read poets of Roman classical literature. His works, especially the *Metamorphoses* and *Heroides*, are a storehouse of retellings of classical Greco-Roman **myth**s and **legend**s and remain a major source for modern retellings. Ovid was regarded as preeminent among his contemporary poets for twenty years but was, for obscure reasons, suddenly banished from Rome by the Emperor Augustus. He lived the last ten years of his life among a semibarbaric people in Tomis on the Black Sea.

The *Heroides* is a collection of twenty-one epistles in elegiac verse. It begins with fifteen letters addressed by heroines of legend or mythology to their absent or unfaithful lovers and concludes with three pairs of letters between a man and a woman. Although some scholars argue that only the first fourteen epistles were written by Ovid, the framing strategy of giving a voice to women elsewhere peripheral to well-known stories of male heroes enabled an important slant on classical mythology. The collection has often been read as a literary game as, through his engagement with great precursors such as Homer (for Penelope) and Virgil (for Dido), Ovid draws readers into intertextual readings against the speakers' points of view. More recently, Efrossini Spentzou has argued that the concentration on the emotional point of a story preceding its outcome bestows greater interpretive weight on the speaker's hopes and desires.

Both as a work of art and as a repository of mythology, the *Heroides* has been overshadowed by the *Metamorphoses*, Ovid's version of a Roman **epic**. The *Metamorphoses* remained an anomaly within the epic genre, however, since it lacks the principle of a central, unifying hero. Instead, Ovid unifies the 250 myths retold in fifteen books by exploring the theme of change as a principle underlying all things, by framing this within a chronology that begins with a story of creation and ends with the reign of Augustus, and by a complex process of transition between stories, such as embedding stories within other, thematically linked stories.

Later generations have nevertheless tended to treat the work as a compendium of stories, and many of the myths best known to the modern world are derived from the *Metamorphoses*: for example, Pyramus and Thisbe, Echo and Narcissus, Pygmalion, and the Fall of Icarus. Although Ovid did not invent these stories but retold them from earlier literary, educational, and mythographic sources, his combination of creativity and comprehensiveness has had an inestimable influence on Western **art** and literature, from medieval allegorizers (who argued that the myths he retold anticipated truths of Christian theology) to a modern focus on sociopolitical issues and constructions of **gender** in **transformation** myths involving the loss of human form or human agency. Stories from the *Metamorphoses* retold by Geoffrey **Chaucer**, the Ovidian movement of the English Renaissance, and the innumerable versions of the Pygmalion story in the nineteenth and twentieth centuries offer examples of the wealth of story that Ovid's writing has transmitted to the Western world. *See also* Classical Antiquity; Middle Ages.

Further Readings: Galinsky, G. Karl. *Ovid's Metamorphoses: An Introduction to the Basic Aspects.* Berkeley: University of California Press, 1975; Spentzou, Efrossini. *Readers and Writers in Ovid's "Heroides": Transgressions of Genre and Gender.* Oxford: Oxford University Press, 2003.

John Stephens

P

Pacific Island Tales

Covering one-third of the earth's surface, the Pacific Ocean is the largest geographical feature on the planet. Scattered across this wide expanse of water are hundreds of islands that are home to a large and diverse range of people and cultures. Although different and unique, the many island nations that make up the region are connected not only by *Moana Nui a Kiwa*, the Pacific Ocean, but also by the rich storehouse of stories that have grown out of the very human need to explain how the world came into existence, why nature behaves the way it does, and the role humans play in the grand scheme of things. For most oral cultures, the distinctions between history, **myth**, **legend**, and **folktale** blur, and the imposition of these labels weakens the validity and authenticity of the long histories people have transmitted orally for hundreds of generations. Moreover, conventional approaches to folktale, based typically on Anglo-European ideas about narrative traditions, do not always apply to Pacific Island stories. Therefore, this entry is written from within an indigenous perspective and presents stories of the Pacific with the understanding that they are as much history as folktale. What follows is a representative selection of the infinite number of stories from the vast Pacific.

Genesis

Many Pacific Island stories are **etiologic tale**s. They tell of how the islands came into being and how they were populated with humans, animals, fish, birds, insects, plants, rocks, lakes, rivers, other geographical features, and the elements. To the people of the Pacific, there is no separation between nature and humans, between the past and the present, the living and the dead, and the known and the unknown. Everything forms a continuum. Pacific people also believe that life is circular, rather than linear, with no beginning and no end. Everything is interconnected. These connections render all relationships sacred because all are bound together by the same life force. The function of many Pacific Island stories and much **folklore** is to explain how and why these relationships came into being and why they must be nurtured, honored, and retained.

Whakapapa, genealogy, is the sacred bond connecting human beings with ancestors and the gods, and Pacific Islanders' most important and sacred **incantation**s and rituals reiterate this connection. Those individuals able to recite their tribe's genealogy back to the origins of the gods and human beings, including the names of all those who have performed great and noteworthy deeds, are held in high esteem; the knowledge of a tribe's genealogy is sacrosanct and must be recited without error. The people of the Pacific face the past, the known, as they proceed into the future, which is unknown, allowing them to draw on the wisdom, strength, and support of their ancestors. The oral transmission of history has enabled the people of the Pacific to retain their tales and heroes in living form, with each new generation learning their stories and, perhaps more importantly, their responsibility to a collective and illustrious past.

The pantheon of Pacific gods forms a family, with Ranginui (Aotearoa/New Zealand), Wakea (Hawai'i), and Tagaloa'alagi (Samoa) the sky father, and Papatuanuku (Aotearoa) and Papa (Hawai'i) the earth mother. Since time began, the parents were locked in an embrace that left little room for their children, who were forced to exist between them without light or space. One

Maui' Hauls Up the Land, illustration by Richard Wallwork in *Myths and Legends of the Polynesians* by Johannes C. Andersen (New York: Farrar & Rinehart, 1928), facing p. 202.

of the first sins in the world, according to mythology, was the separation of the sky father and the earth mother. This shocking act of severance was led by Tane, god of the forest, and sometimes by Tangaroa, god of the sea. In some Pacific cultures, Tane is also the progenitor of human beings, while in others, it is Maui. The separation of **mother** and **father** was strongly opposed by many of Tane's **brothers**; Tawhiri Matea, god of winds and storms for example, was one such dissenter, and he chose to remain with the sky father after separation. The many children of Ranginui and Papatuanuku were divided in the separation of their parents; this is seen as the cause of much of the chaos and discontent in the world today. **Family** disagreements and sibling rivalries are common themes in the folklore of the Pacific region, where respect for parents and all elders is paramount.

Maui—Demigod

One of the preeminent characters in Pacific Island folklore and one common to almost all of Polynesia is Maui; in parts of Melanesia, an equivalent figure is known as Qat. Maui is a demigod born to a solo human mother who throws him into the sea, believing him to be stillborn. He thus becomes a child of Tangaroa, god of the sea, establishing a strong and intimate link between humans and the ocean. Maui is eventually rescued and raised to adulthood by an uncle.

Maui's first quest is to find his family, especially his father. Once he has found his mother and brothers, he tricks her into leading him to his father who resides in the underworld. His penchant for trickery is one of Maui's more endearing qualities, rendering his more audacious acts less offensive. Although attributed with having many godlike abilities, such as changing form, accomplishing dangerous feats, achieving impossible goals, and making fabulous discoveries which benefit all of humanity, it is Maui's skill as a fisherman that identifies him as the most important founding figure in the Pacific. With the help of the magic jawbone of his ancestress, he fishes up land from the ocean, providing a place for humans to live. Maui is also responsible for slowing down the sun as it travels across the sky, allowing more daylight hours for humans to fish, grow crops, erect buildings, build canoes, sing and dance, debate politics, and enjoy constructive and creative lives. It could be said that Maui is the founder of daylight saving time. Maui is also responsible for tricking one of his ancestors into giving up the secret of fire, which can now be found in certain trees.

Like many heroes in other parts of the world, Maui is the youngest child, the *potiki*, who is abandoned by his mother and who must make his own way in the world. As a **trickster**, he also breaks many of the established social contracts, showing little respect for the gods, ancestors, elders, nature, or rigid social structures. However, Maui fails in his most ambitious endeavor when he attempts to conquer **death** by entering the **birth** canal and emerging out of the mouth of Hine Nui te Po, the great lady of the underworld. His failure affirms that, despite his status and achievements as a demigod, he is nonetheless mortal.

Sina—Demigoddess

One of the few female heroes common to many Pacific Islands is Sina (Samoa and Rotuma), Hina (Hawai'i and Tonga), Ine (Aotearoa/New Zealand), and Ina (Cook Islands). Sina is sometimes sister, sometimes mother, sometimes wife to Maui. Among her many deeds, she is cited as being responsible for bringing the coconut palm to the islands. The coconut tree is probably the most important gift from the gods to the people of the Pacific, for this remarkable plant provides drink, **food**, containers for water, material for mats and clothing, shade, firewood, and timber for building houses and canoes. Humans would not have been able to survive on the isolated islands they discovered on their journey across the Pacific had it not been for this incredibly useful plant.

The Samoan version of the origin of the coconut palm tells of Sina, who acquires a pet eel that soon outgrows its container. The eel grows so big that it becomes a threat to its owner; it is both benign and malevolent. The eel is sometimes depicted as being in love with Sina, but, aware of the futility of such feelings, it asks her to cut off its head and bury it. From the head grows the coconut tree, explaining why the coconut, with its three holes, resembles the face of an eel. Stories about Sina appear in various forms in Aotearoa, Samoa, Tonga, Mangaia, New Guinea, Pukapuka, Tuomotu, Atiu, Tahiti, Hawai'i, and Rotuma. In the Cook Islands, one story, of Sina and a shark, is depicted on official banknotes.

Families—Of Gods and Humans

The close connections among gods, humans, and nature take various forms in different parts of the Pacific, but all illustrate the intimate and personal nature of these relationships. The Hawaiians consider the kalo, or taro (one of the most important food plants in the Pacific) to be a god, the older brother of the firstborn human being. In Samoa, Vanuatu, and

Fiji, the kava plant (from which a mild sedative is made) grows out of the body of a brother, and sometimes a sister. Its distinctive leaf, shaped like a human hand, is said to reach up out of the earth to the living sibling. The communal partaking of kava is an ancient, sacred, and highly ritualized custom in many societies in the Pacific.

Although many Pacific cultures share common gods, their power and importance vary according to where they reside. For example, in Aotearoa/New Zealand, which has a large land mass, Tane (Kane in Hawai'i), god of the forest, grew in importance over Tangaroa, god of the sea. In Samoa, Tonga, Tahiti, and other Pacific nations where so much of life depends on the sea and its gifts, Tagaloa'alagi (Tangaroa) rules supreme over all other gods. As so many Pacific Island tales are born of the sea, are about the sea, and include sea creatures, islanders' connections with it are ancient and profound. The ocean is also the pathway by which island connects with island; islanders' long and intimate relationship with it is why they are among the greatest navigators and sailors in the world.

Humans—One with Nature

There are tales of close relationships between humans and sea creatures throughout the Pacific region. At times they are pets, sometimes lovers, and often guardians or guides. There are stories of whales, octopi, turtles, dolphins, stingrays, eels, dugongs (large marine mammals), and sharks, all capable of giving assistance or bringing harm to humans. For example, in Fiji, on the island of Kadavu, there is a shark god named Dakawanga who guards the entrance to the island. There was once a terrible struggle between a giant octopus and the shark, which, upon realizing that it would be strangled in the octopus's tentacles, promised not to harm the people of Kadavu if allowed to go free. The octopus agreed, and to this day, the people of Kadavu have no fear of sharks, who they believe will remain true to this promise.

All Pacific cultures include tales in which humans, plants, birds, and sea creatures coexist and interrelate, reinforcing the close and respectful relationships between nature and humans. In one story, a pet whale is lent to a friend to convey him across the ocean. At the end of the journey, the man kills and eats the whale. The whale's owner learns of this and sends **women**, rather than **men**, to find the culprit. The women are able to identify him by his missing front teeth. With the help of magic, the culprit is brought back to the owner for execution. In Aotearoa, it is a dog rather than a whale that is killed, with the culprit being identified by the dog's flesh caught in his teeth. He too is put to death for his crime. A similar story tells of a man who wishes to travel to a distant island. He begs the owner of some pet turtles to allow him to use them to help make his journey. As in the previous stories, on arrival, the man kills and eats the turtles. The heartbroken owner kills the culprit. The execution of those who have violated a trust, between individuals and between humans and animals, is considered just and correct.

Respect for the Gods

In Hawai'i, Pele, the goddess of volcanoes, has the power to create and destroy land. Pele is both feared and respected, but she is also much loved, for she is continually creating new land. Folklore insists that those who take pieces of Pele's lava without paying due respect and making appropriate offerings will have bad luck. There are many instances of tourists who have returned home with pieces of lava only to suffer great misfortune until the lava is returned to Pele, its rightful owner.

Much Pacific folklore includes warnings to people before they embark on difficult or dangerous enterprises. Before setting off on a quest or a journey, for example, travelers are given specific instructions with warnings that, if not carried out or obeyed, they will be killed or harmed. The travelers almost always disobey and are carried off to the underworld, are killed, or are otherwise used in some terrible way. Those who heed the warnings and obey the instructions are rewarded with a handsome husband or a beautiful wife and many children (see **Punishment and Reward**). Humans are also able to call on the gods for help to defeat enemies or bring down those who have done them wrong, and often the aid comes in the form of a bird, a fish, a reptile, or even insects.

Acts of cruelty, betrayal, and disrespect are cause for retribution and sometimes have unusual consequences. One tale from the islands of Tonga tells how the god Tangaloa lives with a mortal woman for a time, but soon returns to his family in the heavens. Ahoei, Tangaloa's son, is born; when he grows to manhood, he goes in search of his father in the upper world, where he is met by his half brothers. Deeply jealous of the bond between Ahoei and their father, the brothers kill him, cut off his head, and consume his body. When Tangaloa discovers what they have done, he forces them to vomit up their brother, who is then brought back to life. Tangaloa then decrees that Ahoei will be an earthly **king**, ruling over his brothers and all of Tonga forever, thus establishing the royal family that rules Tonga to this day.

Tall Tales

Tales from at least two Pacific cultures tell of a community of women who live without men. They take their pleasure from trees or from plantains but somehow give birth to human children. When it is time for the children to be born, two old men come to cut the child out of the mother, who then dies. This practice ends when a man, a stranger, comes into the community and lives with the leader of the women. He tells her that there is no need for the women to die when they give birth and teaches her how women achieve this in other places. Stories such as these were clearly invented by men but nonetheless have been incorporated into the folktales of certain Pacific communities.

Modern Folktale

In the 1930s, on the island of Tanna, Vanuatu, a modern folk hero emerged. John Frum witnessed the arrival of hundreds of planes laden with material goods being delivered to American troops; he promised the people of Tanna that one day those same goods would be theirs. This has become a religion adopted by many people on the island. John Frum and his beliefs are now firmly embedded in local folklore, with hundreds still waiting for his promises to come true and performing the rituals he is said to have established.

Contemporary Literature

Contemporary English-language writers from the Pacific are contributing to the world's storehouse of literature. In their stories are ways of seeing, of being, and methods of telling tales that reflect the diverse and unique societies that make up the Pacific. Much Pacific literature alludes to the gods and the roles they played, and continue to play, in islanders' lives. Most Pacific writers draw on ancient stories for inspiration, and novelists such as

Patricia **Grace** (Aotearoa/New Zealand) weave old tales into new until the end becomes the beginning and the beginning becomes the end, and all of the stories combine to tell the history of the people. The spiral of life ensures that islanders' never lose sight of the past as they move into the future.

Writers, poets, playwrights, filmmakers, and other artists from Polynesia, Melanesia, and Micronesia are creating new versions of ancient oral stories that may not be widely known in the modern world. Since the early 1970s, writers such as Albert Wendt (Samoa), Hone Tuwhare, Patricia Grace and Witi **Ihimaera** (Aotearoa/New Zealand), Epeli **Hau'ofa** and Konai Helu-Thaman (Tonga), Tom Davis (Cook Islands), and Grace Molissa (Vanuatu) have been writing and publishing in English. The recent popular film *Whale Rider* (2002), based on the novel by Witi Ihimaera, is an example of an ancient oral story retold for the modern world. Pacific writers and artists are presenting the many different aspects of their region and, in turn, the world is discovering that not all stories have yet been heard and that all stories are not the same, as the literary critic Roland Barthes once declared.

Conclusion

The hundreds of cultures making up the Pacific are connected through their folklore and a shared genesis. As humans traveled across the Pacific Ocean, populating the myriad of islands along the way, many of their common stories changed as each newly discovered island presented hitherto-unknown geographies and resources that required new explanations and readings. So, although much folklore and many stories of the Pacific Islands are similar, there are also differences, making each culture unique but still connected to the larger family of *Moana nui a Kiwi*, the Pacific Ocean. ***See also*** Australian and Aotearoan/New Zealand Tales; *Pear ta ma 'on maf.*

Further Readings: Alpers, Antony. *Legends of the South Sea: The World of the Polynesians Seen through Their Myths and Legends, Poetry and Art.* Christchurch, NZ: Whitcombe & Tombs Ltd., 1970; Amadio, Nadine. *Pacifica: Myth, Magic, and Traditional Wisdom from the South Sea Islands.* Sydney: Angus & Robertson, 1993; Andersen, Johannes Carl. *Myths and Legends of the Polynesians.* 1928. Rutland, VT: C. E. Tuttle Co., 1969; Flood, Bo, Beret E. Strong, and William Flood. *Pacific Island Legends: Tales from Micronesia, Melanesia, Polynesia, and Australia.* Honolulu, HI: Bess Press, 1999; Gittins, Anne. *Tales from the South Pacific Islands.* Owings Mills, MD: Stemmer House Publishers, 1977; Reed, A. W. *Fairy Tales from the Pacific Islands.* Sydney: Reed, 1969; ———. *Myths and Legends of Polynesia.* Wellington: Reed, 1974.

Reina Whaitiri

Panchatantra

The *Panchatantra*, or "Five Books," is a Sanskrit composition attributed to around 200 CE. It is in many regards one of the most popular storybooks in history, as well as the classic **frame narrative**, and its diffusion from India west through the early Islamic world and into medieval Europe is associated with the creation of many of the best-known examples of the genre. The text has been reworked and rewritten extensively over time. In 1924, Franklin Edgerton attempted a reconstruction of the basic text of the book based on a collation of known Sanskrit manuscripts. An Arabic translation from a lost Persian compilation, about 750 CE, by Abdullah Ibn al-Muqaffah, expands the original very considerably and was the vehicle for its transmission into Europe until the eighteenth century, when Sanskrit documents began to become available. By that time, the Sanskrit book had also been rewritten as the *Hitopadesa*. The book was translated from a Hebrew version into Latin under the title *Directorium humanae vitae* by John of Capua (c. 1275), but became more popular in the Renaissance under the title *Fables of Bidpai*. Under that title, it is also associated with the name Doni, the Italian who first printed a translation; Bidpai is an alteration of the Sanskrit name *Vidyapati* (chief sage). A later translation from the Persian text, *Anvar al-Suhayli* (*Lights of Canopus*), was used by Jean de **La Fontaine**.

The initial frame is quite simple: a philosopher, Visnu Sarma, is entrusted with the education of three stupid princes, and so devises a course of instruction using stories as a sort of sugarcoated method to educate them. Many of the stories are animal **fable**s and are set up to illustrate various ethical and moral principles (*nitishastra*, or a code of conduct in Sanskrit); the book is thus also an early example of the *speculum principis* (the "mirror of the prince," that is, a book intended to teach statecraft). The framing is complex rather than sequential: stories (and many verses) are embedded within each other, rather than being presented in an orderly schema such as that used in the *Decameron* (1349–50) of Giovanni **Boccaccio** (ten days, ten narrators). Unifying narratives link individual books: in the first, two jackals bring about a friendship between a lion and a bull, and then cause an estrangement of the two after they become concerned about the bull's influence on the lion (the Arabic version adds a trial for one of the jackals). The second book deals with a friendship between four different animals; the third with a war between the crows and the owls. The names of the two jackals of the first book become the work's title in Arabic: *Kalila and Dimna*. In the Arabic version, the text expands to fifteen books, although the later books are much shorter than the main first three books.

Many of the stories are not fables, but rather **folktale**s: how a weaver won a **princess** by impersonating the Hindu god Vishnu; how a merchant's son, reciting a line of poetry at different occasions, wins the hand of a princess (and, as in Geoffrey **Chaucer**'s "Reeve's Tale," sleeps with several women in the course of one night). The story of the gullible carpenter in book three also echoes the theme of Chaucer's "Merchant's Tale" (ATU 1423, The Enchanted Pear Tree): the wife, aware that her husband is hidden nearby, tells her lover that their union is ordained by a goddess to save the husband's life. A Brahmin has glorious plans for his wealth, which come to nothing (ATU 1430, The Man and His Wife Build Air Castles). One of the most notable inclusions is the story of the "Brahmin and the Mongoose" (ATU 178A, The Innocent Dog), in which a Brahmin kills a mongoose that has in fact saved the Brahmin's son from a deadly serpent; in Europe, the mongoose is a dog, and the story in fact became a **saint's legend** behind a pilgrimage site in France. This **motif** recurs with a happy ending in the Walt **Disney** film, *The Lady and the Tramp* (1955).

The transmission of the *Panchatantra* from India to the Middle East is also the subject of a **legend**: Buzurjmihr, doctor to Khusrau Anushirwan (the idealized **king** of the Sassanian dynasty in Persia, which immediately preceded the advent of Islam) went to India seeking an herb of healing and immortality and brought back the book of fables. This allegorical reading sets the tone for the interpretation of the stories that are incorporated. From the time of the book's translation into Arabic, it became the inspiration for a widespread but under-recognized genre of medieval moral literature. *See also* South Asian Tales.

Further Readings: Edgerton, Franklin, ed. and trans. *The Panchatantra Reconstructed*. 2 volumes. New Haven, CT: American Oriental Society, 1924; Irving, Thomas Ballantine, ed. and trans. *Kalilah and Dimnah: An English Version of Bidpai's Fables Based upon Ancient Arabic and Spanish Manuscripts.*

Newark, DE: Juan de la Cuesta, 1980; Naithani, Sadhana. "The Teacher and the Taught: Structure and Meaning in the *Arabian Nights* and the *Panchatantra*." *Marvels & Tales* 18 (2004): 272–85; Ryder, Arthur, trans. *The Panchatantra*. Chicago: University of Chicago Press, 1925; Visnu Sarma. *The Panchatantra*. Translated by Chandra Rajan. New Delhi: Penguin Books India, 1993.

Stephen Belcher

Pantomime

A form of popular **theater** that frequently features fairy-tale characters and plots, loosely adapted, pantomime developed in England but has gained some currency in performance traditions throughout Great Britain and the Commonwealth, the United States, western Europe, and the former British colonies. Despite its roots in the gestural performance tradition of *commedia dell'arte*, modern pantomime is far from silent. With its musical numbers, dance routines, slapstick comedy, broad humor, audience participation, topical references, mockery of authority figures, and **cross-dressing** feature performers, pantomime reveals its indebtedness to vaudeville and the English music hall. Generally staged during the Christmas season (or, less commonly, at Easter), pantomime may also be regarded as a modern carnivalesque seasonal ritual. Noisy, boisterous, and playfully risqué, pantomime is considered family entertainment, often serving as children's introduction to the world of theater and forming a significant (if frequently overlooked) part of a cultural repertoire of fairy tales. Among pantomime's enthusiasts are writers who have experimented with the **literary fairy tale**: Charles **Dickens**, John **Ruskin**, Lewis **Carroll**, and, more recently, Angela **Carter**.

Conventions of characterization, costuming, and plot in modern British pantomime are distinctive. The standard roles include the Dame, a lusty and sometimes miserly older woman played by a garishly dressed man; the Principal Boy, a lowborn, thigh-slapping young hero traditionally played by a woman in heels, tunic, and tights; and the Principal Girl, the young heroine and love interest, also played by a woman. To varying degrees, pantomime productions have highlighted themes of **sex**, **gender**, and social class in their romantic storylines. Conventions of pantomime plot structure bring the story to a close with the **marriage** of the Principal Boy and Girl, sometimes joined by unlikely pairings of other characters. Pantomime is also expected to include an opening chorus of townspeople or other common folk, a humorous "slop scene" midway through the production, and a final presentation of performers in their most elaborate or outrageous costumes. The content and style of a pantomime's source text must thus be adapted or radically altered to fit the generic conventions of this theatrical form.

Pantomime is generally viewed as distinctly British, and despite Victorian critiques of the form (as uncouth or immoral), its appeal has endured and crossed boundaries of age, class, gender, race, nation, and ideology. As one of many marginalized and relatively unregulated forms of **performance**, pantomime emerged in eighteenth-century England—combining **music**, **dance**, and the highly stylized gestures of the Italian *commedia dell'arte* tradition popularized in the court of Charles II. These early English productions united the basic story of a popular tale or classical **myth** (the basis for the first part of the pantomime) with Anglicized versions of *commedia*'s stock characters, including the lovers Harlequin and Columbine, Clown, and the miserly *pater familias* Pantaloon. The dramatis personae from the opening were transformed into *commedia*'s stock figures by a good **fairy**, after which they would engage in an acrobatic comic chase. This sequence, the harlequinade, offered a burlesque (re)vision of the opening scenes, contrasting its own grotesqueries and physical comedy to the seriousness established at the outset. Like the many troupes of Italian and French fair performers who appeared in London in the early years of the eighteenth century, using their plays to mock the canonical theatrical repertoire, early English pantomimes were fundamentally satirical. The subjects of modern pantomime's satire often include both social and generic conventions, as audiences are invited to laugh at behavior within and beyond the theater, both on and off the stage.

By the early decades of the nineteenth century, English pantomime's stock of story lines and characters had shifted away from the mythological, expanding to include those from nursery rhymes (Humpty Dumpty, Boy Blue, Jack and Jill), English lore (Dick Whittington, Jack and the Beanstalk), popular literature (Robinson Crusoe), and French **literary fairy tale**s (the Yellow Dwarf and the White Cat were borrowed from Marie-Catherine d'**Aulnoy**; **Cinderella**, **Sleeping Beauty**, **Bluebeard**, and **Puss in Boots** were adapted from Charles **Perrault**; and Antoine **Galland**'s popular treatment of the *Arabian Nights* inspired numerous pantomime **Aladdin**s and **Sindbad**s). In turn, pantomime interpretations of fairy tales left their mark on print and material culture, as successful productions inspired toy theaters, souvenir scripts, and books such as Benjamin Tabart's *Cinderella; or, The Little Glass Slipper* (1804)—which represented scenes from a production at London's Drury Lane Theatre. It is also during this period that the fairy-tale extravaganzas of English playwright, translator, and costume historian James Robinson **Planché** emerged, drawing on French literary tales and *folies féeriques* but rejecting the lowbrow humor associated with pantomime.

With the relaxation, in 1843, of the theatrical licensing laws that had previously limited the performance of spoken drama to a small number of English patent theaters, pantomime ceased to be marginalized. Highly profitable Christmas-season pantomimes (with considerably relaxed performance structures) appeared at both major patent theaters and minor houses. As pantomime entered the mainstream of mid-nineteenth-century British theater, the former emphasis on gestural and improvised comedy began to share the spotlight with elaborate set mechanics and costume design, showiness, and spectacle.

By the turn of the twentieth century, the harlequinade was offered as a nostalgic novelty rather than as the core of the pantomime structure. Nevertheless, topical humor, social commentary, broad satire, punning, double entendres, improvised wisecracks, and slapstick comedy have remained central to English pantomime throughout its history. *See also* Adaptation.

Further Readings: Holland, Peter. "The Play of Eros: Paradoxes of Gender in English Pantomime." *New Theatre Quarterly* 13 (1997): 195–204; Mayer, David. *Harlequin in His Element: The English Pantomime, 1806–1836.* Cambridge, MA: Harvard University Press, 1969; O'Brien, John. "Harlequin Britain: Eighteenth-Century Pantomime and the Cultural Location of Entertainment(s)." *Theatre Journal* 50.4 (1998): 489–510.

Jennifer Schacker

Parable

A parable is a brief narrative that presents an implicit **moral** or lesson by depicting events and characters that correspond to the ideas and values that are being taught. The parable often stands between the **fairy tale** and **fable** in terms of narrative complexity. Literary critic Northrop Frye compared the simplicity of the fable to that of the **riddle**, since presenting the moral at the end of the fable is the equivalent of guessing the answer to a riddle. The parable, however, lacks the fable's summarizing moral. Instead of explicitly declaring its lesson, the parable requires some decoding, as if it were an extended metaphor or allegory. Nonetheless, its meaning is usually easy to grasp. In fact, the parable typically strives to make an abstract idea understandable through the concretization of a fictive illustration. The parable is well represented in the teachings of Jesus, and it is used to clarify theological concepts. Modern parables, such as those by Franz **Kafka**, may obscure rather than clarify a moral.

Unlike the fairy tale and fable, the parable does not typically anthropomorphize animals. Instead, parables are usually mundane and realistic, employing principally human characters and situations that are familiar to their audience. Exceptions exist, such as Jesus' parable of "sheep and goats" (Matt. 25.31–46), but are relatively rare. *See also* Bible, Bible Tale; Didactic Tale; Exemplum, Exempla; Religious Tale.

Further Reading: Frye, Northrop. *Anatomy of Criticism.* 1957. Princeton, NJ: Princeton University Press, 1990. 300–01.

R. Seth C. Knox

Parody

As a form that imitates earlier texts for comic or burlesque effects, parody is a logical outgrowth of the **intertextuality** that characterizes the fairy-tale tradition. As revisionists, rather than copiers or translators, authors of the **literary fairy tale** distance themselves from the narrative antecedents they rework. Dissociation thus goes hand in hand with association. Through his persistent use of exaggeration and sarcasm, the seventeenth-century Italian writer Giambattista **Basile** ridicules the homely energies of the folk materials he retells for a more sophisticated audience. But when he recasts the **Puss in Boots** story previously told by a sixteenth-century literary predecessor, Giovan Francesco **Straparola**, he intensifies his detachment. The tongue-tied youngster whom Straparola had called "Constantino Fortunato" becomes "Cagliuso," a maladroit ingrate whom Basile exposes as an unworthy recipient of a devoted **cat**'s crafty scheming. The cat's final disgust with the boor she has elevated allows Basile to expose the arbitrariness of Straparola's happy ending. His ironic closure mocks a predecessor whose clumsy resolution of the plot has made him as much of a bumbler as Cagliuso. The fine tale that Straparola has marred, Basile implies, requires the superior art that only he (and, after him, Charles **Perrault**) can provide.

For his part, Perrault flirts with parody when, at the end of "La belle au bois dormant" (1697)—his version of "**Sleeping Beauty**"—he slyly injects a counterpoint to the cynical finale of Basile's "Sole, Luna e Talia" ("Sun, Moon, and Talia," 1636). Whereas Basile's brutal **king** had no compunction in burning his wife on a bonfire she had intended for his mistress, Perrault's indecisive counterpart is uneasy about the grisly demise of the demonic woman who has tried to murder his own lovely sleeper. Perrault's narrator coyly reminds us that the young king could not help pitying a murderess who, in this version, happens to be his very own **mother**. Yet, in an abrupt turn, the narrator also assures us that this orphan was "quickly consoled" by domestic delights he can now enjoy unimpeded. Perrault's distancing from Basile, however, is not free of a self-mockery that stems from his relation to readers whose sensibilities he considers to be less sophisticated and more sentimental than those of Basile's audience.

Perrault's levity was adopted by parodists who recast his fairy tales in the nineteenth and twentieth centuries. George **MacDonald** has fun with Perrault's "Sleeping Beauty" in "The

Light **Princess**" (1864) and "Little Daylight" (1868). But his mockery of features that had become literary conventions is enlisted to signify his dissociation from ossified social conventions of his own time. After informing us that the "great forest" into which a **prince** has wandered in "The Light Princess" gives him an "advantage" over "princesses, who are forced to marry before they have had a bit of fun," MacDonald's narrator protests: "I wish our princesses got lost in a forest sometimes." An equal irreverence marks the characterization of the uninvited **fairies** who propel the plots of "The Light Princess" and "Little Daylight," for their literary transgressiveness again serves MacDonald's ideological ends. In "The Light Princess," the spurned **sorceress** Makemnoit "despised all the modes we read of in history, in which offended fairies have taken their revenges." Similarly, in "Little Daylight," the cackling bad fairy who appears at the baptismal font forces the good fairies into a substantial revision of precedents established in "Sleeping Beauty." Offsetting not one, but two curses, the fairies who "had been wise to keep two in reserve," make it possible for a young prince to kiss the "withered lips" of a decrepit crone who is none other than the "young princess" he adores. Cured of her spell, she returns his kiss far more gratefully than Perrault's hundred-year sleeper.

Good fairies, especially **Cinderella**'s godmothers, are among the figures most playfully transformed by parodists. Victorian fairies such as Blackstick in William Makepeace **Thackeray**'s *The Rose and the Ring* (1855) or the tiny godmother in Juliana Horatia **Ewing**'s "Timothy's Shoes" (1870) curtail their magic to allow immature wards to grow up on their own. Such comic agents were further altered in modern America. When the sly godmother in Shelley **Duvall**'s *Faerie Tale Theatre* production of "Cinderella" (1984) pretends that her magic wand is broken, she starts a game of "gotcha" that Cindy quickly masters. Cast as an aging Southern belle, this godmother (played by Jean Stapleton) is as comically effective as the New York bag lady (played by Pearl Bailey) in "Cindy Eller"—a 1985 episode of *ABC After School Special*—who steers another young *naive* toward self-confidence.

Our awareness of a text before its comic refashioning is crucial to a parody's success. The pleasure we derive from "fractured" fairy tales on **television** stems from their toying with materials amply familiar to the viewer. In a 1980s *Sesame Street* episode, Kermit the Frog, as television reporter, invites the audience to witness a dotty godmother's attiring of Cinderella. After three unproductive wand-wavings, the petulant teenager strides off, her faith in fairy-tale magic broken. But a lovely pink gown has replaced the trench coat and hat formerly worn by the frog, who is now hoisted on a palace-bound carriage. A scene that began with a horse that "used to be a mouse" and now ends with a Cinderella that used to be a male frog can delight both young and older viewers. But the latter may savor intertextual nuances of little interest to the former. How *will* the prince react to a green amphibian dressed in a pink gown? Will he be smitten, as demanded by "Cinderella" conventions, or will he emulate "The **Frog King**" by dashing this potential mate against a wall?

Yet parodies can be much harsher than such playful extensions of Perrault. The poems in Anne **Sexton**'s *Transformations* (1971) relentlessly satirize **Grimm** fairy tales as embodiments of a brutal patriarchal culture. Why is the "good and kind" monarch in "The Maiden without Hands" so invested in an amputee who is helpless to feel herself, pull down her own pants, or brush her own teeth? Has mutilation become a fetish? Sexton persistently resituates the Grimm texts within a bleak modern context. "The final solution," the mother of **Hansel and Gretel** assures their **father**, is to leave unwanted children in the forest. But even after Gretel, "seeing her moment in history," shuts and locks the oven and sets it on "bake," her return to her father's table cannot erase "the smell of the cooking **witch**." In *Transformations*, parody has lost all levity. The laughter it exacts is heavy. Distancing is necessary, but decidedly painful, for readers in a post-Holocaust world. *See also* Metafiction; Postmodernism.

Further Reading: Ennis, Mary Louise. "Fractured Fairy Tales: Parodies for the Salon and Foire." *Out of the Woods: The Origins of the Literary Fairy Tale in Italy and France*. Edited by Nancy L. Canepa. Detroit: Wayne State University Press, 1997. 221–46.

U. C. Knoepflmacher

Parrish, Maxfield (1870–1966)

Maxfield Parrish was an American painter, muralist, commercial artist, and illustrator, some of whose most famous pictures feature fairy tales. Although his works have the bright glowing colors of the art nouveau style, he enjoyed an extraordinarily long career and worked until the 1960s. Born in Philadelphia, Pennsylvania, to an artist father, he studied with noted writer and illustrator Howard Pyle. He first worked as a commercial artist, making pictures for advertisements and illustrating the covers of such periodicals as *Harper's Weekly* and *Century Magazine*. His first commission was L. Frank **Baum**'s first book, ***Mother Goose** in Prose* (1897). He also soon illustrated Kenneth Grahame's *The Golden Age* (1899) and *Dream Days* (1902). His pictures adorn a number of childhood classics and collections of folktales, including Eugene Field's *Poems of Childhood* (1904) and *The **Arabian Nights*** (1909). In addition, Parrish produced a notable series of *Hearst Magazine* covers based on such fairy tales as "The Frog Prince" and "**Sleeping Beauty**." His almost hyperrealistic style is based upon bright luminous colors, especially blues, red, and gold, which are especially appropriate to murals; a characteristic "Parrish blue" was named for him. His paintings often include nude androgynous figures posing in elaborate landscapes with glowing clouds. In his late life, Parrish concentrated on painting fine arts landscapes. His colors and style continue to influence artists, and his work is widely disseminated through posters. *See also* Art; Illustration.

Further Reading: Ludwig, Coy L. *Maxfield Parrish*. New York: Watson-Guptill, 1973.

George Bodmer

Pasolini, Pier Paolo (1922–1975)

The writer, poet, filmmaker, and critic Pier Paolo Pasolini hailed from the northeastern Friuli region of Italy but spent the bulk of his professional life in Rome, where he became one of Italy's greatest men of letters and public intellectuals of the twentieth century. He had a lifelong interest in **folk** and dialect traditions, deeming them authentic expressions of the culture of the lower classes in which a preindustrial and prebourgeois consciousness remained preserved.

In 1953, Pasolini published *Canzoniere italiano* (*Italian Songbook*), an anthology of "popular" **poetry** and other folkloric forms such as lullabies, **riddle**s, games, and military songs from Italy's various regions. In the substantial introduction, he reviewed the study of folk poetry over the preceding century, concentrating especially on those who conceptualized it as a "specimen of an idealized collectivity, and therefore coincident with the discovery of the 'nation.' "His novels of 1955, *Ragazzi di vita* (*The Ragazzi*) and 1959, *Una vita* *violenta* (*A Violent Life*), expressionistically employ Roman dialect to depict life in the subproletariat *borgate*, or slums, that were beginning to encircle Rome in the 1950s. Pasolini was equally prolific as a poet in these years and after, producing *Le ceneri di Gramsci* (*The Ashes of Gramsci*, 1957) and other collections; and his career as a filmmaker began in 1961 with *Accattone* (*Beggar*). In 1975, he was violently murdered under circumstances that still remain unclear.

Pasolini's closest creative encounters with folktale and fairy-tale narrative traditions came in the form of his Trilogy of Life, three films based on classic medieval tale collections: *Il Decameron* (1971), inspired by Giovanni **Boccaccio**; *I racconti di Canterbury* (*The Canterbury Tales*, 1972), from Geoffrey **Chaucer**; and *Il fiore delle Mille e una nottte* (*Flower of the **Arabian Nights***, 1974; also known as simply *Arabian Nights*) from the fifteenth-century anonymous compilation of Persian and other Middle Eastern tales. The films share an interest in the question of mass acculturation and popular resistance to it; the celebration of an unreined **sexuality** that figures vitality in its purest form; and most of all, an investigation of the nature and structure of narration and the essential human need to tell stories and to be an audience to telling.

Pasolini's *The Arabian Nights* opens with the citation, "Truth does not lie in a single dream, but in many dreams." Thus, although his version may prefer the realistic stories of the original *Nights* to its many folktales and fairy tales, the overall model of unlimited narration offered by the source text is highlighted, as is the life-affirming and mesmerizing nature of tale-telling. Pasolini does away with the **frame narrative** of **Sheherazade** and King Shahriyar, instead adapting a number of tales as framing devices that form a complexly embedded "Chinese box" narrative structure only in part present in the original. The overarching container story is the "Tale of Zumurrud and Nur ed Din," which is then interlaced with other narratives, some of whose elements and characters in their turn reappear in later tales. This intricate, nonlinear structure of Pasolini's *The Arabian Nights*, featuring unbounded and multiple entanglements among its characters and situations, runs parallel to and in some cases underlines its revelry in uninhibited erotic delights as well as its polemical mythicization of third world, preindustrial society. *See also* Arabian Nights Films; Erotic Tales; Film and Video.

Further Reading: Rumble, Patrick. *Allegories of Contamination: Pier Paolo Pasolini's* Trilogy of Life. Toronto: University of Toronto Press, 1996.

Nancy Canepa

Pear ta ma 'on maf (*The Land Has Eyes*) (2004)

Directed by Vilsoni Hereniko, this 2004 Pacific Island film tells the story of a Rotuman girl, Viki, who loses her father and eventually finds her way to making a new life for herself. While featuring belief narratives (legendary origin tales), the film has a coming-of-age **folktale** structure and is centered on the theme of **storytelling**. In folktale fashion, the protagonist's **transformation** requires a broader change that reestablishes social order, and the story is told in a simple and yet highly metaphoric style. When faced with loss and shame, Viki finds inspiration in the stories her father used to tell her, especially the tale of an ancestral **woman warrior**. With her (super)natural helpers, Viki fights for justice and obtains it. Building on the Rotuman proverb "the land has eyes, the land has teeth, and knows the truth," *The Land Has Eyes* exemplifies the power that stories have to transform individuals and situations.

Written and directed by Rotuma-born playwright Vilsoni Hereniko, *The Land Has Eyes* is the first feature-length movie by an indigenous Fijian. (Rotuma is a small island in the South Pacific that is politically part of Fiji and culturally close to Tonga and Samoa.) The dialogue is in Rotuman with English subtitles, and most of the cast consists of Rotumans who had, in many cases, never seen a movie before. At the 2005 inaugural Waiora Maori Film Festival in New Zealand, where *Whale Rider* (2002) was named best feature film, *The Land Has Eyes* won the best overall entry award. *See also* Australian and Aotearoan/New Zealand Tales; Film and Video; Ihimaera, Witi; Pacific Island Tales; Proverbs.

Further Readings: *The Land Has Eyes.* http://www.thelandhaseyes.com; Rotuma Web site. 2006. http://www.rotuma.net/.

Cristina Bacchilega

Peasant

Most traditional folktales and fairy tales originated in an agricultural age. The peasant or farmer depicted in such tales serves as a generic everyman—a person without special resources or benefits. Preindustrial storytellers and listeners could identify with the peasant **family**, taking vicarious pleasure at their successes and laughing at their foibles. Folktale peasants represent a full spectrum of human qualities and social situations. They are depicted variously as sly heroes blessed with natural wit and common sense, or they appear as hapless **simpleton**s, easy victims for **trickster**s and swindlers. Some are impoverished and exploited by powerful overlords, while others are wealthy and quite capable of abusing their own servants and neighbors.

Lacking formal education, folktale peasants are ready targets for confidence artists, leading to situations that provide plots for countless **jest**s. A good example is "De os die burgemeester werd" ("The Ox That Became Mayor"; ATU 1675, The Ox [Ass] as Mayor) as recorded by J. R. W. Sinninghe in his *Volkssprookjes uit Nederland en Vlaanderen (Folktales from the Netherlands and Flanders*, 1978). In this tale, a wealthy but stupid peasant, having no children of his own, takes an ox to the university to be educated. A quick-witted student takes possession of the ox, and in return for a substantial payment promises to have the ox educated. The tale ends with the peasant thinking his ox has become mayor of Amsterdam, because coincidentally the mayor's name is indeed Ox.

Innumerable trickster stories feature peasants as naïve dupes. One such **tale type** (ATU 1563, "Both?") tells how a peasant unwittingly surrenders his wife and daughter(s) to the sexual abuse of a servant. "Pedro Animales Fools His Boss" from Yolando Pino-Saavedra's *Folktales of Chile* (1967) follows the pattern set by its many European antecedents. In this story, Pedro Animales (also known as Pedro de Urdemalas) is employed by a rancher. Needing three tools, the rancher tells Pedro to fetch them from the house. At the house, Pedro tells the owner's wife and two daughters that the master has ordered the three of them to give themselves to him. Not believing him, they refuse, upon which Pedro calls to the master, "Didn't you say all three?"—"Yes, all three!" he shouts back; so the three **women**, ever obedient to husband and **father**, submit to the trickster. It is noteworthy that in these stories the farmhand takes revenge on the master by abusing the latter's wife and daughters, not the farmer himself. American counterparts to tales of type ATU 1563 are the popular "farmer's daughter" jokes which characteristically feature a naïve farmer who unwittingly surrenders his daughter to a stranger (often a traveling salesman).

For each peasant depicted as a hapless dupe, another appears as a clever and fearless hero ready to face down any opponent, even a supernatural **ogre**. A good example is J. M. Thiele's "En bonde narrer en trold" ("A Peasant Tricks a Troll"; ATU 1030, The Crop Division), as recorded in *Danmarks Folkesagn* (*Denmark's Folk Legends*, 1818–23). A peasant enters into a contract with a troll through which they agree to share harvests. The peasant will take everything growing aboveground, and the troll everything growing below the ground—alternating each year. The peasant plants grain the year he gets everything aboveground and carrots when he is to receive everything belowground. Thus the troll receives only worthless grain roots and carrot tops. Elsewhere, for example in France, the same tale depicts the peasant entering into a contract with the **devil**. It is noteworthy that in folktales a simple peasant can outwit the devil himself, a concept quite contrary to official theological views.

A large family of folktales with worldwide distribution (ATU 1060–1114) describes various contests between an ordinary person (typically a peasant, **soldier**, or **tailor**) and an ogre, again often identified as the devil. Many of these events involve agricultural skills, for example a threshing contest (ATU 1089) or a mowing contest (ATU 1090). Needless to say, the peasant always wins, and usually through trickery. For example, in a typical mowing-contest tale, the peasant secretly plants iron rods in the portion of the field to be mowed by the devil, causing the latter to damage his scythe and lose the contest.

A number of traditional tales reflect the view that even poor peasants—armed with common sense, daring, and a measure of good luck—can compete with the educated and the powerful. Such tales typically not only praise the simple virtues of ordinary people, but they also place into question the credentials of the **clergy**, scholars, judges, and other educated classes.

Exemplary is the tale known generically as Doctor Know-All (ATU 1641). This story originated in India, but has worldwide distribution. European versions usually feature a peasant as the charlatan-hero. "Crab" from Thomas Frederick Crane's *Italian Popular Tales* (1885) is typical. A **king** loses a valuable ring and offers a reward to anyone who can recover it. A poor peasant, although he has no special knowledge, brazenly claims to be a great astrologer and thus gains an audience with the king. He has himself installed in a room within the castle where he spends days poring over a large book and scribbling notes, although in truth he can neither read nor write. This intense labor so unnerves the king's servants who stole the ring that they surrender it to the peasant, who is forthwith proclaimed the greatest astrologer in the world.

Other members of peasant families also prove themselves able to compete with the well-born and highly educated, and none more so than daughters, featured prominently in tales of type ATU 875, The Clever Farm Girl. Told around the world, these stories depict various circumstances that enable a peasant's daughter to prove herself the equal of a king. Typically, two peasants are engaged in a dispute, which the king attempts to resolve by giving them **riddle**s. The one peasant solicits help from his clever daughter and easily solves the riddles. Discovering the source of the winning peasant's clever answers, the king asks to meet the daughter. Impressed with her beauty and cleverness, he marries her. *See also* Folk.

Further Reading: Röhrich, Lutz. "The Social Milieu." *Folktales and Reality.* Translated by Peter Tokofsky. Bloomington: Indiana University Press, 1991. 184–98.

D. L. Ashliman

Peau d'âne (Donkey Skin) (1970)

Directed by French filmmaker Jacques Demy, this musical fairy-tale **film** from 1970 is based on Charles **Perrault**'s 1694 verse tale but follows more closely the apocryphal version of 1781. Demy gives the tale a kitschy, even psychedelic twist by using bright and often-clashing colors, flamboyant costumes, and the eccentric Lilac **Fairy** (played by Delphine Seyrig), blending classicism with the culture of the 1960s. Most famous for *Les parapluies de Cherbourg* (*The Umbrellas of Cherbourg*, 1964), Demy cast its star, Catherine Deneuve, as the **princess**; and his choice of Jean Marais to play the incestuous **king** clearly pays homage to Jean Cocteau's ***La Belle et la Bête*** (*Beauty and the Beast*, 1946). The film playfully integrates intertextual references not only to the classical fairy tale but also to the *Grand Siècle*—the seventeenth century—in which the genre emerged (see **Intertextuality**).

Demy's retelling of this **incest** tale undoes the morality of Perrault's version, in which an incestuous **father** desires his virtuous daughter, who escapes his claws by disguising herself in a donkey skin, and who performs menial chores until she marries a **prince**, much like **Cinderella**. This princess, however, is not quite sure why she should not marry her father. When Donkey Skin seeks counsel from the Lilac Fairy, the latter dissuades the princess from marrying her father not for moral reasons but out of rivalry, which becomes evident in the last scene of the film. The morality of the original story gets suspended in this amoral if not immoral version of the tale. Although the princess does ultimately get her prince, one is left to wonder whether she would have found greater happiness had she gotten her king.

The film often juxtaposes the classical and the modern with numerous intertextual references. When the king tries to seduce his daughter with poetry, he quotes Cocteau's "Ode à Picasso" and Guillaume Apollinaire's "L'amour." The first poem is attributed in the film to the Lilac Fairy, who represents modernity in her dress (she is more of a sexy pixie than a classical fairy), language, and means of transportation (she arrives at Donkey Skin's wedding in a helicopter). Allusions to other fairy tales abound: the king sits on a throne that resembles a white **cat**, the title of a tale by Marie-Catherine d'**Aulnoy**; the carriage that whisks Donkey Skin away recalls the one in Cinderella; and the old woman who spits frogs recalls the bad girl in Perrault's "Les fées" ("The Fairies"). Often the noble names used in the film refer to literary or actual figures of the classical period: "la Ségur" refers to the writer Sophie, Comtesse de **Ségur**; "la

Catherine Deneuve and Jacques Perrin in the 1970 French film *Donkey Skin/Peau d'âne*. [Janus Films/Photofest]

Clève" perhaps to the main character of Madame de Lafayette's classic novel; and "La princesse Pioche de la Vergne," to Madame de Lafayette herself. *Donkey Skin* truly is a celebration of the classical fairy tale with a thoroughly modern twist. *See also* French Tales.

Further Reading: Taboulay, Camille. *Le cinéma enchanté de Jacques Demy.* Paris: Cahiers du cinéma, 1996.

Anne E. Duggan

Pedagogy

The fairy tale becomes a tool of pedagogy when it is deliberately used to teach values, norms, behaviors, skills, or other lessons. The term "pedagogy" typically denotes formal instruction, such as the kind that takes place in schools, but it can also refer to teaching that occurs outside institutional settings. The fairy tale has lent itself to pedagogical uses because of its association with children and because of its kinship with other didactic forms such as the **exemplum**, **fable**, **parable**, and **cautionary tale**. Some of the earliest antecedents of fairy tales were tales of religious or spiritual instruction, such as the **Jātaka**s (which are tales illustrating virtues based on the Buddha's former lives and thought to be among the oldest existing folk narratives) or **Bible tale**s.

One early European example of the fairy tale's role in pedagogy involves a story in Latin verse that may be a forerunner of the cautionary tale "**Little Red Riding Hood**." As the scholar Jan M. Ziolkowski has pointed out, the story—titled "De puella a lupellis seruata" ("About a Girl Saved from Wolf Cubs")—was included in *Fecunda ratis* (*The Richly Laden Ship*, c. 1022–24) by Egbert of Liège, a teacher in the cathedral school. Egbert prepared *Fecunda ratis* as a schoolbook with an instructional purpose, and the tale about the girl saved from **wolf** cubs because she wears a red wool tunic given to her by her grandfather on her baptismal day was included to provide a religious lesson.

The use of the fairy tale as a pedagogical instrument is linked especially to the development of **children's literature** in the eighteenth and nineteenth centuries, which itself reflects changes in the concepts of **childhood and children**. The notion that children needed to be subjected to the civilizing process and to a system of education generated the need for pedagogical tools, and the fairy tale was soon enlisted in the service of teaching children. For example, Jeanne-Marie **Leprince de Beaumont**, who worked as a governess in England, published a series of pedagogical works targeting specific ages and social classes, such as *Le magasin des enfants* (1756; translated into English as *The Young Misses' Magazine* in 1759) and *Le magasin des adolescentes* (1760), which included **didactic tale**s intended to teach children social values and virtues.

In nineteenth-century Germany, Jacob and Wilhelm **Grimm** conceived their *Kinder- und Hausmärchen* (*Children's and Household Tales*, 1812–15) as a tool of national pedagogy. The Grimms viewed their collection of fairy tales as part of a project to reaffirm the cultural identity of the German **folk**, and when they described their collection of fairy tales as an "*Erziehungsbuch*"—an "educational manual"—they meant not only that their tales conveyed useful social, moral, and even religious lessons for children, but also that they were intended to educate the German people about German character and culture. Because of their multiple pedagogical purposes, the Grimms' tales became a model for children's literature and were included in school readers; and by the end of the nineteenth century, after Germany had achieved nationhood, the *Children's and Household Tales* became part of the Prussian school curriculum. In the twentieth century—during the Third Reich—Nazi pedagogy took advantage of the tales' place in the educational system and their close association with the idea of German national character. Conscripted into the service of Nazi pedagogy, Grimms' tales were used to teach National Socialist ideology, with the result that, after World War II, occupation forces in Germany removed fairy tales from the school curriculum.

Despite such abuses, the pedagogical use of fairy tales is a double-edged sword. For example, shortly after the Russian Revolution, radical pedagogues in Russia sought to suppress fairy tales as remnants of the old power structure, but the imaginative and satirical writer Kornei **Chukovsky** dissented, claiming that the playful genre had a significant role in the education of children. Similarly, following the pedagogical abuse of fairy tales during the Third Reich, both East and West German pedagogues and children's advocates debated the role of fairy tales in children's literature and education. While some argued against their use, others identified in them the possibility for a liberating pedagogy. Reevaluation of the fairy tale's pedagogical role and potential occurred not just in Germany but internationally in tandem with the emergence of the children's rights movement in the 1960s. Teachers and writers found new ways of reutilizing fairy tales to challenge conservative ideologies and to encourage critical thought among children. The Italian pedagogue Gianni **Rodari**, for example, not only wrote innovative fairy tales of his own but also developed techniques and methods that teachers could use to revitalize the liberating potential of **storytelling** and **fantasy**. Rodari's pedagogical theories and techniques have influenced schools and teachers around the world, who use his work to empower children with imagination and storytelling skills.

On yet another level, the fairy tale—especially because of its simple language—is frequently used by teachers in foreign-language instruction, and many pedagogical articles have been written describing how individual teachers use fairy tales to teach specific skills and grammatical principles. *See also* Moral; Nationalism.

Further Readings: Bastian, Ulrike. *Die "Kinder- und Hausmärchen" der Brüder Grimm in der literaturpädagogischen Diskussion des 19. und 20. Jahrhunderts.* Frankfurt a.M.: Haag und Heerchen, 1981; Kamenetsky, Christa. *Children's Literature in Hitler's Germany: The Cultural Policy of National Socialism.* Athens: Ohio University Press, 1984; Rodari, Gianni. *The Grammar of Fantasy: An Introduction to the Art of Inventing Stories.* Translated by Jack Zipes. New York: Teachers and Writers Collaborative, 1996; Tatar, Maria. *Off with Their Heads! Fairy Tales and the Culture of Childhood.* Princeton, NJ: Princeton University Press, 1992; Tomkowiak, Ingrid. *Lesebuchgeschichten: Erzählstoffe in Schullesebüchern, 1770–1920.* Berlin: Walter de Gruyter, 1993; Ziolkowski, Jan M. "A Fairy Tale from before Fairy Tales: Egbert of Liège's 'De puella a lupellis seruata' and the Medieval Background of 'Little Red Riding Hood.' "*Speculum* 67 (1992): 549–75; Zipes, Jack. "The Struggle for the Grimms' Throne: The Legacy of the Grimms' Tales in East and West Germany since 1945." *The Brothers Grimm: From Enchanted Forests to the Modern World.* 2nd edition. New York: Palgrave MacMillan, 2002. 231–69.

Donald Haase

Pérez Galdós, Benito (1843–1920)

One of the three greatest novelists of Spanish literature and one of the most controversial dramatists of nineteenth-century Spain, the realist writer Benito Pérez Galdós also wrote a number of *cuentos fantásticos* (fantastic tales). His treatment of child characters in these tales is especially notable and recalls Hans Christian **Andersen** and Charles **Dickens**. Galdós's "La mula y el buey" ("The Mule and the Ox," 1876) relates the aftermath of the **death** of a little girl named Celinina. Having desperately wanted the figurines of a mule and an ox for her crèche at Christmas, in her new existence she grows wings, removes both fig-urines from another family's crèche, and flies off to heaven with other children who had come down to frolic during the holidays. However, because she cannot take the figurines from Earth, she has to fly back and leave them. The next day, her household awakes to see her in her coffin clutching the clay mule and ox. "La princesa y la granuja" ("The **Princess** and the Street Urchin," 1877) tells the story of seven-year-old Pacorrito Migajas, a Madrile-nian orphan who falls in love with a doll displayed in a shop window. After a series of mis-haps, he marries her, but since he had to abandon his human state to do so, he wakes on New Year's morning without physical sensations to find himself in a shop window, now a doll like his "princess." *See also* Spanish Tales.

Further Readings: Fedorchek, Robert M., trans. *Stories of Enchantment from Nineteenth-Century Spain.* Lewisburg, PA: Bucknell University Press, 2002; Pattison, Walter T. *Benito Pérez Galdós.* Boston: Twayne, 1975.

Robert M. Fedorchek

Performance

"Performance" became a key term in **folklore** studies in the United States during the 1960s and 1970s as the discipline moved in a new direction—from **collecting** and categoriz-ing texts toward an understanding of the artists who crafted them. Viewed in this new light, folklore was no longer understood as a disembodied text but as a process at the crossroads of performer, situation, setting, audience, and society, all of which constitute a complete **context** necessary for comprehending cultural expressions.

Critically reevaluating the distinction between "competence" and "performance" that was typical of the classical school, the performance-based approach recognized that not all per-formances are equal. Thus, this new approach focused attention on the rendering of texts and attributed crucial importance to the artfulness of each performative event. The aesthetic sensibilities manifest in a given performance were recognized to be a function of the area's culture, language, speech patterns, generic expectations, and other localized factors. Also known as "ethnopoetics," the study of the expressive uses of language, this approach dem-onstrates the possibility of representing oral texts on the printed page. The rhythms, repeti-tions, and other stylistic features of an oral performance could be made apparent in print by transcribing pauses, volume, and patterns of speech, and by discerning various communica-tive functions.

One of the pioneers of the performance approach in folklore, Dell Hymes demonstrated the "moment" of performance in his study of an Indian storyteller when he explained that the performance of his **informant** reached a moment of "breakthrough." By situating stories in respect to this particular moment, he called for greater attention to formal elements of textual representation and credited the narrator, who assumed full responsibility for his per-formance. Building on the work Hymes had done, Richard Bauman contributed to perform-ance studies by distinguishing among the concepts of story, performance, and event. Bauman defined performance "as a mode of spoken verbal communication [that] consists in the assumption of responsibility to an audience for a display of communicative competence" (Bauman, *Verbal Art as Performance*, 11).

Although U.S. scholars recognized the importance of the performance approach in the late 1960s, the significance of performance was evident to scholars in Russia and Eastern Europe well before then. Precursors of the performance-centered approach can be traced back to the Prague School linguists: in the notion of "performance" over "competence," there is a dichotomy similar to that in the distinction between *la langue* and *la parole*. However, the performance approach formulated a new framework that emphasized "competence in performance."

Another influence on the performance approach was the oral-formulaic theory of Milman Parry and Albert B. Lord, both of whom described the complex technique of oral composition by which lengthy **epic**s are composed and recomposed in performance by means of "formulas" that express a particular idea. In this context, "formula" refers to any group of words regularly employed under the same metrical conditions.

John Miles Foley has shown that the roots of the oral formulaic theory came from European scholars who preceded Lord and Parry. For example, Mark Azadovskii's *Eine sibirische Märchenerzählerin* (1926; translated as *A Siberian Tale Teller*) examined not only the role of the narrator's **gender** but also the role of personality and psychology in performance. Likewise, Linda **Dégh**—trained in the German school of folkloristics—presented several articles in *Narratives in Society: A Performer Centered Study of Narration* (1995) that emphasized the personal role of the storyteller. She took folk narrative as a vehicle of worldview and explained the processes of narrative transmission over time by calling attention to the contemporary world and the more conversational genres of narrative. Dégh claimed that the American school of performance had in praxis still paid too much attention to the text, despite the theoretical emphasis on the folklore event as performance. Dégh's approach delineates a social and functional angle to folk narrative, namely what German scholars call *Märchenbiologie* (fairy-tale biology), an approach that also focuses on the performance of folktales and fairy tales. The tale's repetitive elements and its structure may constitute a "text," but the oral text does not have a fixed and absolute form. It has as many versions as there are performances of it. It emerges and is created, even though the verbal text maintains its core structural elements. In 1923, another folklorist, Walter **Anderson**, had emphasized the role of the storyteller and the community's reception of the oral performance when he posited the Law of Self-Correction and maintained that the erratic features of stylistic variation were corrected by a communal aesthetic.

The concept of performance has had wide-ranging implications the study of folktales and fairy tales. For example, considerations of performance figure significantly in the collecting and **editing** of folktales. The tension between the individuality and integrity of performance on the one hand and the permanence and cultural authority of print on the other is an issue that collectors and editors must take into account in recording and reproducing oral texts. Likewise, contemporary **storytelling** festivals, which are the products of the self-conscious storytelling revival movement, force questions about **authenticity** and tradition in respect to texts, contexts, and performances. Feminist research on folktales and fairy tales has been critical of performance contexts, arguing that they favored genres of male expressive culture and that field researchers sought materials from female informants only when no male was available. *See also* Ethnographic Approaches; Fieldwork; Linguistic Approaches; Oral Theory; Oral Tradition.

Further Readings: Azadovskii, Mark. *A Siberian Tale Teller.* Translated by James R. Dow. Austin: University of Texas, 1974; Bascom, William R. "Verbal Art." *Journal of American Folklore* 68 (1955): 245–52; Bauman, Richard. *Story Performance and Event.* 1986. Cambridge: Cambridge University Press, 1992; ———, ed. *Verbal Art as Performance.* Prospect Heights: Waveland Press, 1977; Ben-Amos,

Dan, and Kenneth S. Goldstein, eds. *Folklore: Performance and Communication.* The Hague: Mouton, 1975; Foley, John Miles. *The Theory of Oral Composition.* Bloomington: Indiana University Press, 1988; Hymes, Dell. *"In Vain I Tried to Tell You": Essays in Native American Ethnopoetics.* New edition. Lincoln: University of Nebraska Press, 2004; Lord, Albert B. *The Singer of Tales.* 2nd edition. Edited by Stephen Mitchell and Gregory Nagy. Cambridge, MA: Harvard University Press, 2000.

Hande Birkalan-Gedik

Perodi, Emma (1850–1918)

The writer and journalist Emma Perodi, born in Florence, Italy, dedicated most of her professional life to **children's literature**. She produced numerous original tale collections, edited scholastic texts, and assumed editorial direction of one of the most important children's journals of the time, *Giornale per i bambini.* Her interest in the fairy tale expressed itself more in a creative re-elaboration of folk narrative than in the "archeological" bent and **collecting** activities of her contemporaries Giuseppe **Pitrè** and Vittorio **Imbriani**. Her collections include *Al tempo dei tempi ... Fiabe e leggende del mare, delle città e dei monti di Sicilia* (*In Days of Old ... Fairy Tales and Legends of the Sea, Cities, and Mountains of Sicily,* 1909), *Fate e fiori* (*Fairies and Flowers,* 1909), *Il paradiso dei folletti* (*The Paradise of Elves,* 1911), *Le fate d'oro* (*The Golden Fairies,* 1892), and her best-known work, *Le novelle della nonna* (*Grandmother's Tales,* 1892).

The *Novelle* includes forty-five tales, many incorporating fairy-tale or fantastic **motifs**, and has a realistic **frame narrative** about a year in the life of a Tuscan **peasant** family, the Marcuccis. The tales are told by the **family** matriarch, grandmother Regina ("Queen"), an idealized model of the storytellers so prized as sources by folklorists of the period. The fantastic dimension of Regina's tales is regularly punctuated by the Marcuccis' everyday vicissitudes, which include **marriage**s, changes in employment, and **food** shortages; and tales are often chosen on the basis of how effectively they may offer instruction or moral solace to the family. Stylistically, too, the tales are marked by an expressive interplay between the real and the fantastic, and by a predilection for the macabre and the paradoxical, which to some degree undermines, ultimately, any straightforward didactic function that the tales purport to have. *See also* Italian Tales.

Further Reading: Faeti, Antonio, ed. and introd. *Fiabe fantastiche: Le novelle della nonna.* By Emma Perodi. Turin: Einaudi, 1993.

Nancy Canepa

Perovsky, Aleksei. *See* Pogorel'sky, Antony

Perrault, Charles (1628–1703)

One of the most influential fairy-tale writers in French literary history, Charles Perrault spent much of his life as a dedicated civil servant. After studying law and serving as secretary to his brother Pierre, Charles went to work for Jean-Baptiste Colbert, the most powerful minister under Louis XIV. In 1663, Colbert appointed Charles Perrault secretary of the Petite Académie, later to be known as the Academy of Inscriptions and Belles-Lettres, responsible for the inscriptions of monuments and medals honoring the Sun King. By 1671, the year he became a member of the French Academy, Perrault was a well-established and highly positioned bureaucrat within Louis XIV's administration. However, around 1676, tensions arose in his relations with Colbert, and upon his patron's death in 1683, Perrault lost his position as Surveyor General of the King's Works and was excluded from the Petite Académie.

In his youth, Perrault had tried his hand at burlesque poetry and later composed odes in honor of the king's reign. After his fall from grace, Perrault focused his attentions on the work of the French Academy. In January 1687, the abbot of Lavau read before the academy Perrault's "Le siècle de Louis le Grand" ("The Century of Louis the Great"), which sparked the famous Quarrel of the Ancients and the Moderns. Leading the charge of the Moderns, Perrault followed up on his poem with his *Parallèle des anciens et des modernes* (*Parallel of Ancients and Moderns*, 1688–97), in which he articulated the different positions of the quarrel. Perrault questioned the contemporary veneration of the writers of antiquity and sought to free authors from the imperative to imitate the Ancients and their genres, and he did so via two main strategies. First, Perrault conflated scientific progress with literary and artistic progress to argue for the superiority of the Moderns. Second, he supported the modernist position by using the judgment of **women** as a common measure for what is natural, clear, and refined in art. This move made the Quarrel not only about Ancients and Moderns, but also about the role of women in French society.

In 1694, Nicolas Boileau, the spokesman for the Ancients, published his *Satire X*, in which he mocked both the modernist position as well as the women who were supposed to legitimate that position. This fueled a series of responses by Moderns such as Jacques Pradon, Jean-François Regnard, and Jean Donneau de Visé, founding editor of the literary review, the *Mercure galant*. Of course, Perrault published his own response, in the form of his *Apologie des femmes* (*Apology of Women*, 1694), a problematic text in which it becomes evident that Perrault used the authority of women only to legitimate the modernist position, having no intentions of allowing women to actually exercise real power in the public sphere. One only needs to consider the history of his first published tale "Griselidis" ("Griselda," 1691) for this to be clear.

Inspired by Giovanni **Boccaccio**'s and Petrarch's versions of the story, Perrault must also have been familiar with versions of "Griselda" printed in collections of *Miroirs des dames mariées* (*Mirror of Married Ladies*), widely published pedagogical manuals. "Griselda" concerns a thoroughly masochistic wife who unconditionally subjugates herself to her sadistic husband, who claims to be testing her virtue. While Petrarch proposed the tale was an allegory for the believer's relationship to God, its proliferation in manuals aimed at newly married women tells another story. Perrault's version of "Griselda," a subdued and domesticated woman, only anticipates the place Perrault reserved for his female characters in his fairy tales.

The second tale published by Perrault, "Les souhaits ridicules" ("The Foolish Wishes"), first appeared in the *Mercure galant* in 1693. In structure it resembles the **fable** "La mort et le bûcheron" ("Death and the Woodsman," 1668) by the Ancient Jean de **La Fontaine** and marks Perrault's attempt to promote the modernist cause through the genre of the fairy tale. Although Marie-Catherine d'**Aulnoy** published the first fairy tale in 1690 as part of a **novel**, Perrault is the first of the seventeenth-century fairy-tale writers to publish a collection of tales in 1694, which included "Griselda," "Foolish **Wish**es," and "Peau d'âne" ("Donkey Skin"). By the end of 1695, these *Contes en vers* (*Verse Tales*) already had gone through five editions.

In February 1696, the *Mercure galant* published "La belle au bois dormant" ("**Sleeping Beauty**"). A year later, this story would open Perrault's most famous collection of tales, *Histoires ou contes du temps passé, avec des moralités* (*Stories or Tales of Times Past, with Morals*, 1697), which also included: "Le petit chaperon rouge" ("**Little Red Riding Hood**"), "La barbe bleue" ("**Bluebeard**"), "Le maître chat ou le chat botté" ("The Master Cat, or **Puss in Boots**"), "Les fées" ("The **Fairies**"), "Cendrillon ou la petite pantoufle de verre" ("**Cinderella**, or The Glass Slipper"), "Riquet à la houppe" ("Riquet with the Tuft"), and "Le petit poucet" ("Little **Thumbling**"). Like his contemporaries d'Aulnoy and Henriette-Julie de Castelnau, Comtesse de **Murat**, Perrault drew from **Italian tales** by Giovan Francesco **Straparola** and Giambattista **Basile**, and he modified them to downplay female agency. To cite one example, Straparola used an enterprising female **cat** in "Constantino Fortunato," the source for Perrault's "Puss in Boots," in which the cat is male. As Perrault frequented **salon**s run by his fellow tale writers, intertextual references to each others' stories abound. The existence of three distinct versions of "Riquet" by Catherine **Bernard**, Perrault, and his niece Marie-Jeanne **Lhéritier de Villandon** even suggest the possibility of tale competitions within the salon.

The history of film **adaptation**s of Perrault's tales is quite rich. Under the direction of Albert Capellani, the Pathé-Frères movie company produced *Peau d'âne* (1904 and 1908), *Cendrillon* (1907), *Riquet à la houppe* (1908), *Le chat botté* (1908), and *La belle au bois dormant* (1908). In 1929, the Brazilian director Alberto Cavalcanti adapted *Le petit chaperon rouge* to the French screen, with the renowned actor-director Jean Renoir playing the **wolf**. While Walt **Disney**'s *Cinderella* (1950) and *Sleeping Beauty* (1958) represent rather domesticated versions of these tales, Jacques Demy's ***Peau d'âne*** (1970) is playfully kitsch and stars Catherine Deneuve, who also plays the **queen** in the recent version of *Le petit poucet* (2001), directed by Olivier Dahan. Still widely read in France and around the world, Perrault is part of the pantheon of quintessential fairy-tale writers, along with Jacob and Wilhelm **Grimm** and Hans Christian **Andersen**. *See also Conte de fées*; Film and Video; French Tales; Literary Fairy Tale.

Further Readings: Duggan, Anne E. *Salonnières, Furies, and Fairies: The Politics of Gender and Cultural Change in Absolutist France*. Newark: University of Delaware Press, 2005; Hannon, Patricia. *Fabulous Identities: Women's Fairy Tales in Seventeenth-Century France*. Amsterdam: Rodopi, 1998; Lewis, Philip. *Seeing through the Mother Goose Tales: Visual Turns in the Writings of Charles Perrault*. Stanford, CA: Stanford University Press, 1996; Seifert, Lewis C. *Fairy Tales, Sexuality, and Gender in France 1690–1715: Nostalgic Utopias*. Cambridge: Cambridge University Press, 1996; Soriano, Marc. *Les contes de Perrault: Culture savante et traditions populaires*. 1968. Paris: Gallimard, 1977.

Anne E. Duggan

Peter Pan Films

Sir James Matthew **Barrie**'s *Peter Pan* (1904) is usually thought of as quintessentially British, yet the major cinema and **television** versions are all American. One was silent monochrome live action; another used hand-drawn **animation** and Technicolor; some turned it into a musical; and modern approaches have employed a combination of live action and computer-generated imagery.

Despite the play's huge success on stage, it was twenty years before the cinema tackled it. When director Herbert Brenon took the plunge, in 1924, Barrie himself adapted his text and approved the casting of boyish eighteen-year-old newcomer Betty Bronson as Peter, carrying on the stage tradition of having a girl play the principal role. Accompanying Bronson's name above the title was the seventeen-year-old Chinese-American Anna May Wong (fresh from playing opposite Douglas Fairbanks in *The Thief of Bagdad*, 1924) as Tiger Lily. Complementing these two youngsters were veterans such as eye-rolling Ernest Torrence as Hook and George Ali recreating a performance of Nana that he had given many times on stage.

Most other elements of the film, including the use of wires for the flying scenes, likewise followed stage versions closely, the major difference being that, whereas onstage, Tinker Bell is represented simply by a darting spot of light, in the film she was fleshed out by Virginia Brown Faire, miniaturized by multiple-exposure techniques.

Thirty years later, live-action screen flying still relied on wires and, since flying is essential to *Peter Pan*, Walt **Disney** saw a chance to exploit the potential of animation to make difficult things look natural. The song sung by the Darling children as they master the trick and take off effortlessly for Neverland ("I can fly! I can fly!! I can fly!!!") celebrates this life-changing achievement.

Overall, Disney (1953) updates Barrie for a 1950s U.S. family audience: the dialogue is rewritten; the humor is slapstick rather than whimsy; Hook's chosen instrument of intended **death** for Peter is an exploding clock rather than a bottle of poison (thereby denying Tinker Bell the chance to save him by drinking it all herself); and the whole Neverland story takes place inside a dream of Wendy's on the last night before she has to move to a room of her own. This framework necessitates a significant alteration to Barrie's ending: when Wendy, Peter, and John return from Neverland, the Lost Boys stay behind with Peter (rather than being adopted by the Darlings, as in the original) because if they all turned up in the flesh in London, that would mean they were real, not just a dream.

The next time Peter flew into view was on American television, in color, singing "I've Gotta Crow!" in March 1955. This was a modified live performance of a mammoth Broadway musical that had opened the year before, to great acclaim. Structured around Mary Martin as Peter, giving a loud and lithe performance in her forties, it contained fifteen big song-and-dance numbers (for example: "I'm flying, I'm not trying," and "It's not on any chart, you must find it in your heart") plus an overture. This musical element was the dominant factor in the film, and the narrative and dialogue were reduced to accommodate it.

It was the right blend to give *Peter Pan*, at the age of fifty, an appeal to a wide television audience. It was rebroadcast live the following year; then remounted, rebroadcast, and captured on video when technology made this possible in the 1960s; it was shown twice more in the 1960s, once in the 1970s, and once in the 1980s, and then became available on DVD at the end of the century. Other actors also took the part of Peter, in this version or another, but through the power of performance and imagination, it was middle-aged Mary Martin who became, for many millions, The Boy Who Would Not Grow Up.

In the 1980s and 1990s, it seemed that production companies saw no future in a straight screen Barrie—but vast potential profits in *Pan* spin-offs. In 1989, a Japanese anime television series in forty-one episodes, *Peter Pan no bōken* (*The Adventures of Peter Pan*) began and ended like Barrie, but the other thirty-nine episodes added science-fiction elements (giant robots and lizards), **fantasy** creatures (the Neverbird), and new characters such as the **Queen** and **Princess** of Darkness. At the same time, in the United States, Fox Broadcasting Company was animating a sixty-five-episode series, *Peter Pan and the Pirates* (1990), which rang all possible changes out of the interplay between the various Barrie characters, especially the youth/**age** antinomy embodied by Pan and Hook. Next came Steven Spielberg's big-screen *Hook* (1991), which starts from the premise that when Peter brought the Darlings back to London, he stayed and grew up to become a Los Angeles businessman and **father**; lured back to Neverland by Hook, who has kidnapped his children, he is easily outfought because, as an adult, he can no longer fly. Finally, another sequel, the **Walt Disney Company**'s 2002 *Return to Neverland*, shifts the background to World War II and starts when Hook mistakes Wendy's daughter Jane for Wendy herself, and abducts her; Peter rescues her soon enough, but cannot get her back to London because, forced by the war to grow up quickly, she does not believe in **fairies**, and therefore she cannot fly.

Such divergences ended when director P. J. Hogan decided that the way to bring Peter Pan to a twenty-first-century audience was not to abandon the original but to imagine how Barrie would recreate it if he had the full panoply of modern filmmaking resources at his disposal (*Peter Pan*, 2003). Peter is now played on screen by a real boy—real in body as well as voice—for the first time. This change brings out the latent **sexuality** between Peter and Wendy (clearly implied in Barrie's text). At the beginning, Peter does not know what a kiss is; in the middle, he dismisses feelings as boring; but at the end, his life is saved, literally, by Wendy's kiss of love and farewell, which enables him to think happy thoughts again, regain his cleverness, and see off Hook—no longer a pantomime villain but a frightening obsessive. The film finds a cinematic way to reinvent Barrie's famous theatrical device of giving the audience the chance to save Tinker Bell's life by clapping to affirm their belief in fairies.

This could be the definitive screen *Peter Pan*; but with 2007's increased relaxation of the copyright control Barrie gave to London's Great Ormond Street Hospital, it seems likely that Peter will be having big adventures for years to come. ***See also*** Childhood and Children; Film and Video; Silent Films and Fairy Tales; Theater; Thief of Bagdad Films.

Further Readings: Allan, Robin. *Walt Disney and Europe: European Influences on the Animated Feature Films of Walt Disney*. London: John Libby, 1999; Birkin, Andrew. *J. M. Barrie and the Lost Boys*. 1979. New Haven, CT: Yale University Press, 2003; Dunbar, Janet. *J. M. Barrie: The Man behind the Image*. London: Collins, 1970.

Terry Staples

The Piano (1993)

Jane Campion's 1993 Academy Award-winning **film** *The Piano* was acclaimed for its **gender** politics and criticized for its racial stereotyping. The familiar story line (embedded in a larger critique of **colonialism** and patriarchal privilege) of **family** dysfunction and **violence** underlain by Freudian romance has clear links to fairy tales—most notably to "**Bluebeard**" (ATU 312, Maiden-Killer; 312A, The Rescued Girl) but also to "**Beauty and the Beast**" (ATU 425C) and "The Maiden Without Hands" (ATU 706). The plot, the sexual repression and violence, the underlying sense of horror, as well as the isolated, remote location, stark landscape, the imprisonment, and the utter dependence of the heroine on a man she neither knows nor loves are also reminiscent of gothic romances, particularly *Wuthering Heights* and *Jane Eyre*. But this feminist reworking, rather than reinforcing gender roles, subverts them, and becomes a tale of female sexual **initiation**, self-determination, and knowledge.

Unwed, mute, and with an illegitimate daughter, Ada McGrath is married off by her father in Scotland to a man she has never seen—Alisdair Stewart, who has emigrated to New Zealand with the hopes of converting virgin forests into cultivated farmlands. Upon the **women**'s arrival upon an isolated beach, Stewart, a host of Maori, and George Baines, Stewart's Englishman-turned-native interpreter, meet them and prepare to transport them and their cargo to Stewart's encampment. It is at this initial meeting that the impossibility of the union becomes clear: Ada, although mute, "speaks" through her piano, which is clearly her emotional double. Having been transported across the ocean and deposited onto the beach, the piano is immediately dismissed by Stewart as being without utility, and, over Ada's protests, he leaves it on the beach. Later, in the second negotiation over Ada's (surrogate) body, Baines negotiates a trade with Stewart—the piano for land.

At this point, the traditional story line begins to bifurcate, and the film is no longer a simple rendering of "Beauty and the Beast" or "Bluebeard." Ada, while still in Stewart's house as his wife, moves back and forth to Baines' house deep in the forest, far from the cultivated sphere, to give him piano lessons. These lessons have been arranged and insisted upon by Stewart, but, in the third negotiation over Ada's body, she agrees to let Baines do certain sexual things to her during the lessons to buy back her piano, key by key. It is in this **forbidden room** that Ada's initiation into her own sexual awareness occurs.

Of all the fairy-tale referents, none is more striking than that of "Bluebeard." Stewart is the older, forbidding, violent husband, to whom she is married for economic reasons and dislocated from her home, surroundings, and family. When Stewart discovers that the piano lessons have become sexual encounters, he forbids Ada going to Baines and, in fact, imprisons her in the cabin. When he discovers the tell-tale marked (piano) key, onto which Ada has inscribed her love for George, Stewart, in a fit of rage, flies at her, brandishing an axe, and brutally cuts off her finger. This act of mutilation and symbolic murder (silencing her piano playing) is enacted in the name of patriarchal authority but in fact displays its total unraveling. As if to underscore the relationship to "Bluebeard," the tale is also inserted as a mise-en-scène in which the local colonials perform Charles **Perrault**'s tale as a shadow play. And yet, despite the fairy-tale connections, Campion has transformed the tale from one that condemns female curiosity to one in which the knowledge that Ada seeks and finds is a means by which she becomes whole, no longer dependent on her piano as her voice, and no longer a victim of male authority. Campion has also made more complex the nature of interpersonal relationships. There are no stock good and evil characters, but there are people dramatically capable of a range of actions and emotions, set against a colonial backdrop that has enveloped them all into a violent sphere. *See also* Feminism; Feminist Tales; Sex, Sexuality.

Further Readings: Bacchilega, Cristina. "'Be Bold, Be Bold, But Not Too Bold': Double Agents and Bluebeard's Plot." *Postmodern Fairy Tales: Gender and Narrative Strategies*. Philadelphia: University of Pennsylvania Press, 1997. 104–38; Coombs, Felicity, and Suzanne Gemmell, eds. *Piano Lessons: Approaches to the Piano*. London: John Libbey, 1999.

JoAnn Conrad

Pig

When Lewis Carroll, in *Alice's Adventures in Wonderland* (1865), has Alice discover that the human baby she wrested away from the sadistic duchess has turned into a grunting pig, he recreates a metamorphic event dramatized in a succession of **literary fairy tale**s that hark back to Giovan Francesco **Straparola**'s "The Pig Prince" from *Le piacevoli notti* (*The Pleasant Nights*, 1550–53). These earlier stories, however, had reversed the order of **transformation** that so greatly disturbs Alice. In them, it is not a human who turns into a pig but rather a pig who can assume the human shape of his parents only after he has mated with a willing bride. Still, the capricious twist of fate that thwarts Alice's desire to nurture a baby boy also affects the female characters in these earlier fairy tales. The girl's revulsion is shared, first, by **mother**s who had hardly expected that meddling **fairies** would force them to present their royal husbands with such an objectionable heir, and, subsequently, by the young **women** these mothers have bribed to accept the sexual advances of a smelly partner.

Whether cast as potential humans who are eager to shed their natal pigskin (by writers such as Straparola and by his major two successors, Marie-Catherine d'**Aulnoy** and Henriette-Julie de Castelnau, Comtesse de **Murat**) or as anthropomorphized animals with distinctly human feelings (like Wilbur in E. B. White's *Charlotte's Web*, 1952), pigs seem to offer fabulists prime vehicles for reflections about the vicissitudes of "destiny." Even the curious hybrid featured in Jacob and Wilhelm **Grimm**'s "Hans mein Igel" ("Hans My Hedgehog," 1815) is associated with the pigs he breeds in a forest before he, too, weds a **princess**. And swinishness acts as a mask that allows an impoverished **prince** to test an aloof princess in Hans Christian **Andersen**'s "Svinedrengen" ("The Swineherd," 1842).

There seem to be multiple reasons for this recurrent identification. Though cast as malodorous, unrestrained, overly voracious, wallowing in filth and mud, swine also strike us as charming, especially when they are small; their intelligence makes them educable; and their smiling countenance seems to betoken a cheerful acceptance of their hapless fate as foodstuff. Their resemblance to humans thus makes us uneasy. This ambivalence is immediately apparent in tales that open with the dubious responses of royal parents to the freakish fairy gift of a human baby who looks like a pig.

The deliberately crude plot of Straparola's "The Pig Prince" plays with the confusion of a **king** who wants to "have his son killed and cast into the sea," yet also acknowledges that this creature, "whatever he might be, was of his own blood." Straparola delights in this incongruity. He feels no need to account for a third fairy's arbitrary subversion of the good wishes of her sisters, but mocks the "saintly" **queen** who indulges her grunting, "dirty," "dreadfully" stinking, and sexually frustrated son even after he kills the first two wives she provides for him. When the queen finds her third "daughter-in-law cheerful and content" even though the groom has just defecated on their wedding bed, a smirking Straparola hints that this new wife, Meldina, values the performance of a virile lover who has impregnated her before rushing "out into the pasture to eat." For the Italian writer, the prince's final assumption of a handsome human shape seems almost as negligible as the role played, at the outset, by the three fairies who have spun his fate. It is only in d'Aulnoy's and Murat's retellings that such female spinners control the entire narrative. D'Aulnoy's "Le prince marcassin" ("The Wild Boar," 1698) and Murat's "Le roy porc" ("The Pig King," 1699) significantly refine and complicate Straparola's story. Both women writers reject his emphasis on chance by giving prominence to fairies whose narrative control patently mirrors the deliberateness of their own authorial design. But whereas d'Aulnoy tries to excuse the maternal laxity Straparola had mocked and to justify the prince's intemperate killing of a scheming wife as a self-defensive act, Murat removes these remnants of the earlier plot. Instead, the dramatic struggle between two competing fairies, Bienfaisante and Rancune, now reflects her own rivalry with d'Aulnoy. By supervising the pig prince's maturation, Bienfaisante replaces his inadequate biological mother. She educates this "milky-white pig" in a palace of her own, cures him of his infatuation with two unworthy mates, and then leads him into an underground bower that holds the bride she has chosen for him, a princess abducted by Rancune. Bienaisante's matchmaking thwarts the designs of Rancune and her male allies, a powerful **sorcerer** and a river god. After soaring through the air to ferry the prince's parents to his wedding, she and another sister destroy the deforming pigskin. Revered by his subjects as a wiser ruler than the **father** who had been unaware of his existence, King Pig owes his eminence to the fairy mentoria who executes Murat's own revisionist design.

Johann Wilhelm Wolf's "Das wilde Schwein" ("The Wild Pig," 1845) and Josef Haltrich's "Das Borstenkind" ("The Bristly Child," 1885) may well be genuine folktales and, as such, be free of the self-conscious **intertextuality** that shaped Murat's literary fairy tale. But it seems likely that subsequent stories of humanized pigs cannot escape the mark of the **archetype**s introduced by Straparola, d'Aulnoy, and Murat. Before writing *Charlotte's Web*, E. B. White had created a story about an animal-child inexplicably born to American middle-class parents. Unlike Stuart Little the mouse-boy, however, Wilbur the piglet is not a freakish hybrid. No prince, he is simply a common pig adopted by female caretakers of other species. Saved from her ax-wielding father by the girl who names him after one of the Wright brothers, he is granted a higher destiny by an airy weaver who assumes the role played by d'Aulnoy's and Murat's maternal caretakers. D'Aulnoy's queen had told her son that she might secure him a wife by falsely proclaiming him as "fairer than love itself"; Murat's Bienfasante went even further when she compelled the princess to fall in love with a "charming" portrait of the prince's nonporcine incarnation. By her own clever acts of advertising "some" ordinary product as "terrific" and "radiant," Charlotte the spider becomes E. B. White's version of the fairy Bienfaisante. Wilbur needs no bride to secure everlasting happiness. By guarding this unaging child, Charlotte's daughters and granddaughters ensure his reign, though "humble" and "close to the ground," as a perennial object for our identification. ***See also*** Animal Bride, Animal Groom; Sex, Sexuality.

Further Readings: Komins, Benton Jay. "Western Culture and the Ambiguous Legacies of the Pig." *CLCWeb: Comparative Literature and Culture: A WWWeb Journal* 3.4 (December 2001). http://clcweb-journal.lib.purdue.edu/clcweb01-4/komins3-01.html; Zipes, Jack, ed. *The Great Fairy Tale Tradition: From Straparola and Basile to the Brothers Grimm.* New York: Norton, 2001. 51–99.

U. C. Knoepflmacher

Pitrè, Giuseppe (1841–1916)

Largely responsible for establishing **folklore** as an independent discipline in Italy, Giuseppe Pitrè produced a vast collection of Sicilian and Italian folk traditions and scholarship covering nearly every genre, including **folktale**s and **fairy tale**s, **legend**s, festivals, folk songs, **riddles**, **anecdote**s, and oddities. He attempted to make the study of folklore a scientific work, and over more than four decades of **collecting**, research, and publication, he made many important contributions to both Italian and international folkloristics.

Pitrè was born in 1841 to a fisherman's family in the Santa Lucia neighborhood of Palermo, Sicily. He started studying classics at age thirteen, and at the age of nineteen, he began studying medicine in the Faculty of Medicine and Surgery at the University of Palermo. After graduating, he practiced medicine in the communities of Borgo and Kalsa, poor neighborhoods of Palermo, for more than thirty years. Pitrè appeared to be conflicted about his twin callings of medicine and folklore, yet he recognized that his profession as a doctor opened opportunities for him as a folklorist. Indeed, it was from among the peasants of the Borgo that Pitrè collected much of the folklore that he published.

In 1884, Pitrè was one of the founding members of the Italian Folklore Society, and in 1897 he was made an honorary member of the American Folklore Society. He founded a museum of ethnography, Il Museo Etnografico-Siciliano (Sicilian Ethnographic Museum), which was established in Palermo in 1910. More commonly know today as the Pitrè Ethnographic Museum, its collection holds more than 20,000 items of Sicilian traditional material culture. The museum's library houses Pitrè's papers and correspondence and serves as a center for research and folklore study. Pitrè realized his goal to have folklore recognized as an independent discipline when he became the chair of "demopsychology" (that is, the study of the psychology of a people, or **folk**) at the University of Palermo in 1911, where he taught until 1915, when he was appointed as a senator.

Most important of Pitrè's major works is the twenty-five-volume *Biblioteca delle tradizioni popolari siciliane* (*Library of Sicilian Folk Traditions*, 1871–1913), which documents traditional Sicilian life through a variety of folklore genres, including folk songs, folktales, games, festivals, beliefs, and folk medicine. Most volumes of the *Biblioteca* begin with prefaces and introductory essays that provide important contextual, historical, and critical perspectives about the area of study. Along with the Salvatore **Salomone-Marino**, Pitrè cofounded and edited the first major Italian folklore journal, *Archivio per lo studio delle tradizioni popolari* (*Archives for the Study of Folk Traditions*), which was published in twenty-four volumes from 1882 until 1906. Pitrè also published the *Bibliographia delle tradizioni popolari d'Italia* (*Bibliography of Folk Traditions from Italy*, 1885–99), a book-length bibliography of Italian folklore materials. This seminal work has approximately 6,680 entries and provides bibliographic references up to the early 1890s. A sixty-volume "national edition" of Pitrè's complete works was released in Italy, the *Edizione nazionale delle opere di Giuseppe Pitrè* (*National Edition of the Works of Giuseppe Pitrè*, 1998), which includes thirty-seven edited volumes, nineteen unedited volumes, and nine volumes of correspondence.

Many volumes of Pitrè's collected materials are folk narratives. The most important is *Fiabe, novell, e racconti popolari siciliani* (*Fairy Tales, Novellas, and Popular Tales of Sicily*, 1875), a collection of 300 folktales, which was published as volumes 4 through 7 of his *Biblioteca*. An extended annotation providing commentary and known variants in collections of oral tales or **literary fairy tale**s follows each tale. Volumes 18, 22, and 24 of the *Biblioteca* are also devoted to narratives; volume 18 is a collection of 158 texts and variants of folktales and legends, and volumes 22 and 24 both contain legends. Pitrè also published a collection of Tuscan folktales, *Novelle popolari toscane* (*Popular Tuscan Novellas*, 1885). Between 1885 and 1899, he founded and edited a sixteen-volume collection of traditional folk oddities, *Curiosità popolari tradizionali*, in collaboration with another Sicilian folklorist, Gaetono di Giovanni. Many of the works in this series were based on library research and existing publications, rather than on ethnographic **fieldwork**.

Pitrè made two important contributions to the methodology of collecting folktales. Like many of his predecessors, he believed that the spirit of the people was contained in folk poetry, folktales, and other forms of expressive culture. Pitrè placed priority on the sanctity of the text and maintained that it was necessary to capture the exact words spoken by his **informant**s. This meant recording and publishing folklore in Sicilian, as spoken by his informants, rather than translating these materials into Italian. Recording folklore in Sicilian presented numerous challenges. Not a written language, Sicilian lacked a standard orthography—an issue that Pitrè had to resolve to record and publish materials consistently. Pitrè also recognized that folk traditions came not just from the anonymous folk but from individuals who added their own expressions of creativity to the stories they told. Accordingly, he documented the source of each tale he collected, capturing basic information about his narrators, including their names, ages, occupations, and where they lived.

The vast majority of Pitrè's collected materials are published in Sicilian, which makes it difficult for scholars who lack the necessary language skills to access his folklore collections. Unlike the better-known collection of folktales by Jacob and Wilhelm **Grimm**, most of Pitrè's collection has not yet been translated into English or other languages, although a few of his folktales appear in English in T. F. Crane's *Italian Popular Tales* (1885) and in Italo **Calvino**'s *Italian Folktales* (1980, originally published in Italian in 1956 as *Fiabe italiane*). This situation is slowly changing; in 1991, fifty narratives from Pitrè's collection were translated into German and published under the title *Märchen aus Sizilien* (*Fairy Tales from Sicily*), and at the time of this writing, Jack **Zipes** was translating some of Pitrè's texts into English. *See also* Busk, Rachel Harriette; Gonzenbach, Laura; Italian Tales.

Further Readings: Cesaresco, Evelyn Martinengo. "Giuseppe Pitrè." *Folklore* 27 (1916): 314–16; Cocchiara, Giuseppe. "The Lesson of Pitrè." *The History of Folklore in Europe*. Translated by John N. McDaniel. Philadelphia: Institute for the Study of Human Issues, 1981. 351–71; ———. *Pitrè la Sicilia e il folklore*. Messina: Casa Editrice G. Anna, 1951; Gentile, Giovanni. *Giuseppe Pitrè*. Florence: G. C. Sansoni, 1940.

Linda J. Lee

Pitzorno, Bianca (1942–)

One of the most important Italian authors of **children's literature**, Bianca Pitzorno addresses critical realities of modern society through her surrealistic tales. Defying categorization as fairy tales, Pitzorno's stories are neither populated by traditional character types nor situated in faraway lands during unspecified eras. Rather, her characters demonstrate modern sensibilities and often inhabit contemporary times.

The majority of Pitzorno's **novel**s are written for preteens who can relate to the trials of her protagonists. Young readers might reflect upon their own destinies as they encounter on the page issues of everyday life from conflict in the family to the eternal struggles between adults and children, boys and girls, and the powerful and oppressed.

Occasionally, Pitzorno revisits a **literary fairy tale** before sweeping her unsuspecting reader off in a wildly different direction. *L'incredibile storia di Lavinia* (*The Incredible Story of Lavinia*, 1994) recounts the misfortunes of a hungry, cold little match girl who faces certain **death** on Christmas Eve, much like Hans Christian **Andersen**'s character. Pitzorno parodies the original tale by introducing a **fairy** who arrives by taxi and gives Lavinia a magic ring that transforms objects into excrement.

From the search for a modern witch in *Streghetta mia* (*My Little Witch*, 1997) to the imaginative story of Cora, whose foray into metropolitan magic causes wings that adults cannot see to sprout on her little brother's back (*La voce segreta* [*The Secret Voice*], 1998), Pitzorno in her stories carefully negotiates the blurry line between magic and reality from the innocent point of view of children. *See also* Childhood and Children; Italian Tales.

Further Reading: Salvadori, Maria Luisa. "Apologizing to the Ancient Fable: Gianni Rodari and His Influence on Italian Children's Literature." Translated by Alessandra Asteriti Mathys. *Lion and the Unicorn* 26.2 (2002): 169–02.

Gina M. Miele

Piumini, Roberto (1947–)

Italian author of **children's literature**, **poetry**, and tales, Roberto Piumini creates original narratives and preserves traditional stories through his modern, illustrated versions of Italian and European folktales and fairy tales. From 1995 to 2005, Piumini published *Fiabe Siciliane* (*Sicilian Folktales*, 1995), *Fiabe lombarde* (*Folktales from Lombardy*, 1995), *Fiabe toscane* (*Tuscan Folktales*, 1998), *Fiabe Venete* (*Venetian Folktales*, 1999), *Fiabe del Lazio* (*Folktales from Lazio*, 2002), *Fiabe d'Italia* (*Italian Folktales*, 2004), and *Fiabe Piemontesi* (*Piedmontese Folktales*, 2005). Borrowing narratives from nineteenth-century **folklore** collections, Piumini retold regional Italian fairy tales selected by editor Lella Gandini and illustrated by Anna Curti. Such popular **motif**s as seven-headed wizards, underwater palaces, statues that transform into maidens, magical feathers, and enchanted flutes all figure into these tales.

Piumini also rescripted the popular **Italian tales** "La favola del mercante" ("The Merchant's Fable," 2004); "L'ovo di Giotto" ("Giotto's Egg," 1988), a Tuscan tale rewritten by Piumini in ten scenes; and "Giovannin senza paura" ("Dauntless Little John," 2005), hailed by Italo **Calvino** in *Italian Folktales* (1956) as one of the simplest and most beautiful of folktales.

For the book series *C'era una fiaba . . .* (*Once upon a Fairy Tale . . .* , 2005–06), Piumini revisited classic fairy tales from "The Three Little Pigs" and "The Princess and the Pea" to **Aesop**'s "The Cicada and the Ant" and Giambattista **Basile**'s "The Cat **Cinderella**." Piumini's *Fiabe per occhi e bocca* (*Fairy Tales for Eyes and Mouth*, 2001) adds musicality to **"Little Red Riding Hood," "Hansel and Gretel,"** and **"Puss in Boots"** by presenting the tales in the *rima baciata* ("kissing rhyme").

Piumini partnered with Bianca **Pitzorno** on *Gli amici di Sherlock* (*Sherlock's Friends*, 2002–03), a series of mystery novels, and *Tre fiabe d'amore* (*Three Fairy Tales of Love*, 2005).

Further Reading: Salvadori, Maria Luisa. "Apologizing to the Ancient Fable: Gianni Rodari and His Influence on Italian Children's Literature." Translated by Alessandra Asteriti Mathys. *Lion and the Unicorn* 26.2 (2002): 169–02.

Gina M. Miele

Pizarnik, Alejandra (1936–1972)

An Argentinean poet of Russian immigrant parents, Alejandra Pizarnik was concerned in her **poetry** with a sense of exile and orphanhood and sought roots within literature. Among the sources she drew upon were folktales and fairy tales, particularly those from the European tradition.

In her work, Pizarnik picks out individual folktale **motif**s which then become key images in her poetry. Characters such as **Little Red Riding Hood** or the **wolf** are utilized for their fairy-tale associations of innocence or wickedness. Her work also alludes to orphans, babes in the wood, buried pirate treasure, and **princess**es. These fairy-tale elements help to build up a distorted picture of an idealized fairy-tale world into which the poet vainly tries to escape. Pizarnik mentions Hans Christian **Andersen**'s "paper palaces" in her notebooks; images such as his paper maiden in "The Steadfast Tin Soldier" are echoed in the tiny paper figures that populate some of Pizarnik's poems, for example, "Noche compartida en el recuerdo de una huida" ("Night Shared in the Memory of Fleeing," 1968), in which a little paper doll inhabits a tiny paper house.

From a specifically eastern European tradition, Pizarnik draws on the talismanlike doll and the figure of Lady **Death**. In the poems "Devoción" ("Devotion," 1967), "A tiempo y no" ("In Time and Not," 1968), and "Tragedia" ("Tragedy," 1971), these fairy-tale figures enter into absurd dialogues and are taken out of their fairy-tale context to be placed in a modernist setting reminiscent of Eugène Ionesco or Samuel Beckett.

Little Red Riding Hood provides the basis for the poem "La verdad del bosque" ("The Truth of the Wood," 1971). Here the poet equates her journey through **childhood** with Little Red Riding Hood's passage through the wood. This vision of innocence is self-consciously linguistic; the wood is described as being green only in the poet's mind. In this way, Pizarnik highlights clichéd forms of fairy tales that depend on the repetition of key recognizable elements for their meaning. The version in which both grandmother and child are eaten by the wolf is given an existential twist; for Pizarnik, we are all devoured through language itself. The wolf is then pasted into the poet's jotter, giving a visual equivalent of the linguistic borrowing operating in Pizarnik's use of fairy tales.

The wolf-woman or wolf-child is one folkloric role found in specifically eastern European folktales and used by Pizarnik in "Extracción de la Piedra de Locura" ("Extraction of the Stone of Folly," 1968). In traditional tales, the wolf-woman collects the bones of wolves and rebuilds the skeleton. She then sings, and the power of her song fleshes out the bones; the wolf runs away, transformed into a laughing woman. This life-giving and transforming power is what attracts Pizarnik to the image, since it expresses what her poetry aims for: words that are actions and have a quasi-incantatory power like the wolf-woman's song. *See also* Transformation.

Further Reading: Mackintosh, Fiona. "Babes in the *Bosque:* Fairy Tales in Twentieth-Century Argentine Women's Writing." *Fairy Tales and Feminism: New Approaches.* Edited by Donald Haase. Detroit: Wayne State University Press, 2004. 149–67.

Fiona J. Mackintosh

Planché, James Robinson (1796–1880)

English playwright, poet, and scholar James Robinson Planché wrote twenty-three musical extravaganzas based on fairy tales and also translated several **French tales** into English, especially those of Charles **Perrault** and Marie-Catherine d'**Aulnoy**. Beginning as a playwright in 1818, Planché occasionally treated **fairy** themes in **pantomime**s, melodramas, and **opera**s, but he did not write his first fairy-tale extravaganza until 1836, assisted by Charles Dance. The pair had already created five musical comedies based on Greek **myth**. Their first fairy-tale piece adapted the same theatrical form. This extravaganza, *Riquet with the Tuft*, was a **translation** of a French work, *Riquet à la houppe* (1811), by Antoine-Jean-Baptiste Simonnin. Prior to that time, English theatricals based on fairy tales were usually broad burlesques, incorporating characters and action unconnected with the original tale. Simonnin, however, had stayed close to Perrault's original story and written the dialogue to be consistent with the characters. The translation proved to Planché that such works could please English audiences. *Riquet* remained the only fairy extravaganza he ever translated; the others were original creations. Two more—**Puss in Boots** (1837) and **Blue Beard** (1839)—were written with Dance; the rest were solely Planché's.

For two decades, Planché wrote new fairy extravaganzas about once a year. Most had runs of several months, at the time a sign of considerable success. Although he wrote a great deal more, the fairy extravaganzas became so closely identified with Planché that critics regularly referred to him as "d'Aulnoy's cavalier." Most of the extravaganzas were produced and directed by the comic actors Charles James Mathews and Lucia Vestris. These productions won acclaim for their playful but consistent treatment of the characters and dialogue. They also featured increasingly elaborate stagings, with lavish costumes, ornate scenery, large orchestras, and cleverly contrived stage effects.

Planché grew increasingly ambivalent about such spectacle in his extravaganzas, for he felt that the lush visual and auditory elements detracted from the acting and the story. However, in the 1850s, he found an actor he considered ideal, Frederick Robson, whose powerful acting overshadowed any spectacle. Unlike Mathews and Vestris, Robson could evoke the darker emotions of the fairy stories as well as the humor. Many consider Planché's masterpiece, *The Yellow Dwarf* (1854), to be a vehicle created expressly for Robson. Even critics who normally dismissed extravaganza lauded Robson's performance, which made the grotesque title character both laughable and disturbing.

Also in the 1850s, Planché translated two volumes of fairy tales, the first containing the works of Perrault and a few others, and then a volume dedicated solely to d'Aulnoy. His translations are remarkable for their scholarly concern with documenting the nuances of references in the stories, for instance, identifying the toys and fashions of 1695 in abundant and detailed endnotes aimed at serious readers. Planché also created one final fairy-tale work after retiring, an 1865 verse **adaptation** of "**Sleeping Beauty**" titled *An Old Fairy Tale Told Anew*. *See also* Theater.

Further Reading: Buczkowski, Paul. "J. R. Planché, Frederick Robson, and the Fairy Extravaganza." *Marvels & Tales* 15 (2001): 42–65.

Paul James Buczkowski

Plays. *See* Theater

Poetry

There exists a long tradition of retelling folktales and fairy tales as **novel**s, dramas, and poems. A well-known folktale like "The Pied Piper of Hamelin" has been retold and illustrated in the form of poetic children's books innumerable times. Robert Browning in particular popularized the prose tale in his long poem "The Pied Piper of Hamelin" (1842), and the artist Kate Greenaway added thirty-five splendid **illustration**s to it in 1888. But before that, Johann Wolfgang von **Goethe** had already referred to the pied piper in his poem "Der Rattenfänger" ("The Rat-Catcher," 1804), and, about a century later, Ambrose Bierce published his poetic version "The Pied Piper of Brooklyn" (1910), in which the famous pied piper is transplanted to New York and changed into the preacher Henry Ward Beecher. In 1941, Bertolt Brecht went so far as to depict Adolf Hitler in his prophetic and satirical poem "Die wahre Geschichte vom Rattenfänger von Hamelin" ("The True Story about the Pied Piper of Hamelin"). Here, the piper (Hitler) first appears as a savior who excites the people because of his powerful piping (rhetoric, promises), but as he deceives the people, he is driven to madness by his own music (power) and eventually killed. There are many more poems in various languages that play off the pied-piper **motif**, indicating the universal appeal of this ambiguous figure. Even though the folktale is not retold in these poems, the mere allusions to the pied piper suffice to call into memory the message of this **cautionary tale**.

Fairy tales have received a similar treatment by many poets from different cultures. They do not always retell the traditional tale as such, but they certainly include many allusions to fairy tales, often basing their poems of numerous stanzas on a particular motif, which is interpreted in a new light. For a long time, poets have delighted in rephrasing the plot of traditional fairy tales in charming poetic versions. These poems were especially popular in the nineteenth century, and German authors such as Ludwig Uhland, August Heinrich Hoffman von Fallersleben, Heinrich Heine, Eduard Mörike, and Wolfgang Müller von Königswinter attained considerable recognition for their poetic ability of changing the prose tales into poetry. Numerous Anglo-American poets of that time were equally intrigued and influenced by the *Kinder- und Hausmärchen* (*Children's and Household Tales*, 1812–15) of the Brothers **Grimm**, notably Alfred, Lord **Tennyson**, Samuel Rogers, Bret Harte, Frances Sargent Osgood, Ethel Louise Cox, John Greenleaf Whittier, James N. Barker, Tom Hood, and Guy Wetmore Carryl. Their lengthy poems are usually nothing more than poetic variations of the traditional fairy tales, and they do not offer new interpretations or insights into the symbolic or psychological meaning of fairy tales.

Beginning with the twentieth century, poets lost their interest in retelling fairy tales in rhymed stanzas. These modern authors recognized the magical fairy-tale world, but they were interested in offering new interpretations of the symbolic messages of fairy tales that concern themselves with general human problems and dreams. After all, fairy tales deal with people as social beings who have some very basic experiences in common, as for example **birth**, maturation, courtship, **marriage**, work, advancing **age**, and **death**. In addition, the narratives contain such emotions as love, hate, distress, happiness, rivalry, and friendship, with many fairy tales presenting life's joys and tribulations in such contrasting pairs as good versus evil, success versus failure, poverty versus wealth, victory versus defeat, compassion versus harshness, humility versus pride—in short, black versus white. Since much of this is expressed metaphorically, it should not be surprising that poets feel themselves drawn toward these universal symbols of human behavior. There is, however, one major difference between the actual fairy tales and most of the modern poems. While the tales promise a happy end with joy for a much better life in the future, the poems usually stress the problems and imperfections of human existence, leaving the reader with a feeling of despair and pessimism. Nevertheless, the mere fact that poets react to the miraculous stories of the past is a sign that they too are interested in a better world. By juxtaposing fairy tales with modern social problems, they imply at least indirectly that solutions might just be found even if they are not as perfect as the endings of fairy tales.

Such disenchanted interpretations of fairy-tale motifs have become the norm in modern fairy-tale poetry, a subgenre of lyric poetry that has received considerable attention from scholars, notably because of poetry collections like *Disenchantments: An Anthology of Modern Fairy Tale Poetry* (1985) and *The Poets' Grimm: 20th Century Poems from Grimm*

Fairy Tales (2003). Some poets, such as Olga **Broumas**, Hayden Carruth, Roald **Dahl**, Franz Fühmann, Günter **Grass**, Ulla Hahn, Sara Henderson **Hay**, Randall **Jarrell**, Sarah Kirsch, Anne **Sexton**, and James Whitcomb Riley, have gained much scholarly recognition for their fairy-tale poetry. But there are literally countless poets who have written at least one if not two fairy-tale poems. In fact, one could perhaps go so far as to say that there is hardly a single poet who has not at least alluded to a traditional fairy tale in a poem. A few more names that deserve to be mentioned at least in an alphabetical list of German and Anglo-American poets are Julia Alvarez, Bruce Bennett, Elizabeth Brewster, Robert Gillespie, Louise Glück, Albrecht Goes, Robert Graves, Debora Greger, Donald Hall, Brenda Hillman, Marie Luise Kaschnitz, Galway Kinnell, Karl Krolow, Maxine Kunin, Eli Mandel, Roger Mitchell, Lisel Mueller, Howard Nemerov, Wilfred Owen, Robert Pack, Dorothy Lee Richardson, Eva Strittmatter, Phyllis Thompson, David Trinidad, and Edith Weaver. As these names indicate, it would be a mistake to delineate fairy-tale poetry along gender lines. Both female and male poets draw on fairy-tale motifs, with **women** occupying themselves somewhat more with issues inspired by **feminism**.

Very few poems maintain the happiness and harmony reached at the end of the original narratives. With the exception of some humorous or nonsensical poems, most modern poetic reactions to fairy tales are critical or satirical with plenty of irony also coming into play. One could in fact categorize many of these poems as **anti-fairy tale**s with a definite message of social criticism intended to encourage the reader to reevaluate questionable social norms and behavior. It could be argued that poets perhaps hope that their innovative anti-fairy tales will bring about transformations in human relationships and mores. Even though the critical stance of poets is expressed through the indirect messages of fairy-tale motifs, it is quite obvious that they are often making moral statements. And yet, that is not to say that there are not quite a few fairy-tale poems that reach truly lyrical heights of linguistic beauty and philosophical depth, as for example in Louise Glück's poem "Gretel in Darkness" (1975) and the end of Wilfred Owen's short poem "The **Sleeping Beauty**" (1963), where the speaker withdraws from the sleeping woman, having recognized that it was not his "part / To start voluptuous pulses in her heart."

The subject matter of fairy-tale poems is concerned with all aspects of life, including the interplay of love and hate, marriage and divorce, **gender** and **sexuality**, war and peace, and **politics** and economics, to name a few. The titles of the poems are frequently identical to those of the original fairy tales, thus immediately bringing to mind the happy ending of the narrative. However, the poem usually contradicts that perfect world by confronting it with a reality check, as in Mary Blake French's short poem "Ella of the Cinders" (1975), where the speaker—contradicting the fairy-tale stereotype—declares: "I am not physically perfect." But there are also those titles that do not reveal that the poem is in fact a reaction to a fairy tale, as for example Noelle Caskey's "Ripening" (1979; based on "**Sleeping Beauty**"), Sara Henderson Hay's "The Name" (1963; based on "Rumpelstiltskin"), and Barbara Unger's "Breasts" (1973; based on "Snow White and Rose Red").

Overall, sexual themes and sexual politics dominate fairy-tale poetry, something that is quite understandable if one considers the many erotic motifs in the traditional tales (see **Erotic Tales**). Especially well-known poets like Sexton, Broumas, and Helin Chasin have dealt with questions of feminism, gender issues, sexuality, sexual politics, and emancipation. While their poems might be shocking and aggressive at times, they are without a doubt important lyrical reinterpretations of Grimm tales. They raise many questions, as can be seen from "**Snow White**" (1976), a poem by Chasin in which the speaker admits how easy it is to "make do" by being beautiful, virtuous, and passive, waiting and dreaming to be saved.

There are many poems that are based on such themes as beauty, materialism, egocentricity, dishonesty, and vanity. Adults looking at fairy tales simply do not automatically buy into their perfect world. Randall Jarrell, the author of a number of philosophical fairy-tale poems, summarized the frustrations of people with a world void of happy endings. One of the best examples is his poem "The Märchen (Grimm's Tales)" from about 1945. Realizing that fairy tales deal with constant **transformation**s, Jarrell in this poem calls upon his reader to face the necessity of change in the modern world. That is perhaps the basic message of most fairy-tale poems commenting on social and human imperfections. Fairy tales are based on the principle of hope, and their poetic mutations, despite their pessimism and cynicism, cling to the proverb that "Hope springs eternal."

In addition to the dozens of fairy-tale poems that allude to specific tales, there are also those poems that deal in general with the meaning of fairy tales in the modern world. Alfred Corn's poem "Dreambooks" (1974), for example, reflects on modern life as the "Grim fairy tale" and its "Once upons." Another more general group could be termed fairy-tale collages, which combine a number of fairy-tale allusions into one poem. Gail White's poem "Happy Endings" (1978) is a telling example of such a poetic tour de force in its series of allusions to more than a dozen characters, motifs, and situations from "**Little Red Riding Hood**," "**Hansel and Gretel**," "Sleeping Beauty," and "**Cinderella**" all in the space of twenty-one very short lines.

The fairy tales from the *Children's and Household Tales* that have been dealt with most often by modern poets are primarily "The **Frog King**," "Rapunzel," "Hansel and Gretel," "Cinderella," "Little Red Riding Hood," "Sleeping Beauty," "Snow White," "Rumpelstiltskin," "Snow White and Rose Red," "The Maiden without Hands," "The **Fisherman and His Wife**," "The Juniper Tree," "Foundling," "The Goose Girl," and "Brother and Sister." Hans Christian **Andersen**'s well-known fairy tales "The Princess on the Pea" and "The Emperor's New Clothes" have also been dealt with in poems by Rolf Haufs, Maurice Lindsay, Christoph Meckel, Paul Muldoon, Gerda Penfold, Jane Shore, and Carolyn Zonailo. The Canadian poet Joy Kogawa includes similar themes as those found in the poems based on fairy tales from the Brothers Grimm in her poem beginning "I think I am that fabled princess" (1967).

All of these poems draw on some of the best-known fairy tales, thereby assuring meaningful communication with readers. A fairy-tale **aphorism** by Elias Canetti from 1943 represents a fitting summary for the purpose of the entire subgenre of fairy-tale poetry: "A closer study of fairy tales would teach us what we can still expect from the world." Indeed, these poems express the fact that modern life is unfortunately no fairy tale. The world is rather disenchanting most of the time, but perhaps modern anti-fairy tale poems might just bring back some of the enchantment of the traditional tales by reawakening the wish and hope for a more humane world. *See also* Ballad; Cante Fable; Duffy, Carol Ann; Marie de France; Pizarnik, Alejandra; Pushkin, Aleksandr; Rossetti, Christina Georgina.

Further Readings: Beaumont, Jeanne Marie, and Claudia Carlson, eds. *The Poets' Grimm: 20th Century Poems from Grimm Fairy Tales*. Ashland, OR: Story Line Press, 2003; Bechtolsheim, Barbara von. "Die Brüder Grimm neu schreiben: Zeitgenössische Märchengedichte amerikanischer Frauen." Dissertation. Stanford University, 1987; Hay, Sara Henderson. *Story Hour*. Fayetteville: University of Arkansas Press, 1982; Horn, Katalin. "Heilserwartung im Märchen und ihre Spiegelung in einer Auswahl moderner Lyrik." *Neophilologus* 73 (1989): 108–18; Hösle, Johannes. "Volkslied, Märchen und moderne Lyrik."

Akzente 7 (1960): 570–77; McClatchy, J. D., ed. *Anne Sexton: The Artist and Her Critics*. Bloomington: Indiana University Press, 1978; Mieder, Wolfgang, ed. *Disenchantments: An Anthology of Modern Fairy Tale Poetry*. Hanover, NH: University Press of New England, 1985; ———, ed. *Grimms Märchen—modern: Prosa, Gedichte, Karikaturen*. Stuttgart: Philipp Reclam, 1979; ———, ed. *Mädchen, pfeif auf den Prinzen! Märchengedichte von Günter Grass bis Sarah Kirsch*. Köln: Eugen Diederichs, 1983; ———. *Tradition and Innovation in Folk Literature*. Hanover, NH: University Press of New England, 1987; Ostriker, Alicia. "The Thieves of Language: Women Poets and Revisionist Mythmaking." *Signs* 8 (1982): 68–90; Sexton, Anne. *Transformations*. Boston: Houghton Mifflin Company, 1971; Zipes, Jack, ed. *Don't Bet on the Prince: Contemporary Feminist Fairy Tales in North America and England*. New York: Methuen, 1986.

Wolfgang Mieder

Pogorel'sky, Antony (1787–1836)

Antony Pogorel'sky, the pseudonym of Aleksei Perovsky, left behind a small but impressive literary heritage. He is usually regarded as the initiator of the fantastic tale within Russian prose and was clearly inspired by E. T. A. **Hoffmann** and Ludwig **Tieck.** Born out of wedlock, he nevertheless enjoyed a splendid education, followed by studies in philosophy and linguistics at the University of Moscow, from which he graduated in 1808. Rapidly becoming a participant of the progressive cultural movement of his time, Pogorel'sky launched his literary career with the translation of Nikolai Karamzin's sentimental novel *Bednaya Liza* (*Poor Liza*, 1796) into German in 1807. In 1825, he published his first fantastic tale, "Lafertovskaya makovnitsa" ("The Lafertovsky Poppy Cake"), in which he elaborates the well-known **motif** of a man who sells his soul to the **devil.** Using all the characteristics typical of the genre, Pogorel'sky also adds humor to his tale. Thereby he reveals a sense for parody as well as for mystification, which makes him a brilliant storyteller. It is, however, *Chyornaya kuritsa ili podzemnye zhiteli* (*The Black Hen or the Underground People*, 1829), his only story for children, that has become one of the earliest classics of Russian **children's literature.** The amusing and yet moralistic story presents a two-world structure, combining the realistic world of a boy named Alyosha in St. Petersburg of the 1790s with an underground world inhabited by little people. It was originally written for Pogorel'sky's nephew, the future writer Aleksei Tolstoy. *See also* Fantasy.

Further Reading: Berry, Thomas. "Aleksei Alekseevich Perovsky (Antonii Pogorel'sky)." *Russian Literature in the Age of Pushkin and Gogol: Prose*. Edited by Chrisine Rydel. Detroit: Gale, 1999. 256–63.

Janina Orlov

Politics

The *Oxford English Dictionary* defines "politics" as a plural noun signifying activities associated with governing, a particular set of political beliefs and principles, activities aimed at gaining power within an organization, and principles inherent in a sphere or activity. The significance of the word "politics" in folktales and folktale research exists in all four of these senses.

Folktales encompass a large number of narratives that are quasi-historical in their content. Many **legend**s and **epic**s recount reigns of particular monarchs and their ways of governance. Many performative folk genres are also related to particular political events, such as the coronation of medieval kings or the oral records of military campaigns. Very often, medieval histories were encapsulated in the narratives of the bards. Historical details are mixed with **fantasy**, and it is the job of the researcher to disentangle the two. The information obtained from this is often of a general nature, but one does gain an impression of the kind of popularity, or lack thereof, that rulers had in the mind of the general populace.

Folktales themselves reflect particular political beliefs and principles. Every narrative presents a worldview, and since folktale texts contain many layers of changes within them, this worldview is supposed to be that of many people. Analyses of the political beliefs of folktales have been the subject of much research. Folktales are often accused of being dominated by stories of **kings** and **queens**, but seen from another perspective, folktales exhibit the kinds of rulers that the **folk** appreciate or decry. Folktales of almost every cultural and linguistic zone contain images of just and ideal rulers, and also of the most brutal and tyrannical leaders.

Folktales narrate innumerable stories about individuals or groups and their activities to gain power within an organization. This may be a home, village, region, or country, and the protagonist may be male, female, a child, or even an animal. Folktales narrate the tasks that people undertake to gain power, and they tell of the knowledge that increases their power and of the physical attributes that make someone powerful. The narratives often narrate how power comes to a helpless individual due to certain acts, including their devotion to God.

Since politics are also the principles inherent in a sphere or activity, we need to understand how the folktale is itself political. The act of narration implies representation of reality. As such, the narration itself is a political act, that is, an act associated with governance, with political beliefs, and with gaining power. By such an act, a narrator immortalizes certain realities and his or her own perception of those. This representation and the perception are shared between the narrator and the listener and have the potential to be spread further. Propagation and communication of perspective constitute an essential political act, and therefore politics are inherent in the existence and narration of folktales. What makes the inherently political nature of folktales and fairy tales both interesting and threatening is that folktales have a wide range of recipients and therefore have the potential to influence political opinions on a vast scale.

"Politics" is also a very important idea in folk narrative research and fairy-tale studies. This concerns not the politics of the folktale or fairy tale per se but the politics of the **collectors**, **editors**, and scholars. Ever since the pioneering work conducted by the Brothers **Grimm**, the politics of collectors have been an important element in determining the kind of materials they gather and the ways in which they then edit and narrate oral texts in writing. Almost all shades of political opinion have been reflected in folktale research, but the influence of nationalist politics in the nineteenth century and of Marxist, fascist, and anticolonial politics in the twentieth century was most pronounced. Each of these different and sometimes contradictory ideologies found folktales to support its own brand of politics. The "fantastic" elements of the folktale make its relationship to reality difficult to decode and leads to multiple interpretations. Some scholars celebrate the power of this fantasy, while other see it as an escape from reality. In folktales, a poor girl can and does marry a **prince**, as if narrators were oblivious to the (un)reality of such an alliance and of their own class consciousness. However, one might also see this as a discourse that is counter to social reality and, as such, a critique of it. Scholars' politics have also caused new evaluations of folktales. For example, since the 1970s, feminist scholars have criticized the brand of **gender** politics reflected in folktales and fairy tales, especially very popular canonical tales like "**Cinderella**," "**Snow White**," and "**Little Red Riding Hood**." According to this view, the gender politics of folktales and fairy tales have perpetuated patriarchal values and power structures.

It is not possible to talk of the politics of folktales and fairy tales in general. They represent a vast repertoire of narratives that are not unified by an individual author or a common sociohistorical context. The diverse politics reflected in folktales and fairy tales are not universal but specific, whether the political exists at the level of the narrator, within the text, or in the interpretation of the text by scholars. *See also* Feminism; Nationalism.

Further Readings: Duggan, Anne E. *Salonnières, Furies, and Fairies: The Politics of Gender and Cultural Change in Absolutist France*. Newark: University of Delaware Press, 2005; Haase, Donald. "German Fairy Tales and America's Culture Wars: From Grimms' *Kinder- und Hausmärchen* to William Bennett's *Book of Virtues*." *German Politics and Society* 13.3 (1995): 17–25; Irwin, Robert. "Political Thought in *The Thousand and One Nights*." *Marvels & Tales* 18 (2004): 246–57; Kamenetsky, Christa. "Folklore as a Political Tool in Nazi Germany." *Journal of American Folklore* 85 (1972): 221–35; *Politique du conte*. Special issue of *Féeries* 3 (2006); Zipes, Jack. "Might Makes Right: The Politics of Folk and Fairy Tales." *Breaking the Magic Spell: Radical Theories of Folk and Fairy Tales*. Revised and expanded edition. Lexington: University Press of Kentucky, 2002. 23–46.

Sadhana Naithani

Polívka, Jiří (1858–1933)

Jiří Polívka, the pseudonym of Bohdan Kamiński, was a Slavic scholar, literary historian, ethnologist, collector, and writer. Polívka studied Slavic philology in Prague, received his doctorate in Vienna in 1882, and in 1884 qualified as a university professor in Prague. In addition to teaching the Czechoslovakian language at Czech universities, he chaired of the department of Slavic philology in Prague (from 1895) and served as vice president of the Czechoslovakian Academy of Sciences from 1920 to 1932.

Polívka authored numerous studies on philology, the history of Slavic literature, and Slavic ethnology. He was founder and editor of *Národopisný věstník českoslovnský* (*Journal of Czechoslovakian Ethnography*) and served as the editor of *Věstník slovanské filologie a starožitností* (*Journal of Slavic Philology and Relics of the Past*). In collaboration with Johannes **Bolte,** he published the monumental *Anmerkungen zu den Kinder- und Hausmärchen der Brüder Grimm* (*Annotations to Grimms' Children's and Household Tales*, 5 volumes, 1913–32), which updated and significantly expanded the notes and commentary that Jacob and Wilhelm **Grimm** had published with their tales. Polívka also produced the four-volume *Súpis slovenských rozprávok* (*Catalogue of Slovakian Fairy Tales*, 1923–1932), the largest scholarly edition of Slovakian fairy tales. *See also* Slavic Tales.

Further Reading: Gašparíková, Viera. "Polívka, Jiří." *Enzyklopädie des Märchens*. Edited by Kurt Ranke et al. Volume 10. Berlin: Walter de Gruyter, 2002. 1145–50.

Mojca Ramšak

Polygenesis

Polygenesis is an explanation for the occurrence of similar cultural traits in different cultures. The hypothesis of polygenesis proposes that similar cultural items—such as artifacts, ideas, and customs—may arise independently, in different parts of the world and at different times. Other ways of explaining similar cultural traits in different cultures are inheritance from a common ancestor and **diffusion** through borrowing. While these views share a quasi-historical outlook, the hypothesis of polygenesis is distinctly psychological in that it focuses on the unity of the human mind. The underlying assumption is that, given the fundamental unity of the human psyche, similar needs in comparable situations eventually yield similar inventions.

Andrew **Lang** was perhaps the most vocal nineteenth-century champion of "the theory of similar minds working on similar matter" to explain the wide recurrence of fairy-tale themes. But even Lang reserved "independent invention" for **motif**s, which he believed were evolved from human fancy everywhere, and acknowledged that recurrence of specific fairy-tale plots involves diffusion. More recently, Claude Lévi-Strauss revamped this strain of argument. While agreeing that diffusion and polygenesis need not be incompatible, he argued that folktale borrowings presuppose underlying equivalences between motifs evolved in different cultures. In this view, historical borrowings follow trends laid down by psychic constants—and the human mind is the ultimate enigma. *See also* Monogenesis.

Further Readings: Lang, Andrew. "Cinderella and the Diffusion of Tales." *Folk-Lore* 4 (1893): 413–33; Lévi-Strauss, Claude. *The Story of Lynx*. Chicago: University of Chicago Press, 1995. Chapters 16–17.

Francisco Vaz da Silva

Popeye the Sailor

An American animated cartoon, *Popeye the Sailor* originated as a newspaper comic strip created by Elzie Crisler Segar and first appeared in 1916. By 1933, *Popeye the Sailor* was picked up by Fleischer Studios, which introduced the animated character in an episode of *Betty Boop*. Fleischer Studios went on to produce the first Popeye series, which rivaled Mickey Mouse in popularity, until 1942. Thereafter *Popeye* was produced by Famous Studios (1942–57), King Features Syndicate (1960–61), and Hanna-Barbera Cartoons (1978–83). *Popeye* made its way back to the silver screen as a full-length live-action feature with Robert Altman's *Popeye* (1980), starring Robin Williams and Shelley **Duvall**.

Among the most important Fleischer Studios' Popeye films were three Technicolor featurettes drawing on the **Arabian Nights**: *Popeye the Sailor Meets Sindbad the Sailor* (1936), *Popeye Meets Ali Baba's Forty Thieves* (1937), and *Aladdin and His Wonderful Lamp* (1939). An honorable merchant and sailor in Antoine **Galland**'s version of the tale, **Sindbad** becomes, in the hands of Fleischer Studios, a piratelike figure played by Bluto. In Fleischer's version of "**Ali Baba**," Popeye is a member of the U.S. Coast Guard and receives a call warning of the ravages of Abu Hassan (the name of another character from the *Arabian Nights*) and his forty **thieves**. Popeye, Olive Oyl, and Wimpy sail across the globe to an Arab country—where camels fill up on gasoline—to save the local population. While *Popeye Meets Ali Baba's Forty Thieves* is fascinating in its pro-American and imperialist ideology, Fleischer Studios' version of "**Aladdin**" is of interest for its creative narrative technique. In the first scene, Olive Oyl is busy typing her own version of "Aladdin" in which she plays the role of the **princess** and Popeye that of Aladdin. At the end of the film, however, Olive Oyl learns that her story has been rejected, and the film concludes with Olive Oyl surrounded by scraps of paper. Interestingly, the production of these three films corresponds to the discovery of oil in the Persian Gulf in the 1930s. In 1950 and 1952,

Famous Studios reinscribed footage from Fleischers' *Ali Baba* and *Sindbad* in *Popeye Makes a Movie* and *Big Bad Sindbad*, framing the stories with Popeye as the storyteller.

In the short period between 1960 and 1961, King Features released a plethora of Popeye cartoons influenced by fairy tales. Jack Kinney, director of Walt **Disney**'s *Pinocchio* (1940) and a Mister Magoo version of *Arabian Nights* (1959), produced several of these: *Lil' Olive Riding Hood*, *Popeye and the Spinach Stalk*, *Olive Drab and the Seven Swee'peas*, *The Green Dancin' Shoes*, *Popeye the Ugly Ducklin'*, and *Swee'pea through the Looking Glass*. Paramount Pictures also produced several fairy-tale Popeyes for King, including *Mirror Magic* (a **mirror** informs Brutus he is not the strongest in the land), *Aladdin's Lamp*, and *Popeye Thumb*. **See also** Animation; *Arabian Nights* Films; Film and Video; Television; Thief of Bagdad Films.

Further Reading: Grandinetti, Fred M. *An Illustrated History of E. C. Segar's Character in Print, Radio, Television and Film Appearances, 1929–1993.* Jefferson, NC: McFarland and Company, 1994.

Anne E. Duggan

Portuguese Tales

Portugal is a small rectangle lying at the southwestern corner of both Spain and Europe and has been an independent state since the twelfth century. Portugal has been a proven storytelling country since the thirteenth century. Its southern region was the land of Arabs and Berbers for 600 years, between the eighth and the fourteenth centuries. Portugal grew from the north southward, winning land from occupiers through the thirteenth and fourteenth centuries, which extended to crusadelike conquests in North African countries. The "Moors" were the aliens against whom Portuguese cultural identity was first defined. Menhirs and other prehistoric landmarks still tend to be connected to "the time of the Moors." There are countless **legend**s of Moor women enchanted as snakes and guarding treasures in identifiable wells, brooks, grottoes, and boulders.

The Atlantic lines the southern and western coasts of Portugal, and expansion overseas in the fifteenth and sixteenth centuries was the answer to the people's confinement to a narrow stretch of the Iberian Peninsula. There are a widespread number of officially Portuguese-speaking countries sharing some of their folktales with Portugal, notably Brazil. Moreover, the Portuguese presence can be discerned in tales recorded in African countries such as Mozambique, Angola, São Tomé, Guinea-Bissau, and most particularly in Cape Verde. This same presence can also be detected in folktales from Goa, and the influence of Catholic missions in the **myth**s and legends of East Timor.

Stories with **fairies** can first be found in genealogy books. The *Livro de linhagens do Condo D. Pedro* (*Book of Lineages of the Count Dom Pedro*, c. 1340) includes two intriguing legends of family origins. The first is "The Goat-Footed Lady," the Melusine-type story of a supernatural wife who agrees to marry a human if he promises never to cross himself. When he breaks this promise, she flies away, taking her daughter with her and being forced to leave her son behind. The story proceeds with a meeting in the wilderness between the fairy and her son, in which she gives him a magic horse (Motif B401, Helpful horse) with which he saves his father from the Moors. This tale ends with the vampirical account of the metamorphosed fairy who years later sucks her victims' blood and needs to be appeased with offerings of animal entrails. In the second legend, "Dona Marinha," the fairy is a harmless, mute **undine** who finally speaks when the knight who first ravished her compels her to talk by threatening to throw their child in the fire if she doesn't. She screams, and a piece of flesh is dislodged from her throat. The legend ends like a fairy tale: because she now speaks as a full-fledged human, the knight marries her. Her name—Dona Marinha— becomes the Marinho family name.

In the *Crónica geral de Espanha de 1344* (*General Chronicle of Spain*), a Portuguese adaptation of the Spanish *Crónica general*, there is the intriguing tale of King Rotas, a unique account connected with the foundation of Toledo. King Rotas is a wise man who leaves his kingdom in the east and makes his way to the west. Along the journey, he copies into a book the writings found in seventy cylinders with "all the knowledge and nature of things and how they should be dealt with." While he travels westward, he predicts the fall of Troy and gives Rome its name. He at last settles in a cave as a wild man, befriended by a **dragon**, in what later becomes Toledo. He is found and agrees to marry the **king**'s daughter. Later, he grants the kingdom to his two sons and, after returning to the dragon's cave, he leaves to wander the world once again.

In the fifteenth century, an anonymous monk wrote a book of **exempla** for his sister, a nun, the *Orto do esposo* (*The Orchard of the Spouse*), where one reads tales like The **Death** of a Miser (ATU 760A*), The Treasure Finders Who Murder One Another (ATU 763), Late Revenge (ATU 960B), The **Devil** and the Evil Woman (ATU 1164), The One-eyed Husband (ATU 1419C), and The Wager That Sheep Are Hogs (ATU 1551). Many of these are found earlier in the *Gesta Romanorum* (*Deeds of the Romans*), and some still persist in Portuguese **oral tradition**.

The well-loved playwright Gil Vicente (1465–1536) staged popular folktales such as The Man and His Wife Build Air Castles (ATU 1430), Old Hildebrand (ATU 1360C), and The Old Maid on the Roof (ATU 1479*). These plays exude spontaneity and gusto for life, which were soon to be cut short by repression following the Council of Trent (1545–63). This can be felt in *Contos e histórias de proveito e exemplo,* a collection of forty tales by G. Fernandes Trancoso, all formatted in the exempla tradition and bitterly controlled by the censorship of the Inquisition. Its first edition of 1575 seems to have been wiped out except for one surviving copy, now at the Oliveira Lima Library in the Catholic University of Washington (published in a facsimile edition by the Lisbon National Library in 1982). Three tales of this first edition were banned from later editions—due no doubt to their many magical and marvelous elements—and there would be no trace of their existence had that one copy not survived.

Nevertheless, many oral narratives must have found an underground way to survive. A manuscript by sixteenth-century poet Fernão Rodrigues Lobo Soropita alludes to the Three Citrons of Love appearing in a festive interlude (later published in 1868 in Soropita's *Poesias e prosas inéditas*). This was a good thirty years before Giambattista **Basile** published his Neapolitan version of the tale, "Le tre cetre," in 1636 (ATU 408, The Three Oranges). Furthermore, the seventeenth-century writer F. Manuel de Melo quotes the rhyme "Oh Maria, so sweet in your death, so bitter in life," which is associated with Portuguese versions of The Basil Maiden (ATU 879). The writing down of these tales was likely to have been forbidden by the censorship following the Council of Trent. These early allusions to both tales seem to indicate that they were common knowledge well before they came to be registered and published in the nineteenth century.

Long novelesque tales printed in **chapbook**s and sold at fairs are documented in Portugal since the sixteenth century. Throughout the seventeenth century they proved to be resistant to the onslaughts of censorship, though many have been lost and are only documented in lists. Chapbooks were very popular in the eighteenth and nineteenth centuries, and stories like Robert the Devil, The Grateful Dead (ATU 505), and *Princesa Magalona* (ATU 861A, Abduction at the Rendezvous) had long-lasting fame and were republished until the 1960s. Versified **adaptation**s of such stories are still printed in Brazilian chapbooks.

The earliest transcription of a folktale with a scholarly purpose appeared in 1720 in Rafael Bluteau's *Vocabulario Portuguez & Latino*, with one **joke** on the stubbornness of **women** (ATU 1365B, Cutting with the Knife or the Scissors). But we have to wait another hundred years for further proof of an interest in folk literature, which developed during the Romantic movement through the need to reach the ethnic roots of the nation. In the 1820s, the writer and poet Almeida Garrett published a collection of Portuguese **ballads** (romances) and wrote a long medievalistic poem inspired by one of them. The individual traits of one's own country were easier to find in folk poetry than in the "surprising universality of folktales" (Teófilo Braga's words, in *O Povo Portuguê* [*The Portuguese People*], 1885). Fifty years had to pass for the interest in ballads to extend to folktales, with Teófilo Braga, Adolfo Coelho, and Consiglieri Pedroso. In 1870, Braga published an article on fairy tales—"Os contos de fadas" ("The Stories of Fairies")—in which three Portuguese folktales were published with an ethnographic purpose (ATU 325, The Magician and His Pupil; ATU 408, The Three Oranges; and ATU 563, The Table, the Donkey and the Stick).

The first published collection of folktales, *Contos populares portugueses* (*Portuguese Folktales*), was by ethnographer Adolfo Coelho and appeared in 1879. The collection included seventy-five folktales, preceded by an introduction in which Coelho identifies the **collectors** and most of the **informant**s and declares a preoccupation with accurate transcriptions. The collection, with no variants, was meant to show the scope of Portuguese material, and Coelho's introduction includes an informed comparative study of his corpus with myths and the folktales of other cultures. Coelho's main interests had to do with Portuguese ethnography and educational problems. In 1879, he published a book of Portuguese folktales meant for children, but he did not encourage the **translation** of foreign folktales, since these might endanger the purity of the Portuguese oral tradition. In 1883, Teófilo Braga published *Contos tradicionaes do povo portuguez* (*Traditional Tales of the Portugeuse People*) in two volumes, the first with fifty-seven fairy tales and nearly seventy **novella**s and jokes; the second contained early Portuguese literary sources of folktales followed by legends and **fable**s. The third collection to appear is that of Z. Consiglieri Pedroso, *Portuguese Folk-Tales*, published by the Folklore Society of London in 1882. Although no variants of the same tale were published in the English edition, Pedroso makes a point of presenting several versions of tales widespread in Portugal in his 1910 publication, being well aware of the danger of mistaking a particularly well-told version for what he called a "genetic type." Two large volumes of regional folktales and toponymic legends of the Algarve appeared in 1900 and 1905, collected by F. X. Ataíde Oliveira; these tales are often tinged with an excessive interest to make them clear and likeable (*Contos tradicionais do Algarve*). He also published a curious collection of local legends of enchanted Moor women (*As mouras encantadas e os encantamentos no Algarve*, 1898), in which he describes his endeavors to persuade women to tell narratives that they had silenced for fear of "doubling the enchantment of the Moor women."

Several **folklore** and philological journals with articles about oral traditions and collected folktales also appeared at the end of the nineteenth century. These included the *Revista Lusitana* (1887–1943) and regional journals like *A Tradição* (1899–1904)—with tales collected by Tomás Pires in the region of Alentejo—and *Revista do Minho* (1885–1911), with tales from the northern region of Minho. Several other journals, some of them short-lived, reflect, together with folklore societies, the keen interest in ethnography and folklore in the first decades of the twentieth century.

José Leite de Vasconcellos, who remains the most outstanding scholar in Portuguese folk-loristic studies, is also the last of the old school of specialists in a cluster of then-related subjects, such as philology, anthropology, ethnology, and folklore. The journal *Revista Lusitana*, which he founded, reflects this interdisciplinary outlook. He left behind a huge gathering of folktale material, which came to be published posthumously in two volumes, *Contos populares e lendas* (*Folktales and Legends*, 1964–66), containing a corpus of more than 600 items. Earlier in the twentieth century, the well-loved rewriter of traditional fairy tales for children Ana de Castro Osório created her own publishing company for that sole purpose, with countless publications that included translations of tales by the Brothers **Grimm** and Hans Christian **Andersen**.

Folktale studies in Portugal were practically ignored during the middle third of the twentieth century. Linguists and philologists, on the other hand, did accurate **fieldwork** for their own specific purposes. The folktales found in the studies by linguists and philologists were later assembled and published as *Contos populares portugueses (Inéditos)* (*Portuguese Folktales [Previously Unpublished]*, 1984–86), a collection of 734 previously unpublished folktales. Today, there is an Archive of Portuguese Folktales (APFT) in the Centro de Estudos Ataíde Oliveira (CEAO) at the University of the Algarve (see **Archives**). The tales preserved in the APFT are represented in the *Catalogue of Portuguese Folktales* published by Isabel Cardigos in 2006.

Modern Portuguese writers using the fairy tale as a model for their fiction are mostly women. One notable exception is José Régio, with his metaphorical novel *O príncipe com orelhas de Burro* (*The Prince with Donkey's Ears*, 1942), which was turned into a film by Antonio Macedo in 1978. One can perhaps find two categories of authors of adult fairy tales in Portugal: those, like Régio, who use well-known tales or fairy-tale motifs as a reference on which they impose their own subversive palimpsests; and those who work with the fairy tale's deep resonance with earth magic and the feminine voice. Examples of the first category are Ana Teresa Pereira, an author of gothic horror and vampire stories with strong intertextual links to the world of film and fairy tales; and Sophia Mello Breyner, a poet and writer of children's fairy tales, but also of "A Gata Borralheira" (1984), a severe reflection on the duality of Cinderella. We should add a shocking version of **Little Red Riding Hood** by António Pina (2005) inspired by a series of six paintings by Portuguese artist Paula **Rego**. In the second category, there is *A mãe de um rio* (*The Mother of a River*, 1981) by Agustina Bessa Luís, a notable contemporary woman writer. She tells the story of a **peasant** girl whose golden fingers fate her to inherit the motherhood of a river for a thousand years—one of the three stories in *Inquietude* (1998), a **film** by Manoel de Oliveira. The second category would also include Hélia **Correia**'s *Montedemo* (*Devil's Mountain*, 1983), which brings the voice of legend ("contam," that is, "some say") and the indefinite **time** of fairy tale together with the historical precision of postcolonialism and **tourism**.

In the realm of modern Portuguese media, João César Monteiro was a remarkable filmmaker who experimented with fairy-tale based plots. He first experiments came in films of strong ethnographic appeal and medievalistic auras, such as *Veredas* (*Footpaths*, 1977), based on the tale type known as The Magic Flight (ATU 313); and *Silvestre* (1982)—a confluence of an Iberian ballad ("The Maiden Warrior") and tale of The Robber Bridegroom (ATU 955). Monteiro also made amusing films inspired by The Three Oranges (ATU 408) and The Two Travelers (ATU 613). His last experiment—based on the play *Schneewittchen* (*Snow White*, 1901) by Swiss writer Rober Walser—was *Branca de Neve* (2000), an outrageous innovation with just a voice on a black screen. In the late 1970s, state **television** financed series of shorts on Portuguese folktales, within which interesting pictures were made such as "The Soup Stone" and "The Grain of Corn," two **cartoons** by Artur Correia.

Further Readings: Baubeta, Patricia Anne Odber de. "The Fairy-Tale Intertext in Iberian and Latin American Women's Writing." *Fairy Tales and Feminism: New Approaches.* Edited by Donald Haase. Detroit: Wayne State University Press, 2004. 129–47; Cardigos, Isabel. *Catalogue of Portuguese Folktales.* Helsinki: Academia Scientiarum Fennica, 2006; Consiglieri Pedroso, Z. *Portuguese Folk-Tales.* Translated by Henriqueta Monteiro. 1882. New York: B. Blom, 1969; Donati, Cesarina. *Tre racconti proibiti di Trancoso.* Rome: Bulzoni, 1983; Owen, Hilary. *Portuguese Women's Writing, 1972 to 1986: Reincarnations of a Revolution.* Lewiston: Edwin Mellen Press, 2000. 85–104.

Isabel Cardigos

Postmodernism

"Postmodernism," a notoriously elusive term, tends to be used in one of two closely interrelated ways. First, it is used to indicate a particular type of aesthetic practice evident since the early 1970s in literature, architecture, **music**, **dance**, and the visual **art**s. Postmodernism is in this sense a loosely defined artistic genre, the characteristics of which include stylistic eclecticism, a playfully serious drawing of attention to art's workings, and the deliberate blurring of distinctions between high art and popular culture. Second, postmodernism is used very broadly to indicate a historical period, again beginning roughly in the 1970s, characterized primarily by globalization and the multinational corporation, but also by the second wave of Euro-American **feminism** and the ongoing ramifications of postwar decolonization (see **Colonialism**).

Attendant on postmodernism in both senses of the term has been a powerful wave of social and cultural theory, occupied in particular with ideology: with dominant modes of understanding and living in the modern world, and with those emergent ideologies of the late twentieth century concerned both with critiquing and overturning conventional wisdom. Folktales and fairy tales, as genres of fictional narrative, have been the subject of postmodernist scrutiny, as have most cultural artifacts. There is, however, a more specific reason for the establishment of a relationship between postmodernism and, in particular, the fairy tale. Common to much postmodernist theorizing, especially that produced in the philosophical tradition of continental Europe that takes its bearings from Karl Marx, Sigmund **Freud**, and Friedrich Nietzsche, is an antifoundationalism: that is, a critical attitude to the idea that underpinning our knowledge and understanding of the world and ourselves are certain indisputable principles or truths. (One useful means of distinguishing postmodernism from modernism is to say that modernism believes in the possibility of foundations, while postmodernism is skeptical.) Folktales and fairy tales have been seen at various points in history as offering potent expressions of fundamental facts of life: on questions of morality, of the means to succeed in the world, and of parent/child and male/female relations. Fairy tales, as imbibed by the young, have served to inculcate such facts of life and so have worked as foundations in their own right.

Postmodernism in its various guises proposes a sustained critique of such foundational thinking, as is evident in much of the fairy tale-related work, both creative and critical, produced since the early 1970s. Writing in this vein can be conceived variously as postmodernist: in terms of how it is written—its form—and according to its particular ideological concerns, whether or not the latter are made explicit. It is possible to pick out three recurring and intimately related preoccupations: the self (what tends in academic writing to be termed "the subject"), history, and the text.

The Subject

Ideas and theories about the component parts of our selves—our **gender, race and ethnicity**, social class, **sexuality**, and so forth—tend on the whole to be normative and so to posit fixed models of good and healthy personhood. Folktales and fairy tales offer potent representations of subjects and, in the tales' clear narrative and moral purpose, of how and why certain types of people succeed while others necessarily fail. Postmodernist fairy tales strive to lay bare the workings of such models of subjectivity and so to undermine their truth claims. A classic of the genre is Angela **Carter**'s story collection, *The Bloody Chamber* (1979), in which the alleged norms of fairy-tale personhood—the thrusting hero, the passive heroine, the innocent young girl, and the wicked stepmother—are the subject of sustained scrutiny. Like much of the fairy-tale literature of the 1970s and 1980s, *The Bloody Chamber* offers startling reversals of generic convention: a sexually inquisitive and far-from-passive Beauty (from **"Beauty and the Beast"**) and **Little Red Riding Hood**, for example. To replace one norm with another is not a postmodernist strategy, however, in that the idea of the norm, or foundation, remains in place. Postmodernism is concerned with the ways in which all general and generalized models of behavior and morality are fictions that have acquired the status of truth, a process that requires the denigration or silencing of other competing possibilities—possibilities that are themselves conceived in relation to the norm from which they appear thus to deviate. *The Bloody Chamber*, as a postmodernist work, is at pains to dissect the workings of subject formation, rather than straightforwardly to replace one model with another. Carter's representation of an inquisitive and self-possessed Little Red Riding Hood thus figures within the context of a story concerned with the complex drama of desire that goes to make up, in this case, heterosexual relations, a drama that necessarily involves power but does not necessarily require domination. The same is true of fairy-tale influenced fiction by the likes of Jeanette Winterson (*The Passion*, 1987; *Sexing the Cherry*, 1989) and Emma **Donoghue** (*Kissing the Witch*, 1997), in which the vivid dramas of the genre are harnessed to a contemporary queer (gay and lesbian) aesthetic (see **Gay and Lesbian Tales**). These fictions are not shy of proposing alternative models of behavior. Such proposals are, however, acknowledged as open and provisional rather than closed and fixed, as necessary fictions rather than replacement truths.

In addition to deconstructing conventions of subjectivity, postmodernism calls into question the commonsense notion that the self, while influenced by individual circumstances and experiences, is in part an innate, internal, and private thing, constitutive of a unique and personal identity. The discrete and autonomous self is another foundational **myth**, against which postmodernist theory proposes a subject that is the effect of the social and cultural materials and practices that surround it. Accordingly, folktales and fairy tales do not just reflect meanings out in the world but, as experienced, serve in the forming and maintaining of the self. Such a process is explored at length in the work of Margaret **Atwood**. The **novel** *Lady Oracle* (1976), for example, dramatizes the manner in which the norms of the fairy tale—the fairy-tale romance, in this case—are internalized and so serve to structure the protagonist's sense of her self and of others. However, because the self thus conceived is a manifold fiction and not an extrasocial fact, it is open to change. Atwood represents female protagonists who are able to revise their fictional selves by looking to alternative narrative possibilities. In the case of *Lady Oracle*, she looks to the **Bluebeard tale type** as a dramatization both of the dangers of romantic ideals and of cunning routes to its subversion.

History

Foundational myths are maintained in part via the elision or erasure of their provenance, and so of the details of their particular history. This is strikingly true of folktales and fairy tales, which tend to be thought of in one of two ways: as archetypal expressions of the human **storytelling** impulse, an impulse of universal scope and appeal, or as the relatively pure expression of particular national or ethnic groups. The abstracted and sometimes fantastical environments of the tales lend themselves to ahistorical readings; and the venerable traditionality of the tales in turn serves to authenticate, as age-old wisdom, particular models of morality and patterns of behavior. This is the fairy tale conceived as what Jack **Zipes** calls a "myth."

Folkloristics has long sought to provide a history of aspects of the tale traditions, but the era of postmodernism has witnessed significant developments in **sociohistorical approaches**. While not necessarily postmodernist in any explicitly programmatic sense, the work of a range of scholars can be considered as such in its concern to undermine or overturn the ahistorical or generalizing tendency in thinking about the tales. The work of these scholars insists on the complex historicity of folktales and fairy tales. This has been true particularly in the case of scholarship on the tales of Jacob and Wilhelm **Grimm**. Ideas of unproblematic oral transmission, of the unmediated voice of the "**folk**," of an ethnically pure narrative tradition, and of undoctored transcription have been methodically and extensively dismantled in the work of Heinz Rölleke, Maria Tatar, Ruth B. Bottigheimer, and Linda **Dégh**, among others. As a result, the genre of the folktale as disseminated forcefully by the Grimms, and later through the nineteenth century, emerges in all its historical particularity. The same historicist tendency can be seen in work on early collections of **Italian tales** (by Nancy L. Canepa) and on **French tales** (by Lewis C. Seifert and Catherine Velay-Vallantin), each of which has contributed to an expanded and considerably complicated picture of the rise in Europe of the fairy tale as a literary genre.

An offshoot of this ongoing critical and editorial work has been a greatly expanded body of tales, stretching far beyond the geographically and historically narrow confines of the canon sanctioned by Walt **Disney** on the one hand and the collections of Charles **Perrault** and the Grimms on the other. A large number of newly restored tales has served significantly to discredit all claims to have identified true or authentic folktale types or meanings. What emerges in the case of gender criticism—in the work of Marina **Warner** and Angela Carter, for example—is a far more diverse set of representations of femininity, well beyond the stereotype of the passive heroine. Contemporary revisionist tales thus appear not as inauthentic interpolations but as properly in keeping with a diverse and living narrative tradition.

Similarly, postmodernist fiction demonstrates a persistent interest in history, despite allegations to the contrary. Of particular concern has been the extent to which history is always in part a textual matter, the product of an unavoidably subjective interpretative engagement with the material evidence of the past. Fictional narration and historiography are thus intimately related practices. While few would claim that history is a fairy tale, the generic conventions of such fictions can serve variously to shape conceptions of historical change, as well as to influence profoundly individual expectations at particular historical moments. Such ideas have been explored in a number of influential postmodernist texts. A. S. **Byatt**'s award-winning novel, *Possession* (1990), shuttles between the events and texts of the nineteenth century and scholarly efforts in the late twentieth century to interpret such matters. Embedded in the novel are two nineteenth-century fairy tales, the allure but ultimate resistance of which as historical evidence is emblematic of the novel's postmodernist understanding of history as a matter of ongoing textual construction. In a related vein, Salman **Rushdie**'s *Midnight's Children* (1981) makes extensive use of the **Arabian Nights** to tell its skewed fictional account of Indian independence. In the course of the novel, the tale collection becomes variously a way for an individual protagonist to recount his experiences, a self-consciously fantastical means of dramatizing the epochal events of nation formation, and, in the collection's own complicated cross-cultural life, an allegory of the constitutive mixings of postcolonial history. The *Arabian Nights* is thus woven into a narration of real historical events, an integral part of a novel that mixes fact and fiction in an enactment of the narrative process that is a necessary element of all historical accounting.

The Text

Along with historicity and theories of the subject, postmodernist writing, both critical and creative, pays particular attention to the status of the folktale and fairy tale as text. Rather than treat straightforwardly the content and meaning of the tales, after the manner of a real-life drama, such writing works to draw attention to their textuality—to language, form, generic conventions, and narrative structure. It is in this sense that postmodernist literature is described as **metafiction**: literary prose that parades its own workings, not merely to play games with the reader but to explore the extent to which conceptions of the world and of others, experienced both in fiction and beyond, are always mediated by language. Again, such writing is similar in intent to the historicist scholarship discussed above, in which close attention is paid to subtle changes in the language of the tales across time and in different historical contexts. A detailed reading of the text of the tales can produce surprising results. For example, rather than accept at face value the *moralités* (**moral**s) appended to the tales of Perrault's *Histoires ou contes du temps passé* (*Stories or Tales of Times Past*, 1697), Winfried Menninghaus treats them as linguistic objects in their own right. What emerges from such an analysis is a pervasive slippage between tale and moral, such that the latter no longer appears as a natural or self-evident summary of foregoing events. The mismatch is revealed precisely by a concentration on form and language rather than merely on content.

The formal strategies of postmodernist metafiction are many and varied. Texts such as Robert **Coover**'s *Briar Rose* (1997) present multiple interlocking accounts and **variant**s of the same basic tale ingredients, thereby frustrating any attempt to treat as final a particular version or moral purpose. The same device is evident in Carter's *The Bloody Chamber* and is taken to its logical conclusion in Suniti **Namjoshi**'s *Building Babel* (1996), in which the form of the **Internet**, with its potentially limitless and unforeseen links, is used as a model for postmodernist tale telling. The text is left open and unfinished, with the reader invited to visit a Web site and submit his or her own thoughts and variations, thus undermining the apparent closure of the material text. Perhaps the most eloquent plea for limitless storytelling in this vein is Rushdie's *Haroun and the Sea of Stories* (1990), an allegory against the tyranny of endings that borrows as its model not only the cyclical story feasts of the *Arabian Nights* and the **Kathasaritsagara**, but also the folktale tradition itself, imagined in liquid form as a living stream of story.

The subversion of expectations is another means of unsettling readers and so of drawing attention to the workings of genre. This can be achieved through absurdist **parody**, as in Donald **Barthelme**'s pop art **Snow White** (1967); through the mixing of genres, as in Carter's stories and novels, which swoop from high to folk art, or Coover's *Pinocchio in Venice* (1991), which juxtaposes European art with the *commedia dell'arte*; through frame breaking, whereby characters from one narrative space invade another, as in John Barth's many attempts to grapple with the *Arabian Nights*; and through formal narrative strategies such as the overt manipulation of plot, the sharing of narration between multiple voices, and the use of anachronistic allusions, each of which can be found variously in the work of the writers mentioned here.

Self-referentiality and role reversal are now staples even of **children's literature**, as demonstrated to wonderful effect in the Pocket Postman books by Allan and Janet Ahlberg and the Seriously Silly Stories series by Laurence Anholt. The same is true of **television** and cinema, most flagrantly in the likes of **Shrek** (2001), an endlessly knowing fairy-tale **film** constituted almost entirely from a series of audience-friendly parodies. Yet it is not as self-standing narratives that the folktale and fairy tale are experienced most commonly by young audiences of the twenty-first century, but rather through the subtle, even subliminal allusions that continue to litter the world of television drama and **advertising**. The popular media tend intermittently to invoke the received wisdom of the tales as a means in particular of harnessing the desires and expectations of susceptible viewers. It is against the perpetuation of such myths that postmodernist literature and criticism has directed its attention. Far from being relativist or in thrall to aesthetic pleasure as an end in itself, as is sometimes suggested, the skepticism of postmodernism toward conventional myths and putative truths, coupled with its playful attention to art's designs, requires of its audience a questioning alertness to the workings of language and signification. The folktale and fairy tale as investigated in postmodernist writing are not just objects of critique but the means of imagining new possibilities, both artistic and ideological. As such, postmodernism proposes the tales as viable narratives for the twenty-first century.

Further Readings: Bacchilega, Cristina. *Postmodern Fairy Tales: Gender and Narrative Strategies*. Philadelphia: University of Pennsylvania Press, 1997; Carter, Angela. *The Virago Book of Fairy Tales*. London: Virago, 1990; Menninghaus, Winfried. *In Praise of Nonsense: Kant and Bluebeard*. Translated by Henry Pickford. Stanford, CA: Stanford University Press, 1999; Preston, Cathy Lynn. "Disrupting the Boundaries of Genre and Gender: Postmodernism and the Fairy Tale." *Fairy Tales and Feminism: New Approaches*. Edited by Donald Haase. Detroit: Wayne State University Press, 2004. 197–212; Warner, Marina. *From the Beast to the Blonde: On Fairy Tales and Their Tellers*. New York: Farrar, Straus and Giroux, 1994; Zipes, Jack. *Fairy Tale as Myth/Myth as Fairy Tale*. Lexington: University Press of Kentucky, 1994.

Stephen Benson

Pourquois Tale. *See* Etiologic Tale

Pourrat, Henri (1887–1959)

A French author whose prolific works centered on the **folklore** and people of Auvergne, Henri Pourrat is best known for *Gaspard des montagnes* (*Gaspard of the Mountains*, 1921–31) and the thirteen-volume *Le trésor des contes* (*The Treasury of Tales*, 1948–62). Destined to study agronomy and admitted in 1905 to the prestigious Institut Agronomique in Paris, Pourrat was forced to return to his native Ambert when he was diagnosed with tuberculosis. Because his condition necessitated a calm regime, Pourrat dedicated his time to reading and writing and began publishing various pastoral and comical pieces on local life in the periodicals *Echo de la Dore* and *La veillée d'Auvergne*. The latter, a monthly regionalist revue, published Pourrat's first tale, "Comment saint Martin pêcha au grand jour de Pâques" ("How Saint Martin Fished on the Great Day of Easter") in 1909. Around 1910, Pourrat began to collect popular songs and tales systematically. His work as a collector, however, was not exactly scientific. Pourrat did not transcribe word for word the tales he collected, nor did he document his sources. Rather, he sought to relate the context of the telling, and his collections in fact should be considered retellings.

Pourrat's early **fieldwork** culminated in *Gaspard of the Mountains*, whose first volume won the Prix du Figaro in December 1921, *Le Figaro* publishing the first volume in serial form before Albin Michel issued the full text in May 1922. Organized in four parts, each containing seven *veillées* or evening gatherings, the **novel** attempts to reproduce the oral **storytelling** setting. "La vieille," Old Marie, is the principal narrator who recounts the adventures of the peasant Gaspard, whose story gets interrupted by other *veillées* within the **frame narrative**. References to such figures as Geneviève de Brabant and Little **Thumbling** are scattered throughout. In 1931, the complete two-volume *Gaspard* was awarded the French Academy's Grand Prize for the novel.

Other notable works by Pourrat include *Contes de la bûcheronne* (1936), which consists of eighteen tales recounted by the wives of woodcutters (*bûcherons*); *Vent de mars* (*March Wind*, 1941), awarded the Prix Goncourt; and, of course, his seminal *Treasury of Tales*. Generally, Pourrat blends elements of well-known stories from the **oral tradition** and from collections by writers such as Noël du Fail, Charles **Perrault**, and the Brothers **Grimm**. For instance, Pourrat's "La branche qui chante, l'oiseau de vérité et l'eau qui rend verdeur de vie" ("The Tale of the Singing Branch, the Bird of Truth, and the Water of Youth") resembles tales by Giambattista **Basile** and Marie-Catherine d'**Aulnoy**, which may also have entered into the oral tradition of Auvergne. Through the **collecting** of tales and his approach to retelling them, Pourrat sought to preserve the oral tradition and culture of Auvergne for future generations. *See also* French Tales.

Further Readings: Pupier, Pierre. *Henri Pourrat et la grande question*. Paris: Sang de la terre, 1999; Zipes, Jack. "Henri Pourrat and the Tradition of Perrault and the Brothers Grimm." *The Brothers Grimm: From Enchanted Forests to the Modern World*. 2nd edition. New York: Palgrave Macmillan, 2002. 135–51.

Anne E. Duggan

Pratchett, Terry (1948–)

Best-selling British **fantasy** author Terry Pratchett has written fantasy and science fiction for both adults and children but is known mostly for the roaring success of the Discworld series, an acute and comic ongoing **parody** of both traditional sword-and-sorcery and contemporary culture. While these are highly popular **novel**s, Pratchett is notable for his self-conscious and intelligent awareness of narrative, and a recurring nod to folkloric and fairy-tale patterns can be found across his writing.

Characters in the Discworld series include the stock **archetype**s of both fairy tale and fantasy, most notably **witch**es, trolls, heroes, and talking animals; however, this is simply one aspect of an intertextual project which ranges widely across **myth**, **legend**, literature, history, and popular and mass culture. Pratchett's self-confessed purpose for Discworld's fantasy is to bring a sense of realism to profoundly unrealistic symbols, something he largely achieves. The application of basic common sense to magical situations is productive not only of comic undercutting but also of a humanist ideology that is strengthening as the series develops. His fairy-tale awareness is thus twofold: on one hand, he parodies the expectations of such stock tropes as gingerbread cottages by adding the realities of tooth decay and sticking to the candy-floss doormat (*The Light Fantastic*, 1986); on the other, he is uncompromising in his investigation of the dehumanizing potential of narrative, the overwriting of individual reality with the unrealistic expectations of story. This is seen most strongly in *Witches Abroad* (1991), his most sustained play with fairy-tale forms, in which the three witches, recurring protagonists in the series, encounter and resist the power not only of an evil fairy godmother with a totalitarian grip on tale-telling, but of the narrative itself. The novel's inversions include a **Cinderella** who needs to be prevented from going to the ball, a thoroughly unpleasant **Frog King** who retains his bulging eyes and tendency to catch flies, and a **Sleeping Beauty** irreverently awakened by the witches instead of her **prince**.

In other Discworld novels, fairy tale is a minor but recurring note. One frequent reference is to Black Aliss, the archetypal evil witch who is assumed to be behind many of the stock fairy-tale stories, and who represents the notion of magical and hence narrative power gone astray, to dehumanize and control. Another repeated wry comment is on the saccharine nature of modern **children's literature**, compared knowingly to the Discworld version, the *Grim Fairy Tales*, which are unashamedly bloody. The strong presence of these references in the Discworld children's books, especially *The Amazing Maurice and His Educated Rodents* (2001), is no accident. A companion thread to this is Pratchett's ongoing attack on the twee, sugary Victorian flower **fairies**, mostly notably in the notion of "pictsies," the drinking, fighting, foul-mouthed Nac Mac Feegle.

Pratchett also plays occasionally with folkloric forms, particularly the myths of sacrifice and rebirth in *Hogfather* (1996), the tale of the golem (*Feet of Clay*, 1996), and the predatory, mortal-snatching **elf**-queen of *Lords and Ladies* (1992) and *The Wee Free Men* (2003). *See also* Dwarf, Dwarves; Intertextuality; Metafiction; Postmodernism.

Further Reading: Butler, Andrew M., Edward James, and Farah Mendlesohn. *Terry Pratchett: Guilty of Literature*. Reading: The Science Fiction Foundation, 2000.

Jessica Tiffin

Pretty Woman (1990)

Directed by Garry Marshall, the American film *Pretty Woman* has become a major blockbuster over the last decades, as well as the epitome of the **Cinderella**-type film. It features the story of Edward Lewis (Richard Gere), a ruthless executive who is alone on business for a week in Los Angeles, and Vivian (Julia Roberts), a beautiful and naïve prostitute who works in the red-light district. Edward and Vivian strike up a business arrangement whereby Vivian will become Edward's companion for a week in exchange for $3,000. They both take up residence at a hotel and, as their relationship becomes more and more intimate, they attend a number of social gatherings. Edward behaves as a sort of Pygmalion who molds Vivian into the image of his own desires, thus transforming her into a lovely, opera-loving lady. As a romantic com-

Richard Gere stars as Edward Lewis with Julia Roberts as Vivian Ward in the 1990 motion picture *Pretty Woman*. [Buena Vista Pictures/Photofest]

edy, the film is rounded off with a happy ending. Once the week is over, both characters are deeply in love with each other. Edward declares his love to Vivian and thus rescues her from her humble existence; for her part, Vivian manages to liberate Edward from his Oedipus complex and his sentimental inability to have mature relationships with **women**.

Despite its huge success at the box office, the film has been severely judged by many critics, particularly from the feminist perspective. They argue that the film softens the reality of prostitution, which is shown as a profession that implies little risk for women and virtually no oppression. Its plot is also said to reinforce patriarchal stereotypes that empower men while disempowering women. Thus, Edward is characterized as a wealthy businessman who can ultimately rescue Vivian because he has a good education, power, and money. In contrast, Vivian is absolutely powerless, has received no education, and is virtually destitute; therefore, she has no other way to improve her disadvantageous lot in life but to seek out a rich man who will transform it through marriage. The film has likewise been criticized for its glorification of wealth and consumerism, an aspect that can be seen in a number of scenes in which the main characters boast about their money or achieve supposed happiness by making use of credit cards in their shopping sprees.

Nevertheless, *Pretty Woman* has also been praised as a film that offers lighthearted escapism. Moreover, the role played by Laura San Giacomo as Kit De Luca, Vivian's roommate, introduces some realism into the film, since Kit is a drug addict whose character is coarser and less naïve than Vivian's. ***See also*** Cinderella Films; Feminism; Film and Video; North American Tales.

Further Readings: Greenburg, Harvey Roy. "Rescrewed: *Pretty Woman*'s Co-Opted Feminism." *Journal of Popular Film and Television* 19.1 (1991): 9–13; Kelly, Karol. "A Modern Cinderella." *Journal of American Culture* 17.1 (1994): 87–92; Miner, Madonne. "No Matter What They Say, It's All About Money." *Journal of Popular Film and Television* 20.1 (1992): 8–14.

Carolina Fernández-Rodríguez

Prince

As personifications of wealth, power, and male status, princes feature prominently in fairy tales told around the world. Although "prince" is the favored term in English-language stories and translations for a fairy-tale hero of high rank, other designations are also used, for example **king**, king's son, count, knight, and similar prestigious titles.

Fairy-tale princes are most often heroes in their own right: handsome, youthful, athletic, courageous, skilled in martial arts, and clever. "The Thirteenth Son of the King of Erin" (ATU 300, The Dragon-Slayer) from *Myths and Folk-Lore of Ireland* (1890) by Jeremiah Curtin illustrates all these qualities. This quintessential prince-as-hero tale opens when a king, following the premonition of an old sage, casts out the last of his thirteen sons to return home one evening. The rejected son, called here the thirteenth, is actually the first-born, "the best, the hero of them all." He forthwith sets for himself the task of killing a great serpent that is threatening to devour the daughter of another king. Before entering this battle he must first kill three giants, which he does through cunning trickery and physical prowess. He then slays the serpent but inexplicably refuses to take credit immediately. However, as he rides away, the rescued **princess** manages to pull off one of his boots. The tale ends when the boot proves to fit only him, and he marries the princess.

The hero who makes his first appearance in a story as an animal, revealing himself in his true princely form only after his **marriage** to a human bride, is a stock figure in countless fairy tales, especially ATU types 425–44. Characteristically, the **animal groom** is an enchanted prince whose curse will be broken through his marriage. The disenchantment normally follows one of two patterns. In some tales, the prince's curse is broken when his bride receives him in her bed. Other tales reflect an opposite resolution; the beast turns into a prince precisely when his new bride resists his intimate advances.

An example from the first group comes from Giovan Francesco **Straparola**'s *Le piacevoli notti* (*The Pleasant Nights*, 1550–53). The first tale of Straparola's second night, this story (ATU 441, Hans My Hedgehog) tells how a **queen** gives **birth** to a **pig**. When he comes of age, he seeks a bride, and his **mother** arranges for him to marry the first of three **sisters**. On their wedding night, the bride resists the pig's clumsy attempts at lovemaking, and he tramples her to death. The same thing happens to the second sister, but the third sister meets her pig bridegroom with tender kisses, which forthwith transforms him into a handsome prince.

The second group is exemplified in an episode from the tale "The Girl with Two Husbands" (ATU 433B, King Lindorm) as recorded in Richard M. Dawkins' *Modern Greek Folktales* (1953). A queen gives birth to a snake, and in time a marriage is arranged between the snake and a princess. Acting on the advice of her mother, the bride wears seven shirts on her wedding night. When the groom asks her to undress, she answers, "No, you undress." Six times he pulls off a snake skin, which she throws into the fire. As he removes the seventh skin, he turns into a handsome youth.

In tales told from a female perspective, the prince is often relatively passive, serving primarily to facilitate a royal marriage for the heroine. The tale ATU 310, The Maiden in the Tower, offers an example. Best known in Jacob and Wilhelm **Grimm**'s version "Rapunzel" (1812), the story was first published in 1634 by Giambattista **Basile** in *Lo cunto de li cunti* (2.1). Basile's story depicts a young woman imprisoned in a tower by an **ogress**. A prince happens by and gains access to the tower by climbing up the heroine's long **hair**. The ogress disrupts their tryst. Through the heroine's cunning and courage, she and her lover escape, making their way to the prince's kingdom where they marry and live together happily. This prince, although not himself an active hero, does give the heroine a life of luxury.

Folktales and fairy tales are inconsistent in their depictions of the inherent qualities of royal offspring. Some tales claim that royal **blood** ennobles a person, regardless of his or her environment, admitting no possibility that a commoner might in any way be superior to a person of noble birth. In "The King's Son," a tale from the Caucasus region of Eurasia recorded by Marjory Wardrop in *Georgian Folk Tales* (1894), a blacksmith's wife exchanges her own infant son with a prince whom she has been nursing. Years later, the king shows his assumed son a forest, and the latter responds, "If only we could burn it for charcoal." The king then takes the other boy, who has been raised as a blacksmith's son, into the same forest, and he exclaims, "If this forest were mine, I would double the guards so that it should not be injured." The king thus sees how the smith's wife had tried to cheat him and reclaims his rightful son.

On the other hand, fairy-tale commoners (**peasant**s, **soldier**s, **simpleton**s, **tailor**s, and such) often prove themselves worthy of marrying princesses, thus inheriting kingdoms and advancing to royalty. In some tales, a commoner competes directly with a prince for the hand of a princess. The Polish-Jewish tale "The King's Lost Daughter" from *Yiddish Folktales* (1988) by Beatrice Silverman Weinreich offers an example. A Polish king's daughter disappears, and her father offers her hand in marriage to anyone who can find her. A German prince and a fisherman's son take up the search. They learn that the princess is being held captive by a **witch** atop a glass mountain. The prince is too frightened to climb the mountain, but the fisherman's son pushes onward, kills the witch, and saves the princess. Back at court, the prince takes credit for the rescue. However, the truth comes out. The Polish king gives his daughter to the fisherman's son and has the German prince executed.

Further Reading: Röhrich, Lutz. "The Social Milieu." *Folktales and Reality.* Translated by Peter Tokofsky. Bloomington: Indiana University Press, 1991. 184–98.

D. L. Ashliman

Princess

As translated into English, the word "princess" is used in fairy tales to designate the daughter (or sometimes the wife) of a leading male authority figure: **king**, emperor, monarch, pharaoh, raja, sultan, sheik, tribal chief, or tsar. Princesses appear even in the fairy tales of regions such as Iceland and the Americas, where no tradition of royalty exists. Synonyms are also used. For example, Jacob and Wilhelm **Grimm** often favored the Germanic coinages *Königssohn* and *Königstochter*, literally "king's son" and "king's daughter," over the Latin-rooted *Prinz* or *Prinzessin.*

The title of "princess" also can be assigned to an exceptionally attractive young woman without royal heritage, especially if her **birth** is marked by miraculous circumstances. The Indian tales "Princess Aubergine" and "Princess Pepperina," as recorded in *Tales of the Punjab Told by the People* (1894) by Flora Annie Steel, offer good examples.

To become a princess is the ultimate fairy-tale reward for the leading **women** in stories of many types, most famously ATU 510A, **Cinderella**. These heroines typically come from families of modest means and are mistreated by their stepmothers and stepsisters. The stories conclude with the persecuted woman's elevation to the rank of princess through her

marriage to a **prince**. This leap across social barriers is achieved through a combination of the heroine's long-suffering patience, virtue, inherent beauty, and magic.

The popularity of princess figures in fairy tales derives primarily from this genre's psychological **function** as an aid for **fantasy** escape. Generations of women have felt themselves transformed, if only for the few minutes it takes to tell a story, from household Kates into beautiful women worthy of being swept away by a Prince Charming.

Today's popular culture continues to promote this fantasy. Ordinary women prove to be authentic princesses in such mainstream motion pictures as *The Princess Bride* (1987), *Ever After* (1998), *The Princess Diaries* (2001), and *The Princess Diaries 2: Royal Engagement* (2004). Furthermore, the basic Cinderella plot (a poor and often persecuted young woman, aided by a new wardrobe and a romantic attachment with a princelike boyfriend, dramatically improves her social situation) is central to numerous popular films, including *Sabrina* (1954, 1995), *Working Girl* (1988), *Pretty Woman* (1990), and *Maid in Manhattan* (2002). George Bernard Shaw's drama *Pygmalion* (1913) and its offshoot *My Fair Lady* (stage play 1956, film 1964) follow this same formula.

In many fairy tales, a princess personifies a man's ultimate **reward** for heroic behavior, a prize offered by her **father**, the king, as payment for solving some problem or completing a task. This can be a matter great importance for the realm, such as ridding the kingdom of a **dragon** (ATU 300); or it can be an abstract test of skill, such as climbing a glass mountain (ATU 530) or solving a **riddle** (ATU 851).

In some instances, the princess is both the reward for and the target of an endeavor. In numerous tales (for example, ATU 301, The Three Stolen Princesses), a king offers an abducted daughter to whatever man can rescue her. In other cases, the princess is promised to the man who can correct some perceived flaw in the young woman herself, for example breaking her pride, causing her to laugh, or curing an illness. In such tales, the princess serves first as an adversary in a contest, then as a trophy to be displayed by the winner, rather than as a person to be cherished in her own right. Often, this prize is further enhanced, because in addition to gaining the princess, the hero inherits all or half of her father's kingdom, even if he is from a lower social class.

The question of defining a true princess is humorously treated in Hans Christian **Andersen**'s "Prinsessen på ærten" ("The Princess on the Pea," 1835). A prince will marry only a real princess, so his mother devises a test of sensitivity (ostensibly an indicator of royalty) by placing a pea beneath twenty featherbeds and twenty mattresses on the bed where a potential bride is to sleep. When a woman complains of a horrible lump in her bed, they know that they have at last found a real princess. However, Andersen's final sentence "Now that was a real story!" reveals the author's tongue-in-cheek attitude toward the whole concept of relating royalty to physical sensitivity.

"The Princess and the Bowling Ball" from Jon **Scieszka**'s children's book *The Stinky Cheese Man and Other Fairly Stupid Tales* (1992) goes even further. In this parody of Andersen's familiar tale, a king and **queen** decide that their son should marry only a woman who can feel a pea through 100 mattresses. No woman passes this test, so the prince remains unmarried. Finally, he meets the young woman of his dreams. Not wanting to lose her to the unfair sensitivity test, he secretly puts a bowling ball beneath the mattresses. The next morning, the woman complains about a lump as big as a bowling ball in her bed. The king and queen immediately conclude that she is a true princess, and they approve her marriage to their son. Scieszka may have drawn inspiration for this burlesque from the musical comedy *Once upon a Mattress* (1959), also a **parody** of Andersen's tale wherein the princess test is rigged, in this instance by stuffing the mattresses with weapons.

Sensitivity tests for princesses are treated ironically even in the oldest fairy tales. "The Three Delicate Wives of King Virtue-Banner: Which Is The Most Delicate?" a tale from ancient India recorded in *Vetalapanchavinsati*, translated from the Sanskrit as *Twenty-Two Goblins* (1917) by Arthur W. Ryder, describes a king and his three wives, called princesses (although wives of a king, they are not designated as queens). One princess is wounded when a lotus petal falls on her; the second is burned by moonbeams; the third is bruised by the sound of pestles. The third woman is deemed the most delicate, but this is not an unqualified honor, because the narrator characterizes such extreme delicateness as both a virtue and an inconvenience. *See also* Cinderella Films; Feminism; Feminist Tales; Film and Video.

Further Reading: Lieberman, Marcia R. "'Some Day My Prince Will Come': Female Acculturation through the Fairy Tale." *College English* 34 (1972): 383–95.

D. L. Ashliman

The Princess Bride (1987)

An American film based on William Goldman's 1973 **novel** of the same title, *The Princess Bride* is a classic, swashbuckling, and ironic cinematic take on fairy tales, romance, and the adventure narrative. It was modestly successful upon its first release in 1987 but has since acquired a cult following of devoted fans. Directed by Rob Reiner and scripted by Goldman, the film preserves the novel's self-conscious play with familiar **motif**s, specifically its consciousness of itself as narrative rather than reality.

The novel itself is framed by an apparently autobiographical narrative, which forms an acute investigation of the difference between literary and oral narrative—the novel itself versus the abridged version read to a child. The author, in his own persona, establishes the existence of *The Princess Bride* as an original historical novel by S. Morgenstern, in which the adventure tale is purportedly padded with political and social commentary deeply alienating to a child reader. Goldman's version is apparently abridged to exclude such elements and reduce the story to the exciting oral narrative of his memory. While this background is actually apocryphal, it allows the story to claim the status of an essential reduction of narrative to the terms of symbolic adventure, consciously denying the complexities of the

Robin Wright (Buttercup/The Princess Bride) and Cary Elwes (Westley) star in the 1987 film *The Princess Bride*. [Twentieth Century Fox/Photofest]

literary. At the same time, this works to substantiate the authenticity of the story, allowing certain elements to resonate between the frame and the tale—for example, Morgenstern and the author's father are both supposed to be natives of the mythical kingdom of Florin.

The film retains this element of metafictional play by situating the narrative within a frame involving a child being read the story by his grandfather. Occasional frame-breaks to the child's response emphasize the narrative's construction within the expected and familiar motifs of heroic adventure. *The Princess Bride* is most obviously based on the high-romance/adventure genre, with its elements of swashbuckling swordplay, daring rescues and escapes, pirates, political intrigue, and a villainous **prince**. Its strongest intertexts are the classic adventure films of Errol Flynn. Nonetheless, the story also has obvious fairy-tale elements, including a beautiful **princess**, her heroic suitor striving to be worthy of her, her deception into a false **marriage**, and various encounters with magic, giants, monsters, and perilous forests. The film teeters between active **parody** of such elements through ironic undercutting and an allegiance to a strongly moral and rather sentimental notion of true love. Princess Buttercup's beauty is ultimately insufficient, and she must learn trust and moral courage. Her lover Westley is a parodic hero in another sense, his heroic abilities—swordplay, strength, wit, and persistence—exaggerated to the point where he literally overcomes **death** in the service of Buttercup. The film's tongue-in-cheek parody is affectionate and nostalgic, however, and its conclusion, complete with convenient white horses for the heroes' escape, offers a **utopia**n affirmation of love and a comprehensive defeat of the evil prince. *See also* Fantasy; Film and Video; Frame Narrative; Metafiction.

Further Reading: Henry, Richard, and Deborah F. Rossen-Knill. "*The Princess Bride* and the Parodic Impulse: The Seduction of Cinderella." *Humor: International Journal of Humor Research* 11 (1998): 43–63.

Jessica Tiffin

Propp, Vladimir (1895–1970)

Vladimir Propp was a Russian folklorist whose primary contribution to the study of folktales and fairy tales derives from the ideas in his structuralist work *Morfologiya skazki* (*Morphology of the Folktale*, 1928). However, his nonstructural contributions to the field also had and continue to have an enormous impact on scholars.

A professor first of German, then of **folklore**, at Leningrad University, Propp worked with a sample of **Russian tales** collected by Aleksandr **Afanas'ev** to arrive at his notion of **functions**, articulated in the *Morphology*. Significantly, although Propp criticized Antti **Aarne**'s division of folktales into discrete **tale type**s, Propp limited his analysis to Aarne's types 300–749, specifically, the **wonder tale** (which Propp's editor replaced with "folktale" in the book's title). According to Propp, although characters in a tale are essentially interchangeable, the actions they perform occur in a stable sequence. To illustrate this principle, Propp cites different tales in which various **magic helper**s all aid the hero in travel to a distant land. Propp argues that it is the function of the helper in aiding the hero, rather than the helper's distinct identity, that is important.

Propp then delineates thirty-one separate functions that can potentially appear in any tale, beginning with the absentation of a family member and ending with a wedding. These functions do not, however, appear in every tale. One reason is that Propp's analysis was biased toward tales with male protagonists. Alan **Dundes**, in his structural work based on the 1958 English translation of *Morphology*, further condensed these functions into related pairs such as interdiction/violation, lack/liquidation, and so on. All tale characters are compressed into eight types that are classified by common spheres of action: the villain, donor, (magic) helper, **princess** or sought-after person, her **father**, the hero, and the false hero. This classification is noteworthy for allowing scholars to consider tale characters by what they do rather than who they are.

Much of Propp's other work, including books and articles on **epic**, ritual, and humor, has not been translated into English. Only segments of his *Istoricheskie korni volshebnoi skazki* (*Historical Roots of the Wondertale*, 1946) and selected essays are available to the non-Russian reader. If *Morphology* is largely concerned with the structure of fairy tales, *Historical Roots* is an attempt to connect the content of fairy tales to the rituals and beliefs (especially those surrounding **initiation**s) of pre-Christian, pre-class, and "primitive" social reality. Propp's search for the origin of fairy tales in the material conditions of the people was influenced in part by the political climate of Soviet Russia; he faced censure for relying on the scholarship of folklorists in other countries.

Alternately criticized as a formalist and embraced as the father of structuralist folkloristics, Propp contributed a wealth of scholarship to the study of folktales and fairy tales. *See also* Folktale; Structuralism.

Further Reading: Liberman, Anatoly. Introduction. *Theory and History of Folklore*. By Vladimir Propp. Edited by Anatoly Liberman. Translated by Ariadna Y. Martin and Richard P. Martin. Minneapolis: University of Minnesota Press, 1984. ix–lxxxi.

Jeana Jorgensen

Proverbs

Elements of folk speech in **folktale**s and **fairy tale**s contribute to the style that makes these genres accessible to so many readers and listeners. Formulaic language in the form of rhyming couplets, proverbs, proverbial phrases, and twin formulas appear quite naturally as part of everyday speech and colloquial communication. Especially **didactic tale**s might be based on the wisdom of traditional proverbs that is easily understood and learned. But some tales have also been reduced to a proverbial statement. An especially interesting case is the folktale of "The Pied Piper of Hamelin" with its message that the promise to pay the piper for his services of ridding Hamelin of the rats should have been kept. The German tale appeared in an English translation for the first time in 1605, at a time when such proverbs as "Who pays the piper, calls the tune" and "Those that dance must pay the piper" were already current. The proverbial expression "to pay the piper" was recorded for the first time in 1638, and it thus could be either a shortened version of one of the proverb variants or of the actual folktale. Popular opinion and also many reference works have claimed that the latter is the case, especially since Robert Browning's poem "The Pied Piper of Hamelin" (1842) clearly was instrumental in spreading the phrase of paying the piper. Even if the proverbial phrase might at first have been merely a reduction of one of the longer proverbs, the folktale would still be somewhat of a secondary source for the phrase, since many speakers make the connection to the folktale. Matters are much clearer with the proverb "You have to kiss a lot of toads (frogs) before you meet your handsome prince," which is definitely a proverbial summary of the fairy tale "The **Frog King**." It has gained much currency as a piece of emancipated wisdom on T-shirts, greeting cards, and in the mass media since the 1970s.

Fairy tales actually do not make much use of proverbs and proverbial expressions, but when they appear in Jacob and Wilhelm **Grimm**'s *Kinder- und Hausmärchen* (*Children's and Household Tales*, 1812–15), they take on considerable significance in direct discourse or in the narrative prose. While traditional proverbs add wisdom and didacticism, proverbial expressions, comparisons, and exaggerations are simply part of metaphorical folk speech. However, the fairy tales of the Brothers Grimm contain considerably more proverbial language than tales of other **collectors** in Germany and Europe. It has now been shown that especially Wilhelm Grimm added proverbial texts to his later editions of the *Children's and Household Tales*, having convinced himself that folk speech ought to be part of the verbal imagery of fairy tales.

There is no doubt that both Jacob and Wilhelm Grimm were very interested in proverbial language. They employ them in their letters, they cite them in their volumes of the dictionary of the German language, and they refer to them in their many scholarly publications whenever possible. In fact, it was Wilhelm Grimm who put together a small collection of medieval proverbs and who commented on them in detail in his edition of *Vridankes Bescheidenheit* (1834), a collection of gnomic verses by the poet Freidank. Jacob Grimm was especially interested in the codification of Germanic law in proverbs, as can be seen from the many examples in his legal treatise, *Deutsche Rechtsalterthümer* (*German Legal Antiquities*, 1828). In addition, they had most of the standard German proverb collections in their private library, attesting to their deep-rooted interest in folk wisdom. Wilhelm's preoccupation with proverbial language went so far that he added many traditional phrases to the tales, clearly changing their style to his own preference. As one compares the seven editions of Grimms' fairy tales from 1812–15 to the edition of 1857, one can determine a definite progression in the proverbiality of the fairy tales. But Wilhelm Grimm did not add these proverbs in a manipulative or deceptive fashion. In the introduction to the sixth edition of the *Children's and Household Tales* of 1850, he states openly: "In the sixth edition, too, new tales have been added and individual improvements made. I have been ever eager to incorporate folk proverbs and unique proverbial expressions, which I am always listening for." Having discovered that proverbs and proverbial expressions are part of the traditional fairy-tale style, Wilhelm Grimm saw no particular **authenticity** problem in adding proverbial texts to the *Children's and Household Tales*.

A paragraph in Grimms' "**Hansel and Gretel**" serves as an illustration of Wilhelm Grimm as a proverbialist. In the first four editions, the paragraph in question does not contain a proverb, but in the fifth edition of 1843, Wilhelm finally inserted the proverb "Wer A sagt, muß auch B sagen" ("He who says A, must also say B") to justify at least in part the **father**'s decision to help the **mother** with her evil plan to abandon the children in the woods for a second time. As Wilhelm thought more and more about children as listeners or readers of the fairy tales, he might also have been pleased about the didactic component of this proverb:

> Not long afterward, there was distress everywhere, and the children heard how the mother said to the father in bed at night, "Everything has been eaten up again, we still have a half loaf of bread, after that the song is over. The children must go, we shall lead them deeper into the forest, so that they don't find their way out again; otherwise there is no escape for us." The husband felt sad about it, and he thought, "It would be better that you shared your last mouthful with your children." But the wife did not listen to anything that he said, chided him, and reproached him. If someone begins

something, they have to continue [Wer A sagt, muß auch B sagen], and because he had given in once, he had to do it again.

As can be seen, the proverb is somewhat lost in the translation since there is no good English equivalent proverb, except perhaps, "In for a penny, in for a pound." In the German original, however, Wilhelm's addition of this well-known proverb adds considerable motivational force to the discussion between the parents.

But again, proverbs and proverbial phrases are part of folk narratives in general, as has been shown for tales from other cultures and languages, in which they add a didactic touch and colorful metaphorical language. *See also* Aphorisms.

Further Readings: Bluhm, Lothar, and Heinz Rölleke. *"Redensarten des Volks, auf die ich immer horche": Märchen–Sprichwort–Redensart; Zur volkspoetischen Ausgestaltung der "Kinder- und Hausmärchen" durch die Brüder Grimm.* Stuttgart: Hirzel, 1997; Hasan-Rokem, Galit. *Proverbs in Israeli Folk Narratives: A Structural Semantic Analysis.* Helsinki: Academia Scientiarum Fennica, 1982; Mieder, Wolfgang. *Die Brüder Grimm und das Sprichwort.* Bern: Peter Lang, 1986; ———. "Sprichwörtliche Schwundstufen des Märchens." *Proverbium* 3 (1986): 257–71; ———. "'To Pay the Piper' and the Legend of 'The Pied Piper of Hamelin.'" *Proverbium* 2 (1985): 263–70; ———. "Wilhelm Grimm's Proverbial Additions in the Fairy Tales." *The Brothers Grimm and Folktale.* Edited by James McGlathery. Urbana: University of Illinois Press, 1988. 112–32; Röhrich, Lutz. "Sprichwörtliche Redensarten aus Volkserzählungen." *Ergebnisse der Sprichwörterforschung.* Edited by Wolfgang Mieder. Bern: Peter Lang, 1978. 87–107; Wilcke, Karin, and Lothar Bluhm. "Wilhelm Grimms Sammlung mittelhochdeutscher Sprichwörter." *Brüder Grimm Gedenken* 8 (1988): 81–122.

Wolfgang Mieder

Prøysen, Alf (1914–1970)

Alf Prøysen was a Norwegian poet, songwriter, radio personality, and short-story writer best known internationally for his children's fairy tales about *teskjekjerringa*, a woman who changes to the size of a teaspoon. This "teaspoon woman" (which is the literal meaning of the Norwegian word) is known in English as Mrs. Pepperpot. Prøysen's utilization of the **thumbling** motif became very popular, and the Mrs. Pepperpot books have been translated into many languages.

The first Mrs. Pepperpot book was published in 1956 in Swedish as *Gumman som blev liten som en tesked* (*The Woman Who Became as Small as a Teaspoon*) and did not appear in Norwegian until the following year. But Prøysen had already developed the character in 1955 in a radio program for children. Three other collections of stories about Mrs. Pepperpot followed, among them *Teskjekjerringa i eventyrskauen* (*Mrs. Pepperpot in the Magic Wood*, 1965), a collection of stories including "Teskjekjerringa og Kvitebjørn Kong Valemon" (sometimes translated as "Mrs. Pepperpot in the Magic Wood"). This story incorporates the polar bear from the famous folktale and other characters from Norwegian folk songs. Many of the individual stories from these collections appeared later in picture books by various illustrators. Using simple language and written in the tradition of Norwegian folktales, the Mrs. Pepperpot stories are full of folkloristic **motif**s and characters but also exhibit literary influences. Many of Prøysen's songs and **ballad**s have become part of Norwegian culture, and he is considered a national icon in his native country. *See also* Scandinavian Tales.

Further Reading: Hagemann, Sonja. *Barnelitteratur i Norge, 1914–1970.* Oslo: H. Aschehoug & Co., 1974. 236–54.

Marte Hult

Psychological Approaches

Of the many ways to interpret the meanings of fairy tales, psychological approaches seek to decipher how the symbols in fairy tales relate to the working of the human mind, especially its unconscious layers. Since there is no one unified understanding of the human mind, psychological approaches have different assumptions and methods. Psychological approaches tend to focus on the mental and emotional states of tale characters and narrators rather than the social and historical circumstances that shape the transmission of the tales. This has prompted recent scholars employing **sociohistorical approaches** to challenge the ahistorical trends that permeate psychological approaches. While some authors of psychological studies of folktales and fairy tales utilize clinical evidence to support their interpretations, other psychologists employ tales in their therapeutic practices. Psychological approaches fall predominantly into three categories: those primarily influenced by Sigmund **Freud**, those primarily influenced by Carl Gustav **Jung**, and those that seek alternative understandings and methodologies.

Freudian Approaches

Freud, the so-called father of psychoanalysis, contributed to the psychological study of **folklore** mainly by developing theories that have been used to interpret folklore and by inspiring scholars not only to apply his theories but also to elaborate them for wider applications. Freud and his followers generally interpreted folktales and fairy tales, like dreams, as symbolically coded expressions of subconscious processes. Translating the symbols involved identifying instances of forbidden and repressed desires (such as the Oedipal wish to kill one's same-sex parent and marry the other parent), projection (shifting one's desires onto another), and sexual stages of development (progressing through oral, anal, and genital fixation to maturity). Two further mechanisms for translating unconscious desires are splitting (representing ambivalent feelings through two separate figures) and displacement (transferring an association to a seemingly unrelated object). Freud himself wrote only a few studies of folktales and fairy tales, including "Märchenstoffe in Träumen" ("The Occurrence in Dreams of Material from Fairy Tales," 1913) and "Das Motif der Kästchenwahl" ("The Theme of the Three Caskets," 1913).

Freud's early followers who worked with folktales and fairy tales include Franz Riklin, Ernest Jones, Otto Rank, Erich Fromm, and Géza **Róheim**. Riklin's *Wunscherfüllung und Symbolik im Märchen* (*Wishfulfillment and Symbolism in Fairy Tales*, 1908) posited that the fantastic elements in fairy tales express hidden desires, such as hostility toward oppressive parent figures (as found in the prevalence of wicked stepmothers, for instance). Jones and Fromm each analyzed the sexual meanings of tales such as "The **Frog King**" and "**Little Red Riding Hood**." Fromm's analysis is particularly characteristic of the Freudian lens: in his interpretation of "Little Red Riding Hood," he views the red hood as a symbol of menstruation and hence sexual maturity. The tale ends, according to Fromm, with the triumph of man-hating **women** who mock the **wolf**'s sterility by filling his belly with stones. Thus, the relationship between children and parents dominates Fromm's Freudian analysis. Róheim's interpretation of "Little Red Riding Hood" relied on his interest in dreams. He viewed the tale as an account of a dream experience (sleeping within the stomach/womb) informed by oral aggression. Róheim was notable for his folkloristic training, paired with a critical appreciation for Freudian concepts. He interpreted individual tales and also posited that folk narratives originate in dreams—an intriguing twist on the prior psychoanalytic theories regarding parallels between fairy tale and dream. Rank's *Der Mythus von der Geburt des Helden* (*The Myth of the Birth of the Hero*, 1909) utilized Freud's evolutionary model linking ontogenesis (development of the individual) and phylogenesis (development of the species).

One of the central Freudian works on fairy tales is Bruno **Bettelheim**'s *The Uses of Enchantment: The Meaning and Importance of Fairy Tales* (1976). Bettelheim advocated the view that fairy tales aid children in maturation, for example, in overcoming Oedipal attachments to their parents and developing confidence when faced with sibling rivalries—a view that is alternately popular and provocative. However, feminists and folklorists alike have attacked Bettelheim: the former for uncritically using the sexist tools of Freudian psychoanalysis, and the latter for being ignorant of the variations and sociohistorical contexts that are central to understanding the evolution and transmission of folktales and fairy tales.

The modern champion of Freudian folkloristics, Alan **Dundes**, consistently campaigned for the rigorous application of psychoanalytic concepts to folkloric materials while not losing sight of folkloristic methodologies and goals. Dundes often analyzed folktales and fairy tales, claiming that literal and historical interpretations of the tales rarely were able to account for every feature of the tale. Moreover, Dundes relied heavily on the notion of projection—both internally, among tale characters, and externally, between narrator and character—which theoretically has the advantage of being less sexist and offensive than other Freudian concepts such as penis envy (which Dundes rejected because he saw no evidence for it in folklore). The actual implementation of projection might well be biased, as in Dundes's interpretation of tale type ATU 706, The Maiden without Hands. Rather than viewing the heroine as a passive victim of her **father**'s greed or lust, Dundes believed that the girl projects her Oedipal fantasy of being loved by her father onto him in the tale, making him act as the aggressor. The father claims the girl's hands (as in marriage), which also functions as a punishment for her taboo desires. While this interpretation grants the heroine agency on the unconscious level, it does not address the actual **violence** in the tale's content. The sexism of the Freudian family status quo also remains unquestioned.

One of Dundes's major insights was that fairy tales represent the child's point of view and therefore must be interpreted with attention to relevant developmental processes. An instance of Dundes's style of analysis in keeping with prior examples is his interpretation of tale type ATU 333, Little Red Riding Hood. Dundes again utilized projection to discuss the heroine's unconscious fantasies, relying especially on notions of oral aggression. He additionally brings in Asian cognates of the folktale ATU 123, The Wolf and the Kids. The heroine in some Asian and European variants of both tale types consumes her female relative—sometimes literally breast-feeding—and alludes to defecating in bed, thus relegating the tale's conflict (intergenerational and between two females) and imagery to the realm of **childhood** psychology.

Jungian Approaches

Carl Gustav Jung had been a follower of Freud until breaking away and founding a school of analytic psychology. Jung remained interested in the unconscious while rejecting many of Freud's ideas about infantile sexuality. Some key concepts in analytic psychology include the existence of both personal and collective unconscious symbolic reservoirs; the existence of universal **archetype**s; and the importance of symbols in helping each person to reach maturity and wholeness through the process of individuation. Jung's involvement with fairy tales extended from publishing analyses of the archetypes in the tales and founding a research institute to both inspiring and encouraging others to pursue his brand of archetypal analysis.

Marie-Louise von **Franz** worked with Jung as both an analytic psychologist and scholar, and she continued his work of interpreting folk narratives and archetypes. Much of her work also deals with the balance (or lack thereof) between anima, the female principle, and animus, the male principle, each of which is said to exist within the opposite sex. Lacking integration, an individual will be unbalanced, and fairy tales (and symbolic forms more generally) can help mediate the different aspects of personhood. *The Feminine in Fairy Tales* (1972) is an example of this type of work. In this book, von Franz intersperses textual interpretation with examples from her clinical practices that are reminiscent of fairy-tale themes. This is a common technique among Jungian analysts; Marion Woodman's *Leaving My Father's House* (1992)—which is an analysis of tale type ATU 510B, Peau d'Asne—also includes commentaries from her patients. Von Franz additionally assisted Hedwig von Beit in preparing *The Symbolism of the Fairy Tale* (1952–57), a three-volume work that draws on Jungian archetypes to discuss self-realization within the tales. Both von Franz and von Beit agreed that the wolf and **mother** in the Little Red Riding Hood tale type are both aspects of the mother archetype. Ole Vedfelt of the C. G. Jung Institute added that the heroine represents the Kore, or maiden, archetype, and her rescuer is her animus (Holbek, 311–14).

The writer and scholar Joseph Campbell was not strictly a follower of Jung, but his analyses of folktales and fairy tales—which he often did not distinguish from other genres of folk narrative—fit within a general framework of Jungian symbolism. Consistent with the Jungian approach, Campbell believed symbols cause **transformation**s within the human psyche, whereas Freudians view symbols as effects of psychological dysfunctions. Campbell's book *The Hero with a Thousand Faces* (1949) interprets fairy tales as containing a "call to adventure," whereby an individual can attain wisdom by journeying forth from home. Campbell was not always attuned to context; however, he did acknowledge distinct archetypal-hero pattern among broad genres of folk narrative. Fairy-tale heroes achieve domestic, microcosmic victories, whereas the heroes of **myth** achieve macrocosmic triumphs. Campbell, like other Jungians, has been accused of essentializing not only **gender** but also cultural values.

Alternative Approaches

Although the approaches of Freud and Jung have dominated the overlap between psychological fields and fairy-tale studies, there are alternative attitudes. Some draw on variant psychological schools, while others recast the psychological classics anew.

Jack **Zipes** both poses critical challenges to psychological approaches and suggests alternative interpretations. He demystifies the appeal of writers such as Bettelheim by uncovering their biases and assumptions. Zipes introduced the psychological theories of Jacques Lacan, notably the gaze, to his discussion of **illustration**s and sexuality in *The Trials and Tribulations of Little Red Riding Hood* (2nd edition, 1993). In his introduction to *Don't Bet on the Prince: Contemporary Feminist Fairy Tales in North America and England* (1986), Zipes combines psychological theories of development with feminist critiques of patriarchy to yield a powerful argument for the necessary of revising fairy tales to convey less-repressive gender roles. Zipes is especially critical of pop-psychology analyses of folktales and fairy tales, which tend to result in superficial manuals for life.

Rather than condemning shallow attempts at psychological interpretations and leaving it at that, Zipes offers other suggestions for integrating psychological approaches with rigorous and socially informed perspectives. In his essay "Recent Psychological Approaches with Some Questions about the Abuse of Children," Zipes pays special attention to the works of psychologist Alice Miller. Miller's main argument is that adults use and abuse children, both intentionally and unintentionally, while working through their own internal struggles, which in turn children repress and enact as they mature. The recognition that trauma resulting from manipulation is often real—contrary to Freud and his followers, who often interpreted stories of abuse as fantasy—impacts the study of fairy tales, which frequently involve violence.

Zipes and Maria Tatar both utilize some psychological concepts while critiquing the unreflective adoption of psychological approaches. In *Fairy Tales and the Art of Subversion: The Classical Genre for Children and the Process of Civilization* (1983), Zipes uses Freud's concept of the *unheimlich* (uncanny) to discuss the liberating potential of the fantastic in fairy tales. Tatar, in *The Hard Facts of the Grimms' Fairy Tales* (1987), relies on Freud's idea of the "family romance," whereby neurotics are deluded into thinking that they were actually adopted, their "real" parents being much more noble and exalted than their currently acknowledged families. This wish-fulfillment plot parallels the twin themes of naturalness and illegitimacy in fairy tales. Tatar also uses projection to explain why children's resentment of their parents is transformed in the tales into parental malice toward children. Yet Tatar is skeptical of the tendency to interpret symbols as universal. Instead, she advocates for a context-bound psychoanalysis of tales and tale characters.

Bengt **Holbek** summarizes and synthesizes many psychological approaches in his *Interpretation of Fairy Tales: Danish Folklore in a European Perspective* (1987). He refuses to adhere to any one approach because, according to him, each is flawed in that it results from study of the mind rather than study of the text. Yet he does not discard the possibility that some aspects of the various psychological approaches might be useful in a folkloristic interpretation of fairy tales; hence, he retains concepts such as projection and splitting. Because Holbek's aim is to decode the meaning of the marvelous in fairy tales—those fantastic elements that cannot be explained literally or historically—his decision to utilize elements of symbol-oriented psychological systems is appropriate.

Drawing on both Freud and Jacques Lacan, Shuli Barzilai provides an example of a fairy-tale analysis that privileges psychological theories but does not neglect folkloristic methods. In *Lacan and the Matter of Origins* (1999), Barzilai's chapter on the maternal object examines the representations of the characters in the Little Red Riding Hood tale type. According to Barzilai, the exchange between Little Red Riding Hood and the wolf in bed does not signify the girl's stupidity in mistaking a wolf for her grandmother, but rather depicts the overwhelming power of the paternal order in making her make sense of the situation in a certain way. Additionally, a mechanistic identification with the aggressor could cause the heroine, like any victim, to submit to both psychic and physical **violence**. Barzilai also suggests that the tale is about the splitting of the paternal subject into wolf and hunter, extending Bettelheim's child-oriented analysis to assert that the characters within the tale do not simply reflect the child's perception of the father, but in fact signify a patriarchal desire to both seduce and save the child.

In sum, while psychological approaches to folktales and fairy tales have tended to focus on the relationships among symbol, mind, and text, those relationships are in no way fixed or universal. Some interpretive methodologies run the risk of yielding the most insight into the mind of the individual interpreter or the worldview of a given culture or time period. These interpretations can privilege one version of a tale over all others, thus silencing the polyvocality that makes folktales and fairy tales such potent narrative forms. Other interpretations are illuminating for their capacity to explain the otherwise unexplainable mysteries of these tales. On the whole, psychological approaches are stimulating and thought provoking, much like the phenomena they try to explicate. *See also* Feminism; Sex, Sexuality; Trauma and Therapy.

Further Readings: Barzilai, Shuli. "'Grandmother, what a dreadfully big mouth you have!' Lacan's Parables of the Maternal Object." *Lacan and the Matter of Origins.* Stanford, CA: Stanford University Press, 1999. 199–226; Dundes, Alan. "The Psychoanalytic Study of the Grimms' Tales: 'The Maiden without Hands' (AT 706)." *Folklore Matters.* Knoxville: University of Tennessee Press, 1989. 112–50; Haase, Donald. "Psychology and Fairy Tales." *The Oxford Companion to Fairy Tales.* Edited by Jack Zipes. Oxford: Oxford University Press, 2000. 404–08; Holbek, Bengt. *Interpretation of Fairy Tales: Danish Folklore in a European Perspective.* 1987. Helsinki: Academia Scientarium Fennica, 1998; Laiblin, Wilhelm, ed. *Märchenforschung und Tiefenpsychologie.* 5th expanded edition. Darmstadt: Primus, 1995; Zipes, Jack. "Recent Psychological Approaches with Some Questions about the Abuse of Children." *The Brothers Grimm: From Enchanted Forests to the Modern World.* 2nd edition. New York: Palgrave Macmillan, 2002. 153–85.

Jeana Jorgensen

Pú Sōnglíng (1640–1715)

Pú Sōnglíng, a celebrated short-story writer in the Qing dynasty (1644–1912), was the author of *Liáo Zhāi Zhì Yì* (*Strange Stories from a Chinese Studio*, largely compiled by 1679 and printed in 1766), one of the most influential resources in the repertoire of Chinese folktales. Born into a poor merchant family in Shāndāng province, Pú devoted his early years to the civil service exams. However, he never attained his goal of becoming a statesman, as he failed the tests for fifty years. Pú worked as a private tutor for families of the gentry and maintained close contacts with both literati and commoners. His literary interests and work range from classical poems, essays, and short stories, to folk songs and operas.

His best-known work, *Strange Stories from a Chinese Studio*, consists of almost 500 short stories of the unusual and supernatural (including **anecdote**s). After its appearance, Pú's collection became a popular resource for both amateur and professional **storytelling**, cinema, and **theater** in imperial and modern China, reaching almost every sector of Chinese society. In terms of its popularity and impact in China, it has been compared by some to the **Grimm**s' fairy tales of western Europe.

Stories about fox spirits and ghosts occupy a prominent place in *Strange Stories from a Chinese Studio*, accounting for half of the collection. Fox spirits and ghosts, whether good natured or vicious, interact with humans for various reasons, including karmic retribution, paying a debt of gratitude, intaking a person's essence/soul, or having erotic experiences with and even marrying humans. Praising conventional moral values such as benevolence, justice, filial piety, and loyalty, the stories also reflect a long-standing tradition among literati since medieval China of recording anomalies and marvels. Pú, however, enriches this tradition by depicting a humanized world of supernatural heroines rather than simply by writing about "strangeness." Compared to the passive male protagonists, many of the **women** depicted in these stories are daring, active, and defiant in pursuing love and **marriage**.

The significance of *Strange Stories* for folktale and fairy-tale studies lies in Pú's intertwining of the oral and the literary. Pú's stories are deeply indebted to oral narratives among the masses and the lower level of literati in his time. He was said to offer tea to passersby and travelers in exchange for tales. Folklorists have shown that many of Pú's stories correspond to today's widely circulated Chinese folktales and are useful in studying the transformation and history of **tale type**s. On the other hand, Pú's tales are crafted with literary creativity, and the popularity of his *Strange Stories* greatly expanded the repertoire of Chinese folktales, especially fox spirit tales. *See also* Chinese Tales; Ghost Story.

Further Readings: Barr, Allan. "Disarming Intruders: Alien Women in *Liaozhai Zhiyi.*" *Harvard Journal of Asiatic Studies* 49 (1989): 501–17; Chang, Chun-shu, and Shelley Hsueh-Lun Chang. *Redefining History: Ghosts, Spirits, and Human Society in P'u Sung-Ling's World, 1640–1715*. Ann Arbor: University of Michigan Press, 1999; Johnson, T. W. "Far Eastern Fox Lore." *Asian Folklore Studies* 33.1 (1974): 35–68; Pú Sōnglíng. *Strange Stories from a Chinese Studio*. Translated by Herbert A. Giles. 2 volumes. London, 1880; ———. *Strange Tales from a Chinese Studio*. Translated by John Minford. London: Penguin, 2006.

Jing Li

Puck

A sometimes evil, sometimes mischievous spirit or demon from popular superstition, Puck is best known as the **trickster** fairy in William **Shakespeare**'s *A Midsummer Night's Dream* (1595–6). Nevertheless, Puck—usually regarded as a unique being rather than a spirit type—predates Shakespeare. Although the exact origin of "Puck" (both as a word and as an entity) remains uncertain, it is clear that cognates for the name exist (or existed) in numerous languages, for example in Old English (*puca*), Welsh (*pwca*), Irish (*pooka* or *phooka*), and Swedish (*puke*). The use of the word dates to pre-Christian times, when it referred to a nature spirit tied to particular places, often pools, rocks, and streams. With the introduction of Christianity, the Puck figure was increasingly associated with the **devil**, or taken to be the devil himself, and the words "hobgoblin," "bug," and "boggart" assumed a more dangerous air as time passed.

Over the thousand years of its existence in **folklore**, the Puck figure took on various incarnations as a **fairy**, goblin, imp, or devil. As the term came to refer to a general type of spirit rather than to an individual entity, it described rough, hairy creatures that were capable, at times, of transforming into animals, especially horses. During this time, the Puck figure also went under the names of Robin Goodfellow and Hobgoblin, although it is usually agreed that the conflating of the Puck and Robin figures began with Shakespeare and held fairly firm thereafter. The domain of Puck/Robin was mainly domestic, sometimes aiding and sometimes thwarting such daily human efforts as sweeping, conducting of routine farm chores, and keeping an eye on the coffer or on the servants. A common belief was that the Puck would disappear if offered a new suit of **clothing**. Puck figures were deemed useful but were also known to be quite easily offended and quick to settle a score. They might help one to turn the churn, but they were just as capable of souring its contents or of leading weary travelers from the road at night. Thus, one expression for being lost is "Robin Goodfellow has been with you tonight."

In the popular **broadside ballad**s (and woodcuts) of Elizabethan and Jacobean England, Robin Goodfellow is sometimes depicted as the son of Oberon, the fairy king, and a mortal woman, and his jocularity in those ballads is conveyed with his signature laugh of "Ho! Ho! Ho!" Popular renditions of Puck/Robin appear centuries later, too, perhaps most notably in Rudyard Kipling's *Puck of Pook's Hill* (1906), wherein Puck criticizes the "painty-winged, wand-waving" versions of English fairies. In recent times, he has appeared as a compact superhero in Marvel Comics, as a character in Neil **Gaiman**'s Sandman **fantasy** series (1988–96), and (after a fashion) as Dobby the House **Elf** in J. K. **Rowling**'s Harry Potter books (1997–2007).

Further Readings: Briggs, Katharine M. *The Anatomy of Puck: An Examination of Fairy Beliefs Among Shakespeare's Contemporaries and Successors.* London: Routledge, 1959; ———. *An Encyclopedia of Fairies: Hobgoblins, Brownies, Bogies, and Other Supernatural Creatures.* New York: Pantheon, 1976.

Lori Schroeder Haslem

Pullman, Philip (1946–)

Philip Pullman is a British writer, and the winner of numerous awards, including the Carnegie Medal, the Guardian Award, the Elinor Farjeon Award, the Smarties Prize, the Whitbread Award, and the international Astrid Lindgren Memorial Award. Pullman is best known around the world as the author of the **fantasy** trilogy His Dark Materials, consisting of *Northern Lights* (1995), *The Subtle Knife* (1997), and *The Amber Spyglass* (2000), in which many **folklore** elements are employed, such as the quest, the struggle between good and evil, the descent into the realm of the dead, **magic object**s, and **punishment and reward**. The concept of the **magic helper**, originating from the archaic totem animal, is ingeniously developed in Pullman's trilogy into daemons, external projections of human souls in animal form.

Pullman composed a number of books for younger readers that he himself calls fairy tales. Some of them originate from plays he wrote for his students when he was a schoolteacher. His very first work for children, *Count Karlstein, or The Ride of the Demon Huntsman* (1982), is a gothic tale, employing the common fairy-tale topos of "the depths of the deepest, darkest, gloomiest forest." Another adventure story with folktale overtones is the **graphic novel** *Spring-Heeled Jack: A Story of Bravery and Evil* (1989), set in Victorian London and featuring, in Pullman's own words, a "hero who used to go around rescuing people and catching criminals … before Superman and Batman had been heard of." *Count Karlstein* was reissued as a graphic novel in 1991.

Clockwork, or All Wound Up (1996) is a much more sophisticated horror story, with obvious echoes from the German Romantic writers, not least E. T. A. **Hoffmann**. It involves automatons but does not exclude the presence of evil magical powers and a deal with the **devil**. It also offers intricate metafictional games with the reader, in which the essence of true **storytelling** is reflected upon. Fairy tale and reality are tightly entangled, and characters walk easily in and out of their stories.

I Was a Rat: or The Scarlet Slippers (1999) is a hilarious revision of a fairy tale, in which the main character is one of the rats that **Cinderella**'s fairy godmother turned into pageboys and obviously failed to transform back. This, however, merely provides the starting point of the plot, while the story itself evolves around the tragic fate of an orphan with rodent habits, a kind of feral-child or Kaspar-Hauser narrative (Kaspar is suggested as a possible name for the rat boy before he is named Roger). Cinderella herself, by this time living happily ever after with her **prince**, although not wholly without problems, is portrayed in the story as a benefactor. The book has obvious parallels with present-day Britain and the contemporary media's thirst for sensations. It also explores the fluctuating borders between human and animal as well as the consequences of unconstrained desire.

In *The Firework-Maker's Daughter* (1995), we are transported to an indistinct Oriental country, "a thousand miles ago ... east of the jungle and south of the mountains," a fine example of Pullman's highly individual style and inventive play with language. Here we meet a strong and independent heroine, reminiscent both of the irresistibly charming female *picaro* (rogue) from Pullman's historical juvenile **novel**s (the Sally Lockhart quartet, 1985–94), of Lyra in the His Dark Materials triology, or the brave innkeeper's daughter Gretl in *Clockwork*. *The Firework-Maker's Daughter* is a quest story, with the traditional elements such as trials, supernatural beings, magical water, talking **animal helper**s, and a final contest; however, it has a significant additional dimension dealing with creativity, especially maintaining **women**'s rights to be as creative and skillful as **men**. Lila the firework-maker's daughter proves to be as determined and competent as her **father**, and she wins with her firework display over three male rivals, who are generous enough to celebrate her superiority.

In one of his most recent books, *The Scarecrow and His Servant* (2004), set in a festive atmosphere of a fairy-tale-like Italy, Pullman recycles the century-old figure of an animated scarecrow, turning it into a comical Don Quixote adventure with many philosophical overtones. The plot is recognizable, with its formative journey among villains and friends, but the traditional roles are reversed, as the scarecrow is the master and a young boy his companion and clever advisor. As in most books by Pullman, harsh societal indignation can be discerned between the lines.

Pullman has, with humor and irony, retold several traditional folktales: *The Wonderful Story of **Aladdin** and the Enchanted Lamp* (1995, illustrated by David Wyatt), *Mossycoat* (1998, illustrated by Peter Bailey), and ***Puss in Boots**: The Adventures of That Most Enterprising Feline* (2000, illustrated by Ian Beck). All of these picture books are marvelous new versions wherein Pullman has added many witty details to the text, often changing the point of view and bringing forward unexpected aspects of the well-known stories. In *Puss in Boots*, words are integrated with pictures in the form of clever speech and thought balloons, commenting on the events and revealing the characters' true feelings.

Pullman is a superb storyteller; always adding unexpected twists to traditional fairy-tale plots and creating multifaceted, lovable, unforgettable characters. These archetypal orphans and underprivileged children, indispensable also in modern fairy tales, are strong-minded and strong-willed, yet never straightforwardly good or still less ideal. Pullman's language is colorful and original, enhancing familiar plots with vibrant descriptions and fluent, humorous dialogue. It is to a great extent through language that Pullman creates and explores his own exciting and mystifying worlds, familiar and yet strange, such as the scary medieval atmosphere of *Clockwork*, the shadowy jungles and threatening mountains of *The Firework-Maker's Daughter*, or the pseudo-Mediterranean landscape of *The Scarecrow and His Servant*. All of these spooky and fairy-tale-like environments are, however, easily translated into identifiable contemporary situations.

Pullman has also written historical novels, which he calls historical thrillers, mainly set in Victorian England, as well as psychological **young adult fiction**. *See also* Fantasy; Metafiction.

Further Readings: Lenz, Millicent, with Carole Scott. *His Dark Materials Illuminated: Critical Essays on Philip Pullman's Trilogy*. Detroit: Wayne State University Press, 2005; Tucker, Nicholas. *Darkness Visible: Inside the World of Philip Pullman*. London: Wizard Books, 2003.

Maria Nikolajeva

Punishment and Reward

Justice may be an elusive goal in real life, but it often achieved in the **fantasy** world of fairy tales. A fairy-tale ending, almost by definition, is an outcome that rewards the virtuous while punishing the wicked. Supernatural or fate-driven justice systems underlie **myth**, **legend**, and **folklore** in many cultures. Everyday experience may suggest that "life isn't fair," but if an injustice occurs in a fairy tale, one may reasonably expect that the evildoers will be punished and the good rewarded.

There are exceptions; not all fairy tales have happy endings. For example, in some tales, murder victims must wait until a next life for full justice, although the murderers themselves are often executed. Tales of type ATU 780, The Singing Bone, found around the world, typically depict how a murderer is exposed when a bone of his or her victim, which has been made into a flute, magically sings out the truth. The perpetrator is punished, thus restoring at least a measure of justice, as expected in a fairy tale.

This promise of fairness requires a caveat: fairy tales typically are told only from the hero's or heroine's point of view, so if he or she is rewarded—even at someone else's expense—it is seen as a positive outcome. Furthermore, concepts of fairness can be skewed by prejudice, as reflected in many folktale depictions of racial minorities, certain social castes, and people perceived to be **witch**es, **ogre**s, or outlaws.

Women, especially those living in seclusion or demonstrating behavior outside of conventional social norms, are often suspected of witchcraft, and are thus beyond the protection of ordinary law and morality. Hans Christian **Andersen**'s "Fyrtøjet" ("The Tinderbox," 1835)—a version of ATU 562, The Spirit in the Blue Light—offers a striking example. A **soldier**, homeward bound, meets a disgusting old woman whose lower lip hangs down to her chest. She pays him generously to recover a tinderbox from an underground chamber, but when she refuses to tell him how she is going to use it, he summarily cuts off her head and steals the box. As he later discovers, it controls **magic helper**s that with time facilitate his forceful overthrow of the **king** and **marriage** to a **princess**. The hero thus gains the ultimate fairy-tale reward, all because he killed an ugly old woman.

A similarly amoral tale, this time with the **gender** roles reversed, is "Mally Whuppie" (ATU 327, The Children and the Ogre), recorded in *A Dictionary of British Folk-Tales in the English Language* (1970–71) by Katharine M. **Briggs**. The story opens with the abandonment of three **sisters** by their impoverished parents. The girls find shelter in a giant's house. Mally, the youngest sister, tricks the giant into killing his own daughters and then steals different valuable items from him, thus procuring royal marriages for her sisters and herself. The giant finally captures her and ties her in a bag, intending to beat the bag with a club until she is dead. However, Mally tricks the giant's wife into taking her place in the bag, and the giant beats to **death** his own wife. The three sisters deservedly gain the ultimate fairy-tale reward, but they do so at the expense of a **family** that had nothing to do with their initial misfortune. However, it is a family of giants, marginalized individuals for whom fairy tales show little sympathy.

Other forms of discrimination are often tolerated in folktales as well. In this regard, the story type ATU 592, The Dance among Thorns, has an interesting evolution. Told in Europe since the fifteenth century, this tale—in its earliest versions—depicts a monk who is forced to dance in thorns by a boy with a magic flute or fiddle. Reflecting the anticlerical sentiment of many medieval and Renaissance **jest** books, this tale suggests that the monk well deserves this punishment, for crimes both specified and assumed.

Later versions, most prominently Jacob and Wilhelm **Grimm**'s "Der Jude im Dorn" ("The Jew in the Thornbush," 1815), feature a Jew—instead of the traditional clergyman— as the scapegoat deserving punishment for unspecified crimes. An American version from Kentucky, "The Jew That Danced amongst the Thorn Bushes" from *Tales from the Cloud Walking Country* (1958) by Marie Campbell, includes an apology from her **informant**: "Seems like all the tales about Jews gives the Jews a bad name—greedy, grabbing for cash money, cheating their work hands out of their wages—I don't know what all. I never did know a Jew, never even met up with one."

If folktales sometimes penalize individuals without due process, they also protect individuals who by any rational standard deserve reprimand. Reflecting the patriarchal standards of most traditional cultures, folktales seldom prescribe punishment for **father**s, however heinous their crimes may be. The widespread family of tales known collectively as ATU 510B, Peau d'Asne—or Donkey Skin—from the title of Charles **Perrault**'s version, depicts a father's attempts to marry his own daughter. Although the storytellers virtually always condemn the father's behavior, they almost never describe any punishment, choosing instead to not mention him after the daughter makes her escape.

Similarly, the tale type known as The Maiden without Hands (ATU 706), another widely distributed international tale, depicts a heroine horribly mutilated by her father (or sometimes a brother), but the perpetrator is rarely punished. "The Armless Maiden" from Aleksandr **Afanas'ev**'s *Russkie narodnye skazki* (*Russian Folktales*, 1855–67) presents a case in point. Following the death of their parents, a brother and a sister live together. The brother marries a **sorceress**, who falsely accuses her husband's sister of wicked crimes. Believing his wife, the brother punishes the sister by cutting off her arms and abandoning her in the forest. Following a series of miraculous events, the mutilated woman's arms are restored, and the truth of her sister-in-law's accusations is revealed. The brother avenges his slandered sister by tying his wife behind a horse and dragging her to death. But he, who foolishly believed his wife's lies, and who himself cruelly cut off his sister's arms, escapes all punishment.

Female family members do not fare so well. For example, in the Grimms' "Die zwölf Brüder" ("The Twelve Brothers," 1812; ATU 451, The Maiden Who Seeks Her Brothers), when a king discovers that his **mother** has been slandering his wife, he has the older woman thrown into a barrel filled with boiling oil and poisonous snakes (a curiously redundant punishment).

Another mother tortured to death by her own offspring is the jealous mother/stepmother in the Grimm brothers' "Sneewittchen" ("**Snow White**"; ATU 709). Identified as the heroine's mother in the first edition of their *Kinder- und Hausmärchen* (*Children's and Household Tales*, 1812), the villainous woman is changed to a stepmother in the second edition (1819) and all following editions. After numerous attempts to kill her daughter/stepdaughter, the woman meets her end when Snow White and her new husband force her to put on a pair of red-hot iron **shoe**s, and she consequently dances herself to death. A measure of justice is thus achieved, with the sadistic punishment to some extent fitting the crime. The glowing shoes, an appropriate symbol for her own unbridled envy, bring about her final demise. Snow White herself receives the expected reward: first restoration to life, then marriage to a **prince**.

An additional family related conflict that often results in punishment is adultery. There are, of course, **erotic tales** depicting **sex** as an amoral game with no losers, but in many traditional tales, sexual indiscretion, especially by a female, calls for punishment. Probably the best-known instance of punishment for adultery in the history of **storytelling** is the pivotal **motif** in the **frame narrative** to the *Arabian Nights*. King Shahriyar catches his wife making love with a slave. He not only summarily puts them to death, but vows henceforth to take a new bride every night, and then to protect his honor by having her executed the following morning. This transpires until he marries **Sheherazade**, who saves herself by telling him stories in bed, always leaving one story unfinished until the following evening. After 1,001 nights, the king admits to himself that this wife is indispensable, and he abandons his earlier vow.

Punishment for adultery has been a popular theme in European literary stories since the **Middle Ages**. Two tale types are especially widespread: ATU 992, The Eaten Heart; and ATU 992A, The Adulteress's Penance. Giovanni **Boccaccio** recorded a prominent example of the former in his *Decameron* (1349–50) (4.9). A knight discovers that is wife is having an affair. The aggrieved husband kills his wife's lover and then has the murdered man's heart served to her. Upon discovering what she has eaten, the wife jumps to her death from a castle window. However, in a sense the two illicit lovers are joined in death, for they are laid to rest in a common grave, suggesting that the community does not entirely condemn their affair.

Tales belonging to the type called The Adulteress's Penance (ATU 992A) are similar. Examples come from the *Gesta Romanorum* (*Deeds of the Romans*, no. 56), Marguerite de Navarre's *Heptaméron* (1559) (4.32), and folktale collections from various nations. As typically told, a guest in a knight's castle observes that a certain woman drinks only from a human skull. Later, the host explains that the woman is his wife, caught in adultery, and that the skull is that of her former lover, killed by the husband. The woman is now forced to do penance by drinking from her lover's skull.

Stories from other cultures show similarities. In the Aleutian legend "A Sea-Otter Story," recorded by F. A. Golder in the *Journal of American Folklore* in 1905, a man discovers that his wife and his nephew are having an affair. He cuts off the nephew's head and presents it to her. She jumps into the sea with the severed head, and the husband watches as two sea otters emerge from the spot where she disappeared, then swim out to sea together.

Asian folktales, too, are replete with examples of cruel punishment of women guilty (or suspected) of adultery. For example, in the ancient Indian tale "The Parrot and the Thrush: Which Are Worse, Men or Women?" from the *Vetalapanchavinsati*, translated from Sanskrit as *Twenty-Two Goblins* (1917) by Arthur W. Ryder, an adulterous woman has her nose bitten off by a goblin. She blames her husband, who is then threatened with legal execution for mistreating his wife. The truth comes out, and she is further punished by having her ears cut off as well.

It is not unusual for folktales, reflecting the religious beliefs from which they emanate, to defer certain punishments and rewards until a later existence. Thus, a Hindu or Buddhist tale might depict favorable or negative reincarnations. In Edward B. Cowell's edition of the

Jātaka (1895–1907), the tale "The Headstrong Man" (no. 41) depicts a greedy man who is condemned to numerous miserable rebirths lasting hundreds of thousands of years. He suffers through 500 existences as an ogre, never having enough to eat, then an additional 500 lives as a dog. He finally has a human incarnation, but only as a starving beggar.

Religious tales from other faiths depict punishments and rewards in keeping with their respective value systems. For example, "In Heaven and Hell," a Russian-Jewish tale from Beatrice Silverman Weinreich's *Yiddish Folktales* (1988), tells of a man who violates the Sabbath by making tea and smoking cigars. After his death, he is forced endlessly to drink scalding tea and choke on cigar smoke. Others, who sinned by dancing, are forced by an angel with a whip to dance forever without pause.

Punishments and rewards meted out by supernatural powers are common to all cultures, sometimes reflecting belief systems long since abandoned. For example, **fairies** are common arbiters of justice in European folktales. The widespread tale known generically as **The Kind and the Unkind Girls** (ATU 480) offers a significant example. An early version is Perrault's "Les fées" ("The Fairies") from his *Histoires ou contes du temps passé* (*Stories or Tales of Times Past*, 1697). A girl, while fetching water from a spring, kindly offers a drink to a **peasant** woman, a fairy in disguise. Upon returning home, the girl discovers that with every word she speaks, a flower or precious stone drops from her mouth. Considered logically, this reward may have unwanted consequences (as did, for example, the golden touch of King Midas), but fairy tales transcend ordinary wisdom, and this gift is seen only in positive light.

The girl's mother, wanting the same reward for an older (and more favored) daughter sends the latter to the same spring. This time the fairy uses a different disguise—that of a well-dressed lady—and the older sister treats her rudely. Henceforth toads and vipers drop from the disrespectful sister's mouth every time she speaks. Holding the younger girl responsible for this curse, the mother drives her from the house. She escapes into the woods where a prince discovers her. Attracted by her beauty, as well as the treasure that she generates, he takes her to the palace, thus giving her the fairy-tale reward of a royal marriage.

Magic rewards sometimes go awry because of the beneficiary's carelessness. A case in point is the internationally distributed tale type ATU 750A, The Three **Wish**es. In their basic form, these tales depict an individual given three wishes by a supernatural being. The recipient uses the first two foolishly and must then use the final wish to undo the consequences of the first two. "The Sausage" from *Fairy Tales from the Swedish* (1901) by Gabriel Djurklou is exemplary. An old woman is granted three wishes by a mysterious lady. While fantasizing about what to request, she remembers that it is mealtime, and she carelessly wishes for a sausage. Seeing how she has wasted the first wish, her husband angrily wishes the sausage onto her nose. Now they have no choice but to use the final wish to remove the sausage from the wife's face.

Fables, with their inherent moralizing function, often depict the punishments and rewards brought about respectively by untoward or positive behavior. Although the negative consequences of inappropriate acts typically are more dramatic than are the benefits of good acts, there are fine examples of the latter. "The Lion and the Mouse" (ATU 75, The Help of the Weak), found in Joseph **Jacobs**'s *The Fables of **Aesop*** (1894) and similar collections, carries a message common to many tales: Be kind to the weak, for they may help you in return. In the Aesopic fabl,e a lion, about to eat a mouse, releases him instead. Hunters later capture the lion and bind him to a tree. The mouse, not forgetting his debt to the lion, gnaws through the ropes and frees him. ***See also*** Anti-Semitism; Cautionary Tale; Clergy; Didactic Tale; Violence.

Further Readings: Bottigheimer, Ruth B. "Deaths and Executions." *Grimms' Bad Girls and Bold Boys: The Moral and Social Vision of the Tales.* New Haven, CT: Yale University Press, 1987. 95–100; Jason, Heda. *Whom Does God Favor, the Wicked or the Righteous? The Reward-and-Punishment Fairy Tale.* Helsinki: Academia Scientiarum Fennica, 1988; Mueller, Gerhard O. W. "The Criminological Significance of the Grimms' Fairy Tales." *Fairy Tales and Society: Illusion, Allusion, and Paradigm.* Edited by Ruth B. Bottigheimer. Philadelphia: University of Pennsylvania Press, 1986. 217–27; Tatar, Maria. "Just Desserts: Reward-and-Punishment Tales." *Off with Their Heads! Fairy Tales and the Culture of Childhood.* Princeton, NJ: Princeton University Press, 1992. 51–69.

D. L. Ashliman

Puppet Theater

Puppetry is an ancient art, found in cultures as diverse as those of ancient Egypt, the Bornu of Nigeria, and the Kwakiutl of Canada. The representative forms considered in this entry include the puppetry of China and countries that adopted its techniques, Japan, Hawai'i, and the West.

Puppetry is fully attested to in China in about the fifth century CE. However, archeology and literature suggest that rod and glove puppets, marionettes, and perhaps water puppets originated much earlier. However, the form most associated with China, shadow puppetry, seems to have reached its current form only in the eleventh century CE. Different styles evolved: in northern China, puppets are made with translucent sheets of painted leather, so light shown through them casts colored images; in the south, puppetry uses thicker, more opaque leather to cast darker shadows.

Plays featured subjects taken from mythology, folktales, and classic works of fiction, such as **Wú** Chéng'ēn's *Xī Yóu Jì* (*Journey to the West*, 1592) with its popular character, Sūn Wùkōng, the Monkey King; *Bai shé zhuàn* (*White Serpent*, Féng Mènglóng, seventeenth century, although other versions are also dramatized); and *Mùlán Cí* (*Mulan the **Woman Warrior***). Beginning in the late twentieth century, national Chinese puppet festivals have encouraged both traditional forms and new innovations.

Shadow puppets were introduced to India, where they performed **myth**s and **fable**s, and from there reached Egypt by the thirteenth century, when Muhammad ibn Daniyal wrote three shadow plays. Dialogue in Egyptian shadow plays usually consists of rhyming prose in classical Arabic. Egyptian plays usually convey religious morals, although the stories come from folktales and literature, such as the ***Arabian Nights***. A puppet appears as narrator in the prologue. From Egypt, shadow puppets were adapted in Turkey by the fourteenth century and soon supplanted most native forms of puppetry. In Turkey, plays begin with a prologue in which the scholarly and gentle Hacivat appears and introduces his friend, the uneducated but outspoken Karagöz. Their banter leads to a story, acted out in the body of the play. Turkish puppets spread through most of the Mediterranean: in Arabic, the characters become Hajiwaz and Karakoz, the latter a **trickster** and the former an honest man caught in his friend's schemes. The puppets entered Greek culture in the late nineteenth century, becoming Hadjiavatis and Karagiozis. Mediterranean shadow puppetry waned in popularity during the twentieth century, being replaced by marionettes in most countries.

Shadow puppetry also spread with Hinduism from India throughout Southeast Asia, including Indonesia, where plays dramatize Hindu myths. In Java, highborn or divine characters speak an ancient form of the language, while commoners repeat their words in vernacular and add humorous commentary. Gamelan music plays during the performance.

Another Chinese invention, water puppets (figures manipulated on the surface of a pool of water), also spread to other countries, including Vietnam, where they are a popular means of enacting folktales. Puppeteers stand behind barriers and reach beneath the water's surface to operate the puppets.

In Japan, puppets were introduced from Korea in the eighth century CE. They were used in dramatizations of sacred stories at shrines. Eventually, a uniquely Japanese form evolved, *Ningyō-jōruri* ("puppet-storytelling," usually called Bunraku). In 1734, large puppets were introduced, each worked by three men. All voices are provided by a highly trained singer-narrator performing with a shamisen player. Bunraku puppets also perform Kabuki plays, including fairy tales. Although Bunraku's popularity waned somewhat during the nineteenth century, after World War II, as part of an effort to foster Japan's cultural traditions, the government started granting stipends to Bunraku artists and public interest revived. In 1966, a permanent Bunraku theater was built in Tokyo, and in 1985, the troupe relocated in Osaka.

In Hawai'i, traditional *hula ki'i* (literally, "image dance") treats stock characters, such as boastful but cowardly warriors, crafty seducers, scheming lovers, and stupidly literal-minded royal functionaries. Large jointed puppets are manipulated by puppeteers hiding behind a screen and providing the characters' voices. Narrators who play a hollow-gourd drum called an *ipu* interrogate both the puppets and the viewers for comic effect. The performances usually depict folktales, often ending with the central characters marrying.

In Europe, puppetry appeared in Greece and Rome, depicting folktales and mimes. Medieval puppet shows (called "motions") usually depicted fables or **Bible** stories, although in time, popular plays were adapted for puppets. Narrators usually provided the **frame narratives**; voices were provided by narrators or puppeteers. In Russia, *skomorokhi* (wandering minstrels) also performed with puppets from the tenth century CE into the sixteenth.

Some puppet characters derived from the Italian *commedia dell'arte*, including Punch (originally Punchinello, mispronounced from Pulcinella), first recorded in 1662. Comically misshapen and prone to clubbing other characters, Punch spread throughout Britain and its colonies, for instance reaching Philadelphia in 1742. Other stock characters with similarly caricatured features and also wielding clubs include Guignol in France, Kasperl in Germany, and Petrushka in Russia.

In the early nineteenth century, puppet performances of nursery and fairy tales were widespread. In Britain, a hobby version, the "toy theater," featured cutout figures in an open-topped box with backdrops and curtains. Children often made their own cutouts, but figures also were sold, portraying famous actors in costume. Toy theaters remained popular for most of the century.

By the 1870s and 1880s, evolving stage technology allowed for large-scale productions in major cities, some lasting as long as plays and featuring live actors. Showmen like Walter E. Deaves and, somewhat later, illustrator Tony Sarg, produced elaborate fairy-tale plays using marionettes and other puppets, a late survival being Chicago's Kungsholm Miniature Grand **Opera** in the 1950s.

In recent times, although traditional puppetry is still practiced, new forms continue to develop. For instance, Chinese shadow plays dramatize new stories; troupes such as the Train Theater of Jerusalem tour the world presenting fairy stories in several languages, and Bunraku-style puppets are studied internationally. *See also* Theater.

Further Readings: Blumenthal, Eileen. *Puppetry: A World History.* New York: Harry N. Abrams, 2005; Speaight, George. *Punch & Judy: A History.* Boston: Publishers Plays, Inc., 1970.

Paul James Buczkowski

Pushkin, Aleksandr (1799–1837)

Aleksandr Pushkin stands out as Russia's greatest poet and the founder of modern Russian literature. Born in Moscow, into a cultured but poor aristocratic family, young Pushkin spent a lot of time in his father's library. Entrusted to governesses and French tutors, Pushkin learned Russian mainly from household serfs and his nanny, Arina Rodionovna, who, just like his grandmother, was a great storyteller. At nine years of age, he was already familiar with Homer's the *Iliad* and the *Odyssey* and the writings of Plutarch. They were followed by the classics of French literature and philosophy, which he read in the original language.

Pushkin published his first poem when he was fourteen, by then a student of the prestigious Imperial Lyceum at Tsarskoe Selo. His first attempt in the genre of fairy tale was the unfinished poem *Bova,* 1814. It was based on a popular **chapbook** story, *Bova Korolevich,* which is said to be based on the English romance *Bevis of Hampton* (c. 1200). The **motif** of Bova appears occasionally in Pushkin's works, although it is never fully elaborated. At the Lyceum, Pushkin also began writing the fairy-tale poem *Ruslan i Lyudmila* (*Ruslan and Lyudmila*), which was to become his literary breakthrough. Published in 1820, this satirical verse tale caused confusion among the critics, who thought it was unorthodox and vulgar since Pushkin unified the vernacular and high poetry, including erotic allusions. The common readers, however, were enthusiastic.

In 1822, while exiled in the south of Russia, Pushkin wrote the bawdy *Skazka o tsare Nikite i sorok ego docheryakh* (*The Tale about Tsar Nikita and His Forty Daughters*), which was never published during his lifetime. Apart from its ribaldry, the tale, through its meter (trochaic tetrameter) and setting (the life of tsars), anticipates three of Pushkin's fairy tales in the 1830s.

Between 1824 and 1826, Pushkin stayed at the family estate in Mikhailovskoe, where he made annotations of the fairy tales told by Arina Rodionovna and others. These notes form the stem of *Skazka o tsare Saltane* (*The Tale of Tsar Saltan,* 1831), which was the first of Pushkin's fairy tales to be published. A combination of the European and Oriental fairy-tale tradition unified with the Russian idiom, *The Tale of Tsar Saltan* varies several familiar motifs, of which the **swan maiden** and the banished wife or maiden are the best known. At the same time, the tale is about a son's longing for his **father**. By the time of publication, the status of the **literary fairy tale** and its relation to the genuine **folktale** was being

A painting of Aleksandr Pushkin by Tropinin. [Getty Images]

debated in Russia. Pushkin's fairy tale met with harsh criticism. *The Tale of Tsar Saltan* was described as a poor and artificial imitation of the original Russian folktales. Pushkin, however, continued elaborating the genre, and in 1833 he finished the lyrical *Skazka o mertvei tsarevne i o semi bogatyryakh* (*The Tale of the Dead Princess and the Seven Knights*), a Russian version of "**Snow White**" based on the oral retelling of the famous **Grimm** tale. The slyest of the fairy tales is probably the dystopian and satirical *Zolotoi petushok* (*The Tale of the Golden Cockerel*, 1834). Inspired by the motif of the Arabian astrologer in *Alhambra* by Washington Irving, *The Tale of the Golden Cockerel* is the only one of Pushkin's tales that has a purely literary source. Controversial in its own time, the tale not only questions the responsibility and morals of the tsar, it also becomes a reflection about the Orient versus Russia.

A completely different type of tale is represented by the unfinished *Skazka o medveditse* (*The Tale of the She-Bear*) from 1830. In this allegorical pastiche of folkloric formulas and genres, Pushkin implicitly discusses marriage and procreation, a subject very dear to him at the time, since he was about to get married. The witty and anticlerical approach in *Skazka o pope i o rabotnike ego Balde* (*The Tale of the Priest and His Workman Balda*) from 1830 made publication impossible during the poet's lifetime. Still, of all the fairy tales by Pushkin, considering tone and narration, *Skazka o pope*, renamed after his death and restored to its original version about forty years later, comes closest to the oral **performance**. In *Skazka o rybake i rybke* (*The Tale of the Fisherman and the Fish*, 1833), Pushkin presents a Russian version of the Grimms' tale about the **fisherman and his wife**. Applied to Russian conditions, the last episode with the wife wishing to be Pope is omitted.

Pushkin's fairy tales, all of them written in verse, constituted an indispensable contribution to the establishment of the literary fairy tale in Russia. His interest in and deep knowledge of folk traditions, songs, lyrics, and **proverbs**, as well as **myth**, is also manifested in several poems, as for example in *Rusalka* (*The **Mermaid***) from 1819, *Besy* (*The Demons*, 1830), and *Pesni o Sten'ke Razine* (*Songs about Stenka Razin*, 1826). Folkloric elements appear in the verse novel *Evgeny Onegin* (1831), as well as in the historical novel *Kapitanskaya dochka* (*The Captain's Daughter*) from 1833 and in *Povesti pokoinogo Ivana Petrovicha Belkina* (*The Tales of the Late Ivan Petrovich Belkin*), a collection of short stories from 1830. In *Pikovaya dama* (*The Queen of Spades*), written in 1833, Pushkin develops the conventions of the fantastic tale, a new genre in Russian literature.

While staying in Mikhailovskoe, Pushkin wrote to his brother in November 1824, "In the evening I listen to fairy tales, and thereby I am compensating for the insufficiencies of my accursed upbringing. How charming these fairy tales are! Each is a poem!" Later on, in a conversation on Russian literary language with Vladimir Dal, Pushkin concluded, "Our language is inherently beautiful and nowhere has it such breadth of expression as in folktales. We must learn to speak and love Russian, not simply to admire it in tales." By incorporating common, everyday speech into his texts, Pushkin created a language for Russian literature. *See also* Russian Tales.

Further Readings: Bethea, David M., ed. *The Pushkin Handbook.* Madison: University of Wisconsin Press, 2005; Eimermacher, Karl. "Aspekte des literarischen Märchens in Russland." *Beiträge zur russischen Volksdichtung.* Edited by Klaus-Dieter Seemann. Wiesbaden: Harrassowitz, 1987. 92–111; Mikolchak, Maria. "Misogyny in Alexander Pushkin: Rescuing the Russian Fairy Tale." *Misogynism in Literature: Any Place, Any Time.* Edited by Britta Zangen. Frankfurt a.M.: Peter Lang, 2004. 99–110.

Janina Orlov

Puss in Boots

Puss in Boots (ATU 545B), the popular folktale of a poor young man's social rise—thanks to the cunning manipulations of his animal helper—is found in early influential collections of literary European fairy-tale culture and is documented in both Eastern and Western **oral tradition**s.

The most famous version is *Le maître chat ou le chat botté* in Charles **Perrault**'s *Histoires ou contes du temps passé* (*Stories or Tales of Times Past*, 1697), in which a youngest son inherits a **cat**. On his own initiative, the cat seeks to gain the **king**'s confidence, presenting him repeatedly with gifts allegedly in the name of his rich master, Marquis de Carabas. The king is tricked into providing the young man with royal **clothing** and taking him for a drive with himself and his daughter. The cat runs ahead, threatening herdsmen and farmers to say that herds and farmland all belong to the Marquis of Carabas. The cat then comes to the castle of an **ogre**, whom he flatters into transforming himself into a mouse that the cat devours, making the young man indeed the owner of all. The king, overwhelmed by these riches, offers his daughter in **marriage**. At the end, the young man is the son-in-law of the king, and the cat a great lord.

"Puss in Boots" illustrated by Walter Crane in *The Marquis of Carabas' Picture Book, containing Puss in Boots, Old Mother Hubbard, My Mother, The Forty Thieves* (London: George Routledge and Sons, n.d.), p. 7. [Courtesy of the Eloise Ramsey Collection of Literature for Young People, University Libraries, Wayne State University]

Literary and oral versions have this same rags-to-riches pattern. In literary versions and in most of the oral **variant**s of middle and western Europe and of North and South America, a cat helps a youth. However, in the numerous variants of Eastern and southeastern Europe, the Caucasian region, and central Asia, a fox, a typical **trickster**, is the animal helper (even in some Italian and French variants). In southern Asia and Africa, the helper is an ape, a jackal, or a gazelle; in South America, a cat or rabbit, mouse or ape. The shift from a domestic to a wild animal causes a change in the story opening: the youth helps the wild animal, and it in turn is obliged to help.

The first known version dates from the Italian Renaissance, the story of Costantino Fortunato and his cat in Giovan Francesco **Straparola**'s *Piacevoli notti* (*Pleasant Nights*, volume 2, 1553). Within fifty years, this collection had more than twenty Italian editions and translations in French, Spanish, and German. Here, the cat is female; the castle, which the cat takes over, has no actual owner, so the expropriation goes off smoothly.

Eighty years later, the baroque story of Cagliuso in Giambattista **Basile**'s *Lo cunto de li cunti* (*The Tale of Tales*, 1634–36) keeps the female trickster cat, who manages "legally" to enrich the youth: the property is bought from the dowry. In contrast to literary versions, but similar to many fox variants, Basile has the cat test the sincerity of the young man and then abandon him, bitterly disillusioned. Whether Basile used oral tradition or himself influenced oral narratives remains unclear.

Perrault changed the female cat into an aggressive male with picaresque tendencies, and the boots, a sign of male prestige, are his invention. He also added murder. Though the language of the text is concise, ironic, and subtle, its composition is close to the structure of folktales, including that particular fairy-tale **moral,** where the hero's happiness justifies murder and robbery: in most of the oral fox variants, the owner of the castle is a **dragon,** who is mercilessly burnt, slain, or shot. Perrault's ogre who can transform himself is reminiscent of the **tale type**s ATU 325, The Magician and his Pupil, or ATU 331, The Spirit in the Bottle.

Although Basile and Perrault allude to children as consumers of their tales, they wrote for adults. These literary versions reflect their times of upheaval, when poetic as well as political considerations (for example, the fear of censorship) suggested falling back on folktales. Perrault's text, for instance, realized modernist aesthetic conceptions and analyzed the decline of the absolutist system and the ascendancy of the middle classes of his time for his readers in the aristocratic and bourgeois **salon**s. His cat could be understood as a servant whose advancement depends on the career of his master, the latter as a figure who compromises himself by exterminating his past in tacit conspiracy with his servant, and the king as a corruptible sovereign and an ally of intriguing plebeian elements (the cat).

Perrault's version proved to be extremely forceful, influencing the image of "Puss in Boots" worldwide, and is still a bestseller. The Brothers **Grimm** omitted their own version of the story (originally published in 1812) in their 1819 second edition of the *Kinder- und Hausmärchen* (*Children's and Household Tales*) because it was too close to Perrault's text. In the 1920s, the Dutch colonial administration in Indonesia used **translation**s of the Perrault version for educational purposes. Since the middle of the twentieth century, local fox variants in southeast Europe have been edged out and replaced by the Perrault version.

The tales of Puss in Boots usually include no wonders beyond an anthropomorphized animal and sometimes an ogre with magic qualities. Success is always gained by rational means and relying on a perfect knowledge of social conventions and human flaws. It is interesting to note that oral versions tend toward different kind of genres. Most of the Norwegian variants are classical **fairy tale**s: the cat is an enchanted **prince** or **princess** hoping to be released from his or her animal figure. Variants including the young man's breach of trust are warning examples of ingratitude. In the Caucasian region, "Puss in Boots" became an **etiologic tale**: since the fox helper is disillusioned by the young man's lack of sincerity, foxes in general avoid human beings. Many Bulgarian variants tell the story rather anecdotally, integrating a **Nasreddin anecdote** with scatological features. How the young man copes with the discrepancy between extreme poverty and sudden luxury is often detailed, and the intelligence of the fox is contrasted to the young man's intellectual simplicity. In all variants, the animal helper is the active character, the young man the passive. The animal's dubious strategies have never been an obstacle to the popularity of "Puss in Boots" with children. *See also* Shoe.

Further Readings: Escarpit, Denise. *Histoire d'un conte: Le chat botté en France et en Angleterre.* 2 volumes. Paris: Didier Erudition, 1985; Köhler-Zülch, Ines. "Kater: Der gestiefelte K. (AaTh 545 B)." *Enzyklopädie des Märchens.* Edited by Kurt Ranke et al. Volume 7. Berlin: Walter de Gruyter, 1993. 1069–83; Zipes, Jack. "Of Cats and Men." *Happily Ever After: Fairy Tales, Children, and the Culture Industry.* New York: Routledge 1997. 15–38.

Ines Köhler-Zülch